Eileen Gardner
January 25, 1925–September 26, 2005

Criminal Law

11th Edition / 2012

Thomas J. Gardner | Terry M. Anderson

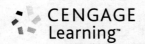

CENGAGE
Learning™

Australia • Brazil • Japan • Korea • Mexico • Singapore • Spain • United Kingdom • United States

Criminal Law: 11th Edition / 2012

Criminal Law, 11th Edition
Thomas J. Gardner | Terry M. Anderson

Executive Editors:
 Maureen Staudt
 Michael Stranz

Senior Project Development Manager:
 Linda deStefano

Marketing Specialist:
 Courtney Sheldon

Senior Production/Manufacturing
Manager:
 Donna M. Brown

PreMedia Manager:
 Joel Brennecke

Sr. Rights Acquisition Account Manager:

 Todd Osborne

Cover Image:
Getty Images*

*Unless otherwise noted, all cover images used by
Custom Solutions, a part of Cengage Learning,
have been supplied courtesy of Getty Images with
the exception of the Earthview cover image, which
has been supplied by the National Aeronautics and
Space Administration (NASA).

For product information and technology assistance, contact us at
Cengage Learning Customer & Sales Support, 1-800-354-9706
For permission to use material from this text or product,
submit all requests online at cengage.com/permissions
Further permissions questions can be emailed to
permissionrequest@cengage.com

This book contains select works from existing Cengage Learning resources and
was produced by Cengage Learning Custom Solutions for collegiate use. As such,
those adopting and/or contributing to this work are responsible for editorial
content accuracy, continuity and completeness.

Compilation © 2011 Cengage Learning

ISBN-13: 978-1-133-15375-7

ISBN-10: 1-133-15375-5

Cengage Learning
5191 Natorp Boulevard
Mason, Ohio 45040
USA

Cengage Learning is a leading provider of customized learning solutions with
office locations around the globe, including Singapore, the United Kingdom,
Australia, Mexico, Brazil, and Japan. Locate your local office at:
international.cengage.com/region.

Cengage Learning products are represented in Canada by Nelson Education, Ltd.
For your lifelong learning solutions, visit **www.cengage.com /custom.**
Visit our corporate website at **www.cengage.com.**

Printed in the United States of America

About the Authors

Thomas J. Gardner, after earning a Bachelor of Science degree in economics, served three years as a naval officer in the South Pacific during and immediately after World War II. He then attended and graduated from Marquette Law School with a Juris Doctor degree in 1949. During the Korean War he worked in procurement for the Air Material Command. He also earned a Master of Arts degree in political science. His long association with the criminal justice system began as a criminal defense lawyer. He then worked as a prosecutor, as a police legal adviser, and in police in-service legal training. He was a member and president of a police and fire commission. For twenty-eight years, he taught courses in Criminal Law, Criminal Evidence, and Arrest, Search and Seizure at the Milwaukee Area Technical College complex of campuses. He lives in Milwaukee, Wisconsin.

Terry M. Anderson, Professor of Law, is a Professor of Law at Creighton University School of Law in Omaha, Nebraska. He was a Visiting Professor at Denver College of Law for the 2002–2003 academic year, and at the University of New Mexico during the 1980–1981 academic year. He received his Bachelor of Arts degree in 1968 and Juris Doctor degree in 1971 from the University of North Dakota, where he was a member of the Order of the Coif and the Case Editor of the *North Dakota Law Review*. After earning a Master of Laws degree from Harvard Law School in 1972, he joined the Creighton Law School faculty. He teaches Contracts, Insurance, and Secured Transactions in Personal Property. E-mail: terryanderson@creighton.edu

Contents in Brief

Contents

Boxed Features

Preface

Goals

The first edition of this text was published more than thirty years ago. Its goal was to introduce law enforcement personnel and others in the criminal justice field to the main principles of American criminal law. In the subsequent editions, including this, the eleventh edition, we have tried to adhere to that goal and at the same time broaden the scope of the text while also keeping it current. As in past editions, we have included recent court opinions and legislative acts that illustrate the current status of those principles of American criminal law. We have also tried to include information we believe to be helpful to the study of criminal law, taken from governmental reports, empirical studies, and news accounts of current criminal cases and developments. We hope these additions and changes in the eleventh edition serve to advance our goal for this text.

We make extensive use of court opinions, especially United States Supreme Court opinions, and case citations in the text. We use these opinions and case citations primarily to illustrate how the majority of courts interpreted and applied criminal statutes within their jurisdiction. We also identify and cite decisions on key points of criminal law so that teachers and students will have a sound basis for doing more extensive research into such points. It has always been our plan to create a text that would prove useful as both a classroom learning tool and a reference book for post-classroom use. We are gratified that users of our text have found that it met that plan in previous editions, and we hope they will conclude the same about this edition.

Features

In this edition we continue to use more detailed case excerpts called Case Close-Ups to examine courts' analyses of difficult or emerging criminal law issues, sometimes including our observations about the possible effect of a court's decision on a particular issue. These case excerpts, of which there are fifteen spread throughout the text, generally include a more detailed factual statement, and a more complete discussion of the court's reasoning, than in the other case excerpts found in the text. In some of the cases, such as *James v. United States* discussed in Chapter 8, we include positions taken by dissenting judges. In Chapter 12, we brought two cases together in one Case Close-Up to illustrate some common problems, the resolution of which might vary from state to state.

Where possible, we chose U.S. Supreme Court cases for the Case Close-Up features. In subject areas where the Supreme Court does not ordinarily issue opinions, we chose opinions of the Federal Circuit courts or the highest state courts. Cases were usually selected because their topics were of current interest, but not necessarily because the opinion represents the majority view on the topic. We hope these closer looks at important cases will add substance to our coverage of the issues framed in those cases.

We continue to make references to specific state and federal criminal statutes, as well as illustrations from the Model Penal Code, which we have expanded in this edition. For example, in Chapter 6, we include excerpts from the Florida "Stand Your Ground" statute, which has been a model for similar legislation in 21 other states.

In this edition we have retained the chapter-opening vignettes, with new vignettes for most chapters. We also retained the chapter-ending "Case Analysis and Writing Exercises" feature. We retained the cases highlighted in some of those exercises, and added new cases in others. In this edition we also continue to use charts, boxes, and lists as supplements to text and case summaries. We intend the textual materials and case summaries to serve as the main exposition of criminal law principles, with the boxes and other tools helping to illustrate specific applications or examples of those principles.

≡ New to This Edition

Reorganization

In addition to the features just discussed, we have made other changes and additions to this edition. Continuing the reorganization begun in the ninth and tenth editions, we shortened the chapter on Jurisdiction and moved it to an earlier part of the book in this edition. It is now Chapter 2. The other chapters are organized by subject matter as in the tenth edition. We have also reorganized the outlines that begin each chapter, with a view to better reflect the relationship of the headings in the outlines to the contents of the chapters. Finally, in each chapter we rewrote the chapter-ending summary to conform to the learning objectives in the beginning of the chapter. As part of that effort, we put each summary in bullet format.

We have always been appreciative of the efforts of those who review our book before we begin work on a new edition. In this edition, as in the past, we have made it a point to incorporate specific suggestions made by our reviewers and others who have taken the time to communicate with us. We thank them and invite all our readers to share their thoughts on the book with us at the e-mail addresses listed in the brief biographies that appear in the front pages of this edition.

New Content

In addition to the reorganization changes discussed above, in the eleventh edition we have made many substantive additions as well. They include:

- **Chapter 1, Criminal Law: Purposes, Scope, and Sources:** We added new material on the SORNA legislation and the *ex post facto* clause; a new Supreme Court case discussing the overbreadth doctrine; new discussions of the Domestic Offender Gun Ban law and Supreme Court cases on the 2nd Amendment and individual's right to own guns.
- **Chapter 2, Jurisdiction Essential Elements of a Crime:** We condensed and shortened discussions of the various jurisdictions that have power to make and enforce criminal laws; we added a section listing federal laws that support state and local law enforcement; we expanded the discussion of the law of the seas and approaches to the continental United States.

- **Chapter 3, Essential Elements of a Crime:** We expanded and reconfigured the section on the proof of mental fault, including a new Supreme Court case on the "knowing" element of a federal crime, and a case from the Military Court of Appeals on a similar element; we also added more examples of the difference between general and specific intent; we added a new key term, "concurrence" with examples, and an expanded discussion of causation in deaths tied to illegal drug distribution. We deleted one Case Analysis Exercise and added a new Exercise that builds on the Supreme Court's discussion of "knowingly" in the new Case Close Up in this chapter.

- **Chapter 4, Criminal Liability:** We added new cases showing liability based on intent under solicitation statutes and the "bomb" hoax statute; we rewrote the conspiracy section, and added new material on the overt act requirement and RICO prosecutions; we added the "Pinkerton" rule used in federal prosecutions for liability of one conspirator for crimes committed by another conspirator, plus a new Case Analysis Exercise on recent applications of the Pinkerton rule.

- **Chapter 5, Criminal Responsibility and the Capacity to Commit a Crime:** We rewrote the introduction sections and explained the difference between lack of capacity as an excuse, and affirmative defenses. We added a discussion of burdens of proof in capacity issues, with new cases and statutes as examples. We also rewrote the insanity sections to better explain the various tests used to determine insanity; we also expanded the discussion of confinement of persons committed after a finding of not guilty by reason of insanity. We expanded the Guilty but Mentally Ill verdicts section by adding state cases and statutes showing how that verdict is reached. We redid a box on civil commitment laws to emphasize their use for confinement of sexual violent predators. Finally, we expanded the diminished capacity section to include a discussion of that defense under federal statutes.

- **Chapter 6, The Law Governing the Use of Force:** This chapter illustrates our efforts to redo the outline to be more in conformity with the subject matter. We eliminated some headings, and added a new heading identifying a new section on the use of tasers in traffic stops. We wrote a new introduction to the chapter, with a hypothetical problem marked for ongoing analysis throughout the chapter; we added a new case in the Stand Your Ground section as those laws apply to passengers in automobiles. We updated the battered women section, bringing in the Gail Owens story. We added a case showing a conviction of a police officer who used excessive force.

- **Chapter 7, Other Criminal Defenses:** We added a new introduction to better explain affirmative defenses and allocations of burdens of proof. The witness immunity section has been expanded to discuss specific federal and state immunity statutes and cases; we also made use and transactional immunity key terms. We added specific cases and statutes on duress as a defense in a murder case, including duress in felony-murder cases. We added a discussion of the necessity defense in federal prosecutions, and expanded the collateral estoppel/double jeopardy section, with a recent Supreme Court case.

- **Chapter 8, Criminal Punishment:** We expanded the discussion of proportionality in non-capital cases, adding 2 new Supreme Court cases to explain the history of proportionality. We added a recent Supreme Court case on the distinction between elements of an offense and sentencing facts for *Apprendi* purposes. We added the recent Supreme Court cases on capital punishment to the box on that subject. We also used the *Graham* juvenile life sentence case as a Case Close Up. We added a Supreme Court case on restitution under the federal restitution act. We expanded the discussion of career criminals, including 2 new Supreme Court cases under the federal Armed Career Criminal Act, as well as a new box on prison populations and recidivism.

- **Chapter 9, Free Speech, Street Crimes, and the Bill of Rights:** We added a new case giving an example of the fighting words doctrine. We expanded the Obscene Communications section to better explain the rules for analysis of content-based laws and content neutral laws. We added recent cases showing application of criminal libel laws. Campaign finance laws have criminal sanctions for violations, and for this reason and the overall importance of the decision we added a box on the 2010 Supreme Court campaign finance case. In the Threats of Violence section we added 5 new case examples of First Amendment analysis of speech that was charged as a threat. We also added a new case example on nuisance speech and the First Amendment. We renamed the gun ownership section in light of the *Heller* and *McDonald* cases, which we discuss. We also added a new section on bullying. Though not a separate crime, the incidence and consequences of bullying behavior seems on the rise.

- **Chapter 10, Homicide:** We rewrote the fetal murder section to add 4 new cases and the federal statute, all of which help to explain the status of the born alive rule. We changed the intent to kill section by adding premeditated to the title, and then included a new paragraph with the federal murder statute, and a Case Close Up interpreting the federal murder statute. We expanded the discussion of deadly weapons, to clarify the connection to murder. We added cases to the transferred intent section to show limits of the doctrine. We added a more compete explanation of the current status of serious bodily harm murder. The felony-murder section has been completely rewritten, with several specific references to state and federal statutes and cases showing the current state of the felony-murder rule. Finally, we updated the assisted suicide section, adding a discussion on internet chat rooms and their role in suicides, and a Montana case allowing doctor-assisted suicide.

- **Chapter 11, Assault, Battery, and Other Crimes Against the Person:** We rewrote the Assault section, updating the cases cited and adding new federal and state cases plus the Model Penal Code showing how the crime is defined. We updated the cases cited in the Simple Assault box to show the current split in the federal courts on that section. In the battery section we added specific state statutes to better explain what constitutes a battery. The aggravated assault section was rewritten to include more specific references to statutory requirements for such assaults. The hate crime section was expanded to include the New York statute as an example, and cases and developments under that law. In the child abuse section we added a new discussion of child abuse and religious beliefs. New cases were added in the kidnapping section to better explain the elements of that crime. The domestic violence sections have been updated by adding specific state statutes defining domestic violence as well as a Supreme Court Case Close Up on a domestic violence-related federal statute. Finally, we added three new key terms, and one new Case Analysis Exercise on aggravated assault.

- **Chapter 12, Sexual Assault, Rape, Prostitution, and Related Sex Crimes:** We updated the federal rape and sexual assault statistics. We added the federal rape-shield rule and recent cases under that rule, plus a case showing application of the rule to a sexual assault on a male victim, and recent cases showing exceptions to the rule in state courts based on prior false reports. We added a new section on AIDS and H.I.V. related crimes, with specific statutes and recent cases showing the current state of prosecutions for such crimes. The international sex trade box was extensively rewritten to show current developments and cases. The child pornography section was updated to include as a Case Close Up the Supreme Court case that upheld child pornography sections of the PROTECT Act. We added "Sexting" to the title of the "Nude Photos" section, and illustrated how it applied in a criminal prosecution.

- **Chapters 13, Theft:** We added new cases in the section defining what property can be stolen to illustrate real estate and services theft. We also added a case showing how "property of another" works in joint checking account situations. We added new cases showing how credit card theft can occur, and how it is prosecuted.

- **Chapter 14, Robbery and Burglary:** We made several organizational changes to this chapter. We changed the title to reflect these changes. We moved "Bribery" to chapter 15, and brought "Trespass" to this chapter. We added 4 new key terms, and changed the learning objectives accordingly. For substantive changes, we mainly added many more specific cases and examples of the crimes discussed, such as carjacking, home invasion, purse snatching, and extortion. We did rewrite the robbery section and extortion section to incorporate statutes and cases.

- **Chapter 15, White Collar Crime, Cyber Crime, and Commercial Crime:** We rewrote many of the subsections in the fraudulent practices section, and added specific statutes and cases to show how those practices work and are prosecuted. We added a new box on scams and fraud schemes, including the Bernie Madoff case. The bribery section, moved here from chapter 14, has been extensively expanded and includes new cases and statutes, as well as a discussion of the connection between bribery and extortion. We discuss the Supreme Court's recent "honest services fraud" case in the section on financial markets. We extensively rewrote the identity theft section, and include several recent state and federal cases on that topic. The Computer/Cyber Crime section was updated by including federal computer crime statutes and recent cases under those statutes. The Arson section was rewritten to include state and federal arson statutes showing the basis for degrees of arson.

- **Chapter 16, Drug Abuse and Alcohol-Related Crime:** We extensively rewrote the introductory material on the drug problem, incorporating reports, studies, and news stories about the drug trade. We added a new box on meth labs, and cited a study on youth usage of drugs, including Adderall. We also rewrote the section on possession of controlled substances, adding several recent cases under state and federal controlled substances acts. We expanded the "usable amount" section to include recent cases considering that issue. We updated the status of medical use of marijuana with recent cases and positions taken by the U.S. Attorney General on drug prosecutions. We added two new sections: one on the use of drugs in religious ceremonies, and the other on elements and defenses in drunk-driving offenses. Finally, we added two new key terms.

- **Chapter 17, Terrorism:** We added a new section on terrorism prosecutions and the results since 2001. We also added two new boxes: one on the continuing battle against terrorism, and the other on the Torture Act and the first prosecution under that act. We expanded the terrorism under state law section by adding new state cases and statutes. We also expanded the section on other criminal charges by adding new cases, including one under the federal seditious conspiracy statute.

- **Chapter 18, Organized Crime and Gangs:** We extensively updated the section on organized gangs to include recent reports and statistics on gang violence in the United States. We added a new box, "Making Gang Members Pay", with statutes showing how gang membership increases the penalty for a crime. We added the recent Supreme Court case under the RICO statute on the meaning of a "criminal enterprise". We extensively rewrote the money laundering section, creating a new section on transactions covered by money laundering statutes, with several recent cases including two Supreme Court cases on the elements of money laundering under the federal statutes. We added statutes and cases to the currency transactions section to better explain the elements of the crimes discussed there, in particular "structured transactions".

- **Chapter 19, Immigration Crimes, Contempt, and Other Crimes Against the Government:** We extensively added to and updated the sections on immigration to bring in recent developments, including the Arizona statute directed at illegal immigrants. We added a new box on the "Secure Communities" program. We expanded the section on criminal charges for illegal immigration, adding several statutes and cases dealing with removal of illegal aliens. We rewrote the contempt sections to better explain the kinds of contempt, and added cases illustrating the differences. We also added material on the relationship between criminal contempt convictions and the Double Jeopardy clause.

≡ Supplements

A number of supplements are provided by Wadsworth to help instructors use *Criminal Law*, Eleventh Edition, in their courses and to aid students in preparing for exams. Supplements are available to qualified adopters. Please consult your local sales representative for details.

For the Instructor

Instructor's Resource Manual An improved and completely updated Instructor's Resource Manual with Test Bank has been developed by Valerie Bell at Loras College. The manual includes learning objectives, detailed chapter outlines, chapter summaries, key terms, discussion topics, and student activities. Each chapter's test bank contains questions in multiple-choice, true–false, fill-in-the-blank, and essay formats, with a full answer key. The test bank is coded to the chapter objectives that appear in the main text and includes the page numbers in the main text where the answers can be found. Finally, each question in the test bank has been carefully reviewed by experienced criminal justice instructors for quality, accuracy, and content coverage. Our "Instructor Approved" seal, which appears on the front cover, is our assurance that you are working with an assessment and grading resource of the highest caliber.

Online Lesson Plans From Scott Rudeen, Globe Education Network, the instructor-created lesson plans bring accessible, masterful suggestions to every lesson. Each lesson plan includes a sample syllabus, learning objectives, lecture notes, class discussion topics, in-class activities, a detailed lecture outline, and assignments. Lesson plans are available on the instructor website.

WebTutor™ on Blackboard® and WebCT® Jump-start your course with customizable, rich, text-specific content within your Course Management System. Whether you want to web-enable your class or put an entire course online, WebTutor delivers. WebTutor offers a wide array of resources, including media assets, test bank, practice quizzes linked to chapter learning objectives, and additional study aids. Visit www.cengage.com/webtutor to learn more.

The Wadsworth Criminal Justice Video Library So many exciting new videos—so many great ways to enrich your lectures and spark discussion of the material in this text. Your Cengage Learning representative will be happy to provide details on our video policy by adoption size. The library includes these selections and many others.

- *ABC*® *Videos.* ABC videos feature short, high-interest clips from current news events as well as historic raw footage going back 40 years. Perfect for discussion starters or to enrich your lectures and spark interest in the material in the text, these brief videos provide students with a new lens through which to view the past and present, one that will greatly enhance their knowledge and understanding of significant events and open up to them new dimensions in learning. Clips are drawn from such programs as *World News Tonight, Good Morning America, This Week, PrimeTime Live, 20/20,* and *Nightline,* as well as numerous ABC News specials and material from the Associated Press Television News and British Movietone News collections.
- *Cengage Learning's "Introduction Criminal Justice Video Series"* features videos supplied by the BBC Motion Gallery. These short, high-interest clips from CBS and BBC news programs—everything from nightly news broadcasts and specials to CBS News Special Reports, CBS Sunday Morning, 60 Minutes, and more—are perfect classroom discussion starters. Designed to enrich your lectures and spark interest in the material in the text, these brief videos provide students with a new lens through which to view the past and present, one that will greatly enhance their knowledge and understanding of significant events and open up to them new dimensions in learning. Clips are drawn from BBC Motion Gallery.
- *Films for the Humanities.* Choose from nearly 200 videos on a variety of topics such as elder abuse, supermax prisons, suicide and the police officer, the making of an FBI agent, and domestic violence.

ExamView*® *Computerized Testing The comprehensive *Instructor's Resource Manual* described above is backed up by ExamView, a computerized test bank available for PC and Macintosh computers. With ExamView you can create, deliver, and customize tests and study guides (both print and online) in minutes. You can easily edit and import your own questions and graphics, change test layouts, and reorganize questions. And using ExamView's complete word-processing capabilities, you can enter an unlimited number of new questions or edit existing questions.

Online PowerPoint Slides These handy Microsoft PowerPoint slides outline the chapters of the main text in a classroom-ready presentation and will help you make make your lectures engaging, as well as assist you in reaching your visually oriented students. The presentations are available for download on the password-protected website and can also be obtained by e-mailing your local Cengage Learning representative.

Classroom Activities for Criminal Justice This valuable booklet, available to adopters of any Wadsworth criminal justice text, offers instructors the best of the best in -criminal -justice classroom activities. Containing both tried-and-true favorites and exciting new projects, its activities are drawn from across the spectrum of criminal justice subjects, -including introduction to criminal justice, criminology, corrections, criminal law, policing, and juvenile justice, and can be customized to fit any course. Novice and seasoned instructors alike will find it a powerful tool to stimulate classroom engagement.

For the Student

Careers in Criminal Justice Website This unique website gives students information on a wide variety of career paths, including requirements, salaries, training, contact information for key agencies, and employment outlooks. Several important tools help students investigate the criminal justice career choices that are right for them.

- *Career Profiles*: Video testimonials from a variety of practicing professionals in the field as well as information on many criminal justice careers, including job descriptions, requirements, training, salary and benefits, and the application process.
- *Interest Assessment*: Self-assessment tool to help students decide which careers suit their personalities and interests.
- *Career Planner*: Résumé-writing tips and worksheets, interviewing techniques, and successful job search strategies.
- *Links for Reference*: Direct links to federal, state, and local agencies where students can get contact information and learn more about current job opportunities.

Handbook of Selected Supreme Court Cases, Third Edition This supplementary handbook covers almost forty landmark cases, each of which includes a full case -citation, an introduction, a summary from West Law, excerpts from the case, and the decision. The updated edition includes *Hamdi v. Rumsfeld*, *Roper v. Simmons*, *Ring v. Arizona*, *Atkins v. Virginia*, *Illinois v. Caballes*, and much more.

Coursemate Cengage Learning's Criminal Justice CourseMate brings course concepts to life with interactive learning, study, and exam preparation tools that support the printed textbook. CourseMate includes an integrated eBook, quizzes mapped to chapter Learning Objectives, flashcards, videos, and more, and EngagementTracker, a first-of-its-kind tool that monitors student engagement in the course. The accompanying instructor website offers access to password-protected resources such as an electronic version of the instructor's manual and PowerPoint® slides. The webquizzing was developed by Cornel Plebani of Husson College.

Criminal Justice Media Library

Cengage Learning's Criminal Justice Media Library includes nearly 300 media assets on the topics you cover in your courses. Available to stream from any Web-enabled computer, the Criminal Justice Media Library's assets include such valuable resources as; Career Profile Videos featuring interviews with criminal justice professionals from a range of roles and locations, simulations that allow students to step into various roles and practice their decision-making skills, video clips on current topics from ABC® and other sources, animations that illustrate key concepts, interactive learning modules that help students check their knowledge of important topics and Reality Check exercises that compare expectations and preconceived notions against the real-life thoughts and experiences of criminal justice professionals. The Criminal Justice Media Library can be uploaded and used within many popular Learning Management Systems. You can also customize it with your own course material. The Criminal Justice Media Library can be uploaded and used within many popular Learning Management Systems. You can also customize it with your own course material. The Criminal Justice Media Library can be uploaded and used within many popular Learning Management Systems. You can also customize it with your own course material. You can also purchase an institutional site license. Please contact your Cengage Learning representative for ordering and pricing information.

CLeBook

Cengage Learning's Criminal Justice e-books allow students to access our textbooks in an easy-to-use online format. Highlight, take notes, bookmark, search your text, and, for most texts, link directly into multimedia. In short, CLeBooks combine the best features of paper books and ebooks in one package.

Current Perspectives: Readings from Infotrac® College Edition These readers, designed to give students a closer look at special topics in criminal justice, include free access to InfoTrac College Edition. The timely articles are selected by experts in each topic from within InfoTrac College Edition. They are available free when bundled with the text and include the following titles:

- *Cyber Crime*
- *Victimology*
- *Juvenile Justice*
- *Racial Profiling*
- *White-Collar Crime*
- *Terrorism and Homeland Security*
- *Public Policy and Criminal Justice*
- *Technology and Criminal Justice*
- *Ethics in Criminal Justice*
- *Forensics and Criminal Investigation*
- *Corrections*
- *Law and Courts*
- *Policy in Criminal Justice*

Terrorism: An Interdisciplinary Perspective Available for bundling with each new copy of *Criminal Law*, Eleventh Edition, this eighty-page booklet discusses terrorism in general and the issues surrounding the events of September 11, 2001. The booklet examines the origins of terrorism in the Middle East, focusing on Osama bin Laden in particular, as well as issues involving bioterrorism, the specific role played by religion in Middle Eastern terrorism, globalization as it relates to terrorism, and the reactions and repercussions of terrorist attacks.

≡ Acknowledgments

We would like to thank the reviewers of the tenth edition for their helpful comments as we prepared this eleventh edition:

Yury Cheryachukin, California State University, Stanislaus

Megan Cole, Brown College

Howard Jordan, Hostos Community College

Thomas McAninch, Scott Community College

Amy Pinero, Baton Rouge Community College

Robert Simpson, Champlain College

Thomas J. Gardner

Terry M. Anderson

Criminal Law

CHAPTER 1

Criminal Law: Purposes, Scope, and Sources

The criminal justice system in the United States includes several levels and kinds of courts, including federal and military courts, state courts, and local or county courts. Trials in criminal cases are held in the court that has jurisdiction over the crime charged. Pictured here is the historic Green Lake County Courthouse in Green Lake, Wisconsin. In most states, prosecution for some state crimes, usually those carrying the possibility for lesser sentences, might be brought in county courts like this one, while more serious crimes might be prosecuted in state district courts.

OUTLINE

LEARNING OBJECTIVES

In this chapter we introduce criminal law and the role it plays in the American legal system. The learning objectives for this chapter are:

- Identify the branches of government, and their relationship to the criminal law.

- Describe the difference between public law and private law, including the difference between criminal law and tort law.

- List the reasons people commit crimes, and why they do not.

- Understand the four generally recognized goals of the criminal justice system.

- Know the meaning of police power.

- Identify the general limitations on the exercise of the police power by government.

- Know the meaning of the phrase *nulla poena sine lege.*

- List and describe five specific constitutional limitations on the power to create a criminal law.

- Define circumstances that would make a criminal law a status crime.

- Trace the origin of the common law to its place in criminal law today.

Wynford Murray was convicted of first-degree sexual assault of a 3-year-old child in New York in 1997. In 2006 he was convicted in Virginia of failure to register as a sex offender. In 2008 Murray was arrested in Redondo Beach, California, after a much-publicized police search for Murray, based on reports by a former girlfriend that Murray was in possession of graphic depictions of sex with infants. He was convicted of failure to register as sex offender as required by California law. In April 2009 Murray was sentenced to 25 years to life in prison under California's "three-strikes" law (see Chapter 8).

Most states and the federal government have passed laws making it a crime for convicted sex offenders like Murray to fail to register in a state's sex offender registration program. Thus, a person convicted of designated sex offenses must register in a state database in any state in which that person resides, or relocates. Many of the state laws, and the federal law making it a federal crime to travel between states without registering, were passed in the last few years. As a result, some persons, like Murray, prosecuted for failure to register as sex offenders, were convicted of sex offenses before the registration acts were passed. Many of these persons raised a constitutional challenge to their convictions, relying on the Ex Post Facto Clause in the U.S. Constitution. They contended they were being punished for actions taken before the failure-to-register crimes were enacted, making their convictions unconstitutional. These contentions raise the issue of what constitutes "punishment" for purposes of the constitutional prohibition against *ex post facto* laws. In this chapter we examine the basis for the power of states and the federal government to pass criminal laws, and the constitutional limitations on that power.

≡ Important Concepts in Criminal Law

Crime has been part of the human condition since people began to live in groups. Ancient documents indicate that conduct we now call murder, theft, or robbery was identified as criminal by civilizations that existed thousands of years ago. Criminal laws regulate human conduct and tell people what they cannot do and, in some instances, what they must do under certain circumstances. Though their content may have differed, all societies have had criminal codes regulating conduct.

Democracies have always sought to translate their basic principles and ideals into achievable goals through a system of laws that balance the rights of individuals with the compelling needs of society as a whole. These goals include public order, domestic tranquility, and protection of the basic rights of individuals.

Because governments in democracies are the servants and not the masters of the people, laws are seen as the product of the will of the people. Criminal justice systems in democracies operate most successfully when the majority of the people believe that laws are fair and that the system can operate efficiently and effectively.[1]

The issue of what laws should be enacted often causes intense public debate. Laws are enacted by elected representatives of the people. They are enforced, administered, and interpreted by civil servants and elected officials in other branches of government.

In the United States, those branches are as follows:

1. *The legislative branch:* Laws (including criminal laws) are enacted by the legislative branch. The chief executive officer participates in the legislative process by signing or vetoing proposed laws. State governors and the U.S. president provide leadership on many proposed laws by either supporting or opposing them and by providing information about proposed laws.

2. *The executive branch:* Agencies within the executive branch of government administer and enforce laws. Law enforcement agencies are found within the executive branch of government and are charged with the enforcement of criminal laws, in addition to the performance of other duties.

3. *The judicial branch:* People who are charged with crimes have a right to be tried before a judge or a jury in a court in the judicial branch of government. Fact finders

(jury or judge) determine the issues in cases presented to them, including the issue of guilt or innocence. Judges in the United States have the power of judicial review in determining the constitutionality of laws or ordinances.

In the United States each state has its own judicial system, and the federal government has its judicial system. These systems are generally independent of one another. Each state has a tier of trial courts, where jury trials take place. After a defendant has been convicted of a crime, the conviction may be appealed to the state's appellate courts. Many states have a two-tiered appellate court plan: a first tier, generally called the court of appeals, and a top tier, generally called the supreme court. Appeals of convictions for violation of criminal law proceed first in the state's appellate court system.

Once a conviction has been affirmed by the highest state court, it is usually final. However, if the defendant raises an issue about the constitutionality of the conviction, under the U.S. Constitution he or she is entitled to ask the U.S. Supreme Court to review that issue. The defendant would do so by asking the Supreme Court to issue a writ of **certiorari**, a discretionary writ issued by the Court to review the decision of a lower court. Writs of certiorari are infrequently granted. If the writ is denied, the conviction is final. Limited post-conviction review is possible under state post-conviction review laws, and through use of the writ of **habeas corpus**, discussed later in this chapter.

In the federal system, federal district courts serve as trial courts. The United States is divided into eleven judicial circuits, plus the District of Columbia Circuit and the Federal Circuit (which handles special areas such as patent law). The judicial circuits each have a court of appeals, which hears appeals from the federal district courts located in the circuit. Decisions of the circuit courts may be reviewed by the Supreme Court through the certiorari process, though here also such review occurs infrequently.

As discussed more fully later in this chapter, criminal law in the United States traces its beginnings to the criminal law and its development in England. In early England, actions we now define as crimes, such as robbery, murder, and theft, were classified as private matters. As a result, victims were responsible for remedying their own problems. Victims and their families usually responded with violence if they knew or suspected the identity of the offender. They also had the option of bringing the matter before a civil court, but such courts were few and the chances of success minimal. During the reign of Henry II (1154–1189), English law began to recognize that crime was more than a personal affair between the victim and the perpetrator and that punishment should not be left to individuals.

Today, criminal law in England and the United States is part of each nation's **public law**. The criminal law applies to all persons within each country, and it is enforced by public officials rather than the victims of criminal conduct. Apprehension and prosecution of criminals are public matters. Public law enforcement agencies, public prosecutors, courts, jails, and correctional institutions make up the criminal justice systems in both countries.

Because the same action can be a violation of the criminal law and a civil wrong known as a **tort**, victims of a crime may bring civil actions in civil courts to seek compensation from the offender. The crimes of sexual assault, battery, theft, or criminal libel are examples of actions that may be prosecuted as crimes under public law, and serve as a basis for a civil action. If the victim obtains a judgment in the civil action, the victim is responsible for collecting that judgment from the offender. The tort laws governing such a civil action are examples of private law. Private law deals with relationships between individuals in matters such as divorce, contractual issues, real estate law, and private inheritance.

Criminal law in the broadest sense refers to the many laws and statutes that define and regulate criminal conduct. These laws and statutes are called substantive criminal law. In addition, criminal law in this sense includes many rules and statutes designed to

certiorari A form of review of lower court decisions by the Supreme Court. Certiorari is discretionary with the Court, and most petitions requesting it are denied. Traditional legal doctrine is that no conclusion can be drawn from a denial of certiorari.

habeas corpus A writ that compels the authority holding a person in confinement to explain the basis for that confinement. Used frequently as a method for state and federal prisoners to attack the constitutionality of their imprisonment. Both the federal government and states have some form of a habeas corpus law, often called post-conviction relief laws.

public law Laws or statutes that apply to all people within a state or nation. Criminal laws in England and the United States are examples of public law.

Tort A noncontractual civil wrong.

set out and regulate the steps that are followed from the criminal incident through punishment and release of the offender. This part of criminal law is called criminal procedure. Many of the rights guaranteed by the U.S. Constitution in criminal investigations and prosecutions serve as limitations on the process used by the government in those investigations and prosecutions. For example, the well-known *Miranda* rule requiring police to inform a suspect of his rights at the time of arrest stems from the Fifth Amendment. The requirement that police obtain a search warrant based on probable cause is found in the Fourth Amendment; the rights to have the assistance of counsel and confront witnesses against an accused are contained in the Sixth Amendment. There are also many statutory rules in both the federal and state criminal codes regulating the procedures that must be followed in criminal investigations and prosecutions. Because of the immense scope and complexity of the criminal procedure rules and principals, it is generally treated as a subject distinct from substantive criminal law. *See, e.g.,* Gardner & Anderson, *Criminal Evidence* (7th edition, Cengage/Wadsworth Learning, 2010). Thus, while this chapter discusses many of the constitutional limitations on the power of governments to define and punish conduct, such as the Ex Post Facto Clause, or the "overbreadth doctrine," it should be remembered that a significant part of the constitutional and statutory limitations on the investigation and prosecution of criminal conduct must be learned by studying criminal procedure.

Criminology and criminalistics are fields that are separate from but related to substantive criminal law. **Criminology** is the sociological and psychological study of the causes of crime, the control of crime, and the conditions under which criminal law developed. Criminalistics is the professional and scientific discipline directed to the recognition, identification, individualization, and evaluation of physical evidence by application of the natural sciences. Criminology is a branch of sociology; criminalistics is the application of science to criminal investigation and encompasses forensic science.

criminology The sociological and psychological study of the causes, development, and control of crime, as well as the conditions under which criminal law developed.

Substantive Criminal Law

Substantive criminal law is an important branch of public law. It defines the standards of conduct that the society and the community require for the protection of the community as a whole. It establishes the standards necessary to preserve public order and to protect property rights. It seeks to protect the right of individual privacy and the right to move about freely without fear of molestation. It does this primarily by defining conduct that is unacceptable and punishable.

In ancient times and on the frontiers in America, people had to protect themselves and often moved about armed with weapons. If the law could not (or would not) punish an offender, the victim or the victim's family and friends would punish the offender themselves. Such retaliations could trigger blood feuds that went on for years between families and clans.

With the establishment of a system of laws and the growth of public confidence in the ability of the criminal justice system to preserve ordered liberty, people have generally ceased taking the law into their own hands. Public confidence that the government, as an agent of the people, has the ability and the desire to maintain public order is an indispensable ingredient of a successful criminal justice system.[2]

Not all legal wrongs come under substantive criminal law. Some legal wrongs are only civil violations. A *civil wrong* is a private wrong, such as a tort or a contract violation, done to a person or property and involves only the private individuals affected by the wrong. A *criminal wrong* is one in which the state and the public have declared an interest. Ordinarily, when a private wrong occurs, only the injured party or the party's representative may seek civil redress in a civil court of law. Nearly every large American community has three or four times as many civil courts, which hear civil cases of alleged

WHY SOME CONDUCT MAY OR MAY NOT BE DESIGNATED AS CRIMINAL

Reasons a Legislative Body Might Designate Specific Conduct as Criminal

- The conduct may be designated criminal to protect the public from violent or dangerous conduct.
- The conduct may be designated criminal to protect public health.
- The conduct may be designated criminal to maintain public order.
- The conduct may be designated criminal to protect the right of privacy of individuals.
- The conduct may be designated criminal to protect public morality.
- No other apparent way to promote a desired public policy is available.

Reasons a Legislative Body Might Not Designate Specific Conduct as Criminal

- The government does not have constitutional power to prohibit such conduct.
- The conduct in question is constitutionally protected.
- No influential public or private groups or individuals have demanded the regulation of such conduct.
- Enforcing a law criminalizing such conduct would not be economically feasible.
- Passing a law criminalizing such conduct would not be politically popular.

RIGHTS OF CRIME VICTIMS

A majority of states have amended their state constitutions to include a guarantee of rights for crime victims. This guarantee, which is often posted on courtroom doors, generally includes provisions such as the following:

- The right to notification of all court proceedings related to the offense.
- The right to be reasonably protected from the accused offender.
- The right to have input at sentencing, such as a victim impact statement.
- The right to information about the conviction, sentencing, imprisonment, and release of the offender.
- The right to an order of restitution from the offender.
- The right to notice of these rights.
- The right to enforce these rights.

Source: See FS 00301, United States Office for Victims of Crime, April 2002.

private wrongs, as criminal courts, which hear criminal cases involving public wrongs. In cases of public wrong, the state may begin a criminal action in a criminal court or take the alleged public wrong to a civil court, or both, as is done occasionally in obscenity, antitrust, or consumer fraud cases.

Criminal Law and Moral Law

Criminal laws are strongest when they reflect the moral and ethical beliefs of the society. Murder, for example, is considered morally wrong, and most people would not murder another person even if it were not forbidden by all jurisdictions in the United States. Murder, then, is forbidden not only by the criminal law but also by the moral law. This moral or ethical commitment to the law is known as the *law behind the law*. The importance of the law behind the law is that it compels most people to conform to

---

DISTINGUISHING CRIME, TORT, AND MORAL WRONG

Type of Wrong		Court Determining Wrong
Crime	A public wrong against society	Criminal court
Tort	A private wrong against an individual	Civil court or individuals
Moral wrong	Violation of a moral or religious code	No punishment unless the moral wrong is also a crime or tort

A crime may also be a tort and a moral wrong. For example, murder is a crime, a tort, and also a moral wrong.

FACTORS INFLUENCING WHETHER TO COMMIT A CRIME

Why a Person Would Not Commit a Crime	Why a Person Would Commit a Crime
Moral or ethical commitment to obey the law	Insufficient moral or ethical restraints ("law behind the law")
Fear of arrest and punishment	Belief in ability to get away without detection, arrest, and punishment
Social and peer pressures of friends, associates, family, and community	Peer pressure
Fear of embarrassment to self, family, and friends	Belief that detection and associated embarrassment can be avoided
Lack of motive or compelling drive to commit crime (no compelling desire to steal, murder, assault, rape, and so on)	Compelling desire or motive to achieve illegal objective (narcotic addiction, for example, provides motive for a person who would probably not otherwise commit a crime)
Lack of opportunity, or lack of capacity or skill, to commit crime	Opportunity combined with capacity and skill
Fear of economic sanction, such as loss of job or promotion, lawsuit and damages, or loss of license (driver's license, liquor license, credentials for lawyer, doctor, nurse, and so on)	Sees crime as a quick, easy way of obtaining money, drugs, power, or other objectives. (Even if caught, the odds are good that the person will not go to prison. Few persons convicted of nonviolent felonies go to prison.)

---

standards necessary for public order regardless of whether a police officer is watching them. Public order is not possible without the law behind the law, because not enough police officers are available to enforce criminal law without this moral and ethical backing.

The standards set by moral laws are generally higher than those set by criminal laws. Moral law attempts to perfect personal character, whereas criminal law, in general, is aimed at misbehavior that falls substantially below the norms of the community. Criminal conduct is ordinarily unjustifiable and inexcusable.

Criminal law alone cannot bring all conduct into conformity with the standards expected by the community. Society uses many sanctions besides criminal law to encourage people to behave properly. Civil law judgments, licensing regulations and revocations, loss of employment, or simple peer pressure are examples of the ways a society can use sanctions other than the criminal law to control offensive conduct.

≡ Goals and Purposes of Criminal Law

People in all societies have the inherent right to protect their society and those living in that society from acts that threaten either the society or the people. Societies throughout history have exercised this inherent right and have had either written or unwritten laws forbidding and punishing acts or omissions considered detrimental to the group or the individual.

From colonial days through World War I, the criminal codes of the various American states were generally small and usually embodied only those crimes that were considered serious wrongs against the society. Because these criminal laws were used to define and enforce public morality, the traditional attitude of lawyers and judges was that a crime was essentially a moral wrong and should primarily be enforced through family, religious, and social pressures.

The first decades of the twentieth century saw the rapid change of the United States from an agricultural society to an industrial one. This transformation, plus the unbelievable array of economic, social, and political changes that accompanied it, hastened the arrival of the mass industrial society. These changes reduced the influence of American religious institutions, the community, and the home in molding and shaping behavior (particularly of the young) to the standards expected by society. To compensate for this change, many new criminal laws were enacted. The burden of maintaining public order and public safety gradually shifted to local, state, and federal governments, so that today the U.S. criminal justice system is both large and complex and assumes a greater role in shaping conduct than ever before.

The U.S. Constitution is the supreme law of the United States. Its preamble states that the purposes of the U.S. Constitution are to "establish Justice, insure domestic Tranquility, ... promote the general Welfare, and secure the Blessings of Liberty to ourselves and our Posterity."

The U.S. Supreme Court stated that the "most basic function of any government is to provide for the security of the individual and his property," *Lanzetta v. New Jersey*, 59 S. Ct. 618 (1939).

The generally recognized goals and purposes of the criminal justice system are to

- Discourage and deter people from committing crimes
- Protect society from dangerous and harmful people
- Punish people who have committed crimes
- Rehabilitate and reform people who have committed crimes

The U.S. District Court for the District of Columbia expressed the objective and purpose of criminal law in these terms in the first-degree murder case of *United States v. Watson*:

> The object of the criminal law is to protect the public against depredations of a criminal. On the other hand, its purpose is also to prevent the conviction of the innocent, or the conviction of a person whose guilt is not established beyond a reasonable doubt. The Court must balance all these aims of the trial. This view was eloquently stated by Mr. Justice Cardozo in *Snyder v. Commonwealth of Massachusetts,* 291 U.S. 97, 122, 54 S. Ct. 330, 338, 78 L. Ed. 674: " ... [J]ustice, though due to the accused, is due to the accuser also. The concept of fairness must not be strained till it is narrowed to a filament. We are to keep the balance true."[3]

In forbidding burglary, assault, rape, robbery, and other crimes, criminal laws protect the right of privacy of individuals. The U.S. Supreme Court recognized this

Architect of the Capitol

The signing of the U.S. Constitution, the supreme law of the United States.

important function in the 1967 case of *Katz v. United States* (88 S. Ct. 507), when the Court wrote:

> The protection of a person's general right of privacy—his right to be left alone by other people—is, like the protection of his property and his very life, left largely to the laws of the individual States.

Many factors contribute to the causes and prevention of crimes. The criminal laws passed by the state and federal governments are intended to affect, and do affect, decisions by citizens to commit crimes. Other factors are also present. Statistics collected by the U.S. Bureau of Justice Statistics (BJS) show that the number of violent crimes and major property crimes committed in the United States decreased by over 30% between the years 1994 and 2004. The FBI Uniform Crime Reports, Violent Crimes report released in September, 2010, the FBI stated that violent crimes fell 5.2% from 2005 levels. In 2009 an estimated 1,318,398 violent crimes were committed, which is down 5.3% from the number of violent crimes in 2008. The BJS noted in a report titled "Cross-National Studies in Crime and Violence" (BJS, 2004) that the drop in violent crime since 1994 was due not only to more and harsher criminal laws, but also to factors such as the aging of the population, or falling unemployment rates. Declines in drug and alcohol use also played important roles in lowering the crime rates.

The Permissible Scope of Criminal Laws in the United States

Criminal laws have been used by totalitarian governments, from Hitler's Nazi Germany to the rule of the Taliban in Afghanistan, as a means to control their citizens by brute force and terror. In a government like that of the United States, criminal laws and the criminal justice system are essential parts of the democratic system, serving to strike a balance between maintaining public order and preserving basic freedoms. To prevent misuses of the criminal justice system, in the United States constitutional limits are placed on the power of government to regulate the conduct and lives of its citizens through the use of criminal laws. Some of these constitutional limitations are presented in this chapter. Other limitations are presented in Chapters 5, 6, 7 and 8 of this book.

The Use and Limitations of the Police Power to Maintain Public Order

Each state is responsible for the maintenance of public order and public safety within that state. To do this, states enact criminal laws and establish a criminal justice system under the police power of that state. The **police power** is an inherent power vested in each state. The Tenth Amendment of the U.S. Constitution provides that "[t]he powers not delegated to the United States by the Constitution, nor prohibited by it to the States, are reserved to the States respectively, or to the people."

police power The inherent power of every state and local government, subject to constitutional limits, to enact criminal laws.

The term *police power* refers to the broad legislative power of a state to pass laws that promote the public health, safety, and welfare. In the 1949 case of *Kovacs v. Cooper,* the U.S. Supreme Court stated:

> The police power of a state extends beyond health, morals and safety, and comprehends the duty, within constitutional limitations, to protect the well-being and tranquility of a community. A state or city may prohibit acts or things reasonably thought to bring evil or harm to its people.[4]

In the 1974 case of *Village of Belle Terre v. Boraas,* the U.S. Supreme Court sustained a zoning ordinance restricting land use to single-family dwellings, stating:

> The police power is not confined to elimination of filth, stench, and unhealthy places. It is ample to lay out zones where family values, youth values and the blessing of quiet seclusion, and clean air make the area a sanctuary for people.[5]

In enacting criminal laws through the use of the police power, the state is regulating the conduct of citizens within the state by telling them what they may not do or what they must do. However, the police power is not absolute. In addition to limitations placed on the police power by the U.S. Constitution or state constitutions, the state may not regulate conduct capriciously or arbitrarily.

In enacting criminal law, the state must be able to show

- A compelling public need to regulate the conduct the state seeks to regulate, and that the power to regulate is within the police power of the state. The U.S. Supreme Court held in *Lawton v. Steele* that "it must appear, first, that the interests of the public generally.... require such interference; and, that the means ... are not unduly oppressive upon individuals."[6]
- That the law does not contravene the U.S. Constitution or infringe on any of the rights granted or secured by the U.S. Constitution or the constitution of that state.
- That the language of the statute or ordinance clearly tells people what they are not to do (or what they must do) and that the law prohibits only the conduct that may be forbidden.

To understand these limitations, suppose some of the states create the following offenses as misdemeanors:

- State A enacts a law requiring that all people in the state go to a church of a specific religion every Sunday.
- State B enacts a law forbidding skateboarding.
- State C enacts a law forbidding the sale, use, or possession of any tobacco product.
- State D enacts a law requiring operators and passengers of motorcycles to wear protective headgear.[7]

Not only would State A violate First Amendment rights to the freedom of religion by passage of a law of this nature but also this statute is not within the police power of a state because it serves no valid function of government.

Regulation of skateboarding could be done by governmental units, such as cities and school districts, for public safety reasons and to minimize interference with pedestrian and motor vehicle traffic. But no compelling public need exists to completely forbid such conduct because of public health, safety, or morals; therefore, such regulations could hardly stand under attack. The right to be free from interference by government was stated as follows in 1975:

> No right is more sacred, or is more carefully guarded, by the liberty assurance of the due process clause than the right of every citizen to the possession and control of his own person, free from restraint or interference by the state. The makers of our Constitution conferred, as against the government, the right to be let alone—the most comprehensive of rights and the right most valued by civilized man.

>   * * *

> However, personal freedoms are not absolute, and the liberty guaranteed by the due process clause implies absence of arbitrary interferences but not immunity from reasonable regulations.[8]

State C could show that its regulation is within the police power of the state because medical studies show that the use of tobacco products does affect people's health. As of September 2009, 16 states have adopted a total ban on smoking, which includes public buildings, government buildings, private workplaces, child care centers, and food service centers. The other states have prohibited smoking in some but not all these locations. Enforcement of a complete ban has not been advocated by any group because it would be difficult if not impossible to enforce. A total ban on smoking could lead to the kind of lawlessness associated with attempts to outlaw alcohol in the 1920s.

☰ The Principle of "No Punishment Without a Law for It"

nulla poena sine lege
The principle of legality; no act should be made criminal or punished without advance warning in the form of legislative act.

A basic principle of both English and American law is that no one can be lawfully punished for his or her conduct or omission unless that conduct or omission has been clearly made a crime by statutory or common law of that jurisdiction. The Latin maxim **nulla poena sine lege** ("no punishment without law") long ago established this principle.

This principle, generally known as the *principle of legality*, was made part of American law in 1791 by the enactment of the Fifth Amendment of the U.S. Constitution, which provides that "No person shall be ... deprived of life, liberty, or property without due process of law."[9]

In American jurisprudence the principle of legality has two main tenets: one, it prohibits retroactive definition of criminal behavior by judicial decision, and two, it requires statutory definitions of crimes to be sufficiently clear and precise so as to enable reasonable people to understand what conduct is prohibited. By the end of the nineteenth century, it was generally accepted in this country that courts lacked the power to "create" crimes that had not previously existed under statute or common law (see later in this chapter). Most states have passed statutes similar to section 720 ILCS 5/1-3 of the Illinois Criminal Code, which states:

> Applicability of Common Law. No conduct constitutes an offense unless it is described as an offense in this Code or in another statute of this State.

The second tenet of the principle of legality requires that a statute must define criminal conduct clearly enough that people affected by the statute will receive adequate notice of the behavior prohibited. If the statute is too vague, courts might construe the statute to include conduct not reasonably understood to be prohibited, thus effectively creating a new crime. The "void for vagueness" doctrine is discussed in more detail later in this chapter.

Although the "prior notice" doctrine requires that fair warning be given in language that the ordinary person will understand, it does not require that the statute list in detail the many ways in which a forbidden wrong may be committed. The following example illustrates this:

EXAMPLE: Criminal homicide can be committed by many different unlawful acts such as using a gun, knife, poison, a crowbar, a truck, or other vehicle; pushing off a cliff or a bridge or down stairs; or strangulation. Murder statutes do not have to list the hundred or more ways of committing murder. Such statutes forbid the defined evil and clearly provide notice as to the act or acts forbidden.[10]

Therefore, in view of the principle of "no punishment without a law for it," the following questions must be asked before any person is arrested, charged with a crime, or convicted: What has the person done that violates the statutes of the state? Was the person legally (not just morally) obligated to act, and then failed to perform this legal (not moral) duty?

≡ Classifications of Crimes

Many acts have been designated as criminal offenses in the United States. The President's Commission on Crime reported in 1966 in *The Challenge of Crime in a Free Society* (p. 18) that the federal government alone has designated more than 2,800 offenses as crimes and noted that "a much larger number of State and local" offenses exist.

The large number of crimes in the United States may be classified as follows:

- According to their sources, as statutory, common law, administrative, or constitutional crimes (see later in this chapter).
- As felonies or misdemeanors, which determines the method in which they are tried and, in many states, affects the law of arrest for such offenses. Many states classify felonies and misdemeanors as class A, class B, and so forth. In this way, punishment can be standardized: a class B felony is generally a 20-year felony; a class C felony is a 10-year felony, and so on (see the following section "Felony and Misdemeanor").
- According to the harm or wrong that occurs (see individual state criminal codes for classifications of crime, such as "crimes against the person" or "crimes against property").

Felony and Misdemeanor

felony The most serious grade of crime; usually includes possibility of prison sentence.

The felony/misdemeanor classification is the most common and most important classification of crime. A **felony** is the most serious crime and generally is punished by one year or more in prison or a penitentiary. Most states and the federal government have laws providing for the death penalty for a few very serious felonies.

misdemeanor Offenses that carry punishment of a degree less than felonies. Usually misdemeanor crimes do not involve prison sentences.

A **misdemeanor** is a less serious offense and may be punished by imprisonment in the local jail or house of correction for a period of time less than a year (e.g., 30 days, 60 days, or longer lengths of time) (Figure 1.1). An offense that does not provide for possible jailing or imprisonment is generally not classified as a crime but rather as a civil offense. For example, ordinary speeding is punished by a fine and loss of points but is not a crime.

QUALITY-OF-LIFE CRIMES AND THE BROKEN WINDOW THEORY

Many veteran law enforcement officers subscribe to the broken window or quality-of-life theory of crime. This theory holds that small quality-of-life crimes will eventually encourage greater lawlessness. For example, if graffiti and broken windows are tolerated, more serious property damage and other crimes will follow. If prostitution is tolerated, other crimes will follow since prostitution often fuels illegal drug activity. With prostitution and illegal drug activity come purse snatchings, robbery, theft, burglary, and other felonies.

Law enforcement officers believe a community should be concerned and take action when the first signs of a breakdown in the quality of life appear, such as the abandoned building with broken windows, loud drunken bar patrons out on the street after closing hours, or the presence of street gangs.

WHEN FAILURE TO ACT IS A CRIME

State and federal criminal codes usually identify and prohibit specific, affirmative actions, called crimes of commission. Examples of these crimes are the prohibitions against murder, robbery, and similar crimes where the crime consists of taking defined actions.

A small percentage of crimes in criminal codes are crimes of omission—failure to act when a duty or obligation is imposed upon persons under certain circumstances. The following are examples of crimes of omission that can be found in state criminal codes. Using the statutes from your state's criminal code, find a section that defines and makes criminal the following crimes of omission.

1. Failure to report the death of a child.
2. Failure to report the location of a human corpse.
3. Failure by a parent or guardian to provide adequate food, clothing, shelter, or medical care to a child under the person's care and supervision.
4. Failure to submit to a Breathalyzer or other similar test when lawfully requested to do so by a police officer.
5. Failure of one involved in an accident to remain at the scene.
6. Homicide by omission.

Whether a crime is a felony or a misdemeanor is important for the following reasons:

1. Conviction of a felony would, in most states, stand in the way of some types of employment, affect credit rating or the ability to adopt a child, and prevent a person from entering the armed forces, becoming a law enforcement officer, or obtaining a license as a nurse, doctor, lawyer, and so on, unless a pardon is obtained.[11] A misdemeanor conviction would not ordinarily have these effects.
2. People charged with felonies have the right to a preliminary hearing or a "presentation or indictment of a grand jury."[12]
3. The law governing making an arrest for a felony differs from the law governing making an arrest for a misdemeanor in the following ways:
   a. There is broad authority for law enforcement officers to make a felony arrest; however, law enforcement officers in states using the "in presence" requirement cannot arrest for misdemeanors unless the misdemeanor is committed in their presence or unless other statutory or common law authority exists.
   b. "Citizen's arrest" is generally limited to felonies committed in the presence of the citizen unless the statutes or common law of a state provide additional authority.[13]

FIGURE 1.1 Government May Regulate Conduct by Making the Conduct Either a Criminal or a Civil Offense

[a]Felonies are punished by possible imprisonment for one year or more in state prison. Misdemeanors are punished by possible imprisonment for up to one year in a jail or a detention center. Both felonies and misdemeanors may also be punished by fines and forfeitures. Capital felonies can be punished by death in most states.
[b]Fill in maximum imprisonment in your state.

VICTIMLESS CRIMES

The term *victimless crimes* is used to designate crimes that do not directly inflict personal or property harm on another person in the sense that murder, robbery, rape, and theft do. The term is controversial when applied to crimes such as drug violations because the deadly drug trade in the United States results in many victims.

Examples of Victimless Crimes[a]

Possession or use of a small amount of a drug such as marijuana

Public drunkenness (decriminalized by many states)

Prostitution

Gambling (many forms of gambling are now legal)

Obscenity offenses involving consenting adults

Fortune-telling

Examples of Victimless Crimes that Have Been Abolished by Many States

Fornication

Adultery

Cohabitation

Examples of Crimes that Have Crimes[a] Been Declared Unconstitutional

Use of contraceptives (even by married couples)—*Griswold v. Connecticut*, 381 U.S. 479 (1965)

Drug addiction as a crime in and of itself—*Robinson v. California*, 370 U.S. 660 (1962)

Possession of or reading obscene material in privacy of one's home—*Stanley v. Georgia*, 394 U.S. 557 (1969)

Homosexual relations between consenting adults in privacy of one's home—*Lawrence v. Texas*, 123 S. Ct.2472 (2003)

[a]Some people take the position that society is the victim of many of these offenses.

≡ General Constitutional Limitations on Criminal Laws

The U.S. Supreme Court has stated that "[b]roadly speaking, crimes in the United States are what the law of the individual States make them, subject to (constitutional) limitations."[14] States, therefore, have broad authority to create criminal laws.

The authority to enact criminal laws cannot be exercised in a manner that violates the rights of persons guaranteed by the U.S. Constitution or the constitution of a state. In succeeding chapters we discuss some of these rights in detail: States cannot criminalize conduct protected by the First Amendment freedom of speech, freedom of religion, or freedom to move about freely (see Chapter 9). Nor may states impose a punishment that violates the Eighth Amendment prohibition against "cruel and unusual punishment" (see Chapter 8). Chapters 6 and 7 on defenses also present other constitutional limitations. The following materials present some of the general, constitutional limitations on criminal laws and the exercise of the police power.

Ex Post Facto Laws

ex post facto Criminal law made retroactive to punish prior conduct not criminal when done. Prohibited by Article I, Sections 9 and 10, of the Constitution.

Article I, Sections 9 and 10, of the U.S. Constitution forbid the U.S. Congress and all states from enacting "**ex post facto**" (after the fact) laws. Therefore, no state or the U.S. Congress can create a new crime in November and make the law retroactive so as to punish conduct that was lawful in September or October of that year. Most state constitutions also forbid ex post facto laws. Ex post facto restrictions apply only to criminal laws and not to civil laws such as tax laws. The ex post facto restriction also only limits the power of state and federal legislative bodies; it does not apply to the judicial branch of government. See U.S. Supreme Court case of *Rogers v. Tennessee*, 532 U.S. 451 (2001).

The Ex Post Facto Clause forbids the following:

1. Creating a criminal law and making it retroactive so as to make conduct before the enactment of the law a criminal violation.
2. Laws that aggravate a crime retroactively (e.g., making a misdemeanor a felony as of a date six months before the enactment of the legislation).
3. Laws that increase the punishment for a crime retroactively.
4. Laws that alter the legal rules of evidence and permit conviction on less or different evidence than the law required at the time of the commission of the offense.[15]

The Ex Post Facto Clause does not necessarily apply every time a statute incorporates past behavior into a new designation of criminal conduct. For example, in 1996 Congress enacted the Domestic Violence Offender Gun Act, which amended the 1968 Federal Gun Control Act, 18 U.S.C. § 921. The 1968 Act prohibited convicted felons from owning or possessing firearms. The 1996 amendment made it a violation of the Act for any person convicted of a "misdemeanor crime involving domestic violence" to own or possess a firearm. A person convicted of a domestic violence misdemeanor in 1990, for example, could lawfully possess a firearm prior to the 1996 amendment. After 1996, however, that same person could be convicted under the amended Act. This is not an Ex Post Facto Clause problem because the amendment did not make past conduct criminal; rather, it provides that the future action of possessing a firearm after the amendment's effective date by persons convicted of misdemeanor domestic violence crimes is now a crime. Since people are presumed to know the law, those affected by the amendment were under a duty to avoid ownership or possession of firearms after the Act became applicable to them. The U.S. Supreme Court considered the meaning and applicability of the

Domestic Violence Offender Gun Ban in *United States v. Hayes*, 129 S. Ct. 1079 (2009), discussed in chapter 11.

The applicability of the Ex Post Facto Clause to statutes of limitation was discussed by the U.S. Supreme Court in the 2003 case of *Stogner v. California*, 123 S. Ct. 2446. Most crimes, except murder and some other violent crimes, have limitation periods for prosecution. If prosecution does not occur during the statutory period, it is barred. Courts have often held that the Ex Post Facto Clause does not prevent a state from increasing the limitation period for future offenses, or offenses that were not time-barred when the increased limitation period became law. Thus, an offender who committed a crime that had a 5-year limitation period when committed cannot raise an ex post facto objection if the legislature increases the limitations period to 10 years during the initial 5 years after the crime was committed. In *Stogner,* the California legislature increased the limitation period for sexual crimes committed against children and expressly made the increased period applicable to offenses that had become time-barred under existing limitation periods prior to the time the statute increasing the limitation was adopted. The Supreme Court held the statute unconstitutional under the second part of the test, concluding the statute aggravated the crime of sexual assault retroactively.

In order to run afoul of the Ex Post Facto Clause a statute must have the effect of retroactively "punishing" an offender. When is a law "penal" and subject to the Ex Post Facto Clause? In the 2003 case of *Smith v. Doe*, 538 U.S. 84, the U.S. Supreme Court held that the Alaska Sex Offender Registration Act (so-called Megan's Law, see Chapter 12) was not punitive in nature, and thus the ex post facto limitations did not apply. The defendants contended that because they committed their crimes before the act was passed, its registration requirements could not be applied to them. The Supreme Court disagreed. Because the act was intended by the Alaska legislature to set up an administrative system to track sex offenders, the Court held it was civil and nonpunitive in nature. Though the act did contain information about sex offenders that might "taint" those forced to register, the Court held such forced registration was not a penal law because the information was already a matter of public record.

Bill of Attainder

bill of attainder
Legislative act that inflicts punishment without trial; prohibited by Article I, Sections 9 and 10, of the Constitution.

Article I, Sections 9 and 10, of the U.S. Constitution also forbid Congress and the states from enacting any bill of attainder. A **bill of attainder** is a legislative act that inflicts punishment without the person (defendant) already having had a trial in a court before a judge. In 1965, the U.S. Supreme Court stated the history of the bill of attainder in *United States v. Brown*, 381 U.S. 437:

The bill of attainder, a parliamentary act sentencing to death one or more specific persons, was a device often resorted to in sixteenth-, seventeenth-, and eighteenth-century England for dealing with persons who had attempted, or threatened to attempt, to overthrow the government. In addition to the death sentence, attainder generally carried with it a "corruption of blood," which meant that the attained party's heirs could not inherit his property. The "bill of pains and penalties" was identical to the bill of attainder, except that it prescribed a penalty short of death, e.g., banishment, deprivation of the right to vote, or exclusion of the designated party's sons from Parliament. Most bills of attainder and bills of pains and penalties named the parties to whom they were to apply; a few, however, simply described them.

A contemporary example of a bill of attainder is the congressional act declared unconstitutional in *Foretich v. United States*, 351 F.3d 1198 (D.C. Cir. 2003). In a child

IS SORNA "PUNITIVE" WHEN APPLIED TO JUVENILE OFFENDERS?

After Congress passed the Sexual Offender Registration and Notification Act, 42 U.S.C. §16901 (SORNA) in 2006, young persons charged with sexual offenses and adjudicated delinquents under the Federal Juvenile Delinquency Act, 18 U.S.C. §5031 can be required to register as sex offenders. In *United States v. Juvenile Male*, 590 F.3d 924 (9th Cir. 2010) a district court ordered a juvenile to register as a sex offender under SORNA based on sexual offenses committed prior to the adoption of SORNA, and for which the juvenile was adjudicated a delinquent under the federal act. The juvenile appealed the decision, contending that SORNA as applied to him was a violation of the Ex Post Facto Clause, because the registration requirement was retroactive punishment. The Ninth Circuit Court agreed, and held that SORNA's registration requirement for juvenile offenders violated the Ex Post Facto Clause.

Can this case be distinguished from the holding in *Smith v. Doe*, the U.S. Supreme Court case discussed earlier in this chapter? Does sex offender registration present different issues for juvenile as opposed to adult offenders, as the Ninth Circuit concluded? Should other courts reach similar decisions in juvenile registration cases? In February 2010, the United States filed an application for certiorari in the Supreme Court, seeking review of the Ninth Circuit's decision. The Supreme Court granted the application for certiorari, but rather than deciding the issue raised, it certified a question to the Montana Supreme Court on the continued necessity of the juvenile's registration requirement under the Montana registration law. The Court reserved judgment on the ex post facto issue because it may have been rendered moot by the juvenile's completion of his supervision sentence. See *United States v. Juvenile Male*, 2010 WL 2243707.

In a related case under the federal SORNA statute, the U.S. Supreme Court in 2010 held that a defendant who was convicted of a criminal sexual offense and who traveled in interstate commerce, both of which occurred before SORNA was passed, could not be convicted of failing to register as a sex offender. SORNA states that any convicted sex offender who travels in interstate commerce must register under applicable state sex offender laws. Failure to do so is a federal offense. The defendant traveled to a new state without registering, but did so before SORNA was passed. The Court found the Act inapplicable and reversed the conviction because SORNA by its terms only applied to sex offenders who traveled in interstate commerce after the Act was passed. The Court therefore did not resolve any ex post facto issues raised by a conviction under SORNA for failure to register based on a pre-2006 sex offender conviction. See *Carr v. United States*, 2010 WL 2160783 (June 1, 2010).

custody case that received national attention Dr. Foretich and his ex-wife Dr. Morgan fought over custody of their daughter. Dr. Morgan persistently ignored court orders to allow Dr. Foretich visitation rights, based on her unproved claims Dr. Foretich was guilty of criminal sexual abuse of their daughter. Because of her refusal to obey court orders, Dr. Morgan served over 2 years in jail for contempt of court, and ultimately fled the country with her daughter to New Zealand to avoid visitation rights. Congress then passed the Elizabeth Morgan Act, which severely limited the visitation rights of any parent where a child "asserts that [the parent] has been sexually abusive with the child." When Dr. Foretich challenged the Act as an unconstitutional bill of attainder, the Court of Appeals for the District of Columbia agreed with him. It held that Congress singled out Dr. Foretich for legislative punishment based on the judgment of Congress that he had committed criminal acts of child abuse. That determination violated the bill of attainder clause, the court held.

In forbidding bills of attainder, the U.S. Constitution and state constitutions limit legislatures to the task of writing laws (rule making). Persons charged with a crime must be brought before a court to determine guilt or innocence.

The Second Amendment and Gun Control

Before 2008 it was unclear whether the Second Amendment to the U. S. Constitution created an individual right to "bear arms," or if it only recognized a "public" right to keep an armed militia. However, in *District of Columbia v. Heller*, 128 S. Ct. 2783 (2008) the Supreme Court held that the Second Amendment protected an individual's right to own and possess firearms, at least as applied to federal criminal laws. As a result, the Court held that the District of Columbia's prohibition on gun ownership must comply with the Second Amendment's right to bear arms. The *Heller* case and the limits placed on federal gun control laws are discussed in more detail in Chapter 9, as is the opinion of the U.S. Supreme Court in the case of *McDonald v. City of Chicago*, 2010 WL 2555188 (2010) on the applicability of the Second Amendment to state laws.

Due Process, "Void for Vagueness," and the "Overbreadth" Doctrine

due process The constitutional guarantee that criminal arrests and trials must meet certain minimum standards of fairness (procedural due process) and that laws not violate constitutional rights (substantive due process).

The Due Process Clause of the Fourteenth Amendment prohibits a state from depriving a person of life, liberty, or property without **due process** of law. In some situations, the Due Process Clause works to prohibit a state from making protected conduct criminal.

For example, it is clear a state could not make it a crime for a person to leave the state, because the right to travel is a protected right. A state could make leaving the state an offense if it aggravated some other crime, such as abandonment of a child. See *Jones v. Helms*, 452 U.S. 412 (1981). In 2003 the U.S. Supreme Court applied the Due Process Clause to invalidate a Texas sodomy statute. In *Lawrence v. Texas*, 123 S. Ct. 2472, two adult men were convicted of engaging in homosexual conduct in the privacy of their home. The Texas statute provided: "A person commits an offense if he engages in deviate sexual intercourse with another individual of the same sex." The statute defined "deviate" sexual intercourse as including contact between genitals of one person and the mouth or anus of another. The Court held the statute violated the Due Process Clause because it deprived the defendants of their liberty interest under the Fourteenth Amendment: "The State cannot demean their existence or control their destiny by making their private sexual conduct a crime. Their right to Liberty under the Due Process Clause gives them the full right to engage in their conduct without intervention of the government." In doing so, the Court reversed the decision reached in *Bowers v. Hardwick*, 478 U.S. 186 (1986), which upheld a Georgia sodomy statute.

"void for vagueness" doctrine The constitutional law doctrine that invalidates criminal laws written in such a manner as to make it unreasonably difficult for a defendant to know whether or not conduct is prohibited by the law.

In writing a criminal statute or ordinance, the Due Process Clause of the U.S. Constitution also requires that a legislative body must use clear and precise language that gives fair and adequate notice of the conduct that is forbidden or required. If the language of a statute or ordinance is vague, it may be held unconstitutional under the **"void for vagueness" doctrine**.

The "void for vagueness" test asks whether a statute or ordinance on its face or as applied to a particular defendant "is so vague that men of common intelligence must guess at its meaning and differ as to its application."[16] A vague criminal statute or ordinance creates uncertainty as to what the law requires and may have some or all of the following results:

1. It may trap those who desire to be law-abiding by not providing fair notice of what is prohibited.[17]
2. It may cause arbitrary and discriminatory enforcement because those who enforce and apply the law have no clear and explicit standards to guide them.[18]
3. When a vague statute "abut(s) upon sensitive areas of First Amendment freedoms, it operates to inhibit the exercise of (those) freedoms. Uncertain meaning inevitably leads citizens to steer far wider of the unlawful zone ... than if the boundaries of the forbidden areas were clearly marked."[19]

A case illustrating the "void for vagueness" doctrine is *Washoe County, Nev. Sheriff v. Burdg,* 59 P.3d 484 (Nev. 2002), *cert. denied* 123 S. Ct. 2279 (2003). In *Burdg,* a Nevada statute made it illegal to "possess a majority of the ingredients required to manufacture or compound a controlled substance other than marijuana." The Nevada Supreme Court held the statute was unconstitutionally vague because it failed to specify what constituted "ingredients," encouraged arbitrary enforcement, and was incapable of any valid application.

"overbreadth" doctrine
The constitutional law doctrine that invalidates laws that regulate conduct so broadly as to interfere with individual freedoms.

Criminal statutes and ordinances may also be held to be unconstitutional if the manner in which they are written violates the **"overbreadth" doctrine**. In 1967, the U.S. Supreme Court stated that overbreadth "offends [when the words of a statute or ordinance] ... sweep unnecessarily broadly and thereby invade the area of protected freedoms."[20] A vague statute or ordinance may be overbroad if its uncertain boundaries leave open the possibility of punishment for protected conduct and thus lead people to avoid such protected activity in order to steer clear of violating the uncertain law.[21] However, a clear and precise statute may also be overbroad if it prohibits constitutionally protected conduct.

The "void for vagueness" test and the "overbreadth" test are separate and distinct. However, when First Amendment rights are at issue, the U.S. Supreme Court uses the two tests in a manner that makes them virtually one doctrine. From the cases, it can be stated that statutes and ordinances that regulate conduct must comply with the following requirements:[22]

- Fair and adequate notice must be given of the conduct that is forbidden or required.
- A precise standard of conduct must be specified in terms of results that can reasonably be expected.
- The statute or ordinance cannot permit or encourage arbitrary and discriminatory law enforcement that may result in erratic and arbitrary arrests and convictions.
- The statute or ordinance cannot violate or infringe on rights that are secured or granted by the U.S. Constitution.

Status Crimes

A state may regulate and control the use of such drugs as heroin, cocaine, and crack in a number of ways. The government may and does forbid the importing or manufacturing of the drugs; the law forbids possession and transportation of the forbidden drugs; the sale, use, or possession of such drugs is also forbidden. All of these specific acts (conduct) have been determined to be harmful to others or to the society as a whole. But can a state make addiction to heroin, cocaine, or crack, by itself, a crime?

To do something about its increasing heroin problem in the late 1950s, California passed a law making heroin addiction, by itself, a crime. The issue before the U.S. Supreme Court in the 1962 case of *Robinson v. California* was whether a person could be arrested and convicted for what he or she is or was.[23] The U.S. Supreme Court considered the question of whether a state could make a **"status"** or a "chronic condition" a crime in itself.

status crime Criminal laws that punish a status, such as drug addiction, with no act requirement.

In pointing out the many ways in which government may legitimately attack the evils of narcotics trafficking, the U.S. Supreme Court reversed the defendant's conviction.

In holding that a state law that made the "status" of narcotic addiction a criminal offense for which an offender might be prosecuted and imprisoned at any time, the Court held that such a criminal statute inflicted a "cruel and unusual punishment" in violation of the Eighth and Fourteenth Amendments of the U.S. Constitution. The Court stated that "even one day in prison would be a cruel and unusual punishment for the 'crime'

CASE CLOSE-UP

United States v. Stevens
United States Supreme Court
2010 WL 1540082 (April 20, 2010)

Defendant Stevens was charged with violation of 18 U.S.C. §48, which makes it a crime for anyone who knowingly "creates, sells, or possesses a depiction of animal cruelty" if done for commercial gain. A depiction of animal cruelty is defined in the act as one "in which a living animal is intentionally maimed, mutilated, tortured, wounded, or killed" if the act violates state or federal law. The legislative history of the statute makes it clear Congress was intending to punish those who create, sell or possess so-called "crush videos," where women are filmed while crushing small animals such as cats, monkeys, or mice with either their bare feet or wearing high heels. Such videos were often accompanied by the sounds of anguish emitted by the animals, or dominatrix patter by the women.

Stevens was convicted of violating §48 based on sales he made of videos showing pit bull dogfights, and attacks made by pit bulls on other animals. The trial court dismissed Stevens's claim that the statute violated the First Amendment, holding that depictions defined in §48, just as in the case of child pornography and obscenity, were not protected by the First Amendment. On appeal, the Third Circuit Court of Appeals reversed the conviction, holding that the conduct covered by §48 was covered by the First Amendment. It then held that the statute could not survive a First Amendment strict scrutiny analysis because it regulated content-based speech, was not narrowly tailored, and lacked a compelling governmental interest. It concluded the statute was unconstitutional.

On appeal, the Supreme Court affirmed. It rejected the government's argument that animal cruelty depictions should be treated the same as child pornography, and not protected by the First Amendment. [See the discussion of United States v. Williams, 553 U.S. 285 (2008), where the Court declined to apply the overbreadth doctrine to a child pornography statute. That case is discussed in Chapter 12., pages 337–339] The Court decided the case based on the "overbreadth" doctrine. The Court stated that Stevens's objection to the statute was based on its "facial" overbreadth, that is, that the statute as written can be applied to conduct that is clearly lawful and ordinary, and by making such conduct a crime violates the overbreadth doctrine. The Court agreed, noting that under the statute a depiction of any "killing" or "wounding" of an animal would be a violation, so long as the conduct was unlawful in the state where the sale or possession of the depiction occurred. The statute does not require that such "killing" or "wounding" be done cruelly. As a result, the Court said, the statute would make criminal the "humane slaughter" of a stolen cow, or a video depicting killing an animal during recreational hunting that was legal in the state where the killing occurred, but illegal where the depiction was sold or possessed. The United States argued that prosecutions would be limited to "crush" video depictions, noting that President Clinton issued a signing statement when he signed the bill into law that prosecutions should be limited to depictions of wanton cruelty to animals to appeal to prurient interests in sex. The Court rejected that argument, stating that notwithstanding the signing statement, here the prosecution was based on depictions that had no prurient sexual connotations. Because lawful, protected conduct could be made criminal under the terms of the statute, the overbreadth doctrine rendered the statute unconstitutional. The Court did suggest that a statute properly limited to apply to "crush" videos might pass constitutional muster.

"VOID FOR VAGUENESS" AND "OVERBREADTH" DOCTRINES

The Due Process Clause of the U.S. Constitution, made binding on states by the Fourteenth Amendment, requires that criminal legislation clearly identify prohibited conduct so as to give a reasonable person fair notice of that conduct. A criminal statute written so broadly as to invade the area of constitutionally protected rights, like free speech, is unconstitutional under the "overbreadth" doctrine. The following are representative cases on the "void for vagueness" and "overbreadth" doctrines.

Vagueness

Coates v. City of Cincinnati Supreme Court of the United States 402 U.S. 611 (1971)

Ordinance made it illegal for three or more people gathered on a sidewalk to "annoy" passersby. Because what annoys one person may not annoy another, the Court held that "[t]hus the ordinance is vague ... in the sense that no conduct is specified at all."

Papachristou v. City of Jacksonville Supreme Court of the United States 405 U.S. 156 (1972)

Ordinance making being a "vagrant" a crime and defining vagrants as "rogues and vagabonds," "dissolute persons," or "common night walkers" held unconstitutional. The ordinance did not give fair notice of prohibited conduct.

Warren v. State Florida Supreme Court 572 So.2d 1376 (1991)

Statute making it a crime to keep a "house of ill fame" unconstitutionally vague.

State v. Lara Kansas Court of Appeals 853 P.2d 1168 (1993)

Statute making criminal "excessive and unusual" motor vehicle noises held not void for vagueness.

State v. Bohannon Washington Court of Appeals 814 P.2d 694 (1991)

Statute making it a crime for causing a minor to engage in "sexually explicit conduct" held not void for vagueness.

Overbreadth

City of Houston v. Hill Supreme Court of the United States 482 U.S. 451 (1987)

Ordinance making it unlawful to "interrupt policeman in execution of his duty" held overbroad, because it made otherwise protected speech a violation of the ordinance. (A citizen who interrupted a police officer to tell the officer of a bank robbery could lawfully be arrested under this ordinance.)

---

of having a common cold." In the 1968 case of *Powell v. Texas,* the defendant was an alcoholic with approximately 100 arrests for acts of public intoxication.[24] In this case, the defendant argued that because he was compelled to drink and because he could not control his "status," the state did not have the power to punish him for his acts of public intoxication.

The U.S. Supreme Court, however, affirmed Powell's conviction, holding that he was arrested and convicted for what he did (being drunk in a public place) and that Powell was not convicted for what he was (status). In refusing to extend the rule of law that had been established in the case of *Robinson v. California,* the Supreme Court held:

Traditional common-law concepts of personal accountability and essential considerations of federalism lead us to disagree with appellant. We are unable to conclude, on the state of this record or on the current state of medical knowledge, that chronic alcoholics in general, and Leroy Powell in particular, suffer from such an irresistible compulsion to drink and to get drunk in public that they are utterly unable to control their performance of either or both of these acts and thus cannot be deterred at all from public intoxication.

Application of the "status" versus "acts" distinction of *Robinson* and *Powell* has been difficult. In *Jones v. City of Los* Angeles, 444 F.3d 1118 (9th Cir. 2006), *vacated based on settlement agreement* 505 F.3d 1006 (2007), the Ninth Circuit Court of Appeals held that a Los Angeles ordinance making it a crime for a homeless person to sleep or lie in a public street or sidewalk violated the Cruel and Unusual Punishment Clause. The city argued that *Powell* applied, because the ordinance punished the act of sleeping on a public street, not the status of being homeless. The Court rejected that argument, finding that because the city or other sources did not provide adequate shelter for the homeless, they had no choice but to sleep in public places. As a result, the ordinance punished their status as homeless people, not their voluntary actions.

Equal Protection of the Laws

If a state made the crime of burglary in that state applicable only to males, the first man charged with burglary in that state would challenge the statute, arguing that it violated the Fourteenth Amendment requirement of "equal protection of the laws." Women could commit burglary in that state, but for the same conduct a man could be convicted and sent to jail.

The Equal Protection Clause of the Fourteenth Amendment requires that states must treat all people alike, not only in enacting criminal and civil laws but also in enforcing rules. For example, probably all states have consanguinity laws forbidding marriages between brothers and sisters and other close relatives. Consanguinity laws apply to all persons, regardless of status, race, or religion.[25] They represent a valid exercise of the police power of a state because children born to closely related parents are more apt to have abnormalities.

But can a state make it a crime for blacks to marry whites, or for people of different races to live together? In the early 1960s, some states had such laws, which forbade marriage between persons of different races (miscegenation laws).[26] The following is a famous case that came before the U.S. Supreme Court and which involved the challenge to convictions under a Virginia miscegenation law.

Loving v. Virginia

Supreme Court of the United States (1967) 388 U.S. 1, 87 S. Ct.1817

Richard Loving, a white man, and Mildred Jeter, a black woman, were lawfully married in Washington, D.C. They then moved to the state of Virginia, which forbade interracial marriages. The Lovings were criminally indicted and pleaded guilty to the charges. They were sentenced to one year in jail. However, the trial judge suspended the sentence on the condition that the Lovings leave Virginia and not return for 25 years. The convictions and sentences were appealed to the U.S. Supreme Court. The Court noted that "Virginia is one of 16 States which prohibit and punish marriages on the basis of racial classifications." In declaring such laws unconstitutional, the U.S. Supreme Court held:

These statutes ... deprive the Lovings of liberty without due process of law in violation of the Due Process Clause of the Fourteenth Amendment. The freedom to marry

> *has long been recognized as one of the vital personal rights essential to the orderly pursuit of happiness by free men.*
>
> *Marriage is one of the "basic civil rights of man," fundamental to our very existence and survival.... To deny this fundamental freedom on so unsupportable a basis as the racial classifications embodied in these statutes, classifications so directly subversive of the principle of equality at the heart of the Fourteenth Amendment, is surely to deprive all the State's citizens of liberty without due process of law. The Fourteenth Amendment requires that the freedom of choice to marry not be restricted by invidious racial discriminations. Under our Constitution, the freedom to marry or not marry a person of another race resides with the individual and cannot be infringed by the State.*
>
> On June 12, 2007, Mildred Jeter Loving made this statement marking the 40th anniversary of the Supreme Court's decision:
>
> Surrounded as I am now by wonderful children and grandchildren, not a day goes by that I don't think of Richard and our love, our right to marry, and how much it meant to me to have that freedom to marry the person precious to me, even if others thought he was 'the wrong kind of person' for me to marry. I believe all Americans, no matter their race, no matter their sex, no matter their sexual orientation, should have the same freedom to marry.
>
> Richard Loving died in 1975, killed by a drunk driver. Mildred died in 2008.

≡ Sources of Criminal Law

Substantive criminal law can be found in the following sources, each of which is discussed in the next sections:

- Criminal law, on rare occasions, can be found today in the common law of some states.
- Most criminal law is found in the statutes of each state and in the statutes of the federal government.
- Criminal law can also be found in commercial, sanitation, health, financial, and tax administrative regulations that have criminal sanctions. These regulations are enacted by state and federal administrative and regulatory agencies.
- A few sections of state constitutions and one section of the U.S. Constitution contain criminal law. Treason is the only crime defined by the U.S. Constitution. For material on treason, see Chapter 17 on terrorism.

Common Law Crimes

common law The earliest type of law. Common law was created by judges based on custom, usages, and moral concepts of the people. Most law today is statutory law enacted by legislative bodies.

Because the **common law** was the first and earliest source of criminal law, it is presented first here. And because the historic source of U.S. criminal law lies in the common law of England, a review of the development of criminal law in England and in the American colonies is necessary.

When the English kings gained control of the whole of England in the Middle Ages, royal judges began deciding civil and criminal cases throughout all of England, thus supporting the Crown by preserving the peace and dispensing justice. Few people in those days could read or write, and England was not a democracy. The king, the judges, and the ecclesiastical authorities played important roles not only in creating (sometimes inventing) criminal laws but also in defining the elements and the scope of the criminal offenses. Judges became familiar with the general customs, usages, and moral concepts of the people and based judgments on them. In doing so, the judges determined which customs and moral concepts should prevail as law.

common law crime
Crime created by
judges.

By the early 1600s, with only a few criminal statutes, the criminal law of England was composed primarily of the mandatory rules of conduct laid down by the English judges. In formulating the **common law crimes** of England, the royal judges believed that their decisions represented the best interests of the king and of the country as a whole. These decisions became the common law of England. As authoritative precedents, they were followed and applied in future cases wherever English common law was used and followed.

During this period of development of the criminal law in England, the English Parliament enacted a few criminal statutes, such as embezzlement, false pretense, and incest. The English ecclesiastical courts (religious courts) both defined and punished offenses, such as private acts of fornication, adultery, and seduction, that were held to be violations of the moral code, but were not public offenses. The English settlers who began colonizing North America in the early 1600s brought with them the English common law. This formed the basis of the law in each of the individual colonies. Modifications and adjustments were made to meet the needs of each colony. A great deal of discretion was vested in colonial governors, councils, and judges with respect to the enforcement and scope of offenses and with respect to the creation of new laws. However, for the most part, English common law crimes continued as the common law crimes in each of the American colonies.

During the American Revolution and for some time after it, a great deal of hostility was directed toward the English in America; this hostility extended to the common law. Justice Hugo L. Black of the U.S. Supreme Court referred to this situation in his 1958 dissenting opinion in *Green v. United States,* in which he stated:

> Those who formed the Constitution struck out anew free of previous shackles in an effort to obtain a better order of government more congenial to human liberty and welfare. It cannot be seriously claimed that they intended to adopt the common law wholesale. They accepted those portions of it which were adapted to this country and conformed to the ideals of its citizens and rejected the remainder. In truth, there was widespread hostility to the common law in general and profound opposition to its adoption into our jurisdiction from the commencement of the Revolutionary War until long after the Constitution was ratified.[27]

American lawyers and judges knew the value of many of the English common law principles, which at that point had been developing for more than 200 years. But the public wanted American law for Americans, and many changes were thus made by the new state legislative bodies, which transformed English common law into statutory law.

Common Law Crimes in the U.S. Federal Courts In 1812, the case of *United States v. Hudson and Goodwin* came before the U.S. Supreme Court.[28] The defendants were charged with the common law crime of criminal libel because they wrote in a newspaper that the president of the United States and the Congress had secretly voted to give $2 million as a present to Napoleon Bonaparte. No federal statute made libel a crime, but criminal libel was a common law crime.

The Supreme Court pointed out that state courts could punish a person for a violation of the common law crime of libel under their police power if they chose to adopt and incorporate the offense as part of the crimes of that state. But the Supreme Court held that federal courts had only that power and jurisdiction given to them by the U.S. Constitution and the Congress and had no power to adopt common law crimes. The rule that there are no federal common law crimes has since been affirmed many times over the years. In 1949, Justice Robert H. Jackson wrote that "it is well and wisely settled that

IMPORTANT DOCUMENTS OF THE ENGLISH-SPEAKING WORLD

Magna Carta, 1215 A civil war in England forced King John to sign the **Magna Carta** ("great document"), which provided:

- There will be no criminal "trial upon … simple accusation without producing credible witnesses to the truth therein."
- "No freeman shall be taken, imprisoned … except by lawful judgment of his peers or the law of the land."

The signing of Magna Carta in 1215 was the first step toward democracy in England, because it was the first time that a king relinquished some of his power to the people. Until Magna Carta, English kings ruled with almost absolute power under the concept of "divine right of kings," and the people had only the little freedom the kings chose to give them.

The writ of habeas corpus developed in English common law to protect the new rights of English people under Magna Carta. In 1679, the English Parliament enacted the first habeas corpus statute. The U.S. Constitution of 1788 guarantees and protects the writ of habeas corpus in Article I, Section 9. All of the original 13 states guaranteed the writ in their original constitutions. Today, people who believe they are being illegally detained can use the writ of habeas corpus to challenge their imprisonment.

Mayflower Compact, 1620 As the Mayflower rode at anchor off Cape Cod, some of the passengers threatened to go out on their own, without any framework of government. To avoid this threat of anarchy, the Mayflower Compact agreed that "We … doe … solemnly and mutually … covenant and combine our selves together into a civil body politike for our better ordering and preservation … and by vertue hereof to enact … such just and equal laws … unto which we promise all due submission and obedience."

English Bill of Rights, 1689 Because of numerous attacks on personal liberty, the English Parliament forced King James II to abdicate, and Parliament produced a Bill of Rights. This document served as a guide for Americans and provided:

Magna Carta The document signed by King John in 1215 giving certain rights to his nobles. Successive kings affirmed this charter before Parliament.

there can be no judge-made offenses against the United States and that every federal prosecution must be sustained by statutory authority."[29]

Common Law Crimes in State Courts   Many states have abolished criminal common law crimes, but all states have continued to use common law rules of criminal procedure. Some states, however, have not abolished common law crimes and continue to allow prosecution for common law crimes. In those states, prosecution is rare and not often successful.

For example, Dr. Jack Kevorkian, the medical doctor who championed assisted suicides, was charged in Michigan with the common law crime of assisting two suicides. Angry over being charged with an "unwritten" law, Dr. Kevorkian shouted a number of times in court during his trial, "This is not a trial! This is a lynching! There is no law! No law!" The jury acquitted Dr. Kevorkian of the common law charges. (Later, using the Michigan criminal code, Dr. Kevorkian was charged and convicted of murder in 1999 and sentenced to 10 to 25 years in prison. He was paroled in 2007.)

Because of the difficulties and limited success of prosecuting for common law crimes, prosecutors use the modern statutory crimes that are available in the criminal codes of their state.

- "Suspending laws … without consent of Parliament is illegal"
- "Keeping a Standing Army within the Kingdom in Time of Peace unless it be with Consent of Parliament is against the law"
- "Election of Members of Parliament ought to be free"
- "Freedom of Speech … ought not to be impeached or questioned."

Declaration of Independence, July 4, 1776 After King George declared the American colonies to be in a state of rebellion and the English Parliament forbade all trade with the colonies, an eloquent statement of the American democratic creed was made in the Declaration of Independence:

> *We hold these truths to be self-evident, that all men are created equal, that they are endowed by their Creator with certain unalienable Rights, that among these are Life, Liberty and the pursuit of Happiness.—That to secure these rights, Governments are instituted among Men, deriving their just powers from the consent of the governed,—That whenever any Form of Government becomes destructive of these ends, it is the Right of the People to alter or to abolish it, and to institute new Government, laying its foundation on such principles and organizing its powers in such form, as to them shall seem most likely to effect their Safety and Happiness.*

U.S. Constitution, ratified 1788 Because of the failure to achieve a workable government under the Articles of Confederation, delegates from the American states met in Philadelphia in 1787. George Washington presided for months over the debates and arguments that led to the adoption and ratification of the Constitution that has been used by the United States since that time.

The Bill of Rights The first ten amendments were made part of the U.S. Constitution in 1791. See the appendix of this book for applicable sections of the U.S. Constitution.

Statutory and Administrative Crimes

After the American Revolution, the new state legislatures began converting common law crimes to statutory form. Through the police power of the state, they had the power to amend, affirm, change, extend, abolish, modify, or alter any common law crime or rule.

In many instances, state legislatures kept the common law crime intact by merely restating the law in statutory form. In other instances, legislatures created new crimes by forbidding and punishing conduct that was not a crime in common law. In still other instances, they redefined the common law crime by changing elements of the crime or removing common law limitations and extending the crime to cover conduct not included in the common law crime. If the common law punishment was considered too severe, changes were made in the degree or form of punishment. Attempts were made to clarify areas of doubt or uncertainty in common law crimes.

Practically all criminal laws that are enforced today are statutory laws enacted by legislative bodies. Many of today's statutory crimes were unknown in common law. Most of these criminal laws were enacted to meet the problems of a mass industrial society.

In the early twentieth century Congress began passing laws creating administrative agencies whose responsibility was to adopt and enforce regulations to further the purposes of federal laws. Some of the regulations adopted could be enforce by the imposition of criminal penalties, the question of the authority of administrative agencies to make criminal laws was raised. In 1911, that issue came before the U.S. Supreme Court in the case of *United States v. Grimaud*.[30] Congress had passed a statute authorizing the secretary of agriculture to make regulations to preserve and maintain government forests as forest reserves. Congress made violation of these regulations a criminal offense. The defendant (Grimaud) had continued to graze his sheep on U.S. forest lands without obtaining permits as required under the new regulations. Because the federal courts were divided on the question of whether a violation of such regulations constituted a crime, the government appealed the case to the U.S. Supreme Court.

The Supreme Court held that Congress may constitutionally delegate to an administrative agency the power to make regulations that are enforced by criminal penalties established by that legislative body. The Court stated that the secretary of agriculture did not exercise the legislative power of declaring the penalty or fixing the punishment for grazing sheep without a permit, but the punishment is imposed by the act itself. The offense is not against the secretary but, as the indictment properly concludes, is "contrary to the laws of the United States and the peace and dignity thereof."

Today, established practice allows Congress and most state legislatures to delegate to an administrative agency the power to make rules, and the legislature may provide by statute that such rules may be enforced by criminal penalties. In a few states, this procedure has been held to be unconstitutional. But in the majority of states, criminal laws may be created by the legislature establishing the framework and by the administrative agency providing the specific regulation or rule within that framework. The delegation of such authority is constitutional in the majority of the states if

administrative crime
Crime created by government administrative agencies under specific authority and guidelines granted to the regulatory or administrative agency by law of that state or the federal government.

- The legislative act sets forth sufficient standards to guide the administrative agency, and the act provides for criminal penalties for the violation of the administrative regulations created within the guidelines, and if
- The administrative agency stays within the guidelines established by the legislative body in creating rules enforced by the criminal penalties, but
- The rules of the administrative agency "must be explicit and unambiguous in order to sustain a criminal prosecution; they must adequately inform those who are subject to their terms what conduct will be considered evasive so as to bring the criminal penalties of the Act into operation,"[31] and

COMMON LAW, STATUTORY, AND ADMINISTRATIVE CRIMES

Common Law Crimes (used in the early days of the United States)	Custom, usage, or moral values, and concepts of a community built up over a period of many years	Plus	Adoption by judges of these customs or concepts in court decisions as crimes
Statutory Crimes (make up the vast majority of crimes today)	Enactment of bills by a legislative body	Plus	Signing of the bills by the chief executive officer (governor or president)
Administrative Crimes (used in the fields of health, drugs, stock market, taxation, and other areas the government must regulate)	Enactment of sufficient guidelines by a legislative body that are signed into law by the governor or president	Plus	Authorized regulatory agencies that create rules within the guidelines established by law

- The determination (adjudication) of whether a violation of the **administrative crime** has occurred is made by a court with proper jurisdiction and is not made by the administrative agency.

Summary

- In American jurisprudence, legislatures make criminal law, and the judicial branch determines when the criminal law has been violated
- Criminal laws, as public laws, are applicable generally to every person within the jurisdiction of the law. Private law, such as tort or contract laws, apply only to the individuals affected by conduct of other individuals
- The reason for making conduct criminal are closely tied to the goals of the criminal law, which are to deter prohibited behavior, protect society from dangerous individuals, and both punish and reform those convicted of a crime.
- The police power of a state can be broadly used to define criminal conduct, but it is subject to many constitutional limitations. Among these limitations are the principle of legality (*nulla poena sine lege*), the Ex Post Facto Clause, the bill of attainder clause, the "void for vagueness" and "overbreadth" doctrines, and the due process and equal protection clauses.
- A "status" crime is a statute that makes a condition or character trait a crime without any requirement of a criminal act. Such a crime inflicts a cruel and unusual punishment in violation of the Constitution.
- Common law crimes, those without a specific statute defining the criminal conduct, were at one time the predominant source of criminal laws. By the twentieth century virtually all criminal law was statutory, and under federal law no conduct may be adjudged criminal without a specific statutory authority.

Key Terms

certiorari, p. 5
habeas corpus, p. 5
public law, p. 5
tort, p. 5
criminology, p. 6
police power, p. 11
nulla poena sine lege, p. 12

felony, p. 13
misdemeanor, p. 13
ex post facto, p. 16
bill of attainder, p. 17
due process, p. 19
"void for vagueness" doctrine, p. 19
"overbreadth" doctrine, p. 20

status crime, p. 20
common law, p. 24
common law crime, p. 25
Magna Carta, p. 26
administrative crime, p. 28

Case Analysis and Writing Exercises

1. Pestinikas and his wife verbally agreed to provide food, medicine, and other necessities to a sick and elderly 92-year-old man. Unfortunately, Pestinikas and his wife failed to provide the food and medical care they had been paid to provide. The state can prove that the 92-year-old man's death was caused by this failure and that the man died of malnutrition and exposure.

   Under the criminal code of your state, could criminal charges be brought against Pestinikas? What possible charge could be issued? *Commonwealth v. Pestinikas,* 617 A.2d 1339 (Pa. Super. 1992). For a discussion of criminal liability for negative acts, see Perkins, *Criminal Law,* 2nd ed. (Mineola, NY: Foundation Press, 1969).

2. Michael was almost 18 years old. Around midnight on a summer's night, he approached a 16½-year-old girl, Sharon, and her sister as they waited at a bus stop. The girls had been drinking. Michael and Sharon moved away from the others and began to kiss. When Sharon objected to Michael's sexual advances, Michael struck her in the face. Sharon then submitted to sexual intercourse.

   If the California prosecutor had charged Michael with rape, the state would have had a difficult time obtaining a criminal conviction.

Therefore, based on the statements of the parties and witnesses (and other evidence), Michael was charged with violating California's statutory rape law. This California law forbade sexual intercourse with a female under 18 (who is not the wife of the perpetrator).

Another term for this offense is SIWAC (sexual intercourse with a child). Because the statute makes men alone criminally liable, Michael attacked the statute as violating equal protection of the laws. Does California have a valid state interest in enacting a statutory rape law and making it applicable to men only? Explain. See *Michael M. v. Superior Court of Sonoma County,* 450 U.S. 464, 101 S. Ct. 1200 (1981).

3. Creek was charged with the crime of kidnapping a child. During the entire kidnapping, the child, Adam, remained asleep. Under relevant state tort law, Adam could not recover damages from Creek for the tort of false imprisonment, because to do so, a victim must be conscious during the imprisonment.

Creek contended that because he could not be held liable for the tort of false imprisonment, he could not be guilty of kidnapping where the victim was asleep or unconscious. Was he correct? Are the goals of tort law and criminal law the same? Should different goals produce different results here? See *Creek v. State* (588 N.E.2d 1319 (Ind. App. 1992)).

4. Under the reasoning of *Robinson v. California* and *Jones v. City of Los Angeles,* discussed in this chapter, may the city of Chicago pass an ordinance that permits the police to order a homeless person found sleeping in an airport seating area to leave, and if that person does not, arrest the homeless person? Is this ordinance the same or different from the ordinance declared unconstitutional in *Jones*? In what way or ways? See *Benson v. City of Chicago,* 2006 WL 2949521.

Notes

1. Polls taken in recent years report that Americans have less confidence in the criminal justice system than they do in other institutions, such as public schools, the medical system, big business, news services, and organized labor. Only 23 percent of white and 25 percent of black respondents expressed confidence in the criminal justice system. By contrast, 61 percent of those polled expressed confidence in the police, and 51 percent felt confident in the Supreme Court. See *NIP Journal,* 2002, no. 248. A 2009 report by the Pew Institute indicated that only 48% of Hispanics and 36% of blacks believed the police would not unfairly use force in confrontations with members of these minorities.

2. Failure to protect citizens breeds crime. When the government fails to protect citizens, some persons are likely to take the law into their own hands. An example of private justice (vigilantism) may have occurred in a New York City subway in December 1984. Bernhard Goetz told New York police that he believed he was about to be robbed and that he produced a gun, shot his presumed assailants, and then left the scene. A New York grand jury would not indict Goetz for the shooting but did indict him for the illegal possession of a handgun. He was convicted and punished for that offense.

3. *United States v. Watson,* 146 F. Supp. 258, 262 (D.D.C. 1956), *judgment reversed,* 249 F.2d 106 (C.A.D.C. 1957).

4. *Kovacs v. Cooper,* 336 U.S. 77, 69 S. Ct. 448 (1949).

5. *Village of Belle Terre v. Boraas,* 416 U.S. 1, 94 S. Ct. 1536 (1974).

6. *Lawton v. Steele,* 152 U.S. 133 (1894).

7. State laws that require motorcycle operators and passengers to wear protective headgear have generally been upheld by state and federal courts as being a valid use of the police power of the state.

The Supreme Court of Nebraska reviewed these cases in *Robotham v. State,* 488 N.W.2d 533 (1992), in which the Nebraska motorcycle helmet law was upheld.

However, some motorcycle groups have mounted considerable political opposition to state helmet laws. In Wisconsin, for example, hundreds of motorcyclists converged on the state capitol building in Madison to protest the Wisconsin helmet law. The motorcyclists slowly drove around Capitol Square in downtown Madison, tying up traffic for blocks in all directions. After a number of such demonstrations in which motorcycle drivers and passengers did not wear helmets, the state legislature repealed the Wisconsin law requiring drivers and passengers on motorcycles to wear protective headgear.

8. *Bykofsky et al. v. Borough of Middletown,* 401 F. Supp. 1242, *affirmed* (3d Cir. 1976), 535 F.2d 1245, *review denied,* U.S. Supreme Court, 97 S. Ct. 394 (1976).

9. See the appendix of this text for applicable sections of the U.S. Constitution.

10. See the case of *United States v. Bass,* 404 U.S. 336, 92 S. Ct. 515 (1971), in which the U.S. Supreme Court held that "a fair warning should be given … in language that the common world will understand."

11. When good reasons are given, state governors are likely to grant a pardon for a felony or misdemeanor conviction. The pardon will wipe the slate clean for the person. Depending on the law of the state, governors have the authority and power to grant clemency in different ways. They may grant a pardon, or commute or modify a sentence. Such clemency could be conditional if authorized by the state law.

12. Fifth Amendment to the U.S. Constitution.

13. Some states authorize store employees to arrest persons for shoplifting, which in most cases is a misdemeanor or is charged as an ordinance violation. The shoplifting statutes of other states authorize the store employees to detain the suspect until the police or sheriff arrives.

14. *Rochin v. California,* 342 U.S. 165, 168, 72 S. Ct. 205, 207 (1952).

15. See the May 2000 U.S. Supreme Court case of *Carnell v. Texas,* 529 U.S. 513, where the sexual assault conviction of the defendant was reversed because a Texas law retroactively reduced the amount of proof necessary to support the sexual assault conviction in violation of the Ex Post Facto Clause.

16. *Connally v. General Construction Co.,* 269 U.S. 385, 46 S. Ct. 126 (1926).

17. See *Papachristou v. City of Jacksonville,* 405 U.S. 156, 162, 92 S. Ct. 839, 843 (1972); and *United States v. Harriss,* 347 U.S. 612, 617, 74 S. Ct. 808, 811 (1954).

18. See *Coates v. City of Cincinnati,* 402 U.S. 611, 614, 91 S. Ct. 1686, 1688 (1971); and *Shuttlesworth v. City of Birmingham,* 382 U.S. 87, 90–91, 86 S. Ct. 211, 213–214 (1965).

19. *Grayned v. City of Rockford,* 408 U.S. 104, 109, 92 S. Ct. 2294, 2299 (1972).

20. *Zwickler v. Koota,* 389 U.S. 241, 250, 88 S. Ct. 2294, 2299 (1972).

21. See *Grayned v. City of Rockford,* 408 U.S. 104, 109, 92 S. Ct. 2294, 2299 (1972); and *Dombrowski v. Pfister,* 380 U.S. 479, 486, 85 S. Ct. 1116, 1120 (1965).

22. See 119 S. Ct. 1849 (1999).

23. 370 U.S. 660, 82 S. Ct. 1417 (1962).

24. 392 U.S. 514, 88 S. Ct. 2145 (1968).

25. State statutes also often provide that marriage licenses may be issued to women beyond childbearing age who wish to marry a close relative. Under such statutes, two first cousins could marry if the woman meets the requirements of the state statute.

    The results of six major medical studies reported in 2002 concluded that only small medical risks are seen in children born to first cousins who marry. The report recommended that the term *incest* should not apply to sexual relations between cousins—only to sexual relations between siblings and between parents and children. (See the *New York Times* article "Few Risks Seen to the Children of First Cousins," April 4, 2002.)

26. It is reported that there are now more than 1 million married interracial couples living in the United States. For example, U.S. Supreme Court Justice Clarence Thomas is a black man and is married to a white woman.

27. *Green v. U.S.,* 356 U.S. 165, 78 S. Ct. 632 (1958).

28. *U.S. v. Hudson and Goodwin,* 11 U.S. (7 Cranch) 32, 3 L. Ed. 259 (1812).

29. *Krulewitch v. U.S.,* 336 U.S. 440, 69 S. Ct. 716 (1949).

30. *U.S. v. Grimaud,* 220 U.S. 506, 31 S. Ct. 480 (1911).

31. *M. Kraus & Bros., Inc. v. U.S.,* 327 U.S. 614, 66 S. Ct. 705 (1946).

CHAPTER 2

Jurisdiction

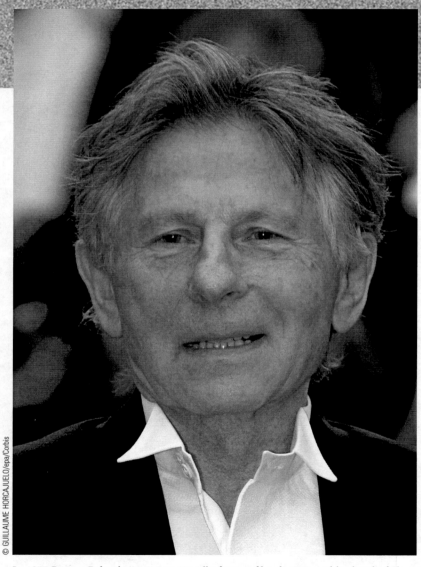

© GUILLAUME HORCAJUELO/epa/Corbis

In 1977 Roman Polanski, an internationally famous film director and husband of Sharon Tate, the actress killed by the Charles Manson cult, was charged in Los Angeles with rape. He subsequently pled guilty to a lesser charge of unlawful sex with a minor, but in 1978 fled the United States to Europe prior to sentencing. Polanski, who holds French citizenship, lives in France, which refuses to extradite French citizens. In 2009, while visiting in Switzerland to accept a directing award, Polanski was arrested by Swiss authorities, and held for extradition. Switzerland has an extradition treaty with the United States. In July of 2010 Swiss authorities refused the extradition request made by the United States. Polanski is now free to return to France.

LEARNING OBJECTIVES

In this chapter we discuss the basis of the power of a court to try a defendant charged with a crime. The learning objectives for this chapter are:

- Explain why a state has general power to make criminal law and to prosecute those who violate the law.

- List the specific powers granted to the federal government to make criminal laws.

- Draw the boundaries for congressional power under the Commerce Clause to regulate actions through criminal laws.

- Identify the ways a state can obtain jurisdiction over the person of a defendant charged with violation of a criminal law.

- Explain the basis for an international court to claim jurisdiction over a person charged with a violation of international law.

- Describe the "Federal Domain."

- Identify the jurisdiction of military courts.

- Describe the jurisdiction of Indian Tribal Courts.

In the morning of May 30, 2008, after a night of ingesting various kinds of drugs and alcohol, Ravis Key drove his car on roads within the Fort Hood Military Base in Texas. At the intersection of Tank Destroyer Boulevard and Clark Road, Key's vehicle struck a vehicle driven by Sergeant Andre Araijo. Key's vehicle was travelling at a speed in excess of 75 MPH, and no skid marks were found to indicate Key made any effort to stop his vehicle before the collision. The collision caused a massive head injury that killed Sergeant Araijo. Military Police summoned to the accident scene tested Key and found him to be intoxicated. Subsequent blood tests found evidence of cocaine, MDMA, and marijuana in Key's body at the time of the collision.

Federal authorities charged Key with the crime of "Intoxicated Manslaughter" under Texas Penal Code § 49.08, which carries a possible sentence of 20 years in prison. While Key could have been charged under the federal involuntary murder statute, which carries a maximum possible sentence of 8 years in prison, the federal prosecutors elected to charge him under the Texas statute on the theory the Federal Assimilative Crimes Act, 18 U.S.C. § 13 (ACA) assimilated the Texas statute into federal law. The ACA permits the federal government to apply state laws on federal preserves, like military bases, unless Congress has indicated federal criminal statutes were intended to preempt such state laws. Key was convicted and sentenced to 216 months in prison. On appeal, a Federal Court of Appeals held that assimilation was proper, and it affirmed Key's conviction under the Texas law. *United States v. Key*, 599 F.3d 469 (5th Cir. 2010). In this chapter we discuss the various jurisdictions in the United States with the power to make criminal laws and apply them to persons who act in violation of those laws. In some situations, like the *Key* case, one jurisdiction may "assimilate" criminal laws passed by another jurisdiction.

The most extensive criminal codes therefore are found in the criminal codes of each of the 50 states and the federal government. It is reported that these 51 criminal codes consist of more than 3,000 crimes each. The Code of Military Justice for the U.S. Armed Forces (also written by the U.S. Congress) is less extensive, as it is limited to the U.S. military.

≡ Jurisdiction of the Federal Government to Enact Criminal Laws

The American Criminal Justice System is a huge, complex system serving over 300 million people living in thousands of cities, counties, and parishes in the 50 states and territories. Under the American system of federalism, states have the primary responsibility of maintaining public order and safety within each state while the U.S. Congress has the responsibility of creating a federal criminal code within the power granted to the federal government by the U.S. Constitution.

Because the states have the primary responsibility to maintain public order and security in their state, they have broad authority to create criminal law under the police power of each state. The U.S. Supreme Court stated, "… crimes in the United States are what the law of the individual state makes them, subject to (constitutional) limitations" (*Rochin v. California*, 72 S. Ct. 204, 1952). The federal government does not have inherent police power to create criminal law and is limited to the powers granted to the federal government in the U.S. Constitution.

jurisdiction Power to regulate conduct and punish an offender.

The power to regulate "Commerce … among the several states" found in Article I of the U.S. Constitution is the basis of a great part the authority the federal government has to enact criminal laws. If an activity (e.g., legal or illegal drug trade) involves more than a single state, Congress may regulate it by either criminal or civil laws.

On the other hand, an activity that is solely within a single state (e.g., local state schoolyards) can be regulated by states and local communities but not by the federal government.

EXAMPLE: The federal conviction of a Texas schoolboy for carrying a gun on a Texas schoolyard was held invalid by the U.S. Supreme Court in the 1995 case of *United States v. Lopez*, 115 S. Ct. 1624. As schoolyards are not ordinarily part of interstate commerce, the U.S. Congress may not enact criminal laws regulating them. Texas and the school may punish Lopez for carrying a gun on a schoolyard, but the federal government may not. Most states make this conduct a specific crime.

Federal crimes fall into the following three classes, which reflect the power of the federal government under the constitution to pass criminal laws:[1]

1. Crimes that affect interstate or international travel or communication, such as the Travel Act (interstate travel or use of U.S. mail, telephone, and so on to facilitate a crime), the Wire Fraud Act (interstate transfer of stolen or illegal funds), the National Stolen Property Act (interstate transfer or possession of stolen property), the Fugitive Felon Act (fleeing across state lines to avoid prosecution), the Mann Act (interstate prostitution), the Hobbs Act (extortion), and the Lindbergh Act (interstate kidnapping).
2. Crimes committed in places beyond the jurisdiction of any state. These include crimes committed in the District of Columbia and crimes committed overseas by the military or on U.S.-controlled ships or aircraft.
3. Crimes that interfere with the activities of the federal government.[2] Because the federal government's scope of activities is broad, this category of federal crimes is broad. It includes fraud by use of the U.S. mails, robbery of federally insured banks or savings and loan associations, violation of the federal income tax laws, and attempted overthrow of the U.S. government.

Situations in which the federal government has jurisdiction over a criminal homicide include the following:[3]

- Within the special maritime and territorial jurisdiction
- When death results from terrorism, sabotage, or certain cases of reckless or negligent destruction of "federal" transportation facilities
- When the victim is the president of the United States, the vice president, or successors to the office[4]
- When the victim is engaged in performing federal functions
- When the victim is killed "on account of the performance of his official duties"
- When death occurs in connection with a federally punishable bank robbery
- When the homicide occurs during an offense defined by the Civil Rights Act of 1968 (18 U.S.C.A. § 245)
- When an American citizen is killed anywhere in the world under the Comprehensive Crime Control Act of 1984

Federal Crimes Frequently Used to Support State and Local Enforcement

The power of state and local law officers is limited to their jurisdictions. Federal jurisdiction, however, is not limited to the borders of a state. For example, a child is missing and may have been kidnapped. If the child is not recovered after a few days, the FBI will presume that the child has been transported to another state, which will give the FBI jurisdiction to become involved in the case. In such cases, federal laws and agencies serve as important forces in complementing state and local law enforcement.

The following are some of the many federal crimes that are of particular and frequent interest to state law enforcement officers:

Unlawful Flight Statute (Fugitive Felon Act) (18 U.S.C.A. 1073): This law permits federal agencies to assist in locating state fugitives who may have fled from one state to another. The fugitive may be seeking to avoid prosecution for a felony or may be a potential witness in a felony case. If apprehended by a federal agency, the person will be returned to the state from which he (or she) fled. There is seldom federal prosecution under the law.

Federal Kidnapping (18 U.S.C.A. 1201): Kidnapping or abduction of any person for reward or ransom when interstate transportation, or use of special maritime or territorial jurisdiction of the United States is involved.

Interstate Transportation of Stolen Motor Vehicles (18 U.S.C.A. 2312, 2313), **of Stolen Property** (18 U.S.C.A. 2314): These are large areas of criminal activity. More than one million vehicles are stolen every year in the United States and more than 3 million vehicles are entered for valuables or accessories. Proof of interstate transportation is needed and proof of $5,000 or more of goods, wares, merchandise, security, or money known to be stolen, converted, or taken by fraud. See Chapters 13 and 14 for further material on theft offenses.

Mail Thefts and Forging and Uttering of U.S. Treasury Checks (18 U.S.C.A. 1708 and 495): Every month millions of Social Security, pension, and other checks are sent through the mails, as well as packages and other materials. Many of these items are stolen, often coupled with the crimes of forging and uttering of regular checks and U.S. Treasury checks. See Chapter 12 for further material.

Federal Conspiracy (18 U.S.C.A. 371): The federal crime of conspiracy makes it illegal for 2 or more persons to "combine or conspire" either to commit any offense against the laws of the United States or defraud the government of the United States. As there are a vast number of "laws of the United States" on the books, this covers a vast amount of territory. See Chapter 4 for material on the law of conspiracy.

RICO (Racketeer Influence and Corrupt Organization) (18 U.S.C.A. 1963 and 1964): See Chapter 18 for the history and wide use of this federal statute. State RICO statutes are commonly called "Little RICOs."

Mail Fraud (18 U.S.C.A. 1341): This crime prohibits the use of the mail as part of a scheme to defraud. Traditionally, the mail fraud statute has been aimed at con men, dummy corporations, fraudulent franchise schemes, and other frauds. It is sometimes used against corrupt public officials. Sending an extortion, bribery, blackmail, or demand for a ransom letter in a kidnapping case through the mail would ordinarily be held to justify federal jurisdiction. The mail fraud statute has been extended not only to mail but to any facility in interstate or foreign commerce.

The Travel Act This provides that "Whoever travels in interstate … commerce or uses any facility in interstate … commerce including the mail, with intent to …"

3) … promote, manage, … carry on … any unlawful activity … shall be fined not more than $10,000 … or imprisoned for not more than five years, or both."

b) … "unlawful activity means 1) any business activity … (involving and including) prostitution offenses in violation of the laws of the State in which they are committed …"

See Chapter 18 for further material on the Travel Act.

The Federal Domain—1/3 of America

The federal government owns and controls up to 1/3 of all of the land in the United States in the form of territories and federal enclaves.[5] *The U.S. Constitution (Art. IV, Sec. 3) states that "In the Territories of the United States, Congress has the entire dominion and sovereignty … and has full legislative power over all subjects…."*

As the District of Columbia (Washington, D.C.) is one of the territories of the United States, Congress has full police power and has enacted a full criminal code necessary to maintain public order and security in this large American city.

Federal Enclaves Territories and the Assimilative Crimes Act

federal enclaves
Federally owned and controlled lands.

Federal enclaves are federally owned and controlled lands. They can be found in all states. Military installations—such as Army posts, Navy yards, Air Force bases, Coast Guard stations, and Marine bases—are enclaves if they are within the borders of states. National parks and forests and federal buildings, such as post offices, federal court buildings, and federal office buildings, can under certain circumstances also be enclaves.

Before 1948, some of the enclaves had a degree of autonomy, which created some problems throughout the United States. In 1948, Congress passed the Assimilative Crimes Act (ACA) (18 U.S.C.A. § 13) to incorporate, by reference, the state criminal law of the surrounding state in force at the time of the defendant's conduct. In the case of *United States v. Sharpnack,* the U.S. Supreme Court held that the ACA was constitutional.[6] In that case, the defendant, who was a civilian, was convicted of committing sex crimes involving two boys at the Randolph Air Force Base, a federal enclave in Texas. In affirming the conviction, the Court stated:

> There is no doubt that Congress may validly adopt a criminal code for each federal enclave. It certainly may do so by drafting new laws or by copying laws defining the criminal offenses in force throughout the State in which the enclave is situated. As a practical matter, it has to proceed largely on a wholesale basis. Its reason for adopting local laws is not so much because Congress has examined them individually as it is because the laws are already in force throughout the State in which the enclave is situated. The basic legislative decision made by Congress is its decision to conform the laws in the enclave to the local laws as to all offenses not punishable by any enactment of Congress. Whether Congress sets forth the assimilated laws in full or assimilates them by reference, the result is as definite and as ascertainable as are the state laws themselves.

However, the ACA will not operate to incorporate a state law making conduct a crime if the federal government has already passed a statute or regulation that makes the same conduct a federal crime. For example, in *Lewis v. United States,* 118 S. Ct. 1135 (1998), the Supreme Court reversed a conviction of defendants for first-degree murder of a child under Louisiana law, which the district court held applicable under ACA. Because Congress had passed a second-degree murder statute that would apply to the murder of a child on an Army base in Louisiana, the Supreme Court said that law should have been the basis for the defendants' conviction and sentencing.

extradition The surrender of an accused criminal under the provisions of a treaty or statute by one authority to another having jurisdiction.

In *United States v. Palmer,* 956 F.2d 189 (9th Cir. 1991), the court held that because the National Park Service had adopted regulations governing the meaning and punishment of drunk driving within a national park, California's stricter laws on punishment for repeat offenders could not be applied under the ACA.

≡ Nation-to-Nation Jurisdiction

Nations long ago realized that the world could not afford criminal jurisdictional gaps between nations. An alarming situation would exist, for example, if a person could commit a murder in the middle of the Atlantic or Pacific Ocean, with no nation having criminal jurisdiction. Because of this, the jurisdiction of each nation was extended to follow its ships over the high seas. The English common law gave jurisdiction to English courts over crimes committed on British ships and over crimes committed by British subjects on foreign ships.

Today, statutes in both the United Kingdom and the United States give each country jurisdiction over crimes committed not only on ships but also on aircraft controlled by

USE OF EXTRADITION AND FORCIBLE ABDUCTION TO BRING FUGITIVES BEFORE COURTS

Extradition is the removal of a person from one jurisdiction to another so that he or she can face charges in the requesting jurisdiction. **International Extradition.** The United States has more than eighty treaties in force with foreign countries which allow for extradition of fugitives between sovereign nations. A compilation of these treaties can be found in the notes following 18 U.S.C.A. Section 3181. There are many interesting and newsworthy international extradition cases, including:

General Manuel Noriega (former dictator of Panama)

Because Panama was the center of illegal drug and money laundering activities, the United States invaded Panama in 1990 in what was called the "biggest drug bust in history." More than two hundred people were killed and a billion dollars in property damage occurred. With the consent of the new Panama government, General Noriega was taken to Miami, Florida, and was convicted in a U.S. federal court as a prisoner of war of drug charges (746 F. Supp. 1506). After completing his sentence in Florida, Noriega was extradited to France in 2010 where he had been convicted *in absentia* of money laundering. Panama is also seeking extradition. The U.S. Supreme Court turned down Noriega's appeal in 2010 (*Noriega v. Pastrana*, No. 09-35).

Rendition and the War on Terror

In November 2009, twenty-three Americans, almost all C.I.A employees, were convicted *in absentia* in an Italian court for kidnapping Abu Omar, an Egyptian cleric in Milan, Italy, in 2003. The cleric was then flown to another country for questioning (rendition). In 2007, one American was given an 8-year sentence, and the other 22 were sentenced to 5 years, making them fugitives under Italian law. (See *New York Times* article [11/05/09] "Italy Convicts 23 Americans, Most Working for C.I.A., of Abducting Muslim Cleric.")

Duane "Dog" Chapman (A&E series, "Dog, The Bounty Hunter")

As a bounty hunter, Chapman seized Andrew Luster, convicted rapist and heir to the Revlon fortune in Puerto Vallarta, Mexico, and returned him to the United States in 2003. Mexico requested extradition of "Dog" on kidnapping charges. "Dog" was arrested in Hawaii and released on bail. A Mexican court dismissed the charges and a U.S. Magistrate in turn dismissed the extradition proceedings against "Dog" in 2007.

Roman Polanski (Hollywood film director)

In 1977 Polanski was charged with drugging and raping a 13-year-old girl. He pleaded guilty to lesser charges but fled to France prior to his sentencing. After being a fugitive for years, he was taken into custody by Swiss

United Nations Convention An agreement between nations on a specific subject, such as piracy at sea

each country. By virtue of the international convention ratified by the Tokyo Convention Act of 1967, the courts of any country in the world may try piracy (armed violence at sea committed on a surface ship or an aircraft), even though the piracy was not committed within that country's territorial waters.[7] In addition to piracy, international conventions of nations have sought the elimination of slave trading, war crimes, hijacking and sabotage of civil aircraft, genocide, and terrorism.

Because of the statutes giving many nations jurisdictions over crimes, situations could exist in which a number of nations have concurrent jurisdiction (that is, the same crime could be tried in the courts of another nation).

EXAMPLE: A Romanian man was on an American airliner flying from Europe to New York City. While in the air, the man placed his hand on the genitals of a 9-year-old Norwegian girl. It was held that jurisdiction existed to try the man for sexual assault in a New York federal court under the federal "special aircraft jurisdiction."[8]

authorities on an international arrest warrant and was held in 2010 pending extradition requested by Los Angeles prosecutors.

Interstate Extradition. Article IV, Section 2 of the Constitution, as well as 18 U.S.C.A. Section 3182 and the Uniform Criminal Extradition Act,[a] provide that fugitives who flee to another U.S. state can also be extradited back for trial.

Forcible Abductions. Two significant United States Supreme Court Cases on forced abductions of criminal defendants are the following:

Case	Year	Facts	Ruling
Ker v. Illinois, 119 U.S. 43	1886	The defendant was forcibly abducted from Peru in South America to face trial for robbery in Illinois.	The U.S. Supreme Court affirmed the robbery conviction, holding that the forcible abduction was "no sufficient reason why the defendant should not answer" for the robbery charges.
United States v. Alvarez-Machain, 112 S. Ct. 2188	1992	Because the defendant was believed to be involved in the torture and murder of a U.S. Drug Enforcement Administration (DEA) agent, Dr. Alvarez was snatched from his office in Mexico and flown to Texas, where he was arrested.	The U.S. Supreme Court held that while the kidnapping may be "shocking," it did not violate the Mexican–U.S. treaty, and thus, the rule of Ker applied. Note: A federal court acquitted Dr. Alvarez.

[a]Courts in the United States have held that the Uniform Criminal Extradition Act (adopted in many states) has changed the common law. Bail bond agents and law enforcement officers can be sued civilly for violations in failing to comply with the Uniform Criminal Extradition Act in forcing a person to return to another state without that person's consent. For cases involving bail bond agents, see *State v. Lopez*, 105 N.M. 538, 734 P.2d 778 (App. 1986), *review denied* 107 S. Ct.1305, 40 CrL 4173 (1987), and *Loftice v. Colorado*, (Colo. Ct. App. 1988), *review denied* 490 U.S.1047, 109 S. Ct.1957, 45 CrL 4025 (1989). However, in many states bail bond agents continue to have greater arrest power than private citizens. See *Shifflett v. State*, 319 Md. 275, 572 A.2d 167 (1990).

In a 1998 unanimous decision, the U.S. Supreme Court held that states have essentially no discretion and must extradite as long as proper procedures are followed and the wanted person's identity and fugitive status are confirmed. See *New Mexico v. Reed*, 118 S. Ct. 1860 (1998).

International Criminal Law

Article I, Section 8, of the U.S. Constitution provides that "The Congress shall have Power ... to define and punish Piracies and Felonies committed on the high Seas, and Offenses against the Law of Nations." Over the years, the United States has participated with the other nations of the world to define international criminal law—*offenses against the law of nations*—by international treaties and international conventions. In 1928, sixty-three nations, including Germany and Japan, outlawed aggressive warfare by signing and agreeing to the Kellogg-Briand Pact. The brutalization of civilians and the deportation of people from their homeland to slave labor camps were defined and forbidden by the Geneva Convention of 1897.

After the end of World War II, the Allied nations tried some of the Nazi and Japanese military and civilian leaders for war crimes in trials held at Nuremberg, Germany,[9] and Tokyo, Japan. Special temporary criminal courts were created to try these leaders for crimes like ethnic cleansing, deportation of thousands of people to slave labor camps, use of slave labor in German and Japanese war factories, and the killing of millions of people.

CRIMES AGAINST SHIPS AND AIRCRAFT	
Piracy or Hijacking	The seizure of a ship or aircraft while it is underway. This is a federal crime and also a crime against the law of nations. (See *United States v. Palmer*, 3 Wheat. 610, 4 L. Ed. 57.)
Mutiny	When the crew (or some of the crew) seize an aircraft or ship and revolt against lawful authority, the crime of mutiny is committed. In military law, the crime also includes an insurrection of soldiers against lawful authority.
Barratry or Barretry	Unlawful acts committed by the captain or officers of a ship that are contrary to their duties. The term is also used for the offense of frequently exciting and stirring up quarrels or lawsuits.

Other temporary criminal courts were established in 1993 to sit at The Hague, Netherlands, to try persons charged with crimes committed during the civil war in the former Yugoslavia (Bosnia).[10] A similar court was established in Africa after the slaughter of half a million Tutsi and Hutu people.[11]

The Treaty of Rome, which was ratified in July 2002, created the world's first permanent war crimes court, the International Criminal Court (ICC), which sits at The Hague. This court has the power to investigate and prosecute people accused of genocide, war crimes, and crimes against humanity. The court's jurisdiction extends to all countries that ratified the treaty and to crimes committed in countries that ratified the treaty. The United States did not ratify the treaty and is currently negotiating for immunity from prosecution by the ICC for the U.S. military. Great Britain did ratify the treaty and was the subject of a claim brought against British troops for activities in Iraq. The ICC has jurisdiction, even though Iraq did not ratify the treaty, because Great Britain did.

Jurisdiction of the Sea Approaches to the Continental United States

Each nation has established territorial jurisdiction in the waters and airspace around it. In 1983, the United States claimed sovereignty over waters extending 200 nautical miles from the United States and its possessions.[12] Vessels within these waters or on the high seas may be stopped under any of the following circumstances:

1. When there is reasonable suspicion or probable cause to believe that contraband such as illegal drugs exists or other criminal activity is occurring[13] or

2. If a ship or vessel is without nationality (stateless) or "a vessel on the high seas whose nationality (is) unclear"[14] or

3. With consent or a statement of no objection from the foreign nation where the vessel is registered: *United States v. Pretel*, 939 F.2d 233 (5th Cir. 1991); *United States v. Robinson*, 843 F.2d 1 (1st Cir. 1988), *review denied* 488 U.S. 834, 109 U.S. 93 (1988) or if the ship meets the statutory definition of a "hovering vessel": *United States v. Cariballo-Tamayo*, 44 CrL 2401 (1989); *United States v. Gonzalez*, 875 F.2d 875 (1989).

Maritime jurisdiction
Jurisdiction of the United States over actions within territorial waters of the United States on U.S. ships, or stateless vessels on the high seas.

Under maritime jurisdiction, criminal laws can be created to govern the conduct of persons (either Americans or aliens) aboard American ships or aircraft in the territorial waters, on the high seas or elsewhere. The United States has jurisdiction of crimes committed on aircraft or vessels of whatever nationality in its internal waters and territorial seas and waters. Under maritime jurisdiction, the United States has asserted jurisdiction over stateless vessels on the high seas (*United States v. Henriquez*, 731 F. 2d 131, 2d Cir., 1984).

The Crimes of Piracy, Felonies Committed on the High Seas, and Offenses against the Law of Nations

When the U.S. Constitution was written, the Barbary Pirates were a problem that led to sending the U.S. Marines to " … the shores of Tripoli" (Marine hymn). The authority for this action is found in Article I, Section 8 of the U.S. Constitution, which provides, "The Congress shall have Power … to define and punish Piracies and Felonies committed on the high Seas, and Offenses against the Law of Nations."

In 2008 Somalian pirates seized the U.S.S. Maersk Alabama off the Horn of Africa in one of the world's busiest waterways. The American captain was rescued in a daring Navy SEAL operation. Forty-seven other hijackings occurred in 2008 and 68 successful pirate hijackings occurred in 2009. Corporations and nations have paid hundreds of millions of dollars to the pirates to get their ships, cargos, and crews back. Warships from Europe, Russia, China, Japan, and other nations patrol the vast sea area to protect their ships and destroy the pirates.

In 2010, twelve Somali men were being tried in U.S. federal courts in Norfolk, VA, and in New York for attacks not only on American cargo ships but also on U.S. Navy warships. The pirates have invested in fleets of fast ships and modern weapons plus state-of-the-art electronic gear. Ships with valuable cargo have been seized by the pirates more than a thousand miles off the Arabian and African coasts.

≡ The Military, Martial, and War Powers Jurisdiction of the Federal Government

The constitution and Congressional acts give the federal government the power to raise and maintain a military force, to declare and conduct war, and in certain circumstances to use military forces within the several states. Incident to this power is the need for federal laws and courts to oversee the military forces, and those associated with the military forces.

Jurisdiction of Military Courts[15]

A person who enters U.S. military service becomes subject to the Uniform Code of Military Justice.[16] Over the years, hundreds of thousands of military personnel have been tried for many offenses, ranging from "military" crimes such as desertion, unauthorized absences, willful disobedience of orders, and drunkenness on duty to "civilian" crimes, such as rape, murder, and drug violations that took place on leave.

From 1969 through 1987, U.S. military courts did not have jurisdiction over offenses that were not "service connected" and were committed off-base or off-post. In 1987, military courts were given back the authority and jurisdiction they lost in 1969. The U.S. Supreme Court abandoned the "service connection" requirement that was established in the 1969 case of *O'Callahan v. Parker*.[17]

In the 1987 case of *Solorio v. United States*, the U.S. Supreme Court held that the military justice system has jurisdiction to try a member of the armed service for *any* crimes committed (on- or off-base) as long as the accused was a member of the military service at the time of the alleged offense.

When U.S. Citizens or Military Are in a Foreign Country

Americans who commit crimes in foreign countries are subject to prosecution before foreign courts, whether they are military personnel or tourists. U.S. civilians have been sentenced to serve long prison terms in Turkey, Mexico, and other countries for narcotics violations—a grim reminder that sentences in some countries are quite severe.

U.S. military personnel are stationed in many countries throughout the world. A service person who commits a crime while off-base, while off-duty, and in a foreign country is subject to the jurisdiction of the laws of that country. Under the status of forces agreement (SOFA), or visiting forces agreement, that many countries have with the United States, the military person could be tried by the courts in the host country.[18] However, in many instances the prosecutor in the foreign country waives jurisdiction and turns the offender over to the U.S. military authorities for trial before a military court.

Examples of crimes that American service personnel were charged with are murder of a West German taxi driver and desertion (*Plaster v. United States*),[19] murder of a Mexican prostitute (*United States v. Newvine*),[20] and rape of a German woman (*Bell v. Clark*).[21]

Because foreign countries in the past generally wanted a continued U.S. military presence, they often waived criminal prosecution. However, in November 1995, Japan did not waive jurisdiction to try three U.S. servicemen for the rape of a 12-year-old schoolgirl on the island of Okinawa. Before a Japanese court, one serviceman pleaded guilty, and the other two admitted assisting in the rape. Thousands of Okinawans demonstrated to demand the removal of U.S. military bases from Okinawa and removal of the 47,000 U.S. troops from Japan.[22] In 2006, the governments of the Philippines and Italy asserted their right to try American military personal for crimes committed in their countries.

Martial Law and the Use of Military Forces in the Continental United States

martial law A state of military control over civilian populations as declared by state or federal government.

In attempting to define **martial law** in 1946, the U.S. Supreme Court made the following statements in the case of *Duncan v. Kahanamoku*:

> The term martial law carries no precise meaning. The Constitution does not refer to "martial law" at all and no Act of Congress had defined the term. It has been employed in various ways by different people and at different times. By some it has been identified as "military law" limited to members of, and those connected with, the armed forces. Others have said that the term does not imply a system of established rules but denotes simply some kind of day-to-day expression of a General's will dictated by what he considers the imperious necessity of the moment.... In 1857 the confusion as to the meaning of the phrase was so great that the Attorney General in an official opinion had this to say about it: "The Common Law authorities and commentators afford no clue to what martial law, as understood in England, really is.... In this Country it is still worse." ... What was true in 1857 remains true today.[23]

Military forces have been used many times in the history of our country to maintain public order and enforce laws. In 1787, the year when the Constitution was formulated, the governor of Massachusetts used the militia to cope with Shays' Rebellion. President Washington sent federal troops into Pennsylvania to suppress the Whiskey Rebellion of 1794. Federal troops were used by President Lincoln to prevent the withdrawal of the southern states from the Union and to maintain public order. Federal troops remained in the South until the 1880s. During some of this time, martial law was in effect in the southern states where federal troops remained.

Federal troops were used by President Eisenhower to secure compliance with Supreme Court school desegregation orders in Arkansas in 1957 and by President Kennedy in Mississippi in 1962 and in Alabama in 1963. In the 29-month period between January 1968 and the end of May 1970, National Guard troops were called

---

GENERAL JURISDICTION REQUIREMENTS

To charge a person with a crime, the state or federal government must

- Charge under a statute or ordinance that is constitutional on its face.
- Charge in the county or place in which the crime is alleged to have occurred.
- Produce the person to be charged before the court that will try him or her.

Indians who commit crimes while not within their reservation or Indian country are subject to the jurisdiction of the state or government, just as non-Indians who commit crimes while on their reservation or within Indian country can be tried (1) by their tribal court and punished by not more than one-year imprisonment and/or a $5,000 fine (25 U.S.C.A. § 1302(7)) or (2) before a U.S. federal court for the 14 serious crimes under the federal Major Crimes Act (18 U.S.C.A. §§ 1153 and 3242).

Non-Indians charged with committing crimes against other non-Indians in Indian country are subject to prosecution under state law.[a]

U.S. military personnel may be tried by a military court for all crimes they commit while they are in the military service, whether the offense was committed on or off a military base, ship, aircraft, and so on.

People who commit crimes on federal enclaves can be tried before

- A federal court, using the criminal code of the surrounding state under the Assimilative Crimes Act (18 U.S.C.A. § 13)
- A military court, if the person was a member of the U.S. armed services

[a]See *United States v. McBratney*, 104 U.S. (14 Otto) 621 (1881); *United States v. Antelope*, 430 U.S. 641, 97 S. Ct. 1395 (1977), footnote 2.

---

upon 324 times to cope with urban riots and disorders and unrest on college campuses.[24] In all the incidents in the 1950s, 1960s, and 1970s, troops and National Guard units provided assistance to civilian law enforcement agencies that had the primary responsibility for preserving public order. People arrested or taken into custody were brought before federal and state courts, where they were advised of their constitutional rights.

The Crime of the Improper Use of National or State Guard Troops

Posse Comitatus Latin, meaning "power of the country." In the U.S. it generally refers to the military forces.

Federal and state National Guard troops (and other military) can lawfully be used in disaster assistance, search and rescue missions, domestic terrorist events, civil disturbances, and other specific circumstances when they are needed to protect constitutional rights or to support a request from a state, or to enforce federal authority.

But the 1878 Posse Comitatus Act imposes limits upon the use of military troops in civil law enforcement. This law was enacted after federal troops left the southern states after the Civil War and after the Reconstruction Period. It also must be remembered that Ohio National Guard troops fired upon and killed four unarmed college students in 1970. The students were lawfully protesting against the Vietnam War. The Posse Comitatus law, which forbids direct military involvement with civilian law enforcement activities, states that:

Whoever, except in cases and under circumstances expressly authorized by the Constitution or Act of Congress, willfully uses any part of the Army or Air Force as a posse comitatus or otherwise to execute the laws shall be fined under this title or imprisoned not more than 2 years, or both.[25]

FIGURE 2.1 Who Backs Up the Police Officer on the Street?

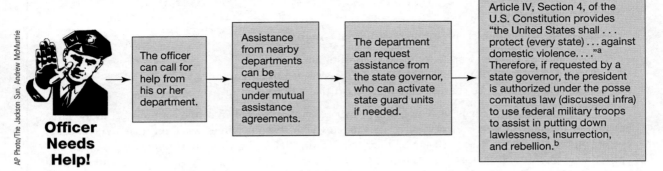

[a]States may not maintain armed forces without the consent of the U.S. Congress: Article I, Section 10, of the U.S. Constitution provides that "No State shall, without the Consent of Congress ... keep Troops, or Ships of War in Time of Peace." (See the appendix of this text for applicable sections of the U.S. Constitution.)

[b]The 2006 "in the dead of night" amendment to the posse comitatus law is unanimously opposed by state governors, because it makes it easier for a president to override local control of law enforcement and declare martial law. During the Vietnam War period, federal troops were used to quell student demonstrations against the war, and at Kent State University federal troops fired into the demonstrators, killing four students. In an editorial on February 19, 2007, the *New York Times* reported that a bipartisan posse comitatus bill is pending before Congress.

The FBI Law Enforcement Bulletin article, "Military Support of Domestic Law Enforcement: Working Within Posse Comitatus," of December 2001 (http://www.fbi.gov) lists specific circumstances where U.S. military forces may be called upon to directly perform domestic law enforcement duties.

Figure 2.1 demonstrates the power that stands behind the neighborhood police officer in the United States.

Indian Tribes within the United States

Of the almost 1.5 million Native Americans in the United States, more than half live on reservations located mainly in 17 states. The U.S. Supreme Court has pointed out that the 310 recognized Indian tribes in the United States "possess those aspects of sovereignty not withdrawn by treaty or statute, or by implication as a necessary result of their dependent status."[26]

In 1975 and again in 1977, the U.S. Supreme Court held that

Indian tribes are unique aggregations possessing attributes of sovereignty over both their members and their territory, Worcester v. Georgia, 31 U.S. 6 Pet. 515, 557 (1832), they are "a separate people" possessing the power of regulating their internal and social relations. United States v. Mazurie, 419 U.S. 544, 557, 95 S. Ct. 710, 717 (1975).[27]

Indian tribal governments have Indian tribal courts and Indian police. However, criminal jurisdiction in Indian country and on Indian reservations is complex. Prior to the passage of Public Law 280 in 1953 (and amended in 1968), criminal jurisdiction in Indian country was shared between the federal government and Indian tribal governments.

Public Law 280 changed this and required that in six states, federal authority be transferred to the six states. However, the law permitted the six states to return (if they wished) criminal jurisdiction to the federal government if any of the six states desired. This would have to be done with the approval of the local tribe members.

The National Institute of Justice Report #229886 of 2010 states that polls among tribal members rated the performance of tribal police higher than that of state, county, or federal law officers. Interestingly, a good number of tribal police are non-Indian and often these officers are deputized not only as tribal police officers but also as state and federal officers. To learn more of this complicated Indian criminal justice system, go to http://www.ojp.usdoj.gov/nij/topics/tribal-justice/welcome.htm.

Indians who commit crimes while not on or within their reservation or Indian country are subject to the laws of the state or government where the crime was committed. Indian tribal courts have jurisdiction for crimes punished for not more than one-year imprisonment and/or a $5,000 fine (25 U.S.C. § 1302 (7)). The Federal Indian Major Crime Act is found at 18 U.S.C. § 1153 and 3242. Non-Indians charged with committing crimes against other non-Indians in Indian country are subject to prosecution under state law. (See *United States v. Antelope*, 430 U.S. 641 1977, footnote 2.)

Self-Government by Indian Tribes

In various treaties between the U.S. government and many Indian tribes, some signed more than 150 years ago, the tribes relinquished their rights to vast amounts of land in exchange for a "special relationship" with the federal government. Among other obligations, the federal government was required to provide the tribes such services as health care and education. That special relationship exists today but is in the process of change.

The tribes are seeking, with the approval of the U.S. Congress, to eliminate their dependence on the Bureau of Indian Affairs (BIA), which together with the tribal councils has managed Indian affairs since 1824. Recent studies show that Indian reservations have received only about eleven cents out every dollar appropriated to the BIA by Congress.

Indian tribes now operate more than 100 casinos and large-scale bingo halls in 23 states. Agreements are generally negotiated with the local, state, and federal government about the type of gambling and the location of the gambling facility. With the revenues from gaming, Indian tribes can finance community projects for their people and move toward self-government. In 2005, Indian tribes made payments of $1.2 billion to states and cities where they operate casinos.

Summary

- Each state has general power to make criminal laws. The federal government has only the power delegated to it in the U.S. Constitution.
- The federal government has specific power to make laws including criminal laws under parts of the Constitution such as the Commerce Clause, as well as power to make criminal laws for federal territories, enclaves, military posts, and as applied to crimes against federal employees or officers.
- The Commerce Clause gives the federal government power to regulate actions by use of criminal laws only if the actions involve or affect interstate commerce.
- International conventions, treaties, and other agreements between nations can confer power on the federal government to make criminal laws. All countries, including the United States, have the power to regulate their shores and the sea area around those shores.
- The federal domain consists of substantial land areas within the United States, Puerto Rico, and other territories and enclaves. It also includes sea and air approaches to the United States.
- U.S. citizens serving in the military may be prosecuted for crimes in military courts, including when they are serving in foreign countries.
- Indian tribal courts have power to try Indians charged with crimes on an Indian reservation. Crimes committed by Indians outside a reservation are subject to state or federal prosecution.

Key Terms

jurisdiction, p. 34
federal enclaves, p. 37
extradition, p. 37

United Nations Conventions, p. 38
maritime jurisdiction, p. 40

martial law, p. 42
posse comitatus, p. 43

Case Analysis and Writing Exercises

1. In 18 U.S.C. Section 931, Congress made it a federal crime for any convicted felon to possess body armor. The defendant, a convicted felon, was charged under this statute when he was found wearing a bulletproof vest. The vest was manufactured in another state but had been moved to the defendant's state before he bought it. Neither the defendant nor the vest had any other connection to interstate commerce. Does Congress have authority under the Commerce Clause to pass this statute? Does it satisfy any of the tests in *Lopez*? See *United States v. Patton*, 451 F.3d 615 (10th Cir. 2006), *cert. denied* 127 S. Ct. 1247 (2007).

2. Wheeler, a Navajo tribal member, was convicted in tribal court of contributing to the delinquency of a minor. He was subsequently indicted in federal court for statutory rape arising out of the same incident.
   a. If the above occurred in the same jurisdiction, would it violate the Double Jeopardy Clause?
   b. Should the indictment be dismissed? See *Wheeler v. United States*, 435 U.S. 313 (1978).

3. Kasi was convicted in Virginia State Court for the murder of three CIA employees outside CIA headquarters in Langley. After the killings, Kasi escaped from the United States and returned to his native Pakistan. Four years later, FBI agents discovered Kasi in Pakistan and forcibly abducted him back to the United States to face criminal charges.

Pakistan and the United States have a mutual extradition treaty, and Kasi's abduction was not in accordance with that treaty. Kasi claims the Virginia State Court lacked jurisdiction over him because his return to this country was not in compliance with the Pakistan–United States treaty. Is he right? What should a court look for in the extradition treaty? See *Kasi v. Angelone*, 300 F.3d 487 (4th Cir. 2002).

4. In 2007 the U.S. Supreme Court decided *Gonzales v. Carhart*, 127 S. Ct. 1610 (discussed in Chapter 9). In that case, the Court held that the Partial-Birth Abortion Ban of 2003 was constitutional. In a short concurring opinion, Justice Thomas noted that the question of the power of Congress under the Commerce Clause to pass the act was not briefed in the case, and thus not presented to the Court. Assume that under the act a physician who performed abortions only in one town, in one state, and only for residents of that town, was charged with violation of the act. Under *Lopez* and *Raich*, discussed in this chapter, does Congress have the authority to make this purely intrastate activity a federal crime? Why or why not? Putting aside (for now; see Chapter 9) the Second Amendment, does the Commerce Clause give Congress authority to pass a law that makes ownership of all guns unlawful? Are these cases different in any significant way?

Notes

1. In the 1995 case of *United States v. Lopez* (115 S. Ct. 1624, 57 CrL 2031), the U.S. Supreme Court stated that

   > We have identified three broad categories of activity that Congress may regulate under its

   commerce power.... [First] "[T]he authority of Congress to keep the channels of interstate commerce free from immoral and injurious uses has been frequently sustained, and is no longer open to question." Second, Congress is *empowered to regulate and protect the instrumentalities of interstate commerce, or persons or things in interstate commerce, even though the threat may come only from intrastate activities.*

... [F]or example, the destruction of an aircraft (18 U.S.C. § 32), or ... thefts from interstate shipments (18 U.S.C. § 659). Finally, Congress' commerce authority includes the power to regulate those activities having a substantial relation to interstate commerce, Jones & Laughlin Steel, 301 U.S., at 37, that is, those activities that substantially affect interstate commerce.

2. If federal property is intentionally damaged or destroyed, the federal government ordinarily has jurisdiction over the matter. When state property is intentionally damaged or destroyed within that state, the state government has jurisdiction. What about a situation in which the property is internationally owned, such as the United Nations building in New York City? In the 1976 case of *People v. Weiner* (85 Misc. 2d 161, 378 N.Y.S.2d 966), the defendant was charged with criminal mischief for having sprayed red paint on the outside wall of the UN headquarters. The New York Criminal Court held that it had jurisdiction over the person of the defendant and the offense.

3. This material was presented in the *Working Papers of the National Commission on Reform of Federal Criminal Laws*, vol. 2, p. 832.

4. At the time of the assassination of President Kennedy, only the state of Texas had jurisdiction to try the homicide charges.

5. The *National Geographic* magazine article "To Use or to Save" (October 1996) states that the federal domain "covers a third of the nation, more than 700 million acres, a public trust unmatched in the world."

6. 355 U.S. 286, 78 S. Ct. 291 (1958).

7. *United States v. Georgescu*, 723 F.Supp. 912 (1989).

8. U.S. Supreme Court Justice Robert H. Jackson represented the United States at the Nuremberg trials. He wrote as follows:

No half-century ever witnessed slaughter on such a scale, such cruelties and inhumanities, such wholesale deportations of people into slavery, such annihilations of minorities. The terror of Torquemada pales before the Nazi inquisition.... Goaded by these facts, we have moved to redress the blight on the record on our era.... We should

not overlook the unique and emergent character of this body as an International Military Tribunal. It is no part of the constitutional mechanism of internal justice of any of the Signatory nations. Germany has unconditionally surrendered, but no peace treaty has been signed or agreed upon. The Allies are still technically in a state of war with Germany, although the enemy's political and military institutions have collapsed. As a Military Tribunal, it is a continuation of the war effort of the Allied Nations. As an International Tribunal, it is not bound by the procedural and substantive refinements of our respective judicial or constitutional systems, nor will its rulings introduce precedents into any country's internal civil system of justice. As an International Military Tribunal, it rises above the provincial and transient and seeks guidance not only from International Law but also from the basic principles of jurisprudence which are assumptions of civilization and which long have found embodiment in the codes of all nations.

9. See the *New York Times* article, "Trying to Make Sure That War Crimes Aren't Forgotten or Go Unpunished," September 22, 1997.

10. The first person convicted for Balkan war crimes was a Croat. See the *New York Times* article, "Croat Is First to Be Convicted (in The Hague) by Balkan War Crimes Panel," June 1, 1997. The article points out that of 76 people charged with Balkan war crimes, only 9 were in custody.

A Bosnian Serb who returned to live in Germany was sentenced to life imprisonment by a German court for war crimes committed in Bosnia. After the man was arrested in Germany, the German government agreed to try him under German law because the United Nations War Crimes Tribunal in The Hague stated it was overburdened. See the *New York Times* article "Bosnian Serb Is Sentenced to Life Term for Genocide," September 27, 1997.

11. Ships are free to travel in territorial waters, if their passage is "innocent." *Innocent passage* is defined by the Law of the Sea Treaty as follows: "Passage is innocent so long as it is not prejudiced to the peace, good order or security of the coastal state."

12. During Prohibition in the 1920s (when the consumption and sale of alcoholic beverages were illegal in the United States), European ships would sell liquor to Americans in "Rum Row,"

international waters off the East Coast of the United States. The U.S. Supreme Court upheld a Coast Guard vessel coming alongside Lee's ship and observing illegal whiskey on the deck. Lee's conviction was affirmed in the case of *United States v. Lee,* 47 S. Ct. 746 (1927).

13. *Singleton v. United States,* 789 F. Supp. 492 (D. Puerto Rico 1992).

14. Article I, Section 8, of the U.S. Constitution provides (in part) that

    The Congress shall have Power ... To define and punish Piracies and Felonies committed on the high Seas, and Offenses against the Law of Nations; To declare War ... and make Rules concerning Captures on Land and Water; To raise and support Armies; ... To provide and maintain a Navy; To make Rules for the Government and Regulation of the land and naval Forces; To provide for calling forth the Militia to execute the Laws of the Union, suppress Insurrections and repel Invasions; ... To make all Laws which shall be necessary and proper for carrying into Execution the foregoing Powers, and all other Powers vested by this Constitution in the Government of the United States, or in any Department or Officer thereof.

    Article II of the U.S. Constitution provides in part that

    Section 1. The executive Power shall be vested in a President of the United States of America....
    Section 2. The President shall be Commander in Chief of the Army and Navy of the United States, and of the Militia of the several States, when called into the actual Service of the United States.

15. 10 U.S.C.A. Sections 801–940 (Supp.V. 1970) amending 10 U.S.C.A. Sections 801–940 (1964).

16. 395 U.S. 258, 89 S. Ct. 1683 (1969).

17. 483 U.S. 435, 107 S. Ct. 2924 (1987).

18. The best known SOFA (status of forces agreement) is that with the NATO countries, where there has been a large U.S. military commitment since 1945 in a continuous effort to keep the peace.

19. 720 F.2d 340, 34 CrL 2154 (4th Cir. 1983).

20. 14 CrL 2387 (1974).

21. 437 F.2d 200 (4th Cir. 1971).

22. See the *New York Times* article, "One Pleads Guilty to Okinawa Rape; 2 Others Admit Role," November 8, 1995.

23. 327 U.S. 304, 66 S. Ct. 606 (1946).

24. From the testimony of Major General Wilson, chief of the National Guard Bureau, before the President's Commission on Campus Unrest, 116 Cong. Rec. 27, 339.

25. 18 U.S.C. Section 3243. This act is titled the Kansas Act.

26. 430 U.S. 641, 645 (1977).

27. The Posse Comitatus Act, 18 U.S.C. Section 1385 (1878), forbids the use of the military to enforce civilian laws. Federal law 10 U.S.C. 375 requires the secretary of defense to establish regulations to ensure against direct participation by members of the military in the enforcement of civilian laws. The act provides: Whoever, except in cases and under circumstances expressly authorized by the Constitution or this Act of Congress, willfully uses any part of the Army or the Air Force as a posse comitatus or otherwise to execute the laws shall be fined not more than $10,000 or imprisoned not more than two years, or both.

THE COMMERCE CLAUSE AND FEDERAL CRIME

Article I of the U.S. Constitution gives Congress the power to regulate "Commerce … among the several states." Called the Commerce Clause, it is the basis for a great part of the authority the federal government has to pass criminal laws. Where activity involves more than a single state, Congress may regulate it, including by the passage of criminal laws. On the other hand, activity that is solely within a single state cannot normally be regulated under the Commerce Clause. Identifying the difference between interstate and intrastate activity has varied over the years.

In 2005 the U.S. Supreme Court decided *Gonzalas v. Raich*, 545 U.S. 1. In that case the Court upheld the authority of Congress under the Commerce Clause to make purely intrastate use and possession of marijuana a federal offense. A California resident who used marijuana solely for medical purposes, as permitted under the California Compassionate Use Act, claimed that the Commerce Clause gave Congress power to regulate marijuana only if it was used or produced in interstate commerce, an argument that appeared to be supported by the Lopez decision. The Court rejected that argument, stating that the presence of a permitted local market for an illegal drug could adversely affect efforts by Congress to control the interstate market for that drug. Thus, Congress could constitutionally regulate the purely local market under the Commerce Clause.

The decision in *Raich* may be treated as a more expansive view of the authority given Congress under the Commerce Clause than was the decision in *Lopez*. For example, in *United States v. Maxwell*, 446 F.3d 1210 (11th Cir. 2006), *cert. denied* 127 S. Ct. 705 (2007), the court reversed an earlier decision in which it had held that Congress had no authority to make the purely intrastate possession of child pornography for personal use a federal crime. The court reasoned that if Congress had power to regulate the intrastate use of marijuana because of its potential impact on the interstate drug market, then Congress also had power to regulate the purely personal, intrastate possession of child pornography because of the potential adverse affect such use might have on the control of the interstate market in child pornography.

The court made this statement about the effect of *Raich*, a statement that might be an accurate prediction of the future. The Raich decision:

> *leaves some doubt as to whether, in the Commerce Clause context, an as-applied challenge may ever be sustained so long as Congress may constitutionally regulate the broader class of activities of which the intrastate activity is a part.*[a]

[a]446 F.3d at 1215.

CHAPTER 3

Essential Elements of a Crime

Oscar Sosa for The New York Times

In one of the more controversial applications of the felony murder rule (discussed in Chapter 10), in 2004 Ryan Holle, then 20 years old, was convicted of first-degree murder after he loaned his car to three men with whom he had been partying. The three men drove the car to the house of a drug dealer, and during a burglary killed the drug dealer's daughter. The three killers were each sentenced to life in prison without parole. Holle, who contended he thought the men were going to get food, received the same sentence as the actual killers under accomplice liability and the felony murder rules.

OUTLINE

Crimes Requiring Proof of Mental Fault

Actus Reus: The Forbidden Act or Omission

Mens Rea: The Guilty Mind

Proving Criminal Intent or Criminal State of Mind

The Requirement of Scienter

The Motive for Committing a Crime

Strict Liability Crimes

Strict Liability Laws That Seek to Protect Children

Proximate Cause or Causation

Possession Alone as a Crime

The Possession of Illegal Contraband Inference

The Use of Presumptions and Inferences in Criminal Law

Functions of Presumptions and Inferences

In June 2010 Mahmoud Reza Banki was convicted by a New York Federal Court jury of several crimes related to a money-transfer system called "hawala." Banki, an Iranian immigrant, used this informal system to transfer millions of dollars between the United States and Iran. Such transfers violate the Iran trade embargo laws. Banki contended he was innocent, and that while he helped transfer money, it was all done with relatives, and he didn't know the money was going to Iran. He lacked the necessary intent to commit a crime, he contended. Is that intent necessary?

Criminal laws focus on prohibited behavior. People usually cause harm by their actions, not just their thoughts or intentions. However, in many situations it is appropriate to punish prohibited actions (called the *actus reus*) only if they are accompanied by a required mental state (called the *mens rea*). As the old saying goes, "even a dog knows the difference between being kicked and stepped on." Often, the required mental state for the crime to occur is "knowledge" about some aspect of the crime. For example, it is a federal crime to "knowingly" use a fake identity belonging to another person. What must the defendant "know"? That an identity card is faked? That the identity belongs to another person? Or, under the laws in virtually all states making it a crime for a convicted felon to "knowingly" possess a firearm, when does a person "know" he is in possession of a firearm? What if a passenger in his car has a firearm in his possession? In this chapter we discuss the elements of crimes, focusing on both the physical acts, the *actus reus*, and the mental state, the *mens rea*.

True Crimes and Strict Liability Crimes

From the development of common law until modern times, all crimes had two essential elements: (1) the physical act or omission and (2) a mental requirement known as criminal intent or purpose. Some writers refer to such crimes as *true crimes.* Today, true crimes continue to make up a considerable number of crimes in any criminal code.

In the 1920s and 1930s, state legislatures began creating criminal laws that did not require the mental element essential to true crimes. This relatively new type of crime is called a *strict liability crime,* or regulatory offense. Strict liability crimes can be found in criminal laws pertaining to traffic violations, narcotics, liquor, sanitation, hunting, and pure-food requirements. In strict liability crimes, the government does not have to prove intent or purpose and must show only that the accused performed the act or omission charged or brought about the results that are alleged and shown .Most crimes have some form of mental requirement as an element of the crime. The various forms of mental requirement found in those crimes are discussed in the following section.

Crimes Requiring Proof of Mental Fault

Before a person may be convicted of a crime that requires proof of mental fault, the government must prove the following elements beyond a **reasonable doubt**:

reasonable doubt
Proof beyond a reasonable doubt means that it is not enough to prove it was more likely than not that an element of the crime was true. The proof must be such that a reasonable person could not conclude the element was not true.

actus reus The criminal act.

mens rea The criminal intent or state of mind.

- *The external physical act:* That the conduct or act forbidden by the law of the jurisdiction was in fact committed by the defendant.
- *The internal mental element:* That the act or omission was accompanied by a state of mind required by the criminal statute.

The Latin term **actus reus** ("guilty act") is used by the courts and writers to describe the essential physical act, and the term **mens rea** ("guilty mind") is used to describe the essential mental requirement. State statutes vary on how they define the degrees of criminal intent. That is, with respect to an element of the offense, the mental state of the defendant as to that element can have various formulations. For example, to be convicted of the crime of possession of stolen property, probably all state statutes require that the defendant have knowledge that the property was stolen. The *actus reus* is the physical possession of the property; the *mens rea* is the intent (specific or general) to possess the property; the scienter (knowledge) element is knowledge that the property was stolen. (Scienter is discussed later in this chapter.) Other crimes might require only that the defendant was negligent about an element of the crime. For example, in most states the crime of vehicular homicide can be established by proof that the defendant unintentionally caused the death of another, while operating a motor vehicle recklessly or with gross negligence.

Model Penal Code (MPC) Proposed criminal law developed by the American Law Institute, a group of lawyers, judges, and teachers. Many states have modeled their criminal codes on the Model Penal Code.

The **Model Penal Code (MPC)** is a proposed criminal code drafted by the American Law Institute, a group of lawyers, judges, and law professors. Many states use parts of the MPC when drafting their own criminal codes. Section 2.02 of the MPC suggests the following formulation of the mental element:

Minimum Requirements of Culpability. Except as provided in Section 2.05, a person is not guilty of an offense unless he acted purposely, knowingly, recklessly, or negligently, as the law may require, with respect to each material element of the offense.

The U.S. Supreme Court has never created or announced a doctrine requiring proof of *mens rea* in all crimes and in all cases before an accused can be held accountable for his or her acts.[1] Therefore, the states are generally free to create criminal laws that do not require proof of *mens rea* or to create criminal laws requiring different degrees of mental fault or mental guilt. But if a degree of mental guilt is made an element of the crime by law, the prosecutor must then prove this essential element of the crime, as well as prove the acts taken together with this mental element.

Thinking of committing a crime without performing a criminal act is not a crime. If a person with criminal thoughts does nothing to carry out those thoughts, no crime has occurred. Government cannot punish thoughts alone. To show that a true crime has occurred, the state must show that the external physical act and the internal mental state essential to that crime occurred at the same time. Even crimes such as conspiracy, in which two or more people share their thoughts about a crime, generally require that the conspirators do at least one physical act in furtherance of the conspiracy (see Chapter 4).

In some instances, an act without the required mental state (guilty mind) is no crime. For example, a person incapable of entertaining the required criminal mind because of legal insanity has not committed a crime. A student who picks up someone else's book or briefcase by mistake has performed a physical act, but without the guilty or criminal state of mind necessary for the crime of theft, no crime has been committed. However, suppose that the student keeps the book or briefcase for two days and then, realizing the mistake, decides to keep the property. The taking and keeping of the property for two days has been a continuous act in the eyes of the law. The crime of theft occurred when the intent to deprive the true owner of permanent possession concurred with the act of taking and retaining possession.

Concurrence The requirement in crimes requiring proof of mental intent that the forbidden act and guilty mind must occur at the same time or otherwise be linked. For example, trustees, guardians, and lawyers might have possession of another person's money (physical act). For the crime of embezzlement to occur they must intentionally and wrongfully misappropriate this money (forbidden act and guilty mind).

The requirement that the mental fault and prohibited act must both be present in crimes requiring mental fault is usually called "concurrence." **Concurrence** requires a connection between the mental fault and the forbidden act, in the sense that the mental fault "drives" or "actuates" the forbidden act. For example, one who innocently enters a residence of another, but once inside decides to steal the occupant's property cannot under most state statutes be convicted of burglary, because that crime requires the mental intent to enter the house for the purpose of committing a crime. The forbidden act occurred, but there was no concurrence of the required mental fault. Or, a person may both desire and make plans for the death of another, but if he subsequently and inadvertently kills that person in an automobile accident he can't be guilty of murder. His mental state of wanting to kill the other person did not "drive" or "actuate" the act that caused the death.

Although the forbidden act and the guilty mind must concur, the resulting harm need not take place at the same time.

EXAMPLE: While A is on vacation, X rigs a spring gun to A's front door (forbidden act), setting it with the intention that A be killed when he opens the door (guilty mind). Two weeks after the spring gun is set in place, A returns from vacation and is shot and killed when he opens his door.

In the example given, the *actus reus* and the *mens rea* concurred, but the results did not occur until A opened the door two weeks after the act with intent to kill was performed.

Actus Reus: The Forbidden Act or Omission

Most criminal laws forbid specific acts, and a few punish the failure to carry out a legal duty. The act forbidden or commanded by the law is described in the definition of each particular offense, usually in terms of the harm or the wrong that occurs. In the crime of murder, the death of the victim caused by the defendant's forbidden act or omission is the harm and the wrong. In the crime of larceny, the loss of personal or movable

ELEMENTS OF A CRIME

Crimes may consist of combinations of the three human activities of thought, communication, and actions (or conduct):

1. *Thoughts* alone cannot be punished as crimes; however, thoughts can constitute the required mental element (*mens rea*) for verbal offenses or acts that have been designated as crimes.
2. *Communications* (spoken or written words, symbols, and so on) may be offenses in themselves or may be combined with either thoughts or actions to constitute crimes (see Chapter 9).
3. *Human acts* alone can sometimes constitute a crime, without a showing of a mental element. These crimes, in which the state is required to show only that the defendant committed a forbidden act or omission, are usually called *strict liability crimes*. When the state is required to prove a specific mental element (*mens rea*), it must then prove the required intent, purpose, or knowledge that is an essential element of the crime.

property caused by the defendant's wrongful taking and carrying away is the harm and the wrong.

The manner in which the harm or wrong can be caused varies considerably. A murder can be committed by use of a gun, a knife, a blow, poison, or by any one of many different acts. The harm or the wrong done usually varies from crime to crime, but sometimes two crimes embody the same harm or wrong.

All criminal homicides share the same harm or wrong, which is the death of a person. Homicides can differ from one another primarily because of the differing states of mind of the offenders at the time they cause the harm or wrong, which is the death of another person. Both murder and manslaughter involve the death of a person, but because of the different mental states required for a conviction, they are different crimes.

Just as different mental states may result in different crimes charged, so too may different acts be made criminal where more than one person is a party to a crime. As a result, the *actus reus* may be different for each party's involvement in the crime. A *party to a crime* could be (1) a person who actually and physically commits the crime, (2) a person who conspires in the planning of the crime or orders that the crime be committed, or (3) a person who aids and assists in the commission of the crime. All state criminal codes define parties to a crime and make each of the parties to a crime equally liable for the crime (see Chapter 4).

The different *actus reus* for parties to a crime are illustrated by the following example:

EXAMPLE: A hires B and C to murder X. A tells B and C how and where she wants X to be murdered. B is the vehicle driver and lookout while C commits the murder. A hired and ordered the killing.

C's act in killing X is the *actus reus* of the direct commission of the crime. B's acts as aider and abettor are the *actus reus* of assistance. A jury could easily find that all three parties (particularly A) conspired and agreed in the planning of the murder, which is the *actus reus* of agreement.

The state has the burden of proving beyond a reasonable doubt the *actus reus* element of every offense, and the jury must unanimously agree that the state has proved the *actus reus* elements before they may find a defendant guilty.

Because the *actus reus* element for each category is different, the jury must agree unanimously on which *actus reus* or which category the state has proved.

Mens Rea: The Guilty Mind

A cardinal principle of criminal law pertaining to true crimes was long ago expressed in Latin as *actus non facit reum nisi mens sit rea* ("an act does not make a person guilty unless the mind is guilty").

The term *mens rea* means evil intent, criminal purpose, and knowledge of the wrongfulness of conduct. It is also used to indicate the mental state required by the crime charged, whether that be **specific intent** to commit the crime, recklessness, guilty knowledge, malice, or criminal negligence.

Criminal liability usually requires "an evil-meaning mind [and] an evil-doing hand."[2] However, while the phrase *evil-meaning mind* suggests an evil purpose for doing the evil act, a mind can be "guilty" without such evil purpose. For example, doing an act recklessly, but without the "evil" intent to harm another, may lack the *mens rea* for one crime but nonetheless satisfy the *mens rea* requirement of another. One's state of mind can range from being "purposeful"—that is, intending a particular result or consequence—to merely negligent—that is, failing to be aware of the probable results or consequences of an act.

The following example illustrates situations in which the harm done is the same in all cases, but the mental element varies:

EXAMPLE: X, a construction worker, is working on the fourth floor of a building under construction in the downtown area of a city. His conduct caused the death of W, who was hit on the head by a crowbar as she was walking on the sidewalk past the building.

1. deliberately dropped the heavy crowbar so as to hit W on the head.
2. did not want to kill anybody but wanted to see the people scatter when he dropped the crowbar to the sidewalk.
3. threw the crowbar at another worker in a fight, but missed. The crowbar fell, killing W on the sidewalk below.
4. came to work drunk and accidentally pushed the crowbar off the edge of the building.
5. Another worker called for the crowbar and X threw it to him, but the throw was bad and the crowbar hit W on the sidewalk below.
6. was knocked unconscious when a crane collapsed, causing him to drop the crowbar, which hit and killed W.

Assuming a jurisdiction uses the mental fault classification similar to that suggested by the MPC, set forth earlier in this chapter, what crimes, if any, could X be charged with in each of these examples? What arguments are available to X based on his degree of mental fault?

While the classification system suggested by the MPC distinguishes between each level of mental state, the distinction does not always make a difference. See *United States v. U.S. Gypsum Co.,* in which the U.S. Supreme Court stated that in the case of most crimes, "the limited distinction between knowledge and purpose has not been considered important."[3]

In *United States v. Bailey,* the U.S. Supreme Court stated that in a "general sense, 'purpose' corresponds loosely with the common-law concept of specific intent, while 'knowledge' corresponds loosely with the concept of 'general intent.'"[4]

The concepts of "general intent" and "specific intent" referred to in the *Bailey* decision were the common law's attempt to isolate and identify the different mental states required for various crimes. At common law, "general intent" referred to the intent of the defendant to do the forbidden act. If the act was done intentionally, it did not matter

specific intent The intent necessary for one or more elements of an offense. Murder, for example, requires the specific intent that the act be done intentionally or purposely.

CASE CLOSE-UP

Flores-Figueroa v. United States
United States Supreme Court
129 S. Ct. 1886 (2009)

Flores-Figueroa, a Mexican citizen, unlawfully entered the United States. In order to secure employment, Flores-Figueroa presented an employer with a counterfeit Social Security and alien registration card ("green card"). The cards used his real name, but the numbers on the documents belonged to other people. Flores-Figueroa was charged with various immigration crimes, and was also charged with "aggravated identity theft" under 18 U.S.C. §1028A(a)(1), which upon conviction provides for a mandatory two years imprisonment to be added to the sentences for the underlying crimes. Section 1028A(a)(1) states that it is a crime if one "knowingly transfers, possesses, or uses, without lawful authority, a means of identification of another person."

Flores-Figueroa was convicted of all charges, and he appealed the conviction and increased sentence under the aggravated identity theft statute. He alleged the prosecution failed to prove that he knew the numbers on the counterfeit cards belonged to "another person." Flores-Figueroa contended that §1028A(a)(1) required the government to prove he "knowingly" violated every element of the statute, including the use of a number belonging to another person. The trial court and Court of Appeals disagreed, and the Supreme Court granted review on that specific question. The Supreme Court agreed with Flores-Figueroa, and it reversed his conviction under the aggravated identity theft statute.

The government contended that "knowingly" modified only the actions of transferring or possessing counterfeit documents, and that doing so was without lawful authority. It did not require, the government contended, knowledge that the counterfeit numbers belonged to "another" person. The Court rejected the government's position, mainly based on the way the statute was worded:

"There are strong textual reasons for rejecting the Government's position. As a matter of ordinary English grammar, it seems natural to read the statute's word 'knowingly' as applying to all the subsequently listed elements of the crime.... In ordinary English, where a transitive verb has an object, listeners in most contexts assume that an adverb (such as knowingly) that modifies the transitive verb tells the listener how the subject performed the entire action, including the object as set forth in the sentence." (129 S. Ct. at 1890). Since the object of the sentence was the means of identification of "another person," the Court concluded the government must prove Flores-Figueroa knew the documents he used belonged to "another person." Since it did not, the conviction was reversed.

Justice Alito, in a concurring opinion, expressed concern that the majority decision was an "overly rigid rule of statutory construction." He identified some statutes where the lower federal courts had interpreted statutes differently, because of the context of the statute. For example, 18 U.S.C. § 2423(a), which makes it a crime to "knowingly" transport an individual under 18 years of age across state lines for the purpose of prostitution, has uniformly been interpreted by the Courts of Appeals as not requiring proof the defendant knew the individual transported was under 18 years of age. In the appropriate context, Justice Alito stated, such an interpretation would be correct. He concluded, however, that the present case did not have such a context, and thus agreed with the result.

At least one lower federal court has adopted Justice Alito's understanding of the limited holding in *Flores-Figueroa*. In *United States v. Cox*, 577 F.3d 833 (7th Cir. 2009), decided shortly after *Flores-Figueroa*, the Seventh Circuit Court of Appeals held that 18 U.S.C. § 2423(a) does not require proof that the defendant knew the individual transported was under the age of 18.

if the defendant had any particular purpose for doing the act. For example, manslaughter (and second-degree murder) was a general intent crime, since all that was required for conviction was proof that the acts leading to the death of the victim were done intentionally. No proof of a particular purpose or plan to cause the death was required.

"Specific intent" referred to the intent not only to do the forbidden act, but also to the intent to do some other identified act, or with some specific purpose in mind. For example, the crime of burglary not only required the general intent to do the forbidden act, unlawfully entering the premises of another, but also the specific intent to steal or otherwise commit a felony within the premises. Other illustrations of the difference between general intent and specific intent might include the crime of "indecent exposure," which requires only the intent to do the forbidden act. It does not require the specific intent that any particular person should see the act. The crime of false pretenses requires not only the general intent to make a false statement, but also the specific intent to use the false statement to defraud another person of money or property.

In *United States v. Bailey,* the U.S. Supreme Court stated that in "common law, crimes generally were classified as requiring either 'general intent' or 'specific intent.' This ... distinction, however, has been the source of a good deal of confusion."[5]

This confusion, the Court pointed out, had led to a movement away from the common law classifications of *mens rea*. Citing Section 2.02 of the MPC, presented earlier in this chapter (and LaFave and Scott's *Criminal Law,* 2nd ed., Belmont, Calif.: West/Wadsworth, 1986), the Court suggested a better method would include using the following categories "in descending order of culpability: purpose, knowledge, recklessness, and negligence."

Proving Criminal Intent or Criminal State of Mind

When criminal intent or another mental element is an essential element of a crime, the state has the burden of proving the required *mens rea*. Proof of the mental element may be made by

- Showing the acts of the defendant and the circumstances that existed at the time of the crime. Because most people know what they are doing and also know the natural and probable consequences of their acts, a judge or jury may reasonably infer that the defendant intended the natural and probable consequences of his or her deliberate acts.[6] Thus, a person who pointed a loaded gun at another person and pulled the trigger knew what he or she was doing and desired the natural and probable consequences of the acts.
- Producing evidence to show the statements of the defendant at the time of the crime, as well as statements made after the crime. Statements of a defendant before or after a crime may be incriminating and may include admissions or a confession of guilt.

Only rarely is written evidence of the intent or purpose of a defendant available to the state. The following jury instruction on intent was approved by the Fifth Circuit Court of Appeals in the 1975 case of *United States v. Durham:*

> It is reasonable to infer that a person ordinarily intends the natural and probable consequences of his knowing acts. The jury may draw the inference that the accused intended all the consequences that one standing in like circumstances and possessing like knowledge should reasonably have expected to result from any intentional act or conscious omission. Any such inference drawn is entitled to be considered by the jury in determining whether or not the government has proved beyond a reasonable doubt that the defendant possessed the required criminal intent.[7]

Although one can reasonably infer that a person ordinarily intends the natural and probable consequences of his or her knowing and deliberate acts, one cannot extend that inference to conclude that a person intends results that are not the natural, reasonable, or probable consequences of a voluntary act. Moreover, this

On November 9, 2009 Army Major Nidal Hasan, a psychiatrist, shot and killed 13 soldiers and civilians at a military medical center at Fort Hood, Texas. Hasan was shot by police officers, and is paralyzed as a result. Hasan is being held in a military jail awaiting trial at Fort Hood while his defense attorneys' obtain a psychiatric evaluation. The investigation has shown that on many occasions before the rampage Hasan visited a shooting range to practice target shooting with the guns used in the killings. Such evidence may be used to show Hasan's intent in the killings.

inference has sometimes been rejected as a basis for convicting a defendant who is charged with accomplice liability, such as aiding and abetting another in the commission of a crime, if the underlying crime requires a showing of specific intent. (Vicarious liability of aiding and abetting is discussed in Chapter 4). Courts have held that convicting one who aids another person who has committed such a crime, based only on the inference that the accomplice could foresee the commission of the crime, is not permitted, unless it is shown the accomplice intended to further the commission of the crime. See, e.g., *United States v. Hill*, 55 F.3d 1197 (6th Cir. 1995). In *Wilson-Bey v. United States*, 903 A.2d 818 (D.C. 2006) the court reversed the conviction for first-degree murder on an aiding and abetting theory because the government did not prove the aider had the specific intent to kill required by the statute.

Major Nadil Malik Hasan was charged with 13 counts of premeditated murder as the initial criminal charges arising out of the brutal and wild shootings that occurred at the Fort Hood, Texas, U.S. Army base in 2009. Many eyewitnesses and victims, who attempted to flee the building by throwing chairs and tables at Major Hasan, will testify about the actions taken by the gunman, making proof of the *actus reus* easy. However, since premeditated murder is a specific intent crime, requiring proof beyond a reasonable doubt of the specific intent to kill, how will the military prosecutors prove that specific intent? Do the prosecutors need to prove Major Hasan's motive for the wild, deadly shooting spree? Is motive a necessary part of *mens rea*? Why or why not?

The Requirement of Scienter

scienter A form of specific intent requiring a showing that the actor knew of the existence of certain facts. For example, one cannot be guilty of possession of stolen property if one does not know property is stolen.

Scienter is sometimes made an essential element of a crime that the state must prove beyond a reasonable doubt. **Scienter** is a legal term meaning a degree of knowledge that makes an individual legally responsible for the consequences of his or her acts. Scienter is alleged in a criminal complaint through charging that the accused person had sufficient knowledge to know that his or her act was unlawful. Examples of crimes in which state statutes most often require scienter include the following:

- In battery or assault on a law enforcement officer, knowledge that the victim is a law enforcement officer
- In refusing to aid a law enforcement officer, knowledge that the person requesting assistance is a law enforcement officer
- In obstructing a law enforcement officer, knowledge that the person obstructed is a law enforcement officer
- In receiving stolen property, knowledge that the property received is stolen property
- In possession of obscene material, knowledge of the nature of the material
- In bribery of a public official or a juror, knowledge that the person is a public official or juror
- In harboring or aiding a felon, knowledge that the person aided is a felon

EXAMPLE: As you are driving your car down a busy street, you see a hitchhiker. You pick up the hitchhiker, and a mile down the road you are stopped by police. The hitchhiker had committed an armed robbery of a store minutes before you picked him up in your car.

What scienter element must be shown to justify your arrest and conviction for either the offense of being party to the crime of armed robbery or the harboring and aiding a felon?

ESSENTIAL ELEMENTS OF A TRUE CRIME

To obtain a conviction, the state must prove the following essential elements when charging a *true crime*:

- *The act element:* The forbidden act (or failure to act).
- *The mental element:* The state of mind required for the crime (the guilty mind); usually proved by use of inferences drawn from the acts of the defendant.
- *The harm element:* The wrong done (killing, physical injury, property damage, loss, and so on).
- *The cause element:* The harm done was the natural and probable result of the wrongful act.

Some crimes require proof of additional essential elements, such as scienter and possession (actual or constructive).

INNOCENT ACTS THAT, IF DONE WITH FORBIDDEN INTENT, ARE CRIMES

Innocent Acts	Forbidden Intent	Resulting Crimes
Possessing a tool or other instrumentality	To use such a device to break into a depository or building and steal therefrom	Possession of burglarious tools
Traveling in interstate or foreign commerce	To avoid prosecution for a state felony or to avoid giving testimony in such a prosecution	Fugitive felon or witness violation; 18 U.S.C.A §§ 1073 & 1074 (a)
Traveling in interstate or foreign commerce	For the purpose of engaging in nonmarital sexual activity with a person under 18 years of age (21 countries now permit police to arrest for this offense in an effort to stamp out the sex trade in children between nations)	Mann Act; 18 U.S.C.A § 2423
Traveling in interstate or foreign commerce	With intent to incite a riot (statute requires an overt act, but such act could be a lawful act)	18 U.S.C.A § 2101 (a)(1)
Using U.S. mail, telephone, or interstate wire facilities	To participate through racketeering in a criminal enterprise	RICO violation; 18 U.S.C.A §§ 1961–1968 (see Chapter 18)
Using U.S. mail	To advance a fraudulent scheme	Mail fraud; 18 U.S.C.A § 1341
Using a fictitious name or address	To further a fraudulent mail scheme	18 U.S.C.A § 1342
Association with other people or organizations	Knowing they advocate the overthrow of our government and that they intend to use force or violence to bring it about	18 U.S.C.A § 2385
Entering a train	With intent "to commit any crime or offense against a person or property thereon"	18 U.S.C.A § 1991
Going on "any military, naval, or Coast Guard reservation, post, fort, arsenal, yard, station, or installation"	"For any purpose prohibited by law or lawful regulation"	18 U.S.C.A § 1382
Teaching or demonstrating the use, application, or making of a firearm, or making of a firearm, explosive, or incendiary device, or a technique capable of causing injury or death	"Intending that the same will be unlawfully employed for use in, or in furtherance of , a civil disorder which may in any way or degree obstruct, delay, or adversely affect commerce" or the performance of any federally protected function	18 U.S.C.A § 231(a)(1)

The following cases on this topic have appeared before the U.S. Supreme Court or lower federal courts in recent years.

United States v. Feola

Supreme Court of the United States (1975) 420 U.S. 671, 95 S. Ct. 1255

Feola and others assaulted two men. Feola argued that he did not know the men he assaulted were undercover federal agents, and, for that reason, his convictions of assaulting federal officers should be reversed.

While most state "assault on law enforcement officer" statutes require proof of scienter (knowledge that the victim was a law enforcement officer), the U.S. Congress did not put this element into the federal crime of assaulting or battering a federal officer.

In *Feola* the U.S. Supreme Court refused to read the scienter element into the federal crime as written by the U.S. Congress. The Court pointed out that the defendants may have been surprised when their victims turned out to be federal officers, but they knew from the beginning that the planned course of conduct was unlawful. The Court held: "A contrary conclusion would give insufficient protection to the agent enforcing an unpopular law, and none to the agent acting under cover."

United States v. Falu[8]

Federal Court of Appeals, Second Circuit (1985) 776 F.2d 46, 38 CrL 2142

The federal "schoolyard statute," 21 U.S.C.A. Section 860(a), provides for doubling the sentence of a person convicted of selling drugs within 1,000 feet of an elementary or secondary school. The federal statute does not require the government to prove that a defendant had knowledge of the school's proximity.

Perez sold heroin to a federal undercover agent brought to him by his friend, Falu. The sale occurred within 1,000 feet of a public school that could not be seen from the location where the sale occurred. Perez and Falu were convicted of "knowingly or intentionally" selling the heroin. Perez directly committed the crime, and Falu was an aider and abettor to the crime. Increased penalties were given to both defendants under the schoolyard statute, as Congress's clear purpose was to deter drug distribution in and around schools. The Court of Appeals affirmed the convictions and increased penalties, stating:

> *The defendant argues that without a requirement that a defendant be aware of the key element under the schoolyard statute, namely, proximity to a school, the statute fails to provide fair notice that the prohibited conduct is subject to enhanced penalties. Falu attempts to distinguish the schoolyard statute from a statute like 18 U.S.C.A. § 111, which makes assaulting a federal officer a federal offense regardless of the defendant's knowledge of the victim's identity. See U.S. v. Feola, 420 U.S. 671, 684 (1975). Section 111, he argues, seeks to effectuate the legislative aim—protection of federal officers—directly, while the schoolyard statute operates only indirectly to benefit school children.*

The court rejected that argument, concluding that Congress intended to create a "drug-free" zone around schools, and as a result intended to eliminate any need for proof that the defendant knew he was engaged in criminal behavior near a school.

> The same result was reached in *United States v. Harris*, 313 F.3d 1228 (10th Cir. 2002), where a defendant engaged in a drug deal ran from police and entered a schoolyard, where he attempted to throw away the drugs he was holding. The Court upheld his conviction under 21 U.S.C. § 860(a), even though no evidence proved his intent to distribute drugs on the schoolyard. The court held it was enough under the statute that the defendant intended to distribute drugs somewhere, and was within 1,000 feet of the school.

United States v. Thomas

United States Court of Appeals for the Armed Forces, 65 M.J. 132 (2007)

A defendant was charged with violation of 10 U.S.C. § 911, 912(a), which makes it a crime to "wrongfully introduce" illegal drugs into a military installation. The prosecution did not prove the defendant knew he was entering a military installation, but contended that knowledge was not required, citing cases like *Falu* and *Harris*. The court of military appeals disagreed, finding that while Congress intended strict liability in the federal officer assault statute and the drug-free zone statute, by adding the requirement of "wrongful" to 10 U.S.C. § 911, 912(a), Congress intended to apply the statute only to those who knew they were introducing illegal drugs to a military installation.

The Motive for Committing a Crime

Intent and *motive* are sometimes thought of as being one and the same. However, the law contains a clear distinction between the two. **Intent** is the mental purpose or design to commit a specific act (or omission), whereas **motive** is the cause, inducement, or reason why an act is committed.

intent The mental purpose or design to commit a specific act (or omission).

motive The cause, inducement, or reason why an act is committed.

EXAMPLE: A man entered a crowded tavern. When the man saw the person he was looking for, he went up to him and killed him by plunging a large knife into his body.

When this case was tried, the state easily proved intent to kill through the many eyewitnesses to the crime (i.e., the jury easily inferred intent to kill from the action of the defendant). However, the state had no admissible evidence as to motive (why the defendant sought out and killed the victim). The state did have inadmissible hearsay evidence that the victim had sold the defendant a bad batch of heroin. The heroin caused the defendant to become ill. As soon as the defendant could get on his feet, he went out and killed the supplier of the heroin.

Intent is an essential element of many crimes and must be proved beyond reasonable doubt when required. Motive, however, is seldom made an essential element required for a criminal conviction.[9] For example, in the 1991 case of *State v. Famiglietti*,[10] the Supreme Court of Connecticut held that the state did not have to prove the motive or reason the defendant set fire to his store after it was shown that the fire was intentionally set by the defendant.

Motive, however, is always relevant evidence that, if available to the state, can be used to show why the person committed the crime. In this sense, motive can be used to help prove intent or another degree of *mens rea* in that it provides the trier of fact with more information and may remove doubt by answering the question "Why?" Motive alone is

FIGURE 3.1

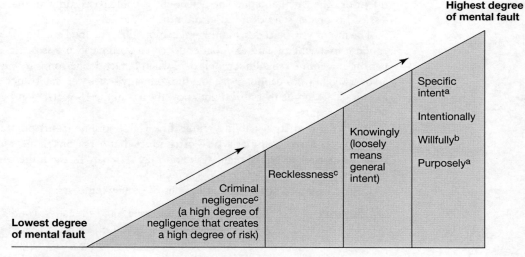

FIGURE 3.1

[a]See pages 244–255 of *Criminal Law* by LaFave (Belmont, Calif.: West/Wadsworth, 2003) for a discussion of general intent and specific intent.
[b]The English police officer's handbook (Moriarty's Police Law, 28th ed., Butterworths, 1972) states on page 5 that "when a person of his own free will does an act he is said to do it willfully."
[c]See pages 261–272 of *Criminal Law* by LaFave for a discussion of recklessness and negligence.

not sufficient to convict; however, a person may be lawfully convicted even if there is no motive or if a motive cannot be shown.

Criminal homicides are committed for various motives, such as hatred, anger, greed, and revenge. However, homicide and other offenses may be committed for "good" motives. Robbing a bank to give the money to the poor and needy is still a crime, even if the stolen funds are used for a good purpose.

Motive can be important evidence in determining punishment or sentencing. An elderly man who kills his terminally ill wife because of her great pain and suffering is charged and sentenced differently than a man who brutally kills an innocent person while committing a crime such as rape or robbery. Figure 3.1 illustrates the different degrees of mental fault.

≡ Strict Liability Crimes

In enacting statutes to enforce rules having to do with public safety—such as traffic, liquor, purity of food, hunting, and narcotics offenses—modern legislative bodies often choose not to create "true" crimes, but rather to enact statutes that do not require any proof of *mens rea*. In these areas, the legislature's interest in promoting public safety justifies strict regulation of acts that threaten that public safety. In such cases, the statute may dispense with the need to prove a defendant was aware his or her actions violated the statute or regulation. These statutory crimes are usually called **strict liability crimes**.

Except for narcotics offenses, the penalties for strict liability offenses are usually lighter than "true" crimes. The offenders are often not considered "criminals" in the full sense of the word, and the state is not required to carry the burden of proving criminal

strict liability crime
Crime that does not require proof of the mental element essential to true crimes.

intent or other mental fault. The defendant is liable based only on the acts taken, regardless of his or her state of mind at the time of the acts.

The motor vehicle codes, hunting regulations, and the food and liquor laws of most states contain strict liability statutes. A bartender cannot ordinarily use as a defense the fact that the person to whom he sold liquor looked 22 when in fact the person was only 17. The driver of an overweight truck cannot argue that the company scales were faulty, nor can an adult male, in most states, argue that he did not know the age of the 15-year-old girl with whom he had sexual intercourse.

In referring to strict liability crimes, the U.S. Supreme Court pointed out that "Congress has rendered criminal a type of conduct that a reasonable person should know is subject to stringent public regulation and may seriously threaten the community's health or safety."[11]

Courts sustained strict liability laws in the following cases:

Firearms	Unregistered hand grenades. *United States v. Freed*, 91 S. Ct. 1112 (1971); unregistered machine guns, *United States v. Evans*, 978 F.2d 1112 (9th Cir. 1992); the offense of carrying a concealed weapon, *People v. Combs*, 408 N.W.2d 420 (Mich. 1987).
Motor vehicle safety laws	Defective headlight. *Queen v. State*, 189 Ga. App. 161, 375 S.E.2d 287 (1988); running a red light, *Hoffer v. State*, 192 Ga. App. 378, 384 S.E.2d 902 (1989).
Intoxicating liquor or beer	Sale to underage person. *State v. Jones*, 57 Ohio App. 3d 155, 567 N.E.2d 313 (1989).
Drug-related deaths	A number of states have enacted so-called Len Bias laws that make people who illegally manufacture, distribute, or dispense illegal drugs strictly liable for drug-related deaths. See *State v. Ervin*, 242 N.J. Super. 584, 577 A.2d 1273 (1990), in which the defendant's girlfriend died of cocaine she obtained from the defendant. His conviction for the New Jersey crime of causing a drug-induced death was affirmed.
Public health laws	Corporation officers can be convicted of Federal Food and Drugs Act violations even when "consciousness of wrongdoing [is] totally wanting." See *United States v. Dotterweich*, 64 S. Ct. 134 (1943), in which adulterated and misbranded drugs were shipped.
Other laws	Prior to discharge from service, an Air Force colonel negotiated for a civilian job and was involved in contract negotiations that violated the laws against taking government action while having conflicting financial interest. *United States v. Hedges*, 912 F.2d 1397 (11th Cir. 1990).

In the case of federal criminal statutes, the U.S. Supreme Court has stated that strict liability crimes are not preferred and that Congress must make it clear if it intends that the *mens rea* requirement has been eliminated from a criminal statute. For example, in *Staples v. United States*, 511 U.S. 600 (1994), the Court held that in a prosecution under the National Firearms Act (26 U.S.C. § 5801), which requires registration of automatic weapons meeting the definition of "firearms" under the act, the prosecution must prove that a defendant knew the weapon he or she possessed constituted a firearm under the act. The defendant was in possession of an automatic rifle, which qualified as a firearm

EXAMPLES OF CONDUCT MADE CRIMINAL UNDER STRICT LIABILITY LAWS

Statute	Conduct	Case
Minnesota prohibited "promoting, employing, using, or permitting a minor (to engage in) a sexual performance" (Minn. Stat. 617, 246).	After checking the identity of a young woman, Eve White hired her to dance nude on her bookstore dance floor. The young woman was only 17. White could not argue that she honestly believed the girl was 26.	*Minnesota v. White*, 464 N.W.2d 585, *review denied* U.S. Supreme Court, 112 S. Ct. 77 (1991)
To protect minors from the illegal drug trade, Congress enacted 21 U.S.C.A. § 861,[12] which forbids an adult to "employ, hire, [or] use" a minor to avoid detection or apprehension in committing a drug crime or to "receive a controlled substance" from a minor other than an immediate family member.	Convictions were affirmed in the Chin and Cook cases, in which the defendants argued that they did not know their drug suppliers were minors. Proof of knowledge of age is not required for conviction.	*United States v. Chin*, 981 F.2d 1275, *review denied* U.S. Supreme Court, 113 S. Ct. 2377 (1993) *United States v. Cook*, 76 F.3d 596 (4th Cir. 1996)
The White Slave Traffic Act increases the punishment for transporting a minor for immoral purposes in interstate or international commerce. Proof is required to show knowledge that the person is being transported for immoral purposes, but proof is not required to show knowledge that the person transported is a minor.	Hamilton could not argue that he did not know the person he was transporting was a minor, or that he made an honest mistake of fact.	*United States v. Hamilton*, 456 U.S. 171, *review denied* U.S. Supreme Court, 92 S. Ct. 2051 (1972)

that must be registered under the act. The prosecution argued that because the statute stated simply that it was a crime to possess or receive a firearm that was not registered, the prosecution did not have to prove the defendant knew the weapon in his possession qualified as a firearm under the act. The Supreme Court disagreed. It held that where the act, possession of a rifle, was not clearly dangerous, the statute should be construed as requiring that the defendant know the weapon in his possession was one that must be registered. The Court distinguished the *Freed* case, discussed above, on the basis that any person would know that a grenade was something inherently dangerous and liable to be the subject of regulations. That is not the case, the Court reasoned, for more standard weapons.

While the maxim "ignorance of the law is no excuse" is applicable to strict liability crimes, in some situations knowledge that an act is unlawful may be an element of the crime. This was the case in *Liparota v. United States*, 471 U.S. 419 (1985). There the Supreme Court held that to be convicted under 7 U.S.C.§2024(b)(1) for the unlawful

If the young people shown above are not old enough to be drinking alcoholic beverages under the state laws setting the minimum drinking age, the bar or store that sold them the alcohol could be criminally liable under the state underage drinking laws, even if the bar did not know the young people were underage and even if the young people presented false identification showing them to be drinking age. Underage drinking laws are examples of strict liability laws, which have no requirement that the person charged with violation of the law possess any particular mental state.

use of food stamps, the prosecution must prove the defendant knew that his use of food stamps was not authorized under the statute.

Strict Liability Laws That Seek to Protect Children

The age of a minor is an essential element of such crimes as SIWAC (sexual intercourse with a child), contributing to the delinquency of a child, violating liquor laws or child pornography laws, or giving or selling a minor a pistol, drugs, cigarettes, and so on. Such laws seek to protect children. To provide further protection to children, many states take away the defense of "mistake of age" from some or all of the offenses that seek to protect children. When this defense is taken away, defendants cannot argue that they made an honest mistake about the age of a child. (See Chapter 7 for a discussion of the defenses of honest mistake of law or fact.)

By taking away the defense of honest mistake as to the age of a child, the state then makes the offense a strict liability offense, and defendants can be proved guilty by showing only that they committed the forbidden act.

EXAMPLE: An adult has sex with a minor. The state has to show only that the sex occurred and the age of the parties. Consent cannot be used as a defense by the adult, as the minor is incapable of giving consent. Mistake as to the age of the minor cannot be used if this defense is prohibited by state law.

☰ Proximate Cause or Causation

Crimes are defined in terms of conduct that is forbidden or required and the mental state existing at the time of the forbidden act or omission. Crimes can also be defined in terms of the harm done or the wrong that occurs.

In crimes in which a harm has occurred, the state must prove that the defendant's wrongful act or omission was the ordinary and probable cause of the harm that resulted. The harm to the victim could occur immediately, such as a bloody nose resulting from a blow to the face or death from being shot at point-blank range. In other instances, a victim could be dangerously injured in a chain of events in which the victim's death does not occur until days or weeks after the crime. In all such cases, the state must prove beyond reasonable doubt that the unlawful and wrongful act of the defendant was the ordinary and probable cause of the harm that resulted. The following cases illustrate court rulings in which the victim's death did not occur immediately.

proximate cause The ordinary and probable cause of a result.

- In the 1992 case of *People v. Roberts* (826 P.2d 274), a prisoner attacked another prisoner with a knife. Death did not occur immediately following eleven stab wounds, and before dying the victim seized the knife from the defendant and attacked a guard. The guard also died, and the defendant was charged with murder for both deaths. The Supreme Court of California pointed out that **proximate cause** of a death is "a cause which, in natural and continuous sequence, produces the death, and without which the death would not have occurred" (CALJIC #8.55). The court pointed out that California follows the old rule, holding:

  If a person inflicts a dangerous wound on another, it is ordinarily no defense that inadequate medical treatment contributed to the victim's death.

  * * *

  To be sure, when medical treatment is grossly improper, it may discharge liability for homicide if the maltreatment is the sole cause of death and hence an unforeseeable intervening cause.

  The Court also held that the defendant could be held to have caused the death of the guard if he could have foreseen that his actions might lead to the attack on the guard.

- The highest court in New York State held in 1993 that a gunshot to the victim's head was a sufficient, direct cause of the victim's death two months later to establish causation beyond a reasonable doubt. In the case of *People v. Velez*, 159 Misc. 2d 38, 602 N.Y.S.2d 758 (1993), the victim pulled out his feeding tube, refused food, and ingested only ice water and other liquids. The defense lawyer argued that the victim committed suicide, but the court held that the victim's acts did not operate as an intervening act excusing criminal liability.[13]

- In the case of *McKinnon v. United States*, 550 A.2d 915 (D.C. 1988) the defendant was convicted of first-degree murder after he slashed his girlfriend's throat. The woman died six weeks later from the injury and from hepatitis, which experts testified probably was caused by blood transfusions or the drug therapy necessary to treat the wound. Neither this case nor the California *Roberts* case presented any claims that medical treatment was grossly improper.

In some situations a person who violates a criminal law and in the process harms another person can be charged with crimes related to the harm. One example of this is the so-called felony-murder rule, which applies when a defendant accidentally or unintentionally causes death while committing a felony of violence (robbery, rape, arson, and so on). Examples of causation in felony murder cases are presented in Chapter 10.

Many cases present situations in which unintended harm occurs while a defendant is committing a misdemeanor or other offense. This often results in a charge of involuntary manslaughter, a lesser offense than felony-murder, as many of the cases in the box on page 47 illustrate. For a prosecutor to charge and a jury or fact finder to convict, the state must be able to prove that the harm was the natural and probable consequence of the wrong done by the defendant.

When the death or injury of a victim is not a foreseeable risk of a defendant's illegal act, courts will not permit a manslaughter or other felony conviction to stand. The following cases illustrate:

- The defendant stole money from a church collection plate—a misdemeanor. One of the members of the church had a heart attack and died from it as he chased the defendant in his car. In reversing the defendant's conviction of manslaughter for the victim's death, a Florida Court of Appeals held in 1992 that

  the petty theft did trigger a series of events that concluded in the death [of the victim] … and was, in that sense, a "cause" of death…. [But] the petty theft did not encompass the kind of direct, foreseeable risk of physical harm that would support a conviction of manslaughter (*Todd v. State*, 594 So. 2d 802).

- The defendant was a capable driver and had been driving for some years but did not have a driver's license. The victim's death occurred when an intoxicated passenger grabbed the wheel from the defendant, causing the car to go out of control. In holding that not having a driver's license was not the proximate cause of the death, the court reversed defendant's manslaughter conviction. *Frazier v. State*, 289 So. 2d 690 (Miss. 1974).

The proximity between the distribution of illegal drugs such as cocaine or heroin and drug overdose deaths has led to state criminal statutes making the person who distributed the illegal drugs responsible for the resulting overdose death. For example, section 782.04(1)(a)(3) of the Florida Statutes (2001) states that a person who distributes illegal drugs that cause death by overdose of the drugs is guilty of first-degree murder. In *Armuller v. State*, 944 So. 2d 1137 (Fla. App. 2006), *review denied*, 956 So. 2d 455 (2007) a drug distributor convicted of murder under this statute contended his actions were not the proximate cause of the overdose death because he sold the drugs (heroin) to friends of the victim, who then helped the victim to inject the drug. The court rejected his "intervening cause" argument, holding that the defendant initiated the distribution of the heroin, and that was sufficient under the statute to satisfy the causation requirement.

The Ancient Year-and-a-Day Murder Rule

One causation problem that can arise in a homicide is a significant lapse of time between the criminal act and the victim's death. At common law, courts applied a rule that a murder conviction required the victim's death within a "year and a day" of the criminal act. The year-and-a-day rule goes back hundreds of years in the law to 1278, when medical science was primitive.[14] Before the American Revolutionary War, Sir William Blackstone described the rule as follows: "In order … to make the killing murder, it is requisite that the party die within a year and a day after the stroke (blow) received, or cause of death administered; in the computation of which the whole day upon which the hurt was done shall be reckoned the first."[15]

CASES OF UNINTENDED HARM RESULTING FROM A MISDEMEANOR OR OTHER MINOR OFFENSE

Conduct of Defendant	Resulting Harm/Criminal Conviction	Case
Repeatedly allowing vicious animals to run loose.	Vicious dogs killed a jogger/ Involuntary manslaughter.	*State v. Powell*, 109 N.C. App. 1, 426 S.E.2d 91 (1993), *aff'd*, 46 S.E.2d 266 (1994)
Permitting an inexperienced youth or intoxicated person to drive his or her vehicle.	Death of child or other person/ Involuntary manslaughter.	*State v. Travis*, 497 N.W.2d 905 (Iowa App. 1993) and other cases
Leaving cocaine in a place where a child could easily obtain it.	Infant daughter died after eating cocaine/Manslaughter and drug abuse.	*State v. Grunden*, 65 Ohio App. 3d 777, 585 N.E.2d 487 (1989)
In Howard Beach, New York, six white teenagers (several of whom had weapons) taunted and threatened three black men. Several of the youths chased Michael Griffith, who ran from the threatening teenagers.	Car killed Griffith as he attempted to cross a busy six-lane highway. Defendants could not use as a defense that "Griffith chose the wrong escape route."	Convictions for manslaughter, assault, and conspiracy affirmed, *People v. Kern*, 554 N.E.2d 1235 (1990)
A girlfriend who was being beaten fled defendant to avoid the beating.	Car crushed the fleeing victim/ Third-degree murder conviction affirmed.	*Commonwealth v. Rementer*, 410 Pa. Super. 9, 598 A.2d 1300 (1991) and other cases
Urging a distressed person talking of suicide to go ahead and do it and providing a gun.	Victim committed suicide/ Second-degree manslaughter.	*People v. Duffy*, 79 N.Y.2d 611, 584 N.Y.S.2d 739, 595 N.E.2d 814 (1992)
Leaving infants or children alone for long periods of time.	Babies left at home while mother went out for evening were killed in fire/Involuntary manslaughter.	*Commonwealth v. Skufca*, 321 A.2d 889, *review denied* 419 U.S. 1028, 95 S. Ct. 510 (1974)
During a fight, the defendant hit his brother in the side with a baseball bat, causing the victim to collapse in a hallway. The defendant then kicked his brother several times. The victim died as the result of the injuries.	Defendant charged with second-degree murder but convicted of voluntary manslaughter after seeking a reduction to assault with intent to do great bodily harm.	*People v. Bailey*, 549 N.W.2d 325 (Mich. 1996)
After starting a fight by striking the first blow and causing the victim to fall to a concrete floor, the defendant then kicked the victim one or more times.	Victim died as a result of bleeding inside his head caused by the injury/Manslaughter.	*State v. Jones*, 598 So. 2d 511 (La. Ct. of App. 1992)
Defendant, who was angry over a highway incident, followed a man home and continued to threaten and make menacing gestures to the victim even after being warned that the older man (victim) had a bad heart.	Victim died of a heart attack while his wife was calling the sheriff; the threats and gestures were held to be an assault/ Involuntary manslaughter.	*State v. Nosis*, 22 Ohio App. 2d 16, 257 N.E.2d 414 (1969)
Providing liquor to a minor or an intoxicated adult.	See "dramshop laws" in Chapter 16, which discusses civil and criminal liability for taverns and social hosts for resulting harm.	*Anderson v. Moulder*, 183 W.Va. 77, 394 S.E.2d 61 (1990)

Under the year-and-a-day rule, a defendant could not be convicted of murder if the victim did not die within a year and a day. The rule made sense years ago, when medical knowledge was limited. But with medical science today, the rule serves little purpose. Many states have abolished the rule or increased the time of the rule. In California, the rule is three years and a day.

While some states continue to use the rule where not specifically repealed by statute, many state supreme courts have abrogated the rule under the court's power to develop the common law. For example, in *State v. Picotte*, 661 N.W.2d 381 (Wis. 2003), the Wisconsin Supreme Court reversed a conviction of a defendant for reckless homicide where the victim died more than a year and a day after the defendant's acts. The court held that although the legislature had not specifically repealed the rule, the court could do so under its power to regulate the growth and development of the common law. However, it concluded that the abrogation of the year-and-a-day rule should be prospective only, and thus the defendant in the case before it could not be convicted of the reckless homicide crime.

Most states have no statute of limitations for murder (see Chapter 7), and a murder trial can commence whenever an offender is taken into custody.

≡ Possession Alone as a Crime

All states make the possession of certain objects a criminal offense. Examples of such crimes are possession of illegal drugs, carrying a concealed weapon, possession of an instrument of a crime, possession of stolen property (vehicles, credit cards, and so on), and possession of graffiti instruments (in some cities and states). The following jury instruction defining *possession* is used in federal courts:

> [T]he law recognizes different kinds of possession. A person may have actual possession or constructive possession.... A person who has direct physical control of something on or around his person is then in actual possession of it. A person who is not in actual possession but who has both the power and the intention to later take control over something … is in constructive possession of it.... Whenever the word "possession" has been used in these instructions it includes actual as well as constructive possession.[16]

Because of public safety, virtually all states forbid carrying an unauthorized concealed weapon (see Chapter 9). *Carrying* requires a showing of actual possession. If a pistol is in the trunk of the car and not within the immediate reach and control of a person, it is not within actual possession.

Illegal drugs could be in actual possession of a defendant, or a defendant could have constructive possession of the drugs. The term *constructive possession* is used to indicate control over property and objects that the defendant does not have in actual possession. The object may be in his or her car parked two blocks away, in a desk drawer in the home or office, or in a suitcase stored somewhere for which he or she has a baggage claim check or key. Constructive possession would not be sufficient to sustain a conviction for carrying a concealed weapon, as a showing of actual possession is necessary. However, constructive possession would sustain a conviction for the possession of contraband, such as narcotics.

The mental element that must be proved in possession offenses is generally that of intention or "knowledge." These mental elements are usually easy to prove, because a person with a loaded revolver or two pounds of marijuana in his pocket cannot argue convincingly that he did not know that the contraband was in his actual possession. The intent to possess, then, is a state of mind existing at the time the person commits the offense. In seeking to determine the state of mind of the alleged offender in order

---

WHEN POSSESSION ALONE IS A CRIME

Possession May Be	Possession May Be	Possession of a Controlled Substance May Be
Actual or Constructive (not in actual possession)	In one person (sole); or Joint (in possession of more than one person)[a]	Of a *usable amount*; or Of a *trace amount*; or Within the body of the suspect; or A combination of any of the above

Most states will not permit a criminal conviction for drug possession based only on a showing of illegal drugs within the body of a defendant. Some states will not sustain a conviction of drug possession on only a showing of a trace amount alone. The strongest cases are those in which a usable amount or a large amount (possession with intent to deliver) is proved (see Chapter 16 on drug abuse).

[a]Charges of joint possession are commonly brought in cases in which a large amount of illegal drugs is seized by law enforcement officers. See the U.S. Supreme Court case of *Ker v. California*, 374 U.S. 23, 83 S. Ct. 1623 (1963), for an example of a conviction based on joint possession of illegal drugs by a husband and wife.

---

to decide whether an intent existed, the jury or the court may base its decision on the defendant's acts, conduct, and other inferences that can be reasonably deduced from all the circumstances.

Possession is one of the rights of ownership of property. Criminal statutes do not require that ownership be proved. A person who possesses heroin may or may not be the owner of the heroin. Possession of personal property is presumptive evidence of ownership, and possession accompanied by the exercise of complete acts of ownership for a considerable time is strong evidence of ownership. In the absence of evidence showing otherwise, objects and articles in a vehicle, dwelling, or business place lead to a strong inference that they are in the constructive possession of the person controlling the vehicle, dwelling, or business place. Therefore, heroin found in an apartment searched under the authority of a search warrant is in the constructive possession of the person controlling and occupying the apartment, unless the person can show otherwise (also see Chapter 16 on drug abuse).

The Possession of Illegal Contraband Inference

A strong inference of possession of illegal contraband can be made when the contraband (such as cocaine or an illegal gun) is found (1) under the front seat of a car driven by the owner of the vehicle, (2) in the home of a person who is the sole occupant of the house or apartment, or (3) in other situations in which a reasonable inference of possession can be drawn.

Examples were used by the U.S. Supreme Court in 1994 to illustrate when conclusions of illegal possession could not be inferred. The following innocent persons should not be arrested or charged, as pointed out in the case of *United States v. X-Citement Video, Inc.*:[17]

- "[A] Federal Express courier who delivers a box" containing the illegal contraband.
- "[A] new resident of an apartment receives mail (containing contraband) for the prior resident and stores the mail unopened."
- "[A] retail druggist who returns an uninspected roll of developed film to a customer," unaware that the film is illegal sexually explicit child material.

Because these innocent persons could be improperly charged with the possession of illegal contraband, the Supreme Court forbade making such possessions strict liability crimes.

≡ The Use of Presumptions and Inferences in Criminal Law

Presumptions and inferences have long been hailed as a "staple of our adversary system of fact-finding."[18] Presumptions and inferences enable a fact finder to conclude that because some facts have been proved (usually called *predicate facts*), other facts may be inferred or presumed to be true. For example, if it is proved that a contractor failed to order materials needed to perform a home repair contract, it might logically be presumed or inferred that the contractor never intended to perform the home improvement contract.

In criminal prosecutions, use of presumptions and inferences can present due process problems, if the jury is permitted or required to find facts necessary to a conviction based only on inferences or presumptions drawn on other facts. Because the Due Process Clause requires the prosecution to prove every element of a crime beyond a reasonable doubt, the use of inferences or presumptions can violate that clause, if the facts establishing the element of the crime are the result of a presumption or inference.

The Supreme Court of the United States has generally permitted the use of permissive inferences and permissive presumptions, because the fact finder need not reach the presumed conclusion. As a result, the prosecution continues to bear the burden of proof beyond a reasonable doubt, and the Due Process Clause is not violated. However, mandatory presumptions have been treated differently. Mandatory presumptions, generally referred to as irrebuttable, or conclusive presumptions, can be unconstitutional under the Due Process Clause because the presumption allows the prosecution to avoid proving an element of the crime charged.[19]

Some presumptions direct the fact finder to reach conclusions in favor of the defendant. The best-known presumption, and probably the oldest, is the presumption of innocence until proven guilty. The presumption of innocence until proven guilty is a *rebuttable* presumption, which means it may be overcome by evidence proving otherwise. The presumption of innocence may be overcome by evidence showing that a defendant is guilty beyond a reasonable doubt.

Sometimes a conclusive presumption is stated as a rule of substantive law that cannot be overcome with evidence showing otherwise. Of the few conclusive presumptions of this type, perhaps the best known is the rule of law that a person under a certain minimum age, usually 7 years, has not reached the age of reason and therefore is not capable of committing a crime. (Infancy as a limit on criminal responsibility is discussed more fully in Chapter 4.)

Figure 3.2 illustrates the different elements that may be essential to the proof of a crime.

Functions of Presumptions and Inferences

Both presumptions and inferences play an important role in trials. Presumptions are created to permit orderly civil and criminal trials.[20] The Supreme Court of Pennsylvania and the Supreme Court of Indiana defined the function and legal significance of presumptions as follows:

> A presumption of law is not evidence nor should it be weighed by the fact finder as though it had evidentiary value. Rather, a presumption is a rule of law enabling the

FIGURE 3.2

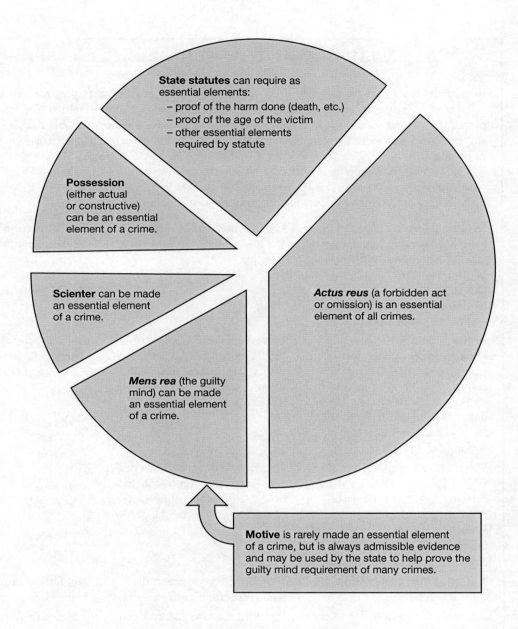

State statutes can require as
essential elements:
– proof of the harm done (death, etc.)
– proof of the age of the victim
– other essential elements
  required by statute

Possession
(either actual
or constructive)
can be an essential
element of a crime.

Actus reus (a forbidden act
or omission) is an essential
element of all crimes.

Scienter can be made
an essential element
of a crime.

Mens rea (the guilty
mind) can be made
an essential element
of a crime.

Motive is rarely made an essential element
of a crime, but is always admissible evidence
and may be used by the state to help prove the
guilty mind requirement of many crimes.

party in whose favor it operates to take his case to the jury without presenting evidence of the fact presumed. It serves as a challenge for proof and indicates the party from whom such proof must be forthcoming. When the opponent of the presumption has met the burden of production thus imposed, however, the office of the presumption has been performed; the presumption is of no further effect and drops from the case.[21]

presumption A rule of law that the trier of fact shall assume the existence of a state of facts without evidence being produced. Presumptions are rebuttable or irrebuttable.

A **presumption** is an assumption the law expressly directs that the trier of fact (jury or judge) *must* make. Because most presumptions may be disputed, they may be outweighed or overcome with evidence showing otherwise. Unless presumptions are overcome with other evidence, judges and jurors *must* accept the presumption as true. It is this aspect of presumptions that creates due process problems in criminal cases, since placing the duty on a defendant to overcome a presumed fact can operate to relieve the prosecution from its duty to prove every element of a crime beyond a reasonable doubt.

PERMISSIBLE AND IMPERMISSIBLE INFERENCES

In criminal trials, fact finders may draw reasonable inferences from facts presented in a case. Stacking of inferences, or basing an inference solely upon another inference, is not permitted. For example, a jury could properly infer that a tire jack used with such force as to cause the victim to fall after being hit in the head and neck area was a deadly weapon and that an intent to kill existed. This particular example was held not to be inference stacking in *State v. Jacks,* 63 Ohio App. 3d 200, 578 N.E.2d 512 (1989).

The leading U.S. Supreme Court case on inferences is *Jackson v. Virginia* and is the basis for the first Case Analysis and Writing Exercise at the end of this chapter.

Following are examples of permissible and impermissible inferences:

Defendant forced a young girl into a secluded area and forced her to take off her clothes and lie on the ground. He threatened her with a gun as he loosened his pants. Nothing was said of his intent, and he fled at this point.	Can an inference be made as to the intention of the defendant?	Yes, conviction for attempted sexual assault affirmed. See *Green v. Connecticut*, 194 Conn. 258, 480 A.2d 526 (1984), *review denied* 469 U.S. 1191, 105 S. Ct. 964, 36 CrL 4178 (1985).
In the middle of the day, police saw defendant walking out of an empty warehouse. Defendant was cooperative, did not run, and had nothing in his possession. He told police that he had to go to the toilet and entered the building looking for a lavatory.	Can an inference of intent to steal be drawn to justify a conviction of burglary (illegal entry with intent to steal)?	No, see *Commonwealth v. Muniem*, 225 Pa. Super. 311, 303 A.2d 528 (1973).
Police with a search warrant stop a United Parcel Service (UPS) truck carrying more than 200 parcels on city delivery. The warrant authorizes the opening of one of the parcels, which was found to contain 2 pounds of heroin.	Can an inference be drawn based on this information to conclude probable cause to justify an arrest of the UPS driver by the police?	No.
X is present in a store while the store was robbed.	Would mere presence at the scene of a crime justify an arrest?	No, further information would be needed.
A murder is committed, and only two people were at the scene of the crime. They could have committed the crime together, or one could be guilty and the other innocent.	Would these facts justify a conclusion that probable cause exists to arrest either or both?	Yes, see Restatement of Torts (2d) Sec. 119 (1965).
Defendant was one of the crew aboard a small boat carrying 22,000 pounds of marijuana on a long trip to the United States. Defendant claims he had no knowledge of the illegal enterprise.	From the facts, can inferences be drawn that defendant was a party to the illegal enterprise?	Yes, see *United States v. Guerrero-Guerrero*, 38 CrL 2235, 776 F.2d 1071 (1st Cir. 1985).

| Police sought to catch a thief who had been stealing property at a Veterans Administration hospital. Money in a wallet was left in a room with invisible dye on the wallet. The dye became visible when it came in contact with moisture. Defendant was seen leaving the room with blue dye on her hands. The money in the wallet was gone. | Are these facts and the inferences drawn from them sufficient to sustain a conviction for petty theft? | Yes, see *United States v. Baker*, 769 F. Supp. 137 (S.D.N.Y. 1991). |
| Defendant was arrested with cocaine in his possession. He also had a scale for weighing the cocaine, baking soda for cutting it, more than $1,000 in $20 bills, and other drug items. At his jury trial, a woman testified that she bought cocaine from the defendant on the day of his arrest. | Would this evidence justify the jury's finding of possession of cocaine with intent to deliver? | Yes, see *Sams v. State*, 197 Ga. App. 201, 397 S.E.2d 751 (1990). |

Inferences of guilt cannot be drawn from the following:

- The fact that a defendant in a criminal case does not get on the witness stand and testify in his or her own behalf. *Griffin v. California*, 85 S. Ct. 1229 (1965); *Carter v. Kentucky*, 101 S. Ct. 1112 (1981).
- A Detroit Police Department policy providing for the automatic arrest of all occupants in a vehicle wanted in connection with a felony. The car in question was stopped 48 hours after a burglary, and all occupants were arrested. The policy based on impermissible inferences was condemned by Michigan courts. *People v. Harrison*, 163 Mich. App. 409, 413 N.W.2d 813, 42 CrL 2153 (1987).
- Prosecutors, judges, and police officers cannot comment on the fact that a defendant asserted his or her Fifth Amendment right to remain silent after being given *Miranda* warnings. *State v. Marple*, 98 Or. App. 662, 780 P.2d 772 (1989).

In a period of six months, four elderly women were sexually assaulted in their homes. The unique pattern of the crimes indicated that a single perpetrator was committing the crimes. After the defendant was arrested, the series of very similar crimes stopped. Most state and federal courts hold that evidence of the inference of guilt drawn from the fact that a series of similar crimes stopped when the defendant was arrested and held in jail was inherently unreliable to prove guilt. See *Commonwealth v. Foy*, 612 A.2d 1349 (Pa. 1992). An Arizona court disagreed with the *Foy* result, and held it was permissible to permit a police officer to testify that crimes fitting the defendant's modus operandi stopped after the defendant was arrested. *State v. Miller*, 156 P.3d 1145 (Ariz. App. 2007).

The purpose of civil and criminal trials is to determine the truth of the issues presented to the fact finder. Criminal trials commence with the presumption that the defendant is innocent. To overcome this presumption, the state must present evidence proving the guilt of the defendant beyond a reasonable doubt in the minds of the jury. Each essential element of the crime charged must be proved beyond a reasonable doubt.

Inference A conclusion or deduction that a jury or judge may draw from a fact or a group of facts presented to them.

An **inference** is a conclusion or deduction that a jury or judge *may* draw from a fact or a group of facts presented to them. Fact finders must use good common sense and their knowledge of everyday life. In their reasoning process, juries and judges must use inferences. A common inference used in criminal trials is that persons intend (desire) the natural and probable consequences of their deliberate acts. The following example illustrates this.

EXAMPLE: X is charged with either attempted assault with a deadly weapon or attempted murder. X is a strong, 30-year-old man who did the following:

Conduct of X	Inferences That Can Logically Be Drawn from X's Conduct
Reliable witnesses testify that X repeatedly attempted to hit Y on or about Y's head with a baseball bat. Bystanders stopped X.	Fact finders can easily conclude that a baseball bat is a deadly weapon in the hands of a strong man who exhibited an intent to kill or seriously injure.
Same facts as stated above, except that X used a rolled-up newspaper to strike at Y.	Fact finders cannot logically conclude that a rolled-up newspaper is a deadly weapon or that the defendant exhibited intent to kill; therefore, neither charge could stand.

The Presumption That All Persons Are Sane, Normal, and Competent

An important presumption assumes that all adults are sane, normal, and competent. Adult witnesses in civil and criminal cases are assumed to be sane, normal, and competent. However, attorneys in civil or criminal proceedings may challenge this presumption if necessary, and show otherwise. Before young children can testify, the trial judge questions them (*voir dire*) and then rules as to whether they meet these requirements of a witness.

California statutes, like those of most states, provide that defendants in criminal cases are presumed to be competent to stand trial. Thus, in most states a defense lawyer challenging this presumption has the burden of coming forward with evidence to prove that a defendant is incompetent and cannot be tried. In a very few states, the prosecution must prove by "clear and credible evidence" that the defendant is competent. See, e.g., Wis. St. Ann., § 971.14(4)(b). In 1992, the U.S. Supreme Court heard the case of *Medina v. California* (505 U.S. 437, 112 S. Ct. 2572), in which defense lawyers sought to have this presumption held unconstitutional. Medina was convicted of three murders committed during robberies and shooting sprees. The U.S. Supreme Court followed the ruling of the California Supreme Court in holding that California Penal Code Section 1369(f), which makes a defendant prove incompetence by a preponderance of the evidence, does not violate any right granted or protected by the U.S. Constitution. However, in *Cooper v. Oklahoma*, 517 U.S. 348 (1996) the Court reversed a conviction because an Oklahoma law required a defendant to prove incompetence by "clear and convincing" evidence, rather than a lesser standard of "preponderance of the evidence."

The *Medina* decision followed the 1952 case of *Leland v. Oregon* (72 S. Ct. 1002), in which the U.S. Supreme Court held that states may require defendants seeking to use the insanity defense to carry the burden of proving the defendant's insanity beyond a reasonable doubt. Most states and the federal government place the burden of proof on the party alleging insanity.

Summary

- *Actus reus* describes the physical acts making up the crime, while *mens rea* refers to any mental requirement for conviction of the crime.
- Not all crimes require proof that a defendant had a specific intent to achieve a specific end. In some cases, all that is required is that the defendant intended to do the prohibited act, sometimes known as general intent.
- An example of a crime that does not require a specific intent might be second-degree murder, which does not require that the defendant act with the specific intent to cause death.
- The Model Penal Code, which some states have followed, lists the mental states for criminal liability as purposely, knowingly, recklessly, or negligently. If a statute requires a showing that the defendant acted purposely or knowingly, the defendant's mental state is an element of the offense.

- Motive is the reason a defendant took action; intent is simply the mental state leading to the action taken.
- Strict liability crimes generally involve areas where a government has a strong interest in regulating conduct to promote public safety, such as food laws, or protect certain persons, such as school children.
- The year-and-a-day rule in murder cases, though overruled in most jurisdictions, is a rule of proximate causation that sets a limit on how far removed in time a death can be from acts causing harm to the victim and still be treated as a murder.
- Since the Due Process Clause requires the prosecution to prove every element of an offense beyond a reasonable doubt, a presumption that operated to mandate a jury finding on an element of an offense without such proof would violate the Due Process Clause. A conclusive or mandatory presumption is one which may not be rebutted by the defendant.

Key Terms

reasonable doubt, p. 52
actus reus, p. 52
mens rea, p. 52
Model Penal Code (MPC), p. 52
Concurrence, p. 53

specific intent, p. 55
scienter, p. 59
intent, p. 62
motive, p. 62
strict liability crime, p. 63

proximate cause, p. 67
presumption, p. 73
Inference, p. 76

Case Analysis and Writing Exercises

1. After the Supreme Court's decision in *Flores-Figueroa*, discussed on page 58, what should be the results in the two following cases on the government's duty to prove what the defendant "knew": For a conviction under the Mann Act, 18 U.S.C. § 2421, which makes it a crime to "knowingly" transport a person in interstate commerce" for prostitution, must the government prove the defendant knew he was transporting across state

lines? See *United States v. Shim*, 584 F.3d 394 (2d Cir. 2009). For a conviction under 18 U.S.C. § 1001, which makes it a crime to "knowingly" make false statements to the government, must the prosecution prove the defendants knew of the law that made their statements unlawful? See *United States v. Starnes*, 583 F.3d 196 (3d Cir. 2009).

2. The defendant, James Jackson, testified at his criminal trial that he had shot and killed his friend,

Mrs. Cole. Jackson also testified that he was not drunk at the time of the shooting but that he had been "pretty high." He testified that Mrs. Cole had taken off some of her clothes and then attacked him with a knife when he had resisted her sexual advances. Jackson testified that he had fired warning shots and then reloaded the gun. When the victim attempted to take the gun from him, it "went off," killing her. Without seeking help for the victim, he drove her car to another state. No other person was at the scene of the shooting, and Jackson argued not only self-defense but also that he was too intoxicated to form the specific intent necessary for conviction of first-degree murder.

A deputy sheriff also testified at the trial. He knew the defendant and Mrs. Cole and had seen them in a restaurant just before the shooting. Because Jackson appeared intoxicated, the sheriff offered to hold Jackson's revolver until Jackson sobered up. Jackson said that this was unnecessary because he and Mrs. Cole were about to engage in sexual activity.

Jackson waived his right to a jury trial and was tried before a judge. The fact finder (the judge) found him guilty of first-degree murder. Should the U.S. Supreme Court hold that the evidence and the inferences drawn from the evidence were sufficient to support the conviction? Explain. See *Jackson v. Virginia*, 443 U.S. 307, 99 S. Ct. 2781 (1979).

3. Inferences can be drawn in the following two situations, but would they be strong enough to justify issuing criminal charges? Would conclusions drawn from these inferences or presumptions violate the Due Process Clause? Why or why not?

a. A state statute states that a person commits an offense "if he or she left a child 6 years of age or younger unattended in a motor vehicle for more than 10 minutes." See *People v. Jordan*, 820 N.E.2d 1083 (Ill. App. 2004), *aff'd, People v. Jordan*, 843 N.E.2d 870 (Ill. 2006). What would the prosecution argue to try to convince the court the presumption was only permissive?

b. After a valid stop by the police for speeding, four men are observed in the car. The officer smelled burned marijuana as he stood next to the vehicle and also saw an envelope marked "Supergold" on the floor of the car between the two men in the front seat. In accordance with the practice of the local district attorney's office, only the driver and owner of the car were charged with possession of marijuana. What defenses might be used by defense lawyers in that case?

4. Most states make it a crime to purchase alcohol for a minor, sometimes called the *shoulder tap crime*, based on the typical manner a request by a minor for an adult to purchase alcohol occurs. These crimes generally do not require proof that the defendant knew the person for whom the alcohol was purchased was under the drinking age. Should the same strict liability apply to the crime of furnishing alcohol to a minor? If so, does a host at a private party that is attended by both adults and minors "furnish" alcohol to both groups? Should a host be able to offer evidence that he reasonably believed a minor was old enough to drink? Would it help your case if the jurisdiction made such a defense available to bars and liquor stores that required buyers to provide proof of age? See *In re Jennings*, 95 P.3d 906 (Cal. 2004).

Notes

1. *Powell v. Texas*, 392 U.S. 514, 535, 88 S. Ct. 2145 (1968).
2. *Morissette v. United States*, 342 U.S. at 252 (see).
3. 444 U.S. 394, 100 S. Ct. 624, 26 CrL 3065 (1980).
4. 438 U.S. at 445, 98 S. Ct at 2877 (1978).
5. 444 U.S. 394, 100 S. Ct. 624, 26 CrL 3065 (1980).
6. See 22 Corpus Juris Secundum Criminal Law, Sections 30–36.
7. 512 F.2d 1281 (5th Cir. 1975).
8. In the 1995 case of *United States v. Lopez* (115 S. Ct. 1624, 57 CrL 2031), the U.S. Supreme Court held that the federal law forbidding the possession of a firearm in a school zone was invalid. The Court held that as the possession of guns near schools did not affect interstate commerce, the federal government did not have the authority to enact the law under the Commerce Clause of the U.S. Constitution. In her concurring opinion, Justice Sandra Day O'Connor pointed out that states have authority to enact gun-free school laws and that 40 states have enacted such statutes.

9. Because motive is the reason and belief that could cause a person to act or refrain from acting, motive could be the basis for enhancing or increasing a criminal penalty. Increasing or enhancing a penalty because of motive therefore punishes the person's thought. Antidiscrimination laws prohibit acts committed with a discriminatory motive. Treating a person less favorably than others because of race, color, religion, sex, or national origin is forbidden because of discriminatory motive, which is often proved from the inference drawn from difference in treatment.

10. 595 A.2d 306 (Conn. 1991).

11. See pages 242–250 of LaFave and Scott, *Criminal Law*, 2nd ed. (Belmont, Calif.: West/Wadsworth, 1986).

12. The Comprehensive Drug Abuse Prevention and Control Act of 1970, as amended.

13. In the 1991 case of *Dill v. State* (600 So. 2d 343), the victim was shot in the head during a robbery but did not die until nine months later, when he pulled out his feeding tube and suffered dehydration. The conviction for capital murder was affirmed, with the Court holding that the victim's death was caused by the gunshot wound. For further cases and material on causation, see pages 277–299 of LaFave and Scott, *Criminal Law*, 2nd ed. (Belmont, Calif.: West/Wadsworth, 1986).

14. See *People v. Stevenson*, 416 Mich. 383, 331 N.W.2d 143 (1982).

15. Blackstone, *Commentaries*, 197.

16. See *United States v. Winchester* (916 F.2d 601 (11th Cir. 1990)), having to do with people who cannot possess a firearm under the Federal Gun Control Act of 1968.

17. 115 S. Ct. 467 (S. Ct. 1994).

18. *County Court v. Allen*, 442 U.S. 140 (1979).

19. *Sandstrom v. Montana*, 442 U.S. 510 (1979).

20. Because taxpayers have possession of their tax records, the burden of proof is on the taxpayers to prove the accuracy of their tax returns. Federal courts have held for many years that rulings of the commissioner of the Internal Revenue Service are presumed to be correct. See *Welch v. Helvering*, 290 U.S. 111 at 115 (1933). During the debate on the new federal tax code in 1998, changes were urged by members of Congress, and many writers predicted that this presumption and burden of proof would be changed in the new tax law. However, the 1998 Tax Reform Act modifies the old rules only slightly, and the presumption and burden of proof remain practically the same as they have been for many years.

21. *Commonwealth v. Vogel*, 440 Pa. 1, 17, 268 A.2d 89, 102 (1970); *Sumpter v. State*, 261 Ind. 471, 306 N.E.2d 95 (1974).

CHAPTER 4

Criminal Liability

AP Photo/Plymouth County Jail

In 2003 Richard Reid, the "shoe bomber", pled guilty in Federal Court to 8 counts of terrorism based on his failed attempt to blow up a commercial airliner on which he was a passenger by detonating explosives hidden in his shoes. His crime resulted in the requirement that air passengers remove their shoes before going through gate security lines. Reid, a British citizen, is currently serving a life sentence in a Federal super-max prison in the United States.

OUTLINE

LEARNING OBJECTIVES

In this chapter we examine the manner in which criminal liability is assessed, in particular for liability based upon acts and the relationship of those acts to crimes. The learning objectives for this chapter are:

- Identify when conduct has crossed the line between thinking about committing a crime and attempting to commit a crime.

- Explain the function and need of corroborating evidence in solicitation prosecutions.

- Identify the steps that must be taken before one can be guilty of a conspiracy.

- Explain when, if ever, impossibility of committing the completed crime is a defense to a charge of attempt.

- Identify the circumstances when abandonment of the criminal purpose can have an effect on liability for an attempt, or liability for criminal acts done in a conspiracy.

- State the rule for liability of one conspirator for actions of another.

- List the parties who can be treated as principles for purposes of criminal liability.

In the year 2000, Jefferson County, Alabama, began a $3 billion sewer and waste treatment project. In 2010, the 11th Circuit Court of Appeals affirmed the convictions and sentences of four Jefferson County officials and several individual and corporate contractors indicted for bribery and conspiracy to commit bribery in violation of federal statutes. The court found that the county officials each received hundreds of thousands of bribes, and the defendants received hundreds of millions in contract proceeds for the sewer work. The individual defendants were sentenced to prison terms ranging from 60 months to 102 months, as well as fines from $300,000 to $19 million. The defendants contended on appeal that they could not lawfully be convicted of both the substantive bribery charge and the conspiracy charge, based on the "Wharton rule" doctrine. The court rejected their contentions, finding the Wharton rule inapplicable to the case.

Criminal laws have long recognized that a person's conduct prior to or leading up to a substantive crime is often by itself blameworthy, even if the substantive crime is not committed. The same is true of actions taken after a crime that in some way aids the criminal, or obstructs law enforcement officers in their efforts to identify and apprehend the criminal. This chapter discusses many of these crimes and the elements that must be proved in the prosecution of them. Crimes such as solicitation, conspiracy, and attempt can be committed and punished quite independently from prosecution and punishment of the crime that was the intended outcome. We discuss many of the limitations on these crimes that have developed over the years, and continue to develop.

In some actions involving two people, such as an illegal drug transaction, the two parties may have earlier agreed between themselves that they would commit that crime. That agreement suggests they have also committed the crime of conspiracy, but as we will see, the Wharton rule prevents them from being convicted of that crime. We learn about this and other limiting doctrines in this chapter.

≡ Preliminary, Anticipatory, or Inchoate Crimes

Professor Wayne LaFave, in his treatise on criminal law, uses the following example to illustrate the varieties of criminal charges that might result from criminal behavior, with the nature of the charge depending on the extent of the behavior:

> Suppose A wants B to kill C. If A hires B to do so, and B does kill C, B is guilty of murder, and so is A, either as an accessory, or as a principal. If B tries to kill C, but fails, A and B are both guilty of attempted murder. If B agrees with A to kill C, but does not attempt the murder, A and B are guilty of conspiracy to commit murder. However, even where B refuses A's request to kill C, and thus cannot be liable for any crime, A can be liable for solicitation.[1]

In this chapter we examine the basis for criminal liability, including liability for the preliminary crimes illustrated in the example above. In prosecutions for preliminary crimes it is not required that the underlying criminal act occurs; it is the planning or attempt to commit that crime that is itself made criminal.

Preliminary crimes are not always present when an underlying crime occurs, because not all crimes are planned in advance. Some crimes are committed impulsively, the decision to commit the crime being made on the spur of the moment or almost simultaneously with the commission of the offense. Nor are all crimes completed. In some instances, the person who has carefully planned to commit a crime decides, for one reason or another, not to do so. Crimes are sometimes not completed because of events that prevent their completion. The problem in preliminary crimes is determining when sufficient planning or attempt has occurred to justify the conclusion a crime has been committed.

In most situations, a person who has formulated the intent to commit a crime, but has taken no actions in furtherance of the crime, has not yet violated any law. He or she may even in some instances vocally express the intention to commit a crime without committing an offense. However, in some instances, such a person may be subject to arrest or to detention for expressing such intentions.

EXAMPLE: 8 U.S.C.A. Section 871 makes it a federal offense to do the following: "(a) Whoever knowingly and willfully ... makes any such threat (to take the life or to inflict bodily harm) against the President, President-elect, Vice President or other officer next in the order of succession to the office of President, or Vice-President-elect, shall be fined not more than $1,000 or imprisoned not more than five years, or both."

It is possible to commit a crime based on a stated intention even though the person making the statement intended a joke or hoax. For example, 18 U.S.C § 35(b), the so-called Bomb Hoax statute, makes it a crime to make a false statement about the presence of a bomb in a civil aircraft. A person making such a statement can be convicted under the act, even if the person never intended to place a bomb on an aircraft, so long as the statement was made maliciously. See *United States v. Hassouneh*, 199 F.3d 175 (4th Cir. 2000).

The examples above illustrate areas where the simple statement of an intention is regarded as sufficiently dangerous or intrusive to justify criminal sanctions. They also demonstrate the need to prevent serious social harm before it occurs. To accomplish this goal courts long ago created the three separate and distinct common law crimes of solicitation, conspiracy, and attempt. Although these offenses are crimes in themselves, each of these acts is **preliminary** or **anticipatory** to a more serious crime that the offender has in mind. These anticipatory crimes are commonly referred to as **inchoate crimes**.

In considering the preliminary offenses, the following questions always arise:

preliminary, anticipatory, or inchoate crimes Criminal acts that lead to or are attempts to commit other crimes.

1. Where and when does noncriminal conduct become criminal conduct by a further act of the suspect?
2. Which of the preliminary offenses, if any, has the suspect committed?
3. When does the commission of the principal offense begin so as to allow the state to charge either the preliminary offense or the principal offense?

Solicitation or Incitement to Commit a Crime[2]

By the early 1800s, English and American courts had recognized solicitation as a misdemeanor under the common law.[3] *Solicitation* may be defined as an attempt to get another person to commit a crime. It may also be described as an attempt to conspire to commit a crime. The solicitation does not have to be successful. The crime of **solicitation** or **incitement** is committed even if the person solicited refuses to cooperate and repudiates the proposal. It is also immaterial, in most instances, whether payment or reward is offered and whether it is accepted or refused. Evidence of the offer of payment or reward, however, can be important in proving solicitation.

solicitation or incitement crimes Attempting to get another to commit a crime.

States commonly have both specific solicitation statutes—such as solicitation of prostitution or bribery—and general solicitation statutes applicable to other conduct. An example of a general solicitation statute is Wisconsin Statutes Annotated, Section 939.30, which states:

(1) Except as provided in sub. (2) and s. 961.455, whoever, with intent that a felony be committed, advises another to commit that crime under circumstances that indicate unequivocally that he or she has the intent is guilty of a Class H felony.

Prosecutions under solicitation statutes require a showing that the defendant has done more than make a casual suggestion that a crime be committed. In many cases the defendant's intent is shown by eliciting incriminating statements that are overheard by the police. For example, in a case prosecuted under the Wisconsin statute cited above, a defendant was charged with solicitation to commit murder. She told a friend that she had hired a co-worker to kill her ex-boyfriend. The friend permitted a police officer to listen in on a telephone conversation with the defendant, where she repeated those statements. Her conviction was upheld based on the testimony of the friend and the police officer, even though the defendant subsequently told the "hit man" not to go through with the crime.[4]

Some state statutes have specific corroboration requirements in the general solicitation statutes. For example, the Texas Penal Code Annotated, Section 15.03(b), states in part that "A person may not be convicted under this section on the uncorroborated testimony of the person allegedly solicited ..."

The following cases further illustrate the crime of solicitation:

- A husband who solicited another person to kill his estranged wife's lover, and who also drove the "hit man" (an undercover police officer) around town showing him where the lover might be found, was properly convicted of both solicitation to commit murder, and attempted capital murder for hire. *Ostrander v. Com.*, 658 S.E.2d 346 (Va. App. 2008)
- A lawyer was convicted of "solicitation of obstruction of justice" because of his request of a store employee to obtain dismissal of shoplifting charges against the lawyer's client. *State v. Clemmons*, 100 N.C. App. 286, 396 S.E.2d 616 (1990)
- An employee of a McDonald's drive-through restaurant told a customer that he would like to have oral sex with her. The employee was convicted of solicitation of oral sodomy. However, the Virginia Court of Appeals reversed the conviction, holding that the statement by the employee was merely a statement of his desire, not an attempt to persuade another to commit the crime. *Ford v. Commonwealth*, 10 Va. App. 224, 391 S.E.2d 603 (1990)[5]

Conspiracy to Commit a Crime[6]

conspiracy crimes An agreement between two or more persons to engage in unlawful acts.

The crime of **conspiracy** is the oldest of the preliminary crimes. It received some legislative recognition as early as 1292, but it was not until the early 1600s that the English Court of the Star Chamber developed the crime of conspiracy into an offense of wide scope, capable of extensive application. This court was created in the late 1500s to try certain high crimes without a jury. Because of the ruthless methods used, the court is sometimes referred to as the *infamous Star Chamber*. Modern critics of the crime of conspiracy sometimes recall the ancient unsavory use of the crime of conspiracy, as did former Justice Robert H. Jackson in his concurring opinion in *Krulewitch v. United States*:

> The crime comes down to us wrapped in vague but unpleasant connotations. It sounds historical undertones of treachery, secret plotting and violence on a scale that menaces social stability and the security of the state itself. "Privy conspiracy" ranks with sedition and rebellion in the Litany's prayer for deliverance. Conspiratorial movements do indeed lie back of the political assassination, the coup d'etat, the putsch, the revolution and seizure of power in modern times, as they have in all history.[7]

The federal government (18 U.S.C.A. § 371) and probably all states have enacted statutes making conspiracy a crime in their jurisdictions. The reasoning behind such legislation generally is that when two or more persons plan a crime together, (1) the extent of potential harm to the society is often increased considerably, (2) the possibility of the abandonment of the criminal plan is greatly reduced, (3) the chances of success in the criminal venture are greater than if only one individual were involved, and (4) their actions can be more difficult to detect than an individual's preparation to commit a crime.

The purpose, then, of criminal conspiracy statutes is to prevent and punish criminal partnerships in crime and to stop, if possible, such criminal combinations of people before attempts to commit substantive crimes are made.

Each state has its own definition of conspiracy, but most have language similar to that found in the Texas Penal Code: "A person commits criminal conspiracy if, with intent that a [crime] be committed: (1) he agrees with one or more persons that they or one or more of them engage in conduct that would constitute the offense; and (2) he or one or more of them performs an overt act in pursuance of the agreement" (V.T.C.A., Penal Code, § 15.02).[8]

Because conspiracy was looked on as a partnership in crime, the traditional view was that the state must prove the involvement of *two or more* guilty persons in the conspiracy.[9] If A and B were charged with conspiracy to murder and the jury found A guilty and B not guilty, the traditional view is that the conviction against A could not stand. The reasoning for the dismissal of the charge and conviction against A is that A could not conspire alone and that two or more guilty persons are necessary for the conviction to stand.

A substantial number of states have limited or rejected the "two or more guilty persons" requirement for the crime of conspiracy. The common-law approach, referred to as the "bilateral" view of conspiracy, has largely been replaced by the "unilateral" view. See, e.g., IC 35-41-5-2 of the Indiana Statutes. Both the National Advisory Committee on Organized Crime and the American Law Institute Model Penal Code, section 5.03(1), have recommended that the rule be changed so that the crime occurs if the defendant agrees with another person, even if that other person is only feigning agreement, or even lacks the capacity to make agreement. This rule would allow a suspect to be charged with conspiracy if the suspect agrees with an undercover officer or an informant to commit a crime. The following example illustrates a conspiracy conviction where an informant only pretended to be a party to a conspiracy to murder:

EXAMPLE: After a New York judge placed a high cash bail on a stockbroker charged with security fraud, the man offered his jail cellmate $35,000 to kill the judge. A New York jury convicted the stockbroker of conspiracy to murder after hearing the testimony of the defendant, the cellmate, and two audiotapes of the conversations between the two men regarding the proposed killing.[10]

Moreover, the conspiracy does not end if one of the conspirators dies before the object of the conspiracy is obtained or an overt act occurs.[11] Conspiracy can also be proved even if the co-conspirator cannot be found or cannot be identified. See *United States v. Thorn*, 348 F.3d 78 (5th Cir. 2003). (All that was required for a conspiracy conviction is that the existence of a co-conspirator is alleged and proved, even if he can't be identified.) Finally, section 5.03(1) of the MPC also states that one conspirator can be convicted of the conspiracy even if an accused co-conspirator is acquitted of the crime.

The Requirement of an Overt Act

Under the common law conspiracy rules, proof of the criminal partnership was all that was required to prove the crime of conspiracy. There was no requirement that the prosecution prove that some overt act was done in furtherance of the conspiracy. Today, most states have written into their criminal conspiracy statutes the requirement of proof of an overt act by a defendant. The Model Penal Code, section 5.03(5) states that a conviction for conspiracy requires proof of an overt act, unless the underlying crime is a "felony of the first or second degree."

Virtually any act in furtherance of the conspiracy will satisfy this requirement. For example, making a telephone call, as in the case *United States v. Fellabaum*, 408 F.2d

220 (7th Cir. 1969), was held to satisfy the overt act requirement. In a 1993 case, the defendants agreed to rob a man. Their overt acts were obtaining guns and ski masks (*Burk v. State*, 848 P.2d 225).

The overt act requirement exists in some federal conspiracy statutes, but not others. The general federal conspiracy law (18 U.S.C. § 371) expressly requires proof of an overt act done in furtherance of the criminal conspiracy that is charged. However, when the U.S. Congress wrote the federal statute (21 U.S.C.A. § 846) forbidding drug conspiracies, the law contained no express requirement of proof of an overt act, but only proof of a criminal conspiracy. In 1994, the U.S. Supreme Court affirmed the defendant's conviction in the case of *United States v. Shabani* (115 S. Ct. 382) and held that the federal drug conspiracy statute was constitutional, stating: "[T]he language (of the federal statutes does not) require that a overt act be committed to further the conspiracy, and we have not inferred such a requirement from congressional silence in other conspiracy statutes."

Conspiracy prosecutions under the Federal Racketeer Influenced and Corrupt Organizations Act (RICO), 18 U.S.C. § 1962, have presented some problems in the overt act requirement. The RICO Act (discussed in Chapter 18) punishes persons who form criminal enterprises. Convictions under § 1962(c), require the prosecution to prove that a defendant committed at least two "predicate acts," that is, actions that were themselves criminal violations, in furtherance of the enterprise. When a defendant is charged under § 1962(d) with conspiracy to violate the RICO laws, the Federal Circuit Courts were initially split on the need for proof that the defendant agreed to commit the two predicate acts. Three Circuits required the prosecution to prove the defendant either committed or agreed to commit the two predicate acts stated in § 1962(c); see *United States v. Sanders*, 929 F.2d 1466 (10th Cir. 1991). Eight Circuits took the other view. See, e.g., *United States v. Ruggiero*, 726 F.2d 913 (2d Cir. 1984).

In *Salinas v. United States*, 522 U.S. 52 (1997) the U.S. Supreme Court held that § 1962(d) did not require proof that the defendant committed or agreed to commit the two predicate acts needed for conviction under § 1962(c). Salinas, a deputy sheriff, and his superior the sheriff, were charged with accepting bribes in violation of the federal bribery law, 18 U.S.C. § 666, violation of the RICO law, § 1962(c), and conspiracy to violate the RICO law, § 1962(d). Salinas was acquitted of the substantive violation, but convicted under the conspiracy section. On appeal Salinas contended that because the jury did not find he committed the two predicate acts needed for conviction under § 1962(c), and the prosecution did not prove he agreed to commit such acts, he could not be convicted of conspiracy.

The Supreme Court rejected his argument, noting first that § 1962(d), unlike the general conspiracy statute, had no overt act requirement. As a result, a person could be convicted of the conspiracy without having taken any acts, so long as he agreed to participate in the underlying crime. The Court said that while the underlying crime, the RICO violation, required two predicate acts, Salinas could be convicted under § 1962(d) without himself committing or agreeing to commit those two predicate acts:

> In the case before us, even if Salinas did not accept or agree to accept two bribes, there was ample evidence he conspired to violate subsection (c). The evidence shows that (the sheriff) committed at least two acts of racketeering activity when he accepted numerous bribes and that Salinas knew about or agreed to facilitate the scheme. This is sufficient to support a conviction under § 1962(d) (522 U.S. at 66).

In. *Whitfield v. United States*, 543 U.S. 209 (2005) the Supreme Court held that 18 U.S.C. 1956(h), the money-laundering statute, required no overt act for a conspiracy conviction. In discussing whether a statute has an overt act requirement, the Court in *Whitfield* stated that if the congressional statute was "modeled on 18 U.S.C. § 371" [the general conspiracy statute] it has an overt act requirement, but if it was "modeled on the Sherman Act, 15 U.S.C § 1" [the antitrust statute] it dispensed with such a requirement. Based on this distinction, the federal district court in *United States v. Johnson*, 624 F. Supp. 2d 903 (W.D. Tenn. 2009) held that the federal murder-for-hire statute, 18 U.S.C. § 1958(a), required no proof of an overt act for a conspiracy conviction. However, at least one Federal Court of Appeals has held that if the government alleges the commission of an overt act in an indictment under 18 U.S.C § 1958(a), the overt act must be proved. *United States v. Cope*, 312 F.3d 757 (6th Cir. 2002).

Overt acts are often very convincing evidence of the sincerity of a conspiracy agreement, and almost all strong conspiracy cases have evidence of overt acts.

The Wharton Rule

Some crimes cannot be committed alone but require two or more people. Examples of such crimes are dueling, bigamy, gambling, adultery, incest, pandering for prostitution, receiving a bribe, and distributing illegal drugs. As the crime of conspiracy punishes partnerships in crime because of increased danger to society, the **Wharton rule**, named after Francis Wharton, the author of an early treatise on Criminal Law, states that the crime of conspiracy cannot be charged if the number of people involved are only those necessary to commit the crime. In *Ianelli v. United States*, 420 U.S. 770 (1975), the Supreme Court explained the place of the Wharton rule in federal conspiracy prosecutions. The Court stated it applied, but only for those crimes that required multiple participants for their commission, and subject to clear legislative intent that Congress intended both prosecutions to be permitted. The Court in *Ianelli* held that Congress did intend prosecutions for conspiracy to violate federal gambling statutes, which require the participation of 5 persons, could be maintained together with prosecutions for the underlying crime.

Wharton rule The requirement that crimes needing more than one person for commission, such as bigamy, require three or more people for a conspiracy conviction.

EXAMPLE: To distribute illegal drugs, there must be both a deliverer and a person receiving the drugs. Under the Wharton rule, if two persons engaged in a one-time sale of a small quantity of an illegal drug, the seller and buyer cannot be charged with conspiracy.[12]

Most states and the federal government use the Wharton rule and will not permit a conspiracy charge when only the people necessary to commit the crime are named as defendants. However, if more people than the number necessary to commit the crime are charged with conspiracy, the Wharton rule would not apply. For example, if three people conspire to sell illegal drugs all three can be charged with the conspiracy crime and also the underlying drug offense, if completed.

In the example given above of the drug deal, the Wharton rule could also be defeated if sufficient evidence showed that the buyer and seller have a long-standing criminal relationship involving repeated sales of large quantities of illegal drugs. The evidence would have to show an agreement beyond a simple one-time transaction. Most states would then permit substantive drug charges in addition to the conspiracy charge.

Impossibility, Abandonment, and Withdrawal

What effect, if any, should the impossibility of committing the criminal object of a conspiracy, the abandonment of the conspiracy by all the conspirators, or the withdrawal from the conspiracy of one conspirator have on the conspiracy charge?

In the case of impossibility, the U.S. Supreme Court in 2003 rejected a Federal Court of Appeals rule that included an impossibility defense. In *United States v. Jimenez Recio*[13] the Court reversed a Ninth Circuit Court of Appeals decision that conspirators could not be convicted of the crime if the "object of the conspiracy had been defeated" before the defendants had joined the conspiracy. In *Jimenez*, police officers seized a truck carrying illegal drugs and convinced the truck driver to lure the defendants to the scene. When

MERE KNOWLEDGE OF A CRIME ALONE IS NOT SUFFICIENT TO SUPPORT A CONSPIRACY CONVICTION

Mere association with criminals without agreeing to assist in the commission of a crime is not enough to prove conspiracy. For example, a live-in housekeeper who admitted she knew that drugs were in the house and that the homeowner was involved in large-scale drug trafficking was improperly convicted of drug conspiracy.

On appeal, it was held that there was insufficient evidence to prove she agreed to assist in the crime. *United States v. Vasquez-Chan*, 978 F.2d 546 (9th Cir. 1992).

In the following U.S. Supreme Court cases, both suppliers knew that their product was being used for illegal purposes. One supplied a product difficult to obtain and often used for illegal purposes, whereas the other defendant supplied a product easy to obtain and not often used for illegal purposes.

- *United States v. Falcone*, 311 U.S. 205 (1940). The defendants sold yeast and sugar (lawful products) to a man who was making illegal alcohol (bootlegging). The evidence showed that defendants knew that their products were being used for illegal purposes, but the Supreme Court held that such mere knowledge alone is insufficient to establish guilt of conspiracy. The Court held that to convict of conspiracy, there must be evidence of an agreement between the parties. In this case, there was no evidence of such an agreement.
- *United States v. Direct Sales*, 319 U.S. 703 (1943). The defendant wholesaler continued to supply a small-town doctor with morphine after federal narcotics officials warned the defendant that the doctor was illegally supplying the morphine to addicts. Sales to the doctor continued for a long time and increased to a quantity sufficient for 400 average doses a day. The U.S. Supreme Court held that the defendant had more than mere knowledge of the illegal activity and that the continuous sales established a tacit (unspoken) agreement between the doctor and the defendant wholesaler to illegally distribute a controlled substance (morphine).

they arrived and drove away with the truck, they were arrested by the police. The defendants argued that since the object of the conspiracy, possession of illegal drugs, was made impossible by the drug seizure by the police, the conspiracy was over before it began. The Ninth Circuit Court of Appeals agreed, but the Supreme Court did not. The Court stated that the essence of the crime is the agreement to commit a crime, not the crime to be committed. Citing the LaFave treatise and the Model Penal Code, it rejected the notion that impossibility is ever a defense to a conspiracy charge.

The same reasoning applies to abandonment of the conspiracy or withdrawal by one conspirator. Even if the conspiracy is abandoned or one conspirator withdraws, the crime of conspiracy is nonetheless complete; "since the crime is complete with the agreement, no subsequent action can exonerate the conspirator of that crime."[14]

The Model Penal Code would provide a defense to a conspiracy charge where a conspirator "thwarted the success of the conspiracy, under circumstances manifesting a complete and voluntary renunciation of his criminal purpose." The New York Penal Code, Section 40.10 (4) states: "In any prosecution for criminal solicitation ... or for conspiracy ... in which the crime solicited or the crime contemplated by the conspiracy was not in fact committed, it is an affirmative defense that, under circumstances manifesting a voluntary and complete renunciation of his criminal purpose, the defendant prevented the commission of the crime."

The Crime of Attempt

Attempt is the most frequently charged of the three preliminary crimes because "near" victims and witnesses generally report attempted rapes, robberies, murders, and other

ATTEMPT UNDER THE FEDERAL CRIMINAL CODE

In *United States v. Joyce*, 693 F.2d 838, 841 (8th Cir. 1982), the Court discussed the crime of attempt:

Although there is no comprehensive statutory definition of attempt in federal law, federal courts have rather uniformly adopted the standard set forth in Section 5.01 of the … Model Penal Code … that the requisite elements of attempt are:

1. an intent to engage in criminal conduct, and
2. conduct constituting a "substantial step" towards the commission of the substantive offense which strongly corroborates the actor's criminal intent.

In *United States v. Vigil*, 523 F.3d 1258 (10th Cir. 2008) a state treasurer was convicted of attempted extortion under the Hobbs Act, 18 U.S.C. § 1951(a) based on his actions trying to compel a person negotiating a state securities contract to hire a friend's wife for unreasonable compensation. The treasurer contended he took no action other than the "usual" political patronage customs, but the court disagreed, finding the treasurer persisted in the hiring demand after the contractor refused to do so.

crimes to the police. Moreover, such victims and witnesses are generally more cooperative about appearing in court to testify to the attempted crimes.

attempt crimes Acts that are a substantial step toward the commission of a crime that is not yet completed.

In defining the crime of **attempt**, the New York Criminal Code provides that "a person is guilty of an attempt to commit a crime when, with intent to commit a crime, he engages in conduct which tends to effect the commission of such crime."[15]

Bad thoughts alone cannot be charged as attempt or any other crime. The prosecution must show that the defendant attempted to commit the crime charged, and this requires showing an overt act or acts. The federal courts and many states use the Model Penal Code "substantial step" test in defining the required overt act. Section 5.01(2) of the Model Penal Code defines the "substantial step" as conduct that "is strongly corroborative of the actor's criminal purpose." New York and other states hold that the state must show that the defendant performed acts that carried the "project forward within dangerous proximity of the criminal end to be attained." The following cases illustrate conduct that courts ruled to be attempts to commit the crime charged:[16]

- Defendant pointed a loaded gun at victim's face and pulled the trigger. The gun clicked but did not fire. Conviction for attempted first-degree assault. *State v. Turner*, 24 Conn. App. 264, 587 A.2d 1050 (1991)
- A mother abandoned her 15-month-old infant. When found, the baby was near death and infested with maggots. Conviction of attempted murder. *State v. Klafta, aff'd* 831 P.2d 512 (1992)
- Defendant was alone with a 14-year-old girl and came within 2 feet of her, telling her to lift up her shirt or he would kill her. The girl said no and continued to back up, screaming. Defendant said he was "just joking" and left. Evidence was held sufficient for a jury to find that the defendant took a substantial step toward raping the girl. *State v. Jackson*, 62 Wash. App. 53, 813 P.2d 156 (1991)
- As two girls were preparing to cross a street at an intersection, the defendant stopped his van, leaned out of the window, and said to the girls, "I'll pay you a dollar if you'll come … with me." The defendant was later found in the area and attempted to avoid being seen by police officers. Conviction for attempted kidnapping because if the girls had entered the van, their movements would have been restrained, and also because the young girls could not consent, and once in the van could have been taken to a place where they were not likely to be found.[17] State v. Billups, *62 Wash. App. 102, 813 P.2d 149 (1991)*

ATTEMPT AND THE MENS REA FOR THE COMPLETED CRIME

One element of most states' attempt statutes is the *intent to commit a crime*. What relevance, if any, does the kind of intent required by the crime attempted have to a conviction for the attempt of that crime? That is, if the crime attempted, usually referred to as the base crime, requires a specific intent, must the person charged with attempt have that same specific intent? The answer seems to be yes.

As an example of this, it is usually held that despite the fact that one could be convicted of murder even though the person intended only to inflict serious bodily harm on the deceased, that person could not be convicted of attempted murder if the victim did not die. That is because "attempted murder" requires the intent to bring about the result described in the base crime, murder, which is the death of a person, not merely serious bodily harm.[a]

This rule has led to inconsistent holdings in attempt convictions of crimes that do not have a specific intent. For example, the crime of manslaughter, and in many jurisdictions, the crime of second-degree murder, do not require proof that the defendant intended death to occur. As a result, some courts have held that there can be no crime of attempted manslaughter or second-degree murder, because attempt crimes all require the intent to commit the base crime (death of another).[b] Others have held that proof that the defendant committed an act that would have resulted in death and was evidence of a "depraved mind" (the usual definition of second-degree murder—see Chapter 10), constituted proof of attempted second-degree murder.[c]

In the case of strict liability crimes (see Chapter 3), it would seem logical to conclude that one could not be convicted of strict liability attempt, because attempt is defined as doing an act with the intent to commit a crime. In strict liability, one can be convicted of the crime if one engages in conduct that is made criminal without either knowledge or intent to commit a crime. Merely attempting to engage in that same conduct, the reasoning goes, cannot be an attempt crime, because it lacks the required intent.

Some courts disagree with this conclusion, at least where the strict liability crime has a specific result in mind. In *State v. Chhom*, 911 P.2d 1014 (1996), the Washington Supreme Court held that a defendant could be convicted of the strict liability crime of rape of a child. If the defendant attempted to have sexual intercourse with the victim, he could be convicted of the crime, even though he may have had no intent with respect to the other elements of the crime (age of the victim) as to which there was strict liability.

[a]See Wayne LaFave, *Criminal Law*, 4th ed., Section 11.3b, p. 584 (WestBelmont, Calif., 2003).
[b]See *State v. Coble*, 527 S.E.2d 45 (N.C. 2000).
[c]See *Brown v. State*, 790 So. 2d 389 (Fla. 2001).

Impossibility in Attempt Cases

In 1994, Francisco Duran paced back and forth on the sidewalk in front of the White House in Washington, D.C., until he saw a man he believed to be President Clinton. Duran then pulled an automatic weapon from under his coat and began firing at the man through the White House wrought-iron fence until security forces seized him.

Duran was charged with the federal crime of attempted assassination of the president. Duran contended he could not be charged with the attempt because it was impossible to complete the crime. The man he saw and shot at was not the president, who was in fact not in Washington at the time of the attempt. The federal court rejected this defense and convicted Duran of the attempt charge.[18]

In a somewhat similar case, defendant Benny Curtis was charged with attempting to kill wild deer out of season when he shot at a deer decoy set up by game wardens in response to residents' complaints about illegal deer shootings. Curtis argued that it was impossible to complete the crime because he was shooting at a decoy, and therefore he could not be guilty of the attempt. The Supreme Court of Vermont rejected that contention, and Curtis was convicted of the charge.[19]

Courts formerly categorized impossibility defenses in attempt cases into two classes: factual impossibility and legal impossibility. Attempting to pick an empty pocket is an example of factual impossibility. The only thing that prevents the crime from being completed is the fact that the pocket is empty. Attempting to receive stolen goods that were not stolen has been characterized as an example of legal impossibility. Even if the defendants completed the intended act, they would not be guilty of a crime.

Most state courts and the federal courts have abandoned the distinction between factual and legal impossibility and have rejected the defense in both situations.[20] The Model Penal Code, Section 5.1, also rejects the impossibility defense, whether factual or legal, concluding that the culpability of the defendant should be judged by the circumstances as the defendant viewed them.

The defense of impossibility was rejected in the following cases, and the defendants were convicted of criminal attempt:

*   Attempted armed robbery, even though the victim had no money in his wallet. *Brown v. Commonwealth*, 482 S.E. 2d 75 (Va. App. 1997)
*   Attempted possession of illegal drugs, even though the substance sold was not PCP, as defendant was told. *United States v. Fletcher*, 945 F.2d 725 (4th Cir. 1991), *cert. denied* 502 U.S. 1116 (1992)
*   Attempt to receive stolen property, even though the property the defendant purchased was not stolen.[21] *Commonwealth v. Henley*, 474 A.2d 1115 (Pa. 1984)
*   Attempt to steal trade secrets in violation of 18 U.S.C. § 1832(a)(4), where defendants alleged the procedures and formula they planned to steal were not secret. *United States v. Hsu*, 155 F.3d 189 (3d Cir. 1998)

One form of the impossibility defense in attempt cases remains viable. If a defendant plans to engage in conduct that he believes to be a crime, but the conduct as planned is not a crime, the defendant is not guilty of an attempt. LaFave, in *Criminal Law*, states that under the principle of legality (discussed in Chapter 1 of this text), "the defendant did not intend to do anything which had been made criminal, and what is not criminal may not be turned into a crime after the fact by characterizing his acts as an attempt."[22] For the same reason, one cannot be convicted of a conspiracy to commit a crime if the agreed objective is not criminal. See *In re Sealed Case*, 223 F.3d 775 (D.C. Cir. 2000).

Abandonment of the Criminal Purpose

In attempt, conspiracy, and solicitation, a person usually has time to change his or her mind and decide not to go ahead with the intended crime. The Model Penal Code, Section 501.04, states that it is a defense to the crime of attempt that the actor abandoned the attempt under circumstances "manifesting a complete and voluntary renunciation of his criminal purpose."

Many states now have statutes in their criminal code on abandonment of a criminal effort. Important questions concerning abandonment of a criminal intent include: Has a preliminary crime already been committed (how far along is the criminal effort)? Was the abandonment voluntary or involuntary? What was the reason for the abandonment (did the victim scream or police arrive at the scene or a burglar alarm go off)? The following cases illustrate:

*   A neighbor rang the doorbell of an elderly widow's home and, after being invited in and offered a beer, told the woman, "I am going to have you." After dragging the woman into a bedroom and throwing her on a bed, the defendant forcefully took most of her clothes off. As the defendant began taking his pants off, the woman kneed him in his groin and hit him in the face. Defendant then stopped his efforts,

ATTEMPT CRIMES AND INTERNET CHAT ROOMS

One of the unfortunate side effects of the Internet boom is the use of so-called chat rooms by pedophiles to communicate with children. These sex-related communications are, by themselves, harmful to children and present the real possibility that the conversation could lead to actual contact between the adult pedophile and the child. As a result, states have passed legislation aimed at this conduct, generally making it criminal to entice a child into having unlawful sexual relations. As an example, Section 18.2–374.3 of the Virginia Code Annotated makes it a crime to use a communication system, including a computer, for the purpose of promoting unlawful sex with a child.

Police officers often enter these chat rooms and pass themselves off as young children to others using the chat room. When an adult pedophile connects with the officer, the officer engages in conversations that frequently lead to the arrest of the adult for attempted violations of these enticement statutes. The defense of legal impossibility is often raised by these defendants. Courts virtually always reject that defense, as the courts in the following cases did:

- *U.S. v. Murrell*, 368 F.3d 1283 (11th Cir. 2004), *cert. denied* 125 S. Ct. 439 (2004). Defendant was convicted of attempt to entice a child into having unlawful sexual relations. An investigator posed as the father of a minor child in chat room conversations with the defendant, although in fact no minor child existed. The defendant contended that he could not be convicted because he never communicated with a minor child. The court rejected this argument, saying the attempt crime required only that the government prove the defendant tried to entice a child into having sexual relations. It did not matter that no child ever heard those enticements.
- *Hix v. Com.*, 619 S.E.2d 80 (Va. 2005). The defendant was convicted of attempted indecent liberties with a child, after chat room conversations in which the defendant proposed having sex with the "child." When the defendant agreed to meet the "child" at a McDonald's restaurant, police arrested him. The court rejected his argument that he could not be convicted of the crime of indecent liberties with a child, holding it did not matter that he never actually communicated with a child. It was sufficient, the court held, that he was attempting to do so.

apologized, and pleaded with the woman not to call the police. The Supreme Court of Wyoming affirmed defendant's conviction of attempted sexual assault, pointing out that the defendant did not voluntarily stop his attack and that the crime of attempt had already been completed. *Apodaca v. State*, 796 P.2d 806 (1990)

- A stranger forced a woman back into her home, told her to undress, pointed a handgun at her, shoved her onto a couch, and once threatened to kill her. The woman cried and talked about her little girl, telling the defendant that her little girl's daddy was dead. The defendant then said that if she had a little girl, he would not do anything, and he left in his pickup truck. The Supreme Court of Mississippi reversed defendant's conviction of attempted rape, holding that under the attempt statute of Mississippi that when "a defendant, with no other impetus but the victim's urging, voluntarily ceases his assault, he has not committed attempted rape."[23] *Ross v. State*, 601 So. 2d 872 (1992)
- Under a different name, Staples rented an apartment over a bank. He brought in power tools and equipment and, over a weekend when the bank was not open, drilled several holes through the floor into the ceiling of the bank. Nothing further was done, and at the end of the rental period, the landlord called in the police when he found the equipment and holes in the floor. Staples was arrested and stated that he had abandoned his criminal project. Because the crime of attempted burglary had already been committed, Staples was convicted of that crime. *People v. Staples*, 85 Cal. Rptr. 589 (1970)

PRELIMINARY, ANTICIPATORY, OR INCHOATE CRIMES

Crime	The Crime Consists of Evidence Showing	Other Aspects of the Crime
Solicitation (the preparatory offense charged least often): The invitation or urging to commit a crime.[a]	1. Requesting, encouraging, or commanding another person. 2. To commit a crime (most states restrict general solicitation to felonies).	Because no requirement generally exists for an overt act, the crime is complete when the solicitation is made. If the request to commit the crime is accepted, a conspiracy could exist if the requirements for the crime of conspiracy in that state are met.
Conspiracy (the oldest of the preparatory offenses): The criminal partnership.	1. An agreement between two or more people. (More than half the states now follow the Model Penal Code and do not require two or more guilty people. In these states, proof of guilt of one person is sufficient.) 2. Specific intent to commit a crime, or to obtain a legal goal by criminal acts. 3. Most states now require an overt act in furtherance of the plan be proved for all.	A conspiracy is punishable whether or not it succeeds in its objective (*United States v. Rabinowich*, 238 U.S. 78). In federal courts and some states, convictions for both conspiracy and the completed crime are held not to violate double jeopardy. *Iannelli v. United States*, 420 U.S. 770, 95 S. Ct. 1284 (1975); *Satte v. Barrangan-Sierra*, 196 P.3d 879 (Ariz. App. 2008). The Federal Drug Conspiracy Law does not require proof of an overt act. *United States v. Shabani*, 115 S. Ct. 382 (1994).
Attempt (the inchoate crime charged most often): An attempt often puts a possible victim in fear and apprehension. Many near victims can and do appear as witnesses in criminal trials.	1. That the defendant intended to commit the crime of which he or she is charged, and 2. That he or she did acts that (a) came within "dangerous proximity" of the criminal end or (b) amount to a "substantial step" (§ 5.01 Model Penal Code).	The American Law Institute Model Penal Code recommends the broadening of criminal liability for the crime of attempt. See § 5.01(2) for a discussion of these proposals.

[a]The English call this crime "incitement" and use the term *solicitation* in the crime of solicitation for prostitution.

≡ Parties to the Principal Crime

parties to the principal crime Under common law, persons who either committed the crime, or aided or abetted the commission of the crime or the persons who committed the crime.

At the time of the American Revolution, more than 200 crimes were punished by death in England. Application of the death penalty depended on the degree of criminal participation in the completed crime. The following four common law categories were used to determine the penalty that would be applied after conviction to the **parties to the principal crime**:

1. *Principal in the first degree* was the person (or persons) who actually committed the crime and would receive the death penalty if applicable.

2. *Principal in the second degree* was a person who was present at the commission of the crime, was not involved in the planning of the crime, but aided and abetted in the actual commission of the crime. This offender could not be tried under the common law until the actual perpetrator had been apprehended and convicted of the offense.

3. *Accessory before the fact* was a person who, knowing that a crime was to be committed, aided in the preparation for the crime but was not present at the time the crime was committed.

4. *Accessory after the fact* was a person who knew that the crime had been committed and gave aid or comfort to the person who committed the crime. Neither an accessory before the fact nor an accessory after the fact could be tried until after the conviction of the principal in the first degree.

Today, most states have done away with the four common law categories, as has the federal government. Under 18 U.S.C. § 2 in prosecutions for violation of federal law any person who "commits" the crime or "aids or abets" commission of the crime may be convicted "as a principal." The majority of jurisdictions have statutes that create the following two categories of criminal liability and make all principals or parties to the crime liable to the same punishment:

1. All people who knowingly are involved in or connected with the commission of a crime either before or during its commission are known as *principals or parties to the crime*, regardless of their connection. This category is a combination of the common law principal in the first and second degree and the accessory before the fact.

2. The person or people who render aid to the criminal after the crime has been committed were previously known under the common law as *accessories after the fact*. Legislative bodies have statutes identifying the criminal offenses in this category. This category is discussed in the section on post-crime offenses in this chapter.

The rule has been abolished that neither the principal in the second degree nor the accessories before or after the fact could be forced to trial before the trial of the principal in the first degree. Any participant in a crime may be tried and convicted, even though the person who actually committed the crime has not been apprehended and tried or even identified.[24]

Theories of Criminal Liability

Defendants may be charged as principals or parties to violations of criminal laws either because they committed the forbidden acts themselves, or because some other person did so and they are in some way liable for the acts of the other person. The following sections discuss the various ways one can incur criminal liability based on actions of another person.

aider and abettor One who provides help to the person who commits a crime, either before or after the crime is committed.

conspirator A person who is a party to an agreement to commit an unlawful act.

Criminal Liability as an Aider and Abettor and/or a Conspirator   A person could be criminally liable for the conduct of another if he or she is a party to a conspiracy to commit a crime and hires, urges, counsels, or plans with another to commit a crime. A person is also liable for the conduct of another if he or she is an **aider and abettor** to a person who committed a crime.

Aiders and abettors to a crime are usually at the scene of a crime and rendering aid and assistance to the person committing the crime, but the aid and assistance could also be rendered miles from the crime scene. The aider and abettor may also have been involved in the planning of the crime and therefore would also be a **conspirator**. Or a conspirator could live in London, England (or elsewhere), hire the killing of a person in Los Angeles, and never go near the scene of the crime.

Fact finders (jury or judge) may draw reasonable inferences from the conduct of the offenders and make conclusions as to whether the people were aiders and abettors or conspirators to the crime, or both. In states using the common design rule, fact finders could infer from the facts of the case whether the defendants in a criminal case committed the crime (or crimes) under a common design or plan.

Criminal Liability Under the Common Design or Common Plan Rule Under the common design rule, when people have a common plan to do an unlawful act, whatever is done in furtherance of the **common design or plan** is the act of all, and they can all be punished for that act.

Thus, if one of the parties to an armed robbery wore a mask, then all the parties to the robbery wore a mask, and all are subject to the penalties of committing the crime of armed robbery while concealed. See *Curl v. State*, 162 N.W.2d 77 (Wis. 1968). If one of the parties to a drug-trafficking offense carried a gun, then all the parties are subject to the penalties of carrying a loaded gun while trafficking marijuana. See *United States v. Martinez*, 958 F.2d 217 (8th Cir. 1992).

A common design is a spoken or unspoken conspiracy to commit an unlawful act. Any member of the conspiracy (plan) could be held liable as a principal for any offense committed in the furtherance of the plan or conspiracy while he or she is a member of it. Latecomers cannot be convicted as principals for offenses that were committed before they joined the conspiracy or after they withdrew from the conspiracy.[25]

The following cases are illustrations of the principle **"what one did, they all did"**:

- As a deputy sheriff was walking up to a car he had stopped for a minor vehicle license problem, one of the three men in the car pulled out a gun and killed the officer. The other two men in the car were surprised at what happened, but they, too, pulled out revolvers and began shooting at the remaining deputy sheriff in the squad car. The men fled after wounding the officer but were apprehended the next day. All three of the men were convicted of the murder of the officer and also of attempted murder of the wounded officer. The Wisconsin Supreme Court affirmed the convictions.[26]

- Defendant Watts guarded the parents of a teenage girl while his two friends raped the girl. Watts was convicted of two counts of rape in concert because he aided and abetted both rapes. In affirming the California convictions for these and other crimes, the Federal Court of Appeals held:

  We hold that no violation of due process has occurred in this case.... The ancient and universally accepted principle of accomplice liability holds a defendant legally responsible for the unlawful conduct of others that he aids and abets.[27]

- The California Supreme Court held in 1991 that because the crime of robbery is ongoing through the getaway, a getaway driver who has no prior knowledge of a robbery, but who forms the intent to aid (during the getaway), may properly be found liable as an aider and abettor of the robbery.[28]

- The fact that the defendants provided the following lawful goods and services to drug traffickers—fueled their plane, rented hangar space, stored ammunition and guns, falsely identified conspirators to outsiders, and offered to pay a security guard $20,000 to disappear while the plane was being loaded—was sufficient to affirm their conviction for aiding and abetting.[29]

common design or plan Scope of liability of persons who are party to a conspiracy or other agreement to do an unlawful act.

What one did they all did The rule that all parties to a conspiracy or other agreement to perform an unlawful act are liable for every action taken by any party in furtherance of the conspiracy or agreement.

Civil Liability as an Accomplice or Aider and Abettor

Crime victims sometimes bring actions against an offender in civil court, in addition to or in place of bringing criminal charges. In civil actions the burden of proof is lower, thus making it possible for the victim to obtain money damages even if the defendant is not convicted of criminal charges. The following cases are examples of civil liability of an **accomplice:**

accomplice One who aids another in the commission of a crime. An accomplice is generally treated the same as a principal.

- Four months after her husband kidnapped their child, a Colorado woman learned her husband had appeared on television on the *Phil Donahue Show* to discuss why he kidnapped the child. The company that produced the show had a babysitting service that the father used during the taping of the show, and as result the company would have been able to provide the mother with information to help the mother locate her child. But the company refused the mother's request for help. In a civil action, the mother won $5.9 million in damages from the company for aiding and abetting the kidnapping. The husband was later arrested, and the child was returned to her mother.
- *Soldier of Fortune* magazine was found liable for a $12.4 million civil judgment for publishing a "gun for hire" advertisement. The ad provided the name of a man, who was hired to, and did, kill a businessman.
- A person watching a battery gave verbal encouragement to the assailant, yelling "kill him" and "hit him more." In a civil action, the court held that liability did not require action in concert with the assailant, or even that the injury resulted directly from the encouragement. The court stated that civil liability in the United States for assault and battery is not limited to the direct perpetrators of the assault, but extends to those who, by encouraging the assailant or other means, aid the assailant.

Liability for Crimes Other than the Planned and Intended Offense

When the evidence demonstrates a common design or conspiracy to commit an unlawful act to which all the defendants agreed, whatever is done in the furtherance of the criminal plan is the act of all, if it is a natural and probable consequence of the intended crime. In prosecutions under the various federal conspiracy laws, courts commonly apply the so-called *Pinkerton* rule, taken from the Supreme Court's decision in *Pinkerton v. United States*, 328 U.S. 640 (1946). Under the *Pinkerton* rule a co-conspirator can be held liable for crimes committed by another conspirator, even if the co-conspirator did not know about the other crime, and did not agree to commit the other crime, so long as the crimes were committed in furtherance of the conspiracy and were foreseeable. See *United States v. Silvestri*, 409 F.3d 1311 (11th Cir. 2005).

Pinkerton rule The rule followed in federal courts that one conspirator is liable for crimes committed by another conspirator, if foreseeable and done in furtherance of the conspiracy.

State courts generally apply similar rules. For example, if guns are carried and a shot is fired by one member of the group, that shot is fired by all the defendants, and all of them must answer for the results.[30]

In *People v. Jones*, the California courts held that an accused who knew that his codefendants were armed was responsible for all the consequences when a night watchman was killed in a robbery.[31] The defendant in the *Jones* case was unarmed.

The definition of the natural and probable consequences of the intended crime varies somewhat from jury to jury and court to court. The following example illustrates the problem:

EXAMPLE: X and Y conspire to burglarize a residence. X is the lookout and getaway driver while Y is in the house committing the burglary. Y commits the following additional crimes. Which of the following should X be charged with?

"THE 2009 U.S. SUPREME COURT CASE ON ACCOMPLICE LIABILITY IN DRIVE-BY SHOOTING CASE"

Sarausad, the driver of a vehicle involved in a drive-by shooting near a Seattle school, was convicted of second-degree murder under Washington's accomplice liability law. Sarausad contended he could not be convicted because he did not know that one of his passengers had a gun until after the passenger pulled out the gun and fired it into a group of students, killing one and wounding another. The U.S. Supreme Court, reviewing a lower court's grant of Sarausad's habeas corpus petition, found that the evidence at trial established that the driver "slowed down before the shots were fired, stayed slowed down until the shots were over, and immediately sped up … there was no hesitation, there was no stopping the car. There was no attempt (by the driver) to swerve his car out of the way so that innocent people wouldn't get shot." *Waddington v. Sarausad*, 129 S. Ct. 823 (2009).

The trial court had instructed the jury on Washington's accomplice liability law as follows:

A person is an accomplice in the commission of a crime if, with knowledge that it will promote or facilitate the crime, he or she either:

1. solicits, commands, encourages, or requests another person to commit the crime, or
2. aids or agrees to aid another person in planning or committing the crime.

The U.S. Supreme Court reversed the lower court's grant of the habeas corpus petition, rejecting Sarasaud's argument that the jury instruction confused the jury because it could conclude the prosecution did not need to prove Sarasaud knew about the crime of murder. The Court held that the jury instruction clearly and unambiguously instructed the jury that the prosecution must prove the driver had knowledge that his conduct would promote or facilitate the commission of murder.

In this case the government had no evidence that the driver and his passengers set out to do a drive-by shooting or to commit any other felony such as robbery, burglary, rape, or the like. Because there was no evidence that the driver had any specific intent to commit the murder or any other felony, the government had the burden of proving the driver had knowledge his conduct would promote or facilitate the commission of the murder. The Supreme Court concluded the jury instruction clearly informed the jury of that burden, and as a result the driver was properly convicted.

1. Y is surprised by the homeowner and, in an attempt to get away, kills the man.
2. Y is surprised by an 11-year-old boy who lives in the house and needlessly kills the boy.
3. In addition to stealing, Y comes upon a woman in bed and rapes the woman.
4. After stealing from the house, Y sees a gallon of gasoline in the back hall of the house, spills the gasoline around the house, and burns it down.

Prosecutors could charge X with all the additional crimes, but whether X would be convicted would depend on whether the finder of fact determined that the additional acts were a natural and probable consequence of the burglary. It certainly could be argued in this case that X aided and assisted in all the crimes while acting as the lookout and getaway driver. If X had hired Y to commit the burglary and X was not at the scene of the crime, X's liability would be the same.

X's defense could be that some of the offenses are not the natural or probable consequence of the intended crime of burglary, and therefore X would not be criminally liable for those offenses. In all cases, X would be charged with and convicted of the crime of burglary.[32]

Can Criminal Liability Result from an Accident Criminal liability can result from intentional, reckless, or grossly negligent conduct. However, can criminal liability result

IF THE STATE CAN PROVE ONE OF THE FOLLOWING BEYOND REASONABLE DOUBT, A PERSON CAN BE HELD CRIMINALLY LIABLE

For a preliminary or anticipatory crime:

- Solicitation
- Conspiracy
- Attempt

For the planned and intended crime (if completed):

- As the person who committed the crime, or
- As a person who intentionally aids and abets the person who committed the crime, or
- As a conspirator who advises, hires, counsels, or otherwise procures another to commit the crime

For a post-crime offense relating to the planned and intended crime, states use one of the following theories of liabilities:

- Party to a crime, in which the state would have to prove each person participated in one of the preceding categories
- Common design or plan
- Criminal liability under the complicity, accountability, or accomplice rules

from accidental conduct? Criminals also have accidents. U.S. Supreme Court Chief Justice Roberts noted in the 2009 case of *United States v. Dean*, 129 S. Ct. 1849 that "Accidents happen. Sometimes they happen to individuals committing crimes with loaded guns."

The famous English lawyer and writer Sir William Blackstone answered the question of criminal liability from accidents in his Commentaries, written in 1769, as follows: "[I]f any accidental mischief happens to follow from the performance of a lawful act, the party stands excused from all guilt: but if a man be doing any thing unlawful and a consequence ensues which he did not foresee or intend, as the death of the man or the like, his want of foresight shall be no excuse … he is criminally guilty of whatever consequences may follow from the first misbehavior."

In the *Dean* case a defendant entered a bank carrying a weapon, intending to rob the bank. In the process, the firearm he carried discharged. The defendant was charged with violation of 18 U.S.C. § 924(c)(1)(A), carrying a firearm during the commission of a violent crime. Conviction under that statute results in a 5-year minimum sentence, which is increased to 7 years if the firearm is discharged. The defendant argued the discharge was an accident, but the Court said the enhanced sentence was still proper: "It is unusual to impose criminal punishment for the consequences of purely accidental conduct. But it is not unusual to punish individuals for the unintended consequences of their unlawful acts."

post-crime offenses
Actions taken after a crime has been committed with knowledge that it had been committed that provide aid to the person who committed the crime.

Post-Crime Offenses

Today, all states and the federal government have enacted many statutes regarding **post-crime offenses** meant to assist law enforcement officers in performing their duty of investigating crimes and apprehending criminals. Some statutes punish people who knowingly give police false information with the intent to mislead them. Other statutes are designed to permit the proper and efficient functioning of the courts and the criminal justice system. Some of these offenses existed under the common law, whereas others have been created in modern times. Examples are:

- Refusing to aid an officer while the officer is doing any act in his or her official capacity
- Obstructing or resisting an officer while the officer is doing any act in his or her official capacity (interfering with an officer)[33]
- Obstructing justice
- Compounding a crime: the making of an agreement (for a consideration) to withhold evidence of, or to abstain from prosecuting, a crime of which the accused has knowledge[34]
- False reports to an officer or law agency[35]
- Misprision of a felony (failure to report or prosecute a known felon)[36]
- Harboring or aiding felons
- Committing perjury
- Escaping from custody
- Bribing witnesses
- Jumping bail
- Communicating with jurors with the intent to influence them

Figure 4.1 illustrates the various stages of crimes, from the original idea of the crime to the offenses that can occur after the crime.

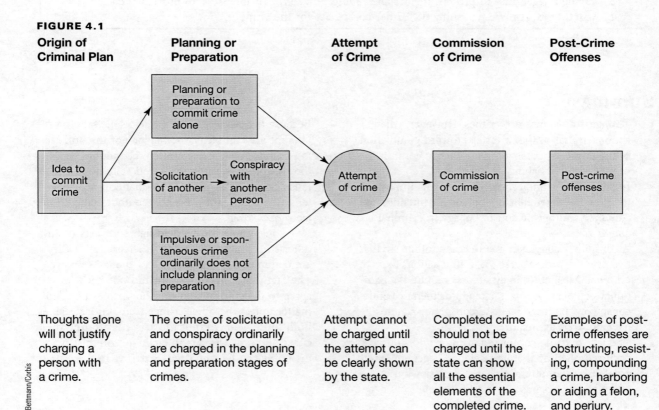

FIGURE 4.1

| Origin of Criminal Plan | Planning or Preparation | Attempt of Crime | Commission of Crime | Post-Crime Offenses |

Idea to commit crime

Planning or preparation to commit crime alone

Solicitation of another

Conspiracy with another person

Impulsive or spontaneous crime ordinarily does not include planning or preparation

Attempt of crime

Commission of crime

Post-crime offenses

Thoughts alone will not justify charging a person with a crime.

The crimes of solicitation and conspiracy ordinarily are charged in the planning and preparation stages of crimes.

Attempt cannot be charged until the attempt can be clearly shown by the state.

Completed crime should not be charged until the state can show all the essential elements of the completed crime.

Examples of post-crime offenses are obstructing, resisting, compounding a crime, harboring or aiding a felon, and perjury.

Bettmann/Corbis

STRICT LIABILITY DISTINGUISHED FROM VICARIOUS LIABILITY

Strict Liability

When a criminal statute imposes liability without requiring proof of mental fault, the offense is called a strict liability offense. If a statute requires proof of a mental element, the offense is not a strict liability offense.

To prove a strict liability offense, the state need prove only that the defendant did the forbidden act. The state does not have to prove a mental fault (mens rea). *Minnesota v. White* (see Chapter 3) came before the U.S. Supreme Court in 1991 and is an example of strict liability. The state proved that White hired a minor to dance nude in her bookstore. After the state proved the forbidden act and the age of the girl, White could not use the defense of mistake of age or consent by the minor.

Vicarious Liability

When a person becomes liable for the criminal act (or acts) of another, the liability is vicarious. Section 2.06 of the Model Penal Code lists the following categories of vicarious liability:

- Causing innocent or irresponsible people to do a criminal act
- Becoming a criminal accomplice of another person by:
  a. Soliciting the person to do a criminal act
  b. Aiding the other person in planning or committing the act
  c. Having a legal duty to prevent the act and failing to take reasonable steps to prevent the act
  d. A statute expressly establishing his or her complicity for the crime

Summary

- Thoughts alone are not crimes. However, when actions are taken that are steps toward completion of the crime, or persuading another to commit the crime, criminal liability is possible.
- In solicitation charges, corroboration is important to show the defendant unequivocally intended to convince another person to engage in criminal conduct.
- A conspiracy conviction requires as a minimum that two or more people agree to commit actions that are criminal. Most conspiracy statutes require the additional step of an overt act taken in furtherance of the conspiracy, but many federal conspiracy statutes have no overt act requirement.
- The fact that the completed crime could not have occurred, the impossibility defense, is generally not a defense to an attempt charge, unless what was being attempted was not a crime at all.

- Because the crimes of conspiracy, solicitation, or attempt are complete whether or not the underlying crimes ever are committed, abandonment of the conspiracy or attempt is generally not a defense. Some states provide an abandonment defense if a defendant prevents the underlying crime from occurring.
- One conspirator can be held liable for acts of another conspirator, including other crimes, if they are committed in furtherance of the conspiracy. The fact that one conspirator did not know of or agree to the commission of other crimes does not matter unless the other crimes were unforeseeable.
- Both those who commit the acts constituting the crime and thus who act to facilitate commission of the crime can be convicted as parties to the crime.

Key Terms

preliminary, anticipatory,
   or inchoate
   crimes, p. 83
solicitation or incitement
   crimes, p. 83
conspiracy crimes, p. 84
Wharton rule, p. 87

attempt crimes, p. 89
parties to the principal
   crime, p. 93
aider and abettor, p. 94
conspirator, p. 94
common design or
   plan, p. 95

What one did they all
   did, p. 95
accomplice, p. 96
Pinkerton rule, p. 96
post-crime offenses, p. 98

Case Analysis and Writing Exercises

1. When one parent abuses a child, may the state charge the other parent with accomplice liability for that abuse? Since most states define accomplice liability in terms of "aiding" another in the commission of a crime, what must the state prove the other parent did? Does the state's definition of *accomplice* make a difference? Compare *Tharp v. Com.*, 40 S.W.3d 356 (Ky. 2000) with *State v. Jackson*, 976 P.2d 1229 (Wash. 1999). Which approach do you think is better? Why?

2. The rule that "bad thoughts alone" cannot constitute an attempt results in the requirement that the defendant must have taken some steps to put the bad thoughts into action. Moreover, these steps must be, in the language of the Model Penal Code, "substantial" enough to "strongly corroborate the actor's criminal purpose." What should be done with the defendant who intends to commit a crime, and takes some act in furtherance of that intent, but the act taken is logically and practically impossible to cause the prohibited result? Sometimes called "inherent impossibility," should a defendant be charged with an attempt when any reasonable person would know the actions taken to complete the crime could not possibly have that result? Minnesota, as part of its attempt laws, has a provision that states:

An act may be an attempt notwithstanding the circumstances under which it was performed or the means employed to commit the crime intended or the act itself were such that the commission of the crime was not possible, unless such impossibility would have been clearly evident

to a person of normal understanding. See M.S.A. § 609.17 (2003).

Assume a prison inmate intends to escape but is apprehended after he has placed a dummy in his bed to confuse prison guards. Can he be charged with attempted escape? If so, does the fact that his plan—to go through five locked doors—is virtually impossible, give him a defense under the statute quoted above? See *State v. Espinal*, 2004 WL 2093508 (Minn. 2004).

3. The defendant planned to kill a woman with whom he had a sexual relationship. He asked a friend to drive the victim and him to an abandoned farm, where he stated he would kill the victim. The friend agreed but instead told the police about the conversation. The police arrested the defendant and charged him with attempted murder and solicitation of murder. Should the defendant be convicted of these crimes? Why or why not? See *People v. Terrell*, 792 N.E.2d 357 (Ill. App. 2003).

4. Assume two people enter into a conspiracy to distribute drugs. One person, A, is a convicted felon. The other, B, is not. During the conspiracy, but unknown to B, A obtains possession of a gun, a violation of a firearms statute prohibiting a convicted felon from owning or possessing a firearm. Can B be convicted of the crime of possession of a firearm by a convicted felon under the *Pinkerton* rule? Do you see problems with applying the rule here? See *United States v. Walls*, 225 F.3d 858 (7th Cir. 2000).

Notes

1. See Section 11.1, Wayne LaFave, *Criminal Law*, 4th ed. (Belmont, Calif.: Thomson/West, 2003).
2. In the United States, the crime is generally called "solicitation"; in England the crime is called "incitement," with the term *solicitation* being used for solicitation for prostitution. See the English *Moriarty's Police Law* (Law and Regulations for the Use of Police Officers), 21st ed. (Butterworths, 1972).
3. The English Parliament enacted the Incitement to Mutiny Act (English armed forces) in 1797. See *Moriarty's Police Law*, p. 12.
4. *State v. Hauk*, 652 N.W.2d 393 (Wis. 2002). Since the crime of solicitation is complete when the solicitation occurs, it does not matter if the defendant later recants the solicitation. Also, as the *Hauk* court held, the usual rule that one cannot be convicted of a crime based only on a confession is inapplicable where the confession is not made to the police, but to a friend. See page 219, Thomas Gardner and Terry Anderson, *Criminal Evidence*, 6th ed. (Thomson/Wadsworth, 2007).
5. The defendant was convicted of the misdemeanor crime of use of abusive language.
6. In 1925, Judge Learned Hand called conspiracy the "darling of the prosecutor's nursery," as prosecutors were using conspiracy as a weapon against organized crime and illegal business practices. See *Harrison v. United States* (7 F.2d 259, 263, 2d Cir. 1925). Today, the federal and state RICO statutes are much more effective in this type of criminal prosecution. See Chapter 18 for a discussion of the RICO statutes.
7. 336 U.S. 440, 445, 69 S. Ct. 716, 719 (1949).
8. The Texas conspiracy statute is actually limited to agreements to commit a *felony*, as opposed to a *crime*. In that respect, Texas is in the minority; most states have statutes making the crime of conspiracy applicable to an agreement to commit any crime. For those states retaining the common law definition of conspiracy, the agreement need only be to achieve some "unlawful purpose." See *Commonwealth v. Hunt* (45 Mass. (4 Metc.) 111, 123 (1842)).
9. Under the old common law, a husband and wife were one person, with the wife being subject to the control and discipline of the husband. (See the discussion on the defense of duress and coercion in Chapter 7.) Because of this relationship, the common law rule held that *because* the husband and wife were one person, they could not conspire together and be charged as the two persons to a conspiracy.

    This old common law rule was rejected by the U.S. Supreme Court in the 1960 case of *United States v. Dege* (80 S. Ct. 1589), in which the Court held that a wife is a person like anyone else and therefore is capable of entering into a criminal conspiracy with her husband or another person. Today, all states would follow this reasoning if the question were before a state court.
10. See "Stockbroker Is Found Guilty of Conspiring to Have a Judge Killed," *New York Times*, December 23, 2000.
11. See *Alleyne v. California*, 98 Cal. Rptr. 2d 737 (2000), *cert. denied* 532 U.S. 958 (2001).
12. See *United States v. Delutis*, 722 F. 2d 902 (1st Cir. 1983). The Wharton rule was held not to apply to the crime of possession with intent to distribute illegal drugs, as one person alone can commit this crime. See *Johnson v. State*, 587 A.2d 444 (Del. 1991).
13. See *United States v. Cohen*, 260 F.3d 68 (2d Cir. 2001).
14. LaFave, *Criminal Law*, 4th ed., p. 652 (Belmont, Calif.: Thomson/West, 2003).
15. Section 110.00, McKinney's *Consolidated Laws of New York, Annotated*, Book 39.
16. Examples of conduct that was mere preparation and did not amount to conduct to attempt to commit the crime charged include:
    - Police officers watching a bank night depository saw two young men park near the depository and remove something from the trunk of their car. The men then walked up near the depository and back. When a car approached, the men hid in nearby bushes. Because no crime occurred, the court held the police had no

probable cause to arrest the men. See *People v. Cradle*, 160 A.D.2d 891, 554 N.Y.S.2d 323 (1990).

- The defendant armed himself and then drove to a nearby city in a stolen cab that he intended to use as a getaway vehicle. The defendant stated he was looking for a jewelry store to rob. The defendant did not find the store he intended to rob. The Supreme Court of Illinois affirmed the defendant's convictions for a number of crimes but reversed the conviction for attempted robbery of the jewelry store, holding that the defendant did not commit a substantial step toward the robbery of the store. See *People v. Smith*, 593 N.E.2d 533 (1992).

17. In the 1992 case of *Commonwealth v. Banfill* (597 N.E.2d 47), the defendant stopped his truck and asked directions from a 13-year-old girl walking on the street. When the girl could not give the defendant information about a street, the defendant told the girl through the open truck window to "get in." The defendant was convicted of attempted kidnapping and appealed.

    The Supreme Judicial Court of Massachusetts reversed the conviction, holding there was insufficient evidence to support the conviction because no overt act is required by the statute. The court pointed out that the defendant did not "make a move toward" the girl in any way, that he did not open the truck door or display a weapon, and that he did not "try to grab out" at the girl.

18. *United States v. Duran*, 884 F. Supp. 577 (D.D.C. 1995). Duran continued to fire his automatic weapon until the clip was empty. While Duran was replacing the empty clip, bystanders seized Duran on the sidewalk outside the White House and disarmed him.

19. *State v. Curtis*, 603 A.2d 356 (Va. 1991).

20. See page 38 of LaFave and Scott, *Criminal Law*, 2nd ed. (Belmont, Calif.: West/Wadsworth, 1986). Legal writers distinguish between legal and factual impossibility. However, the Supreme Court of Pennsylvania states that no American court has recognized factual impossibility as a defense to an attempt charge (*Commonwealth v. Henley*, 474 A.2d at 1116).

In addition to legal and factual impossibility, some courts write of "inherent impossibility." The committee drafting the revised Illinois Criminal Code in 1961 wrote this comment on the defenses of impossibility (Chapter 38, p. 513):

It is the intent of section 8–4(b) to exclude both factual and legal impossibilities as defenses to prosecution for attempt. However, inherent impossibility (attempts to kill by witchcraft such as repeatedly stabbing a cloth dummy made to represent the person intended to be killed) is not intended to be excluded as a defense. [Emphasis in original.]

21. The *Henley* case held that the fact the goods were not stolen provided no defense to an attempt charge. However, if the goods were not stolen, or lost their identity as stolen goods, the defendant could not be convicted of the charge of possession of stolen property. See Chapter 15 for material on the crime of possession of stolen goods.

22. LaFave, *Criminal Law*, 4th ed., p. 600 (Belmont, Calif.: Thomson/West, 2003).

23. In cases such as this, defendants can be charged with other criminal offenses, depending on the criminal code of that state. Possible charges could be home invasion (or burglary), battery or assault, pointing a firearm at another person, and disorderly person (or disorderly conduct).

24. In the 1980 case of *Standefer v. United States* (447 U.S. 10, 100 S. Ct. 1999) the U.S. Supreme Court held that a defendant may be convicted of aiding and abetting the commission of a federal crime, even though the person who actually committed the crime had been acquitted of the offense.

25. The New Jersey accountability and accomplice liability law is presented in the 1992 case of *State v. Bryant*, 607 A.2d 1343 (N.J. 1992), as follows:

N.J.S.A. 2C:2–6a provides that a person is guilty of an offense "if it is committed by his own conduct or the conduct of another person for which he is legally accountable, or both." N.J.S.A. 2C:2–6b provides in part: b. A person is legally accountable for the conduct of another person when:

* * *

(3) He is an accomplice of such other person in the commission of an offense; or

(4) He is engaged in a conspiracy with such other person.

    c. A person is an accomplice of another person in the commission of an offense if:

    (1) With the purpose of promoting or facilitating the commission of the offense, he

    (a) Solicits such other person to commit it;

    (b) Aids or agrees or attempts to aid such other person in planning or committing it; or

    (c) Having a legal duty to prevent the commission of the offense, fails to make proper effort so to do; or

    (d) His conduct is expressly declared by law to establish his complicity.

26. *State v. Nutley*, 24 Wis. 2d 527, 129 N.W.2d 155 (1964).

27. *Watts v. Bonneville*, 879 F.2d 685 (9th Cir. 1989).

28. *People v. Cooper*, 53 Cal. 3d 1158, 282 Cal. Rptr. 450 (1991).

29. *United States v. O'Neil*, 729 F.2d 1440 (2d Cir. 1983), *review denied* 104 S. Ct. 135 (1983).

30. *People v. Bracey*, 249 N.E.2d 224 (1969).

31. 29 P.2d 902 (1934).

32. In the 1991 case of *Ward v. State* (567 N.E.2d 85), no evidence showed that the defendant knew anything about the planned robbery. The defendant drove three men to the store they planned to rob and then left the area. Another car arrived carrying the weapons and ski masks used. During the robbery, a store clerk was killed. The Supreme Court of Indiana reversed the defendant's conviction of felony murder, pointing out that the defendant was not shown to have participated in either the planning or carrying out of the robbery, that he did not remain as a lookout but left the area, that he did not return to aid in the escape, and that he did not receive any proceeds of the robbery.

    In the case of *Mumford v. Maryland*, 313 A.2d 563 (Md. App. 1974), a rape and murder occurred during a burglary. The defendant (a 15-year-old girl) stated that she was elsewhere on the premises when the rape and murder occurred and that she did not know these crimes were being committed. In reversing her conviction for first-degree murder

(felony murder) and ordering a new trial, the court stated:

> There must be a direct causal connection between the homicide and the felony. Something more than mere coincidence in time and place between the two must be shown; otherwise, the felony-murder rule will not be applicable.

(See Chapter 10 for material on the felony murder rule.)

33. Obstructing or interfering with an officer sometimes occurs during an accident or public disaster. Newspaper photographers were convicted in the following cases for seeking to obtain photographs of accidents after being repeatedly told to stay in the area where the general public was permitted. In both disasters, police had cleared the area so that emergency fire and medical vehicles could enter the area, control fire and explosions, and render aid to the injured and dying.

    In the case of *State v. Peruta*, 591 A.2d 140 (Conn. App. 1991), a fatal car accident had occurred. The photographer was convicted of "interfering with an officer" because he repeatedly interfered with rescue efforts.

    In the case of *City of Oak Creek v. King*, 436 N.W.2d 285 (Wis. 1989), a commercial airline had crashed, causing many deaths and injuries. King was convicted of disorderly conduct because he would not stay behind police lines. The Supreme Court of Wisconsin pointed out that reporters do not have special rights that the general public does not have and must obey reasonable police orders at the scene of a public emergency.

34. The South Dakota statute of compounding a crime is as follows:

> *Any person who* accepts or offers or agrees to accept *any pecuniary benefit as consideration for*
>
> 1. *Refraining from seeking prosecution of an offender; or*
> 2. *Refraining from reporting to law enforcement authorities the commission or suspected commission of any crime or information relating to a crime;*

is guilty of compounding. Compounding a felony is a Class 6 felony. Compounding a misdemeanor is a Class 1 misdemeanor.

35. For a false report case that went to the U.S. Supreme Court, see *United States v. Rogers*, 466 U.S. 475 (1984).

36. The drafters of the Model Penal Code state, "In general, our society does not use penal sanctions to compel reporting of crime" (§ 242.5, Comment at pp. 251–252, 1980).

CHAPTER 5

Criminal Responsibility and the Capacity to Commit a Crime

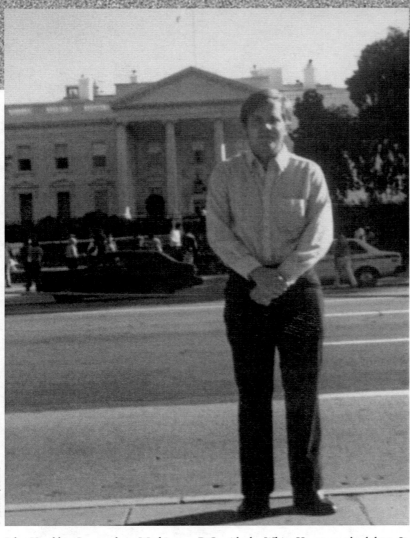

© Bettmann/CORBIS

John Hinckley, Jr., stands in Washington D.C. with the White House as a backdrop. In 1981 Hinckley attempted to assassinate President Ronald Reagan. He wounded the President, and others, including James Brady, Reagan's press secretary. Hinckley was found not guilty by reason of insanity, and while he remains confined to a mental institution, he has over the years been allowed temporary release from the institution. The assassination attempt and resulting trial led to passage of the Brady Law on gun control, and the Insanity Defense Reform Act.

LEARNING OBJECTIVES

In this chapter we consider when a person has the capacity for criminal responsibility. The learning objectives for this chapter are:

- Learn when a child can be held responsible for violation of a criminal law.

- Distinguish between the method of imposing criminal liability upon a child under age 7 and a child of age 14.

- List the two prongs of the *M'Naghten* rule.

- Describe the difference between the *M'Naghten* rule and the "substantial capacity" test.

- Identify the extent, if any, to which the voluntary use of drugs or alcohol may be used as an insanity defense or diminished capacity defense.

- Distinguish the "not guilty by reason of insanity" verdict from the verdict of "guilty but mentally ill" verdict.

- List factors that may present issues of a criminal defendant's competency to be tried on criminal charges.

- Explain why a defendant of questionable competency should not be tried for a criminal violation.

On March 30, 1981, John Hinckley attempted to assassinate President Ronald Reagan. In 1982, he was tried on charges stemming from that attempt and was found not guilty by reason of insanity. Hinckley was ordered confined in a mental hospital, St. Elizabeth's Hospital in Washington, D.C., where he remains today.

Hinckley has appeared in court many times since his confinement to St. Elizabeth's, seeking relaxation of the terms of his confinement. On November 25, 2004, a federal judge denied Hinckley's request for extended, four- to five-day visits to his parents' home in Virginia. That request was denied in part because of Hinckley's relationship with a woman that began after his confinement. Prosecutors were concerned that the breakup of that relationship might result in new violent behavior from Hinckley. The court noted that it was Hinckley's obsession with the actress Jodie Foster that contributed to his past behavior and raised serious questions about the effect on Hinckley of problems in his present relationship. The court did grant Hinckley four additional overnight visits to his parents' home. He had previously had eight such visits. In 2009 a federal judge increased the length of his home visits to 9 days, and permitted Hinckley to obtain a driver's license. In this chapter we examine the rules that determine when persons can be held criminally responsible for their actions. We also learn about the evolution of the insanity defense and its place in criminal law today.

≡ Ancient Concepts of Criminal Responsibility

The law has undergone many changes over the centuries regarding how to determine criminal responsibility and how to assess who has the capacity to commit a crime. At the time of the Norman Conquest of England (1066), for example, trial by ordeal and trial by battle were commonly used to determine criminal responsibility. If a person was of noble birth or was titled, he could demand trial by battle if accused of a crime. In trial by battle, if the suspect or accused came out second, it was then determined that he was guilty of the offense with which he was charged. However, the question of guilt or innocence could become moot, because the accused might be killed or badly injured.

trial by ordeal A test used to determine criminal responsibility in ancient England involving subjecting the individual to a torturous ordeal. These ordeals were essentially appeals to God; surviving the ordeal was viewed as God's judgment of innocence.

In determining criminal responsibility in a **trial by ordeal**, the accused often was required to take a pound weight of red-hot iron into his hands or to plunge his hand, up to the wrist, into boiling water. Ordeal by fire and ordeal by water were also used. Sir James Stephen described trial by ordeal in his *History of the Criminal Law of England*, published in 1883:

It is unnecessary to give a minute account of the ceremonial of the ordeals. They were of various kinds. The general nature of all was the same. They were appeals to God to work a miracle in attestation of the innocence of the accused person. The handling of hot iron, plunging the hand or arm into boiling water unhurt, were the commonest. The ordeal of water was a very singular institution. Sinking was the sign of innocence, floating the sign of guilt. As any one would sink unless he understood how to float, and intentionally did so, it is difficult to see how anyone could ever be convicted by this means. Is it possible that this ordeal may have been an honourable form of suicide, like the Japanese happy despatch? In nearly every case the accused would sink. This would prove his innocence, indeed, but there would be no need to take him out. He would thus die honourably. If by accident he floated, he would be put to death disgracefully.[1]

Another form of superstition involved the concept that individuals deliberately became witches or practiced witchcraft. These individuals were thought to be capable of causing great social harm, such as crop failure, as well as causing serious injuries or illnesses and death to others. Witchcraft first became a crime under the Roman Empire. During the sixteenth, seventeenth, and eighteenth centuries, thousands of people were tried and put to death because they were believed to be either witches or to practice witchcraft. For example, Joan of Arc was charged with being a witch and condemned to death. She was burned at the stake in France in 1431.

Prosecution of such people in the American colonies occurred in Massachusetts, Connecticut, and Virginia. These trials reached a high point in 1692 in Salem, Massachusetts, where 19 persons were executed as witches, and 150 more were sent to prison. The Salem trials were the last American witchcraft trials; the last English witchcraft trials took place in 1712. In 1735, Scotland repealed all laws that made witchcraft a crime in that country.

Today criminal responsibility and capacity are generally seen as potential excuses for the commission of acts that would ordinarily be criminal, as opposed to defenses to criminal liability. That is, if one who commits criminal acts can show he lacked responsibility or capacity, his actions are excused from criminal liability. In this chapter we examine the specifics of the traditional tests for determining responsibility and capacity, mainly as they apply to infancy and insanity. In later chapters we examine the circumstances where one accused of criminal acts might have a defense to criminal liability.

preponderance of the evidence The greater weight of the evidence, though not necessarily the amount needed to remove every reasonable doubt. It is proof sufficient to incline a reasonable person toward one side of an issue rather than the other.

The capacity and criminal responsibility doctrines discussed in this chapter are often labeled affirmative defenses, though if proved they serve not as justification for actions, but excuse of responsibility. In the case of infancy most states have adopted various presumptions about a child's criminal responsibility, as the materials below discuss. In the case of adults, in most states a defense of insanity requires the defendant to prove insanity by a preponderance of the evidence. The U.S. Supreme Court has long held that to require a defendant to prove insanity or other lack of criminal responsibility does not violate the Constitution. *LeLand v. State*, 343 U.S. 790 (1952).

In a few states the prosecution must prove the presence of capacity or sanity, usually beyond a reasonable doubt. See *State v. Johnson*, 636 N.W.2d 391 (N.D. 2001); *Commonwealth v. Keita*, 712 N.E.2d 65 (Mass. 1999). Those states may have been influenced by the Model Penal Code, § 112 (1) and (2) (a), which requires the prosecution to prove an affirmative defense that relates to an element of the crime, once some evidence showing the defense has been introduced.

One aspect of criminal responsibility has seen recent developments. The U.S. Supreme Court held in *Atkins v. Virginia*, 536 U.S. 304 (2002), discussed in Chapter 8, that a mentally retarded person could not be subject to the death penalty. Following that decision, many states passed statutes establishing procedures for determining when a defendant is mentally retarded and thus not subject to the death penalty. Virtually all states placed the burden of proof of mental retardation on the defendant, most requiring proof by a preponderance of the evidence, though a few require proof by "clear and convincing" evidence. See *Pruit v. State*, 834 N.E.2d 90 (Ind. 2005), for a list of state statutes on proof of mental retardation.

Infancy and Criminal Responsibility

infant (child) Under the civil law, a person who has not yet reached the age of majority, whether that age is 18, 19, 20, or 21, as determined by the law of each jurisdiction.

Under the civil law, an **infant (child)** is a person who has not yet reached the age of majority, whether that age is 18, 19, 20, or 21, as determined by the law of each jurisdiction. Although infants, with some exceptions, are not able to enter into contracts, make wills, or vote, the law on children's criminal responsibility for their acts differs from the law governing the children's civil capacity.

The question of the criminal responsibility of children first came before courts in western Europe in the Middle Ages. By the fourteenth century, the common law had determined that children under the age of 7 did not have the capacity to commit a crime. By that time, 7 had been established as the "age of reason" under ecclesiastical law and also as the age of responsibility under Roman civil law. In establishing the age of 7 as the lowest age of criminal responsibility, the common law concluded that a child under the age of 7 did not have the mental capacity to formulate the intent to commit a crime and that, therefore, for children under 7, the threat of punishment would not serve as a deterrent against crime.

Many states have codified some version of the common law rules on children's criminal capacity, though they vary on the age limits adopted.[2] An example of a typical state statute determining children's criminal responsibility is Section 9A.04.050 of the Washington Statutes, which provides in part:

> Children under the age of eight years are incapable of committing crime. Children of eight and under twelve years of age are presumed to be incapable of committing crime, but this presumption may be removed by proof that they have sufficient capacity to understand the act or neglect, and to know that it was wrong.

The age selected by the jurisdiction as the minimum age for a child's criminal responsibility creates a conclusive presumption that a child under that age lacks the capacity to commit a crime. As the presumption is conclusive, evidence to the contrary may not be presented. People over a certain age—in most states, around 14 years of age—are inferred to be capable of formulating the necessary mental frame of mind to commit a crime. Evidence showing otherwise, however, can be used to show incapacity. Moreover, such children may be prosecuted through the juvenile court system, rather than in adult court.

A rebuttable presumption exists under most state statutes and the common law that children between the minimum age (usually around 7) and the maximum age (usually around 14) are presumed to be without criminal capacity to commit a crime. This presumption, however, may be overcome by the presentation of evidence by the state showing that the child has the mental capacity and the ability to formulate the necessary criminal intent.[3]

The U.S. courts look to a variety of factors when the capacity presumption is at issue, and they usually hold that the younger the child, the stronger must be the evidence of mental capacity. The Washington Supreme Court considered the presumption contained in the statute cited above in the 2004 case of *State v. Ramer*, 86 P.3d 132. There, an 11-year-old boy was charged with first-degree rape of a child, a 7-year-old boy. The state unsuccessfully attempted to prove the child had the capacity to understand the nature of

ARE PARENTS CRIMINALLY LIABLE FOR THE CRIMINAL ACTS OF THEIR CHILDREN?

Parents are not generally liable for the criminal acts of their children simply because they are parents. However, most states have laws against contributing to the delinquency of a minor. California, for instance, has a law providing criminal sanctions against parents who fail to "exercise reasonable care, supervision, protection and control over their child." Cal. Penal Code § 272(2). Many states also have civil liability laws which impose financial liability on parents for misconduct by their minor children. For instance, Ca. Civil Codes 1714.1 (for willful misconduct) and § 1714.3 (firearm injury) and Ca. Veh. Code § 17708 (vehicular injuries). For more discussion of this topic, see "Juvenile Justice Reform in the United States 1994-1996," http//www.ojjdp.ncjrs.gov/pubs/reform/ch2-d.html#80.

his acts and that the acts were wrong. In reviewing the trial court's decision that the child lacked such capacity, the Washington Supreme Court stated:

> We have identified seven factors to consider in determining capacity: (1) the nature of the crime, (2) the child's age and maturity, (3) whether the child evidenced a desire for secrecy, (4) whether the child told the victim (if any) not to tell, (5) prior conduct similar to that charged, (6) any consequences that attached to that prior conduct, and (7) whether the child had made an acknowledgment that the behavior is wrong and could lead to detention. (86 P.3d at 136–137)

The court also noted that in sexual charges against children, it is difficult to overcome the presumption, because it is hard to tell if children understand prohibitions on sexual behavior. Based on the testimony of two psychologists, who both stated the child did not understand that his conduct was wrong, the court agreed that the state failed to overcome the presumption of incapacity.

The Juvenile Court System

All states have enacted statutes governing the jurisdiction of children's (juvenile) courts. These courts deal with children who are delinquent and in need of supervision or with children who are neglected and dependent. "Delinquency" is usually defined by statute as conduct by a child that, if committed by an adult, would be a violation of the criminal code of that state. States vary on the maximum age for the jurisdiction of juvenile courts but usually set a limit around 18 years of age. State statutes also generally provide that

IS THE ROLE OF JUVENILE COURTS CHANGING?

When the first juvenile court was established in Cook County, Illinois, in 1899, the idea behind the court was to rehabilitate youths, rather than punish them for their wrongdoings. For the next 50 years or so, this was the guiding philosophy as the states created their own juvenile court systems. These courts tended to be very informal and treated the youths more like wayward children than criminals.

By the late 1960s and early 1970s, two forces began to exert a change on the prevailing juvenile court philosophy. First, in cases like *In re Gault*, 387 U.S. 1 (1967), the U.S. Supreme Court decided that juveniles were entitled to many of the same procedural protections available to adult offenders, such as the right to an attorney, the right to confront witnesses, and the right to remain silent. This change of emphasis from an informal, *in loco parentis* type of proceeding to an adversarial trial caused legislatures to rethink the rehabilitative ideal upon which juvenile courts were based.

Second, the rise of serious, violent juvenile crime in the 1980s and 1990s created an atmosphere of anxiety and fear among the general public. These events caused many state legislatures to modify the juvenile court system, mainly to make it easier for a juvenile to be waived out of the system and into adult court. These modifications took two forms. In one form, states' statutes listed crimes for which the juvenile courts had no jurisdiction. For example, Nevada Revised Statutes, Section 62B.330 (2003), exempts murder, sexual assault, use of a firearm in a crime, or any felony that results in death or serious bodily harm from the juvenile court's jurisdiction. California has a similar provision.[a]

The other way that these modifications came about was that states began expanding the circumstances under which a juvenile could be transferred from juvenile court to adult court. In the article "Mourning the Untimely Death of the Juvenile Death Penalty,"[b] the author notes that by 1999, twenty-nine states had some form of mandatory transfer statute, and that the age of youths transferred had dropped significantly.

[a]Cal. Wel. & Inst. Code, Section 602 (1998 & 2006 Supp.).
[b]42 CAWLR 287, 294 (2006).

juvenile courts may waive jurisdiction to the adult courts of children otherwise under the jurisdiction of the juvenile court.

In most jurisdictions, a juvenile court judge has the discretion to waive the juvenile court's jurisdiction, based on factors such as the age of the juvenile, the crime charged, and the extent of previous offenses. In some states, the prosecutor has the additional discretion to decide to file charges in either the juvenile court or adult court. A few states have "once-an-adult-always-an-adult" rules, where if a juvenile is once transferred to adult court, he will always be treated as an adult in further offenses.

≡ The Insanity Defense

No subject in criminal law has received as much attention and debate as the insanity defense. The questions of what degree of insanity, mental defect, or mental disease renders a person blameless for acts or omissions and what **insanity tests** should be used in determining legal and moral liability have been debated for years.

insanity tests Tests to determine legal and moral liability.

The insanity defense is seldom used by defense lawyers for minor criminal charges.[4] It is most often used in murder cases and for other serious felony charges in which the evidence against a defendant is sometimes so strong that no other defense is available.

Studies have shown that the insanity plea is usually not an easy way out for criminal defendants and that only about 2 percent of defendants charged with serious crimes use the insanity plea.[5] The success rate among defendants using the insanity plea is not high when medical doctors differ as to the sanity of a defendant. Terrible and gross crimes by a defendant are not likely to cause a jury to make a finding of "not guilty by reason of insanity" (NGRI), as was demonstrated in the 1992 Jeffrey Dahmer case, in which a Wisconsin jury quickly found Dahmer sane and criminally liable despite his actions. Dahmer had murdered 15 young men after drugging and performing crude lobotomies on some of them in an attempt to craft zombie-like creatures. Dahmer had sex with some of the corpses and dismembered bodies. He stored hands in a kettle and had a severed head in his refrigerator. A heart from a victim was also saved to be eaten later. (See the *Milwaukee Sentinel* of February 7, 1992.)

In most jurisdictions the burden is on the defendant to prove the insanity defense, usually by a preponderance of the evidence.

Insanity at the Time of the Criminal Incident

The question of insanity (mental disease or defect) may be raised at specific stages during the criminal proceedings. If a defendant is found insane at the time the crime occurred, a judgment of not guilty by reason of insanity is then entered by the court, and the defendant may never again be tried for that offense.

A defendant who is found not guilty by reason of insanity is almost always committed to a mental institution under the laws of that state (or the federal government). Such state and federal laws provide for the length of stay and the conditions under which the person may be eligible for release.[6]

In the 1992 case of *Foucha v. Louisiana*,[7] the defendant was found not guilty of burglary by reason of insanity. After four years in a state psychiatric hospital, a doctor at the hospital stated that Foucha was no longer mentally ill, but declined to certify that the defendant was no longer a danger to himself or others. Under Louisiana law at that time, Foucha had the burden of proving that he was no longer dangerous in order to earn his release from the hospital.

The U.S. Supreme Court held that the Louisiana law violated due process: "the State must establish insanity and dangerousness by clear and convincing evidence in order to confine an insane convict beyond his criminal sentence, when the basis for his original confinement no longer exists." The Court stated that since the State conceded Foucha was no longer insane, the only basis for holding him was his dangerousness. While "dangerousness" by itself can sometimes be a basis for confining a person, the Court said, it must be proved by the State, not disproved by the person confined.

The holding in *Foucha*, where the State conceded the defendant was no longer insane, should be contrasted to the burden of proof required for the release of a person committed after a finding of not guilty by reason of insanity. It is common for commitment statutes to place the burden of proving a person committed is no longer insane on that person, not the government. For example, in *United States v. Weed*, 389 F.3d 1060 (10th Cir. 2004) a defendant was found not guilty by reason of insanity of the murder of a postal worker, a federal offense. Under the federal commitment statute, 18 U.S.C. § 4243, after such a verdict a hearing is held to determine if the defendant should be confined in a mental institution or released, "because no longer dangerous" to others. At that hearing, section 4243(d) requires the defendant to prove by "clear and convincing" evidence that his mental condition does not present a risk to others. The court held that since the defendant had the benefit of a jury trial in which it was found he was insane, sufficient reason existed to confine him, and that it thus became his burden to show that the reason no longer existed.

≡ Tests Used to Determine Insanity

If a state permits a defense to criminal charges based on insanity, it remains to be determined how the insanity decision is made. In *Clark v. Arizona*, 126 S. Ct. 2709 (2006), discussed in more detail in this chapter, the U.S. Supreme Court reviewed the kinds of tests traditionally used to make that determination, and listed the states using the various tests. It noted that states are free to define insanity as they think proper. The Court found that the insanity tests have historically followed one or more of four approaches: (1) cognitive incapacity; (2) moral incapacity; (3) volitional incapacity; and (4) the product-of-mental-illness.

Numbers (1) and (2) combined are the *M'Naghten* rule, number (3) is commonly called the "substantial capacity" rule, and number (4) is usually referred to as the "product" rule. The *Clark* Court stated that 17 states and the federal government have adopted the *M'Naghten* rule. One state has adopted only the "cognitive incapacity" approach, and 10 have adopted only the "moral incapacity" approach. Fourteen states have adopted the "volitional incapacity" approach, most using the Model Penal Code's "substantial capacity" as a model. Two states combine the *M'Naghten* rule with "substantial capacity." Only 1 state, New Hampshire, has adopted the "product-of-mental-illness" approach. The following materials in this section discuss those rules in more detail. The verdict of "guilty but mentally ill" is also discussed in this section, while the "diminished capacity" test appears in the next section.

The *M'Naghten* Case and the "Right and Wrong" Test

"right and wrong" test
An insanity test that claims that defendants are not legally responsible for their acts if, due to a defect of the mind, at the time of the crime they were unable to understand the difference between right and wrong.

It was not until the 1800s that English and American courts considered the question of whether insanity, mental disease, and mental defect should be factors in determining the criminal responsibility of people charged with crimes. The **"right and wrong" test**, which became the most widely used test to determine the question of legal insanity in the United States, was developed in 1843 in the aftermath of the famous English murder case of *Rex v. M'Naghten*, House of Lords, 1843.[8]

Daniel M'Naghten lived in London in the 1840s and believed that the British Home Secretary, Sir Robert Peel, was the head of a conspiracy to kill him. (Peel was the widely recognized founder of the British police, who thus received the nickname "bobbies.") In 1843, M'Naghten shot and killed Edward Drummond, private secretary to Peel, because he mistook Drummond for Peel. At his trial, the defense argued that M'Naghten was insane at the time of the shooting and that he should not be held responsible because his mental delusions had caused him to act as he did. The British jury agreed, and M'Naghten was found not guilty because of insanity.

The "right and wrong" test that emerged from the *M'Naghten* case has become the prevailing standard and test for insanity in U.S. courts. Under the *M'Naghten* rule, defendants are not legally responsible for their acts if at the time they were "laboring under such a defect of reason, from disease of the mind, as not to know the nature and quality of the act he was doing, or, if he did know it, that he did not know that what he was doing was wrong." 8 Eng. Rep. at 722. Under this rule, insanity is present either when a person, because of mental illness, has "cognitive incapacity," that is, does not know what actions he is taking, or "moral incapacity," that is, he does not know the actions taken were wrong.

M'Naghten rule The insanity defense rule requiring proof that because of mental disease or defect defendants did not know the scope or character of their actions.

The ***M'Naghten* rule** established the burden of proof as follows:

> Every man is presumed to be sane and to possess a sufficient degree of reason to be responsible for his crimes, until the contrary be proved to (the jury's) satisfaction; and that to establish a defense on the ground of insanity, it must be clearly proved.

The "Product-of-Mental-Illness Rule" and "Irresistible Impulse"

After courts had used the *M'Naghten* rule to determine insanity, many were critical of the rule. According to its critics, the principal fault of the *M'Naghten* rule was its narrowness and its restricted application to only a small percentage of the people who are mentally ill. The rule does not, critics said, recognize that mental illness is not limited to an inability to *know* that one is doing wrong but includes an inability to control one's acts even if known to be wrong. In response to this criticism, a few states adopted a form of "volitional incapacity" called the "irresistible impulse" and added it to the *M'Naghten* rule.[9] Under this test, defendants must prove that even if they knew what they were doing was wrong, mental illness prevented them from controlling their conduct.[10]

The irresistible impulse rule has not been widely adopted, mainly because courts and legislators have concluded that it lacks precision on the question of what an impulse is and when it is irresistible.

The "product-of-mental-illness" approach has had very limited adoption. In 1954, a form of this approach called the *Durham* product test was adopted by the U.S. Court of Appeals for the District of Columbia in the case of *Durham v. United States*.[11] The court stated that "an accused is not criminally responsible if his unlawful act was the product of mental disease or defect." The *Durham* case established a test for insanity based on a *substantial* lack of mental capacity rather than a complete lack of capacity. It has been criticized on the grounds that it is too broad and gives psychiatrists, rather than the jury, too much discretion in determining the legal issue of insanity. "Criminal responsibility is a legal not a medical question."[12]

In 1984 Congress passed the Insanity Defense Reform Act, 18 U.S.C. § 17. This act establishes a rule for federal criminal prosecutions that is virtually identical to the *M'Naghten* rule. The Act was designed to abolish both the "irresistible impulse" rule and the *Durham* test. Section 17 states: "It is an affirmative defense to a prosecution under any Federal statute that, at the time of the commission of the offense, the defendant, as a result of severe mental illness or defect, was unable to appreciate the nature and quality or the wrongfulness of his acts. Mental disease or defect does not otherwise constitute a defense."

Congress also addressed the criticism that "criminal responsibility" is not a medical question by providing in Rule 704(b) of the Federal Rules of Evidence that a medical expert may not render an expert opinion on the ultimate question of a defendant's sanity under the statute. Most states that considered the "product-of-mental-illness" test ultimately adopted a test modeled on the "substantial capacity" test discussed next.

The Model Penal Code "Substantial Capacity" Test

About a year after the adoption of the *Durham* test by a few jurisdictions, the American Law Institute proposed still another test for determining criminal responsibility. In proposing the new test, the following comment was made:

> No problem in the drafting of a penal code presents larger intrinsic difficulty than that of determining when individuals whose conduct would otherwise be criminal ought to be exculpated (freed of guilt) on the grounds that they were suffering from mental disease or defect when they acted as they did. What is involved specifically is the drawing of a line between the use of public agencies and public force to condemn the offender by conviction.... [T]he problem is to discriminate between the cases where a punitive-correctional disposition is appropriate and those in which a medical-custodial disposition is the only kind that the law should allow.[13]

The final draft of the American Law Institute (ALI) "**substantial capacity**" **test**, found in Section 4.01 of the Model Penal Code, states:

"substantial capacity" test A test to determine criminal responsibility based on whether the defendant could (1) distinguish between right and wrong or (2) conform his or her conduct to the requirements of law.

1. A person is not responsible for criminal conduct if at the time of such conduct as a result of mental disease or defect he lacks substantial capacity either to appreciate the criminality (wrongfulness) of his conduct or to conform his conduct to the requirement of law.

2. As used in the Article, the terms *mental disease* or *defect* do not include an abnormality manifested only by repeated criminal or otherwise antisocial conduct.

The Model Penal Code test (or the ALI "substantial capacity" test) reportedly has now been adopted by about half the states.

While the *M'Naghten* rule requires a defendant to show total mental impairment, the "substantial capacity" test puts less of a burden on defendants. Under the "substantial capacity" test, even if defendants "knew" what they had done, they are permitted to attempt to show that they did not have the "substantial capacity to conform their conduct to the requirements of law."

EXAMPLE: In March 2002, using the Texas version of the *M'Naghten* rule, Andrea Yates was found sane and guilty of the murder of her five young children in Houston, Texas. After an appeal to a Texas Appellate Court, her conviction was overturned because a prosecution witness gave false testimony. Yates was retried in 2006, and on July 26th of that year she was found not guilty by reason of insanity. She was committed to a state mental institution until it was determined she was no longer a "threat to society."

Because of the publicity surrounding many recent uses of the insanity defense, some states that have used the Model Penal Code "substantial capacity" test have returned to the stricter standards of the *M'Naghten* rule. In addition, five states—Idaho, Montana, Kansas, Nevada, and Utah—have passed legislation that abolished the insanity defense

In 2001 Andrea Yates confessed to the crime of filicide (the murder of a child by a parent). Despite the testimony of doctors that she was psychotic when she drowned her five children, a jury in Houston, Texas, initially found her sane under the M'Naghten rule. In July 2006, she was retried and found not guilty by reason of insanity.

and now permit the admission of evidence of mental disease only to negate the mental state required for conviction of the crime charged.

In 1994, the Montana Supreme Court held that the abolishment of the insanity defense did not violate the Constitution (*Montana v. Cowan*).[14] The U.S. Supreme Court denied certiorari.[15] The Supreme Courts of Idaho, Kansas, and Utah[16] all reached the same result. However, in 2001 the Nevada Supreme Court reached the opposite conclusion and held the Nevada statute abolishing the insanity defense unconstitutional.[17] Nev. Rev. Stat. § 194.010 (2004) now follows the *M'Naghten* rule.

With or without an insanity defense, the state must prove mental fault *(mens rea)* in crimes that have as an element of the crime a specific intent, for example, first-degree murder. If mental illness or mental defect prevents a defendant from forming the required *mens rea,* a conviction for that crime could not be obtained, and the defendant could be found not guilty. Even the states identified above that have abolished insanity as a general defense each have statutes permitting evidence of insanity to negate a specific mental intent required for conviction of a crime. See, e.g., 18-207 Idaho Code, and K.S.A. § 22-3220.

The Plea and Verdict of Guilty but Mentally Ill[18]

The incidence of people who are found not guilty because of insanity who then go on to commit other violent crimes after release from mental hospitals has caused 13 states to adopt the plea and verdict of **guilty but mentally ill.**[19] Often called "GBMI" laws, the Michigan legislature was the first to do so in 1975 when it enacted Mich. Comb. Laws § 768.36, after several defendants committed additional murders after being found not guilty because of insanity on earlier murders.

guilty but mentally ill A defendant may be found guilty but mentally ill if all the following are found beyond a reasonable doubt: (1) defendant is guilty of offense; (2) defendant was mentally ill at time offense was committed; (3) defendant was not legally insane at time offense was committed.

DEFENDANTS WHO WERE FOUND NOT GUILTY BECAUSE OF INSANITY

John Hinckley

In 1981 John Hinckley attempted to kill President Reagan. In a wild shooting spree in downtown Washington, Hinckley wounded the president and several other people. Hinckley entered a not guilty plea and a not guilty because of insanity plea.

At that time, the federal courts had broken away from the majority rule in the United States, and the government had the burden of showing that people such as Hinckley were sane and normal. Because of Hinckley's wild, bizarre behavior, the government was not able to carry the burden of showing that Hinckley was sane and normal, and Hinckley was found not guilty because of insanity. Within a short time, Congress passed a law changing the procedure, and now defendants pleading insanity have the burden of coming forward with evidence proving mental disease or defectiveness.[a]

Lorena Bobbitt

Lorena Bobbitt was charged with malicious wounding in 1993. She testified to repeated rapes, beatings, and sodomizing by her husband. On the night of the crime, she testified that her husband came home drunk, tore off her clothes, and forced himself on her. She said that her mind went blank and that only later did she realize that she had sexually mutilated her husband by cutting off his penis, which she threw in a field.

A Virginia jury found Mrs. Bobbitt not guilty under Virginia's insanity test, which holds that a defendant may be held blameless for an act he or she knows is wrong if "his [or her] mind has become so impaired by disease that he [or she] totally is deprived of mental power to control or restrain his [or her] act." After a four-week stay, Mrs. Bobbitt was released from a Virginia mental hospital on the condition that she get therapy. Her husband, John, had been acquitted earlier of marital sexual abuse.

[a]John Hinckley continues to be held in a Washington, D.C., hospital. He has requested permission to spend a limited number of three- and four-day visits at his parents' home outside Washington, D.C., and those requests have been granted by a federal judge. However, in June 2007 a federal judge denied Hinckley's request for a month-long visit at his parents' home.

The public outcry over the insanity defense can be illustrated by events arising in an insanity defense case in Illinois. In that case, Thomas Vanda killed a girl when he was 18 years old. While undergoing psychiatric treatment in Chicago, he was released and killed another girl. He was found not guilty because of insanity. When doctors concluded that his psychosis had disappeared, he was again released over objections from the trial judge and his own defense attorney. In 1978, when he was 25 years old, Thomas Vanda was again charged with murder. The third victim was a 25-year-old woman.

Illinois enacted a guilty but mentally ill statute in 1981. Former Illinois Governor James R. Thompson described the new statutory procedure as follows:

> Under this procedure, when an insanity defense is raised, the court, if the evidence permits, may instruct the jury on the alternative verdict of guilty but mentally ill.
>
> When a person is not legally insane, he or she may be found guilty but mentally ill if, at the time of the offense, he or she suffered from a disorder of thought or mood that does not represent a condition amounting to insanity in the legal sense. When a guilty but mentally ill verdict is returned, the court may impose any sentence that could have been ordered for a conviction on the crime charged. However, the prison authorities must provide necessary psychiatric or psychological treatment to restore the offender to full capacity in an appropriate treatment setting. If the mental illness is cured, the offender must be returned to prison to serve out his or her sentence.

CASE CLOSE-UP

Clark v. Arizona
Supreme Court of the United States
126 S. Ct. 2709 (2006)

As stated earlier in this chapter, the Supreme Court denied review in the cases from state courts that ruled on the constitutionality of abolishment of the insanity defense. In *Clark* the Court considered the claims by a defendant convicted of murder under Arizona law that the Arizona insanity defense statute violated the Due Process Clause. Prior to 1993 Arizona had adopted both alternatives of the *M'Naghten* rule: a defendant could establish the insanity defense if a mental defect left the person unable to know what he or she was doing, the so-called cognitive capacity part; or, the defendant could establish the defense if the person did not know what he or she was doing was wrong, the so-called moral capacity part of the rule. In 1993 the Arizona legislature changed the law so that only the second part of the *M'Naghten* rule could be used to establish the insanity defense.

The Arizona Appellate Courts rejected the defendant's claim that narrowing the grounds for establishing the insanity defense violated due process. The Supreme Court affirmed, holding that states have the traditional power to define crimes and defenses, and that the *M'Naghten* rule had not been elevated "to the level of fundamental principle."[a] Moreover, the Court concluded, as a practical matter, evidence of a defendant's inability to know the nature of his or her actions would be relevant and admissible on the issue, "Did the defendant know what he or she was doing was wrong?" If the evidence showed a mental defect prevented a defendant from knowing what he or she was doing, the Court concluded, that same evidence should establish the insanity defense under the Arizona statute: "In practical terms, if a defendant did not know what he was doing when he acted, he could not have known that he was performing the wrongful act charged as crime."[b] As a result, the Court concluded, the Arizona insanity statute did not deprive Clark of due process.

The Court also held that Arizona's court-made rule—that expert evidence of a defendant's mental disease or defect was not admissible on the question of *mens rea*—did not violate due process. Under the Arizona rule, so-called observational evidence was admissible on the question of a defendant's ability to have the necessary *mens rea* required for a crime. Evidence of the defendant's actions, or what he or she said or did, are examples of admissible evidence on the defendant's mental state. However, expert psychological testimony about the effect of a defendant's mental disease on his or her capacity to form the required *mens rea* was excluded. The Court addressed many claims a defendant might have for the admissibility of relevant evidence, but it ultimately held that Arizona's interest in preserving the integrity of the form of the insanity defense it had chosen justified excluding expert testimony evidence, which would otherwise be admissible on the insanity defense, when the question was the defendant's ability to form the required *mens rea*.

Finally, the Court stated it was not passing on the constitutionality of state statutes that abolished the insanity defense altogether: "We have never held that the Constitution mandates an insanity defense, nor have we held that the Constitution does not so require. This case does not call upon us to decide the matter."[c]

[a]126 S. Ct. at 2719.
[b]126 S. Ct. at 2722.
[c]126 S. Ct. at 2722, fn. 20.

Insanity determinations under existing law deal in absolutes; a defendant must be found totally sane or totally insane. This fails to reflect reality. It does not allow the jury to consider the degree of an individual's mental impairment, the quality of the impairment, or the context in which the impairment is operative. A mental impairment does not necessarily eradicate the state of mind required to make a person guilty of a crime, and the jury should be permitted to consider the gradations of a defendant's mental state.

The guilty but mentally ill verdict does not abolish the insanity defense. It simply recognizes that there are gradations in the degree of mental impairment; it provides accountability, promotes treatment, and eliminates the need to manipulate the system.

Most important, it is designed to protect the public from violence inflicted by people with mental ailments who previously slipped through the cracks in the criminal justice system.[20]

In most states, the statute authorizing a GBMI verdict allocates the burden of proof as follows: First, the prosecution must prove beyond a reasonable doubt that the defendant committed the crime charged. Second, the jury must determine if the defendant was legally insane. Typically, the defendant must prove insanity by a preponderance of the evidence standard, though a few states place the burden or proving sanity on the prosecution. If the jury finds the defendant was not legally insane, it must determine if the defendant was mentally ill, that is, whether the defendant suffered from some mental impairment that affected his ability to control or understand his behavior, but did not amount to insanity. In most jurisdictions, the prosecution must prove mental illness beyond a reasonable doubt. See, e.g., Ga. Code Ann. § 17-7-131. A few jurisdictions demand only proof by a preponderance of the evidence. See, e.g., *Commonwealth v. Rabold*, 951 A2d 329 (Pa. 2008).

Defendants' convicted with GBMI verdicts have frequently attacked the GBMI statute as unconstitutional under the Due Process Clause, contending the presence of the GBMI option permits the prosecution to effectively convict a defendant without proving guilt beyond a reasonable doubt. To date, no court has declared a GBMI statute unconstitutional. See 2 *Wharton's Criminal Law* § 105 (15th Ed. 2007).

Opponents of the guilty but mentally ill verdict argue that it is nothing but a nice name for "guilty and going to prison." The National Alliance for the Mentally Ill opposes such legislation "because it would stigmatize insane offenders with a criminal conviction, compounding the handicaps already faced by those persons in obtaining employment and social acceptance."[21]

Mental Conditions That Do Not Satisfy the Insanity Defense

Many mental conditions do not rise to the level of "insanity" and thus do not provide a defense to criminal conduct. For example, the battered woman syndrome, discussed in Chapter 6, has rarely been successfully raised as a mental disease. Nor have claims like television intoxication, premenstrual syndrome, or so-called cultural defenses. The voluntary use of drugs or alcohol does not qualify as a mental disease, even if the drugs or alcohol make defendants unable to appreciate the nature or quality of their acts.

Defendants sometimes use the compulsive gambling defense against criminal charges such as theft, bank robbery, and embezzlement. They argue they would not have committed such crimes but were compelled to do so because of their gambling urges.[22] For example, in the case of *United States v. Lynch,* the defendant stole $7.5 million and unsuccessfully used compulsive gambling in an attempt to be found not guilty on his insanity plea.[23]

Prosecutors argue that accepting compulsive gambling as an insanity defense could set a dangerous precedent. In any state that would allow such a defense, thieves could claim kleptomania as a defense, arsonists could claim pyromania, perjurers could claim pathologic lying, drunk drivers could claim alcoholism, and prostitutes could claim nymphomania.

In all the reported cases, defendants using compulsive gambling as a defense have failed to be found not guilty because of insanity. There is no showing of acceptance in the mental health field that a compulsive gambler is unable to resist the impulse to steal or to commit other crimes.

≡ The Defense of Diminished Capacity

diminished capacity defense A defense for criminal responsibility based on the fact that because of mental or emotional conditions, the defendant did not possess the required *mens rea* for conviction of crime charged.

In some states a defendant is permitted to assert what is usually called the **diminished capacity defense**. It applies when a defendant has introduced evidence of mental incapacity which does not satisfy the requirement for a finding of insanity under the relevant statute. A court may consider the evidence on the issue of the defendant's requisite *mens rea* for crimes that require a specific intent. Under this defense, it is possible that a defendant was not insane at the time he committed the crime charged, but that his mental condition made it impossible to entertain some specific intent required for conviction. This basis for this defense and its consequences were discussed in the case of *United States v. Fishman* as follows:

> The defense of "diminished capacity" is simply a label that identifies evidence introduced by a defendant to support a claim that he did not commit the crime charged because he did not possess the requisite *mens rea*. A diminished capacity defense varies from a legal insanity defense in several important respects. Whereas following a successful legal insanity defense the court retains control of the defendant and may order involuntary commitment, a successful diminished capacity defense results in a complete acquittal.[24]

The diminished capacity defense under the Federal Insanity Defense Reform Act, 18 U.S.C. § 17, is generally permitted in federal prosecutions. Section 17(a) of the Act adopts a test for insanity which is essentially the *M'Naghten* rule, and identifies it as an affirmative defense, which under § 17(b) the defendant must prove by clear and convincing evidence. Section 17(a) also states that except as set forth for the insanity defense, "Mental disease or defect does not otherwise constitute a defense." Courts applying this sentence to the diminished capacity defense generally conclude that Congress intended only to exclude evidence of mental incapacity as proof of any other test for insanity. Congress did not intend to exclude evidence of mental incapacity less than legal insanity on other issues, such as the absence of the required *mens rea* in a crime. See, e.g., *United States v. Bennett*, 161 F.3d 171 (3d Cir. 1998), *cert. denied* 528 U.S. 819 (1999).

While voluntary intoxication or drug abuse can sometimes serve as a partial diminished capacity defense by eliminating the defendant's ability to form a required specific intent (see Chapter 7), most states reject such voluntary acts as a basis for the insanity defense. For example, in the 2006 case *State v. Sexton*, 904 A.2d 1092, the Vermont Supreme Court held that a defendant who suffered a psychotic episode caused by a two-month LSD binge could not use that mental state as proof of the insanity defense. The court noted that some states permit the insanity defense where voluntary intoxication or drug use has created a "settled" psychotic mental state, that is, where prolonged use of drugs or alcohol has permanently altered the defendant's mental condition. The court held that a two-month period of drug use did not amount to a "settled" psychotic state. The court did, however, permit evidence of the defendant's mental state on the issue of his diminished capacity to form the specific intent required under the Vermont murder statute.

TESTS OR PROCEDURES USED TO DETERMINE CRIMINAL RESPONSIBILITY[a]

Test or Procedure	Year When First Used	Type of Test	Current Extent of Use
M'Naghten "right and wrong" test	1843	Based on ability of defendant to know the difference between right and wrong.	Used by practically all U.S. courts until the 1970s. Now used, with variations, by about half of the states.
Model Penal Code "substantial capacity" test	1955	Did defendant have the "substantial capacity" to (1) distinguish between right and wrong or (2) conform his or her conduct to the requirements of law?	Used by many states, but California and the federal government returned to the *M'Naghten* rule after using this test. See *U.S. v. Carmel*, 801 F.2d 997 (1986); and *People v. Skinner*, 39 Cal.3d 765, 217 Cal. Rptr. 685, 704 P.2d 752, 38 CrL 2002 (1985).
Guilty but mentally ill alternative verdict and plea	1975	Defendant may be found guilty but mentally ill if all the following are found beyond a reasonable doubt: (1) defendant is guilty of offense; (2) defendant was mentally ill at time offense was committed; (3) defendant was not legally insane at time offense was committed.	Used in thirteen states with either the *M'Naghten* rule or the "substantial capacity" test.
Diminished capacity defense	1957	Defense seeks to introduce evidence showing that because of mental or emotional conditions, the defendant did not possess the required *mens rea* for conviction of crime charged.	A finding that the state failed to prove the mens rea for the crime charged could result in a finding of not guilty.

[a]Civil commitments and plea bargains are also used when it is apparent that a defendant has serious mental problems. For example, a civil commitment was agreed on when a minister set fire to his own church. Members of the church were relieved that the matter was handled in this manner instead of through a contested public trial for arson.

The following cases illustrate circumstances under which courts have been asked to submit the issue of diminished capacity to a jury:

- In a 1986 case, the court held that the following statement did not justify a jury instruction on diminished capacity: "Defendant had been drinking and had a lot of cocaine ... [and] was talkative and really hyper." *People v. Rodriguez* (726 P.2d 113)
- Some organic brain dysfunction that resulted in a lowered intellectual function and capacity and some antisocial behavior were held insufficient to instruct the jury on diminished capacity. *State v. Friberg*, 252 Kan. 141, 843 P.2d 218 (1992)
- Emotions such as jealousy, fear, anger, and hatred are not mental disorders under the diminished capacity defense. *State v. Davis*, 64 Wash. App. 511, 827 P.2d 298 (1992)
- The defendant in a 1991 case confessed that he killed the young woman with whom he lived, took her child, stole a car and money from the woman's parents, and fled to Florida. The defendant entered an insanity plea to charges of murder, kidnapping, and burglary. At his trial, he offered evidence that he suffered from schizophrenic tendencies, was hyperactive and disruptive, and had been abused as a child.

SEXUAL VIOLENT PREDATOR LAWS AND INVOLUNTARY CIVIL COMMITMENT LAWS

Type of Law	Examples
Sexual violent predator laws used to detain persons likely to be sexually violent	Sexual violent predators are persons who have been convicted of a sexual violent crime. Once released from confinement, such persons often revert to their previous violent actions. In May 2010 John Gardner, a convicted sexual offender released on parole in California, was sentenced to life imprisonment for the rapes and murders of Chelsea King, 17, and Amber DuBois, 14. In response to cases like this, most states have adopted Sexual Violent Predator Laws (SVP Laws) that permit states to bring civil commitment proceedings against the offender based on a showing the person is a sexual violent offender, and poses a substantial risk of future violent sexual actions. In *Crane v. Kansas*, 534 U.S. 407 (2002), the U.S. Supreme Court held that in civil commitment proceedings under SVP statutes the state must prove not only that the person is a sexual violent offender who is a danger to others, but also that the offender lacks significant control over his actions. In *United States v. Comstock*, 2010 WL 1946729 (May 2010) the U.S. Supreme Court held that Congress possessed the power to pass a law permitting federal officials to bring civil commitment proceedings to keep dangerous sex offenders confined after their prison sentences have been served.
	The U.S. Supreme Court has repeatedly affirmed state sexual violent predator laws that permit a state to hold for an indefinite period of time anyone "who has been convicted or charged with a sexual violent offense and who suffers from a mental abnormality or personality disorder which makes the person likely to engage in predatory acts of sexual violence." *Kansas v. Hendricks,* 117 S. Ct. 2072 (1997)
	If such laws are civil and not criminal, and not punitive in nature, they do not violate due process, ex post facto, or double jeopardy. As treatment is not a constitutional requirement for civil commitment, such laws do not have to provide for treatment. See also *Allen v. Illinois,* 106 S. Ct. 2988, (1986).
Emergency mental detention laws and civil commitment to mental hospital laws	States have emergency mental detention laws under which persons who appear dangerous to themselves or others or are unable to care for themselves may be detained for mental observation for a short period of time, as provided by the statutes of that state. For example, a person who has attempted to commit suicide could be detained for medical observation for a time as provided by the statute of that state.
	Involuntary civil commitment laws establish the procedure by which a person may be committed to a mental institution. In the case of *State v. Johnson*, 843 P.2d 985, 1992, a 21-year-old pregnant homeless woman with a history of drug and alcohol abuse was found on a cold day, naked, in front of a bus station. The involuntary commitment order by the trial court was affirmed, holding that the woman was unable to meet her basic needs for food and shelter due to her mental disorder, despite findings by two examiners that the woman was not mentally ill.

- The Supreme Court of New Jersey held that in New Jersey the defendant was entitled to have this evidence presented to a jury to be considered either with respect to the insanity defense or as part of the defendant's defense of diminished capacity. *State v. Breakiron* (532 A.2d 199)

≡ The Requirement of Competency to Stand Trial

A defendant must be competent (mentally fit) before the government can force him or her to go to trial on criminal charges. The U.S. Supreme Court has stated: A person whose mental condition is such that he lacks the capacity to understand the nature and object of the proceedings against him, to consult with counsel, and to assist in preparing his defense may not be subjected to a trial.[25]

competency to stand trial Defendants must have the ability to co-operate with their attorneys and the ability to understand the charges and proceedings against them.

The test for **competency to stand trial** originated in the common law and now has been codified in state and federal statutes. For example, 18 U.S.C. § 4241 provides procedures for determining competency for persons charged with federal crimes. When either the defendant or the prosecution request, the court may order the defendant to submit to examination to determine competence. If the court finds by a preponderance of the evidence that the defendant lacks competence to stand trial, the defendant can be hospitalized for up to 4 months to try restore competence. If that does not happen, the defendant may be hospitalized for a longer period under 18 U.S.C. § 4246(d). Under that section, the court must find by clear and convincing evidence that the defendant has a mental defect that creates a substantial risk that the defendant might harm another person. If so, the defendant may be confined until he no longer presents such a risk.

U.S. Supreme Court has repeatedly held that it is a violation of due process to try to convict a mentally incompetent person. Because most states place the burden on the party challenging the presumption of competency, the standard of proof on defendants to prove incompetency is that of the "preponderance of the evidence."[26]

A translator or an attorney who can speak the language of a defendant could solve the problem of a defendant who does not understand English. People skilled in sign language could communicate for a deaf person. But what about a defendant with the mental ability of a 5-year-old child or a defendant who is spaced out and in a semi-stupor because of excessive use of drugs or alcohol? If they do not understand the charges and

---

A DEFENDANT MAY BE FOUND MENTALLY COMPETENT TO STAND TRIAL BUT INCOMPETENT TO ACT AS HIS OR HER OWN LAWYER

In the 1975 case of *Faretta v. California*, 422 U.S. 806, the U.S. Supreme Court held that a criminal defendant has a constitutional right to act as his or her own attorney. Denial of that right is reversible error unless it is shown (1) the request was untimely, (2) the defendant abused the right of self-representation, (3) the request was made solely for the purpose of delay, (4) the case is so complex that it requires the assistance of a lawyer, or (5) the defendant is unable to voluntarily and intelligently waive his or her right to an attorney.

This issue was before the Supreme Court again in 2008 in the case of *Indiana v. Edwards*, 171 L. Ed. 345. Edwards was charged with attempted murder, two additional felonies, and a misdemeanor. He was first found to be incompetent to stand trial, but after being committed to a state hospital he was found to be competent. However, he requested the right to represent himself at his trial.

The trial court found that while Edwards was competent enough to stand trial, he was not competent to act as his own attorney in a criminal case that could become a very complicated legal proceeding.

Edwards went to trial with an appointed lawyer representing him and was convicted of all charges. Edwards did not claim his attorney was ineffective or inadequate, but rather that under *Faretta* he had the right to represent himself at his trial. The Indiana Supreme Court ordered a new trial for Edwards, and the state of Indiana appealed. The U.S. Supreme Court sustained the trial court's ruling that Edwards was incompetent to act as his own attorney but competent to stand trial. The criminal convictions were affirmed.

proceedings against them and cannot cooperate with the defense lawyers, they would be determined to be incompetent at that time.

A person could be incompetent (and unfit) to stand trial for a short time (a few weeks or months), or a defendant could be permanently incompetent, and the state could never force the person to go to trial on criminal charges. When a court makes a finding that a defendant lacks competency (is incompetent), the criminal proceedings must then be suspended. The defendant, in accordance with the statutes of that state, is placed in an institution.

If, after a few weeks or months, the defendant is found to be competent and fit to go to trial, criminal proceedings may again continue. But if a defendant is never going to become competent, can the state indefinitely hold this person in a mental institution?

In the 1972 case of *Jackson v. Indiana*, the U.S. Supreme Court held that such defendants could not be held for longer than a "reasonable period of time" to determine whether they will regain their competence and capacity to stand trial.[27] Some courts have held that this reasonable period of time is a period no longer than the maximum sentence for the crime charged or, at the longest, 18 months. After this period of time, the state may either

- Try the defendant, if he or she is found competent and capable of standing trial.
- Dismiss the charges.
- Commence civil proceedings against the person for the purpose of committing him or her to a mental institution if he or she remains incompetent and cannot be tried criminally.[28]

MAY THE GOVERNMENT FORCE A DEFENDANT'S COMPETENCY?

In federal prosecutions, a defendant who has been found to be incompetent to stand trial because of his or her mental condition can be transferred to a medical facility for examination and treatment, for a period not to exceed four months.[a] If the defendant has a condition that is treatable by medications, may the government force the defendant to take those medications in order to render the person competent to stand trial?

In *Sell v. United States*, 539 U.S. 166 (2003), the U.S. Supreme Court held that although a defendant has a constitutional right to be free of involuntary medical treatment, medications can be forced on a defendant to render him or her competent if (1) the treatment is medically appropriate, (2) the medications will not have side effects that undermine the fairness of the trial, and (3) the medications are necessary to advance an important government interest.

Two recent cases illustrate how the Sell rule is applied in federal courts. In *U.S. v. Algere*, 396 F. Supp. 2d 734 (E.D. La. 2005), the court ordered a defendant charged with being a felon in possession of a firearm to be involuntarily medicated to make him competent to stand trial. The court concluded that the medicine for treating the defendant's condition, schizophrenia, was appropriate and would work, that it had no unmanageable side effects, and that prosecuting the defendant on the weapons charge was an important government interest. The defendant had a history of violence and had previously been convicted of manslaughter.

In *U.S. v. Rodman*, 446 F. Supp. 2d 487 (D. S.C. 2006), the court refused to order the involuntary medication of a defendant charged with threatening an attempt on the life of the president of the United States. The court noted that while prosecuting an attempt on the president is a serious government interest, here the defendant had been confined for almost as long as he could have been sentenced for the crime charged. It thus concluded that the best approach would be to take steps to consider the possibility of a civil commitment for the defendant.

[a]18 U.S.C. Section 4241 (d).

Can Amnesia Be the Grounds for a Finding of Incompetency?

Amnesia is the total or partial loss of memory regarding past experiences. Brain injury, disease, mental disorder, shock, and excessive use of alcohol or drugs are some of the many factors that can cause amnesia.[29] Although people with amnesia ordinarily have no difficulty comprehending the nature of the criminal proceedings against them, they would not necessarily remember what occurred at the time of the alleged crime.

In the case of *Ex parte Thompson*, the defendant could understand the crime charged and the factual proceedings against her and could assist counsel in her defense.[30] The court held that she was not rendered incompetent to stand trial by her alleged amnesia with respect to the commission of the crime.

Courts generally have held that partial amnesia does not render a defendant incompetent to stand trial, nor does it deny a defendant a fair trial. In the case of *Morrow v. State*, the defendant was the driver of one of the vehicles in a bad two-car accident.[31] The defendant's passenger was killed. The court held the defendant to be competent to stand trial, pointing out that the defendant was aware of the trial events and was able to consult with and assist his lawyer. However, the defendant claimed not to remember the automobile accident because of head injuries. The court wrote:

> The practical effects of expanding the definition of incompetency to include amnesia must be considered. Several courts have indicated that they were unwilling to hold that limited amnesia was an adequate ground for a determination of incompetency because the effect of such a holding would be to free, without trial, persons against whom prima facie criminal cases had been established. (See *State v. Johnson*, 536 P.2d 1035, 1036 (Ariz. 1975); *Commonwealth v. Price*, 218 A.2d 758, 763 (Pa. 1966).) It has been noted that, if amnesia were held to render an accused incompetent and if the amnesia were permanent, the accused would never be competent and could never be tried; at the same time, because limited amnesia cannot be considered a mental defect or disease, an amnesiac accused could not be hospitalized or institutionalized. (See *Commonwealth v. Price*, 218 A.2d at 763.) Thus permanent amnesia as to the circumstances of the crime charged would be a permanent bar to the imposition of criminal responsibility. This is especially significant in light of "the extreme difficulty—often impossibility—of distinguishing real from feigned amnesia" (71 *Yale L.J.* at 123); "an attempt to verify all but the most patently phony claims of amnesia is at best a difficult and time-consuming task; at worst it is a hopeless one" (at 124).[32]

Even where the evidence of amnesia is convincing, courts may nonetheless find a defendant competent to stand trial. In *State v. Foster*, 2006 WL 3491883 (Conn. Sup. 2006), a defendant was shot in the head during a fight in which his victim died. In his subsequent prosecution for murder, the court found that the defendant did in fact have amnesia covering the period when the crime occurred. However, because the court found the defendant was otherwise able to remember events without difficulty, and thus able to participate in his defense, the court concluded he was competent to stand trial.

Faking Insanity or Incompetency

Every large U.S. city has had criminal cases in which the defendant has successfully been faking insanity or incompetency. The court in the case of *United States v. Carter* stated that the defendant had "bamboozled the U.S. Attorney."[33] Doctors later determined that the defendant was "without mental disorder." In the case of *Thompson v. Crawford*, the defendant fooled psychiatrists and was later discovered.[34] The Florida court vacated the judgment of acquittal and permitted the state of Florida to proceed again with criminal charges.

In the 1991 case of *United States v. Prince,* 938 F.2d 1092 (10th Cir.), the defendant was convicted of bank robbery and unlawful use of a firearm during the robbery and later admitted that he "acted out" the following conduct in the courtroom:

> The defendant exposed himself and began to urinate in the courtroom. A few minutes later, the defendant was brought back into the courtroom and while the trial judge was sternly warning him as to his conduct, the defendant began moaning loudly. This was followed by moans with screams. Five marshals were needed to take the struggling defendant from the courtroom.

> Arguments were made that this conduct showed that the defendant was incompetent to stand trial, but the Federal Court of Appeals affirmed the defendant's conviction, holding that the trial court correctly continued with the trial.

≡ The Criminal Liability of Corporations

A corporation is a legal entity created under the laws of a state or the federal government. Although a corporation is not a living person and thus would seem to lack the "capacity" to commit a crime, it acts through human beings. Thus, for a crime committed by a person to be attributable to the corporation, the person must be in control of the corporation's affairs or in the employment of the corporation.

criminal liability of corporations The rules for making corporations liable for actions taken by officers, directors, or employees. Corporations can be vicariously criminally liable for actions of their agents if the offense is minor, a duty is specifically assigned to a corporation, a statute explicitly creates vicarious criminal liability, or the person committing the crime is acting in the interest of the corporation and is a high managerial agent.

Regarding the **criminal liability of corporations**, Sir William Blackstone wrote in his eighteenth-century *Commentaries* that "a corporation cannot commit treason or felony or other crime in its corporate capacity, though its members may in their distinct individual capacities."[35] Blackstone's statement reflected the early common law thinking that because a corporation had no mind of its own, it could not formulate a criminal intent, and because it had no body, it could not be imprisoned or executed. The early common law view was understandable because relatively few corporations existed in those days, and other ways were available to handle crimes that were committed in the names of corporations. The corporate officers (or employees) who committed the act (or acts) could be criminally charged. The corporation was civilly liable for the acts of its officers and employees, and therefore civil suits for damages could be brought. In addition, a corporation that had committed *ultra vires* acts (acts that are beyond the scope of the corporate charter or that violate the laws of the state) could have its corporate charter revoked by the state.

This common law view changed as corporations became more numerous and as it became apparent that corporations should be made criminally responsible for some types of criminal acts. Today, corporations may be charged with many but not all crimes. The Model Penal Code, Section 2.07(1)(a)-(c), provides that corporations can have criminal liability for (1) specific duties assigned to a corporation, (2) violations of minor offenses that carry only a fine, and (3) an offense authorized or performed by a "high managerial agent."

Many states have reached similar conclusions. As a example, in *People v. Hock Shop,* 681 N.W.2d 669 (Mich. App. 2004), a corporation was charged with the crime of knowingly selling a firearm to a convicted felon. An employee of the corporation sold a firearm to a person known by the employee to be a convicted felon. The Michigan Court of Appeals held that though the corporation was a "person" for purposes of the criminal law, it could not have vicarious criminal liability for the acts of an employee who was not a high management agent unless the statute specifically imposed such liability, or the board of directors authorized or permitted the employee's acts. The state statute did not provide for criminal liability for violation of the firearm law, and the corporation's board of directors was not aware of the sale of the firearm to the felon, so the court affirmed a dismissal of the criminal charges.

Even if a state permits criminal liability for corporations based on authorized acts of employees, courts have held that the prosecution must prove an individual employee could be liable for the offense with which the corporation is charged. In *Com. v. Life Centers of America*, 926 N.E.2d 206 (Mass. 2010) a nursing home corporation was charged with involuntary manslaughter in the death of a nursing home resident. The elderly resident wheeled her wheelchair through the home's entrance doors, and fell down 8 steps to her death. The victim had a history of tying to exit the home, and physicians had placed orders on her chart that she must wear a "WanderGuard" device that automatically locks exit and entrance doors when approached by the wearer. Due to combination of factors, including staff changes and unclear directives about auditing residents' charts, the duty nurses on the night in question did not know the resident was supposed to be wearing the safety device. As a result, the resident was able to exit the home, with the resulting fatal fall.

The prosecution did not charge any individual employee of the nursing home with involuntary manslaughter, conceding that no one person had been anything more than negligent in performing his or her duties. However, the prosecution charged the corporate owner of the nursing home on the theory of "collective knowledge" of all the employees. Under that theory, the liability of a corporation can be based on aggregating the knowledge and actions of multiple employees.

The Massachusetts Supreme Judicial Court held the corporation could not be liable under the collective knowledge theory. The Court reasoned that since involuntary manslaughter was a crime that required "wanton or reckless" conduct, unless at least one individual acted in such a fashion, the corporation could not be liable. While many of the nursing home employees were negligent in connection with the death, multiples of simple negligence to not constitute "wanton or reckless" conduct, the court concluded. If no individual employee could be convicted of involuntary manslaughter, the court held, neither could the corporation.

Under a standard such as the Model Penal Code, it would be hard to imagine how a corporation could be charged and convicted of a crime such as rape, or theft. On the other hand, corporations and individual corporate officers can be convicted of crimes such as violations of the criminal provisions of environmental laws, like the Clean Air Act or the Comprehensive Environmental Response, Compensation, and Liability Act (CERCLA). See, for example, *Hansen v. United States*, 262 F.3d 1217 (11th Cir. 2001).[36] More material on criminal liability of corporations is presented in Chapter 15.

Summary

- Children below a certain age, usually 7 or 8, cannot be convicted of a crime. Children between the minimum age and about 12–14 are presumed to lack capacity to commit a crime, but the presumption may be overcome.
- A child under the minimum age may not be convicted of a crime regardless of the evidence of his mental state. A child of 14 could be convicted if it can be shown the child had the mental ability and understanding to formulate the required criminal intent.

- The first prong of the *M'Naghten* rule requires a showing the defendant did know what he was doing (the cognitive capacity prong); the second prong requires a showing the defendant did not know what he was doing was wrong (the moral incapacity prong).
- The *M'Naghten* rule differs from the substantial capacity test primarily on the magnitude of the defendant's understanding of events that made up the crime charged. The *M'Naghten* rule applies only if the defendant did not "know" the nature of his acts and that they were wrong. The substantial

capacity test applies whenever the defendant cannot "appreciate" the nature of his acts, or that they were wrong, a lesser requirement.

- Voluntary intoxication or drug use is almost never the basis for the successful assertion of the insanity defense. However, in most states the defendant's intoxication or drug use may serve as the basis for a claim for diminished capacity.
- A verdict of not guilty by reason of insanity results in an acquittal of the defendant; a verdict of guilty but mentally ill is a conviction, but the defendant must be given treatment during his confinement.
- Mental illness, mental retardation, or many forms of physical illnesses may be the basis for finding a person incompetent to stand trial. Unless the condition is cured, the defendant cannot be tried for a crime. Defendants may be confined while competency is determined and treated.
- A person who lacks competency does not have the ability to understand what is happening at trial, and thus lacks the ability to participate in his own defense. Due process requires persons charged with crimes to be given an opportunity to consult with counsel, and assist in their own defense. Lack of competency makes that impossible, and thus trials of incompetent persons violate their due process rights.

Key Terms

trial by ordeal, p. 108
preponderance of the evidence, p. 109
infant (child), p. 109
insanity tests, p. 112

"right and wrong" test, p. 113
M'Naghten rule, p. 114
"substantial capacity" test, p. 115
guilty but mentally ill, p. 116
diminished capacity defense, p. 120

competency to stand trial, p. 123
criminal liability of corporations, p. 126

Case Analysis and Writing Exercises

1. In the 1998 trial of Theodore Kaczynski, who was charged in a California federal court of being the Unabomber, a federal judge ordered Kaczynski to undergo mental evaluation to determine whether Kaczynski was competent to stand trial for the criminal charges. In such cases, what does incompetency mean? Is incompetency the same as not guilty because of insanity? What procedure is used if a defendant is found incompetent to stand trial?

2. Section 4.01 of the Model Penal Code, the "substantial capacity" test, states in subsection 2 that mental disease or defect does not include "an abnormality manifested only by repeated criminal or antisocial conduct." This language was clearly adopted to exclude the psychopath, that is, a person who repeatedly manifests criminal conduct. Why should such a person be excluded? What must a defense lawyer prove to get a "psychopath" back within the test? See LaFave, *Criminal Law,* Section 7.5(b) (Belmont, Calif.: West/Wadsworth, 2003).

3. What exactly must the defendant prove to establish the insanity defense? Is it enough to prove a mental defect or disease? If a defendant charged with possession of a controlled substance with intent to deliver proves he suffered from syphilitic encephalopathy, and that this condition caused him to have delusions about the reason he delivered the controlled substance to an undercover police officer, should the insanity defense apply? See *State v. Atsbeha,* 16 P.3d 626 (Wash. 2001).

4. Should the insanity defense be available for defendants charged with strict liability crimes, or crimes that require no proof of any specific intent? Can the prosecution argue that because the crime has no intent requirement, it should not be relevant that the defendant could not know what he was doing was wrong? See *State v. Curry,* 543 N.E.2d 1228 (Ohio S. Ct. 1989). Should the answer be different if the defendant raises the defense of guilty but mentally ill? See *State v. Olmstead,* 800 P.2d 277 (Or. 1990).

Notes

1. Sir James Fitzjames Stephen, A History of the Criminal Law of England, vol. 1 (Macmillan & Co., 1883), p. 73.

2. An example of a state statute that codifies the common law is Mississippi Code Annotated, Section 43-21-151. This statute provides that no child under the age of 13 can be charged with a crime. Children over that age can be so charged, and apparently there is no presumption about their lack of capacity. See *Clemens v. State,* 733 So. 2d 266 (S. Ct. 1999), where a 14-year-old boy was convicted of killing three people and was given two life sentences, to run consecutively.

3. In 1994, a 10-year-old boy became the youngest child in a maximum-security juvenile prison when he and an 11-year-old were found to have thrown a 5-year-old out of the fourteenth floor of a Chicago housing project building. The 5-year-old, who died in the fall, had refused to steal candy for the older boys.

   See the 1991 case of *In re Devon T.*, 584 A.2d 1287 (Md. App. 1991), for a discussion of this law. Devon T. was almost 14 years old and a middle-school student in Baltimore when 20 plastic bags of heroin were found on his person. The Maryland courts held that the state produced sufficient evidence permitting a reasonable inference that Devon knew the difference between right and wrong and knew the wrongfulness of his acts.

4. A defense lawyer who entered an insanity plea for a client in a minor charge could find the client committed to an institution for a much longer time than if the client were found guilty of the offense charged.

   In *Lynch v. Overholser,* 369 U.S. 705, 82 S. Ct. 1063 (1962), a municipal court refused to accept a former mental patient's plea of guilty to a minor check forgery charge. Instead, the court found the defendant not guilty by reason of insanity. Because the defendant was a first offender, he would probably have not received a jail sentence. After the defendant served two years in a mental institution, the U.S. Supreme Court reversed the trial court's decision, holding that the trial court was not justified in committing the defendant to a mental institution on bare reasonable doubt concerning past sanity.

   Also note that prosecutors sometimes find that it is in the state's best interest to seek a civil commitment of a person when evidence shows that the individual is dangerous to him- or herself or others and in need of treatment.

5. The 1990 study done by Policy Research Associates of Delmar, New York, is one such study.

6. The federal Insanity Defense Reform Act of 1984 requires that a federal criminal defendant found not guilty by reason of insanity may not be released onto the streets. Justice Stevens of the U.S. Supreme Court summarized the act as follows in *Frank v. United States*, 113 S. Ct. 363 (1992):

   It (the federal Act) provides that "the Attorney General shall hospitalize the person [found not guilty by reason of insanity] in a suitable facility" until a state assumes responsibility for his care and treatment or the Attorney General finds that his release would not create a risk of harm to people or property in 18 U.S.C. § 4243(e). The question presented by the petition for certiorari is whether a defendant who has pleaded not guilty by reason of insanity is entitled to a jury instruction explaining the effect of this statute. If such an instruction is not given, there is a strong possibility that the jury will be reluctant to accept a meritorious defense because of fear that a dangerous, mentally ill person will go free.

7. 112 S. Ct. 1780 (S. Ct. 1992).

8. 10 Cl. & F. 200, 8 Eng. Rep. 718.

9. See, e.g., Georgia Code Annotated, Section 16-3-3; *Vann v. Commonwealth,* 544 S.E.2d 879 (Va. 2001).

10. The "irresistible impulse" rule became well known because of the book and film *Anatomy of a Murder.* There, a soldier escapes punishment for the death of his wife by pleading that an irresistible impulse caused him to act.

11. 94 U.S. App. D.C. 228, 214 F.2d 862 (1954).

12. *Sauer v. United States,* 241 F.2d 640, 648 (9th Cir. 1957).

13. Commentary to Section 4.01, Model Penal Code.

14. 260 Mont. 510, 861 P.2d 884 (Mont. 1993).

15. 114 S. Ct. 1371 (1994).

16. Idaho: *State v. Searcy,* 798 P.2d 914 (Idaho 1996); Kansas: *State v. Bethal,* 66 P.3d 804 (Kan. 2003), *cert. denied* 540 U.S. 1006 (2003); and Utah: *State v. Herrera,* 895 P.22d 359 (Utah 1995).

17. *Finger v. State,* 27 P.3d 66, (Nev. 2001) *cert. denied* 534 U.S. 1127 (2002).

18. An heir to the du Pont fortune, John E. du Pont, was found guilty of third-degree murder but mentally ill. World-class wrestlers were using du Pont's Pennsylvania estate for training. John du Pont shot Olympic gold medalist David Schulz three times at point-blank range without any apparent provocation. The defendant was found to be "actively psychotic" and was ordered to be treated in a mental hospital until cured, after which he will be sent to a prison for the remainder of his sentence. Du Pont was the wealthiest murder defendant in the history of the United States.

19. In 1998, the Federal Court of Appeals for the Tenth Circuit upheld the guilty but mentally ill law of New Mexico in the case of *Neely v. Newton* (1998 WL 33423). The court held that in clarifying the distinction between those not guilty by reason of insanity and those mentally ill yet criminally liable, the law serves a legitimate state interest. State court decisions upholding the constitutionality of guilty but mentally ill laws are found in *State v. Neely,* 819 P.2d 249 (New Mex. 1991).

    However, in 1997 an Illinois Appellate Court held that the Illinois guilty but mentally ill law encouraged compromised verdicts in violation of due process and that the law seduced juries into settling on a middle ground between guilty and not guilty when in fact there is no middle ground. See *People v. Robles,* 1997 WL 342483 (Ill. App. 2 Dist. 1997). In *People v. Lantz,* 712 N.E.2d 314 (Ill. 1999) the Illinois Supreme Court reversed the Appellate Court, and found the GBMI act constitutional.

20. *The Journal of Criminal Law and Criminology* 73 (1982), pp. 867–874 contains the entire text of former Governor Thompson's remarks as co-chair of the National Violent Crime Task Force. Governor Thompson stated that "the insanity defense has been described as the chronic scandal of American criminal law."

21. "The Insanity Defense: Ready for Reform?" *Wisconsin Bar Bulletin*, December 1982.

22. A 1997 study conducted by the Harvard Medical School and financed by the gambling industry concluded that 1.29 percent of adults in Canada and the United States have compulsive gambling disorders. However, the percentage of problem gamblers among people with alcohol or drug abuse problems or mental disorders was found to be 14.29 percent.

    The need for money to gamble could cause compulsive gamblers to steal from employers, family, friends, and others. Compulsive gamblers also borrow money from other people, including loan sharks. Children of compulsive gamblers are often deprived of necessities needed for their well-being and education. (See the *New York Times* article "Compulsion to Gamble Seen Growing: Study Finds Legality Spreads the Problem," December 7, 1997.)

23. 699 F.2d 839 (7th Cir. 1982).

24. 743 F. Supp. 713 (N.D.Cal. 1990).

25. See *Drope v. Missouri,* 420 U.S. at 171, 95 S. Ct. at 903–04 (1975); and *Pate v. Robinson,* 383 U.S. at 378, 86 S. Ct. at 838 (1966).

26. See the 1996 U.S. Supreme Court case of *Cooper v. Oklahoma,* 517 U.S. 348 (1996), in which the Supreme Court invalidated laws in Oklahoma, Connecticut, Rhode Island, and Pennsylvania and required these states to use the burden on defendants of "preponderance of the evidence" in proving incompetency. Laws in these states had previously used the higher burden of "clear and convincing evidence."

27. 406 U.S. 715, 92 S. Ct. 1845 (1972).

28. A made-for-television movie aired in 1979 about Donald Lang, an 18-year-old black, totally illiterate deaf-mute. Lang could not talk, write, read lips, or understand sign language. In 1965, he was charged with the murder of a Chicago prostitute (Cook County criminal case #65–3421). Because he could not hear, speak, read, or write, he was declared incompetent to stand trial and was placed in a state mental hospital. After Lang was held for five years, the Illinois Supreme Court ordered him tried or released. Because witnesses were no longer available, he was released. In 1973, Lang was charged with killing another woman. After a conviction for the second murder, he was held to be incompetent and was committed in 1979 to a mental hospital. In 1992, Lang again was found unfit to stand trial and was denied release from the Illinois institution to which he was committed. See *People v. Lang,* 587 N.E.2d 490 (Ill. App. 1992).

29. The only survivor of the automobile crash in 1997 that killed England's Princess Diana and two others has been reported to have a loss of memory of most of the events that occurred. Doctors

believe that his memory of all of the events of the crash is not likely to return.

30. 364 So. 2d 687 (1978), *review denied* 441 U.S. 906, 25 CrL 4018 (Ala. 1978).

31. 423 A.2d 251, (Md. Ct. Special App. 1980).

32. Ibid.

33. 415 F. Supp. 15 (D.D.C. 1975).

34. 479 So. 2d 169 (Fla. 1985).

35. 18 *Commentaries*, section 12.

36. See Section 2.07 of the Model Penal Code on "Liability of Corporations, Unincorporated Associations, and Persons Acting, or Under a Duty to Act, in Their Behalf." See *State v. Christy Pontiac-GMC Inc.*, 354 N.W.2d 17 (Minn. 1984), for case citations on criminal charging of corporations.

CHAPTER 6

The Law Governing the Use of Force

On New Years Day, 2009 Bay Area Rapid Transit officer Johannes Mehserle, left in the above photograph, shot and killed Oscar Grant, who it was claimed, was resisting arrest after being detained with other BART passengers because of a fight on the train. On July 8, 2010 officer Mehserle was convicted after a jury trial of involuntary manslaughter, based on the prosecution's charge that the use of deadly force on Grant was excessive, and a criminal violation. Mehserle will be sentenced in November of 2010. The sentence for involuntary manslaughter in California is 2-4 years in prison, but that term length could be enhanced because of the use of a firearm in the commission of the felony. In July of 2010 the United States Justice Department stated that it had opened a civil rights investigation of Mehserle. In the well-known Rodney King case officers acquitted in a state prosecution of using excessive force on King were subsequently convicted in federal court of civil rights violations. Mehserle could face similar charges, since the Double Jeopardy clause (see Chapter 7) does not prohibit a federal prosecution.

OUTLINE

Definition of an Unreasonable Seizure Today
Use of Force in Resisting an Unlawful Arrest
Cases in Which Force Is Not Legally Justified

The Use of Tasers and Other Force in Traffic Stops
Disciplining Children

LEARNING OBJECTIVES

In this chapter we consider the rules governing the use of force by private persons or police officers. The learning objectives for this chapter are:

- Identify the three key points for determining when force is justified.
- Describe the "castle" doctrine and explain what it says.
- Determine how "stand your ground" laws affect the general rules for using force and the effect such laws have on the "castle" doctrine.

- List the circumstances that justify a police officer using nondeadly force in making an arrest.
- Explain why the Fourth Amendment applies to use of force by a police officer.
- Identify the circumstances that would justify the use of deadly force by a police officer.
- List the people who may use force in the discipline of children.

On March 3, 2010, after the Maryland basketball team defeated Duke, hundreds of students took to the streets to celebrate. Prince George County police were called in, and ultimately arrested 28 persons for disorderly conduct and assault on the police. One of those arrested, Jack McKenna, was listed on police reports as having been injured when he attacked an officer on horseback.

A video taken at the scene showed McKenna approaching the mounted officer, but with his hands free. Before McKenna got to the horse, 3 officers charged him, beating him with their batons. The video shows the defenseless McKenna with his hands up and getting hit more than a dozen times.

The officers involved in the beating have been suspended pending an investigation. The Prince George County police department had been under supervision by the Justice department for prior instances of excessive force.

In this chapter we discuss the rules governing the use of force, including the force law enforcement officers may use to arrest or control criminal suspects.

The use of force by one person against another is a violation of the criminal law unless some justification for the use exists. Justification means that the person using the force had a legally sufficient reason for doing so. Whether or not the use of force is justified often depends on the kind of force used, the person using the force, and the circumstances leading up to the use of force.[1] For example, the rules justifying the use of deadly force are different from those that apply to non-deadly force. The rules justifying the use of force in the protection of property differ from those that justify force to protect persons. Also, the rules justifying the use of force by law enforcement officers reflect the duties and risks facing such officers. As you study the materials in this chapter, consider how they apply to the following hypothetical situation:

A, the owner of a house, throws a graduation party for his daughter, D. B, an uninvited acquaintance of D "crashes" the party by entering A's house. A orders B to leave the house, but B refuses, and starts knocking over party decorations. A twists B's arm behind his back, drags him out of the house, and throws B into the street. Incensed, B goes to his car and grabs a tire wrench, and runs at A. A, mistakenly believing the wrench is a machete, pulls a pistol and shoots B in the arm. B runs off as a police officer arrives at the scene. The officer orders B to stop, and when B refuses the officer fires his service revolver at B, hitting B in the leg.

Force has been used by each of the actors in this hypothetical situation. As you study the materials in this chapter, try to determine which, if any, use was justified.

≡ Self-Defense and the Defense of Others

self-defense The elements to evaluate whether an act of force for self-defense is justified include the unlawfulness of the other's action, the necessity to defend oneself immediately, and the reasonableness of the act of self-defense under the circumstances.

defense of another The elements to evaluate whether an act of force for defense of another is justified include the unlawfulness of the action toward the other, the necessity to defend the other immediately, and the reasonableness of the act of defense under the circumstances.

Section 3.04 of the Model Penal Code provides that force can be used in self-protection "when the actor believes that such force is immediately necessary for the purpose of protecting himself against the use of unlawful force by such other person on the present occasion." In their criminal codes and in their court decisions, all states and the federal government have rules for the use of force. The state of New York, for example, provides in Public Law 35.15 that "one may use physical force upon another when and to the extent he reasonably believes necessary to defend himself or a third person from what he reasonably believes to be the imminent use of unlawful physical force by such other persons." The key points in determining the lawfulness of force in **self-defense** or the **defense of another** are:

- *Unlawfulness:* Is what the other person doing unlawful? If it is not unlawful, force is not justified.
- *Necessity:* Force must be immediately *necessary* to protect the person or another from the use of *unlawful* force or interference by another.
- *Reasonableness:* The amount of force used in self-defense or defense of another must be *reasonable* under the circumstances that exist.

In determining what force is reasonable in self-defense, a court or a jury will take into account the size and age of the parties in relation to one another, the instruments or weapons used, and the aggressiveness of the assault made. Ordinarily, if fists were used in the attack and the parties were about the same size and strength, then fists and the strength of arms and body would be the maximum force that could be used in defense.

Also, so long as the belief is reasonable, it does not need to be correct. Someone who reasonably believes another person is reaching for a weapon to use against her or him may respond with force, even if in fact the aggressor was reaching for something else.

EXAMPLE: A 70-year-old, 100-pound woman becomes angry at a 25-year-old, 200-pound man and begins to hit him with an umbrella. The man may defend himself by taking the umbrella away from the woman, but because he has such physical control of the situation, the amount of force that he would be justified in using against her ends there.

The rules for defense of another person mirror the rules for self-defense. A person may come to the aid of another and use necessary and reasonable force to defend the other person against unlawful force or interference. The person coming to the assistance or defense of another must reasonably believe that the facts are such that the third person would be privileged to act in self-defense and also must reasonably believe that his or her intervention is necessary to protect the third person against unlawful force or interference.

Good Samaritan laws Laws that encourage people to come to the aid of another or to defend another against unlawful force or interference.

Most states have enacted **Good Samaritan laws** that encourage, but do not require, people to get involved when they witness an assault. As an example, the Maryland statute states: "Any person witnessing a violent assault upon the person of another may lawfully aid the person being assaulted by assisting in that person's defense" (Art. 27, § 12A). This statute applies to all people in Maryland and requires that the jury determine whether the defendant believed that an unlawful assault on another person was occurring and whether the defendant made a good-faith attempt to defend against the unlawful assault.

Some states have enacted statutes that require people witnessing an assault to take limited action, such as calling the police. Violations of these laws usually are punished by a small fine.

The Use of Deadly Force in Self-Defense or the Defense of Others

deadly force Force that is likely to cause or is capable of causing death or serious bodily injury.

The rules providing justification for the use of deadly force generally are similar to those governing the use of non-deadly force, with some important differences. **Deadly force** is force that is likely to cause or is capable of causing death or serious bodily injury. Firing a weapon at a person is the use of deadly force, whether the intent is to kill or to wound.

All people, including law enforcement officers, may use deadly force, but only if such force is necessary to prevent imminent death or great bodily harm to themselves or others. Moreover, unlike the use of non-deadly force, where there is no duty to retreat, some states impose such a duty where deadly force is used. Section 3.04 (b)(ii) of the Model Penal Code, for example, states that deadly force is not justified if the actor knows he or she can retreat with "complete safety." (See Chapter 10 for a discussion of imperfect self-defense where unlawful force has been used in self-defense.)

Under the common law, and in some state statutes, a person was not permitted to use deadly force if retreat from an attack was reasonably possible and safe. Thus, even if an unlawful attacker threatened death or serious bodily harm, the law instructed the victim of the attack to "retreat to the wall" before employing deadly force against the attacker.

"stand your ground" laws Recent laws passed in many states that permit using deadly force in response to an unlawful attack rather than the traditional "duty to retreat" policy.

Perhaps because it was dissatisfied with the duty to retreat, in 2005 the Florida legislature passed this country's first **"stand your ground" law.** The Florida law states:

A person who is not engaged in an unlawful activity and who is attacked in any other place where he or she has a right to be has no duty to retreat and has the right to stand his or her ground and meet force with force, including deadly force if he or she reasonably believes it is necessary to do so to prevent death or great bodily harm to himself or herself or another or to prevent the commission of a forcible felony.[2]

In the 2009 case of *Hair v. State*, 17 So.3d 804 (Fla. App. 2009), the court held that a passenger of a car who shot and killed a person who unlawfully and forcibly entered the car could not be charged with a crime under the Florida "stand your ground" law, because the law states that any person making such a forcible entry is presumed to present a threat of imminent harm to the occupants of the car. The court also held that it did not matter that at the time the passenger fired the handgun the intruder was backing out of the car.

Since the Florida statute was passed, at least 29 other states have passed similar laws or are considering such laws. These laws have been criticized as "giving more rights to use deadly force than we give police officers"[3] and are really "shoot first" with a "license to kill."[4] See www.leg.state.fl.us/statutes for the full text of the Florida law.

Loss of Self-Defense Privilege for a Wrongdoer or an Aggressor

Wrongdoers who use unlawful force against another have no privilege of self-defense. The victims of wrongdoers have the privilege of self-defense because of the wrongful conduct of the wrongdoers. In self-defense cases, where the defendant and the victim have engaged in a fight, it becomes important to determine which party was the initial aggressor. The 2003 case in which Alexander Pring-Wilson, a Harvard graduate student, killed a man with whom he was fighting, raised that issue.

At Pring-Wilson's first trial, testimony differed on whether Pring-Wilson or the victim, Michael Colono, started the fight that ended in Colono's death. The defendant's lawyers tried to introduce evidence of Colono's past violent conduct but were prohibited from doing so by the trial judge. At the time of the trial, the Massachusetts self-defense law held that evidence of past violence by the victim was admissible but only if the defendant knew of that past conduct. Since Pring-Wilson did not know Colono before the fight that led to his death, the trial court found the evidence inadmissible.

After Pring-Wilson's conviction, but before his appeal was heard, the Massachusetts Supreme Judicial Court decided another case, *Commonwealth v. Adjutant*, 824 N.E.2d 1 (2005). *Adjutant* changed the self-defense rule so that evidence of a victim's prior violent acts, even if unknown to the defendant, could be admissible on the question of who was the first aggressor. Based on this case, the appellate court in Pring-Wilson's case held that he was entitled to a new trial where evidence of Colono's past violence would be admitted. In 2008 Pring-Wilson pled guilty to manslaughter and was sentenced to 2 years in prison.

State statutes and court decisions recognize two situations in which the aggressor or wrongdoer can regain the right and privilege of self-defense.

1. A wrongdoer (X) begins an encounter with the unlawful use of his or her fists or some nondeadly weapon. The victim, however, unlawfully uses deadly force, which, under the circumstances, is unnecessary and unreasonable. Now, X may use force in self-defense but is not privileged to resort to the use of force intended or likely to cause death unless he or she has exhausted
   - every means of escape (under the duty to retreat) and
   - every means of avoiding death or great bodily harm to herself or himself.
2. A wrongdoer may regain the right of self-defense by withdrawing in good faith from the fight and giving adequate notice to the victim as to the withdrawal. The wrongdoer has a duty to retreat, and his or her right to self-defense could be restored by giving notice (or attempting to) and by retreating.

The "Castle" Doctrine and the Minority Duty-to-Retreat Exception to That Doctrine

People who have been assaulted in their homes by a trespasser have no duty to retreat or flee but may stand their ground and use such force as is necessary and reasonable to

"castle" doctrine The doctrine permitting people who have been assaulted in their homes by a trespasser to stand their ground and use such force as is necessary and reasonable to defend themselves.

"make my day" rules Rules adopted by some states that put no limits on the use of deadly force by the occupant of a dwelling in response to a trespasser.

defend themselves.[5] Because a person's home is his or her "castle," the privilege not to retreat in one's home is known as the **"castle" doctrine.** Even states that require retreat before using deadly force exempt dwellings from the duty, as does the Model Penal Code (see § 3.04(b)(ii)(A)). The U.S. Supreme Court decided in 1895 in the case of *Beard v. United States*, 158 U.S. 550 that under federal law a homeowner had no duty to retreat in the face of an unlawful assault in his home or on his property.

Also, some states have adopted **"make my day" rules,** which put no limits on the use of deadly force by the occupant of a dwelling. In *State v. Anderson,* 972 P.2d 32 (Okla. Cr. 1998), the court interpreted the Oklahoma statute (Tit. 21, § 1289.25) as intended to remove any requirement that the force used must be reasonable under the circumstances. An occupant who reasonably believes the intruder intends to use some force is privileged to use any force, including deadly force.

The "castle" doctrine does not require a lawful occupant of a home to retreat when confronted by a trespasser or a person who does not reside in the home. However, state laws vary when the wrongdoer is also a co-occupant of the home (such as a spouse, live-in or housemate, or family member). A minority of states have an exception to the "castle" doctrine that requires a co-occupant of a home to retreat (if safely possible) before using deadly force in self-defense.

Florida's "stand your ground" law discussed above also changes the law on the force permitted under the "castle" doctrine.[6] The Florida law creates a presumption that a homeowner has a reasonable fear of imminent peril or death whenever another person unlawfully and forcefully enters the dwelling. Under this law it is no longer necessary for the homeowner (or other legitimate occupant) to prove the intruder presented the threat of death or serious bodily harm.

The Supreme Court of New Jersey pointed out in the 1997 case of *State v. Gartland*[7] that New Jersey is now among the minority of states that require a lawful co-occupant to retreat (if possible) before using deadly force against another co-occupant. In the *Gartland* case, a wife was convicted of the crime of manslaughter because she failed to retreat before shooting her husband, who was assaulting her in a bedroom of their home.

The Supreme Court of New Jersey reversed the conviction and ordered a new trial because the question of whether the wife could have safely retreated was not presented to the jury. The New Jersey Supreme Court stated:

Exactly where could she retreat? As we understand the record, there was no other way out of the bedroom other than the doorway where her assailant stood. The (jury) charge should have asked whether, armed with a weapon, she could have safely made her way out of the bedroom door without threat of serious bodily injury to herself.

Battered Women and Domestic Homicides

The National Clearinghouse for the Defense of Battered Women states that every year 500 to 750 women kill men who abused them and that "our prisons are filled with women with long histories of abuse, linked to the crimes they're in prison for."[8] The clearinghouse also estimates that a woman is abused in the United States every 13 seconds.

These estimates indicate the high levels of anger, fear, hatred, and humiliation in the households where such conditions prevail. Battered women (and those who allege they were abused) can be found in the prisons of every state. They are serving sentences ranging from assault and battery to voluntary manslaughter and first-degree murder.

To lawfully use deadly force in self-defense, a real or reasonable fear of imminent death or great bodily harm must exist. If no immediate threat is present, then, the law

DEFENSE OF DWELLINGS

More than 4 million burglaries occur in the United States each year, plus millions more vehicle break-ins and thefts. The magnitude of this problem has probably contributed to the number of states that have enacted the "stand your ground" laws discussed earlier in this chapter.

In the defense of dwellings, while each state's laws would determine the force that may be used, there generally is no duty to retreat from an intruder in your home, though doing so might be a wise choice. The list below includes two states' responses to this problem as well as complications that might flow from such laws:

- *The Colorado "Make My Day" Law*: Sections 18–1–704(3) of the Colorado Statutes became effective in 1986. It immediately became known as the "make my day" law (Clint Eastwood's taunt to a felon in a movie). The backers of the law want it to be known as the "homeowner's protection" law and point out that it is not a "license to kill" law. The law provides homeowners with immunity from prosecution for force used against a person making an unlawful entry into the home.[a]
- *The California Home Protection Bill of Rights*: Section 198.5 of the California Penal Code permits a presumption that a person using deadly force on an intruder acted in reasonable fear of death or great bodily harm to himself or herself or to a member of the household. (However, the presumption could be overcome with evidence showing otherwise.)
- *Shootings Receiving National Attention*: A young Japanese exchange student dressed for a Halloween party was told to "freeze" as he approached the wrong house. The student did not understand and was shot to death in Baton Rouge, Louisiana. A criminal jury found the homeowner innocent, but in 1994 a civil court awarded $650,000 for the killing.
- *Mistaken-for-a-Burglar Shootings*: These occur every year in the United States. In 1994, a young Scottish businessman who was out on the town in Houston, Texas, became lost and pounded on the door of the wrong house at 4 a.m. The homeowner mistook the Scot for a burglar and shot and killed him.
- *Police Responding to a Burglary-in-Progress Call*: This can create a dangerous situation. An armed homeowner, either inside or outside the home, may mistake the officer for the burglar, with deadly consequences.

[a]See the 1992 case of People v. Young, 825 P.2d 1004 (Colo. App.), in which the Colorado courts held that immunity from criminal prosecution would not be granted under the Colorado law for shootings of people on a porch of a home.

believes, other alternatives are available to abused women, such as going to a shelter for battered women or going to family members for help.

EXAMPLE: A wife or girlfriend is terrified as her husband or boyfriend comes toward her in a rage, screaming that he will use the knife in his hand to kill her. Witnesses state the woman had no opportunity to retreat but that she was able to grab a gun, which she used to kill the man. Her action was held to be lawful use of force in self-defense.

battered woman defense Evidence of past abuse offered by women charged with violence against their abusers to show its psychological effects as part of their claim of self-defense.

EXAMPLE: After years of beatings and many other abuses, Mrs. Norman killed her husband with a handgun as he was taking a nap. Her husband had been drinking for two days, and Mrs. Norman believed he would beat her again when he finished his nap and resumed drinking. The killing was held to be "imperfect self-defense," and Mrs. Norman went to prison for voluntary manslaughter. (See the case of *State v. Norman* in Chapter 10.)

A 2007 trial in Tennessee that received national attention involved a **battered woman defense.** The defendant, a 33-year-old wife of a minister, was charged with murder after

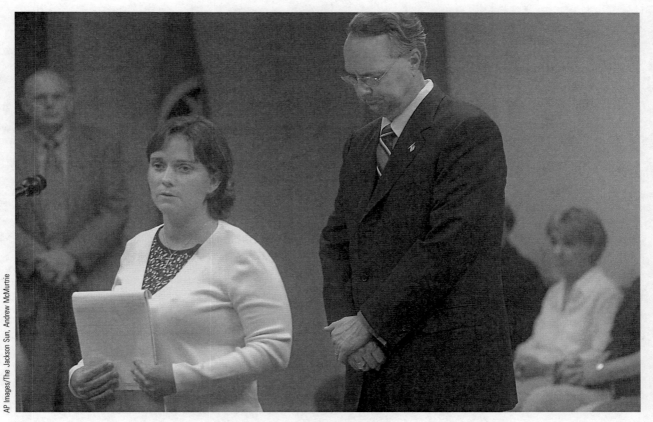

AP Images/The Jackson Sun, Andrew McMurtrie

Mary Winkler (left) was accused of murdering her husband, a preacher, with a shotgun, and was tried for first-degree murder. At her trial she admitted shooting her husband but testified in her defense that her husband psychologically and sexually abused her. The jury found her guilty of voluntary manslaughter on April 19, 2007. Winkler was sentenced to three years in prison, which under state law required her to serve at least 210 days. The defense of spousal abuse, although usually not a complete defense to a crime charged, can often lead to a reduced charge or conviction for a lesser crime, as it did in Winkler's case.

shooting her husband with a shotgun. She testified in her own defense and stated that her husband had abused her physically and sexually during their marriage. She also testified that the shotgun went off accidentally. The jury of ten women and two men convicted her of voluntary manslaughter, with a possible sentence of three to six years or less, instead of murder, with a possible sentence of twelve years to life. One of the men, the jury foreman, after expressing skepticism about the abuse claims, told reporters after the trial that "It was a room of 10 ladies … 10 ladies were going to have a tendency to see [the defendant's] view." In response, one of the female jurors stated, "You shouldn't kill, but you also shouldn't beat your wife."[9]

Many states now permit abused women charged with violence against their abusers to introduce evidence of their abuse and its psychological effects as part of their claim of self-defense. Women in prisons who were abused or who claim they were abused have appealed to state governors for clemency. Gail Owens, who was given the death penalty for the arranged murder of her husband, was scheduled to be executed on September 28, 2010, which would have made her the first woman executed in Tennessee in nearly 200 years. Owens had claimed she suffered from "battered wife" syndrome, though she did not introduce evidence of abuse at her trial. On July 14, 2010 Tennessee Governor Phil Bredesen commuted Owens' sentence to life imprisonment. With credit for time served,

---

WHEN FORCE *CANNOT* BE USED

Force in self-defense or in the defense of another person cannot be used under the following circumstances:

- The force is not immediately necessary.
- The amount of force is unreasonable.
- The other person's actions are lawful. (Force in self-defense or the defense of another must be immediately necessary to protect against unlawful force.)[a]
- The force used cannot be based on a fear that another person means to do harm sometime in the future if there is no immediate fear of harm. *State v. Buggs,* 806 P.2d 1381 (Ariz. App. 1990)

In addition, force cannot be used to punish or to retaliate for past harm or past injury, such as a sexual assault in the past. See *State v. Reid,* 747 P.2d 560 (Ariz. 1987).

A shoot-on-sight order would be unlawful unless the order was within the guidelines established by the U.S. Supreme Court and state courts for the use of force in self-defense, in the defense of another, or when force can lawfully be used to stop a fleeing felon. In the Ruby Ridge siege, deadly force was used to kill a fleeing 14-year-old boy and an unarmed woman.

[a]A minority of states hold that a duty to retreat exists before deadly force can be used against another co-occupant of a home (such as a spouse, live-in, or family member).

Owens will be eligible for parole in the spring of 2012. Governor Bredesen stated that part of the reason for his decision to commute Owens' sentence was the outcome in the Mary Winkler case, pictured above. Winkler, who also alleged the "battered wife" defense, was convicted and served only 67 days in a mental health facility.

Governors in all states receive many requests for pardons and clemency each year. Parole boards and governors review the records of women requesting clemency because they were abused. Chapter 10, on homicide, contains further material on battered women who kill.

≡ The Use of Force in the Defense of Property

A person is privileged to threaten to or intentionally use non-deadly force to protect property that is lawfully in his or her custody or care. In some instances, a verbal request is all that is needed to stop the interference with the property.

The interference with the property must be unlawful. Force may be used only when necessary to terminate the interference, and the amount of force must be reasonable under the circumstances.

EXAMPLE: Y, a store employee, observes X snatch merchandise and run out of the store. Y may use *necessary* and *reasonable* force to prevent the *unlawful* taking of merchandise by X.

EXAMPLE: X snatches W's purse and runs off. Y, who observed the crime, would be justified in using necessary and reasonable force to recover the purse. Theft from the person (or robbery, if force is used) is a felony in most, if not all, states, which would authorize Y, in most states, to make a citizen's arrest. Force could also be used under these circumstances under the state law governing the use of force in making an arrest.

Deadly force was at one time commonly used to protect property. On the American frontier, deadly force was often used by farmers or ranchers to prevent the theft of their horses, cattle, or farm equipment. This force was necessary in those times, because law enforcement officers were seldom readily available.

Today all states forbid the use of deadly force in the defense of property. The reasons for the change in the law can be summarized as follows:

1. On the frontier, a horse and many other items of property were important for survival. Today, few items of property are vital to survival because they can be replaced within a few days.
2. Today, many items of personal property (such as a car) are ordinarily insured against loss by theft. On the frontier, insurance was unknown, and the loss of major or personal items could be a tragedy to a frontier family.
3. Today, thanks to modern communication and transportation, law enforcement agencies are readily available to assist individuals confronted with theft.

The rule that a person cannot use deadly force to protect property applies whether the owner is present or uses a remote-control device, such as a spring gun, that is triggered by opening a door or attaching a spring to property. Indeed, some jurisdictions, such as Oregon, Wisconsin, and some countries, such as England, go so far as to punish separately the mere setting of a spring gun.

EXAMPLE: A farmer who becomes exasperated because melons are being stolen from his fields is not justified in shooting the thieves with a shotgun. Neither can he set up a shotgun that is discharged when a thief brushes a wire attached to the trigger mechanism.

The common law in probably all states makes the user of such devices civilly liable for the wrongs that occur. The Restatement of Torts (Section 85, p. 180) states:

> The value of human life and limb, not only to the individual concerned but also to society, so outweighs the interest of a possessor of land in excluding from it those whom he is not willing to admit thereto that a possessor of land has, as is stated in Section 79, no privilege to use force intended or likely to cause death or serious harm against another whom the possessor sees about to enter his premises or meddle with his chattel, unless the intrusion threatens death or serious bodily harm to the occupiers or users of the premises.... A possessor of land cannot do indirectly and by a mechanical device that which, were he present, he could not do immediately and in person. Therefore, he cannot gain a privilege to install, for the purpose of protecting his land from intrusions harmless to the lives and limbs of the occupiers or users of it, a mechanical device whose only purpose is to inflict death or serious harm upon such as may intrude, by giving notice of his intention to inflict, by mechanical means and indirectly, harm which he could not, even after request, inflict directly were he present.

In 1990, the owner of a small machine shop in Denver, Colorado, rigged a shotgun booby trap after his business had been burglarized eight times in two years. A teenage burglar was killed by the booby trap. The business owner was convicted of manslaughter. Although the owner received probation, he was held civilly liable in a lawsuit. As a result of the damage award, he could lose his business, his home, and all his assets.[10]

After the Denver shooting, other Denver businesses put up signs on buildings stating that their premises were also booby-trapped. Police officers and firefighters became concerned for their safety and stated they would not enter such buildings until the buildings were determined to be safe. One building having such a sign (but no booby trap) was destroyed by fire when firefighters refused to enter.

SECTIONS OF THE U.S. CONSTITUTION CONTROLLING THE USE OF FORCE BY LAW ENFORCEMENT OFFICERS

Provision of the U.S. Constitution	Limit on Force Used
The 4th Amendment forbids "unreasonable search and seizures"; a "seizure" includes the use of unreasonable force	The use of force, including deadly force by law enforcement officers, must be "objectively reasonable in light of the facts and circumstances confronting (the officer) … judged from the perspective of a reasonable officer on the scene …" *Graham v. Conner*, 490 U.S. 386, 390 (1989)
The 8th Amendment forbids "cruel and unusual punishment."	Once convicted and incarcerated, any use of force on an inmate is viewed as punishment and thus subject to the "cruel and unusual punishment" clause. Where force is used to maintain order in jails or prisons, the question becomes "whether force was used punishment applied in a good faith effort to maintain order … or maliciously and sadistically for the very purpose of causing harm." *Whitley v. Albers*, 475 U.S. 312, 320–321 (1986)
The "due process" clauses of the 5th and 14th Amendments forbid governments from depriving any person of "life, liberty, or property without due process of law."	The U.S. Supreme Court has limited the use of the "due process" guarantee to those circumstances where there is no other source "of constitutional protection against a particular sort of intrusive governmental conduct." *Graham v. Conner*, 490 U.S., at 395 (1989).

≡ The Use of Force in Making an Arrest

Force may not be used legally in making an arrest unless the arrest is a lawful, custodial arrest made in good faith. This does not mean that the arrested person must be found guilty of the charge; however, it does mean that probable cause (reasonable grounds to believe) must exist to authorize the arrest.

In most arrests, force is unnecessary because the person arrested complies with instructions and offers no resistance. If force in making arrests should be necessary because of resistance or an attempt to escape, the officer may use only such force as is reasonably believed necessary to

1. Detain the offender, make the arrest, and conduct lawful searches
2. Overcome any resistance by the offender
3. Prevent an escape and retake the person if an escape occurs
4. Protect the officer, others, and the prisoner, if necessary

The tests used in determining whether excessive force was used by a law enforcement officer in making an arrest were established by the U.S. Supreme Court in the 1985 case of *Tennessee v. Garner*, discussed below for the use of deadly force, and the 1989 case of *Graham v. Connor*.[11] In *Graham* the U.S. Supreme Court held:

Today we make explicit what was implicit in *Garner*'s analysis, and hold that *all* claims that law enforcement officers have used excessive force—deadly or not—in the course of an arrest, investigatory stop, or other "seizure" of a free citizen should be analyzed under the Fourth Amendment and its "reasonableness" standard, rather than under a "substantive due process" approach. Because the Fourth Amendment provides an explicit textual source of constitutional protection against this sort of physically intrusive governmental conduct, that Amendment, not the more generalized notion of "substantive due process," must be the guide for analyzing these claims.

Determining whether the force used to effect a particular seizure is "reasonable" under the Fourth Amendment requires a careful balancing of "the nature and quality of the intrusion on the individual's Fourth Amendment interests" against the countervailing governmental interests at stake. *Id.,* at 8, 105 S. Ct., at 1699, quoting *United States v. Place,* 462 U.S. 696, 703 (1983). Our Fourth Amendment jurisprudence has long recognized that the right to make an arrest or investigatory stop necessarily carries with it the right to use some degree of physical coercion or threat thereof to effect it. Because "[t]he test of reasonableness under the Fourth Amendment is not capable of precise definition or mechanical application," in *Bell v. Wolfish,* 441 U.S. 520, 559, (1979), however, its proper application requires careful attention to the facts and circumstances of each particular case, including the severity of the crime at issue, whether the suspect poses an immediate threat to the safety of the officers or others, and whether he is actively resisting arrest or attempting to evade arrest by flight. See *Tennessee v. Garner,* 471 U.S., at 8–9, 105 S. Ct., at 1699–1700 (the question is "whether the totality of the circumstances justifie[s] a particular sort of … seizure"). The "reasonableness" of a particular use of force must be judged from the perspective of a reasonable officer on the scene, rather than with the 20/20 vision of hindsight.

The Fourth Amendment is not violated by an arrest based on probable cause, even though the wrong person is arrested, *Hill v. California,* 401 U.S. 797 (1971); nor by the mistaken execution of a valid search warrant on the wrong premises, *Maryland v. Garrison,* 480 U.S. 79 (1987). With respect to a claim of excessive force, the same standard of reasonableness at the moment applies: "Not every push or shove, even if it may later seem unnecessary in the peace of a judge's chambers," *Johnson v. Glick,* 481 F.2d, at 1033, violates the Fourth Amendment. The calculus of reasonableness must embody allowance for the fact that police officers are often forced to make split-second judgments—in circumstances that are tense, uncertain, and rapidly evolving—about the amount of force that is necessary in a particular situation.

Using Reasonable Force to Obtain Evidence of Drunk or Drugged Driving

More than 17,000 persons are killed each year, and more than a million injured, in traffic accidents involving drunk or drugged driving (driving under the influence—DUI). The National Highway Traffic Safety Administration (NHTSA) estimates the annual cost to Americans for alcohol or drug-impaired driving to be $45 billion. More than 1.5 million DUI arrests are made each year, a number exceeded only by drug arrests. In 2002, NHTSA and the Robert Wood Johnson Foundation estimated that more than 9 million people a year drive vehicles while under the influence of alcohol or drugs.

All states make driving under the influence of alcohol or drugs a crime and have laws that require drivers to submit to breath, blood, or urine analysis when police officers have reasonable grounds to believe the driver is impaired. These laws have been upheld as reasonable regulation of an important and potentially dangerous activity. As these courts frequently point out, driving on public streets is a privilege, not a right.

In recent years an increasing number of drivers have refused to submit to standard breath tests. While all states have "refusal to consent" criminal statutes, the penalties for failure to consent are generally less than for a DUI conviction, and defense lawyers might believe defending a refusal to consent charge presents fewer obstacles than a DUI charge.

It is difficult, as a practical matter, to force an uncooperative driver to submit to a breath or urine test. As a result, police and prosecutors have begun taking forced blood samples from these uncooperative drivers. The U.S. Supreme Court upheld the constitutionality of taking a blood sample without the consent of a suspect in *Schmerber v. California,* 384 U.S. 757 (1966) but stated that the sample must be taken under reasonable circumstances. Since *Schmerber*, most courts have held that the police may use reasonable force to get the blood sample, including the use of several officers to subdue a struggling defendant. See, for example, *State v. Worthington*, 65 P.3d 211 (Idaho 2002), in which three officers and two nurses held down a struggling suspect. The court in *State v. Ravotto*, 777 A.2d 301 (N.J. 2001) found the use of force unreasonable when the suspect expressed a fear of needles and offered to take a breath test.

Standards for the Use of Deadly Force Established by the U.S. Supreme Court

Deadly force is force that is likely to cause death or serious bodily injury. The law regarding the use of deadly force in making an arrest varies somewhat from state to state.

Police department regulations also vary in the language used to regulate and instruct officers as to the use of deadly force. State laws and police regulations must conform, however, to the requirements established by the U.S. Supreme Court in the 1985 case of *Tennessee v. Garner* (which follows) and the 1989 case of *Graham v. Connor* (109 S. Ct. 1865).

The question of the reasonableness of the use of deadly force by a law enforcement officer frequently arises in a "1983" action, a civil action brought under 42 U.S.C. § 1983. That statute makes state officials liable if they violated a person's civil or constitutional rights. In the case of deadly force in an arrest, the person killed or injured may assert a cause of action against the officer employing the deadly force under the Fourth Amendment, since the use of force is a "seizure" and violates the Fourth Amendment if it is unreasonable. That was the claim in *Tennessee v. Garner*, which follows.

Tennessee v. Garner

Supreme Court of the United States (1985) 471 U.S. 1, 105 S. Ct. 1694

At about 10:45 p.m. on October 3, 1974, Memphis police officers were dispatched to answer a "prowler inside call." Upon arriving at the scene, they saw someone run across the backyard. The fleeing suspect, Edward Garner, stopped at a six-foot-high chain-link fence at the edge of the yard. With the aid of a flashlight one of the officers was able to see Garner's face and hands. He saw no sign of a weapon. Garner was 17 or 18 years old and about five feet five inches or five feet seven inches tall. While Garner was crouched at the base of the fence, the officer called out "police, halt" and took a few steps toward him. Garner then began to climb over the fence. Convinced that if Garner made it over the fence he would elude capture, Hymon shot him. The bullet hit Garner in the back of the head, killing him.

In using deadly force to prevent the escape, the officer was acting under the authority of a Tennessee statute and pursuant to police department policy. The statute provides that "[i]f, after notice of the intention to arrest the defendant, he either flee or forcibly resist, the officer may use all the necessary means to effect the arrest" (Tenn. Code Ann. § 40-7-108 (1982)). The department policy was slightly more restrictive than the statute but still allowed the use of deadly force in cases of burglary. The incident was reviewed by the Memphis Police Firearm's Review Board and presented to a grand jury. Neither took any action.

Garner's father then brought this action in the Federal District Court for the Western District of Tennessee, seeking damages under 42 U.S.C. § 1983 for asserted violations of Garner's constitutional rights. The complaint alleged that the shooting violated the Fourth, Fifth, Sixth, Eighth, and Fourteenth Amendments of the U.S. Constitution.[12]

> The Federal District Court dismissed the case. The Supreme Court said this about the Court of Appeals decision reversing the District Court:
>
> *It reasoned that the killing of the fleeing suspect was a "seizure" under the Fourth Amendment and thus constitutional only if reasonable. The court concluded that the Tennessee statute failed to distinguish between degrees of felonies, and in the present case the use of deadly force was unreasonable.*
>
> On review the U.S. Supreme Court affirmed the conclusion of the Court of Appeals that "the facts, as found, did not justify the use of deadly force" and further held:
>
> *While we agree that burglary is a serious crime, we cannot agree that it is so dangerous as automatically to justify the use of deadly force. The FBI classifies burglary as a "property" rather than a "violent" crime. See Federal Bureau of Investigation, Uniform Crime Reports, Crime in the United States 1 (1984). Although the armed burglar would present a different situation, the fact that an unarmed suspect has broken into a dwelling at night does not automatically mean he is physically dangerous. This case demonstrates as much…. In fact, the available statistics demonstrate that burglaries only rarely involve physical violence. During the 10-year period … 1973–1982, only 3.8% of all burglaries involved violent crime.*

Definition of an Unreasonable Seizure Today

unreasonable seizure
A seizure made by a government officer that is unreasonable under the circumstances and thus violates the Fourth Amendment.

In most states, an **unreasonable seizure** would occur if deadly force were used by law enforcement officers or private people under any of the following circumstances:

1. Deadly force may never be used to make the arrest of or to prevent the escape of a person who has committed a misdemeanor.

EXAMPLE: Deadly force should not be used to catch a "prowler" seen in someone's backyard in the middle of the night or to halt a shoplifter who has taken a $75 item and cannot be apprehended in any other way.

2. Deadly force may never be used on mere suspicion.

THE SEARCH FOR NONLETHAL WEAPONS

Device	Description
Stun guns, stun shields, and stun belts	Devices deliver electrical charge meant to subdue without killing. The M26 Taser electric stun pistol shoots darts that stick to clothing and deliver up to 50,000 volts of electricity. Law enforcement agencies often use Tasers to incapacitate people without physical restraint. There is usually no long-term injury, though death has occurred in rare occasions.
Chemical sprays such as pepper spray, mace, or tear gas	Devices used to repel but not kill an assailant. Most states permit any person over age 18 to carry these products.
Crowd control devices	Water cannons and tear gas are commonly used, but American law enforcement agencies are reluctant to use "rubber bullets," which can be lethal under some circumstances.

CASE CLOSE-UP

Scott v. Harris
Supreme Court of the United States
127 S. Ct. 1769 (2007)

In March 2001 Harris was spotted driving his car 73 miles per hour in a 55 zone on a Georgia highway, and he was pursued by Scott and other police officers. The chase lasted several minutes and took place mainly on a two-lane county road. Harris's speed sometimes exceeded 85 miles per hour, and at one point during the chase his car bumped a police vehicle. A videotape of the chase showed Harris passing cars in the left-hand turn lane, running red lights, and causing approaching cars to pull over to the curb to avoid being hit by Harris.

Scott radioed his superiors, seeking permission to execute a maneuver called a "precision intervention technique," in which the pursued vehicle is blocked by a police vehicle in a manner that causes it to slide to a stop. Scott was given that permission but determined the conditions did not make the technique possible. Instead, Scott rammed the Harris vehicle, causing it to crash and severely injuring Harris, who was rendered a quadriplegic as a result of the crash.

Harris sued Scott and the county that employed Scott under Section 1983, alleging that Scott's decision to ram his car was an exercise of unreasonable deadly force and violated the Fourth Amendment. The lower federal courts held that Harris had stated a claim against Scott that raised a fact question about the reasonableness of Scott's actions under *Garner v. Tennessee*. The Supreme Court granted review and reversed the Court of Appeals, holding that as a matter of law Scott's actions were not unreasonable and did not constitute use of excessive force under the Fourth Amendment.

The Court first found that no real factual dispute existed about the nature of the police chase. It found, mainly in reliance on the police video of the chase, that no reasonable jury could have found that Harris was driving his car in a manner that did not present a serious risk of harm to other motorists or pedestrians. It then held that even though Scott's decision to terminate the chase by ramming Harris's vehicle with his bumper was a "seizure" under the Fourth Amendment, it did not violate Harris's rights. The Court concluded that the threat to the public created by Harris's actions outweighed the high likelihood that Scott's actions would injure Harris, and that as a result Scott's decision to "seize" Harris was reasonable under the Fourth Amendment. The Court observed that in making the "reasonableness" calculation here it was important to note that while the likelihood of injury to Harris was high, it lacked the near certainty of death created by shooting an escaping felon in the head in *Garner*.

Finally, the Court rejected Harris's argument that Scott should have abandoned the chase and that his failure to do so made his subsequent actions unreasonable. It said it was "loath to lay down a rule requiring the police to allow fleeing suspects to get away whenever they drive so *recklessly* that they put other people's lives in danger."

EXAMPLE: In 1965, two New Orleans police officers fired at an automobile they were chasing because they suspected that the vehicle had been stolen. Mere suspicion does not justify the use of deadly force, and although "fleeing from an officer" is a felony in many instances, it would not justify the use of deadly force, as it ordinarily is a nonviolent offense.[13]

WHAT IS THE NATURE OF THE CONTACT BETWEEN THE POLICE AND THE PEOPLE IN THE UNITED STATES?

The U.S. Congress ordered a study of the nature of the day-to-day contacts between the police and the people in the United States. The results of this 1999 national survey were published by the U.S. Department of Justice in the NCJ 184957 document, reporting that in 1999

- 21 percent of U.S. residents had a contact with police.
- 52 percent of these contacts were traffic stops.
- 19 percent of the contacts were to report a crime.
- Under 1 percent of the contacts involved police use of force.
- 10 percent of white drivers were stopped.
- 12 percent of black drivers were stopped.
- 9 percent of Hispanic drivers were stopped.

The study also stated 84 percent of drivers considered their stop legitimate, and 90 percent stated that the police acted properly during the traffic stop. About 1 percent of the 45 million people who had any face-to-face contact with police had been threatened with the use of force or had force used against them (including being pushed, hit, choked, threatened with a flashlight, restrained by a dog, or threatened with a gun). The survey concluded that in the United States the use of force by police is quite uncommon.

A 2006 report by the Justice Department, NCJ 210296, on complaints against police officers, stated that 37 percent of such complaints were dismissed, 25 percent were unfounded, and 21 percent resulted in the officers' exoneration. Only 8 percent of the complaints were sustained.

EXAMPLE: Late on a hot summer night, a woman is heard screaming, and a man runs out from between two houses and down the street. The man does not stop when ordered to stop by a police officer. The rookie officer (who later retired as a high-ranking officer with the Milwaukee Police Department) had the good sense not to shoot. When the man did stop, the officer found that the man was a boyfriend of the woman who had made advances on his girlfriend, causing her to scream. The officer stated that he woke up in a cold sweat a number of nights thinking what would have happened had he used his revolver in this situation.

3. Deadly force may never be used by law enforcement officers to arrest or prevent the escape of a person who has committed a nonviolent felony.

EXAMPLE: In a 2008 Virginia case, *Couture v. Com.*, 656 S.E.2d 425, a police officer was convicted of manslaughter in the death of a motorist stopped after running a stop sign. The officer and his fellow officer approached the stopped car, and the driver opened his door to exit the car. The officers ordered to driver to get back in the car, and when he did he reached his hands under the front seat. The defendant reached into the car to restrain the driver, and the driver put the car in gear and started it moving. The officer, while struggling with the driver, then pulled his service pistol and shot the driver, whose hands were on the steering wheel. A gun was found under the seat. The court affirmed the officer's conviction, holding his actions were unreasonable and thus not justified.

Use of Force in Resisting an Unlawful Arrest

Under the common law, a person has a legal right to forcibly resist an unlawful arrest. This rule developed hundreds of years ago in England, when safeguards to protect a person from unlawful arrest did not exist. Today, there are many safeguards, and the old rule has been changed by court decisions and statutes in most states. California Penal Code, Section 834a, and Connecticut Statutes, Sections 53a-23, are examples of such statutes. The Connecticut statute is as follows: "A person is not justified in using physical force to resist an arrest by a reasonably identifiable police officer, whether such arrest is legal or illegal." A few states, however, retain the old rule.[14]

Cases in Which Force Is Not Legally Justified

The following cases illustrate situations in which the use of force is not legally justified:

- Words alone never justify the use of force (see the "fighting words" doctrine in Chapter 9). In the 1994 case of *State v. Escamilla* (245 Neb. 13, 511 N.W.2d 58), the defendant claimed he killed the victim because the victim made a homosexual proposition to him. The trial court would not permit evidence of this defense.

USE OF PHYSICAL RESTRAINTS

When law enforcement officers come in contact with a suspect or a person who might become violent, they may decide to use some form of physical restraint to protect themselves or the person restrained. Use of such restraints can in some circumstances be an unreasonable use of force, as the following materials illustrate.

Use of neck choke holds	Could be held to be unreasonable and excessive use of force[a]	The FBI Law Enforcement Bulletin article "Physiological Effects Resulting from Use of Neck Holds" (July 1983) states:[b] Because of the organs involved, neck holds must be considered potentially lethal whenever applied. Officers using this hold should have proper training in its use and effects. Police officers should have continual in-service training and practice in the use of the carotid sleeper. They should not use or be instructed in the use of the choke hold other than to demonstrate its potential lethal effect. Officers should recognize that death can result if the carotid sleeper is incorrectly applied.
Use of handcuffs	When an arrest is made	Generally upheld as reasonable; see *Healy v. City of Brentwood*, 649 S.W.2d 916 (Mo. App. 1983).
Use of handcuffs	When an investigative stop is made	Would be held reasonable if circumstances justified use; see *People v. Johnson*, 199 Colo. 68, 605 P.2d 46 (1980), in which suspects were believed to be armed robbers and murderers. See also *Rhodes v. State*, 945 S.W.2d 115 (Tex. Ct. App. 1997), which lists cases in which handcuffing was held reasonable during investigative stops.
Use of handcuffs	In transporting mental patients	Would be unreasonable if no need to handcuff, but would be justified when there was a reasonable concern for safety.

[a]See the *New York Times* article, "Police Officer Is Dismissed in Choke Hold Case," November 10, 1997. The victim died.
[b]See also the FBI Law Enforcement Bulletin article, "Suspect Restraint and Sudden Death," May 1996, where the risk to prisoners who are hog-tied is discussed.

- In the 1991 case of *People v. Miller* (211 Ill. App. 3d 572, 570 N.E.2d 515), the defendant claimed the victim beat her the night before. The Illinois courts held that this was not legal justification for the shooting the following day, and the conviction of attempted murder was affirmed.
- The father of a high school girl who had been sexually abused by the former high school basketball coach shot the man five times as he left court in Mound City, Illinois. (See the *New York Times* article, "Coach in Abuse Case Is Shot by Girl's Father," October 17, 1993.)
- The mother of a 12-year-old boy who had been sexually abused fired five bullets into the head and neck of the male abuser as he sat in a Sonora, California, courtroom. The mother was sentenced to 10 years in state prison. (See the *New York Times* article, "Mother in a Courtroom Slaying Calls Jail Term Fair," January 9, 1994.)

The Use of Tasers and Other Force in Traffic Stops

When a motorist is stopped by police for a traffic violation, the common procedure is to inform the motorist of the violation, give him a "ticket," and obtain the motorists' signature showing receipt of the ticket. However, when this common, usually peaceful transaction becomes a confrontation, officers sometimes use force on the motorist to compel the motorist to comply with the officer's commands. What level of force is permitted in these situations?

In 2009 and 2010, the 9th Circuit Court of Appeals had occasion to consider two cases where officers used Taser guns to subdue persons stopped for traffic violations. Taser guns use compressed nitrogen to propel aluminum darts (probes) which are connected to wires that deliver a very painful, 1,200-volt electrical charge into the muscles of the person hit, causing pain and temporary paralysis in muscles hit. Subsequently, both motorists brought actions against the officers under 42 U.S.C. § 1983, the civil rights statute. The officers would be liable only if the force they used was "excessive" under the principles discussed earlier in this chapter, so the court was required to evaluate the reasonableness of using Tasers in those cases.

In *Bryan v. McPherson* , 590 F.3d 767 (9th Cir. 2009), the court held that the police use of a Taser gun was excessive force. There, the motorist, Bryan, was stopped by a California police officer for failure to wear a seat belt. Bryan exited his car, wearing only boxer shorts and tennis shoes, and began slapping his thighs, yelling gibberish, and acting agitated. Bryan did not attack the officer, but the officer fired his Taser gun from about 20–26 feet away and struck Bryan, who fell to the ground and fractured 4 teeth. One of the Taser's probes had to be removed with a scalpel. The court found the use of the Taser to be excessive, noting the "traffic violations generally will not support the use of a significant level of force."

In *Brooks v. City of Seattle*, 599 F.3d 1018 (9th Cir. 2010), the court concluded use of a Taser in a traffic stop was not excessive. There, a motorist, Brooks, was stopped by Seattle police for speeding in a school zone. When presented with a ticket, Brooks refused to sign the ticket and tried to grab her driver's license away from the officer. The officer called his supervisor, who came to the scene and instructed Brooks to comply with the officer's commands. Brooks again refused, refused to turn off her car, and refused to exit her vehicle. The officers opened the driver's door and exerted pressure on Brooks's left arm to gain compliance, but Brooks resisted efforts to remove her from the vehicle. The officers then stated they were going to use a Taser gun, but Brooks again refused, informing the officers she was pregnant. The officers then applied the Taser to Brooks's thigh, removed her from her vehicle, and arrested her.

The District Court found the officers had used excessive force. The Court of Appeals reversed, stating that under the circumstances the use of the Taser was not excessive. The court distinguished the *Bryan* case by noting that here, unlike in *Bryan*, the Taser was used in "drive-stun" mode, and applied directly to Brooks's body, causing only temporary, localized pain. In that mode, the court noted, the effect of the Taser was considerably less than in the "dart" mode used by the officer in *Bryan*. The court also noted that the Seattle Police Department Use of Force Training Guideline identified use of a Taser in "drive-stun" mode as a "level 1 Tactic." Since the officers were acting reasonably in arresting Brooks for obstruction, the use of "level 1" force was not excessive.

In a small, informal survey of 10 police departments in five states, published in the September 2007 FBI Law Enforcement Bulletin and titled "The Dynamic Resistance Response Model—A Modern Approach to the Use of Force," the author who conducted the survey found that while most police departments require motorists to sign for tickets, all 10 responded "no" to the question "Would you use a Taser on a motorist who refused to sign a ticket?" Most of the officers stated that their practice was to hold the driver's license, but let the motorist go, assuming the motorist had no outstanding warrants and had proof of registration and insurance.

≡ Disciplining Children

Under common law, parents and people who take the place of parents (*in loco parentis*) have a natural right to the custody, care, and control of their children. They have a duty to provide food, clothing, shelter, and medical care to the children and to educate and discipline them. Under the common law, a parent or a person *in loco* may use a reasonable amount of force in disciplining a child.

A 2001 study[15] reported that the majority of American families discipline their preschool children by using occasional mild to moderate spanking. The study reported no negative effects on children. However, the study also showed that 4 to 7 percent of parents fell into the "red zone" (danger zone) because they disciplined their children frequently and impulsively by such means as verbal punishment, using a paddle, hitting their children in the face or body, or throwing or shaking their child. These children were more likely to have behavioral problems or experience anxiety or depression.

All states have laws requiring school officials, health professionals (nurses, doctors, therapists), and law enforcement officials to report suspected child abuse. In determining the crime of child abuse, the following factors have to be considered:

- The age, size, and health of the child, as force used on a baby or a sick or helpless child is much different than the same force used on a healthy 14-year-old boy.
- The reason for the discipline, because spanking a child for unintentional bed-wetting or throwing up could lead to the conclusion that the parent was out of control and not rational.

The question of what amount of force is reasonable was presented to the Texas Court of Appeals (Houston) in the 1987 case of *Teubner v. State*.[16] The court held:

Texas Penal Code section 9.61 permits the use of force against a child under a "reasonable belief" standard. However, force going beyond that which is necessary for discipline is prohibited. The question in this case is whether the appellants reasonably believed their use of force was necessary to discipline their child.

From the evidence presented, no reasonable person could possibly believe the conduct was justifiable. The child was subjected to a savage beating with a leather belt on two successive nights. On the first night, Victoria Teubner took over the

---

SUMMARY OF THE LAW ON THE USE OF FORCE

Situation	Less than Deadly Force	Deadly Force
In self-defense or in the defense of others	"The use of (reasonable) force upon or toward another person is justified when the actor (reasonably) believes that such force is immediately necessary for the purpose of protecting himself or herself (or another) against the use of unlawful force by such other person on the present occasion."[a]	"The use of deadly force is not justified unless such force is necessary to protect against death, serious bodily harm, kidnapping, or sexual intercourse compelled by force or threat."[b]
In the defense of property	"One may use physical force, other than deadly force such as may be necessary to prevent or terminate the commission or attempted commission of larceny or of criminal mischief with respect to property other than premises."[c]	Under the old common law, deadly force could be used in the defense of property. All states now forbid the use of intentional deadly force in the defense of property.
To apprehend a person who has committed a crime	"When an officer is making or attempting to make an arrest for a criminal offense, he is acting for the protection of public interest and is permitted even a greater latitude than when he acts in self-defense, and he is not liable unless the means which he uses are clearly excessive."[d]	Misdemeanor: Never. Fleeing felon: Deadly force could be used when officers "have probable cause to believe that the suspect (has committed a felony and) poses a threat to the safety of the officers or a danger to the community if left at large" (*Tennessee v. Garner*).
To stop a person for investigative purposes when only "reasonable suspicion" exists	Only such force that is reasonable and necessary under the circumstances that then exist.	Never
Disciplining children (corporal punishment)	Only parents and other people having a status of *in loco parentis* to a child may use reasonable force "reasonably believed to be necessary for (the child's) proper control, training, or education."[e] Other persons (such as strangers or neighbors) may not discipline a child.	Never

[a]Sections 3.04(1) and 3.05(1) of the Model Penal Code.
[b]Section 3.04(2)(b) of the Model Penal Code.
[c]State of New York, Public Law 35.25.
[d]Restatement of Torts, Section 132(a).
[e]Restatement of Torts, Section 147(2), as quoted by the U.S. Supreme Court in *Ingraham v. Wright*, 429 U.S. 975, 97 S. Ct. 481 (1976).

whipping when her husband tired himself. On the second night, they gagged their daughter to stifle her crying. The photographs admitted into evidence offer a grim record of the effects of the beating. The appellants could not have reasonably believed that the degree of force used was necessary for disciplinary purposes. Appellants' second point of error is overruled.

in loco parentis (Latin; "in place of the parents") Any person taking the place of the parents has the duties and responsibilities of the parents and may reasonably discipline a child in his or her care. This category includes legal guardians, foster parents, and public school teachers.

Besides the parents, any person taking the place of the parents and thus classified as ***in loco parentis*** may reasonably discipline a child in his or her care. This category includes legal guardians, foster parents, and public school teachers.

Because of the threats of lawsuits and pressure from anti-paddling groups, many states have forbidden corporal punishment in public schools within those states. In the states that continue to permit corporal punishment, many school boards forbid or limit the use of corporal punishment of students within the school district. In 1977, the U.S. Supreme Court held in the case of *Ingraham v. Wright* that in common law, "a teacher may impose reasonable but not excessive force to discipline a child."[17] The U.S. Supreme Court noted:

Where the legislatures have not acted, the state courts have uniformly preserved the common law rule permitting teachers to use reasonable force in disciplining children in their charge.

Law enforcement officers, neighbors, and other adults who see children misbehave may not discipline a child (or children), although they may use reasonable force to prevent damage to property or injury to other persons or themselves.

Reasonable force to maintain order (as distinguished from discipline) may be used by personnel on airplanes, ships, trains, or buses and by ushers for theaters, sporting events, and other public gatherings. A disorderly child or adult may be ordered to leave if he or she is disturbing other people or has failed to pay the fare or admission fee. The test, again, is that of reasonability. Did the provocation justify the action taken? Was the force reasonable under the circumstances? The Supreme Court of Minnesota held in 1885 that it was not reasonable to force a passenger off a moving train because he had not paid his fare.[18]

Summary

- Use of force is justified only if (1) reasonable, (2) necessary, and (3) in response to unlawful actions by another.
- The "castle" doctrine states that a person in his home is justified in using reasonable force, including deadly force, in response to an assault in his home. There is no duty to retreat under this doctrine.
- The "stand your ground" laws generally give persons the absolute right to refuse to retreat and to respond to an attacker with reasonable force, including deadly force. Such laws change the "castle" doctrine in many states by adopting a presumption

that a homeowner has a fear of imminent peril whenever he is attacked in his home.
- A police officer may use non-deadly force to detain a suspect, prevent his escape, overcome resistance to arrest, or protect the officer or others from harm.
- Actions by police officers using force to arrest a suspect are "seizures" of the suspect, and thus under the Fourth Amendment must be reasonable. State laws or regulations stating how and when police officers may use force must also comply with the Fourth Amendment.

- A police officer may, as may any person, use deadly force when faced with the threat of death or serious bodily harm to the officer or another. A police officer may also use deadly force to prevent the escape of a suspect in serious, violent felony arrests if the officer reasonably believes the escaped suspect presents a serious danger to the public.
- Parents, guardians, and those *in loco parentis* may use reasonable force in disciplining children in their charge.

Key Terms

self-defense, p. 134
defense of another, p. 134
Good Samaritan laws, p. 135
deadly force, p. 135

"stand your ground" laws, p. 135
"castle" doctrine, p. 137
"make my day" rules, p. 137
battered woman defense, p. 138

unreasonable seizure, p. 145
in loco parentis, p. 152

Case Analysis and Writing Exercises

In the following true incidents, was the use of force lawful?

1. Was the use of force justified in the following two situations?
   a. A 19-year-old woman was raped by two men. She subsequently invited them for a return date, at which time she killed one with a shotgun, while the other man fled.
   b. A 62-year-old retired army officer was awakened by noise in his home. He got up, and armed with a pistol, walked into a hallway where he saw two men coming toward him. He fired his pistol, killing both men, who were in the act of burglary. Does it matter if the burglars were unarmed? Would a statute like the Florida "stand your ground" law apply to this situation?
2. Does the "castle" doctrine apply to an area outside the home (called the "curtilage")? See *People v. Riddle*, 649 N.W.2d 30 (Mich. 2002), where a homeowner claimed the "castle" doctrine permitted him to use deadly force against another person in his driveway, without first seeking a safe way to retreat. (When this case was decided, Michigan had a limited duty to retreat before deadly force may be used.) Does M.C.L.A. Section 780.972, enacted in 2006, change the result in *Riddle?* Why?

3. After a high-speed chase, with speeds in excess of 100 mph, police officers forced a vehicle off the road. The driver of the vehicle refused repeated demands by the police officers to exit the vehicle and was forcibly removed by the officers. The driver, a woman, brought a Section 1983 action against the officers, alleging the force used to remove her from the vehicle was excessive. What are the tests used to determine if the police officers used lawful force? See *Clark v. Department of Public Safety*, 431 So.2d 83 (La. App. 1983).
4. The battered woman syndrome has met with mixed success when urged as a defense to charges against the woman for attacks on her abuser, unless the attacks occurred during an incident of abuse. Should the prosecution be able to use the syndrome in the following case? The defendant was charged with murdering his girlfriend. When the woman was asked on her deathbed if the defendant beat her, she said no, that she was hit by a car. The prosecution wants to introduce expert testimony that the woman experienced the battered woman syndrome and that this syndrome caused her to lie about the cause of her injuries. Should they be permitted to do so? See *State v. Townsend*, 897 A2d 316 (N.J. 2006).

Notes

1. When cases go before a criminal court, most states place the burden of proving there was no justification for the force (such as self-defense) upon the state. The U.S. Supreme Court pointed out in the 1987 case of *Martin v. Ohio* (480 U.S. 228, 107 S. Ct. 1098) that only two states continue to follow the common law "that affirmative defenses, including self-defense, were matters for the defendant to prove." Forty-eight states require "the prosecution to prove the absence of self-defense when it is properly raised by the defendant." Ohio and South Carolina continue to follow the common law rule. The Supreme Court held that the rule used in Ohio and South Carolina is constitutional. The Court pointed out that "the Constitution (does not) require the prosecution to prove the sanity of a defendant who pleads not guilty by reason of insanity."

2. Florida Statutes Section 776.013(3).

3. Paul Logli, president of the National District Attorney's Association.

4. See the *New York Times* article, "15 States Expand Victim's Rights on Use of Deadly Force," August 7, 2006.

5. Although there is no legal duty to retreat (flee) from a person who is larger and stronger, in most instances retreat (if possible) is practical and sensible.

6. Florida Statutes Section 776.013 (1)

7. 694 A.2d 564 (N.J. 1997).

8. See the *New York Times* article, "More States Study Clemency for Women Who Killed Abusers," February 2, 1991.

9. *Pensacola News Journal,* April 20, 2007.

10. See the *New York Times* articles, "Denver Machine Shop Owner Gets Probation in Booby Trap Slaying," August 22, 1990; and "Intruder Killed by Trap in House in Burglary-Prone Area of Mobile (Alabama)," December 29, 1989. Similar incidents have occurred in cities throughout the United States. See the 1971 Iowa case of *Katko v. Briney* (183 N.W.2d 657 Iowa) for a further discussion of civil liability and case citations on booby traps.

After his cabin in northern Wisconsin was burglarized three times in eight months, a man rigged a booby trap with a 12-gauge shotgun to the door of a shed housing an ATV (all-terrain vehicle). When a burglar opened the door days later, he received a load of buckshot in his leg. As Wisconsin makes setting a deadly booby trap a misdemeanor, both the cabin owner and the burglar were charged and convicted. (See the *Milwaukee Journal Sentinel* article, "Cabin Owner Jailed for Setting Booby Trap Seeks Pardon from Governor," February 3, 2000.)

11. 490 U.S. 386, 109 S. Ct. 1865.

12. The police officers in the U.S. Supreme Court case of *Tennessee v. Garner* could use the defense known as "qualified immunity." Under this defense, police officers or other public officials who are sued for violating someone's constitutional rights cannot be held liable if either the law at the time of the incident was unclear or if they (the police officers) reasonably believed at the time that their conduct was lawful.

13. *Sauls v. Hutto and Rupert,* 304 F. Supp. 124 (E.D. La. 1969).

14. *Commonwealth v. Moreira,* 388 Mass. 96, 447 N.E.2d 1224 (1983). In the 1998 case of *State v. Hobson* (No. 96–0914), the Supreme Court of Wisconsin also changed the old common law, holding:

> We agree that there should be no right to forcibly resist an unlawful arrest in the absence of unreasonable force. When persons resist arrest, they endanger themselves, the arresting officers, and bystanders…. Justice can and must be had in the courts, not in the streets.

The uniform rule throughout the United States is that force cannot be used to prevent a lawful or unlawful frisk or a search under either a search warrant or some other lawful authority. A person who uses force to resist or obstruct a law enforcement officer in the performance of his or her lawful duties could be charged with a criminal offense in all states.

15. See the *New York Times* article, "Finding Gives Some Support to Advocates of Spanking: Adding Fuel to Bitter Debate on Child Care," August 25, 2001.

16. 742 S.W.2d 57 (Tex. App. 1987).
17. 430 U.S. 651, 97 S. Ct. 1401 (1977).
18. *State v. Kinney,* 34 Minn. 311, 25 N.W. 705 (1885).

CHAPTER 7

Other Criminal Defenses

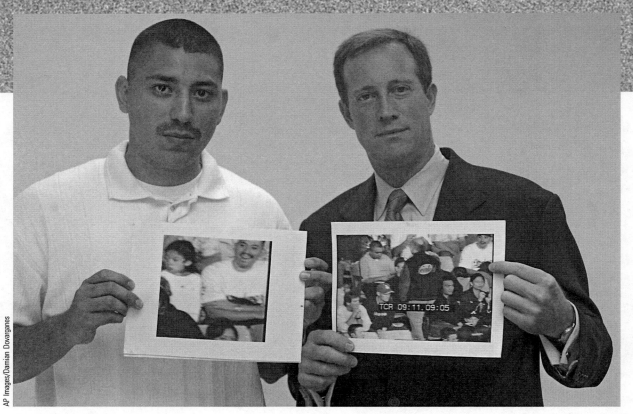

Juan Catalan was charged with murder in a homicide that occurred in San Fernando Valley, California, and served five months in jail after his arrest. He maintained that he and his 6-year-old daughter were attending a Los Angeles Dodgers–Atlanta Braves game at Dodger Stadium, 20 miles away from the murder site, at the time the victim was killed. Here, Catalan and his attorney hold prints from fi lm of the TV show *Curb Your Enthusiasm*, which was shooting scenes during the Dodgers–Braves baseball game. The time-coded fi lm showed Catalan and his daughter at the game, confi rming his alibi. We examine other criminal defenses in this chapter, including alibi defenses like the one successfully raised by Catalan.

OUTLINE

LEARNING OBJECTIVES

In this chapter we present several defenses a defendant may assert in a criminal prosecution. The learning objectives for this chapter are:

- Identify the kinds of immunity to criminal prosecution available, and their limits.

- Determine when, if ever, a mistake of fact or law may provide a defense.

- Distinguish between the defense of duress and necessity.

- State why the Double Jeopardy Clause prohibits successive prosecutions for the same crime.

- Distinguish between a prosecution for the same offense or for a separate offense.

- Learn the difference between *res judicata* and collateral estoppel.

- Identify the tests that determine when government inducements become entrapment.

- List the factors that determine when a speedy trial violation has occurred.

Brian McNamee was a trainer for the Toronto Blue Jays and the New York Yankees. One of the baseball players he worked with was Roger Clemens, an all-star pitcher who has won several Cy Young awards. In 2007 federal investigators interviewed McNamee and told him they had information linking him to the delivery of illegal steroids to many athletes, including Clemens. In return for McNamee's agreement to cooperate with the investigation, the United States Attorney for the Norhtern District of California gave McNamee "use" immunity from prosecution based on any statements made in the investigation. McNamee named Clemens as a person to whom he delivered banned steroids. Clemens subsequently testified before Congress and denied ever taking steroids from McNamee or any other person. In August of 2010 a grand jury indicted Clemens for making false statements before Congress.

In this chapter we discuss the various affirmative defenses to prosecution available to a defendant, including immunity defenses, and the circumstances that must be shown for those defenses to be available.

≡ Affirmative Defenses

corpus delicti In all criminal cases, the government must prove that the crime charged was committed (corpus delicti) and that the defendant was party to the crime (committed the crime or was an accomplice).

affirmative defense A defense to a criminal charge in which the defendant generally admits doing the criminal act but claims an affirmative defense such as duress (he or she was forced) or entrapment.

To prove the guilt of a person charged with a crime, the state must present evidence (1) that a crime was committed (**corpus delicti**) and (2) that the defendant committed or was a party to the crime charged. The U.S. Supreme Court has repeatedly held that "the requirement that guilt of a criminal charge be established by proof beyond a reasonable doubt dates at least from our early years as a Nation" (*In re Winship*, 90 S. Ct. at 1071, 1970).

Defendants in criminal cases may choose to sit quietly if they wish and place on the government the burden of coming forward with evidence proving guilt beyond a reasonable doubt. If the government does carry this burden, a defendant may then produce evidence showing *actual innocence*, justification, or other defenses, usually called affirmative defenses.

An **affirmative defense** is any defense that assumes the complaint or charges to be correct but raises other facts that, if true, would establish a valid excuse or justification or a right to engage in the conduct in question. An affirmative defense does not concern itself with the elements of the offense at all; it concedes them. In effect, an affirmative defense says, "Yes, I did it, but I had a good reason."[1]

Defenses to a criminal charge provide either an excuse for the criminal conduct or a justification for that conduct. The insanity defense, for example, if proved, excuses the behavior that would otherwise be criminal. Self-defense, on the other hand, doesn't excuse the force used; if proved, the defense provides a justification for the use of the force. The distinction between excuse and justification is not of great importance, and the term "affirmative defense" is commonly used to refer to either kind of defense.

It is generally agreed that a state may place the burden of proof for the establishment of an affirmative defense on the defendant. In *Leland v. Oregon*, 343 U.S. 790 (1952) discussed in Chapter 3, the Supreme Court upheld a law that required a defendant to prove the defense of insanity beyond a reasonable doubt. Not all states do so; in the case of the insanity defense, a few states require the prosecution to prove the defendant was sane when the crime was committed.

It is also generally agreed that a state may not shift the burden of proof on an element of the crime to the defendant by designating the element as an affirmative defense. *Mullaney v. Wilbur*, 421 U.S. 197 (1975). However, it is not always clear that the state has made this improper designation. If the state has the power, as states usually do, to define what conduct is criminal, a statute that defines a crime broadly, and then makes affirmative defenses to the crime the burden of the defendant is not a violation of the burden of proof principle. For example, in many states it is a strict liability crime to sell impure food; the prosecution need only prove the food sold was impure. It would be permissible under *Mullaney* for a state to make it an affirmative defense that the seller used reasonable efforts to inspect the food sold, and then place the burden of proof on the defendant to prove the defense. On the other hand, *Mullaney* probably would prohibit a state from defining, as an example, first-degree burglary as any unprivileged entry of a dwelling, and then placing the burden on the defendant to show as an affirmative defense that the entry was not made at night, and thus only a second-degree felony. If "at night" is really an element that makes the burglary a more serious crime (as it is in some jurisdictions, see chapter 14), the state must bear the burden of proving that element.

Affirmative defenses come from various sources. Some, such as immunity or the alibi defense, are the product of state or federal statutes. Others, such as self-defense or duress, have evolved from the common law. Finally, a few affirmative defenses are mandated by the U.S. Constitution. The double jeopardy and speedy trial defenses are examples of defenses with their roots in the Constitution. In this chapter we identify the requirements for many of the affirmative defenses available in state and federal criminal prosecutions.

≡ Immunity as a Defense

Under some circumstances, persons who have committed crimes are exempt from prosecution for their actions, either temporarily or permanently. The basis for their claim to immunity might come from a federal or state statute, an international agreement, or in one case from the U.S. Constitution. The principle forms of immunity are discussed in this section.

Diplomatic Immunity

In 1972 the United States ratified the Vienna Convention on Diplomatic Relations, an international agreement on the status of diplomats stationed in a foreign country. More than a hundred other countries have ratified this Convention. Article 31.1 of the Convention states that a "diplomatic agent" shall enjoy full **immunity** from the criminal jurisdiction of the receiving state (in international law conventions, the word *state* means a "nation or country"). Article 37.1 extends this immunity to members of the diplomat's family. U.S. law (22 U.S.C. § 254(d)) states that any action brought against a person entitled to diplomatic immunity must be dismissed. Two recent federal cases illustrate the scope and limit of diplomatic immunity.

> **immunity** An exemption from criminal prosecution based on the U.S. Constitution, statutes, or international agreements.

In the 2006 case of *United States v. Kuznetsov*,[2] a federal district court denied diplomatic immunity to a Russian citizen employed by the United Nations in New York City. Although the defendant was at one time certified as a member of the Russian Federation Mission, and therefore entitled to immunity, when he became chairman of a UN committee the Russian Mission informed the State Department that the defendant was no longer part of the Mission. The court thus concluded that even though the defendant regarded himself as a "career Russian diplomat," during the years he worked for the UN, when the crimes he was charge with occurred, he was not a "diplomatic agent" and not entitled to immunity. The court also held the defendant lacked immunity under the United Nations Convention on Privileges and Immunities. That Convention applies only to "visiting foreign officials." The court concluded the defendant was not simply "visiting" the UN but was a full-time employee. As a result, the only immunity the defendant enjoyed under the Convention was immunity for acts done in his official capacity. This immunity can be waived by the secretary general of the UN, and it did in this case.

In the 2004 case of *United States v. Al-Hamdi*,[3] a federal court of appeals held that the diplomatic immunity given to members of a diplomat's family ends at age 21. The Vienna Convention leaves it to member states to determine the extent of the family immunity, the court held, and since the State Department issued a regulation setting the

21 years of age limit (23 if enrolled in school), that regulation was conclusive on the issue. The defendant, 26 years old when indicted, was thus convicted of being in possession of a firearm by a nonimmigrant alien.

Diplomatic immunity may be waived by the diplomat's home country, and in the case of serious crimes, the U.S. government frequently requests that waiver. An example of this waiver can be seen in *Van Den Borre v. State*,[4] in which Belgium waived immunity for a diplomat who was then convicted of a double murder.

Immunity for consular officers is not absolute, as it is for diplomats. Article 43 of the Vienna Convention provides that "[c]onsular officers ... shall not be amenable to the jurisdiction of [the host nation] in respect to acts performed in the exercise of consular functions." Criminal acts not so performed expose the consular offices to prosecution. For example, in *United States v. Cole*,[5] a consular officer was successfully prosecuted for smuggling money out of the United States in a diplomatic pouch. The court said the officer was not exercising consular functions.

Legislative Immunity

Article I, Section 6, of the U.S. Constitution provides that U.S. senators and representatives "shall in all cases except treason, felony and breach of the peace, be privileged from arrest during their attendance at the sessions of their respective houses, and in going to and returning from the same." Most state constitutions extend the same or similar privileges to state legislators while the state legislature is in session. Representatives, senators, and state legislators thus have a limited degree of temporary immunity while their legislative bodies are in session. Charges, however, could be held until the legislative body adjourns. Also, state legislators enjoy no immunity from prosecution for federal crimes.[6]

Witness Immunity

Federal and state prosecutors have the power to subpoena witnesses to give testimony to aid the prosecutors in investigations of crimes. Legislative bodies have a similar power. Under the Fifth Amendment, a witness cannot be compelled to testify against himself. A witness summoned to testify may thus refuse to testify by invoking his Fifth Amendment rights. To resolve this conflict, both the federal government and the states have passed various immunity statutes, under which a witness can be given immunity from prosecution and be compelled to answer questions that might be incriminating.

transactional immunity Total or full immunity for the criminal offense to which compelled testimony relates.

The principal federal immunity statute is 18 U.S.C. § 6002, which requires a witness to testify if called before a court, federal agency, or legislative body, on the condition his testimony may not be used against him in a criminal prosecution. Because of statements made by the Supreme Court in the 1895 case of *Counselman v. Hitchcock*, 142 U.S. 47, earlier versions of section 6002 had been interpreted as grants of total or **transactional immunity**. Under transactional immunity the witness cannot be prosecuted for any offense related to the subject matter of his testimony.

use immunity Prohibits prosecutorial authorities from using the compelled testimony in a criminal prosecution, but does not make the witness totally immune from prosecution based on evidence other than the witness's testimony and not derived from that testimony.

Congress was concerned that total immunity hampered federal efforts to combat crime. In 1970 Congress enacted the current version of section 6002, which grants only **use immunity**. Under use immunity, the statements made by the witness may not be used in subsequent prosecutions, but the witness can be prosecuted for the crimes about which they testified if other evidence is used to convict them. The U.S. Supreme Court upheld the constitutionality of section 6002 in *Kastigar v. United States*, 406 U.S. 441 (1972), holding that the statute gives the same protection as the Fifth Amendment, and that is all the protection Congress is required to give a witness.

Many states have enacted both transactional and use immunity statutes, with the prosecution deciding which immunity to request. For example, Illinois has a transactional immunity statute, 725 ILCS 5/106-1, that states after a request by the State a court "may order" a witness to testify by granting immunity from prosecution for the crimes about which the witness testifies. The use immunity statute, 725 ILSC 5/106-2.5, provides that after a request by the State, the court "shall order" a witness to testify with immunity from use of his testimony. In *People v. Ousley*, 919 N.E.2d 875 (Ill. 2009), the Illinois Supreme Court reversed a decision of a district court judge who refused the prosecution's request to grant use immunity. In *Ousley*, three defendants were charged with murder, and the prosecution requested a grant of use immunity to one of the defendants so he could testify against the other two defendants. The trial court refused the request, stating concerns about the effect such testimony might have on the rights of the other defendants. On appeal, the Illinois Supreme Court held that the use immunity statutory was mandatory, and as a result the prosecution's request for an order granting use immunity should have been granted.

☰ Mistake or Ignorance of Fact as a Defense[7]

At times, a mistake of fact can serve as a defense to criminal liability. For example, suppose a man walking out of a restaurant takes the wrong coat from the coat rack. A few minutes later, the true owner of the coat angrily complains to a police officer. The officer stops the man with the wrong coat blocks away and brings him back to the restaurant. Investigation shows that the man does have a coat similar to the coat that he walked away in. Has the man committed a theft, or has he made an honest mistake of fact?

The common law rule is that an honest mistake or ignorance of fact is a defense if it negates the existence of a state of mind essential to the crime. Did the man take the coat with intent to deprive the owner of possession of his coat? The following case also illustrates this rule.

Morissette v. United States

Supreme Court of the United States (1952) 342 U.S. 246, 72 S. Ct. 240

The defendant had been deer hunting in northern Michigan on government property marked "Danger—Keep Out," that had been used as a bombing range. However, the property was used extensively for hunting by people in the area. When the defendant failed to get a deer, he decided to salvage some of the spent bomb casings that had been lying around on the property for years. In broad daylight, he hauled out three truckloads and with much work realized a profit of $84. He was charged with and convicted of knowingly stealing and converting U.S. property. The trial judge would not allow the defense that the defendant believed that the property was abandoned, unwanted, and considered of no value to the government. After the trial court ruled that "this particular offense requires no element of criminal intent," the U.S. Supreme Court reversed the conviction, pointing out that criminal liability generally requires an "evil-meaning mind (and) an evil-doing hand," and held:

> Had the jury convicted on proper instructions it would be the end of the matter. But juries are not bound by what seems inescapable logic to judges. They might have concluded that the heaps of spent casings left in the hinterland to rust away presented an appearance of unwanted and abandoned junk, and that lack of any conscious deprivation of property or intentional injury was indicated by Morissette's good character, the openness of the taking, crushing and transporting of the casings, and the candor with which it was all admitted. They might have refused to brand Morissette as a thief. Had they done so, that too would have been the end of the matter.
> Reversed.

An honest and reasonable belief in circumstances that, if true, would make an act innocent, is thus a defense to a criminal charge. In the following cases, defendants raised the defense of honest mistake of fact:

- *An honest belief that the property a defendant purchased was not stolen property was a good defense because the crime required knowledge.* Willis v. State, 802 S.W.2d 337 (Tex. App. 1991)
- *Defendant's defense that he found the hat he was charged with shoplifting was a good defense because the crime required intent to take property of another person.* Binnie v. State, 1991 WL 1251 (Md.)
- *Defendant was given the baby by a friend, and her belief that the baby was lawfully turned over to her was a defense to a charge of kidnapping of the child.* Miller v. State, 815 S.W.2d 582 (Tex. App. 1991)
- *In a rape charge, a reasonable but mistaken belief that consent to sex was given was a good defense.* People v. Mayberry, 542 P.2d 1337 (Calif. 1975); and People v. Williams, 52 CrL 1350 (Calif. 1993).
- *Honest belief that a shotgun's safety was on was not a good defense to a manslaughter charge, because the crime required only negligence.* People v. Wilson, 877 N.E.2d 761 (N.Y. App. 2009).

Strict Liability Crimes and the Defense of Mistake

When a state legislature or the Congress of the United States creates a strict liability crime, the defense of mistake of fact cannot be used, because criminal liability comes from simply doing the forbidden act without any requirement for the state or government to prove any mental fault (see Chapter 3).

- Statutory rape in which the defendant had sex with an underage child and could not use the defense of honest but mistaken belief as to the age of the child: *Jenkins v. State,* 110 Nev. 865, 1994 WL 389178 (1994); *State v. Stiffler,* 117 Idaho 405, 1990 WL 25145 (1990); *United States v. Ransom,* 942 F.2d 775 (10th Cir. 1991); *Commonwealth v. Knap,* 592 N.E.2d 747 (Mass. 1992); *Garnett v. State,* 322 Md. 571, 632 A.2d 797 (1993).[8]
- In assaulting a federal officer, the defendant cannot use the honest but mistaken belief that he or she did not know the victim was a federal officer: *United States v. Feola,* 420 U.S. 671; 95 S. Ct. 1255 (1975); and *United States v. Goldson,* 954 F.2d 51 (2d Cir. 1992).
- In use of employment of a minor in Minnesota for nude dancing, the honest but mistaken belief as to the age of the child cannot be used: *State v. Fan,* 445 N.W.2d 243 (Minn. App. 1989); and *Minnesota v. White,* 464 N.W.2d 585 (Minn. App. 1990), *review denied* 502 U.S. 819, 112 S. Ct. 77 (1991).

Mistake or Ignorance of Criminal Law

The full scope of the Latin maxim *Ignorantia legis neminem excusat* ("Ignorance of the law excuses no one") may have caused Blackstone to change the phrase in his *Commentaries* (4 *Commentaries,* 27) to "Ignorance of the law which every one is bound to know, excuses no man." Blackstone's statement is a far better expression of the law, because courts will not allow a defendant who has committed an offense that is generally well known to the public to argue ignorance or mistake of that law. Serious offenses, such as murder, rape, robbery, and theft, are violations not only of the statutory law but also of moral and ethical laws. Courts would not seriously consider a defense of mistake or ignorance of such laws. Nor would courts ordinarily permit a person charged with a traffic violation in the state in which he or she is licensed to drive to argue ignorance of the traffic laws of that state. It is presumed that the holder of a license knows the traffic laws when the license is received or renewed.

But what of the hundreds of criminal laws that are not well known? The President's Commission on Law Enforcement and Administration of Justice reported in 1966 in *The Challenge of Crime in a Free Society* that the federal government alone has defined more than 2,800 crimes and observed that state and local governments have defined even more numerous offenses (p. 18). The following U.S. Supreme Court cases illustrate the complexity and great numbers of laws that exist today:

Cheek v. United States

Supreme Court of the United States (1991) 498 U.S. 192, 111 S. Ct. 604

Mr. Cheek was an airline pilot who did not file federal income tax returns for six years. Cheek argued that he did not "willfully" fail to file income tax returns and that he honestly believed his failure to file returns was lawful.

Because of the complexity of the U.S. tax laws, the Supreme Court held that the "willfully" requirement of the criminal charge against Cheek could not be met if the alleged violator was honestly confused about the meaning of the law.

Other courts now view this case as an exception to the general rule that ignorance of the law is no excuse. (See the 1993 case of *Sanford v. State*, 499 N.W.2d 496, reviewing court decisions.)

Lambert v. California

Supreme Court of the United States (1957) 355 U.S. 225, 78 S. Ct. 240

The defendant was charged with and convicted of failing to register as required under a Los Angeles municipal ordinance that requires "any convicted person" who was in the city for longer than five days to register with local authorities. The defendant had been convicted of forgery and had lived in Los Angeles for more than seven years without registering. In a 5–4 decision, the U.S. Supreme Court held that the registration provision of the ordinance violated the due process requirement of the Fourteenth Amendment.

Justice William O. Douglas for the majority stated:

The rule that "ignorance of the law will not excuse" ... is deep in our law, as is the principle that of all the powers of local government, the police power is "one of the least limitable." ... On the other hand, due process places some limits on its exercise. Engrained in our concept of due process is the requirement of notice. Notice is sometimes essential so that the citizen has the chance to defend charges. Notice is required before property interests are disturbed, before assessments are made, before penalties are assessed. Notice is required in a myriad of situations where a penalty or forfeiture might be suffered for mere failure to act....

This appellant on first becoming aware of her duty to register was given no opportunity to comply with the law and avoid its penalty, even though her default was entirely innocent.... Where a person did not know of the duty to register and where there was no proof of the probability of such knowledge, he may not be convicted consistently with due process. Were it otherwise, the evil would be as great as it is when the law is written too fine or in a language foreign to the community.

mistake of law A claim by a defendant that the defendant did not know the action taken violated the criminal law.

Sometimes what appears to be a **mistake of law** may nonetheless provide a defense. For example, in *United States v. Smith*,[9] a government employee was charged with violating the federal Espionage Act. That act makes it a crime to reveal classified information with the intent to cause injury to the United States. The defendant revealed classified information to two individuals the defendant believed were CIA officials. The defendant claimed he believed he was authorized by law to reveal the information to CIA officials, though in fact he was not authorized to do so. The court said his defense, if believed, negated the "intent to harm the United States" element of the crime, and could be raised.

The mistake of law in the previous case provided a defense because the defendant's mistaken belief negated a required mental state, the "intent to harm" the United States. Where the mistake of law is simply that the defendant did not know the actions he or she took were against the criminal law, but the defendant otherwise had the required mental state, it is rare for the mistake to provide a defense.

≡ Intoxication or Drugged Condition as a Defense

Voluntary intoxication or drugged condition as a defense to the commission of criminal acts is frequently raised unsuccessfully. Crimes that require only a general intent, that is, only the intent to do the act, do not permit an intoxication defense. For example, in the 2001 case of *United States v. Sewell*,[10] a defendant charged with robbery attempted to defend by offering evidence that he was high on crack cocaine when he committed the robbery. The court concluded that robbery was a general intent crime and rejected the defense.

Crimes that require a specific intent as to one or more elements of the crime do permit a defense based on voluntary intoxication or drugged condition. To assert the intoxication defense, the defendant must be charged with a specific intent crime, such as intentional murder, kidnapping, or arson. The degree of intoxication must be so great "as to render (the defendant) incapable of purposeful or knowing conduct."[11] *State v. Sexton*, discussed in Chapter 5, is an example of this use of a drugged condition.

Even if the intoxication defense successfully negates a specific intent, the defendant may still be convicted of a lesser offense requiring only general intent. For example, although defendants may lack the specific intent to commit murder, they could be convicted of a lesser, general intent crime, such as second-degree murder or manslaughter.[12]

A few states have eliminated the defense of voluntary intoxication entirely. Montana not only did away with the defense of intoxication but also prohibited any consideration of the defense of intoxication by a fact finder (judge or jury). The Montana law was challenged before the U.S. Supreme Court in 1996. In the case of *Montana v. Egelhoff*, the Supreme Court found that the Montana law did not violate due process protections of the U.S. Constitution.[13]

The involuntary intoxication or drugged condition can be a defense to a criminal charge if the trier of fact (the jury or judge) believes the defendant's story, supported by credible evidence, that (1) he or she did not voluntarily take the drug or intoxicant and instead was tricked or forced into taking the substance and (2) the defendant became so intoxicated or drugged that he or she was not able to mentally form the specific intent necessary for the crime charged but was physically able to commit the crime.

≡ Duress, Coercion, or Compulsion as a Defense

If a person charged with a crime can show his actions were the result of duress, coercion, or compulsion, under some but not all situations, a valid defense would be raised. In attempting to use the defense, defendants must admit that they committed the offense charged but assert that they were forced to do so to avoid death or serious bodily injury to themselves or others. Defining **duress** and coercion in *People v. Sanders,* the court stated:

duress A defense to criminal prosecution on the grounds that the defendant was forced to commit the criminal act.

> In order for duress or fear produced by threats or menace to be a valid, legal excuse for doing anything, which otherwise would be criminal, the act must have been done under such threats or menaces as show that the life of the person threatened or menaced was in danger, or that there was reasonable cause to believe and actual belief that there was such danger. The danger must not be one of future violence, but of present and immediate violence at the time of the commission of the forbidden act. The danger of death at some future time in the absence of danger of death at the time of the commission of the offense will not excuse. A person who aids and assists in the commission of the crime, or who commits a crime, is not relieved from criminality on account of fears excited by threats or menaces unless the danger be to life, nor unless that danger be present and immediate.[14]

One area where duress or coercion is offered as a defense involves escape from prison or other custody. In 1977, the Supreme Court of Delaware held that "intolerable conditions" were not justification for escape from prison, because the defendants failed to give sufficient proof that such justification existed.[15] The court held that the tests used by California courts could be employed in determining justification.

The California tests, established in *People v. Lovercamp,* hold that justification is available as a defense to the charge of escape from prison only when

1. The prisoner is faced with a specific threat of death, forcible sexual attack, or substantial bodily injury in the immediate future.
2. There is no time for a complaint to the authorities or there exists a history of futile complaints that make any result from such complaints illusory.
3. There is no time or opportunity to resort to the courts.
4. There is no evidence of force or violence used toward prison personnel or other "innocent" persons in the escape.
5. The prisoner immediately reports to the proper authorities when he or she has attained a position of safety from the immediate threat.[16]

In 1980, the U.S. Supreme Court ruled as follows in the escape case of *United States v. Bailey:*

> We therefore hold that, where a criminal defendant is charged with escape and claims that he is entitled to an instruction on the theory of duress or necessity, he must proffer evidence of a bona fide effort to surrender or return to custody as soon as the claimed duress or necessity had lost its coercive force. We have reviewed the evidence examined elaborately in the majority and dissenting opinions below, and find the case not even close, even under respondents' versions of the facts, as to whether they either surrendered or offered to surrender at their earliest possible opportunity. Since we have determined that this is an indispensable element of the defense of duress or necessity, respondents were not entitled to any instruction on such a theory. Vague and necessarily self-serving statements of defendants or witnesses as to future good intentions or ambiguous conduct simply do not support a finding of this element of the defense.[17]

Duress or coercion is generally not a defense to a charge of murder. Under the common law, the defense of duress was not available to a defendant in a murder or treason charge. Blackstone stated that the reason for this was that a man under duress "ought rather to die himself than escape by the murder of an innocent."[18] This apparently is the common law today in more than half the states and in the United Kingdom. About 20 states define the defense of duress by statute, and most do not allow the defense in murder cases (and sometimes in other serious crimes). A few states allow the defense in murder cases: *MacKool v. State*, 213 S.W.3d 618 (Ark. 2005); *State v. Heinemann*, 920 A.2d 278 (Conn. 2007). Also, in a few states the defense of duress in a murder charge may be proved for the purpose of reducing the charge of first-degree murder to manslaughter.[19]

Even in those states that do not permit the defense of duress or coercion in murder cases, the defense is generally available to a charge of felony murder (see Chapter 10). In the treatise *Criminal Law* (2nd ed., West/Wadsworth, 1980) § 5.3 b, p. 435-436 La Fave and Scott state, "The law properly recognizes that one is justified in aiding a robbery if he is forced by threats to do so to save his life; he should not lose the defense because his threateners (*sic*) unexpectedly kill someone in the course of the robbery and thus convert a mere robbery into a murder." In *McMillan v. State*, 956 A.2d 716 (Md. App. 2009) the court held that although Maryland does not permit the duress defense in murder cases, where the murder charge is based on the felony-murder rule the defendant may prove duress forced him to participate in the underlying felony. However, the *McMillan* court concluded that the threat of future harm made by gang members who forced the defendant to help them secure entry for a home invasion was not sufficient proof of the "imminent" threat to life required for the duress defense.

Necessity or Choice of Evils Defense[20]

A person who, because of necessity, performs an act that otherwise would constitute a crime may use the justification of **necessity** as a defense if the "harm or evil sought to be avoided by such conduct is greater than that sought to be prevented by the law defining the offense charged."[21]

necessity A defense to criminal prosecution on the grounds that the harm to be avoided outweighed the harm caused by the crime committed. Necessity will not justify taking another person's life.

EXAMPLE: An airplane crashes at night in an isolated area. It is very cold and rescue is not likely until daylight, so the survivors break into a summer cottage and use the food and blankets in the cottage to comfort the injured and sustain themselves until help arrives. In this example, the necessity of breaking into the cottage is obvious and serves as a justification for breaking into the cottage. It is likely the survivors would openly admit what they had done, and the owner of the cottage would be assured of compensation for the damages. Law enforcement officers and the prosecutor would not consider criminal charges, and the matter would not receive further attention.

While the common law recognized the necessity defense, and was thus incorporated into the law of most states, the existence of the defense in federal prosecutions is unclear. In *United States v. Oakland Cannabis Buyers' Co-op*, 532 U.S. 483, 490 (2001), the U.S. Supreme Court stated: "[W]e note that it is an open question whether federal courts ever have authority to recognize a necessity defense not provided by statute." There, the Court did not decide the question, simply holding that even if available, the necessity defense was incompatible with the Controlled Substances Act, and thus not available. A few lower federal courts have held that the defense is available in prosecutions under the felon-in-possession charge under 18 U.S.C § 922(g), though the statute does not expressly state such a defense exists. See *United States v. Alston*, 526 F.3d 91 (3d Cir. 2008).

In 1986, the Eighth Circuit Federal Court of Appeals described the elements of the necessity defense, in those situations where the defense is available:

> A vital element of any necessity defense is the lack of a reasonable alternative to violating the law; that is, the harm to be avoided must be so imminent that, absent the defendant's criminal acts, the harm is certain to occur. *United States v. Bailey*, 444 U.S. 394, 410, 100 S. Ct. 624, 634, 62 L. Ed.2d 575 (1980). As the Tenth Circuit has emphasized: "The defense of necessity does not arise from a 'choice' of several courses of action, it is instead based on a real emergency. It can be asserted only by a defendant who was confronted with such a crisis as a personal danger, a crisis which did not permit a selection from among several solutions, some of which did not involve criminal acts. It is obviously not a defense to charges arising from a typical protest."[22]

Cases in which defendants unsuccessfully used the necessity defense include the following:

- Defendant forced his way into a mobile home because he said he had to use the telephone (other telephones were available nearby). *People v. Haynes*, 223 Ill. App. 3d 126, 584 N.E.2d 1041 (1991)
- A street person broke into a car because he said he had not eaten for a day. *Lightner v. State*, 843 S.W.2d 161 (Tex. App. 1992)
- Unlawful trespass on a naval installation by a protestor who claimed he was attempting to cause the dispersion of nuclear submarines from the naval base and surrounding waters. The protestor unsuccessfully argued that such deployment was the "greater evil" and that his decision to trespass the lesser evil.[23]

The necessity defense, like the duress and coercion defense discussed above, is not available to justify the death of another person.

coercion A person who forces (coerces) another to commit a crime can be charged and convicted of the crime committed in addition to other offenses.

≡ Can One Kill to Save Oneself?

The question of whether a person can kill to save his or her own life came before courts many years ago in the following famous cases.

> ### *United States v. Holmes*
>
> Court of Appeals of the United States (1842) 26 Fed. Cas. 360
>
> The defendant was a member of the crew of a ship that sank, leaving him and many others in an overcrowded lifeboat. Because the ship's mate feared that the boat would sink, he ordered the male passengers thrown overboard, leaving the women and the ship's crew. The defendant assisted in throwing sixteen of the men out of the boat to their deaths. A grand jury refused to indict him for murder, so he was charged with and convicted of manslaughter.

Rex v. Dudley and Stephens

Queen's Bench Division (1884) 14 Q.B.D. 273

The defendants and another man and a boy were shipwrecked and adrift in an open boat for eighteen days. After seven days without food or water, the defendants suggested that the men kill the boy, who was then very weak. When the other man refused, the defendants killed the boy, and all the men fed on the boy's body. Four days later, they were rescued. The jury, by a special verdict, found that the men would probably have died within the four days had they not fed on the boy's body. The jury also found that the boy would probably have died before being rescued. However, the defendants were convicted of murder, with the sentence commuted to six months' imprisonment.

These two cases have been debated by judges, lawyers, and law students throughout the English-speaking world for years. Few people urge that the doctrine of necessity be expanded to full forgiveness instead of the partial forgiveness of manslaughter used in both the cases given. In commenting on the problem, former U.S. Supreme Court Justice Benjamin N. Cardozo observed: "Where two or more are overtaken by a common disaster, there is no right on the part of one to save the lives of some, by killing of another. There is no rule of human jettison."[24]

THE USE OF THE DUDLEY CASE IN ETHICS CLASSES TODAY

The *Dudley* case discussed earlier, while decided in 1884, continues to be used in classrooms throughout the United States today. In 2009, a Public Broadcasting Program featured the case in an ethics discussion with several hundred Harvard University students. The various choices open to the shipwrecked sailors in the lifeboat were discussed, including the ethical and legal implications of each choice.

Using the criminal code of your state, would police and prosecutors likely seek criminal charges today for the following choices made by the persons in the lifeboat?

a.) A lottery was suggested in the *Dudley* case, but not used. Suppose the lottery idea was adopted, and the loser was killed. Would the remaining persons be subject to criminal charges? Would it matter if they did or did not feed on the dead person's body?

b.) Suppose the boy (or another person) agreed to be killed in order to save the others. Would the others be charged with a crime?

c.) In the facts of the *Dudley* case, should all the persons on board the lifeboat be charged, or only those who actually killed the boy?

The attitude of the British courts today is probably reflected by the 1971 case of *Southwark London Borough v. Williams:*

alibi A defense to criminal prosecution on the grounds that the defendant physically could not have committed the crime because at the time the crime was committed, he or she was at another place.

[T]he law regards with the deepest suspicion any remedies of self-help, and permits these remedies to be resorted to only in very special circumstances. The reason for such circumspection is clear—necessity can very easily become simply a mask for anarchy.[25]

≡ Alibi as a Criminal Defense

In using the defense of **alibi**, the defendant is asserting that he or she physically could not have committed the crime, because at the time the crime was committed, he or she was at another place.

EXAMPLE: X is charged with robbery and has been identified by two witnesses and the victim as the man who robbed a liquor store. X uses the defense of alibi and argues that it was physically impossible for him to rob the store because he was at his mother's home 100 miles away at the time of the robbery. His mother and his wife corroborate X's story, stating that they were there also.

Because an alibi can be easily fabricated, it must be carefully investigated. Many states have statutes requiring defendants who plan to use an alibi defense to serve notice on the prosecutor before trial. These statutes are meant to safeguard against the wrongful use of alibis, as they give law enforcement agencies and prosecutors necessary notice and time to investigate the merits of the proposed alibi.

Alibi Notice Statutes

Alibi notice statutes require defendants to make disclosures regarding their cases. Such disclosure includes the place where the defendant claimed to have been at the time the crime was committed and the names and addresses of witnesses to the alibi, if known.

In the 1973 case of *Wardius v. Oregon,* the U.S. Supreme Court held that when a defendant is compelled to disclose information regarding his or her case, the state must also make similar disclosures. The U.S. Supreme Court held:

> [In] the absence of a strong showing of state interests to the contrary, discovery must be a two-way street. The State may not insist that trials be run as a "search for truth" so far as defense witnesses are concerned, while maintaining "poker game" secrecy for its own witnesses. It is fundamentally unfair to require a defendant to divulge the details of his own case while at the same time subjecting him to the hazard of surprise concerning refutation of the very pieces of evidence which he disclosed to the State.[26]

Alibi notice statutes now require disclosure by prosecutors as well as defendants.

An alibi presented to and believed by a jury constitutes a complete defense to the crime charged. Even if the alibi raises only a reasonable doubt in the mind of a jury, it becomes a good defense because the jury cannot convict if a reasonable doubt exists. If only two or three of the jurors believe the alibi, a hung jury may result. The burden is not on the defendant to show that he or she was not at the scene of the crime; it is on the state to show beyond reasonable doubt that the defendant *was* at the scene and committed the crime. Charges of perjury, solicitation to commit perjury, or subornation of perjury have resulted when it has been shown that alibi witnesses testified falsely or that attempts were made to persuade people to testify falsely.

≡ The Defense That the Defendant Was Acting Under the Authority, Direction, or Advice of Another

A person who commits an act that is obviously criminal, such as arson or murder, and then attempts to use as a defense the fact that he or she was acting under the direction of a superior officer or on the advice of an attorney or another person would ordinarily be held fully liable for such an offense. The general rule is that one who performs a criminal act under the advice, direction, or order of another cannot use such a defense.

However, because hundreds of crimes are not well known to the general public, the U.S. Supreme Court, in 1908, quoted with approval a jury instruction stating that when a person fully and honestly lays all the facts before his counsel, and in good faith and honestly follows such advice, relying upon it and believing it to be correct, and only intends that his acts shall be lawful, he could not be convicted of crime which involves willful and unlawful intent; even if such advice were an inaccurate construction of the law. But, on the other hand, no man can willfully and knowingly violate the law and excuse himself from consequences thereof by pleading that he followed the advice of counsel.[27]

In the 1975 case of *Toomey v. Tolin,* the Court held that following the advice of a legal advisor was a complete defense for law enforcement officers involved in a civil suit for false arrest and malicious prosecution.[28] Other cases are:

Cox v. Louisiana

Supreme Court of the United States (1965) 379 U.S. 559, 85 S. Ct. 476

Among other charges, the defendant was convicted of demonstrating "in or near" a courthouse in violation of a Louisiana law modeled after a 1949 federal statute. The U.S. Supreme Court reversed the conviction, stating:

> *The highest police officials of the city, in the presence of the Sheriff and Mayor, in effect, told the demonstrators that they could meet where they did, 101 feet from the courthouse steps, but could not meet closer to the courthouse. In effect, appellant was advised that a demonstration at the place it was held would not be one "near" the courthouse within the terms of the statute.*[29]

Raley v. Ohio

Supreme Court of the United States (1959) 360 U.S. 423, 79 S. Ct. 1257

The U.S. Supreme Court held "that the Due Process Clause prevented conviction of persons for refusing to answer questions of a state investigating commission when they relied upon assurance of the commission, either express or implied, that they had a privilege under state law to refuse to answer, though in fact this privilege was not available to them." The Court stated that this would be to sanction an indefensible sort of **entrapment** by the State—convicting a citizen for exercising a privilege which the State had clearly told him was available to him.

The Defense of "I Acted on the Orders of My Boss"

In the following highly publicized situations, defendants used the defense that "I acted on the orders of others."

- In 1972, U.S. Army Lt. William Calley Jr. was charged with the murder of 22 infants, children, women, and old men in the village of My Lai, Vietnam. Calley used the defense that he acted under orders of his superiors in conducting the search-and-destroy operation in the manner he did. More than 400 Vietnamese women, children, and old men were killed in the operation. *United States v. Calley,* 48 C.M.R. 19, 22 U.S.C.M.A. 534 (1973)[30]
- Some of the high-ranking Nazi officers and officials tried for criminal offenses after World War II used the defense that they were following orders from their superiors.

The Nuremberg Court, composed of judges from the Allied nations, held that this defense was not available when the orders given violated commonly accepted standards of humanity. (See Chapter 2 of this text for more material on the Nuremberg trials.)

- As a result of the Watergate burglary in 1972, criminal charges were issued. Some of the people involved argued that they acted on the authority of others. In the case of *United States v. Ehrlichman,* 546 F.2d 910 (D.C.C. 1976), Ehrlichman failed in his attempt to persuade the court to permit him to use the mistake of law defense.

≡ The Defense of Double Jeopardy

The Fifth Amendment of the U.S. Constitution provides that "no person … shall … for the same offense … be twice put in jeopardy of life or limb." In the 1978 case of *United States v. Scott,* the U.S. Supreme Court, quoting other Supreme Court cases, held that the Double Jeopardy Clause ensures

> that the State with all its resources and power should not be allowed to make repeated attempts to convict an individual for an alleged offense, thereby subjecting him to embarrassment, expense and ordeal and compelling him to live in a continuing state of anxiety and insecurity, as well as enhancing the possibility that even though innocent he may be found guilty.[31]

double jeopardy A defense, stated in the Fifth Amendment, to prosecution on the grounds that the defendant has been tried before on the same charge, and acquitted.

Therefore, **double jeopardy** means that a person who has been acquitted by a judge or a jury may not be tried again, even if subsequent investigation reveals evidence that proves conclusively that the defendant is guilty. If a defendant is found not guilty because of insanity, the person may not be tried again for the same crime, even if the person is later found sane and normal.

The Times When Jeopardy Attaches

In the 1984 case of *Press-Enterprise Co. v. Superior Court of California, Riverside County,*[32] the U.S. Supreme Court pointed out that jeopardy attaches when a jury is sworn.[33] In a nonjury trial, the Court stated that jeopardy attaches when the first witness is sworn.[34]

Prosecution by Both State and Federal Governments

Because most crimes are crimes only against a state, only the state may prosecute. Some crimes, however, are offenses not only against the state but also the federal government. The robbery of a federally insured bank or savings and loan association is an example.

The question of whether the state and federal governments may both prosecute for such offenses has come before the U.S. Supreme Court more than a dozen times. Justice Oliver Wendell Holmes, in noting that both state and federal prosecution in such cases is not in violation of the Fifth Amendment, stated that the rule "is too plain to need more than a statement."[35] The reasoning is presented in the 1959 case of *Bartkus v. Illinois* as follows:

> Every citizen of the United States is also a citizen of a State or territory. He may be said to owe allegiance to two sovereigns, and may be liable to punishment for an infraction of the laws of either. The same act may be an offense or transgression of the law of both. That either or both may (if they see fit) punish such an offender cannot be doubted. Yet it cannot be truly averted that the offender has been twice punished for the same offense; but

OTHER IMPORTANT U.S. SUPREME COURT CASES ON DOUBLE JEOPARDY

Heath v. Alabama

Supreme Court of the United States (1985) 474 U.S. 82, 106 S. Ct. 433 (1985)

Heath hired two men in Georgia to kidnap his pregnant wife from their Alabama home and kill her. The murder then took place in Georgia. Both states convicted the defendant of murder. The Supreme Court affirmed both convictions under the "dual sovereignty" doctrine, holding that it would be shocking to "deny a State its power to enforce its criminal laws because another State has won the race to the courthouse."

United States v. Lara

Supreme Court of the United States (2004), 124 S. Ct. 1628

Conviction in a tribal court was under the tribe's sovereign power and thus did not prevent the government from charging the defendant for the same conduct under federal law in a federal court.

Missouri v. Hunter

Supreme Court of the United States (1983) 459 U.S. 359, 103 S. Ct. 673

Although the Double Jeopardy Clause forbids multiple punishments for the same offense, it does not forbid the imposition, at the same trial, of convictions and punishments for two or more offenses that are specifically intended by the legislature to carry separate punishments. In the Hunter case, the defendant's conviction and punishment for robbery and armed criminal action was affirmed even though the offenses constituted the same crime. Therefore, a defendant may be charged and convicted of multiple crimes arising out of one criminal act if the state legislature intends it.

Green v. United States

Supreme Court of the United States (1957) 355 U.S. 184, 78 S. Ct. 221

The law attaches particular significance to an acquittal. To permit a second trial after an acquittal, however mistaken the acquittal may have been, would present an unacceptably high risk that the government, with

only that by one act he has committed two offenses, for each of which he is justly punishable. He could not plead the punishment by one in bar to a conviction by the other.[36]

In *Bartkus v. Illinois,* the defendant was tried in a federal court and acquitted of robbing a federally insured bank. He was then indicted by an Illinois grand jury and convicted on substantially the same evidence used in the federal court. The Illinois court sentenced him to life imprisonment under the Illinois Habitual Criminal Statute. The U.S. Supreme Court affirmed the conviction, holding that the second trial did not violate the Fifth Amendment of the U.S. Constitution.

Since *Bartkus v. Illinois,* however, many states, including Illinois, have passed legislation that forbids prosecution after another jurisdiction has prosecuted the defendant for the same crime. In such states, the law of the state, and not the Double Jeopardy Clause, forbids prosecution after prosecution in another jurisdiction.[37]

The Meaning of Separate Offense

Double jeopardy does not bar successive prosecutions of a defendant convicted of one offense if the subsequent prosecution involves a different or separate offense.

its vastly superior resources, might wear down the defendant so that "even though innocent he may be found guilty."

Smalis v. Pennsylvania

Supreme Court of the United States (1986) 476 U.S. 140, 106 S. Ct.1745

The Supreme Court held that the granting of a "demurrer was an acquittal under the Double Jeopardy Clause." A demurrer is a finding that as a matter of law, the prosecution's evidence is insufficient to establish the factual guilt of a defendant. Further prosecution is forbidden.

Ball v. United States

Supreme Court of the United States (1985) 105 S. Ct. 1668

When there is a double jeopardy violation, the U.S. Supreme Court ruled that the remedy is to vacate (drop) one conviction and retain the conviction with the "most serious punishment."

Lockhart v. Nelson

Supreme Court of the United States (1988) 488 U.S. 33, 109 S. Ct. 285, 44 CrL 3031

> It has long been settled ... that the Double Jeopardy Clause's general prohibition against successive prosecutions does not prevent the government from retrying a defendant who succeeds in getting his first conviction set aside, through direct appeal or collateral attack, because of some error in the proceedings leading to conviction.
>
> ... This rule, which is a well-established part of our constitutional jurisprudence, ... is necessary in order to ensure the "sound administration of justice."

The Double Jeopardy Clause does not forbid retrial so long as the sum of the evidence, erroneously admitted or not, would have been sufficient to sustain a guilty verdict.

The meaning of *separate* adopted by the U.S. Supreme Court has changed over time. In *Blockburger v. United States*, the Court adopted the following "different offense" rule:

> The applicable rule is that where the same acts or transaction constitutes a violation of two distinct statutory provisions, the test to be applied to determine whether there are two offenses or only one, is whether each provision requires proof of an additional fact which the other does not.[38]

This rule prevented, among other things, prosecutions for so-called lesser included offenses, that is, offenses whose elements were included in the greater offense.

In the early 1990s, the Supreme Court in *Grady v. Corbin* appeared to modify the *Blockburger* "same element" test, holding in one case that successive prosecutions arising out of the "same conduct" were barred by the Double Jeopardy Clause.[39] If the same conduct violated two criminal statutes, successive prosecutions were barred, even though the statutes had different elements. Such a rule would prevent some prosecutions that would be possible under *Blockburger*.[40] However, in 1993, the Supreme Court reversed *Grady v. Corbin* and the "same conduct" rule.[41] It held that the *Blockburger* "same element" test determined double jeopardy questions.

Other Times When the Defense of Double Jeopardy Could Not Be Used Successfully

The defense of double jeopardy could not be used successfully in the following situations:

When one legal action is civil and the other is a criminal action.	The O. J. Simpson case illustrates this principle of law. O. J. Simpson was acquitted of murder charges in a Los Angeles criminal case, but the families of the victims then commenced civil lawsuits against Simpson and won jury awards of more than $34 million.
When a hung jury occurs or in most cases in which a mistrial is declared before jeopardy is attached.	After two all-white juries were unable to reach verdicts in a criminal trial of Byron De La Beckwith, a white supremacist, he was convicted in a third trial for the murder of Medgar Evers, a civil rights activist. The third murder trial was 31 years after the first trial, but neither federal nor state laws have a statute of limitations for murder.
If there is serious fraud in the first trial, a defendant has not been placed at risk, so the defendant cannot claim double jeopardy.	It was shown in the 1997 U.S. Supreme Court case of *Illinois v. Aleman*, 519 U.S. 1128, that an Illinois judge accepted a $10,000 bribe to acquit Aleman of murder. In the first such case in American legal history, the second Illinois trial judge held that Aleman had never been placed in jeopardy and that "absent such risk, the claim of double jeopardy is more imagined than real."
If the prior legal action is an in rem civil forfeiture, the following criminal action is not barred (stopped) by double jeopardy.	The U.S. Supreme Court has held repeatedly that *in rem* (against a thing, a car, a house) civil forfeiture actions are neither "punishment" nor criminal for the purposes of the Double Jeopardy Clause if Congress or the state legislative body meant such actions to be civil and not punitive in form and effect. *United States v. Ursery*, 1996 WL 340815 (1996).
Under the "dual sovereignty" doctrine, different governments may each file separate criminal actions for the same criminal act.	Unless a state statute forbids it, a state may charge and convict a person who has already been charged in a federal court, in another state, or in a foreign country, because the **"dual sovereignty" doctrine** permits different governments to each file separate criminal actions for the same criminal act committed against sovereign governments. In the 1996 case of *United States v. Guzman*, 1996 WL 294401, Guzman violated the drug laws of both the Netherlands and the United States and could be convicted for the same criminal acts by both countries.

"dual sovereignty" doctrine A doctrine that different governments may each file separate criminal actions for the same criminal act.

res judicata The doctrine that prevents a second determination of a charge or issue once it has been judicially determined in a case involving the same parties.

Res Judicata and Collateral Estoppel as Part of the Double Jeopardy Guarantee

Assume Smith has a civil claim against Jones and Baker. She decides to sue Jones. If Smith loses her case, the controversy between the two people has then been adjudicated, and Smith cannot commence a new lawsuit against Jones based on the same issue. The principle of **res judicata** (the issue has been determined) gives Jones a defense to the second lawsuit. Moreover, if Smith decides to sue Baker on the same claim, Baker can

collateral estoppel The doctrine that prohibits a second determination of a fact, when the fact was earlier judicially determined in a case involving the party who advances the doctrine.

use the doctrine of **collateral estoppel** to prevent Smith from retrying factual questions determined in the Smith–Jones trial.

As early as 1916, the principles of *res judicata* and collateral estoppel were made applicable to criminal cases under the Double Jeopardy Clause by the U.S. Supreme Court.[42] The following illustrates the application of *res judicata* and collateral estoppel in a criminal case.

Ashe v. Swenson

Supreme Court of the United States (1970) 397 U.S. 436, 90 S. Ct.1189

In 1960, six men playing poker in the basement of a house were surprised and robbed by three or four masked gunmen. The defendant was arrested and charged with six counts of robbery but was first brought to trial on the charge of robbing only one of the poker players. The jury found Ashe not guilty, after being instructed that the theft of "any money" would sustain a conviction. Six weeks later, Ashe was tried for the robbery of another of the poker players, and this time was convicted. The appeal was from the conviction. In reversing the conviction, the U.S. Supreme Court stated:

> The question is not whether Missouri could validly charge the petitioner with six separate offenses for the robbery of the six poker players. It is not whether he could have received a total of six punishments if he had been convicted in a single trial of robbing the six victims. It is simply whether, after a jury determined by its verdict that the petitioner was not one of the robbers, the State could constitutionally (bring) him before a new jury to litigate that issue again.
>
> In this case the State in its brief has frankly conceded that following the petitioner's acquittal, it treated the first trial as no more than a dry run for the second prosecution: "No doubt the prosecutor felt the state had a provable case on the first charge and, when he lost, he did what every good attorney would do—he refined his presentation in light of the turn of events at the first trial." But this is precisely what the constitutional guarantee forbids.

In a 2009 case the U.S. Supreme Court resolved a split among the Circuit Courts of Appeal on the relevance of a "hung" jury on a multi-count indictment. In *Yeager v. United States*, 129 S. Ct. 2360, the Court considered a collateral estoppel argument made by one of the Enron executives charged with fraud and insider trading under federal laws. Yeager was charged with both fraud and insider trading. A jury acquitted him of the fraud charge but was unable to reach a verdict on the insider trading charge. The prosecution sought to re-try Yeager on the hung jury count, and Yeager contended the collateral estoppel part of the Double Jeopardy Clause prevented his retrial. The Supreme Court held that while retrial after a hung jury on a single-count indictment did not violate the Double Jeopardy Clause, once a jury has acquitted a defendant on one part of a multi-charge indictment, a court must determine if factual questions determined in the acquittal were a necessary part of the retrial. If so, the collateral estoppel doctrine prevents the retrial. The Supreme Court remanded the case to make this determination, and on remand the charges against Yeager were dismissed under the Double Jeopardy Clause. *United States v. Yeager*, 2009 WL 3346589, 334 Fed. Appx. 707 (5th Cir. 2009).

SINGLE OFFENSE OR MULTIPLE OFFENSES?

A defendant, seeking to kill, fires a handgun three times at the victim, missing each time. Should the defendant be charged with one count of attempted murder or three? In a "drugstore" drug case where a defendant had large and small amounts of 10 different illegal substances, what criminal charges should be issued? In a sexual assault case that went on for an hour with a variety of conduct, should multiple charges be issued?

Is a prosecutor justified in issuing (or seeking) multiple criminal charges to obtain a guilty plea in return for dropping one or two of the charges? Victims like this practice. Court calendars are kept smaller, and it saves time.

The following U.S. Supreme Court cases illustrate rulings on whether multiple charges or a single charge is justified. The specific wording of the criminal statute and the legislative intent in each state would generally govern.

Conduct	Ruling	Case
"Whether one who, in the same transaction, tears or cuts successively mail bags of the United States used in conveyance of the mails, with intent to rob or steal any such mail, is guilty of a single offense, or of additional offenses?"	"[I]t was the intent of the lawmakers to protect each and every bag…. Whenever any one mail bag is thus torn, cut, or injured, the offense is complete."	*Ebeling v. Morgan*, 237 U.S. 625, 35 S. Ct. 710 (1915)
Illegal sale of 10 grains of morphine on a specific day, followed by a sale of 8 grains on the following day, and additional morphine at a still later date.	"[T]he first transaction resulting in a sale, had come to an end. The next sale was not the result of the original impulse, but of a fresh one—that is to say, of a new bargain."	*Block burger v. United States*, 284 U.S. 299, 52 S. Ct. 180 (1932)
Cohabiting with more than one woman (old crime of bigamy or adultery).	"It is inherently, a continuous offense, having duration; and not an offense consisting of an isolated act."	*In re Snow*, 120 U.S. 274, 7 S. Ct. 556 (1887)

In the following cases of the 1990s, courts held that the following were multiple and separate offenses that did not violate the Double Jeopardy Clause (one act–one crime):

- Presentation of each bad check was a separate offense. *State v. Pomper*, 620 So. 2d 1098 (Fla. App. 1993)
- Separate convictions for different sex acts upon the same victim are affirmed in many cases throughout the United States.
- Most states permit conviction for both rape and incest based on a single act of child abuse. *Johnson v. Commonwealth*, 292 S.W.3d 889 (Ky. 2009)
- Defendant, who sat next to three young girls in a movie theater and masturbated, could be convicted of multiple charges arising out of the single act. *State v. Jannamon*, 169 Ariz. 435, 819 P.2d 1021 (1991); *Bergen v. State,* 552 So. 2d 262 (Fla. App. 1989)[a]
- Burning three separate apartments in the same building were separate arson offenses. *Richardson v. State*, 326 Md. 257, 604 A.2d 483 (1992)
- Possession of three different drugs with intent to distribute was held to be three separate crimes. *State v. Jordan*, 235 N.J. Super. 517, 563 A.2d 463 (1990)

[a]However, in the 1991 case of Hawkins v. State, 413 S.E.2d 525, the Georgia Court of Appeals held that a lewd act witnessed by two adults was only one crime, because the adult witnesses were not victims of the crime but witnesses to the crime.

Frame-Up as a Defense and as a Crime

frame-up The defense that usually alleges that a law enforcement officer has planted false evidence, or has altered, substituted, or destroyed evidence, in an effort to convict the defendant of the crime charged.

The defense of **frame-up** is seldom successfully raised. When it is, the defense usually alleges that a law enforcement officer has planted false evidence, or has altered, substituted, or destroyed evidence, in an effort to convict the defendant of the crime charged. Planting evidence, or altering or destroying evidence, is a crime in all states.

The defense of frame-up differs from the entrapment defense (see the following section). In entrapment, the defendant admits committing the crime charged but claims law enforcement officers wrongfully enticed him or her in that commission. In frame-up defenses, the defendant denies committing the crime and alleges law enforcement officers or other parties planted, altered, or substituted the evidence against him or her.

The following cases are examples of the frame-up defense:

- A kilogram of cocaine was found in defendant's truck, and at his trial, the defendant alleged that a police officer planted the cocaine in the truck. In affirming the defendant's conviction, the court stated that the defendant's trial strategy was to put the police officer on trial and that such a "strategy is often used and sometimes successful." *United States v. McNatt*, 931 F.2d 251 (4th Cir. 1991)
- The defendant was charged with carrying a concealed weapon and alleged that a police officer "planted" the gun on him when he was stopped and searched. The court permitted the defendant to raise the frame-up defense. *Moore v. United States*, 468 A.2d 1342 (D.C. App. 1983)
- In a Milwaukee case where a high school girl was deliberately shot in the face during a robbery to prevent her from identifying the robber, the defense alleged that the defendant's fingerprints were planted on the counter next to the cash register in the store that was robbed. An investigation showed that there was no merit to the defense, and the defendant's convictions for robbery and murder were affirmed.

Frame-up must be distinguished from *set-up*, where the person doing the set-up is not a law enforcement officer. For example, in *State v. Harris*, 498 P.2d 1222 (Mont. 1972), a bartender obtained the key to the bar safe and gave it to the defendant so he could burglarize the bar. She then informed the police of the planned burglary, and the defendant was caught in the act. The court rejected his claim that he was framed or entrapped, noting that the plan to burglarize the bar originated with the defendant or the bartender, not the police.

Entrapment and Outrageous Government Conduct as Defenses

entrapment The defense that a law enforcement officer used excessive temptation or urging to wrongfully induce the defendants to commit a crime they would not have ordinarily committed.

The defense of **entrapment** was recognized by the U.S. Supreme Court in the 1932 case of *Sorrells v. United States*.[43] In *Sorrells*, the Supreme Court ruled that entrapment occurs "when the criminal design originates with the officials of the government, and they implant in the mind of an innocent person the disposition to commit the alleged offense and induce its commission in order that they (the Government) may prosecute." The defense of entrapment therefore has two elements: (1) improper government inducement of the crime and (2) lack of predisposition on the part of the defendant to engage in the criminal conduct.

Defendants seeking to use the defense of entrapment carry the initial burden of coming forward with evidence of both the government's improper inducement and the defendant's lack of predisposition to commit the alleged offense. If a defendant makes a showing of improper inducement by the government and lack of predisposition by the defendant, the burden then shifts to the government. The government must then show

---

STINGS AND SCAM OPERATIONS

The U.S. Supreme Court stated long ago that American "courts have uniformly held that in waging war against crime … traps, decoys and deception (may be used) to obtain evidence of the commission of the crime." *United States v. Sorrells*, 287 U.S. 435, 454 (1932).

Many of the "sting" and "scam" operations operated every year in the United States are triggered by tips or other information that criminal activity is taking place or being planned. For example, suppose the police are told that a man is offering $5,000 to have his wife or another person murdered. To determine whether this is true, an undercover officer or cooperative person might approach the suspect and pretend to be willing to undertake the murder. If the suspect agrees and solicits the undercover officer, police have sufficient evidence to arrest the man and bring criminal charges. The following are examples of the wide use of stings and scams today:

Pedophile and child enticement or Internet sex scams. These scams are commonly used to identify and apprehend adults who sexually prey on children. Police officers represent themselves, often through Internet chat rooms, as children, and the suspect communicates with them believing that to be the case. If the suspect attempts to entice the "child" into sexual contact, he is arrested. (These scams are discussed more fully in Chapter 12).

Store front stings. Thieves, burglars, robbers, or shoplifters are tricked into bringing stolen goods to the store, where hidden video cameras and microphones record their transactions for subsequent use in criminal prosecutions.

Open-air drug dealing stings. These are set up on streets, alleys, or shopping centers where illegal drug dealing is suspected. Police pretending to be drug dealers offer to sell illegal drugs such as marijuana to persons frequenting the area. These stings are upheld as not being entrapment; see *State v. J.D.W.*, 910 P.2d 1242 (Utah App. 1995).

"readiness" on the part of the defendant and that the "defendant was poised, was likely, to engage in criminal activity."[44]

The U.S. Supreme Court ruled in the 1988 case of *Mathews v. United States*[45] that a defendant "is entitled to an entrapment instruction (to a jury) whenever there is sufficient evidence from which a reasonable jury could find entrapment."

Courts throughout the United States have long recognized that law enforcement officers (or their agents) can properly create ordinary opportunities for a person to commit an offense if the criminal intent or willingness originated in the mind of the defendant. The fact that the officer afforded the opportunity or the facility for the defendant to commit the crime in order to obtain evidence does not constitute entrapment. In *Hampton v. United States*, 425 U.S. 484 (1976), the Court held the entrapment defense was not available to a defendant who sold illegal drugs to undercover police officers, even though a government informer, acting for the government, supplied the drugs sold. The Court said the defendant must prove he did not have the criminal intention until it was implanted by the agent.

A sting operation is not improper inducement to commit a crime if it merely provides an opportunity to commit a crime. Thus, in illegal drug cases the Supreme Court held in *United States v. Russell* in 1973 that infiltration into a drug ring, and supplying some of the items needed to produce the illegal drugs, does not amount to entrapment.[46]

Money-laundering stings. Undercover officers engage in transactions with suspected car dealers, real estate brokers, financial institutions, or other businesses to determine whether they are using the business to launder money obtained from criminal activities. (Chapter 18 discussed money laundering crimes.)

Food Stamp Scams. Undercover police pose as food stamp holders and determine whether suspected persons are using the food stamps for wrongful purposes, like buying alcohol or cigarettes for minors, or whether the food stamps or food stamp debit cards are being wrongfully sold for cash.

Fugitive felons scams. In order to apprehend some of the 1.2 million persons wanted on outstanding warrants, police often use a scam where they send letters or e-mails to addresses where the fugitives might be found, saying they had won a free trip or other prize. When the fugitives show up to collect their "prize," officers are there to arrest them.

FBI stings. The FBI investigates suspected bribes or other wrongdoing by elected state or county officials for violations of federal criminal laws. These stings usually involve an undercover FBI agent offering bribes to an official, which, if accepted, are criminal violations.

Stings to test the integrity of law enforcement officers. Police departments test themselves to make sure officers are acting with integrity. The New York Police Department, which has over 30,000 officers, conducts 600 or more stings designed to test those officers each year. The FBI also does this, but does not report the number and kind of stings it conducts each year.

The use of deer decoys. In states with substantial hunting regions, poaching and other kinds of illegal hunting are often the subject of "decoy" stings. A fake deer or bear is set up, and police arrest persons who shoot the decoy. Entrapment is generally not successful for the charges of trespassing, shooting out of season, or other weapons violation.

However, proof of a sting operation that includes additional conduct by police may amount to sufficient evidence to meet a defendant's burden. For example, in *Jacobson v. United States*, 503 U.S. 540 (1992), the Supreme Court held that repeated attempts by government agents to entice a defendant to purchase child pornography through the mail constituted entrapment: Entrapment occurs, the Court said, "when the Government's quest for convictions leads to the apprehension of an otherwise law abiding citizen who, if left to his own devices, likely would have never run afoul of the law."

Although law enforcement officers may create and present the usual and ordinary opportunities for a person to commit a crime, they may not use excessive urging, inducement, temptations, or solicitations to commit a crime. For example, in the early case of *Sherman v. United States*, 356 U.S. 369 (1958), the Court held that actions by a government informant to entice a drug addict to return to drug use and supply drugs to the informant constituted entrapment.

The Supreme Court quoted another court as follows in the *Sorrells* case:

It is well settled that decoys may be used to entrap criminals, and to present opportunity to one intending or willing to commit crime. But decoys are not permissible to ensnare the innocent and law-abiding into the commission of crime. When the

---

FBI GUIDELINES ON ENTRAPMENT

In the April 1993 issue of the *FBI Law Enforcement Bulletin*, the following guidelines were presented in the article "Undercover Investigations and the Entrapment Defense":

> *To ensure that undercover investigations do not give rise to successful claims of entrapment or related defenses, all law enforcement officers should consider the following three points before conducting undercover investigations. First, while reasonable suspicion is not legally necessary to initiate an undercover investigation, officers should nonetheless be prepared to articulate a legitimate law enforcement purpose for beginning such an investigation. Second, law enforcement officers should, to the extent possible, avoid using persistent or coercive techniques, and instead, merely create an opportunity or provide the facilities for the target to commit a crime. Third, officers should document and be prepared to articulate the factors demonstrating a defendant was disposed to commit the criminal act prior to Government contact.*
>
> *Such factors include a prior arrest record, evidence of prior criminal activity, a defendant's familiarity with the terminology surrounding a particular criminal venture, and a defendant's eagerness to engage in the criminal activity. The most convincing evidence of predisposition will typically occur during the initial Government contacts, which officers should carefully document to successfully defeat the entrapment defense.*

---

criminal design originates, not with the accused, but is conceived in the mind of the government officers, and the accused is by persuasion, deceitful representation, or inducement lured into the commission of a criminal act, the government is estopped by sound public policy from prosecution therefore.

States Are Free to Write Their Own Rules for Entrapment The U.S. Supreme Court has held that the defense of entrapment is not of constitutional dimension. Therefore, the U.S. Congress and state legislative bodies may "adopt any substantive definition of the defense that [they] may desire."[47]

Some states have enacted statutes that define entrapment. Most states, however, use common law definitions created by their courts as the entrapment rules to be used within that state.

Most states and the federal courts use the "origin of intent" test in determining whether the defendant was predisposed to commit the crime charged. The test seeks to determine whether the defendant had the willingness and readiness to commit the crime *and* whether the police or a government agent only provided what appeared to be a favorable opportunity.

Denying the Criminal Act While Using the Defense of Entrapment Until 1988, most states would not permit defendants to plead innocence, while at the same time using an affirmative defense such as entrapment. The innocent plea generally means "I didn't commit the crime," whereas in the entrapment defense, the defendant is pleading, "I wouldn't have committed the crime if it had not been for the improper conduct of the police."

In the 1988 case of *Mathews v. United States*,[48] the U.S. Supreme Court pointed out that such inconsistent defenses have historically been permitted in federal prosecutions. But because it is not a constitutional issue, the Supreme Court held that it is up to each state to determine whether inconsistent defenses would be permitted.

In response to the *Mathews* decision, many states now permit inconsistent defenses (such as entrapment and denying the criminal act), and other states continue to require that criminal defenses be consistent.

A defendant who cannot claim entrapment may still be able to invoke the defense of *outrageous government conduct.* The U.S. Supreme Court first raised the concept of outrageous police conduct in the 1973 case of *United States v. Russell* (discussed earlier in this chapter), in which the Court stated:

> [W]e may some day be presented with a situation in which the conduct of law enforcement agents is so outrageous that due process principles would absolutely bar the government from invoking judicial processes to obtain a conviction…. (at 431–32, 93 S. Ct. at 1642–43).

In the 1976 case of *Hampton v. United States,* Justice Powell stated that "police over-involvement in crime would have to reach a demonstrable level of outrageousness before it could bar conviction."[49]

Outrageous Government Conduct That Violated the Due Process Rights of Defendants   The following conduct was held to fall within the *shock-the-conscience* or *outrageous conduct* exception so as to cause dismissal of the criminal charge:

- Using a defendant's attorney to gather information against him was held to violate not only due process but also the defendant's Sixth Amendment right to an attorney. *United States v. Marshank,* 50 CrL 1205 (N.D. Cal. 1991)
- False statements by law enforcement officers about lineups in a murder case were held to be "outrageous conduct," but because the government case was strong, the charges were not dismissed. *People v. Montgomery,* 1994 WL 642376 (N.Y.A.D. 1994)
- Manufacture of crack cocaine by the police for use in a reverse sting[50] operation caused dismissal of charges by the Supreme Court of Florida. *Metcalf v. State,* 635 So. 2d 11 (Fla. 1994)
- For two-and-a-half years, government agents supplied many materials and showed defendants how to manufacture illegal alcohol, which the agents said they would buy. *Greene v. United States,* 454 F.2d 783 (9th Cir. 1971)
- Intense and extensive police involvement in the manufacture of illegal drugs. *Commonwealth v. Mathews,* 347 Pa. Super. 320, 500 A.2d 853 (1985); and *United States v. Twigg,* 588 F.2d 373 (3d Cir. 1978)

Police Conduct Held Not to Be Outrageous Government Conduct   In the following cases, courts have held that the conduct was not outrageous:

- A civilian working with a police department had sex with a woman to obtain evidence necessary to convict her of prostitution. The Supreme Court of Hawaii affirmed the conviction, holding that it was not outrageous conduct, but it was also not the "ethical standards which law enforcement officials should be guided by." See *State v. Tookes,* 699 P. 2d 983 (1985).
- Paying a defendant's former girlfriend's living expenses while she assisted in building a criminal case against the defendant was held not to be outrageous conduct. See *United States v. Miller,* 891 F.2d 1265 (7th Cir. 1989). One area where such operations are used by police is Internet chat rooms, where police officers present themselves as children in order to lure adults attempting to initiate sexual meetings with children into the police net. These operations have commonly been upheld as appropriate government conduct.
- Sting operations, where police officers use deception to lure criminals into the sting's net, have been upheld by the Supreme Court as legitimate practices in the war on crime. See *United States v. Sorrells,* 287 U.S. 435 (1932).

The Defense That Another Person Committed the Crime

There are a number of ways of proving the wrong person has been charged with or convicted of a crime. Providing exculpatory evidence to the prosecution or investigating officers is the easiest way to accomplish this result, in particular if the evidence is convincing, such as DNA evidence. Showing that an eyewitness wrongly identified the defendant, or committed perjury, can also be good exculpatory evidence. The *Innocence Project*, a national organization that works to free wrongfully convicted persons, estimates that 62% of single-witness identifications are incorrect. See the Innocence Project, Eyewitness Misidentifications, *info@innocenceproject.org*. Another defense that can be used is evidence that another person committed the crime. However, this defense can be abused. Defendants with ample money or power could find another person willing to "confess" to the crime in exchange for money or because of coercion. In a recent case in Milwaukee, Wisconsin, the brother of the defendant charged with murder appeared in the District Attorney's office and asserted he was the person who committed the murder. Also, it is not unusual in criminal cases that receive media attention to find people calling prosecutors and "confessing" to the crimes, just to get attention. Allowing these people to testify would likely confuse the jury.

To deal with this situation, most states have rules similar to Rule 804(b) (3) of the Federal Rules of Evidence. That rule states that before a witness can be allowed to offer evidence to exculpate a defendant, there must be evidence of corroborating circumstances that clearly indicate the trustworthiness of the statement."

The Right to a Speedy Trial as a Defense

In the following Case Close-Up, the U.S. Supreme Court considered the application of a South Carolina rule to control use of exculpatory evidence, holding that the rule as applied to the defendant infringed his right to present a compete defense.

The Sixth Amendment of the U.S. Constitution provides that "in all criminal prosecutions, the accused shall enjoy the right to a speedy and public trial."[51] Most defendants charged with a serious crime do not ordinarily wish either a speedy or a public trial, but unless the right to a speedy trial is waived with the consent of the trial court, the constitutional mandate of a speedy trial must be complied with.

The *four-factor balancing test* used to determine whether a speedy trial violation has occurred was established by the U.S. Supreme Court in the 1972 case of *Barker v. Wingo.*[52] The factors that are weighed are (1) the length of the delay, (2) the reason for the delay, (3) the defendant's assertion of his or her right, and (4) the prejudice resulting from the delay.

In holding that the right to a speedy trial commences when a person "is indicted, arrested, or otherwise officially accused," the U.S. Supreme Court held in *United States v. Marion* that:

> The protection of the Amendment is activated only when a criminal prosecution has begun and extends only to those persons who have been "accused" in the course of that prosecution. These provisions would seem to afford no protection to those not yet accused, nor would they seem to require the Government to discover, investigate, and accuse any person within any particular period of time.[53]

The Court stated that the purpose and "interests served by the Speedy Trial Clause" are as follows:

> Inordinate delay between an arrest, indictment, and trial may impair a defendant's ability to present an effective defense. But the major evils protected against by the

CASE CLOSE-UP

Holmes v. South Carolina
Supreme Court of the United States
547 U.S. 319 (2006)

Holmes was charged with the murder of an 86-year-old woman. The prosecution had substantial forensic evidence connecting Holmes to the murder: the victim's DNA was found on Holmes's clothing, his palm print was found at the scene, fibers from clothing similar to that worn by Holmes were found at the crime scene, and Holmes's shirt had blood stains that matched the victim's blood.

Holmes attempted to introduce evidence that another man committed the murder, specifically, witnesses who were prepared to testify that the other man told them he killed the victim. Holmes also attacked the chain of custody of the forensic evidence. The trial court, applying a court-made rule on introduction of evidence in this situation, held that the evidence that another person committed the murder was inadmissible, because it raised a "bare suspicion" of another's guilt and because of the strength of the evidence against Holmes. Holmes was convicted and sentenced to death, and his conviction was affirmed by the South Carolina Supreme Court.

The U.S. Supreme Court granted certiorari and reversed the conviction. It held that while state and federal courts have broad latitude to determine what evidence may be excluded from a criminal trial, this latitude has limits:

> *Whether rooted directly in the Due Process Clause of the Fourteenth Amendment or in the Compulsory Process or Confrontation clauses of the Sixth Amendment, the Constitution guarantees criminal defendants "a meaningful opportunity to present a complete defense" [citations omitted]. These rights is abridged by evidence rules that "infring[e] upon a weighty interest of the accused" and are "arbitrary" or "disproportionate to the purposes they are designed to serve."*

The Court stated that while evidence that another person committed the crime may constitutionally be excluded if the evidence bears little logical connection to the crime, the South Carolina rule went beyond this standard and made admissibility depend on the strength of the prosecution's case, not the relevance or logical connection of the excluded evidence. If the jury questioned the credibility of the prosecution's evidence, the Court reasoned, it could find the evidence that the other man killed the victim plausible. The Constitution guarantees a criminal defendant this chance, the Court concluded. The conviction was reversed and remanded for a new trial.

speedy trial guarantee exist quite apart from actual or possible prejudice to an accused's defense. To legally arrest and detain, the Government must assert probable cause to believe the arrestee has committed a crime. Arrest is a public act that may seriously interfere with the defendant's liberty, whether he is free on bail or not, and that may disrupt his employment, drain his financial resources, curtail his associations, subject him to public obloquy, and create anxiety in him, his family and his friends.[54]

The U.S. Constitution does not identify a specific number of days necessary to satisfy the speedy trial requirement. Therefore, the federal government and states have enacted statutes establishing their own standards. For example, the federal government in the

Speedy Trial Act, 18 U.S.C. § 3161(c)(1), requires that a person indicted for a felony be tried within 70 days unless the defendant waives his or her right to a speedy trial. Failure to try the person within that time could cause dismissal of the criminal charge if it were shown that the delay prejudiced the defendant under the *Barker v. Wingo* factors. In *Bloate v. United States,* 130 S. Ct. 1345 (2010) the Court held that time delays caused by filing pretrial motions are not automatically excluded from calculating the 70-day period, but can be excluded if the trial court makes a specific finding that the time should be excluded.

Defendants already incarcerated in one state often have pending charges in another state. Obtaining a speedy trial under those circumstances can be difficult, and determining if a Speedy Trial Clause violation has occurred can also be a problem. To deal with this situation most states are party to the Interstate Agreement on Detainers Act. Under this Act, if a person detained in one state makes a request that charges against him pending in another state be brought to trial, the other state must bring the prisoner to trial within 180 days of the request. If that doesn't occur, the charges must be dismissed. The dismissal court has the discretion to make the dismissal with or without prejudice, depending on the circumstances. See, for example *United States v. Ferraira,* 2009 WL 311136.

Because of the danger that a defendant charged with a serious crime might walk free because of a speedy trial violation, great attention is given to time on the speedy trial calendar. If necessary, civil trial judges or retired judges are brought in to try criminal cases that must be tried because of the speedy trial requirement. The following are speedy trial cases that received national attention:

- After a U.S. Army investigation of three murders, charges against a medical doctor were dropped. The doctor left the Army and practiced medicine for five years until he was indicted for the murders and convicted by a federal jury. In holding that no speedy trial violation occurred, the U.S. Supreme Court held:

  Once the charges instituted by the Army were dismissed, MacDonald was legally and constitutionally in the same posture as though no charges had been made. He was free to go about his affairs, to practice his profession, and to continue with his life. *United States v. MacDonald,* 456 U.S. 1 (1982)

- As mentioned earlier, Byron De La Beckwith was tried twice for the 1964 murder of the civil rights leader Medgar Evers. Both trials before all-white juries ended up with hung juries. In 1994, Beckwith was tried for the third time and was convicted. It was held that no violation of speedy trial had occurred. *State v. Beckwith,* 707 So. 2d 547 (1997)

☰ The Statute of Limitations as a Defense

The old English common law adopted the doctrine that "no lapse bars the King"; therefore, statutes limiting the time for criminal prosecutions are rare in England.

However, criminal **statutes of limitations** appeared in America as early as 1652. The federal government adopted time limits for the prosecution of most federal crimes in 1790, and the majority of the states have enacted statutes of limitations for most crimes.

The speedy trial requirements are constitutional mandates and therefore are imposed on all states. Statutes of limitations on criminal prosecutions are optional legislative enactments. Reasons given for limitations on criminal prosecutions are as follows:

statute of limitations A defense to a criminal prosecution based on a statute that sets the maximum time the government has to prosecute a violation of a criminal law.

A limitation statute is designed to protect individuals from having to defend themselves against charges when the basic facts may have become obscured by the passage of time and to minimize the danger of official punishment because of acts in the far-distant past.[55]
* * *

SPEEDY TRIAL, DOUBLE JEOPARDY, AND STATUTES OF LIMITATIONS AS DEFENSES

Double jeopardy and the requirement of a speedy trial are both mandated by the U.S. Constitution and must be complied with.

Speedy trial	Because the U.S. Constitution does not specify the time period within which a defendant must be tried, federal law or the law of each state establishes this time period. Defendants, however, often waive their right to a speedy trial. This is done in open court and most often in writing and signed by the defendant and the defense lawyer.
Double jeopardy	A criminal defendant cannot be retried if jeopardy has attached to the crime with which the defendant has been charged. The U.S. Supreme Court has held that jeopardy attaches when a jury is sworn and, in a non-jury case, when the first witness is sworn.
Statutes of limitations	These are not required by the U.S. Constitution and are optional state legislative enactments. The states of South Carolina and Wyoming have no criminal statutes of limitations.[a]

[a]"The Statute of Limitation in Criminal Law," 102 U. Pa. L. Rev. 630.

The Speedy Trial Clause and the limitations statutes work in tandem to prevent pretrial delay: the statutory period insures against pre-accusation delays and the Sixth Amendment controls the post-indictment time span…. Both provisions shield defendants from endless anxiety about possible prosecution and from impairment of the ability to mount a defense. By encouraging speedy prosecution, they also afford society protection from un incarcered offenders, and insure against a diminution of the deterrent value of immediate convictions, as well as the reduced capacity of the government to prove its case.[56]

Statutes of limitations generally permit a longer period for the prosecution of felonies than for the prosecution of misdemeanors. No time limit is generally placed on prosecution for murder. As discovery of some theft offenses could occur years after the theft, extensions of time are generally given, based on the time of discovery of the offense. The running of time under a criminal statute of limitation could be halted by

- Issuance of an arrest warrant or summons, an indictment, filing of information, or the commencement of prosecution.
- Statute requirement that the person must be a public resident of that state for the time to toll.
- Acts by the suspect to avoid or to frustrate legal proceedings against him or her.

Summary

- Diplomatic immunity is limited to recognized diplomats and certain members of their families. Legislative immunity applies only to active legislators, and only during the time the legislature is in session. Witness immunity can be given to overcome the Fifth Amendment privilege a witness has. The immunity can be for prosecution for any charges related to the witness's testimony, or only for use of that testimony.

- A mistake of fact provides a defense when the mistake is honest and reasonable and nullifies a specific intent necessary for conviction of the crime charged. A mistake of law rarely provides a defense, unless the criminal law defining the offense is generally not known to reasonable people.
- The Double Jeopardy Clause serves as a limitation on the power of government to use its resources to subject a citizen to repeated exposure to the criminal laws, and it also guards against the conviction of innocent persons.
- Two offenses are the "same" for Double Jeopardy purposes if the same facts serve as a basis for each offense. If one offense requires proof of a fact that was not part of the other offense, each charge can be prosecuted. Prosecutions for the same actions under both a state and a federal statute are not prosecutions for the "same" offense under the Double Jeopardy Clause.

- *Res judicata* is the doctrine that states once an issue has been determined between the two parties, it cannot be relitigated by those parties. *Collateral estoppel* is the doctrine that states a fact necessarily found in one trial of a defendant bars proof of the same fact in a second trial. Both doctrines have been made part of the Double Jeopardy Clause.
- Government inducements become entrapment when the actions of law enforcement officers are improper, and the defendant had no predisposition to commit the crimes made the subject of the improper inducements.
- A speedy trial violation has occurred when there has been an excessive delay (made specific in statutes but not in the Constitution), no good reason for the delay exists, the defendant has asserted the right to a speedy trial, and the delay has caused prejudice to the defendant.

Key Terms

corpus delicti, p. 158
affirmative defense, p. 158
immunity, p. 159
transactional immunity, p. 160
use immunity, p. 160
mistake of law, p. 164

duress, p. 165
necessity, p. 166
coercion, p. 167
alibi, p. 168
double jeopardy, p. 171
"dual sovereignty" doctrine, p. 174

res judicata, p. 174
collateral estoppel, p. 175
frame-up, p. 177
entrapment, p. 177
statute of limitations, p. 184

Case Analysis and Writing Exercises

1. Assume a thief steals a credit card and uses the card in several separate instances. Can the thief be charged with multiple violations of a state statute that makes it a crime to "knowingly obtain, possess, use, or transfer a means of identification or financial information of another"? Why or why not? See *State v. Leyda*, 138 P.3d 610 (Wash. 2006).

2. Gorday stopped a motorist parked in a shopping mall, and holding a scissors pointed at the motorist, demanded the motorist's purse. After taking the purse, Gorday took a credit card from the purse and used it to buy gasoline for her car. She was apprehended while doing so and charged with armed robbery, a felony, and unlawful use of a

stolen credit card, a misdemeanor. While awaiting trial on the armed robbery, Gorday considered pleading guilty to the misdemeanor credit card theft charge. Would that be a wise decision for her to make? Why? See *Gorday v. State*, 907 So. 2d 640 (Fla. App. 2005).

3. The police left a car sitting in a parking lot with the keys in the ignition and the driver's door open. The defendant walked by, saw the open door, looked in, saw the keys, and got in the car. As he drove away, the police stopped him and charged him with motor vehicle theft. Does the defendant have a good entrapment defense? Would it make a difference if the police were looking specifically for

this defendant and left the car in the street outside his house? Why or why not? See *People v. Watson*, 990 P.2d 1031 (Cal. 2000).

4. Defendant was charged with murder and with assault with the intent to commit murder. At her trial she claimed that she took the actions because of the demands made by her abusive boyfriend, who told her he would hurt her if she did not do what he demanded. Is the defendant entitled to assert the duress defense to the murder charge? To the assault charge? Why or why not? See *People v. Blue*, 2004 WL 1676165 (Mich. App. 2004), *review denied* 693 N.W.2d 817 (Mich. 2005).

Notes

1. *State v. Cohen*, 568 So. 2d 49 (Fla. 1990).
2. 442 F. Supp. 2d 102 (S.D. New York 2006).
3. 356 F.3d 564 (4th Cir. 2004).
4. 596 So. 2d 687 (Fla. App. 1992).
5. 717 F. Supp. 309 (E.D. Pa. 1989).
6. *U.S. v. Gonzalez De Modesti*, 145 F. Supp. 2d 771 (D.P.R. 2001).
7. The fact that a law enforcement officer made an honest mistake about an important fact in making an arrest would not necessarily invalidate the arrest. In the 1971 U.S. Supreme Court case of *Hill v. California*, 401 U.S. 797, 91 S. Ct. 1106, police made an "honest mistake" in arresting the wrong man. In the 1980 case of *United States v. Allen*, 629 F.2d 51, 27 CrL 2307 (D.C. Cir.), the appellate court held that "the case law establishes that an arrest based on actual assumptions later found erroneous may be valid if there is adequate basis in the record to determine the reasonableness of the officer's conduct in making the arrest."

   The U.S. Supreme Court heard another honest mistake case in 1987. In *Maryland v. Garrison*, 480 U.S. 79, 107 S. Ct. 1013, police officers obtained a search warrant for a search on the third floor of a building, believing that there was only one apartment on that floor. Before they discovered that there were two apartments on that floor, police found heroin and drug paraphernalia in the apartment of another man (Garrison). The Supreme Court held that the evidence was lawfully obtained, adding another case to what is known as the *honest mistake exception*.

   The following three examples are found in the New York Criminal Code Annotated Practice Commentary to Section 15.20, Effect of Ignorance or Mistake Upon Liability:

- A police officer having a warrant for the arrest of A mistakenly arrests B, who resembles A, and holds him in a police station for an hour before ascertaining his mistake and releasing him. The officer is not guilty of "unlawful imprisonment" (Section 135.05) because his mistake of fact "negatives a culpable mental state necessary for the commission of the offense," namely, "knowledge that the restriction is unlawful." Section 135.00(1)

- M has sexual intercourse with F, a mentally ill woman whose condition is not always apparent and is not known to or realized by M. Although M would be guilty of third-degree rape if he had realized F's condition, his unawareness is, by statute, expressly made a defense to the charge. Section 130.10

- During a heated argument between A and B, B, a man with a reputation for violence and rumored to carry a pistol on occasion, suddenly places his hand in his bulging pocket, and A strikes him in the face and breaks his nose. Although B did not have a pistol and was merely reaching for a cigarette, A is not guilty of assault because his factual mistake was of a kind that supports a defense of justification. Section 35.15 (1)

8. In the case of *Garnett v. State*, the Maryland Court pointed out in 1993 that 17 states have laws that permit a mistake of age defense in some form in cases of sexual offenses with underage children (632 A.2d at 802).
9. 592 F. Supp. 424 (E.D. Va. 1984).
10. 252 F.3d 647 (2d Cir. 2001).
11. *State v. Cameron*, 514 A.2d 1302 (1986).
12. *State v. Souza*, 72 Haw. 246, 813 P.2d 1384 (1991).

13. 116 S. Ct. 2013, 59 CrL 2153 (1996).

14. 82 Cal. App. 778, 785, 256 P. 251, 254 (1927).

15. *Johnson v. State,* 379 A.2d 1129 (Del. 1977).

16. 43 Cal. App. 3d 823, 118 Cal. Rptr. 110 (1974).

17. 444 U.S. 394, 100 S. Ct. 624 (1980).

18. Blackstone, 4 *Commentaries,* 30.

19. See Wisconsin Statute 939.46.

20. In the 1980 case of *United States v. Bailey* (444 U.S. 394, 100 S. Ct. 624), the U.S. Supreme Court pointed out the distinctions between the defenses of duress and necessity as follows:

> Common law historically distinguished between the defenses of duress and necessity. Duress was said to excuse criminal conduct where the actor was under an unlawful threat of imminent death or serious bodily injury, which threat caused the actor to engage in conduct violating the literal terms of the criminal law. While the defense of duress covered the situation where the coercion had its source in the actions of other human beings, the defense of necessity, or choice of evils, traditionally covered the situation where physical forces beyond the actor's control rendered illegal conduct the lesser of two evils. Thus, where A destroyed a dike because B threatened to kill him if he did not, A would argue that he acted under duress, whereas if A destroyed the dike in order to protect more valuable property from flooding, A could claim a defense of necessity. See generally LaFave and Scott, *Criminal Law,* 2nd ed. (Belmont, Calif.: West/Wadsworth, 1986), pp. 374–384.

21. Model Penal Code, Section 3.02 (Justification Generally).

22. *U.S. v. Kabat,* 797 F.2d 580 (8th Cir. 1986).

23. *U.S. v. Maxwell,* 254 F.3d 21 (1st Cir. 2001). Protestors violating criminal law frequently argue that the law they are protesting is the "greater evil." Examples of such unsuccessful claims are *Cyr v. State,* 887 S.W.2d 203 (Tex. App. 1994) (abortion); *Troen v. Oregon,* 501 U.S. 1232 (1991) (nuclear power plants); and *State v. Marley,* 509 P.2d 1095 (Haw. 1973) (the Vietnam War).

> One court in *United States v. Schoon,* 955 F.2d 1238 (9th Cir. 1991), has held that necessity can never be a defense in so-called indirect civil disobedience cases. These are cases in which the law violated is not the law being protested. The "greater harm" is thus not caused by the law violated but by some other law or governmental policy. Direct civil disobedience, where the defense of

necessity might be available, occurs when the protestors violate the very law they are protesting. For example, if a law requires citizens to use lead paint on their houses, the harm caused by lead paint would likely exceed the harm caused by violating the law.

24. *Selected Writings of Justice Cardozo,* 390.

25. 2 All E.R. at p. 181 (1971).

26. 412 U.S. 470, 93 S. Ct. 2208 (1973).

27. *Williamson v. U.S.,* 207 U.S. 425, 453, 28 S. Ct. 163, 173 (1908).

28. 311 So. 2d 678 (Fla. App. 1975).

29. The defense lawyer missed the boat on this case. He or she could have also had the statute declared invalid as being "void for vagueness." Everybody has to guess about what is meant by "near." Modern statutes now forbid demonstrations "in" a courthouse or within 200 or 300 feet of a courthouse. Such statutes do not violate "void for vagueness" (see Chapter 1).

30. In affirming Lt. Calley's criminal convictions, the Military Court of Appeals held:

> [There is] ample evidence from which to find that Calley directed and personally participated in the intentional killing of men, women and children who were unarmed and in the custody of soldiers....
>
> [T]he uncontradicted evidence is that ... they were offering no resistance. In his testimony, Calley admitted he was aware of the requirement that prisoners be treated with respect.... [H]e knew that the normal practice was to interrogate villagers, release those who could satisfactorily account for themselves and evacuate the suspect among them for further examination.

31. 437 U.S. 82, 98 S. Ct. 2187 (1978).

32. 464 U.S. 501, 104 S. Ct. 819, 34 CrL 3019 (1984).

33. *Downum v. U.S.,* 372 U.S. 734, 83 S. Ct. 1033 (1963).

34. *Wade v. Hunter,* 336 U.S. 684, 69 S. Ct. 834 (1949).

35. *Westfall v. U.S.,* 274 U.S. 256, 47 S. Ct. 629 (1927).

36. 359 U.S. 121, 79 S. Ct. 676 (1959).

37. In 1993, the United States prosecuted several Los Angeles police officers for civil rights violations arising out of a beating they gave Rodney King. In a previous, very controversial state prosecution, the same officers were acquitted of state criminal charges. Two of the officers, Koon and Powell, were convicted, and two were acquitted. The Double Jeopardy Clause did not prevent those convictions because of the dual sovereignty rule.

The famous videotape of the King beating, which showed that beating in great detail, was extensively used by the federal court in its sentencing decision. See *U.S. v. Koon*, 833 F. Supp. 769 (C.D. Cal. 1993). Koon and Powell were sentenced to 30 months in prison, based on various sentencing guidelines that indicated a downward departure from the 80- to 87-month sentence guidelines for their convictions.

The Ninth Circuit Court of Appeals reversed the downward departure made by the federal district court (see 34 F.3d 1416), but the U.S. Supreme Court essentially restored the original sentences. See *Koon v. United States*, 518 U.S. 81 (1996).

38. *Blockburger v. United States*, 284 U.S. 299, 304 (1932). Thus, a prosecution for auto theft barred prosecution for the lesser offense of joyriding, and vice versa. See *Brown v. Ohio*, 432 U.S. 161 (1977).

39. *Grady v. Corbin*, 495 U.S. 508 (1990).

40. Ibid.

41. *United States v. Dixon*, 509 U.S. 688 (1993).

42. See *United States v. Oppenheimer*, 242 U.S. 85, 37 S. Ct. 68 (1916).

43. 287 U.S. 435, 454, 53 S. Ct. 210, 217 (1932), separate opinion.

44. *Jacobson v. United States*, 503 U.S. 540 (1992).

45. *Mathews v. United States*, 485 U.S. 58 (1988).

46. *United States v. Russell*, 411 U.S. 423 (1973).

47. *U.S. v. Russell*, 411 U.S. 423 (1973).

48. 485 U.S. 58, 108 S. Ct. 883 (1988). Examples of inconsistent defenses that were permitted when the evidence justified it are:

- In an 1896 murder case arising out of a gunfight in Indian Territory, the defense of self-defense was used, along with an instruction on manslaughter. Killing in the heat of passion is inconsistent with self-defense. *Stevenson v. United States*, 162 U.S. 313, 16 S. Ct. 839 (1896)

- In a 1970 rape case, the defendant was permitted to argue that the act did not take place and that the victim consented. *Johnson v. United States*, 426 F.2d 651 (D.C. Cir. 1970), *cert. granted* 400 U.S. 864, 91 S. Ct. 107 (1970)

49. 425 U.S. at 495 n. 7.

50. A reverse buy or reverse sting scheme is one in which the government sells or attempts to sell an illegal drug rather than buy it. Because this conduct by the police could cause defense lawyers to use the entrapment or outrageous government conduct defenses, great caution should be used by law enforcement officers.

51. In the 1992 case of *State v. James* (484 N.W.2d 799), an undercover officer was standing in an area known for high drug activity and "sold" crack only to people who approached him. Eight such locations were used in Minneapolis to discourage buyers who came into high drug activity areas to buy drugs. The Minnesota Court of Appeals affirmed the defendant's conviction, pointing out that the state carried the burden of showing predisposition by the defendant and that the officer did not solicit or encourage the defendant in any way. See also the case of *United States v. Cea*, 963 F.2d 1027 (7th Cir. 1992).

52. The Federal Speedy Trial Act (18 U.S.C.A. 3161) sets a 70-day limit, which begins to run with the date of indictment (§3161(c)(1)). See *Henderson v. United States*, 476 U.S. 321, 106 S. Ct. 1871 (1986).

53. 407 U.S. 514 (1972).

54. 404 U.S. 307, 92 S. Ct. 455 (1971).

55. Ibid. at 320, 92 S. Ct. at 463.

56. See *Toussie v. U.S.*, 397 U.S. 112, 114–115, 90 S. Ct. 858, 859–60 (1970).

57. *United States v. Levine*, 658 F.2d 113 (3d Cir. 1981).

CHAPTER 8

Criminal Punishments

Joe Sullivan, pictured above, was convicted in Florida of sexual battery when he was 13 years old, and sentenced to life imprisonment. In the case of Graham v. Florida, the U.S. Supreme Court held that a state may not sentence a juvenile to life without parole for a non-homicide. Based on that decision, Sullivan is entitled to a new hearing on his sentence.

OUTLINE

LEARNING OBJECTIVES

In this chapter we examine the kinds of punishments that may be imposed for violation of a criminal law, and some limitations on those punishments. The learning objectives for this chapter are:

- Know the text of the Cruel and Unusual Punishment Clause.

- Explain the relationship between the Sixth Amendment and sentencing provisions that permit a judge to determine when an enhanced sentence should be given a criminal defendant.

- State the present status of the Federal Sentencing Guidelines.

- Identify the procedures a school official must follow before imposing corporal punishment on a student.

- Explain why the death penalty was declared unconstitutional in *Furman v. Georgia.*

- Identify at least three groups of persons who cannot be given the death penalty.

- Describe the kinds of evidence that must be produced if the prosecution seeks imposition of the death penalty after a jury has found the defendant guilty of the crime charged.

- Define "three strikes" laws and list the common characteristics of such laws.

In 2001 Cory Saunders was convicted in Massachusetts of the attempted rape of a 7-year-old boy. He was sentenced to prison, and when he was scheduled for release in 2003 authorities concluded he was a "sexually dangerous" offender. As a result, Saunders was detained in prison under the Massachusetts sexually dangerous civil commitment statute. In 2006 Saunders was released from prison. At the time of his release, two psychologists who treated Saunders in prison recommended he not be released.

In 2008 Saunders raped a 6-year-old boy in the Bedford Public Library, New Bedford, Massachusetts, while the boy's mother worked on the library computers. Saunders pled guilty to the rape and was sentenced to life in prison. However, Saunders will be eligible for parole after 15 years. If he is ever paroled, he must stay on probation for the rest of his life.

In this chapter we learn the rules governing the imposition of various kinds of punishments, from simple fines to the death penalty. We will also learn some of the limitations the U.S. Constitution places on punishments for violation of criminal laws.

≡ Punishments Used in Early England

The criminal punishments used hundreds of years ago in England and elsewhere in Europe were very severe. In England alone, more than 200 offenses were punishable by death. Condemned criminals were usually hanged, although occasionally they were beheaded, quartered, or drawn (dragged along the ground by the tail of a horse). Until 1790 burning continued to be the punishment inflicted on women for treason, high or petty (which later included not only the murder by a wife of her husband and the murder of a master or mistress by a servant but also several offenses against the king). In practice, women were strangled before they were burned; this, however, depended on the executioner. In one notorious case, a woman was actually burned alive for murdering her husband, the executioner being afraid to strangle her because he was caught by the fire.[1]

For lesser offenses, various forms of mutilations—such as cropping (clipping of the ears), blinding, amputation of the hand, and branding—were common. The whipping post and the pillory were often used, as were fines and imprisonment. The pillory is a frame erected on a post. The offender's head and hands are placed in the open holes, and the top board is then moved into place, immobilizing the offender in a standing position.

Practices Used in England to Avoid Severe Penalties

For various reasons, including the severity of penalties, England developed procedures to avoid severe penalties. By usage and custom, the following came into practice.

Benefit of Clergy[2]   In the twelfth century, a controversy arose about whether priests accused of felonies should be tried by the royal courts or the ecclesiastical courts. It was decided that the royal courts could try priests but could not put them to death for the first felony conviction. This privilege was known as the **benefit of clergy**, and by the end of the Middle Ages, it was extended to all laypeople who could read.

The test to determine who could claim the privilege of benefit of clergy was a person's ability to recite the first verse of Psalm 51: "Have mercy upon me, O God, after Thy great goodness." This came to be known as the *neck verse* because it saved the accused from hanging. The only punishment that could then be inflicted was imprisonment for one year and an *M* branded on the brawn of the left thumb to prevent the criminal from claiming the privilege again. For many years, only three crimes were excluded from

benefit of clergy A medieval limit on capital punishment. People convicted of a capital crime entitled to claim the benefit of clergy (by the fifteenth century, anyone who could read) could not be executed for their offense. By the end of the eighteenth century, the privilege had been eliminated for most crimes.

The Art Archive/Jarrold Publishing/Picture Desk

Colonial Americans followed the lead of the English in terms of punishment. As punishment for lesser offenses, various forms of mutilations, such as cropping (clipping of the ears), blinding, amputation of the hand, and branding were common. The whipping post and the pillory were often used, as were fines and imprisonment. Stocks like the one shown here were situated in very public places so that shame and ridicule by the community were a strong part of the punishment.

benefit of clergy (high treason, highway robbery, and the willful burning of a house), but in 1769, Blackstone noted that "among the variety of actions which men are daily liable to commit no less than 160 have been declared by Act of Parliament to be felonies without benefit of clergy."[3]

sanctuary In the Middle Ages in England, sanctuary was a religious place where criminals could take refuge. The concept of sanctuary later broadened to include asylum for refugees.

The Law of Sanctuary and the Right of Asylum In the Middle Ages, **sanctuary** was common. The place of sanctuary was generally a church or other religious place. Criminals who were permitted to take refuge in a church or monastery could not be removed from it. Even after sanctuary as an institution was abolished, a system developed in England by which the refugee took an oath of abjuration before a coroner, admitted guilt, and swore to leave the country for life to an agreed-upon place (often the American colonies or, later, Australia). Sanctuary was abolished in England in 1623; however, a modified form reportedly continued in England for another century.[4] Sanctuary never became part of the legal system of the American colonies or of the newly formed United States of America.

The United States, however, recognizes and grants right of asylum to refugees from other countries who can show a "well-founded fear of persecution."[5] Over the last fifty years, the United States has granted asylum to many thousands of refugees. Two famous refugee cases illustrate this practice:

- After the Soviet invasion of Hungary in 1956, the United States gave asylum to Jozsef Cardinal Mindszenty in the American embassy in Budapest for 15 years until the Soviets permitted the cardinal to leave Hungary.
- In 1989, the U.S. embassy in Beijing sheltered for months China's most prominent dissident, Fang Lizhi, and his wife, until China permitted them to leave the country.

Transportation   People convicted of crimes in England could be pardoned if they agreed to be transported to a colony to do hard labor for a number of years. The first convicts were sent abroad to America in 1655. By the time of the American Revolution, England was sending overseas some 2,000 convicts a year.

After the American Revolution, Australia became the principal place to which prisoners were sent under the condition of the pardon. Over the years, approximately 100,000 prisoners were sent to America and an equal number to Australia.[6] Australia and other British colonies strongly objected to the practice of transporting convicts, which was gradually abolished between 1853 and 1864. Imprisonment in England and hard labor on public works were then substituted as punishment.[7]

Punishment Used in Early America

Blackstone points out that English criminal law and punishments, before the American Revolution, were fairly civilized by comparison with those of the rest of Europe. U.S. Supreme Court Justice Thurgood Marshall made the following observations in comparing **capital punishment** in the American colonies with its use in England:

> Capital punishment was not as common a penalty in the American Colonies. "The Capitall Lawes of New-England," dating from 1636, were drawn by the Massachusetts Bay Colony and are the first written expression of capital offenses known to exist in this country. These laws make the following crimes capital offenses: idolatry, witchcraft, blasphemy, murder, assault in sudden anger, sodomy, buggery, adultery, statutory rape, rape, man stealing, perjury in a capital trial, and rebellion. Each crime is accompanied by a reference to the Old Testament to indicate its source. It is not known with any certainty exactly when, or even if, these laws were enacted as drafted; and, if so, just how vigorously these laws were enforced. We do know that the other Colonies had a variety of laws that spanned the spectrum of severity.
>
> By the eighteenth century, the list of crimes became much less theocratic and much more secular. In the average colony, there were 12 capital crimes. This was far fewer than existed in England, and part of the reason was that there was a scarcity of labor in the Colonies.[8]

▬ The Constitutional Limitation on Punishment

The Eighth Amendment of the U.S. Constitution, ratified in 1791 as part of the Bill of Rights, provides that "excessive bail shall not be required, nor excessive fines imposed, nor cruel and unusual punishments inflicted." Two members of Congress opposed passage of this amendment. One stated,

> What is meant by the term excessive bail? Who are to be the judges? What is understood by excessive fines? It lies with the court to determine. No cruel and unusual punishment is to be inflicted; it is sometimes necessary to hang a man, villains often deserve whipping, and perhaps having their ears cut off; but are we in the future to be prevented from inflicting these punishments because they are cruel? If a more lenient mode of correcting vice and deterring others from the commission of it could be invented, it would be very prudent in the Legislature to adopt it; but until we have some security that this will be done, we ought not be restrained from making necessary laws by any declaration of this kind.[9]

About **cruel and unusual punishment**, Justice William J. Brennan stated in 1972 that:

> the Cruel and Unusual Punishments Clause, like the other great clauses of the Constitution, is not susceptible of precise definition. Yet we know that the values and ideals

capital punishment Inflicting deadly injury as punishment for criminal conduct.

cruel and unusual punishment Under the Eighth Amendment, a limitation on punishment for criminal conduct.

it embodies are basic to our scheme of government. And we know also that the Clause imposes upon this Court the duty, when the issue is properly presented, to determine the constitutional validity of a challenged punishment, whatever that punishment may be.[10]

The basis courts used to evaluate the "constitutionality of a challenged punishment" historically has been the **proportionality** principle. In the 1984 case of *Pulley v. Harris,* the U.S. Supreme Court defined the manner of evaluating the appropriateness or proportionality of a punishment for a particular crime:

> Traditionally, proportionality has been used with reference to an abstract evaluation of the appropriateness of a sentence for a particular crime. Looking to the gravity of the offense and the severity of the penalty, to sentences imposed for other crimes, and to sentencing practices in other jurisdictions, this Court has occasionally struck down punishments as inherently disproportionate, and therefore cruel and unusual, when imposed for a particular crime or category of crime. See, e.g., *Solem v. Helm,* 463 U.S. 277 (1983); *Enmund v. Florida,* 458 U.S. 782 (1982); *Coker v. Georgia,* 433 U.S. 584 (1977). The death penalty is not in all cases a disproportionate penalty in this sense.[11]

The *Solem* case cited above by the Supreme Court appeared to have held that the Cruel and Unusual Punishment Clause required courts to conduct a proportionality review in all cases, including those in which there was an imposition of a non-capital sentence. Such a review, *Solem* said, included considerations of (1) the gravity of the offense and the harshness of the penalty, (2) sentences imposed for similar crimes in the same jurisdiction, and (3) sentences imposed for the same crime in other jurisdictions.

Decisions of the U.S. Supreme Court since *Solem* was decided cast some doubt on the status of the proportionality test set forth in that case. In *Harmelin v. Michigan,* 501 U.S. 957 (1991) and *Ewing v. California,* 538 U.S. 11 (2003) the Supreme Court exhibited disagreement on the continued force of the *Solem* holding. Two members of the Court in each case took the position that proportionality review was not required by the Eighth Amendment in non-capital cases. While the other justices disagreed with that position, they nonetheless agreed that before the tests adopted in *Solem* can be applied to a non-capital sentence, a court must first determine that the sentence meets the "grossly disproportionate" test. Only such sentences are then subjected to the tests set forth in *Solem.* Moreover, in *Harmelin* the Court also held that court's reviewing non-capital sentences need not make the kind of inter-jurisdiction comparison suggested by the Court in *Solem.*

Since the decision in *Solem* decisions reversing prison sentences under a proportionality review have been rare, and none have been issued by the U.S. Supreme Court. While the Supreme Court did in 2010 reverse a life sentence imposed on a juvenile offender under an Eighth Amendment analysis, it did not base the decision on proportionality. See *Graham v. Florida,* 130 S. Ct. 2011 (2010), discussed later in this chapter. As a result, though *Solem* has not been reversed, its continued viability is unclear.

Sentencing and Jury Trials

In 2000, the U.S. Supreme Court decided the case of *Apprendi v. New Jersey* (530 U.S. 466). In *Apprendi,* the Court held that any fact that increases the penalty for the crime charged must be submitted to the jury and proved beyond a reasonable doubt. It thus held unconstitutional a New Jersey hate crime statute that permitted the trial judge to increase the sentence of a convicted defendant if the judge found by a preponderance of the evidence that the defendant acted in a manner intended to intimidate the victim.

The *Apprendi* opinion caused many changes in sentencing procedures and also resulted in many reversals of sentences handed down by trial judges. Many state sentencing systems, as well as the Federal Sentencing Guidelines, permitted a judge to make fact

proportionality An objective evaluation of the appropriateness of a punishment for a particular crime.

findings on questions that determined whether the sentence for the crime charged would be enhanced or reduced. After *Apprendi*, judges could make fact findings, but only if they were "sentencing factors", used to determine a sentence within a range provided in the statute establishing the minimum and maximum sentences that could be imposed for the crime charged: "…judge-found sentencing factors cannot increase the maximum sentence a defendant might otherwise receive based purely on the facts found by the jury." *United States v. O'Brien*, 130 S. Ct. 2169, 2175 (2010).

In *O'Brien* the U.S. Supreme Court stated that a fact was a "sentencing factor" only if it was not an "element" of the offence charged. In *O'Brien* defendants were charged with 4 counts in violation of 18 U.S.C. § 924 (c), which prohibits the use or carrying of a firearm in a crime of violence or drug trafficking offense. The minimum sentence for a violation is 5 years in prison. However, § 924(c) (1) (B) (ii) provides that if the firearm is a "machine gun", the minimum sentence is 30 years in prison. The prosecution dismissed one of the counts, the count that alleged use of a machine gun. After the defendants pled guilty to the remaining counts, the prosecution contended the fact that the defendants used a machine gun could be determined by the judge as a "sentence enhancement" factor, and if found by the judge would make the 30 year minimum sentence applicable. The trial judge disagreed, and sentenced the defendants within the 5 year minimum statute.

The prosecution appealed, but the Supreme Court agreed with the trial court. It held the "fact" of the use of a machine gun was an "element" of the offense, and not merely a "sentencing factor". The Court found that the immense danger of a machine gun, the moral depravity of a person choosing to use such a weapon, and the substantial increase in the mandatory minimum sentence meant the use of a machine gun was an element of the offense, and must be proved by the prosecution beyond a reasonable doubt. 130 S. Ct. at 2175.

Blakely v. Washington, 124 S. Ct. 2531 (2004), applied the reasoning of *Apprendi*, which involved specific statutory language that permitted a judge to find facts that increased the maximum sentence for a crime, to state sentencing systems. In *Blakely*, a defendant pled guilty to second-degree kidnapping and use of a firearm. After three days of hearings before the trial judge, the defendant was sentenced to a prison term more than three years longer than the maximum sentence for the crime charged, based on the trial judge's finding that the defendant acted with "deliberate cruelty." Under Washington State sentencing guidelines, a finding of deliberate cruelty permitted the sentencing judge to increase the sentence. The Washington Court of Appeals affirmed the conviction and sentence (47 P.3d 149). The Supreme Court granted certiorari.

The Supreme Court held the sentence was invalid under the Sixth Amendment, because the sentence imposed exceeded the maximum sentence possible based solely on the facts found by the jury. The Court held that the defendant was entitled to a jury trial on the facts supporting the finding that he acted with deliberate cruelty. Because the trial judge, rather than the jury, made the finding that the defendant acted with deliberate cruelty, the resulting sentence was invalid, the Court held.

In 2005 the Supreme Court decided the case of *United States v. Booker,* 125 S. Ct. 738. In *Booker,* the Court held that under the holdings of *Apprendi* and *Blakeley,* the Federal Sentencing Guidelines violated the Sixth Amendment's right to jury trials in criminal cases.

A majority of the Court concluded that the mandatory provisions of the Guidelines, which required judges to enhance sentences when certain facts were found by the judge, such as the quantity of the drug possessed by a defendant in a drug case, were unconstitutional. A different majority held, however, that the non-mandatory provisions of the Guidelines could be used by federal judges as reference points to help the judge reach a sentencing decision.

As a result, sentences may raise a problem under *Blakely* or *Booker* in either of two ways: in one, the sentencing judge may use facts found only by the judge to enhance the

U.S. SUPREME COURT CASES STATING THE CONSTITUTIONAL LIMITATIONS ON PUNISHMENT

Coker v. Georgia

Supreme Court of the United States (1977) 433 U.S. 584, 97 S. Ct. 2861

The defendant escaped from a Georgia prison where he had been serving sentences for murder, rape, kidnapping, and aggravated assault. While committing an armed robbery and another offense, he raped an adult woman. The defendant was convicted of rape, armed robbery, and other offenses and was sentenced to death on the rape charge. The U.S. Supreme Court reversed the sentence of death, holding:

> That question, with respect to rape of an adult woman, is now before us. We have concluded that a sentence of death is grossly disproportionate and excessive punishment for the crime of rape and is therefore forbidden by the Eighth Amendment as cruel and unusual punishment.

State of Louisiana ex rel. Francis v. Resweber

Supreme Court of the United States (1947) 329 U.S. 459, 67 S. Ct. 374

Because of an accidental failure of equipment, the defendant was not executed in the first attempt. The Court held that there was no intention to inflict unnecessary pain, and even though the defendant had been subjected to a current of electricity, this did not prevent the state from executing him in the second attempt. In the 1972 case of *Furman v. Georgia,* the U.S. Supreme Court stated that "had the failure been intentional, however, the punishment would have been, like torture, so degrading and indecent as to amount to a refusal to accord the criminal human status."

Robinson v. California

Supreme Court of the United States (1962) 370 U.S. 660, 82 S. Ct.1417

California enacted a law making narcotics addiction in itself a crime. The defendant received a ninety-day sentence for being a narcotics addict. The Court held that a state may not punish a person for being "mentally ill, or a leper, or … afflicted with a venereal disease" or for being addicted to narcotics. "Even one day in prison would be a cruel and unusual punishment for the 'crime' of having a common cold."

Wilkerson v. Utah

Supreme Court of the United States (1878) 99 U.S. 130, 25 L.Ed. 345

In this case, the Court upheld death by shooting on the grounds that it was a common method of execution in the 1870s.

Roberts v. Louisiana

Supreme Court of the United (1977) 431 U.S. 633, 97 S. Ct. 1993

The Supreme Court held that the fact that the murder victim was a police officer performing his regular duties may be regarded as an aggravating circumstance. The Court held that there is a special interest in affording protection to those public servants who regularly risk their lives to safeguard other people and property. However, a Louisiana statute that provided for a mandatory sentence of death for the crime of first-degree murder of a police officer and that did not allow consideration for particularized mitigating factors was held unconstitutional. The Supreme Court held that such a statute invites "jurors to disregard their oaths and choose a verdict for a lesser offense whenever they feel the death penalty is inappropriate."

Woodson v. North Carolina

Supreme Court of the United States (1976) 428 U.S. 280, 96 S. Ct. 2978

In holding a North Carolina death penalty statute unconstitutional because it provided for an automatic death penalty in all first-degree murder cases, the Court held that "the Eighth Amendment draws much of its meaning from 'the evolving standards of decency that mark the progress of a maturing society.'" The Court concluded that North Carolina's mandatory death penalty statute varied "markedly from contemporary standards."

defendant's sentence; in the other the judge may use the Federal Sentencing Guidelines as mandatory rather than discretionary. The first result is unconstitutional under *Blakely*; the second is prohibited by *Booker*. See, for example, *Villafranco v. United States*, 2006 WL 1049114 (D. Utah 2006).

Lower courts have addressed one question left open in *Booker*, namely, the extent the decision applied retroactively to sentences handed down before *Booker* was decided. While the Court held that the decision was applicable to all sentences that were not final when the decision was handed down, it did not decide what application the decision had for other sentences. Most courts considering the constitutionality of sentences that were final before *Booker* was decided have held the decision was not applicable to such sentences when collateral review was sought under statutes like 28 U.S.C. § 2255, the federal post-conviction relief statute. See, for example, *McIver v. United States*, 2007 WL 860989 (D.D.C. 2007). Generally speaking, when the Supreme Court announces a new rule of constitutional dimension like that in *Apprendi* or *Booker*, unless the Court holds that the rule is retroactive, it is not applicable to cases already final when the rule was announced. See *Tyler v. Cain*, 533 U.S. 656 (2001).

Except for the constitutional dimension limitations on sentencing discussed above, each state has its own system of determining the appropriate sentence for one convicted of a crime. These systems usually give the sentencing judge some discretion within a range set by the legislature. Some common characteristics of state sentencing systems include:

Sentences Can Be

Concurrent or Consecutive Sentences A defendant ordered to serve two years consecutively for conviction of two counts of a crime must serve the sentences one after the other, for a total of four years. If the sentences are to be served concurrently, they are served at the same time, for a total of two years for the two-count conviction.

Determinate or Indeterminate A sentence of a specific period (e.g., 30 days in jail) is a determinate sentence, and must be fully served, less time off for good behavior. A sentence of three to five years in prison is an example of an indeterminate sentence, with the minimum and maximum time to be served.

Suspended Sentence A person receiving a sentence like three to five years in prison could have the sentence suspended based on the person's agreement to commit to the completion of a drug treatment program and not be arrested or convicted of any other crime. Failure to comply with any of the conditions could result in the imposition of the original sentence.

Aggravating and Mitigating Factors Presentence reports prepared by a state agency play an important role in the final sentence. These reports will present the defendant's background and detail aggravating and mitigating factors. A long criminal record would be an aggravating factor while no previous criminal record would be a mitigating factor.

Other Sentencing Laws

Truth in Sentencing Laws In 1984 the federal government passed the Truth in Sentencing law (TIS), which encouraged states, by providing money for prison costs, to pass sentencing laws that guaranteed a defendant sentenced to, for example, a ten-year prison term would serve close to that entire time rather than just a few years. Under TIS laws, parole is abolished and an offender would be given a set determinate prison sentence, followed by a period of extended supervision similar to parole. If a violation of the supervision rules occurred, a re-confinement hearing could be held, and the person could be returned to prison.

The Florida Anti-Murder Act In 2007 Florida passed the Anti-Murder Act, Ch. 2007-2, § 5, Laws of Florida, March 12, 2007. Under the terms of this act, any violent offender on probation who violates the terms of his or her probation or commits another felony is immediately arrested and detained until a hearing is held on the violation. If the violation is upheld, the offender is returned to prison. Florida allocated $21.8 million to pay the expected increases in prison costs this new act would cause over the next three years. The law also expanded the authority of Florida judges to impose maximum prison sentences under Florida sentencing guidelines.

☰ Corporal Punishment

corporal punishment
Inflicting nondeadly
physical injury as pun-
ishment for criminal
conduct.

Corporal punishment was used as criminal punishment in the early history of the United States. Mutilations, such as cutting off ears and various types of branding, were discontinued many decades ago. Whipping, however, continued in some states into the early 1900s. The Eighth Circuit Court of Appeals observed that in 1968 only two states permitted the use of the strap as punishment. As a result of the Eighth Circuit Court's decision in the 1968 case of *Jackson v. Bishop,* whipping as a form of punishment was discontinued in the remaining two states. In the *Jackson* case, the court held:

> We have no difficulty in reaching the conclusion that the use of the strap in the penitentiaries of Arkansas is punishment which, in this last third of the 20th century, runs afoul of the Eighth Amendment; that the strap's use, irrespective of any precautionary conditions which may be imposed, offends contemporary concepts of decency and human dignity and precepts of civilization which we profess to possess; and that it also violates those standards of good conscience and fundamental fairness enunciated by this court in the *Carey* and *Lee* cases.[12]

The Use of Corporal Punishment in Schools

In the 1977 case of *Ingraham v. Wright,* the U.S. Supreme Court considered the relationship between the Cruel and Unusual Punishment Clause and the use of corporal punishment in public schools. The Court first observed that no general rule prohibited corporal punishment in schools: "The prevalent rule in this country today privileges such force as a teacher or administrator 'reasonably' believes to be necessary for [the child's] proper control, training or education."[13]

In holding that the Eighth Amendment Cruel and Unusual Punishment Clause is not applicable to the use of corporal punishment for disciplinary purposes in the public schools, the Court held:

> The schoolchild has little need for the protection of the Eighth Amendment. Though attendance may not always be voluntary, the public school remains an open institution. Except perhaps when very young, the child is not physically restrained from leaving school during school hours; and at the end of the school day, the child is invariably free to return home. Even while at school, the child brings with him the support of family and friends and is rarely apart from teachers and other pupils who may witness and protest any instances of mistreatment.
>
> The openness of the public school and its supervision by the community afford significant safeguards against the kinds of abuses from which the Eighth Amendment protects the prisoner. In virtually every community where corporal punishment is permitted in the schools, these safeguards are reinforced by the legal constraints of the common law. Public school teachers and administrators are privileged at common law to inflict only such corporal punishment as is reasonably necessary for the proper education and discipline of the child; any punishment going beyond the privilege may result in both civil and criminal liability.... As long as the schools are open to public scrutiny, there is no reason to believe that the common law constraints will not effectively remedy and deter excesses such as those alleged in this case.
>
> We conclude that when public school teachers or administrators impose disciplinary corporal punishment, the Eighth Amendment is inapplicable.

Ingraham continues to be the law today, and corporal punishment continues to be meted out in schools. The U.S. Department of Education, Office for Civil Rights, collected data for 2006-2007, and estimates that about 223,190 children are subjected to corporal punishment in public schools each year.

However, in *Sandin v. Conner*, 515 U.S. 472 (1995) the Supreme Court stated that although the Eighth Amendment may not apply to school punishments, where children are sent to public schools "arbitrary corporal punishments represents an invasion of personal security." Since that decision, some lower federal courts have interpreted the *Ingraham* decision as applying only to Eighth Amendment cruel and unusual punishment claims. Other claims based on Fourteenth Amendment procedural and substantive due process may be possible, these courts hold. See, e.g., *Preschooler II v. Clark County Bd. of Trustees*, 479 F.3d 1175 (9th Cir. 2007), where the court held that a teacher's slapping of an autistic child could qualify as excessive force and a violation of the Fourth and Fourteenth Amendments.

procedural due process A claim under the Fourteenth Amendment that there is an absence of fair procedures regulating state conduct.

Procedural due process claims under the Fourteenth Amendment are based on the absence of fair procedures regulating state conduct. For example, if a school district permitted corporal punishment without a prior determination of some violation of school rules by the student, the student's procedural due process rights would be violated.[14] Moreover, even if the school had fair procedures regulating such punishment, procedural due process could be violated if the state had no adequate means for a student to seek redress from a school or teacher who violated those procedures.[15]

substantive due process A claim under the Fourteenth Amendment that state conduct is so brutal, demeaning, and harmful as to shock the conscience.

Substantive due process claims under the Fourteenth Amendment are based on state conduct that is so brutal, demeaning, and harmful as to shock the conscience.[16] Almost all the federal courts of appeal have concluded that excessive corporal punishment by a school official can give rise to a Fourteenth Amendment substantive due process claim.[17]

An example of a substantive due process claim can be found in *Neal v. Fulton County Board of Education*, a 2000 decision of the Federal Eleventh Circuit Court of Appeals. In *Neal*, a student was seriously injured when the varsity football coach struck him in the eye with a metal weight lock as punishment for fighting with another student. The court concluded that the coach intentionally used an excessive amount of force that presented a reasonably foreseeable risk of serious bodily injury.[18]

In *Garcia v. Miera*, the Federal Tenth Circuit Court of Appeals summarized the law concerning school punishments:

> We thus envision three categories of corporal punishment. Punishments that do not exceed the traditional common law standard of reasonableness are not actionable; punishments that exceed the common law standard without adequate state remedies violate procedural due process rights; and finally, punishments that are so grossly excessive as to be shocking to the conscience violate substantive due process rights, without regard to the adequacy of state remedies.[19]

The Use of Corporal Punishment in Prisons

The use of corporal punishment against inmates of prisons is subject to Eighth Amendment cruel and unusual punishment claims. Unlike school students, prison inmates have none of the "community and legal constraints" that provide safeguards against the sort of abuses the Eighth Amendment prohibits.[20]

Eighth Amendment claims by prison inmates have both objective and subjective requirements. The inmate must show that the punishment failed the Eighth Amendment's proportionality test (the objective test) and also that the official administering the punishment possessed the requisite mental intent (the subjective test).[21] An example of such a punishment can be found in *Austin v. Hopper*, 15 F. Supp. 2d 1210 (M.D. Ala. 1998).

In *Austin*, an Alabama prison inmate was chained to a "hitching post" for several hours as punishment for violation of a prison regulation. He was denied food and water and not permitted to use a bathroom. The federal court held that his punishment constituted cruel and unusual punishment. It was excessive and not necessary to enforce the prison regulation and thus failed the objective proportionality test. Also, the official administering the punishment did so with "deliberate indifference to the inmate's health and safety," thus failing the subjective mental intent test.[22]

Capital Punishment

The death penalty was widely accepted at the time the U.S. Constitution and the Bill of Rights were ratified. The only reference to capital punishment in the Constitution is found in the Fifth Amendment, which reads: "No person shall be held to answer for a capital, or otherwise infamous crime, unless...." In the 1972 case of *Furman v. Georgia*, death penalty laws in all states were struck down as "arbitrary and capricious" by the U.S. Supreme Court.[23] The Court required all states wishing to use the death penalty to adhere to the following requirements:

- The issue of whether the death penalty will be used in the state must be submitted to the people of the state in a referendum.
- If a substantial majority of the voters approve the use of the death penalty, the state legislature must enact laws permitting the use of the death penalty.
- The new state statute must determine which crime (or crimes) could be punished by the death penalty, whether it will be the trial judge or jury who will make the decision to impose it, in what method it will be inflicted, and the appellate process used to review the sentence.
- The new statute must require juries or judges considering the death penalty to make findings of statutory **aggravating circumstances** to justify the imposition of the death penalty and also make findings of the **mitigating circumstances** that would weigh against the imposition of the death penalty.

aggravating circumstances A consideration in imposing the death penalty that judges and juries must make a finding of statutory aggravating circumstances to justify the penalty.

mitigating circumstances A consideration in imposing the death penalty that judges and juries must make findings of the mitigating circumstances that would weigh against the imposition of the death penalty.

Death Penalty Laws After *Furman v. Georgia* in 1972

The 1972 case of *Furman v. Georgia* invalidated death penalty statutes in 41 states, as well as federal crimes for which the death penalty could be imposed. In 1984, the U.S. Supreme Court observed that

> In responding to (*Furman v. Georgia*), roughly two-thirds of the States promptly redrafted their capital sentencing statutes in an effort to limit jury discretion and avoid arbitrary and inconsistent results. All of the new statutes provide for automatic appeal of death sentences. Most, such as Georgia's, require the reviewing court, to some extent at least, to determine whether, considering both the crime and the defendant, the sentence is disproportionate to that imposed in similar cases. Not every State has adopted such a procedure. In some States, such as Florida, the appellate court performs proportionality review despite the absence of a statutory requirement; in others, such as California and Texas, it does not.[24]

In 1976, the U.S. Supreme Court reviewed the new death penalty statutes of Georgia,[25] Florida,[26] and Texas.[27] In the 1984 California death penalty case of *Pulley v. Harris*,[28] the U.S. Supreme Court quoted from its 1976 *Jurek v. Texas* decision in affirming the death penalty procedure used by California:

> Texas' capital sentencing procedures, like those of Georgia and Florida, do not violate the Eighth and Fourteenth Amendments. By narrowing its definition of capital murder, Texas has essentially said that there must be at least one statutory aggravating circumstance in a first-degree murder case before a death sentence may even be considered. By authorizing the defense to bring before the jury at the separate sentencing hearing whatever mitigating circumstances relating to the individual defendant can be adduced, Texas has ensured that the sentencing jury will have adequate guidance to

IMPORTANT RECENT U.S. SUPREME COURT DEATH PENALTY DECISIONS

- In *Roper v. Simmons,* 543 U.S. 551 (2005), the U.S. Supreme Court held that the Cruel and Unusual Punishment Clause prohibited a state from executing a juvenile who was under the age of 18 when the capital crime was committed.
- In *Ford v. Wainright,* 477 U.S. 399 (1986), the Court held that the Eighth Amendment prohibits the execution of a prisoner who is insane at the time of the execution.

   Courts differed on what constitutes "insane" for Eighth Amendment purposes, though most followed a two-part test referenced in *Ford:* a defendant is not competent to be executed unless (1) he is aware of the punishment he is about to suffer, and (2) he knows why he is to suffer the punishment. In *Panetti v. Dretke,* 448 F.3d 815 (5th Cir. 2006), the Fifth Circuit Court of Appeals held that a defendant on Texas's death row was not insane, even though he suffered from severe paranoid delusions and believed the state really wanted him executed as punishment for preaching the Gospel. The Court concluded *Ford* did not require that the defendant "rationally understand" the reason for his execution. It is enough, the Court said, that he was "aware" of those reasons. The Supreme Court reversed, holding that the District Court should have considered the defendant's claims of delusions before concluding he was competent and sane. See *Panetti v. Qurterman,* 127 S. Ct. 2842 (2007).
- In *Atkins v. Virginia,* 536 U.S. 304 (2002), the Court held that the Cruel and Unusual Punishment Clause of the Eighth Amendment prohibited imposition of the death penalty on defendants with mental retardation.[a] In 2004, the Court held in *Tennard v. Dretke* (124 S. Ct. 2562) that evidence of mental retardation is inherently mitigating in a capital case, whether or not the defendant has shown a nexus between his mental capacity and the crime committed.
- In *Baze v. Rees,* 553 U.S. 35 (2008) the Court upheld the validity of the lethal injection method of execution. The 37 states using the lethal injection method all use a three-step "cocktail" for the execution. The first drug is an anesthetic, the second causes muscle paralysis, and the third causes cardiac arrest.
- In *Ring v. Arizona,* 536 U.S. 584 (2002), the Court held that a state capital sentencing procedure that permitted the sentencing judge to make the factual determination of the aggravating and mitigating circumstances present violated the Sixth Amendment's right of trial by jury. Factual questions bearing on the imposition of the death sentence or life imprisonment must be decided by the jury, the Court held.

enable it to perform its sentencing function. By providing prompt judicial review of the jury's decision in a court with statewide jurisdiction, Texas has provided a means to promote the evenhanded, rational, and consistent imposition of death sentences under law. Because this system serves to assure that sentences of death will not be "wantonly" or "freakishly" imposed, it does not violate the Constitution.

Polls show that the American public continues to generally support the death penalty. However, the number of death sentences imposed by American juries declined by about 2/3 in the years 1994 to 2009. In the peak year of 1994, 328 death sentences were imposed by juries. In 2008 that number was 111.[29] While American juries are imposing the death penalty less frequently, the number of executions was higher in 2009 because of the backlog of persons waiting on "death row".[30]

Reasons given for the decline in the use of death penalty by juries include:

- Fears by jurors that they are executing the wrong person. Most people are well aware that DNA evidence has proved innocent persons have been convicted in the past.
- States, such as Texas, have passed laws giving juries the option of sentencing the defendant to life without parole. In the past Texas averaged 34 death penalties per year, but in 2009 only 9 death penalties were handed down by juries.

However, in 2004 the Court held in *Schriro v. Summerlin* (124 S. Ct. 2519) that the rule in *Ring* did not apply retroactively and refused to invalidate a death sentence final at the time of the *Ring* decision.

- In *Sattazahn v. Pennsylvania,* 537 U.S. 101 (2003), the Court held that the Double Jeopardy Clause does not bar a state from imposing the death sentence after a defendant convicted of murder and sentenced to life imprisonment appeals the conviction and gets the conviction reversed. On retrial and subsequent conviction, the death sentence may be imposed.

- In the case of *Abdul-Kabir v. Quarterman,* 443 F.3d 441 (5th Cir. 2006), *cert. granted* 127 S. Ct. 432 (2006), the Court considered the jury instructions given to jurors in Texas in capital murder cases. In past cases the U.S. Supreme Court had determined that defendant is entitled to have the jury consider his or her mental condition as a mitigating factor in death penalty cases. (See, for example, *Tennard v. Dretke,* discussed above.) In this case, the question was, Should the jury who sentenced the defendant to death have been given instructions to consider evidence that the defendant had suffered child abuse and suffered from depression? The Supreme Court held that the jury should have been given special instructions on the defendant's mitigating evidence that would enable it to give meaningful relevance to that evidence. See *Abdul-Kabir v. Quarterman,* 127 S. Ct. 1654 (2007).

- In *Kennedy v. Louisiana,* 128 S. Ct. 2641 (2008), the Supreme Court invalidated a Louisiana statute permitting imposition of the death penalty for the rape of a child. Because the rape did not result in death, and was not intended to cause death, the Court said the cruel and unusual punishment did not permit imposition of the death penalty. The Court noted that since Louisiana adopted the statute in 1995, only 6 other states followed suit, indicating a national consensus existed against use of the death penalty in such cases.

[a]The *Atkins* court did not determine Atkins was retarded. Rather, it remanded the case to Virginia State court for a factual hearing on that issue. Atkins committed the murder for which he was sentenced to death in 1996, when he was 18 and had just dropped out of high school, having failed for the third time to pass the tenth grade. When Atkins was tested during his first trial in 1998 he scored 59 on an IQ test used in Virginia criminal cases, well below the cutoff score of 70 used for determination of retardation. However, when tested in November 2004 he scored 76 (the prosecution's test) and 74 (the defense's test). Atkins mental competency was submitted to a jury in 2005, and the jury concluded he was not retarded. In 2006 the Virginia Supreme Court reversed that decision, finding that the trial court erred by admitting improper expert testimony by the prosecution's expert witness, and by telling the jury the consequence of finding Atkins retarded would be to overturn a decision of a another jury to give Atkins the death sentence. The case was remanded for another hearing on Atkins's competency. See *Atkins v. Com.,* 631 S.E.2d 93 (2006). A circuit judge subsequently commuted Atkins' sentence to life imprisonment, which was upheld on appeal.

- In 2009 New Mexico became the 15th state to repeal the death penalty. The governor of New Mexico stated this was due in part to tight budgets and the high cost of death penalty appeals.
- Improved performance by defense counsel, coupled with the U.S. Supreme Court's requirement that juries be told life without parole is an option.
- Concern by juries that lethal injection as a method of execution lacks reliability.

Prosecutors have in the past used the threat of seeking the death penalty to obtain guilty pleas, or information about the crime. For example, when James Earl Ray assassinated Martin Luther King, his crime was extremely well-planned, and enabled him to obtain a Canadian passport in another person's name and escape to Europe before he was apprehended by European police. Prosecutors, believing others might be involved in the assassination, used the threat of the death penalty to try to convince Ray to provide information about the involvement of others. Ray did not cooperate, and prosecutors did not seek the death penalty. Ray never provided any information about a possible conspiracy, and he died in prison after one escape attempt.

FEDERAL CRIMES FOR WHICH THE DEATH PENALTY CAN NOW BE APPLIED

When President Clinton signed the 1994 Violent Crime Control and Law Enforcement Act, the number of federal crimes for which the death penalty could be applied increased significantly. The following is the 1994 list of federal death penalty crimes:

Assassination of the president, vice president, a member of Congress, cabinet member, or Supreme Court justice

Drug trafficking of large amount of drugs

First-degree murder on federal land or property

Genocide

Gun murders during federal crimes of violence and during drug trafficking crimes

Killing a person in a federal witness protection program

Killing (or attempted murder) by a drug kingpin of a public officer or a juror to obstruct justice

Murder at a U.S. international airport

Murder by a federal prisoner or escaped prisoner who is (or was) serving a life sentence

Murder for hire (when federal crime)

Murder in aid of racketeering activity (federal)

Murder in a federal facility involving a firearm

Murder of federal witness, victim, or informant

Murder of a state correctional officer by an inmate

Murder of a U.S. citizen abroad by another U.S. citizen

Murder of a court officer or juror

Murder of a federal law enforcement official

Murder of a foreign official or internationally protected person on U.S. soil

Murder of a state or local official assisting federal law officers

Murder within the special maritime and territorial jurisdiction of United States

Treason and espionage

Where death results:

- Aircraft hijacking (domestic or international)
- Alien smuggling
- Carjacking (federal)
- Destroying federal property with explosives
- Destruction of aircraft, motor vehicles, or their facilities (federal)
- Drive-by shooting (federal)
- Hostage taking (federal)
- Kidnapping (federal)
- Mailing injurious articles (such as explosives)
- Robbery of a federally insured bank
- Sexual abuse (federal)
- Sexual exploitation of children (federal)
- Torture (federal)
- Train sabotage (federal)
- Transporting explosives with intent to kill
- Use of weapons of mass destruction (poison gas, biological, and so on)
- Violating federally protected rights based on race, religion, or national origin

≡ Imprisonment as Punishment

Under early Roman law, imprisonment was illegal as punishment and was used for detention only.[31] Imprisonment is as old as the law of England, but only rarely did statutes in early England provide for imprisonment as punishment for crime. Nearly every English court had its own particular prison, and the right of keeping a gaol (jail) in and for a particular district was a franchise the king granted to certain people, just as he

CASE CLOSE-UP

Graham v. Florida
United States Supreme Court, 2010
130 S. Ct. 2011

In 2003, at the age of 16, Terrance Graham and two friends attempted to rob a restaurant in Jacksonville, Florida. Graham was arrested, and tried as an adult for attempted robbery. He pled guilty, and was sentenced to three years' probation, the first year of which was ordered to be spent in jail. In December 2004, six months after his release from jail and while still on probation, Graham and two friends undertook a home invasion, where they assaulted the homeowner, holding a pistol against his chest while the home was ransacked. Later that night Graham and his friends attempted another robbery, during the course of which one of the friends was shot. Graham took the friend to a hospital, and was subsequently arrested and charged with armed robbery. At the time, Graham was 34 days short of his 18th birthday.

Because Graham was on probation, a court held a hearing on the state's claim that Graham had violated his probation by engaging in criminal conduct and possessing a weapon. The court held him in violation of probation, finding Graham committed the crimes charged. Based on these charges, the judge could impose a sentence from 5 years to life. Although the pre-sentence report prepared by the probation office suggested a 4-year prison sentence, the judge sentenced Graham to life in prison. Because Florida had dropped its parole system, see Fla. Stat. § 921.002, this sentence amounted to a sentence of life without possibility of parole. That meant the only chance for Graham to be released was executive clemency. The Florida appellate courts affirmed the sentence. The U. S. Supreme Court granted certiorari, and reversed.

The Court first stated that the cases on application of the cruel and unusual punishment clause could be divided into those cases where the *particular sentence* given a defendant was under review, and those cases where a *particular type of sentence* was involved. In the former class of cases, the proportionality rules of *Ewing* and *Harmelin* must be followed. Those rules require a preliminary showing that the sentence imposed in that case must be "grossly disproportionate" to the crime committed.

In the second class of cases, the Court said "categorical rules" were applied to decide the cruel and unusual punishment question. Those cases "were different from *Ewing* or *Harmelin* because (they) implicated a 'particular type of sentence' not a "particular defendant's sentence." 130 S. Ct. at 2022-23. As a result, in categorical cases, there is no need to apply the grossly disproportionate test. The Court then concluded that a life sentence without parole given to a juvenile was properly reviewed under the categorical approach. That approach determines the cruel and unusual punishment issue either by the nature of the offense, such as the death penalty for a non-homicide crime, or by the characteristics of the defendant, such as the death penalty for juveniles or the retarded. Here, the Court held, the characteristic of the defendant as a juvenile made a categorical approach appropriate.

The Court stated there are several considerations when considering the cruel and unusual nature of a punishment applied to a juvenile. First among them is the existence of a "national consensus" on the punishment. Even though 37 states and the

United States permit life without parole for juveniles in non-homicide cases, the Court found a consensus against the use of the punishment based on the small number of juveniles who actually receive the sentence. The Court found that nationwide only 127 juveniles were serving such a sentence, and that 77 of these juveniles were in Florida.

As another consideration, the Court found that none of the traditional justifications for punishment; retribution, deterrence, incapacitation, or rehabilitation, supported imposition of life without parole. Moreover, the Court found that because juveniles, unlike adult offenders, lack maturity and have an underdeveloped sense of responsibility, they have lesser culpability than adult offenders.

Finally, the Court noted that the United States is the only country in the world that sentences juveniles to life in prison without parole for non-homicide crimes. It therefore held: "A state need not guarantee the offender eventual release, but if it imposes a sentence of life it must provide him or her with some realistic opportunity to obtain release before the end of that term." 130 S. Ct. at 2035.

Three Justices dissented, two of them based on their belief that the Eighth Amendment's cruel and unusual punishment clause did not apply to term sentences. The Chief Justice concurred in the result, but on the basis that the life sentence without parole was "grossly disproportionate" under existing cases such as *Solem* and *Harmelin*.

In a concurring opinion joined by two justices, Justice Stevens stated this about the cruel and unusual punishment clause: "Society changes. Knowledge accumulates. We learn, sometimes, from our mistakes. Punishments that did not seem cruel and unusual at one time may, in the light of reason and experience, be found cruel and unusual at a later date." 130 S. Ct. at 2036.

granted other rights connected with the administration of justice in England. In addition to the franchise prisons were the Fleet, the prison of the Star Chamber, and the prison of the Court of Chancery.[32]

Because of the filthy, unsanitary conditions of the early English prisons and the corruption and brutality that arose from the franchise system, reform movements began in England as early as 1773, when John Howard became sheriff of Bedfordshire. When he saw the disgraceful conditions in his jail, he proposed that salaried gaolers replace the franchise system. The condition of U.S. prisons has also been the subject of many reform movements, and the use of prisons for the purpose of punishment has been subject to much debate.

Can Indigents Be Held in Jail to Work Off Their Money Fines?

In the 1970 case of *Williams v. Illinois*,[33] the question of whether a person who was indigent (without money) could be imprisoned for the inability to pay a fine was presented to the U.S. Supreme Court. In the *Williams* case, the Illinois courts ruled that Williams would be held in prison and work off his fine at the rate of $5 per day. Williams asked to be released so he could get a job and pay the fine and court costs.

In the case of *Tate v. Short*,[34] the indigent defendant owed fines of $425 on nine traffic offenses and was ordered to serve 85 days in a Texas prison farm to work off the fines at the rate of $5 per day.

The U.S. Supreme Court held that other ways of collecting fines are available and that the Equal Protection Clause of the U.S. Constitution is violated by permitting a person with money to pay fines, whereas a person without money has to work off a fine in jail or prison.[35]

Fines as Punishment

Money fines payable by the convicted offender are frequently used as an alternative to incarceration or together with incarceration. In most states, the maximum fine for any designated criminal act is set by statute. Also, it is common to limit the amount of a fine each level of court within a state may assess against a defendant. A municipal court that handles minor offenses has a lower fine limit than a district court with the jurisdiction to hear major crimes.

Fines must not be excessive. The Eighth Amendment to the U.S. Constitution prohibits "excessive fines imposed" as punishment. Generally, analysis of punishment under the Cruel and Unusual Punishment Clause requires application of the proportionality test. In excessive fines cases, that means comparing the fine assessed with the nature of the offense charged.

Fines can be difficult to collect if the offender is unemployed or has a low-paying job. To improve the rate of collection of fines, some or all of the following methods are used:

- Allowing offenders to pay their fines on an installment plan, which is usually worked out by a clerk taking into account the income of an offender and the amount due.
- Accepting credit cards for payment.
- Computerizing record-keeping systems.
- Telemarketing (use of the telephone to contact people and remind them of payments due).
- Turning collection over to private collection agencies that can pursue debtors across state lines and often have access to databases that allow them to track the movements of an offender. Collection agencies often routinely notify credit bureaus of delinquent accounts, a practice that is reported to be an important factor in recovering overdue fines.

Forfeiture as Punishment

forfeiture Going back to early English law, the concept and use of seizing the property that was used to commit a crime is a strong deterrent to crime, as is seizing the profits of crime a deterrent in crimes committed for profit.

The concept and use of **forfeiture** go back to early English law. Seizing the property that was used to commit a crime is a strong deterrent to crime. Seizing the profits of crime is also a deterrent in crimes committed for profit.

Forfeiture was first used in customs violations such as smuggling. In addition to the traditional criminal punishments of death and fines, the economic sanction of forfeiture was imposed with seizure of ships, implements, and the goods being smuggled.

Forfeiture not only punished the wrongdoers by depriving them of ships (or boats), implements, and goods but also rewarded the king and government, who benefited from the use and sale of these items.

The concept of forfeiture came to America with English common law. It was used over the years in various forms. During Prohibition, forfeiture was used extensively to deter and discourage the manufacture, sale, and use of illegal alcohol.

While forfeiture is not "punishment" for many purposes, such as application of the Double Jeopardy Clause, it remains an important part of law enforcement's efforts to combat crime. Federal statutes today authorize the forfeiture not only of contraband property but also of instrumentalities used in narcotics, gambling, and untaxed alcohol and tobacco. For example, Section 55 of the Uniform Controlled Substance Act, which has been adopted by many states and the federal government, provides for forfeiture not only of controlled substances in violation of the law but also of all raw materials, all vehicles "used, or intended for use," weapons, records and books, and all property, "including money" and profits. Section 55.5 of the act details forfeiture proceedings.[36]

Important recent U.S. Supreme Court cases regarding civil forfeitures are as follows:

- *United States v. Ursery,* 116 S. Ct. 2134 (1996). The Supreme Court held that "in rem civil forfeitures are neither 'punishment' nor criminal for the purposes of the Double Jeopardy Clause"; therefore, the government can commence both a criminal action and a civil forfeiture action without violating double jeopardy.

- *Austin v. United States,* 509 U.S. 602 (1993). The Supreme Court held that the civil forfeiture provision of 21 U.S.C. § 881(a)(4) providing for forfeiture of property used in drug transactions was "punishment" for purposes of the Eighth Amendment excessive fines clause. Whether termed civil or criminal, the Court stated a forfeiture provision is a "punishment" if it has a purpose other than remedial.

- *Bennis v. Michigan,* 116 S. Ct. 994 (1996). In this case, the Supreme Court held that a state forfeiture law could provide for forfeiture (seizure) of property from an owner who was unaware of the illegal use of the property. (Bennis was convicted of a sex act with a prostitute in a car owned by Bennis and his wife, who was unaware of the illegal use of the car.) The U.S. Supreme Court held that under such a state statute, "the innocence of an owner (Bennis's wife) has almost uniformly been rejected as a defense to forfeiture."

- *United States v. 785 Nicholas Ave.,* 983 F.2d 396, *review denied* U.S. Supreme Court 113 S. Ct. 2349 (1993). Under 21 U.S.C.A. Section 881(a)(7), the federal government may seize real estate being used for illegal activity such as drug dealing. To defend against such a forfeiture action, the owners must demonstrate a lack of consent to the illegal activities and that they did all that reasonably could be expected to prevent the illegal activities once they learned of them.

Under federal law today and under the provisions of the forfeiture statutes of many states, the following can now be seized under court order:

- Instrumentalities of the crime (vehicles, watercraft, and the like used in the commission of the crimes)
- Profits of the crime (money from drug dealing, stolen goods, and so on)
- Proceeds of the illegal acts (farms, yachts, cars, homes, and other luxury goods purchased from profits of illegal acts)

The Internal Revenue Service can also seize under court order the property of people charged with or convicted of crimes. Because people involved in the sale of marijuana, cocaine, and narcotics often make huge profits without paying proper taxes, tax liens may be filed against them. Property belonging to such people may be seized for payment of taxes, including homes, furniture, cars, stereo equipment, video games, gems, and real estate.

Under the Mandatory Victims Restitution Act, 18 U.S.C. section 3663A, Federal judges shall order restitution as part of the sentences in certain crimes, such as crimes of violence or fraud, where an identifiable person has suffered a loss. In *Dolan v. United States,* 130 S.Ct. 1047 (2010) the Supreme Court held that while the Act requires a judge to determine the amount of restitution to be paid no later than 90 days after sentencing, the 90 day limit could be extended if the judge determines restitution will be ordered, but cannot within the time limit determine the exact amount to be ordered.

≡ Career Criminals and the Repeat Offender

Law enforcement priorities are most often determined by the crime itself. High priority is most often given when crimes involve injury or death or when important aspects of public interest are involved.

Attention is focused on the person committing the crime rather than on the crime when it is determined that the person is a career criminal or a repeater (or habitual criminal). Recidivism is a major problem in the United States. In a 2009 report published by the Office of Justice Program, Bureau of Statistics, titled "Re-Entry Trend in the United States: Recidivism," statistics showed that nationwide 67.5 percent of persons released from prison in 1994 were rearrested within 3 years of their release. 51.8 percent of those released were back in prison within 3 years.

By taking such offenders off the street, the incidence of crimes can be considerably lessened. Many cities and states have created career-criminal programs. Such programs ordinarily

- Operate under statutes providing additional and longer sentences for repeat offenders.
- Establish special career-criminal units in the offices of police and prosecutors that vigorously investigate frequently committed crimes or crimes following patterns.
- Speed up prosecution of career criminals.
- Discourage plea bargaining, which could lessen prison terms, unless the suspect incriminates associates.

recidivist One who is a habitual criminal.

Several repeater (**recidivist**) cases have come before the U.S. Supreme Court in recent years, with different results. One of the earliest cases was the 1980 Texas case of *Rummel v. Estelle*. In that case a defendant had received a life sentence under the Texas repeater statutes for three nonviolent crimes that netted the defendant a total of $230. The Court affirmed the conviction and sentence, holding that the sentence did not violate the Eighth Amendment.

In 1983 the case of *Solem v. Helm*, 463 U.S. 277, was decided by the U.S. Supreme Court. Helm lived in South Dakota and had a serious problem with alcohol. By 1975, he had committed six nonviolent felonies. In 1979, he pleaded guilty to uttering (passing) a "no account" check for $100 (his seventh felony). Under the South Dakota recidivist statute, his crime was classified as a "class I" felony, and he was sentenced to life imprisonment. Unlike the Texas statutes in the *Rummel* case, South Dakota statutes forbade parole in recidivist cases. Murderers and rapists were eligible for parole in South Dakota, but Helm would never be eligible for parole. The Supreme Court held that the sentence violated the Eighth Amendment as follows:

> The Constitution requires us to examine Helm's sentence to determine if it is proportionate to his crime. Applying objective criteria, we find that Helm has received the penultimate sentence for relatively minor criminal conduct. He has been treated more harshly than other criminals in the State who have committed more serious crimes. He has been treated more harshly than he would have been in any other jurisdiction, with the possible exception of a single State. We conclude that his sentence is significantly disproportionate to his crime, and is therefore prohibited by the Eighth Amendment.

The absence of the possibility of parole appeared to be the basis for the distinction between *Solem* and *Rummel*; the defendant in *Rummel* could be eligible for parole in 12 years, whereas the defendant in *Solem* would never be paroled. However, in *Ewing v. California*, 538 U.S. 11 (2003) the Court upheld a sentence of 25 years to life under the California "Three Strikes" law (discussed in the next section). The statute provided that parole could not be considered until the 25-year term had passed, but the Court did not identify the possibility of parole as the basis of its decision. Rather, the Court held that a state has a legitimate interest in incarcerating repeat offenders who have demonstrated an inability to conform to the criminal laws.

In *Lockyer v. Andrade* (discussed in the next section) a companion case to *Ewing*, the Court upheld a sentence of two consecutive 25 years-to-life terms under the California

PRISONS AND JAILS IN THE UNITED STATES; 2009–2010

Every year thousands inmates are released from U.S. prisons. Unfortunately, many of these inmates are back in prison within a few years of their release. This result, called *recidivism,* has for years been a serious problem in the United States. The causes of this high recidivism rate have been debated for years in Congress and in the states. There is general agreement that two of the major factors contributing to that high rate are the serious mental health problems of about one in six inmates and the scarcity of programs for helping an ex-convict find a job and start a new life.

Because states must spend nearly $30 billion each year to maintain prisons, new efforts are being made to deal with the recidivism problem.

During the 40 years from 1969 to 2009, prison and jail populations have grown every year in the United States, to a present total of about 2 million prisoners. This is far more than the combined total number of inmates incarcerated in the 36 European countries.[a]

At present, each year about 650,000 inmates are released from prisons, but unfortunately between ½ and 2/3 of these inmates are back in prison within a few years of their release. *Recidivism* continues to be a very serious problem in the United States, and state and federal officials are very concerned about that problem. U.S. Attorney General Eric Holder stated before the American Bar Association in 2009 that "[t]here is no doubt that we must be tough on crime. But we must also commit ourselves to being smart on crime … we need to adopt what works."[b]

There were, however, some surprising changes in 2009. State prison populations fell nearly 6 percent. The average state cost for each prisoner is about $25,000 per year, which amounts to about $1 in every $15 from a state's general fund. New York had a 20 percent reduction, and New Jersey had a 19 percent reduction. California is sending fewer low-risk parolees back to prison for parole violations, and Texas is increasing its residential and community-based treatment programs.

There remain important questions to answer. Will crime rates go up because of unemployment and other problems in the United States? Will recidivism continue at the present high rates? How will the state and federal governments react to these situations?

[a]See the *New York Times* article of 4/23/08 entitled "U.S. Inmate Count Far Exceeds Those of Other Nations."
[b]See the *New York Times* op-ed article of 8/15/09 entitled "Getting Smart on Crime."

three strikes law. While dissenting justices noted that a 50-year minimum sentence for a 37-year-old defendant amounted to life without parole, the majority did not make the presence or absence of parole the basis for its decision.

"Three Strikes" Laws

For many years, most states and the federal government have had laws that provided for increased punishment for multiple felony convictions. For example, The Armed Career Criminal Act, 18 U.S.C. § 924(e)(1), mandates a sentence of 15 years in prison for any felon convicted of violation of 18 U.S.C. § 922 (g)(1), the felon in possession of a firearm statute, if the felon had three previous convictions for drug offenses or "violent crimes." In *Begay v. United States*, 453 U.S. 137 (2008) the U.S. Supreme Court held that "violent crimes" under § 924(e)(1) did not include previous fourth-offense convictions for drunken driving, even though treated as a felony under state law. The Court reasoned that Congress intended to limit the kind of prior felonies that resulted in the increased sentence to crimes which were in their nature violent or created to possibility of violence. For similar reasons, the Supreme Court held in *Johnson v. United States*, 130 S. Ct. 1265 (2010) that a conviction under the Florida battery statute, which defines the crime as "actually and intentionally touching" another person, was not a violent felony under the ACCA.

ALTERNATIVES TO PRISONS FOR OFFENDERS BELIEVED TO BE NONVIOLENT

Alternative Punishment	Description	Probable Use
House arrest or confinement with electronic monitoring	Monitoring is done with an ankle or wrist bracelet or a telephone device that monitors the detainee's presence in the house.	Used as a mixture of penalties tailored to the offender. Person must agree as condition of parole, probation, or work release program.
Agreement to take a drug such as Antabuse or to commit to a drug treatment program	When the cause of the criminal conduct is alcohol abuse, drugs are available to suppress or eliminate the urge to drink. Drug and alcohol treatment programs are available in all states.	Person agrees to take suppressant medication "voluntarily" as condition of probation or parole, usually to avoid imprisonment.
"Intensive sanctions" or "shock" probation or parole	Usually used for nonviolent, non-drug user. Can be sentenced by court or enter a program from a correctional institution. Used in overcrowded jails or prisons to free space for new inmates.	The overcrowding of jails and prisons causes use of this type of program.
"Therapy courts"	There are about two thousand "therapy courts" in the United States dealing with drug, alcohol, and spousal abuse problems. A few courts dealing with gambling addiction have recently been formed.	Because of lack of adequate home facilities, house arrest is not used. Persons committing crimes caused by their addictions or to fund their addictions are likely to be repeat offenders unless they successfully complete treatment programs. In these courts, they are given the choice of correcting their problems or going to prison.
Mandatory deportation	Under stricter immigration laws enacted by the U.S. Congress, immigrants who have been convicted of a broad range of felonies (from murder to drug possession) must be deported to their country of origin.	In 1997, more than 40,000 people were deported to free up prison space and lower crime rates.[a]
Banishment to another city or state	Giving an unwanted person the choice to "get out of town" or go to jail was not uncommon fifty years ago. Some cities even provided bus fare. Another practice was to suspend a criminal sentence if the defendant joined the military. It was much easier to get into the military in those days.	Today, the banishment order must be reasonably related to the offense and to rehabilitation. In the 1991 rape case of *McCreary v. State* (582 So. 2d 425), the Supreme Court of Mississippi reviewed cases from other states where banishment was part of a punishment package that the defendant agreed to (usually in a plea bargain agreement).

[a]The eventual success of the program is discussed in the *New York Times* article, "U.S. Deports Felons but Can't Keep Them Out,"August 11, 1997.

CASE CLOSE-UP

James v. United States
Supreme Court of the United States
127 S. Ct. 1586 (2007)

In 18 U.S.C. Section 924, the Armed Career Criminal Act (ACCA), the federal government has established enhanced penalties for persons convicted of federal offences where firearms are involved. Where convictions for previous offenses involved violence, Section 924 provides for enhanced sentences based on the number of those previous convictions.

James was convicted of possession of a firearm after a felony conviction in violation of 18 U.S.C. 922(g)(1). At his sentencing the prosecution argued James should be sentenced under Section 924(e) of the ACCA, which provides for an enhanced sentence of 15 years if the defendant has previously been convicted of three violent crimes in state or federal court. The act defines a "violent crime" as a crime that carries a punishment of more than one year in prison, and (1) has as an element of the crime the threat or use of physical force, or (2) is burglary, extortion, arson, use of explosives, "or otherwise involves conduct that presents a serious potential risk of physical injury to another."

James argued the act did not apply to him, because one of his past convictions was for attempted burglary in Florida. James contended that not every attempted burglary involved violence, and as a result a conviction for attempted burglary did not qualify for inclusion under the act. The Federal District Court disagreed and sentenced James to the minimum 15-year term, and the Court of Appeals affirmed his conviction. The Supreme Court granted certiorari, and in a 5-4 decision affirmed the Court of Appeals.

The Supreme Court first rejected James's argument that not every attempted burglary involved the potential for violence. The Court noted that the Florida Supreme Court had limited convictions for attempted burglary under the statute to attempts that included an act directed toward entering a dwelling. Thus, merely being in possession of burglary tools could not, under Florida law, be enough to convict for attempted burglary. The Supreme Court then reasoned that because attempted burglary under Florida law required an act directed toward unlawfully entering a dwelling, every attempted burglary created the risk that the burglar might encounter another person while doing so and might result in violence. The likelihood of violence was one of the reasons Congress included burglary in the listed crimes that qualified as violent crimes, the Court said, and attempted burglaries carried that same risk. Indeed, the Court observed, attempted burglary might well carry a greater risk of violence, since by definition every person charged with attempted burglary in Florida must have encountered another person during the attempt and been arrested. As a result, the Court held that attempted burglary under Florida law constituted a crime that met the ACCA's residual definition of "violent crime," that is, conduct that "presents a serious potential risk of physical injury to another," and it affirmed James's sentence under the ACCA.

The dissenting justices were critical of the majority because it failed to give any basis for determining when the potential for physical injury was serious enough to satisfy the "violent crime" definition. As a result, they believed, lower federal courts sentencing under the ACCA would have no real guidelines for determining when a defendant fit within the act's coverage.

In the mid-1990s laws called "three strikes and you're out" laws gained prominence when the U.S. Congress incorporated a "three strikes" provision into the Violent Crime Control and Law Enforcement Act of 1994. Many states followed suit.[37]

"three strikes" laws
Laws that impose increased penalties for multiple felony convictions.

In November 1994, California voters adopted Proposition 184, a "three strikes" law, in part as a response to the murder of Kimberly Reynolds, an 18-year-old fashion student, by a paroled drug dealer with a long history of violent crime. California's law is among the harshest **"three strikes" laws** for three reasons: (1) the third or "trigger" conviction may be any felony, not necessarily one for a violent crime; (2) the first two strikes may be convictions for any "serious" felony, though not necessarily a violent crime; and (3) a sentence of 25 years to life must be assessed on each count, with multiple counts served consecutively. Parole may not be considered until the entire mandatory sentence is served.[38]

In 2003 the U.S. Supreme Court decided *Lockyer v. Andrade*, 538 U.S. 63. Andrade was convicted under California's "three strikes" law and sentenced to two terms of 25 years to life, meaning Andrade would not be eligible for parole until 2046. The crimes Andrade committed to invoke the "three strikes" law were mainly minor theft crimes, not crimes of violence. The Ninth Circuit Court of Appeals found the "three strikes" statute unconstitutional, because the sentence was so disproportionate to the crimes committed it violated the Eighth Amendment. The Supreme Court reversed the Ninth Circuit, holding that under established law the sentence was not grossly disproportionate as to violate the Eighth Amendment.

The *Andrade* decision provides no clear answer to the "gross disproportionality" problem for sentences under "three strikes" laws. However, the last paragraph in the majority opinion suggests the approach the Supreme Court will take to that problem when presented again: "The gross disproportionality principle reserves a constitutional violation for only the extraordinary case."

SENTENCE ENHANCEMENT STATUTES

All states and the federal government use sentence enhancement statutes that increase criminal penalties. The following are some of the usual conditions that cause enhancement:

- The crime is a hate crime, or the victim is elderly or handicapped.
- The person is a repeat offender (habitual criminal statute).
- A dangerous weapon is used committing the crime.
- A bulletproof garment is used in committing the crime.
- Concealment of identity (such as a mask) is used.
- Drugs or a weapon is used or sold within 1,000 feet of a school.

Another form of enhancement used to protect people having duties within the criminal justice system increases a misdemeanor battery to a felony battery if committed against:

- A law enforcement or fire-fighting officer if the officer is acting in an official capacity
- A witness or juror
- A public official or officer
- A prison guard, another prisoner, visitor, and so on by a prisoner
- In the 1997 case of *United States v. Gonzales*, 1997 WL 525410 (C.A.5 Tex.), the defendant carried a machine gun during a drug transaction. The 30-year additional sentence enhancement under the federal enhancement statute (18 U.S.C.A. § 924[c]) was held not to violate the Eighth Amendment because machine guns are uniquely associated with drug trafficking and crimes of violence and present a grave danger to the public.

State courts may, notwithstanding the holding in *Lockyer v. Andrade*, overturn a sentence under state constitutional provisions. California, as an example, has a "cruel or unusual" prohibition in its state constitution, Article 1, section 17. In *People v. Carmony*, 26 Cal. Rptr. 3d 365 (2005), the court held a 25-to-life sentence under the California three strikes law for failure to register as a sex offender within 5 days of a defendant's birthday violated the state constitution.

Summary

- The text of the Eighth Amendment prohibits excessive bail, excessive fines, and cruel and unusual punishment.
- The Sixth Amendment requires that factual findings made for the purpose of enhancing a sentence must be made by a jury.
- The Federal Sentencing Guidelines are no longer mandatory, but federal courts imposing sentences must consider the guidelines and the factors stated in the Federal Sentencing act, 18 U.S.C. § 3553 when imposing a sentence.
- School officials may impose corporal punishment on a student only if (1) it is not excessive, and (2) results after a prior determination that the student violated a school rule.
- *Furman v. Georgia* held that imposition of the death penalty without an established procedure to determine which defendant should live and which die was arbitrary and capricious, and thus a violation of the Eighth and Fourteenth Amendments. It was not the death penalty that was unconstitutional, but the "lightning-like" way it was imposed that violated the Constitution.
- Mentally retarded defendants, juveniles under the age of 18, and insane persons may not be given the death penalty.
- State statutes must identify "aggravating circumstances" and the jury must find such circumstances exist before the death penalty may be imposed. Jurors must also be instructed on "mitigating" factors to be integrated into the decision to impose the death penalty.
- "Three strikes" laws provide for the automatic enhancement of a prison sentence, often to life imprisonment, upon the conviction of a third felony or violent crime. Parole generally is not available until the minimum term or years are served.

Key Terms

benefit of clergy, p. 192
sanctuary, p. 193
capital punishment, p. 194
cruel and unusual
   punishment, p. 194

proportionality, p. 195
corporal punishment, p. 199
procedural due process, p. 200
substantive due process, p. 200
aggravating circumstances, p. 201

mitigating circumstances, p. 201
forfeiture, p. 207
recidivist, p. 209
"three strikes" laws, p. 213

Case Analysis and Writing Exercises

1. Were the sentences in the following well-publicized cases appropriate in achieving the goals of the criminal justice system?

Person	Offense Convicted of	Sentence
Pete Rose (baseball player and manager)	Failed to report and pay income taxes on $354,968	Five months in jail, three months at a halfway house, 11,000 hours of community service, $50,000 fine.
Joseph Hazelwood (former captain of the oil tanker *Exxon Valdez*)	Was drinking the night his ship caused the biggest oil spill in the history of Alaska	Sentenced to scrub oil-soaked beaches in Alaska for 1,000 hours (25 weeks).
Leona Helmsley (hotel owner)	Failed to report and pay taxes on $ .8 million	Four years in prison and a fine of $7.1 million.
Zsa Zsa Gabor (actress)	Slapped a motorcycle officer during a valid traffic stop in Beverly Hills, California	Three days in jail, 120 hours of community service in a homeless shelter for women, $13,000 fine.
Lawrence Singleton (raped a 15-year-old California hitch-hiker and then hacked her forearms off in 1978; released after serving eight years of a fourteen-year sentence)	Moved to Florida after being run out of several California towns; convicted in 1991 in Florida of petty theft and obstruction (lying to police as to his identification)	The *Singleton* case caused California and other states to increase manda-tory sentences for violent crimes. In 1997, Singleton was convicted of the murder of a Tampa, Florida, prosti-tute and sentenced to death. He was 69 years old at the time. (Singleton died of cancer in 2001 while on death row in Florida.)
John du Pont (the wealthiest murder defendant in the his-tory of the United States)	Without provocation, shot and killed Olympic gold medalist Dave Schultz	Found guilty of third-degree murder but mentally ill in 1997. After re-ceiving the mental treatment he needs, du Pont will serve the balance of his sentence of five to ten years.
Daniel Rostenkowski (as chair-man of the House Ways and Means Committee, was one of the most influential members of the U.S. Congress)	Federal charges of mail fraud in a scandal in the House Post Office and using federal money for personal expenses	Lost his reelection bid after his conviction in 1994 and served a 15-month sentence, followed by two years of probation. Will keep his

2. Bajakajean ("B") was convicted of the federal crime of willful transportation of U.S. currency in excess of $10,000 outside U.S. borders. B had $357,144 in his possession and was about to board a plane for Italy when arrested. He was sentenced to three years' probation and fined $15,000.

The United States sought forfeiture of the $357,144 under a law that stated the sentencing court "shall order that the person forfeit ... any property ... involved in the offense."

a. If the sentencing court orders forfeiture of the $357,144, is it a "fine"?

b. If so, would it violate the Excessive Fines Clause of the Eighth Amendment? How is "excessive" to be determined in such cases? See *United States v. Bajakajian,* 524 U.S. 321 (1998).

3. Many states use a lethal injection system for execution of convicted killers. California is one of those states. What issues are raised when an inmate facing lethal injection contends that the method is unconstitutional because the procedure causes unusual pain and suffering? How should they be resolved? See *Morales v. Hickman,* 438 F.3d 926 (9th Cir. 2006), *cert. denied* 126 S. Ct. 1314 (2006).

4. One form of punishment permitted, but not often used, is banishment from a particular location for a specific time. What are some of the issues that might arise if a defendant objects to such a punishment? Which of the two banishments imposed in the following cases should be upheld?

a. *State v. Schimelpfenig,* 115 P.3d 338 (Wash. App. 2005): Convicted murderer banned for life from residing in county where victim lived and family still lived.

b. *People v. Brockelman,* 933 P.2d 1315 (Colo. 1997): Defendant convicted of assault of former girlfriend banned from visiting town where girlfriend lived.

Notes

1. *A History of the Criminal Law of England* (three volumes) by Sir James FitzJames Stephens, Judge of High Court of Justice, Queen's Bench Division (England 1883) 1: 477.

2. In 1996, John Silber, president of Boston University, wrote an op-ed article for the *New York Times* titled, "Students Should Not Be Above the Law: Judging Crimes Is a Job for Courts, Not Colleges" (May 9, 1996). He pointed out that colleges and universities are "circumventing the courts (to) bury serious criminal cases in their own judicial systems." Because crime victims are talked out of reporting their cases to the police, students are receiving special treatment, just as people did who qualified under the "benefit of clergy" exception centuries ago. Silber cited as an example a man who graduated in 1996 from Miami University in Ohio, a private university. After the man was accused of sexually assaulting an 18-year-old freshman as she was sleeping, the man was allowed to graduate on "student conduct probation" instead of having Ohio police and prosecutors handle the matter.

3. Blackstone 4 *Commentaries,* 18.

4. *A History of the Criminal Law of England,* chapter 13, pp. 491–492.

5. Refugees from Cuba, Haiti, Mexico, Central America, and other parts of the world have been a continuing problem in the United States. The Immigration and Naturalization Service (INS) most often concludes that the refugees are fleeing from poverty in their countries and thus are not eligible for legal entry into the United States. Transporting, smuggling, or harboring aliens in violation of the Refugee Act of 1980 (Public Law 96–212) is a criminal offense. The defendants in the case of *United States v. Aguilar et al.,* 871 F.2d 1436 (9th Cir. 1989), *opinion amended and suspended* 883 F.2d 662 (9th Cir. 1989), ran a "modern-day underground railroad" that smuggled Central Americans across the border between Mexico and Arizona. The defendants in the *Aguilar* case were convicted of violations of the immigration laws (smuggling, transporting, and harboring aliens) arising from their participation in a "sanctuary movement."

6. Radzinowicz, *A History of English Criminal Law and Its Administration* (London: Stevens, 1948); and Chute and Bell, *Crime, Courts, and Probation* (New York: Macmillan, 1956).

7. "Transportation" was used by a number of countries. The Roman Empire transported prisoners to Romania; the Soviet Union transported hundreds of thousands of political prisoners to Siberia. In addition, the frontiers of the world have always been used as a refuge by people fleeing from the law or political trouble.

8. *Furman v. Georgia,* 408 U.S. 238, 92 S. Ct. 2726 (1972).

9. Annals of Congress, 782 (1789).

10. *Furman v. Georgia,* 408 U.S. 238 at 258, 92 S. Ct. 2726 at 2736.

11. *Pulley v. Harris,* 465 U.S. 37, 104 S. Ct. 871, 34 CrL 3027 (1984).

12. 404 F.2d 571 (8th Cir. 1968), where the court presents reasons why whipping is unconstitutional as a punishment.

13. 429 U.S. 975, 97 S. Ct. 481 (1977).

14. Most school districts permitting corporal punishment require it to be administered only after the principal approved it, in the presence of another adult, and not with an instrument that could cause physical injury to the student.

15. See *Garcia v. Miera,* 817 F.2d 650, 656 (10th Cir. 1987).

16. *County of Sacramento v. Lewis,* 523 U.S. 833 (1998).

17. *Neal v. Fulton County Board of Education,* 229 F.3d 1069, 1075 (11th Cir. 2000).

18. Ibid. at 1076.

19. 817 F.2d 650, 656.

20. *Ingraham,* 429 U.S. 975 (1977).

21. Because of state and federal sentencing guidelines, a convicted defendant is very unlikely to be sentenced by a court to receive corporal punishment. Such a sentence would be judged solely by the objective proportionality test of the Eighth Amendment. Other unusual sentences can run afoul of the Eighth Amendment. For example, in *Williams v. State,* 505 S.E.2d 816 (Ga. App. 1998), a convicted sex offender was required to walk in the area where he committed his crime while wearing a sign that said, "BEWARE HIGH CRIME AREA." The appellate court said this sentence constituted cruel and unusual punishment because the defendant was put in harm's way from other criminals frequenting the designated area.

22. This is the test established by *Farmer v. Brennan,* 511 U.S. 825 (1994). Had the prison official administered the corporal punishment in order to quell a riot, the test would have been whether the official was acting in a "good faith effort to restore discipline or order." See *Whitley v. Albers,* 475 U.S. 312 (1986).

23. 408 U.S. 238, 92 S. Ct. 2726 (1972).

24. In the 1984 case of *Pulley v. Harris,* the Supreme Court defined and explained the use of proportionality.

25. *Gregg v. Georgia,* 428 U.S. 153, 96 S. Ct. 2909 (1976).

26. *Proffitt v. Florida,* 428 U.S. 242, 96 S. Ct. 2960 (1976).

27. *Jurek v. Texas,* 428 U.S. 262, 96 S. Ct. 2950 (1976).

28. 465 U.S. 37, 104 S. Ct. 871, 34 CrL 3027 (1984).

29. See the *New York Times* articles, "Death Sentences Decline, and Experts Offer Reasons," December 15, 2006, and "Death Sentences Dropped, But Executions Rose In 2009," December 18, 2009.

30. *Id.*

31. Rubin, *The Law of Criminal Corrections* (St. Paul, Minn.: West, 1963).

32. England also had debtors prisons in which people who owed civil debts could be imprisoned until the civil debt was paid. England abolished the practice of debtors prisons in 1869. Such imprisonment would not be lawful under the U.S. Constitution, and some state constitutions specifically forbid this form of imprisonment. Most of the democratic world has abolished the practice.

33. *Williams v. Illinois,* 90 S. Ct. 2018 (1970).

34. 915 S. Ct. 668 (1971).

35. In footnote 19 of the *Williams* case, the Court stated: " We wish to make clear that nothing in our decision today precludes imprisonment for willful refusal to pay a fine or court costs. See *Ex parte Smith,* 97 Utah 280, 92 P.2d 1098 (1939)." Therefore, a person who has money or an income may be imprisoned for refusal to pay either a fine or court costs.

36. Other federal statutes having forfeiture provisions are the Controlled Substance Act, 21 U.S.C.A. Section 881; Organized Crime Control Act of 1970, 18 U.S.C.A. Sections 1963 and 1955(d); Copyrights Act, 17 U.S.C.A. Sections 506(b) and 509(a); and Child Protection Act of 1984, 18 U.S.C.A. Sections 2253 and 2254.

37. A driver's license may be revoked (or suspended) not only for traffic violations but also, depending on state law, for sex crimes, failure to pay child support, failure to pay nontraffic fines, underage drinking, truancy, or other reasons specified by the law of the state.

38. Between 1993 and 1995, twenty-four states enacted "three strikes" laws. See *State v. Oliver,* (745 A.2d 1165, 1169 (N.J. 2000).

39. California Penal Code Section 1170.12.

CHAPTER 9

Free Speech, Street Crimes, and the Bill of Rights

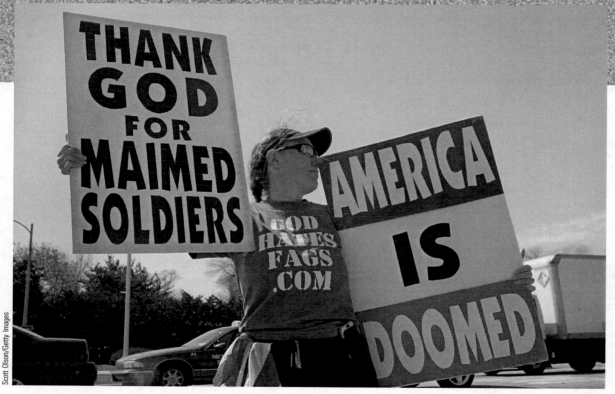

These members of a religious group that is avowedly anti-homosexual make it a practice to demonstrate or protest at funerals of soldiers killed in Iraq or Afghanistan. The group's leader, Rev. Fred Phelps, has been sued by the father of a marine killed in Iraq. Phelps and his followers contend the soldiers are killed because they serve a country that permits homosexuality. A jury initially gave the father a judgment of $5 million against Phelps, but that was reversed on appeal by a federal circuit court. In October the U.S. Supreme Court heard oral argument on the First Amendment protection, if any, Phelps and his followers should receive.

OUTLINE

LEARNING OBJECTIVES

In this chapter we examine the extent to which the Bill of Rights, mainly the First Amendment, serves as a limit on the power of government to make criminal laws regulating conduct, such as speaking or assembling in public places. The learning objectives for this chapter are:

- Read and remember the First Amendment.
- Identify the difference between fighting words and merely rude language.
- Define a "clear and present danger."

- List the circumstances that permit government to regulate speech based on content.
- Define obscenity.
- State when a threat becomes a "true threat."
- Describe some ways one person might stalk another person in violation of a criminal law.
- Identify when an assembly becomes unlawful.
- State the basis for the Supreme Court's decision that the Second Amendment is binding on the states.

In 1998 two U.S. citizens and six domestic organizations filed suit in federal court, challenging a federal law, 8 U.S.C. § 2339B(a)(1), that makes it a criminal offense punishable by up to 10 years in prison for a person to give "material support to a foreign terrorist organization." The group wished to provide humanitarian assistance and advice to Kurdistan Workers Party (PKK) and the Liberation Tigers of Tamel Eelam (LTTE), foreign organizations that had been designated terrorist organizations under 8 U.S.C.§ 1189(a)(1). The group argued that the law prohibited them from giving advice to the organizations about legal activities, such as appearing before the United Nations or other international bodies. This prohibition violated their First Amendment right to free speech, they contended.

In 2010 the U.S. Supreme Court upheld section 2339B, stating that Congress had a compelling interest in limiting support of terrorist organizations, and that included prohibiting conduct that involved speech such as advice or training. The Court rejected the group's argument that the Act couldn't validly prohibit them from giving the terrorist organizations advice about legal activities, noting that such free advice would make it possible for the terrorist organizations to devote more assets to the terrorist activities. *Holder v. Humanitarian Law Project*, 2010 WL 2471055 (U.S. Supreme Court, 2010).

The relationship between the rights of free speech—as well as the freedom of assembly, privacy, and religion—and criminal laws is very important but very complicated. In this chapter we learn about the extent to which governments can pass laws that make certain kinds of speech or assembly a crime, or criminal laws that invade a person's rights of privacy or religion. Also discussed are many of the limits placed on such criminal laws by the U.S. Constitution.

Crimes such as those against the person, or against property rights, rarely present conflicts with other private or public goals. That is, there generally is no accepted policy or goal that is advanced by assaulting an innocent person or stealing his or her property. That is not the case with many of the crimes presented in this chapter. Some of them involve the written or spoken word, and thus raise First Amendment issues. Others are "street crimes"—that is, criminal statutes or ordinances that seek to maintain public order by regulating the activities of persons on public streets and property and that rub against the freedom of movement. This chapter examines the power of government to use the criminal laws to regulate these activities, and the limitations placed on that power by the U.S. Constitution.

≡ Belief—Speech—Action: When Speech May Be Regulated

The First Amendment of the U.S. Constitution provides that "Congress shall make no law … abridging the freedom of speech, or of the press." Courts have repeatedly pointed out that "freedom to speak one's mind is not only an aspect of individual liberty—and thus a good unto itself—but also is essential to the common quest for truth and the vitality of society as a whole."[1]

Human communications take many forms. Pure speech includes words spoken face-to-face or through one of the many media. Written communication includes books, magazines, newspapers, billboards, bumper stickers, and so on. Picketing, protest marches, and boycotts are also forms of communication. Symbolic speech such as uniforms, religious garb, black armbands, and hand gestures express messages and ideas and are protected by the First Amendment.

Speech and other forms of communication are not absolute rights, as they can seriously clash with the rights of others and the need for public order. The U.S. Supreme Court has pointed out that such regulation is necessary or the freedoms of an organized society could be "lost in the excesses of unrestrained abuse."[2]

In creating the "narrowly limited classes of speech" that can be forbidden and punished, the U.S. Supreme Court has repeatedly stated that "the line between speech unconditionally guaranteed and speech which may be regulated, suppressed, or punished is finely drawn."[3] The following are five categories of speech that the First Amendment does **not** protect:

1. Obscenity, when identified by a state, can be punished as a crime.
2. Fighting words.
3. Inciting or urging unlawful conduct (including "true" threats that clearly and unequivocally threaten the life or safety of another person).
4. Defamation (libel or slander).
5. Public nuisances, which require a "showing that substantial privacy interests are being invaded in an essentially intolerable manner"[4] (for example, loud noises in the middle of the night while others are sleeping).

☰ The "Clear and Present Danger" Test

"clear and present danger" test The test used to judge government restrictions on speech.

The principal test used for government restriction of speech based on its content is the **"clear and present danger" test**. Local, state, or federal governments in the United States cannot forbid or suppress speech and punish the speaker unless the speech is likely to bring harm to people or property. Justice Oliver Wendell Holmes announced the "clear and present danger" doctrine in the 1919 case of *Schenck v. United States*:

> The most stringent protection of free speech would not protect a man in falsely shouting "Fire" in a crowded theater, causing panic. It would not even protect a man from an injunction against uttering words that may have all the effect of force. The question in every case is whether the words are used in such circumstances that are of such a nature as to create a clear and present danger that they will bring about the substantive evils that Congress has a right to protect. It is a question of proximity and degree. When a nation is at war many things that might be said in time of peace are such a hindrance to its efforts that their utterances will not be endured so long as men fight and that no court could regard them as protected by any constitutional right.[5]

Using Justice Holmes's example, one could yell "fire" in an open field of a public park without fear of prosecution, because anyone hearing the words would feel no need for panic. The words would thus not present a "clear and present danger" of harming anyone. On the other hand, communicating a threat to take the life of the president is inherently dangerous, so much so that Congress passed 18 U.S.C. § 871(a), which makes it a federal crime to knowingly threaten the life of the president.[6]

Fighting Words

disorderly conduct Loud, obnoxious, or other offensive conduct in a public place.

fighting words Speech that, because it will likely incite immediate violence, is not protected by the First Amendment.

All states and cities have enacted laws and ordinances that are called disorderly persons, **disorderly conduct**, breach of the peace, or disturbance of the peace laws. These laws and ordinances forbid speech or conduct that either causes a public disorder or tends to cause a public disorder. **Fighting words** are communications that could either cause a public disorder or tend to cause a public disorder.

In 1942, the U.S. Supreme Court defined *fighting words* as "those words which by their very utterance … tend to incite an immediate breach of the peace."[7] If a case came before a judge or a jury, a decision would have to be made to determine if the

CRIMINAL CONVICTIONS FOR WORDS ALONE

Words Causing Conviction or Sanction

"Fuck the Draft" written on the back of a jacket worn in a Los Angeles courthouse. The defendant was arrested and convicted of disorderly conduct.

During an anti–Vietnam War demonstration, streets were blocked and traffic was stopped. As sheriffs were clearing the streets, Hess was heard to say, "We'll take the fucking street later." Hess was immediately arrested and convicted of disorderly conduct.

"They holler at us to get an education … and now … my draft classification is 1-A…. If they ever make me carry a rifle the first man I want in my sights is LBJ" (President Lyndon Johnson). The 18-year-old student was convicted of threatening the life of the president of the United States.

"… If our president, our Congress, our Supreme Court continues to suppress the white Caucasian race, it is possible that there might have to be some revenge taken.…" The Ku Klux Klan leader was convicted of inciting violence.

A group of American Nazis sought to march and demonstrate peacefully in the village of Skokie, Illinois, where more than half of the population were Jewish. A parade permit was refused on the grounds that the swastika and storm trooper uniforms amounted to fighting words to many of the residents. An injunction was issued forbidding "displaying the swastika … in the course of a demonstration, march or parade" in the village.

Students held up a banner that said "Bong Hits 4 Jesus" while the Olympic torch passed by a group of students excused from classes to watch the event. When the student who brought the banner refused to take it down, the school principal grabbed the banner and immediately suspended the student from school for ten days.

U.S. Supreme Court Ruling

As the words were not addressed to any specific person and did not create or tend to create a public disorder, the defendant's conviction was thrown out. *Cohen v. California*, 91 S. Ct. 1780 (1970)

The U.S. Supreme Court held that Hess's words "were (not) intended to produce and likely to produce imminent (immediate) disorder." As it was held that there was no "clear and present danger," Hess's conviction was reversed. *Hess v. Indiana*, 94 S. Ct. 326 (1973)

Watts v. United States, 394 U.S. 705 (1969).[a]

In reversing the conviction, the Supreme Court held that the language was not "directed to inciting or producing imminent lawless action." *Brandenberg v. Ohio*, 89 S. Ct. 1827 (1969)

The Illinois Supreme Court held that the swastika is symbolic political speech and not "fighting words." It was held that the village did not meet its "heavy burden" necessary to justify a prior restraint on speech. (Villagers who would become angry at the Nazis could stay home or go somewhere else the day of the parade.) *Village of Skokie v. National Socialist Party of America*, 373 N.E.2d 21 (1978), *review denied* U.S. Supreme Court.

The Ninth Circuit held that the suspension violated the student's free speech rights. *Frederick v. Morse*, 439 F.3d 1114 (2006). The Supreme Court granted certiorari, *Morse v. Frederick*, 127 S. Ct. 722 (2006), and in June 2007, in a 5–4 decision, the Court reversed the Ninth Circuit and upheld the action of the school principal, stating the principal reasonably believed the banner promoted illegal drug use. *Morse v. Frederick*, 127 S. Ct. 2618.

[a]In *Watts*, the Supreme Court held that federal or state criminal laws that prohibited "pure" speech must distinguish between "true threats" and constitutionally protected speech. The Court held that Watts's statements were not "true threats" but only "political hyperbole" and that Watts's only offense was a "kind of very crude, offensive method of stating political opposition to the president." The Court did not establish a bright line rule for distinguishing a true threat from protected speech, leaving the lower federal courts and the state courts to establish such tests. These various tests for identifying true threats generally require not only that the threat clearly threatens harm but also that a reasonable person hearing the threat would believe the person making the threat had the intent and ability to carry through on it.

The ancient Romans called it *digitus impudicus* ("the imprudent fi nger"). Here, former vice president of the United States Nelson Rockefeller stated he was "responding in kind" to hecklers during an appearance for Senator Robert Dole (background). Courts may call the gesture distasteful and vulgar, but only in very rare circumstances could it be held to be fighting words.

insulting or vulgar language amounted to fighting words. The following examples illustrate the fighting words doctrine:

EXAMPLE: One resident of a neighborhood kept a large RV parked in his yard. Other neighbors complained, but he refused to move the vehicle. The neighbors then convinced the town council to pass an ordinance banning the practice. While the ordinance was pending, the resident placed several mock tombstones in his yard, graphically and rudely describing the "deaths" of the complaining neighbors. A town police officer ordered the resident to remove the tombstones. He refused, and a fight broke out between the neighbors. The resident was arrested for disorderly conduct. He subsequently sued the police officer, alleging a civil rights violation under 42 U.S.C. § 1983, claiming his arrest and the order to remove the tombstones violated his First Amendment rights. The trial court applied the fighting words doctrine, and found for the police officer. On appeal, the circuit court held that the fighting words doctrine did not apply, because while the words on the tombstones might be likely to cause injury to the neighbors, they were not the kind of words that would incite a breach of the peace. Thus, the tombstones were protected under the First Amendment, and could not be ordered to be removed. *Purtell v. Mason*, 527 F.3d 615 (7th Cir. 2008), *cert. denied* 129 S. Ct. 411 (2008).

EXAMPLE: During an angry exchange of words in a Washington restaurant, a 35-year-old man called (70)-year-old Texas Congressman Henry Gonzalez a "communist." Gonzalez "nailed the man with his fist," causing a black eye and facial cuts. Both men were cited for disorderly conduct. Calling a congressman a communist at the height of the Cold War (as was done in this example) was very provocative, and most juries in those days would probably find that a fighting word violation had occurred.

But one wrong does not justify another wrong, and Gonzalez committed a misdemeanor battery when he struck the other man. The police properly issued citations to both men, as two crimes had occurred.

To prove a fighting word violation, the city, county, or state would have to prove the following in most jurisdictions:

- That the defendant addressed very insulting and abusive language,
- To another person face-to-face; words sent in an e-mail, or spoken over the telephone, would not be fighting words;
- Causing a likelihood that "the person addressed will make an immediate violent response."[8]
- If the charge is a public disorder, then the statute or ordinance would probably require a showing that the offense occurred in a public place.

When Does Vulgar, Insulting Language to a Police Officer Constitute Fighting Words?

Many state courts have imposed higher standards for words directed at police officers, reasoning that police officers are expected to exercise greater restraint when foul, insulting language is directed toward them. After reviewing hundreds of state cases, the *FBI Law Enforcement Bulletin*[9] listed the following generally accepted concepts to assist law enforcement officers in deciding whether to arrest for speech directed at them:

1. Direct threats to the safety of an officer "generally constitute 'fighting words' unprotected by the first amendment." However, if the speech falls short of a direct, outright threat and is only harassing and nasty, state courts have held that such communications do not fall under the threat exception.

2. When a crowd is present and the *speech is likely to incite the crowd* (or some of the people in the crowd) to violence, state courts will hold that such speech is not constitutionally protected.

3. Speech that obstructs and hinders police in the performance of their duty generally has been held to justify an arrest. Probably all states have codified the common law crime of obstructing and hindering police officers in the performance of their public duty. However, state statutes vary considerably in defining the crime of obstruction. A few states limit the crime to "resisting." Other states use the words *resist, obstruct,* or *oppose,* and still other states use *resist, obstruct,* or *abuse.*

Some states hold that verbal acts alone cannot constitute obstruction and that physical acts are also required. However, other states hold that verbal communication can amount to obstruction. Obstructing or hindering law enforcement officers in the performance of their duty could occur while officers are making an arrest, while a roadside sobriety test is being conducted for drunk driving,[10] while the officers are investigating a major crime of violence,[11] while the officers are questioning witnesses, or in many other situations such as the failure of a material witness to a major crime or serious accident to properly identify himself or herself.

VERBAL OFFENSES

Type of Verbal Offense	To Constitute the Verbal Offense, There Must Be
Fighting words[a]	1. Insulting or abusive language 2. Addressed to a person face-to-face 3. Causing a likelihood that "the person addressed will make an immediate violent response"
Obscenity	1. A communication that, taken as a whole, appeals to the prurient (lustful) interest in sex 2. And portrays sexual conduct in a patently offensive way 3. And the communication, taken as a whole, does not have serious literary, artistic, political, or scientific value
Inciting or urging unlawful conduct	1. Language or communication directed toward inciting, producing, or urging 2. *Imminent* lawless action or conduct, or 3. Language or communication likely to incite or produce such unlawful conduct
Obstruction of a law enforcement officer or of justice	1. Deliberate and intentional language (or other communication) that hinders, obstructs, delays, or makes more difficult 2. A law enforcement officer's effort to perform his or her official duties (the scienter element of knowledge by the defendant that he or she knew the person obstructed was a law enforcement officer is required) 3. Some states require that "the interference would have to be, in part at least, physical in nature" (see the New York case of *People v. Case*)
Abusive, obscene, or harassing telephone calls	1. Evidence showing that the telephone call was deliberate 2. And made with intent to harass, frighten, or abuse another person 3. And any other requirement of the particular statute or ordinance
Loud speech and loud noise	Cities and states may: 1. Forbid speech and noises meant by the volume to disturb others, and 2. Forbid noise and loud speech that create a clear and present danger of violence

[a]Many state courts apply a higher fighting words standard to law enforcement officers.

☰ Obscene Communications

obscenity Communication that the average person, using contemporary community standards, would find appeals to the prurient interests or depicts sexual conduct in a patently offensive manner and, taken as a whole, lacks serious artistic, literary, political, or scientific value.

Obscenity is not protected by the First Amendment and may be forbidden by government. Defining obscenity, however, has been the subject of many court rulings and debates. The U.S. Supreme Court established the following guidelines for American courts to define obscenity in the 1973 case of *Miller v. California* (93 S. Ct. 2607):

- Whether "the average person applying contemporary community standards" would find that the work, taken as a whole, appeals to the prurient interest.[12]
- Whether the work or communication depicts or describes, in a patently offensive way, sexual conduct specifically defined by the applicable state law.
- Whether the work or communication, taken as a whole, lacks serious literary, artistic, political, or scientific value.

Criminal statutes that have some effect on speech raise First Amendment issues. Generally speaking, if a statute is directed at the content of the speech (e.g., banning a book, a film, or a photograph) it is presumptively invalid under the First Amendment, and subject to strict scrutiny. Under strict scrutiny, the state must show a "compelling interest" served by the statute, and that the means used to achieve that interest are the "least restrictive" possible. However, if the statute is "content-neutral" it violates the First Amendment only if the government lacks a substantial interest in adopting the statute. For example, so-called adult movies and books generally cannot themselves be outlawed because of the limitations of the obscenity test. A statute banning specific books or videos would be directed at the content of those books or videos. However, reasonable

---

THE FORMER CRIMES OF BLASPHEMY, PROFANITY, AND INDECENT LANGUAGE

Prior to the 1970s, most American cities and counties had ordinances that made it an offense to use profanity or vulgar language in a public place. The 1970 ruling of the U.S. Supreme Court in the case of *Cohen v. California* made major changes in this area of criminal law.

Cohen was arrested in the Los Angeles courthouse because he was wearing a jacket with "Fuck the Draft" printed on the back to protest the Vietnam War. Cohen would not have been arrested if he had voiced his opposition with the message "Darn the Draft" or "To Heck with the Draft." The U.S. Supreme Court reversed Cohn's conviction for disorderly conduct, ruling that a state "may not, consistent with the First and Fourteenth Amendments, make the simple public display here involved of this single four-letter expletive a criminal offense."

The Cohen case established the following two concepts regarding the public use of vulgar, profane, or indecent language:

1. The U.S. Supreme Court defended Cohen's use of the admittedly vulgar word *fuck*. The Court refused to allow a state "to cleanse public debate to the point where it is grammatically palatable to the most squeamish among us," because, the Court concluded, "one man's vulgarity is another's lyric." This ruling makes it difficult to define any vulgar, profane, impolite, or other language as a crime, in and of itself.

2. The U.S. Supreme Court also held that people "in the Los Angeles courthouse could effectively avoid further bombardment of their sensibilities simply by averting their eyes." In the 1975 case of *Erznoznik v. City of Jacksonville*, the Supreme Court held that "the burden normally falls upon the viewer to avoid further bombardment of [his] sensibilities simply by averting his eyes."[a]

The following bumper sticker cases illustrate the efforts in a few states to regulate language seen on bumper stickers:

■ The state of Georgia attempted to stop use of a bumper sticker stating "Shit Happens." The Georgia Supreme Court held that the statute used was overbroad, because it regulated protected speech as well as unprotected speech. The court held that because people were not compelled to look at the bumper sticker and could turn their eyes away, there was no captive audience. And because the law was not written to protect children, the relaxed standard of review for the protection of children could not be used. See *Cunningham v. State*, 400 S.E.2d 916 (1991).

■ The 1991 case of *Baker v. Glover*, 776 F. Supp. 1511 (M.D. Ala.), concerned an Alabama law forbidding obscene bumper stickers and signs. "Warning tickets" were issued for the first violation of the new obscenity statute. Baker was a truck driver and received a warning for a bumper sticker on his truck that read "How's My Driving? Call 1–800-EAT-Shit." After Baker was warned that he would be fined if he did not remove the bumper sticker, he commenced a lawsuit in federal court alleging violation of his First Amendment right of freedom of expression. The federal court held that because the message on the bumper sticker did not appeal to a "prurient interest," the state could not forbid the message as obscene. The bumper sticker also was held to have a serious literary or political value as a protest against the Big Brother mentality of urging the public to report bad driving by truck drivers.

[a]91 S. Ct. 1788.

regulations on the location or number of adult bookstores or theaters could be content-neutral, and not a violation of the owners' First Amendment rights. In the case of *City of Los Angeles v. Alameda Books, Inc.*, 535 U.S. 425 (2002) the U.S. Supreme Court upheld a city ordinance that prohibited more than one adult bookstore to be located in the same building. The Court said that like a zoning law, the purpose of the ordinance was to control congestion and other conduct associated with multiple adult entertainment businesses in a small area; it was called a "secondary effect" regulation.

≡ Inciting and Urging Unlawful Acts

inciting The offense of urging another to commit an unlawful act.

Inciting or urging other people to commit a crime or perform an unlawful act was a misdemeanor at common law. The offense is committed even though the other person does not commit the suggested act. Speech and other forms of communication that encourage others to commit crimes are not protected by the First Amendment. To be unlawful, the speech or other communication must be "directed to inciting or producing *imminent* lawless action and [must be] likely to produce such action."[13]

The U.S. Supreme Court cases of *Hess v. Indiana* and *Brandenberg v. Ohio* were presented earlier in this chapter. The U.S. Supreme Court held that the words of the defendants in both cases did not urge imminent (immediate) lawless action, and therefore neither defendant could be convicted of disorderly conduct or inciting. In neither case did the words of the defendant constitute a clear and present danger.

Defamation: Libel and Slander

The crime and the civil offense of defamation goes back more than seven hundred years in the law. As early as 1275, the English Parliament enacted a libel statute that forbade false news and tales. The colonies and the original thirteen states undoubtedly all had laws concerning libel and slander. Over the years, the laws of England and the United States developed into the libel, slander, and defamation laws of today.

defamation The offense of injuring the character or reputation of another by oral or written communication of false statements. Defamation consists of libel (written offense) or slander (oral offense).

Defamation is the offense of injuring the character or reputation of another by oral or written communication of false statements. Defamation consists of the twin offenses of *libel* and *slander*. Libel is generally a written offense, whereas slander is generally an oral offense. Although most states probably have one or more criminal defamation or libel statutes, charges under these statutes are rarely filed, in part because of the First Amendment conflicts and the Supreme Court's decision in *Garrison v. La.*, 379 U.S. 64 (1964), which struck down a Louisiana criminal libel statute as unconstitutional. A recent case illustrates some aspects of the problems in filing criminal libel prosecutions.

Colorado has a criminal libel statute, Colo. Rev. Stat. § 18-13-105, that makes it a class 6 felony to utter false statements about a person with the intent to damage his reputation or hold the person up to public ridicule or contempt. In *Mink v. Suthers*, 482 F.3d 1244 (10th Cir. 2007) a college student was arrested based on a complaint that the student had violated this statute by publishing rude and false stories about a professor in the student's Internet magazine. Because of First Amendment concerns, the state prosecutor decided not to prosecute the student, although the prosecutor did authorize the issuance of a search warrant. The Court of Appeals upheld the student's right to bring a case for damages against the district attorney for her decision to authorize a search warrant to seize the student's computer.

States have sometimes repealed criminal libel statutes after a court has found the statute to be overbroad. In *Parmelee v. O'Neil*, 186 P.3d 1090 (Wash. App. 2008) a court of appeals held the Washington Criminal Libel statute, RCW p.58.010, unconstitutional as overbroad and a violation of the First Amendment. In 2009 the Washington legislature repealed the statute.

Most victims choose to rely primarily on the civil actions of libel and slander that are available to them. Money awards can be obtained through the civil suits to both compensate and punish. The burden of proof is also lower in civil actions.

The crime of fighting words is limited to face-to-face confrontation involving a communication that either causes violence or tends to cause a violent reaction by a person to whom the words are addressed. The law of defamation requires that the communication be made to people other than the victim and that the victim's reputation be lowered in the esteem of any substantial and respectable group. It is possible that words spoken could not only be fighting words but also the basis for civil libel and slander suits.

Law enforcement officers and other public officials carry a heavier burden if they file a lawsuit for defamation. Law enforcement officers have been defined by case law as public officials. To succeed as plaintiffs in a defamation proceeding, as public officials they must plead and prove that the person or newspaper publishing the defamation did so with a reckless disregard as to the truth or falsity of the statements.[14]

▤ Symbolic Speech and the First Amendment

Symbols, along with gestures, conduct, and speech, have always been used to communicate between human beings. The symbol can be used alone or with other forms of communication.

symbolic speech Nonverbal expressions that convey a belief or idea.

Uniforms and the way people dress are types of symbols. People often communicate by their dress who they are, what their lifestyles are, and, to some extent, what they think and believe. The following **symbolic speech** case came before the Supreme Court in 1969:

During the Vietnam War, a group of Iowa students wished to communicate their opposition to the war by wearing black armbands in school. However, the high school principal forbade the armbands, which led to the lawsuit *Tinker v. Des Moines Independent Community School District,* 89 S. Ct. 733 (1969). Because the black armbands did not disrupt classes or school, the U.S. Supreme Court in *Tinker* sustained the students' action, holding:

> The wearing of an armband ... was closely akin to pure speech, which we have repeatedly held is entitled to comprehensive protection under the First Amendment. Students or teachers [do not] shed their constitutional rights of freedom of speech or expression at the schoolhouse gate.

Flag Burning and Cross Burning as Symbolic Speech

Flags are symbols. The American flag has symbolic meanings that are cherished by most Americans. This, however, has sometimes caused protesters and demonstrators seeking to make a political statement to burn or otherwise defile an American flag in an attempt to communicate the message.

In past years, states had statutes that made this type of defilement of the American flag a crime. If the demonstrators burned their own flag as a means to communicate a political message, the symbolic act was held to have the protection of the First Amendment in the two U.S. Supreme Court cases of *Texas v. Johnson,* 109 S. Ct. 2533 (1989) and *United States v. Eichman,* 110 S. Ct. 2404 (1990).

Cross burning can also be a symbolic act that seeks to communicate a message, and therefore it can also have First Amendment protection. A statute that prohibited all forms of cross burning would be unconstitutional. In the 1992 case of *R.A.V. v. St. Paul, Minn.* (112 S. Ct. 2538), the U.S. Supreme Court struck down a St. Paul ordinance making it a crime to burn a cross[15] with an intent to communicate a hate message. The Court found the ordinance invalid because the ordinance forbade the symbolic conduct "based on its [the ordinance's] hostility to the underlying (hate) message."

However, in the 2003 case of *Virginia v. Black,* 538 U.S. 343 (2003), a majority of the Supreme Court held that a Virginia statute that made it criminal to burn a cross on public property or property of another "with the intent of intimidating any person or group of persons" was not unconstitutional on its face. The Court distinguished *R.A.V.* because there the focus of the ban on cross burning was the content of the message intended to be communicated by the burning. In *Black* the ban on cross burning focused on the intended intimidating effect the burning had on people, regardless of the content of the message the cross burners intended. Taking action, even though it might involve symbolic speech, with the intent to intimidate another is not a protected activity. The Court also concluded, however, that the Virginia statute was unconstitutional as applied, because the statute contained a provision that made burning a cross prima facie evidence

CAMPAIGN FINANCE AND THE FIRST AMENDMENT

The issue of campaign finance for national elections has been debated for years, and has been the subject of federal and state statutes, including criminal laws. One concern legislators voiced early on was the role of corporations, and in some cases labor unions, in campaign financing. At various times Congress and state legislatures passed laws restricting or prohibiting corporations or unions from participating in campaign financing. Corporations and unions objected to those laws, claiming their First Amendment rights were violated. Starting in 1990, the U.S. Supreme Court decided three principal cases on this issue.

In *Austin v. Michigan Chamber of Commerce,* 494 U.S. 652 (1990) the U.S. Supreme Court upheld the constitutionality of the Michigan Campaign Finance Act, Mich. Comp. Laws § 169.254(1). That statute made it a felony for a corporation, including a non-profit corporation, to make independent contributions to the campaign of a candidate for state office. A Federal Court of Appeals held the act unconstitutional, but on appeal the Supreme Court reversed, holding that a state had compelling reasons for prohibiting corporations from direct participation in state elections. *Austin* was read as standing for the rule that political speech may be banned based on the corporate status of the speaker.

In *McConnell v. Federal Election Commissioner,* 540 U.S. 93 (2003) the Supreme Court upheld the constitutionality of most parts of the Bipartisan Campaign Reform Act of 2002 (BCRA), 2 U.S.C. § 441(b). That Act, which was the first major federal campaign finance legislation since the 1971 campaign finance act, prohibited corporations or labor unions from using corporate treasury funds for independent direct or indirect contributions to candidates for federal offices. Under the act it was a felony to, among other things, use corporate funds for "electioneering communications," such as network or cable television ads in favor of or against an identifiable candidate. The Supreme upheld the Act, mainly in reliance on the holding in *Austin.*

In 2010 the Supreme Court reconsidered the constitutionality of BCRA as applied to a so-called documentary film made by a non-profit corporation. The film, which made derogatory remarks about Senator Hillary Clinton, was designed to be released over cable networks during the presidential primary race in 2008. In *Citizens United v. Federal Election Commission,* 130 S. Ct. 876 (2010) a deeply divided Court found BCRA's ban on independent expenditures on electioneering communications unconstitutional. The Court specifically overruled *Austin* and the parts of *McConnell* that permitted statutory prohibitions on corporate speech. It held that corporations were privileged under the First Amendment to express political views during the election process, just as ordinary citizens can. The Court rejected the reasoning in *Austin* that corporate wealth had a "distorting effect" on election results. It also rejected arguments that corporate spending would lead to corruption, or that shareholders would be compelled to support positions not shared by them. The Court did uphold the sections of BCRA relating to disclosure of the source of funding for communications.

of an intent to intimidate another person. This provision, the Court said, invites a jury to punish based solely on the fact of the cross burning, without specifically finding an intent to intimidate.

≡ Threats of Violence as Crimes

A threat becomes a crime if it is explicit and likely to result in imminent lawless action. Threats can be charged as various crimes, such as disorderly conduct, inciting violence, or even racketeering if made repeatedly (see Chapter 18). If accompanied by "physical menace," the Model Penal Code, Section 211.1(1)(c), makes **threats of violence** an assault.

threats of violence
Statements or actions that unequivocally convey the message that violent actions will be taken.

true threat A serious expression of an intent to inflict bodily harm.

Many states have specific statutes making "terroristic threats" a crime.[16] The First Amendment provides no protection for threats of violence because the purpose of the speech is not to communicate ideas but to put another person in fear of imminent physical harm.

In the following examples courts considered if speech was a **true threat** and not protected by the First Amendment, or protected speech:

- *Threats against public officials:* In particular, threats against the president of the United States. Such threats are a violation of federal law; 18 U.S.C. § 471. That statute requires only that the threat be made, and does not require proof that the defendant had the ability or intent to carry out the threat. *United States v. Dysart*, 705 F.2d 1247 (1983). Most states have laws making it a crime to threaten a state official, and require proof similar to the federal statute. In *Abbott v. State*, 989 A.2d 795 (Md. App. 2010), the court reversed a conviction under Md. C.L. § 3-708, threats against public officials. The defendant sent a threatening e-mail to the website maintained by the governor of Maryland, which solicited comments from citizens. The court found that the trial court did not properly instruct the jury on whether a reasonable person would have believed the threat was serious. In *United States v. Stewart*, 420 F.3d 1007, 1015 (9th Cir. 2005) a defendant was convicted for threatening to "target a judge" and "string the m----- up and cut his throat."
- *Threats by schoolchildren against teachers or other students:* Because of the number of school killings in recent years, officials have begun taking students' threats very seriously. However, to be the basis of a criminal conviction (as opposed to school discipline), the threat must be a "true threat." In *In re Douglas D.*, 626 N.W.2d 725 (Wis. 2001), the Wisconsin Supreme Court overturned the conviction of a high school student under Wisconsin's disorderly conduct statute. The student wrote an essay in class in which the main character (clearly the student) stated he would come to school the next day and cut off the teacher's head. The court held the essay was not a true threat, because the student could not reasonably understand that a reasonable person would view the statement as a serious expression of an intent to inflict bodily harm, which is the definition of a "true threat."
- In *Fogel v. Collins*, 531 F.3d 824 (9th Cir. 2009) the court held that painting a sign on the back of a van that said "I am a f-----g suicide bomber communist terrorist" was not a true threat, and thus was protected speech. The court stated that a reasonable person viewing the van, which was covered with clearly political statements, would not find the "threat" to be a serious expression of intent to inflict bodily harm.
- *Terrorist threats:* Since the events of September 11, 2001, state and federal governments take terrorist threats seriously. The Model Penal Code, Section 211.3, makes it

a third-degree felony to make threats designed to cause the evacuation of public buildings or public conveyances. Many states have also passed "false bomb report" laws, which make it a crime to give a false statement to a police officer or airline employee about concealing a bomb. In *Levin v. United Airlines*, 70 Cal. Rptr. 3d 535 (Cal. App. 2008) the court held that Cal. Penal Code § 148.1 was constitutional and required only that a person making a false statement about a concealed bomb do so knowing the statement was false. The court stated that "true threat" rules did not apply, because the statute was not directed to the content of the statement, but simply made the **act** of making the false statement a crime. The statute in effect was a codification of Justice Holmes's famous example of yelling "fire" in a crowded theater, the court said.

- *Violations of restraining orders:* Restraining orders directed against former spouses, boyfriends, girlfriends, and family members are routinely issued in an attempt to prevent violence and harassment. Violation of a restraining order can subject the violator to a contempt charge or other criminal liability. In *Cobble v. State*, 2004 WL 1688773 (Ga. App. 2004), a defendant was convicted under the Georgia terroristic threat statute when he stood outside his former girlfriend's house and yelled obscenities directed at her. When the police arrived and subdued him, the defendant stated that as soon as he was released, he would return and kill the girlfriend. Even though the girlfriend did not hear those threats, the court found the defendant guilty under the terroristic threat statute.

Using the U.S. Mail, Telephones, the Internet, or E-Mail to Threaten Another Person

Whether speech constitutes a threat is usually a question of state law. However, when the threat is made by U.S. mail, telephones, or other interstate communication devices, the threat can also result in a federal charge. For example, a defendant was convicted of knowingly transmitting a threat in interstate commerce when he telephoned a bank and said, "You all better have my personal items to me by 5 o'clock or it's going to be a lot of hurt people there," *United States v. Cox*, 957 F.2d 264 (4th Cir. 1992). Using the mail to convey a threat is a violation of 18 U.S.C. § 1201(c).

Using e-mail to express a threat of violence is also a federal crime. In *United States v. Alkhabaz*, 104 F.3d 1492 (6th Cir. 1997), a defendant was charged with violating 18 U.S.C. § 875(c), using interstate communications to threaten kidnapping or violence. The defendant communicated with the victim via e-mail and gave graphic accounts of violent sexual acts directed against females. The Circuit Court of Appeals reversed his conviction, saying his e-mail messages did not constitute true threats because they were directed against females in general, not the victim in particular.

In 1995, the Florida Supreme Court upheld the constitutionality of Florida Statute 365.16, which makes it a crime to use telephones with the intent to "abuse, threaten or harass." The U.S. Supreme Court denied certiorari.[17] Other unlawful uses of a telephone can constitute a federal crime. For example, the Comprehensive Drug Abuse Prevention and Control Act forbids the use of a telephone to facilitate narcotic transactions and money laundering.[18]

Many states have passed statutes making it a crime to use e-mails or the Internet to harass a person. In *Massimo v. State*, 144 S.W.3d 210 (Tex. App. 2004), a defendant was convicted of violation of Texas Penal Code Section 42.07(a)(2), unlawful harassment by electronic communication, when she sent repeated e-mails to a former friend threatening to kill her and her children.

Bullying: Not a Crime, but It Can Consist of Criminal Conduct

In 2010 the State of New York became the 43rd state to enact an "anti-bullying" law. This law requires schools to ban bullying practices, train their staffs to combat bullying, and to formulate anti-bullying programs. While bullying itself is not a crime, the conduct associated with bullying can be criminal.

The U.S. Department of Justice, Office of Community Oriented Policing Services (COPS), defines bullying as having two components:

1. Repeated harmful acts which involve physical, verbal, or psychological attacks of intimidation,
2. Directed against victims who cannot properly defend themselves because of size or strength, or because they are outnumbered or less psychologically resilient.

The Director of COPS stated that while bullying was once viewed as harmless adolescent behavior, it is now known that bullying can have a long-term effect on both the bully and the victim, and can lead to other forms of violence. The increased use of the Internet has also created cyber-bullying, which can exacerbate consequences. In the legislative history to § 814, McKinney's New York Education Statutes (2008), the New York legislature cited a U.S. Department of Justice survey that found 1 out of every 5 children ages 10 to 17 received sexual exploitation advances over the Internet. The survey also quoted findings by I-SAFE, a non-profit youth Internet safety organization, that 42 percent of children using the Internet have been subjected to bullying when online.

Municipal and county law enforcement offices regularly respond to calls from local schools, and they often place officers within schools to monitor student conduct and enforce state laws. Under the U.S. Supreme Court ruling in *Tinker v. Des Moines School District*, discussed in this chapter, schools may impose discipline on students when the student's speech or conduct, including bullying behavior, substantially interferes with the school's educational mission. However, schools cannot control the bullying that occurs outside of school, or on the Internet.

The consequences of a combination of in-school bullying and Internet harassment can be deadly. On January 14, 2010, Phoebe Prince, a 15-year-old student at South Hadley (Mass.) High School, hanged herself after months of bullying at school and over the Internet. Five of her classmates have been charged with crimes ranging from assault to stalking as a result of her death. In March 2010 Alexis Skye Pilkington, a 17-year-old Long Island, N.Y. high school student, killed herself after receiving vicious attacks on the social networking website FormSpring.me.

Additional material on bullying in schools can be found on the U.S. Department of Justice COPS website, at http/www/cops.usop.gov/files/RIC/Publications/e07633414-guide.pdf.

≡ Loud Noise or Nuisance Speech

In 1989, the U.S. Supreme Court stated that "it can no longer be doubted that government has a substantial interest in protecting its citizens from unwelcome noise" (*Ward v. Rock Against Racism,* 109 S. Ct. at 2756). The *Ward* case upheld a New York City regulation that gave city officials broad authority to regulate sounds from Central Park performances.

City ordinances regulating private parties often present both First Amendment and overbreadth problems. In *U.R.I. Students v. Town of Narragansett*, 2010 WL 785328 (D. R.I. 2010) a federal court upheld a town ordinance that imposed criminal penalties on owners and users of private property where loud or drunken parties were held.

Students at the nearby University of Rhode Island often rented housing in Narragansett, and then had loud parties. The City Council passed an ordinance that provided that once a property had been "posted" for a loud gathering, a subsequent loud gathering on the property was a crime punishable by a fine. The landowners and student renters claimed the ordinance violated their First Amendment and Due Process rights, but the district court disagreed. It said the ordinance was valid because it required as a pre-condition to liability a showing that persons at a gathering had violated some other law, such as public intoxication, or public urinating.

In *Kovacs v. Cooper,* the Court upheld a city ordinance that prohibited the use of sound trucks that emitted "loud and raucous" noise on city streets, stating:

> City streets are recognized as a normal place for the exchange of ideas by speech or paper. But this does not mean the freedom is beyond all control. We think it is a permissible exercise of legislative discretion to bar sound trucks with broadcasts of public interest, amplified to a loud and raucous volume, from the public ways of municipalities.[19]

≡ Regulating the Use of Public and Private Places

The First Amendment guarantees "the right of the people peacefully to assemble and to petition the Government for a redress of grievances." First Amendment freedoms and the rights of expression in public places, however, are not absolute. They may be limited

---

PERJURY, SUBORNATION OF PERJURY, AND THE FEDERAL FALSE STATEMENT ACT

The crime of perjury consists of knowingly and materially testifying falsely while under oath. The crime of subornation of perjury is committed when a person induces, urges, or knowingly permits another to testify falsely. In 1968, the President's Commission on Crime stated that perjury has always been widespread and that there should be more effective deterrents against perjury to ensure the integrity of trials.

People who lie to a federal investigator can be charged with a crime under the Federal False Statement Act, even if they are not under oath. In the 1998 case of *Brogan v. United States* (118 S. Ct. 805), federal investigators from the Labor Department and the Internal Revenue Service asked Brogan during an investigation whether he had received any illegal cash or gifts in the matter they were investigating. Brogan was not in custody, nor did the federal agents intend to take him into custody. But the federal agents did know and had evidence that Brogan had received illegal payments.

When Brogan denied receiving illegal payments and said no to the question of the federal investigators, his lie became the basis for federal prosecution under the Federal False Statement Act, which forbids "false, fictitious, or fraudulent statements or representations." Brogan's statement was found to be a deliberate falsehood, and he was convicted of violating the act.

Martha Stewart was questioned by federal investigators in regard to her sale of stock just prior to the collapse of the stock's price. Based on her answers, she was charged with the crime of making false statements to the investigators. In 2004, she was convicted of that crime, and sentenced to five months in prison, five months of home confinement, and a $30,000 fine.

In 2007 I. Lewis "Scooter" Libby, former chief of staff to Vice President Cheney, was convicted by a federal jury of four felony counts of obstruction of justice, giving false statements to the FBI, and committing perjury before a federal grand jury. Libby was accused of obstructing the investigation of who leaked secret information that led to the public identification of a covert CIA agent.

OBEYING LAWFUL POLICE ORDERS

Failure to obey a lawful, valid police order is probably punished as an offense in all states. For example, Section 843.02 of the Florida Criminal Code forbids resisting an officer: "Whoever shall obstruct or oppose any such officer … in the execution of legal process or in the lawful execution of any legal duty … shall be guilty of a misdemeanor of the first degree."

A defense to the charge of refusal to obey a police order is an attack on the lawfulness of the order. If the order is not lawful, there would be no duty to obey. In the first two cases presented below, prosecutors issued the wrong criminal charge and the defendants were convicted of crimes they did not commit.

Case	Facts of Case	Ruling
Gregory v. City of Chicago, U.S. Supreme Court, 89 S. Ct. 946 (1969)	Comedian Dick Gregory was leading a peaceful and orderly demonstration to the home of the Chicago mayor. Police officers accompanied the marchers, and things went very well until people in a large crowd near the mayor's home began throwing rocks and eggs at the demonstrators. Tough, foul language was directed toward them. Because the situation was dangerous and becoming riotous, the senior police officer asked and then ordered Gregory to discontinue the march and lead the demonstrators out of the area. After repeated refusals, Gregory and others were arrested for disorderly conduct (not the charge of refusal to obey a police officer) and fined $200. The U.S. Supreme Court reversed the convictions, holding:	"[Dick Gregory and others] were convicted not for the manner in which they conducted their march but rather for their refusal to disperse when requested to do so by Chicago police. However reasonable the police request may have been and however laudable the police motives, petitioners were charged and convicted for holding a demonstration, not for a refusal to obey a police officer. As we said in *Garner v. Louisiana*, 368 U.S. 157, 164, 82 S. Ct. 248 (1961): '[I]t is as much a denial of due process to send an accused to prison following conviction for a charge that was never made as it is to convict him upon a charge for which there is no evidence to support that conviction.'"
Norwell v. City of Cincinnati, U.S. Supreme Court, 94 S. Ct. 187 (1973)	The defendant, a 69-year-old man, was walking home from work about 10:45 p.m. on Christmas night in a high-crime neighborhood. A police officer approached the defendant because he had been notified of a "suspicious man" in the neighborhood. When the officer asked the defendant if he lived in the area, the defendant looked at him and walked on. The officer then stopped the defendant twice, but each time the defendant threw off the officer's arm and protested, "I don't tell you people anything." The defendant would not stay in the officer's presence and would not answer any of the officer's questions. The defendant was charged and convicted of disorderly conduct	"Upon this record, we are convinced that petitioner was arrested and convicted merely because he verbally and negatively protested Officer Johnson's treatment of him. Surely, one is not to be punished for nonprovocatively voicing his objection to what he obviously felt was a highly questionable detention by a police officer. Regardless of what the motivation may have been behind the expression in this case, it is clear that there was no abusive language or fighting words. If there had been, we would have a different case. See *Chaplinsky v. New Hampshire*, 315 U.S. 568 (1942)."

Case	Facts of Case	Ruling
	(not refusal to obey a police officer).The U.S. Supreme Court reversed the conviction, holding:	
City of Oak Creek v. King, Wisconsin Supreme Court, 436 N.W.2d 285 (1989)	When a commercial airline crashed near an airport, the site was sealed off so that emergency equipment and personnel could assist the injured and dying. The defendant and other employees of a newspaper were repeatedly ordered to leave the area, but the defendant wanted to take pictures of the crash site and stated that he would not leave unless he was arrested. The defendant was arrested and convicted of disorderly conduct (not the charge of refusal to obey the police order). The Wisconsin Supreme Court affirmed his conviction and $40 fine.	"We conclude that the appellant's repeated refusal to obey Detective White's reasonable order, combined with his continued penetration into a nonpublic restricted area in the presence of the general public, was conduct of a type which tends to cause or provoke a disturbance, under the circumstances as they then existed. Therefore, we affirm the decision of the circuit court finding the appellant guilty of disorderly conduct."
Georgia v. Storey, Court of Appeals of Georgia, 351 S.E.2d 502, *review denied* U.S. Sup. Ct., 41 CrL 4023 (1987)	The defendant and others disrupted the Georgia legislature by shouting opposition to the death penalty. They then refused to obey orders of police and security persons to leave the state capitol building.	Convictions for disrupting the legislature and refusal to obey orders were affirmed, and review was denied by the U.S. Supreme Court.
State v. Jaramillo, New Mexico Supreme Court, 498 P.2d 687 (1972)	The defendants sat and lay on the floor in the governor's waiting room. They refused to leave when the office closed at 5:00 p.m. and refused to leave when the building closed at 6:00 p.m. They were convicted under the New Mexico "wrongful use of public property" statute.	The convictions were affirmed, and the statute was held to be constitutional. The court stated: "There is no question but that a State may regulate the use and occupancy of public buildings."
Daniel v. Tampa, Florida, Federal Court of Appeals, 11th Cir., 38 F.3d 546, *review denied* U.S. Sup. Ct., 57 CrL 3065 (1995), 515 U.S. 1132	Because of serious crime problems in public housing projects, canvassing was forbidden. Defendant was warned and refused to leave the building. Conviction for trespass was affirmed.	Florida's trespass-after-warning statute was sustained, and because this was a neutral restriction on speech, it was held to be a reasonable means of combating crime in the public housing project. No First Amendment violation occurred.

FIGURE 9.1 Balancing Tests Used by Courts to Determine the Limits of First Amendment Freedoms

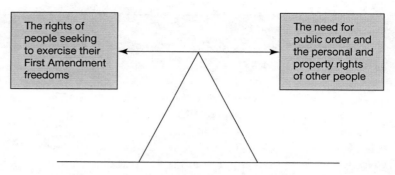

Conflicting rights and needs must be balanced

or restricted in order to insure public safety and order. Figure 9.1 illustrates the balance that must be maintained between First Amendment freedoms and public welfare. When a city, state, or federal agency restricts or limits conduct, it must show that:

1. The government has significant interest (or good reason) based on the nature of the property or some other source.
2. The restriction or limitation can be no greater "than is essential to the furtherance of that (substantial) interest." See *United States v. O'Brien,* 391 U.S. 367 (1968).
3. The federal and state governments may regulate property "under its control for the use for which it is lawfully dedicated" *Adderley v. Florida,* 385 U.S. 39 (1967), where defendants trespassed in an area of a jail closed to the public.
4. Where there is communication (for example, yelling at a basketball game in a public arena as distinguished from yelling in a library or during a city council meeting), the U.S. Supreme Court has said, "[T]he crucial question is whether the manner of expression is basically incompatible with the normal activity of a particular place at a particular time." See *Grayned v. City of Rockford,* 408 U.S. 104, 92 S. Ct. 2294 (1972).[20]

Under these guidelines, governments may regulate picketing, whether it be a city hall, a factory, or an abortion clinic; demonstrations, whether against some government action or in celebration of winning the World Series, parades;[21] and door-to-door canvassing and passing out hand-bills, whether for political or commercial purposes. The next sections in this chapter discuss some of the crimes charged under a city or state's power to regulate streets and public places.

The Crimes of Unlawful Assembly and Rioting

Under the common law, an **unlawful assembly**[22] was a gathering of three or more people for any unlawful purpose or under such circumstances as to endanger the public peace or cause alarm and apprehension.

An unlawful assembly became a **riot** under the old common law when those assembled began to execute their enterprise by a breach of the peace. A riot was a tumultuous disturbance of the peace by three or more people assembled with a common purpose to do an unlawful act.[23] Riot was a misdemeanor in common law, with all persons who encouraged, promoted, or took part in it being criminally liable.

States have by statute adopted one or both of these common law crimes. The state of New York, for example, has enacted the following offenses:[24]

- Section 240.10 Unlawful assembly (class B misdemeanor)
- Section 240.08 Inciting to riot (class A misdemeanor)
- Section 240.06 Riot in the first degree (class E felony)
- Section 240.05 Riot in the second degree (class A misdemeanor)

unlawful assembly Under the common law, a gathering of three or more people for any unlawful purpose or under such circumstances as to endanger the public peace or cause alarm and apprehension.

riot Under the common law, a tumultuous disturbance of the peace by three or more people assembled with a common purpose to do an unlawful act.

The present Federal Riot Control Statute, Section 2102, Title 18, United States Code Annotated, provides in part as follows:

As used in this chapter, the term "riot" means a public disturbance involving (1) an act or acts of violence by one or more persons part of an assemblage of three or more persons, which act or acts shall constitute a clear and present danger of, or shall result in, damage or injury to the property of any other person or to the person of any other individual or (2) a threat or threats of the commission of an act or acts of violence by one or more persons part of an assemblage.... where the performance of the threatened act or acts of violence would constitute a clear and present danger of, or would result in, damage or injury to the property of any other person or to the person of any other individual.

In *United States v. Markiewicz*, 978 F.2d 786 (2d Cir. 1992) the Court upheld the conviction under the Riot Act of 6 members of the Oneida Indian tribe. The defendants gathered on tribal lands to confront other tribal members over control of a bingo parlor on tribal property, and subsequently burned down the hall.

▤ Obstruction of the Law Enforcement Process

The crime of obstruction can be committed in many different ways. Failure to identify one-self when there is a legal obligation to do so is a frequent problem. In 2004 the U.S. Supreme Court upheld a state statute that required individuals to identify themselves when they were the subject of a lawful investigative detention or police stop. There, a police officer who was investigating a report of an assault on a woman asked the suspect, Hiibel, eleven times to identify himself. When Hiibel, who appeared intoxicated, refused to do so, he was arrested and later convicted of the crime of "willfully resisting, delaying, or obstructing a public officer in discharging ... any duty of his office."

The U.S. Supreme Court held that "stop and identify" laws go back hundreds of years and were a staple of English and American law. In affirming Hiibel's conviction, the Court stated that it had never had an obstruction of justice case come before it in which disclosure of a person's name would violate the Fifth Amendment right to remain silent.[25]

The following are some of the many incidents that could result in a charge of obstruction or other similar crime:

- A witness to a felony or serious accident refuses to identify himself when questioned by the police investigating the crime or accident.
- Making false material statements or providing false information to a law enforcement officer or other investigation (18 U.S.C. § 1038 makes this a federal crime).
- Tampering with a witness, victim, or informant is a federal crime: 18 U.S.C § 1512.
- Giving false identifying information to an officer that obstructs a computer records search.
- Obstruction of a crime scene, such as destroying evidence (e.g., erasing fingerprints), planting false evidence, or altering evidence to make the incident appear to be an accident.
- Failure to identify a known offender. For example, a Wisconsin attorney had a friend drive her home in her car from a late-night party because she had been drinking. The friend drove the car on a sidewalk, and when police spotted the car, the friend drove off at high speeds to evade arrest, a felony. The friend ultimately ran off, and the attorney refused to identify him. However, when faced with a contempt charge, the attorney identified the driver, who was arrested and convicted of fleeing from the police.

≣ Public Nuisances as Civil or Criminal Offenses

Under common law, a public nuisance was a civil offense. More than two hundred years ago, Blackstone, the famous English lawyer, described *nuisances* as "anything that unlawfully worketh hurt, inconvenience, or damage" (Blackstone 3 *Commentaries*, 216).

Today, cities and states continue to use the civil law of public nuisances to correct problems. By going into a civil court and filing a civil lawsuit, cities can petition the court to declare a public problem to be a nuisance and urge civil remedies. Public nuisance laws have been used to:

- Seize and tear down crack houses and property owned by slumlords who allow their properties to be used by gangs or drug dealers.
- Seize and take title to the motor vehicles of people who commit offenses such as having sex with a prostitute on a public street.[26]
- Obtain court orders against repeat offenders such as people who blocked the entrances to abortion clinics. After some people were arrested more than 50 times, a Wisconsin court issued a court order forbidding this conduct and made violations of the court order punishable by a fine of up to $5,000 and a jail sentence of up to one year.
- Obtain court orders against prostitutes with five or more convictions, ordering them not to loiter in specific areas of a city or to flag down cars. Violation of the court order is a much more serious offense than the conviction for prostitution or loitering for the purpose of prostitution and can be punished by a larger fine and longer jail sentences.
- An apartment building, a bar, or other building can be declared a "chronic nuisance" if law officers are repeatedly called to quell a disturbance at the premises. Many ordinances permit the city to bill the owner of the building for the cost of the police calls and other necessary city or county services performed.

≣ The Crime of Stalking and Violation of Protective Orders

stalking A crime involving activities such as spying on the victim, following the victim, or attempting to communicate with the victim through the telephone or mail. Cyber stalking through the Internet is also a crime.

Stalking has become a serious problem in the United States and in Europe. Stalkers have attacked John Lennon, tennis star Monica Seles, and some former U.S. presidents. Margaret Mary Ray, the woman who for years stalked David Letterman, committed suicide in 1998 by kneeling in front of a speeding train. Often stalking involves offenders who had a previous relationship with the victim. Stalking has now been made criminal in most states, whether or not the stalker ever commits some other crime against the victim, such as assault or battery. Activities such as spying on the victim, following the victim, or attempting to communicate with the victim through the telephone or mail can be charged as stalking.[27]

Authorities encourage victims to carefully document the stalker's activities, such as in a daily log or journal. This makes it possible for the police to conclude a crime is being committed and gives evidence to the prosecution to satisfy its burden to prove to a court the crime was committed.

Cyber stalking, or using the Internet to stalk or harass a person, is a variation on the usual physical acts in stalking. The case of *State v. Askham*, 86 P.3d 1224 (Wash. App. 2004), *review denied* 103 P.3d 201(Wash. 2004) provides an example of this crime. The defendant was unhappy that his former girlfriend ended their relationship and began seeing another man. The new boyfriend held a position of responsibility at a university, and the defendant began an extensive course of e-mail messages to the man's superiors, claiming that the man was involved in Internet pornography using university computers. While the e-mail messages were anonymous, police tracked them to an account the defendant had at a library. Using this evidence, the defendant was convicted of felony stalking and harassment.

State courts have the power to issue protective orders in the appropriate circumstances, such as in a divorce case where one spouse will not leave the other spouse alone. Stalking or harassing a person would be another appropriate situation where a protective order could be obtained. Some states have passed statutes specifically directed at stalking, such as the Kansas Protection from Stalking Act, which permits a person who proves the elements of stalking or harassment set out in the statute to obtain a protective order. In 2007 Gwen Wentland, the 2005 U.S. indoor high-jump champion, used this act to obtain a protective order against John Uhlarik, who stalked Wentland for years.

In the 1997 California case of *People v. Grams*,[28] a court had issued a protective order against Grams. Grams was charged with violating the order by stalking his estranged girlfriend.

The California law provided that protective orders remained enforceable, notwithstanding the acts of the parties, until the order was changed by order of the court. Grams argued that he could be entrapped if his girlfriend invited him over and then called the police. The California appellate court held that the California legislature could reasonably provide that only the court could lift the order, as the victim's consent is often misguided. (For further material on harassment and protective orders, see Chapter 11.)

≡ Crime on City Streets

City governments, understandably enough, wish to minimize the amount of street crimes that occur. The use of criminal laws directed at conduct or persons believed to be related to criminal acts is common, but they must be tailored to avoid infringing on individual rights. Some such laws include:

- *Anti-cruising laws:* Fines for prohibited cruising—driving cars on designated routes on certain streets during late night hours—can be as high as $1,000 in some places and may also include short jail sentences. The *Milwaukee Journal Sentinel* reported on April 24, 2007, that the city's new anti-cruising laws resulted in the issuance of 658 tickets, and 86 arrests in one weekend. Four shootings occurred in that same weekend.

- *Truancy arrests or detentions:* State laws vary on the treatment of truancy, but in many states authorities are authorized to detain a school-age child not attending school and in some cases obtain criminal convictions of the child's parents. Enforcement of truancy laws has been shown to cut down on crimes such as burglary, criminal damage to property, theft, and criminal graffiti.

- *Juvenile curfew laws:* Daytime curfew laws are aimed at keeping children in school, while nighttime curfews seek to minimize teen drinking, drug use, fighting, vandalism, and gang activities. Such curfews have generally been upheld, if they are not overbroad, that is, written to prohibit conduct that is permitted, like attending school or church events in the evening.

- *Laws directed at homeless persons:* There are close to a million homeless persons on our cities' streets. Some of their conduct can violate criminal laws, such as disorderly conduct, public drinking, or unlawful panhandling. Laws directed specifically at homeless persons—such as prohibitions against sleeping on public streets or parks or in public buildings such as libraries—are generally upheld. (See Chapter 1) for material on homeless persons and status crimes.)

This man is purchasing a firearm for personal use, which under recent Supreme Court decisions discussed in this chapter is his right under the Second Amendment. While he has the "right to bear arms", the right is not absolute. States and the federal government can pass reasonable laws regulating firearms; for example, if this man is ever convicted of a felony he may lose the right to own firearms.

≡ Gun Ownership and Registration Laws

The federal government, the states, and local governments all have power, to some degree, to regulate the ownership, registration, and use of guns, including through the criminal law. All have done so. For example, 28 U.S.C. § 5841 requires the registration of weapons with silencers, sawed-off shotguns, and similar weapons, on the reasoning that these weapons are much more likely to be involved in crimes than other, more ordinary, guns. Violation of this statute can result in a prison sentence of up to ten years. California Penal Code Section 12280(b) bans ownership of assault weapons. The District of Columbia Code Section 7–2502.02(a)(4) barred registration of handguns, except for retired D.C. police officers.

Prior to 2008 there was uncertainty in courts and legislatures about the limits, if any, on state or federal power to regulate firearms by the Second Amendment to the U.S. Constitution. That amendment states "A well regulated Militia, being necessary to the security of a free State, the right of the people to keep and bear arms shall not be infringed." Some regarded this as a private right available to all citizens, while others viewed it as a public right, available only to state governments.

In *District of Columbia v. Heller*, 128 S. Ct. 2783 (2008), the U.S. Supreme Court held that the Second Amendment was a private right, and that as a result the District of Columbia could not ban the possession or ownership of handguns. The Court stated, however, that the District of Columbia could pass reasonable regulations on firearms, such as barring convicted felons from possessing firearms, or laws aimed at controlling the sale of firearms.

In *McDonald v. City of Chicago*, 2010 WL 2555188 (S. Ct. 2010) the Court held that the Second Amendment applied to the states under the Fourteenth Amendment, because the right to bear arms was "firmly rooted" in our nations history, and was thus

DOES YOUR STATE HAVE GUN CONTROL LAWS REGULATING THE FOLLOWING? IF SO, ARE THE LAWS CONSTITUTIONAL AFTER THE *HELLER* AND *MCDONALD* DECISIONS?

Statute #

Forbidding possession by

- a minor? (pistol only?) ⎯⎯⎯⎯
- a person convicted of a felony?[a] ⎯⎯⎯⎯
- a person who is intoxicated? ⎯⎯⎯⎯
- a person who is committing a crime? ⎯⎯⎯⎯
- a person going into or who is in a public building? ⎯⎯⎯⎯
- other? ⎯⎯⎯⎯

Statutes providing "add-on" prison terms for

- committing a crime with use of (or threat of) a dangerous weapon:
  misdemeanor? ⎯⎯⎯⎯
  felony? ⎯⎯⎯⎯
- use of bulletproof garment while committing crime? ⎯⎯⎯⎯
- concealing identity while committing crime:
  misdemeanor? ⎯⎯⎯⎯
  felony? ⎯⎯⎯⎯
- repeater or habitual criminal statute for person who has previously committed:
  misdemeanors? ⎯⎯⎯⎯
  felonies? ⎯⎯⎯⎯
- other? ⎯⎯⎯⎯

Forbidding possession, sale, use, or transportation of

- short-barreled ("sawed-off") rifle or shotgun? ⎯⎯⎯⎯
- machine gun? ⎯⎯⎯⎯
- bomb, hand grenade, shell, projectile? ⎯⎯⎯⎯
- switchblade knife? ⎯⎯⎯⎯
- silencer? ⎯⎯⎯⎯
- electric weapon (stun gun)? ⎯⎯⎯⎯
- mace, tear gas, and/or other chemical sprays? ⎯⎯⎯⎯
- other? ⎯⎯⎯⎯

Statute #

Forbidding the following conduct

- carrying a concealed weapon (CCW)? ⎯⎯⎯⎯
- pointing a firearm at or toward another person? ⎯⎯⎯⎯
- discharging a firearm on the land of another? ⎯⎯⎯⎯
- discharging a firearm within a municipality? ⎯⎯⎯⎯
- discharging a firearm into a vehicle or building? ⎯⎯⎯⎯
- setting a spring gun (trap)? ⎯⎯⎯⎯
- selling or giving a pistol to a minor? ⎯⎯⎯⎯
- reckless use of a weapon? ⎯⎯⎯⎯
- possession or transportation of firearm in:
  a watercraft (motorboat)? ⎯⎯⎯⎯
  an aircraft? ⎯⎯⎯⎯
  a motor vehicle? ⎯⎯⎯⎯
- brandishing a firearm? ⎯⎯⎯⎯
- possession of an unlicensed gun in a home or place of business? ⎯⎯⎯⎯
- other? ⎯⎯⎯⎯

Regulating purchase and use of firearms

- persons excluded (insane, convicted of felony, and so on)? ⎯⎯⎯⎯
- waiting period for purchase of?
  waiting time? ⎯⎯⎯⎯
- instructional program on safe use of firearms? ⎯⎯⎯⎯
- other? ⎯⎯⎯⎯

Requiring firearm owners

- to store firearms in a place that is reasonably inaccessible to children or to use a gun lock that makes the gun inoperable:
  loaded firearms only?
  loaded or unloaded?
  ammunition also covered? ⎯⎯⎯⎯
- To report the loss or theft of a firearm within a short time ⎯⎯⎯⎯

[a]Federal Law 18 U.S.C. Section 922(g)(1) forbids a person convicted of a felony from possession, distribution, or receiving a firearm or ammunition. See the 2002 case of *United States v. Bean* (154 L. Ed. 2d 483).

a "fundamental right" made binding on states by the Due Process Clause. The Court struck down a Chicago ordinance that (1) banned possession of a firearm without a registration certificate, and (2) then prohibited virtually all citizens from registering handguns. The *McDonald* Court reiterated the statements in *Heller* that reasonable regulation of gun use and ownership was permitted. Because of its virtual prohibition of gun ownership, the Chicago ordinance was not reasonable, the Court said.

The most recent survey of state laws published in Wikipedia, "Concealed Carry in the United States," reports that 48 states permit law-abiding residents to carry concealed handguns. Most do so by requiring applicants to obtain permits, though 3 states allow residents to carry without a permit. Only Illinois, Wisconsin and the District of Columbia prohibit the issuance of a permit.

Both the states and the federal government have laws making it a crime, usually a felony, for a convicted felon to possess a firearm. Federal laws also regulate the interstate sale and shipment of firearms. Regulations such as these are permitted under *Heller* and *McDonald*, and lower federal courts have held such regulations permissible under the reasoning of those cases: *United States v. Rene E.*, 583 F.3d 81 (1st Cir. 2009)[federal ban on juvenile possession of handguns]; *United States v. White*, 593 F.3d 1199 (11th Cir. 2010) [federal crime for person convicted of misdemeanor domestic violence crime to possess firearm].

The National Rifle Association (NRA) has led the fight at federal and state levels of government against gun control laws. The NRA has about 2.8 million members and more than $70 million in annual revenues. It has consistently pushed NRA programs with members of the U.S. Congress and of state legislative bodies, obtaining support from legislators from both political parties.

In January 2007 a coalition of over fifty mayors, calling themselves "Mayors Against Illegal Guns," met in Washington, D.C., to urge Congress to crack down on the trade of illegal firearms and pass laws getting more information to law enforcement officers on the origins of guns used in crimes. The mayors complained that even if their city passed strict gun control laws, it was easy for criminals to go to another city with softer laws and avoid the strict laws. A 1994 federal law, banning the sale of assault weapons, was allowed to lapse in 2004.

At an earlier meeting of the group in 2006, a Harvard University professor and an expert in the field of gun violence stated, "We [in the United States] are not an aberrant country in terms of crime or in terms of violence. The only difference is homicide, where we are way out of whack. We have more handguns and much weaker gun laws than any other country."[29]

The Centers for Disease Control and Prevention report that there are 30,000 gun deaths per year in the United States. The *New York Times* reported in an editorial titled "A Day Without Guns," January 30, 2007, that 38 states have passed laws allowing citizens to carry concealed weapons. That number has since increased.

≡ The Free Exercise of Religion

> The U.S. Supreme Court stated in 1990: *"We have never held that an individual's religious beliefs excuse him from compliance with an otherwise valid law prohibiting conduct that the State is free to regulate."*[30]

Freedom to believe is absolute; freedom to act is not. The U.S. Supreme Court has stated that it has never held that an individual's religious belief excuses compliance with an otherwise valid law regulating conduct. When a statute forbids a specific action or conduct, one who engages in that action or conduct because of a religious belief may be prosecuted for the violation. The following chart illustrates some of the conduct not protected by the freedom of religion clause:

Conduct Not Protected[31]	Case
Multiple marriages in violation of state polygamy laws (crime of bigamy).	*Reynolds v. United States,* U.S. Supreme Court (1879) 98 U.S. 145, 25 L. Ed. 244
Handling poisonous snakes in a public place in violation of the state law[32] as part of a religious ceremony.	*State v. Massey,* North Carolina Supreme Court (1949) 229 N.C. 734, 51 S.E.2d 179
Requirements at airports, state fairs, and so on that religious, political, and other groups distribute or sell literature only from booths provided for that purpose.	*Heffron v. International Society for Krishna Consciousness,* U.S. Supreme Court (1981) 452 U.S. 640, 101 S. Ct. 2559
Violation of child labor laws.	*Prince v. Massachusetts,* U.S. Supreme Court (1944) 321 U.S. 158, 64 S. Ct. 438
An Air Force officer continued to wear his yarmulke (Jewish skullcap) after repeated orders to remove it. He was dropped from the service. Affirmed for Air Force.	*Goldman v. Weinberger,* U.S. Supreme Court (1986) 475 U.S. 503, 106 S. Ct. 1310
Members of the Old Order Amish, who do not use motor vehicles but travel in horse-drawn buggies, would not obey a state law requiring reflecting triangles on the rear of all slow-moving vehicles. Held not exempt from complying with this highway safety law.	*Minnesota v. Hershberger,* U.S. Supreme Court (1990) 495 U.S. 901, 110 S. Ct. 1918, *vacating* 444 N.W.2d 282

≡ The Right of Privacy

The U.S. Constitution has no explicit right of privacy. However, the Supreme Court has in various cases found such a right to exist by implication from notions of personal liberty found in the Constitution. Where a right to privacy exists, governments may not pass criminal laws that impinge upon the right, unless the laws have a reasonable, legitimate government purpose and are tailored to advance that interest with the least restriction on the right. In other words, like the freedom of speech, the right of privacy is not absolute.

Some criminal laws were found to unlawfully impinge on the right of privacy. In *Griswold v. Connecticut*, 381 U.S. 479 (1965), the case where the right of privacy was first articulated, the Court struck down a state statute that prohibited providing medical information to a married woman on birth control. In *Lawrence v. Texas*, 123 S. Ct. 2472 (2003), the Court struck down a Texas statute that made criminal consensual homosexual acts done in private, holding that the concepts of personal liberty in the Fourteenth Amendment prohibited the statute.

The right of privacy or personal liberty also resulted in the famous abortion decision, *Roe v. Wade*, 410 U.S. 113, 153 (1973). In that case the Court declared a state abortion law unconstitutional as a violation of a woman's right of privacy. It said:

This right of privacy, whether it be founded in the Fourteenth Amendment's concept of personal liberty and restrictions on state action, as we feel it is, or, as the District Court determined, in the Ninth Amendment's reservation of rights to the people, is broad enough to encompass a woman's decision whether or not to terminate a pregnancy.

The Court also held, however, that the right was not absolute: "We, therefore, conclude that the right of personal privacy includes the abortion decision, but this right is not unqualified and must be considered against important state interests in regulation."

The Court then held that during the first trimester of a pregnancy the abortion decision was solely up to the woman; after the first trimester and before viability the state could regulate the abortion procedures, but could not ban abortions, and after viability the state could ban abortions, so long as an exception was made for the mother's health.

About 1.3 million abortions are performed in the United States each year. Of those abortions, about 85–90 percent are performed during the first trimester, where the woman's right to choose an abortion cannot be regulated by government.

The decision in *Roe v. Wade* has been passionately debated since its announcement. States, and Congress, have passed laws attempting to regulate abortions by use of the criminal laws, many of which have been declared unconstitutional based on *Roe*. Most recently, in the 2007 case of *Gonzales v. Carhart*, 127 S. Ct. 1610 (2007), the Court upheld the constitutionality of the federal "partial birth" abortion law. This law made it a criminal act for a physician to perform an abortion that involved substantially extracting a live fetus from a woman before killing the fetus. It did not provide any criminal penalty for the woman having the abortion.

Opponents of the statute claimed it was invalid under *Roe* because it banned procedures during the second trimester and did not have an exception for the health of the mother. The Court disagreed. It stated that the statute only banned a particular procedure, so-called intact dilation and evacuation (D & E), and since other procedures, including a D & E that did not result in the removal of an intact fetus, were routinely available in the second trimester, the statute did not unreasonably regulate abortions performed during that period.

For postviability abortions, where the state has power to regulate abortions, the Court held the statute constitutional. It stated that although the statute had no exception for the health of the mother, it did not bar other procedures, and given the absence of consensus in the medical community about the necessity of the particular procedure, that failure did not render the statute unconstitutional.

Summary

- The First Amendment protects the freedom of religion, speech, free assembly, the press, and petitioning government for redress of grievances.
- Fighting words differ from ordinary rude language because they carry the possibility of inciting another to violence. It is not enough that the words cause injury.
- A clear and present danger is the possibility that some speech or conduct will bring harm to people or property immediately, not some time in the future.
- Laws directed at the content of speech are subjected to strict scrutiny, meaning the government must have a compelling interest in achieving some goal, and that the limit on the speech is necessary.
- Obscenity is speech or other communication that appeals to a reasonable person's prurient interest, describes in an offensive manner specific defined sexual conduct, and has no redeeming social value.

- A true threat is a threat that a reasonable person would believe was a serious expression of the intent to take violent, unlawful actions.
- A person can stalk another by physically intruding into the other person's life, by sending harassing messages or telephone conversations, or through the Internet.
- An assembly becomes unlawful when three or more people gather and make a public disturbance, including acts that present a clear and present danger of harming people or property.
- The basis for finding the Second Amendment binding on the states was the Due Process Clause of the Fourteenth Amendment. Under the Supreme Court's incorporation rules, a right that was deeply embedded in our nation's history and was a fundamental right is made binding on the states.

Key Terms

"clear and present danger" test, p. 221
disorderly conduct, p. 221
fighting words, p. 221
obscenity, p. 225

inciting, p. 227
defamation, p. 227
symbolic speech, p. 228
threats of violence, p. 230
true threat, p. 230

unlawful assembly, p. 236
riot, p. 236
stalking, p. 238

Case Analysis and Writing Exercises

1. The defendant and his girlfriend were arguing, and the defendant punched the girlfriend. Neighbors saw the punch and called the police. As they were arriving, the defendant left in his car. While the police were talking with the woman, the defendant called her on her telephone. The police officer held the phone and heard the defendant say, "If you get a warrant on me, bitch, I will kill you." The defendant was arrested and charged with making a terrorist threat. Do you see any problems with getting a conviction? Can they be overcome? See *Drew v. State*, 568 S.E.2d 506 (Ga. App. 2002).

2. A man stood outside a dentist's office and near a church where children were being dropped off for day care. Believing the church supported abortion rights, the man yelled at the children, "Why are you going in there? They kill babies." Many of the children were visibly upset by the man's words. He was arrested and charged with public disorder. Can he be convicted based on the "fighting words" doctrine of *Chaplinsky v. New Hampshire*, discussed in the text? Which prong of the *Chaplinsky* test provides the better support for a conviction? See *City of Owosso v. Pouillon*, 657 N.W.2d 538 (Mich. App. 2002).

3. Massachusetts General Law c. 269, Section 1, first passed in 1750, states: "If five or more persons,

being armed with clubs or other dangerous weapons, or if ten or more persons, whether armed or not, are unlawfully, riotously, or tumultuously assembled in a city or town ... any member of the [police] shall go among the persons so assembled ... and ... command all persons so assembled immediately to disperse ..."

The defendant was among a group of people protesting the war in Iraq who refused to disperse when told to do so by police. He was arrested and charged under this statute. How does the prosecution prove the defendant was "unlawfully" assembled? Where does the definition of "unlawful" come from? Is the statute unconstitutional? See *Comm. v. Abramms*, 849 N.E.2d 867 (Mass. App. 2006), *review denied* 854 N.E.2d 441 (2006).

4. The city of Monrovia, California, passed an ordinance that prohibited school-age children from being in public places during school hours on school days. Citations were issued by police who discovered children in violation of the ordinance. Is this a truancy law? If so, would it be valid in California? If it is not a truancy law, what is it? Is it valid? See *Harrahill v. City of Monrovia*, 128 Cal. Rptr. 2d 552 (Cal. App. 2003), *review denied* March 19, 2003.

Notes

1. *Hustler Magazine v. Falwell*, 485 U.S. 46 (1988), quoting *Bose Corp v. Consumers Union*, 466 U.S. 485 (1984).
2. *Cox v. New Hampshire*, 312 U.S. 569 (1941).
3. *Speiser v. Randall*, 357 U.S. 513 (1958).
4. *Hustler v. Falwell.*
5. 249 U.S. 47 (1919).
6. *Watts v. United States*, 394 U.S. 705 (1969).

7. *Chaplinsky v. New Hampshire,* 315 U.S. 568 (1942).

8. Ibid.

9. *FBI Law Enforcement Bulletin,* "The Fighting Word Doctrine," April 1992.

10. *State v. Manning,* 370 A.2d 499 (N.J. 1977).

11. *People v. Cooks,* 58 Cal. Rptr. 550 (Cal. App. 1967).

12. The term *prurient interest* is generally defined as appealing "to a shameful, unhealthy, unwholesome, degrading ... interest in sex." *County of Kenosha v. C&S Management Inc.,* 588 N.W.2d 236 (1999).

13. *Brandenburg v. Ohio,* 89 S. Ct. 1827 (1969).

14. See *New York Times v. Sullivan,* 376 U.S. 254 (1964).

15. Many communities have ordinances regulating the manner and time burning can occur. Burning a flag could also be cited as a violation of these ordinances.

16. See, for example, West's Georgia Code Annotated Section 16-11-37(a) and Nebraska Revised Statute Section 28-311.01 (1995).

17. *Gilbreath v. Florida,* 650 So. 2d 10 (Fla. 1995), *cert. denied* 115 S. Ct. 1996 (1995).

18. 21 U.S.C. Section 403(b), 843(b).

19. 336 U.S. 77 (1949).

20. In the case of *Grayned v. City of Rockford,* 408 U.S. 104, 92 S. Ct. 2294 (1972), the U.S. Supreme Court held:

   The nature of a place, "the pattern of its normal activities, dictates the kinds of regulations of time, place, and manner that are reasonable." Although a silent vigil may not unduly interfere with a public library, making a speech in the reading room almost certainly would. That same speech should be perfectly appropriate in a park. The crucial question is whether the manner of expression is basically incompatible with the normal activity of a particular place at a particular time. Our cases make clear that in assessing the reasonableness of regulation, we must weigh heavily the fact that communication is involved; the regulation must be narrowly tailored to further the State's legitimate interest. "Access to [the streets, sidewalks, parks, and other similar public places] for the purpose of exercising [First Amendment rights] cannot constitutionally be denied broadly." Free expression "must not, in the guise of regulation, be abridged or denied."

21. Ku Klux Klan demonstrations and parades cost local communities a lot of money. Fewer than two dozen Ku Kluxers generally show up, but many more people will appear to protest against the Ku Klux Klan. The likelihood of violence and disorderly conduct is very great. Therefore, adequate police protection must be provided, which means allocating sufficient money for the necessary extra law enforcement and other costs.

   Because of such additional expenses, some communities passed laws and ordinances permitting the imposition of a fee, based on anticipated costs. This would mean that a local administrator would have to estimate the costs for a specific group. The U.S. Supreme Court struck down an ordinance that provided for a fee in the case of *Forsyth County v. Nationalist Movement* (a Ku Klux Klan group), 112 S. Ct. 2395 (1992). The U.S. Supreme Court pointed out that to estimate the fee, the local official had to consider who the group was and the contents of the message they were communicating.

   Requiring prepayment of an $85 fee for the processing of a parade permit application and the cost of traffic control was upheld by the courts in the case of *Stonewell Union v. City of Columbus,* 931 F.2d 1130 (6th Cir. 1991), *review denied* U.S. Supreme Court 112 S. Ct. 275 (1991).

22. States generally statutorize the crime of unlawful assembly, as does Florida in Section 870.03 of the Florida Criminal Code. But some states provide that the crime of unlawful assembly is committed when the person gathered in the unlawful assembly fails to leave the area after law enforcement declares the gathering to be an unlawful assembly and orders the group or crowd to disperse and leave the area.

23. Under the old common law, if a number of people met together and suddenly quarreled and fought among themselves, this would constitute an "affray." An affray differs from a riot in that an affray is not premeditated. Under the old common law, a riot required three or more people, whereas an affray required two or more.

24. Under New York statutes, four or more people plus the person charged are needed for the crime of "unlawful assembly." To convict a person of any of the riot offenses, it must be shown that there were ten or more people gathered, plus the person charged.

25. *Hiibel v. Sixth District Court of Nevada*, 542 U.S. 177 (2004).
26. In the case of *Bennis v. Michigan*, 134 L. Ed. 2d 68 (1996), Mr. Bennis's vehicle was forfeited after he was convicted of this offense. But Mrs. Bennis was an innocent co-owner of the car and appealed to the U.S. Supreme Court. The Supreme Court held that as the vehicle was an abatable nuisance, it could be forfeited without an offset for the innocent co-owner and without a showing that the innocent co-owner knew or consented to the public misuse of the vehicle.
27. California's stalking statute, Penal Code Section 646.9, reads: "Any person who willfully, maliciously, and repeatedly follows or harasses another person, and who makes a credible threat with the intent to place the person in reasonable fear of death or great bodily injury is guilty of the crime of stalking."
28. 60 Cal. Rptr. 2d 423 (Cal. App. 2d 1997).
29. See the *New York Times* articles, "15 Mayors Meet in New York to Fight Against Gun Violence," April 26, 2007, and "52 Mayors Unite to Curb Illegal Firearms," January 24, 2007.
30. *Employment Division v. Smith*, 494 U.S. 872 (S. Ct. 1990).
31. The Freedom of Religion Clause could not be used as a defense for destroying government property (760 F.2d 447), extortion and blackmail (515 F.2d 112), racketeering (695 F.2d 765, *review denied* 460 U.S. 1092), refusal to testify before a grand jury (465 F.2d 802; see 409 U.S. 944), refusal to be photographed after being arrested (848 F.2d 113), putting a logging road through an area sacred to Native American tribes (108 S. Ct. 1319), refusal to have children vaccinated (25 S. Ct. 358), and refusal to participate in the Social Security system (102 S. Ct. 1051), although in 1988 Congress enacted 26 U.S.C. § 3127, which permits members of certain religious groups, such as the Amish people, to elect to opt out of the employee portion of Social Security taxes.
32. According to the New Testament in Mark 16:16–18, "He that believeth and is baptized shall be saved…. [T]hey shall speak with new tongues; they shall take up serpents; and if they drink any deadly thing, it shall not hurt them." In *State v. Massey*, the defendant was convicted of handling poisonous snakes in a religious ceremony, taking literally these words from the New Testament. The Court ruled that the state law forbidding the handling of poisonous snakes was a valid use of the police power of the state of North Carolina and held that the public safety factor outweighed the right to religious freedom.

CHAPTER 10

Homicide

Gene Blevins/LA DailyNews/Corbis

Dr. Conrad Murray has been charged with manslaughter in the death of Michael Jackson. Murray is accused of administering lethal amounts of an anesthetic to Jackson. Prosecutors do not allege Murray intended to kill Jackson, but by his negligent or reckless actions caused Jackson's death, which would not be murder but manslaughter.

OUTLINE

Murder
Intent-to-Kill and Premeditated Murder
The "Deadly Weapon" Doctrine
Transferred Intent
Intent-to-Do-Serious-Bodily-Harm Murder
Depraved-Mind or Depraved-Heart Murder
Felony Murder
Manslaughter
Definition of Manslaughter

Voluntary Manslaughter
Heat of Passion Manslaughter
Imperfect or Unlawful Force in Self-Defense
Charged as Manslaughter
Involuntary Manslaughter
Suicide, Assisting Suicide, and Euthanasia
Murder, Assisted Suicide, or Neither?
The Oregon "Death with Dignity" Law

LEARNING OBJECTIVES

In this chapter we discuss the various kinds and degrees of criminal homicide. The learning objectives for this chapter are:

- Know the meaning of corpus delicti and its role in criminal prosecutions.

- State the current status of the year-and-a-day rule and why its acceptance has waned.

- Identify the "born alive" requirement.

- Explain the doctrine of transferred intent.

- List the homicides that do not require proof of intent to kill.

- Identify which deaths that occur during the commission of a felony qualify as felony murder.

- State the difference between voluntary and involuntary manslaughter.

- List circumstances that could be sufficient to reduce a charge of murder to manslaughter.

- Explain why the U.S. Supreme Court upheld the Oregon Death with Dignity Law.

On September 3, 2006, Nina Reiser disappeared after dropping off her two children at her estranged husband's home in Oakland, California. Although Nina's body had not been found, prosecutors charged her husband, Hans Reiser, a computer programmer and creator of the Reiser FS file system, with first-degree murder. Using circumstantial evidence, such as a sleeping bag with Nina's blood on it, Reiser's car with the passenger seat missing and the floor covered with water, and Reiser's own confusing testimony, in April 2008 a jury convicted Reiser of first-degree murder. In July 2008 Reiser, under a deal with the prosecution that in exchange for his leading police to Nina's body, the charges against him would be reduced to second-degree murder, Reiser took police to a shallow grave where Nina's body was buried. In August 2008 Reiser was sentenced to 15 years to life in prison. He will be eligible for parole in 13 years. In January 2009 Reiser was attacked and beaten by other inmates at the San Quentin prison.

In this chapter we learn the various charges that may be brought against a person or persons when a homicide occurs and what the prosecution must prove in order to obtain a conviction on those charges. We learn what different mental states and circumstances can surround a particular homicide that could result in a charge of murder, or of voluntary manslaughter, or of involuntary manslaughter. We will also learn about the evolving treatment of cases such as assisted suicide and euthanasia.

≡ Homicide in General

homicide The killing of one human being by another. There are three types of homicide: justifiable, excusable, and felonious.

Homicide, the killing of one human being by another, is not always criminal. Sir William Blackstone wrote in the eighteenth century that there were three kinds of homicide—justifiable, excusable, and felonious. He wrote that the first involved no guilt, the second involved little guilt, and the third was the worst crime that humans were capable of committing against the law of nature.

Justifiable homicide is defined in the common law as an intentional homicide committed under circumstances of necessity or duty without any evil intent and without any fault or blame on the person who commits the homicide. Justifiable homicide includes state executions, homicides by police officers in the performance of their legal duty, and self-defense when the person committing the homicide is not at fault.

Excusable homicide is the killing of a human being, either by misadventure or in self-defense, when there is some civil fault, error, or omission on the part of the person who commits the homicide. The degree of fault, however, is not enough to constitute a crime.

Criminal (or *felonious*) *homicide* occurs when a person unlawfully and knowingly, recklessly, or negligently causes the death of another human being. The common law and the states have divided criminal homicide into the crimes of murder, manslaughter, and negligent homicide.

This chapter deals with criminal homicide and the circumstances that give rise to specific charges. Criminal homicide encompasses a wide variety of acts. The acts and the intent with which they were committed determine whether the homicide is intentional or unintentional. Such determination is relevant, because penalties are more severe when the killing was intentional rather than as a result of recklessness, negligence, or carelessness.

≡ The Corpus Delicti Requirement

Corpus delicti means the body or substance of the crime (proof that a crime has been committed). The prosecution must prove in all criminal cases that the crime charged has been committed. For example, if the prosecution cannot prove a fire was deliberately set or that a building actually burned, it cannot prove arson. If it cannot prove the death was not accidental, it cannot prove murder. If both parties were competent adults and consented to sex, rape or sexual assault has not occurred.

In some cases the principal evidence against the defendant is a confession. If no other evidence exists to corroborate the confession, courts often hold that the defendant cannot be convicted of the crime that is charged. Court decisions have noted that confessions can be the result of mistake, mental problems, coercion, or even a friend trying to take the blame for another person. Courts differ on the kind and quality of the evidence sufficient to prove that the crime charged did occur. See *People v. Jennings*, 807 P.2d 1009 (Cal. 1991), where the court held that the state had produced sufficient corroborative evidence to verify "bragging" by the defendant that he had murdered prostitutes and then took back the money he had given them.

Proving Corpus Delicti in "No Body" Cases

Every large American city has active cases of persons reported missing. The city of Washington, D.C., usually has an active list of 100 to 150 missing persons. Most missing persons are missing for a short period of time, or they are living elsewhere and not communicating with their families and friends. Some, however, are victims of murders and other crimes.

Usually, if no body is found, there is no criminal case to prosecute, because evidence needed to prove corpus delicti is ordinarily proved in homicide cases by evidence obtained from the body of the victim or from witnesses to the crime. Corpus delicti can also be proved by circumstantial evidence or by confessions that have been corroborated and affirmed by other evidence.

In the following two "no body" cases, the body of the victim was not found, but corpus delicti was proved by circumstantial evidence. In each case, a murder conviction was affirmed.

People v. Lipsky

Court of Appeals of New York (1982) 57 N.Y.2d 560, 457 N.Y.S.2d 451, 443 N.E.2d 925

While the defendant was in custody on an assault charge in Utah, he confessed that he had murdered a prostitute in Rochester, New York. The victim, Mary Robinson, had been reported missing, but her body had not been found. To corroborate the confession, the state showed that the victim's purse, sandals, wallet, glasses, identification card, and other personal effects were found in an apartment that the defendant had rented in New York within a week of her disappearance. Although the defendant had registered to go to college in New York, he left the state a week after the victim's disappearance and appeared emotionally overwrought. Then, while he was in prison in Utah, he wrote a poem indicating that he had killed another person. In affirming the defendant's conviction and holding that sufficient evidence justified the jury's verdict of guilty, the court held:

> The evidence reviewed above, when read with defendant's confession, the poem he composed and his admissions to his two Provo co-workers, sufficiently establishes both Mary Robinson's death and defendant's strangulation of her as the cause of it to take the issues to the jury. More is not required.

Epperly v. Commonwealth

Supreme Court of Virginia (1982) 224 Va. 214, 294 S.E.2d 882

The victim was last seen leaving a dance with the defendant. Her body was never found, but her blood-soaked clothes and car were found, and there was evidence of a violent struggle at a house on Claytor Lake, where the defendant was seen after the dance. Dog-tracking evidence corroborating some of the state's allegations was permitted at the defendant's trial. The defendant also made incriminating statements.

In affirming the defendant's conviction, the court held:

> *We think the evidence was sufficient to warrant the jury in finding, to the full assurance of moral certainty, that Gina Hall was dead as the result of the criminal act of another person. The jury was entitled to take into account, in this connection, her sudden disappearance, her character and personal relationships, her physical and mental health, the evidence of a violent struggle at the house on Claytor Lake, her hidden, blood-soaked clothing, and the defendant's incriminating statements—particularly his reference to "the body" before it was generally thought she was dead.*

ATTEMPTS TO IDENTIFY AND MINIMIZE VIOLENCE AGAINST CHILDREN

Experts state that about 50,000 children die each year in the United States. It is estimated that of these deaths about 2,000 are caused by child abuse or neglect. Forty percent of the child abuse victims are under 1 year old, and the majority are under the age of 5. The following systems have been created to deal with violence against children:

Child Death Review Teams

The United States (all 50 states), Australia, and Canada now have child death review teams to review deaths of children from violence, child abuse or neglect, motor vehicle accidents, child suicide, and natural or undetermined causes.

Safe Haven Laws for Unwanted Babies

For years, tragic stories of illegally abandoned babies found dead or in unsafe places have appeared in the news. Because of the continuing, sad, attention-getting cases, states began to enact safe haven laws to save the lives of babies. These laws allow a person (usually the mother) to leave an unwanted baby (anonymously and without fear of prosecution) at a hospital, a fire station, or other designated place. Most states (if not all) have now enacted safe haven laws.

Mandatory Child Abuse Reporting Laws

Most states have laws that require persons who "know or have reasonable cause to suspect" child abuse, abandonment, death, or neglect to report that information to authorities. Under the Florida statute, for example, hotlines are established for communicating the information, and failure to do so is punishable as a misdemeanor.

Body Without Proof of the Cause of Death Cases

The body of the deceased is available in most criminal homicide cases. But if doctors are not able to testify specifically that the cause of death was an unlawful act, corpus delicti has not been proved. Unexplained deaths are unusual but not rare in medical history. If doctors are unable to determine the cause of death, or if they are uncertain and unable to state whether the death resulted from criminal acts or from natural causes, then a reasonable doubt may have been created.

Corpus delicti has historically been difficult to prove in sudden infant death syndrome (SIDS) deaths of babies between 2 months and 1 year old because doctors did not know the reason for the cause of death in many of the cases. Today, with more medical knowledge, physicians and medical journals have called into question the SIDS explanation for the deaths of some infants, particularly when multiple deaths occurred in one family. Prosecutors in many states reopened the death investigations of some infants that earlier had been classified as SIDS. For example, a woman in New York was convicted of the murder of five babies, which earlier had been classified as SIDS deaths, and in Philadelphia a woman was charged with the deaths of eight babies, which had earlier been thought to be SIDS deaths.[1]

The testimony of doctors that they "suspected" or had a "hunch" that a criminal act was the cause of death is not sufficient to prove corpus delicti. The following case illustrates the corpus delicti requirement that proof of the cause of death must be established:

People v. Archerd

Supreme Court of California (1970) 3 Cal. 3d 615, 91 Cal. Rptr. 397, 477 P.2d 421

During the period from 1947 to 1966, the defendant married a series of women. After each woman took out a large life insurance policy, she died after being in a coma for a number of hours. It was suspected in each case that a massive injection of insulin was the cause of death. But it was not until 1967 that doctors were able to testify with certainty that the brain tissues of the victims showed this was true. The defendant was suspected of killing six women but was charged and convicted of three deaths. A movie was made of the trial and conviction of the defendant, and a detailed account of the investigation can be found in the FBI Law Enforcement Bulletin article by Sheriff Pitchess, "Proof of Murder by Insulin—A Medico-Legal First" (January 1969).

The Common Law "Born Alive" Requirement and the Crime of Feticide (Fetal Murder)

Under the common law, the killing of a fetus (unborn baby) was not a homicide. Because most criminal homicide statutes prohibited only the killing of a "person" or a "human being," these statutes did not include the killing of a fetus, which was not a person under the common law. In the leading case of *Keeler v. Superior Court*, 470 P.2d 617 (1970) the California Supreme Court said the "born alive" rule prevented a conviction for the death of a fetus. After the *Keeler* decision California statutes were amended to define murder as the "unlawful killing of a human being, **or a fetus**, with malice aforethought" (Title 8, Section 187). This statute made the killing of a fetus in California "with malice aforethought" murder and changed the common law. In 1994, the California Supreme Court held that the state could punish fetal murder without regard to the viability of the fetus. *People v. Davis*, 872 P.2d 591.

In response to cases like *Keeler*, at least 30 states have abandoned the "born alive" requirement, and make the death of a fetus in a mother's body a homicide. The question of whether or not the fetus must be "viable" for conviction under such a statute often depends on the statutory scheme adopted. For example, the Ind. Code, § 35-42-1-1 (4) defines "murder" to include killing a fetus "that has attained viability." It is a Class A felony. Ind. Code § 35-42-1-6 makes it a crime to unlawfully "terminate a pregnancy" and requires no showing of viability of the fetus. It is a Class C felony. Many states have adopted similar "feticide" statutes, which treat the death of an unborn fetus outside the usual definitions of homicide. Under these statutes, there is no requirement that the fetus be born alive, or in most cases even be viable. The Arizona statute, for example, punishes as manslaughter anyone who "Knowingly or recklessly causes the death of an unborn child by any physical injury to the mother." A.R.S. § 13-1103.

In 18 U.S.C. § 1841, passed in 2004, the federal "Protection of unborn children" statute makes it a crime separate from murder to unlawfully take the life of a child that is "*in utero*," *In utero* is defined as "a member of the species homo sapiens, at any stage of development, who is carried in the womb." However, if the circumstances show an intention to kill the fetus, the defendant can be charged under the general murder statute, 18 U.S.C. §1111.

"born alive" requirement To be able to charge homicide of a newborn baby, the prosecution must be able to prove that the child was living at the time it was killed.

feticide Murder of an unborn child.

Eighteen states still have the "born alive" rule, and in most of those jurisdictions some showing that the fetus was alive when it left the mother's body must be made. In *State v. Lamy*, 969 A.2d 451 (N.H. 2009) the court reversed a manslaughter conviction because the state could not show the fetus had any signs of living on its own without life-support machines, and thus did not prove the fetus was born alive. In *State v. Couchesne*, 2010 WL 2244120 (Conn. 2010) the Connecticut Supreme Court remanded a capital murder conviction for a determination of whether an infant kept alive for 42 days on life support after the defendant stabbed her mother to death was "alive."

☰ Proof That the Victim Was Alive at the Time of the Defendant's Unlawful Act

Because criminal homicide is the unlawful killing of a living human being, the state has the burden of showing that the victim was alive at the time of the unlawful act. All people have a right to life, and whether they have 10 minutes or 10 years left to live makes no difference in the eyes of the law.

However, if the victim had already died of illness or injuries at the time of the defendant's unlawful act, criminal homicide was not committed. In the 1973 murder trial of a New York doctor, he was charged with causing the death of a dying cancer patient by injecting a lethal dose of potassium chloride. The patient was in a coma and was not expected to live longer than two days. During the 12-day trial in New York City, the defense attorney argued that the deceased was already dead of natural causes when the injection was made. The state failed to show conclusively that the deceased was still alive at the time of the injection, and the jury acquitted the doctor of homicide.

Whether or not the victim was alive when a sexual assault occurred is sometimes an issue in felony murder cases. In felony murder, discussed in more detail later in this chapter, a defendant convicted of one crime can also be convicted of murder if a person dies as a result of the crime. In such cases, it is necessary for the prosecution to prove the original crime, usually called the "predicate" crime. If for some reason the defendant cannot be convicted of the predicate crime, he or she cannot be convicted of felony murder.

In sexual assault cases, some jurisdictions hold that one cannot be guilty of sexual assault if the victim was dead at the time the assault occurred. See *People v. Hunter*, 530 N.W.2d 174 (Mich. App. 1995), where a conviction for first-degree felony murder was reversed because the victim was dead when sexual penetration occurred. Other jurisdictions hold that so long as the victim was alive when a sexual assault began, it does not matter for felony murder purposes whether the person was alive when sexual penetration occurred. See *State v. Jones*, 705 A.2d 805 (N.J. App. 1998), where a felony murder conviction was affirmed even though the victim may have died before sexual penetration occurred.

When Is a Person Legally Dead?

Until the 1950s and 1960s, the heart was considered the body's most vital organ, and therefore death was defined in terms of cessation of heart and respiratory functions. When doctors became able to keep the heart and other organs alive for transplanting to other patients, medical science recognized that the body's real seat of life is the brain.

Court and state legislative bodies followed the medical profession in defining death in terms of "brain death." For example, the Indiana Supreme Court in 1981 defined death as the "permanent cessation of all brain function" and joined other states in holding that "for the purposes of the law of homicide proof of the death of the victim may be established by proof of the irreversible cessation of the victim's total brain function."[2]

End-of-Life Decisions   On an average day in the United States, more than 6,000 people die. Doctors estimate that at least several hundred of these deaths occur after doctors, patients, and family members agree to withhold life-sustaining treatment and allow the inevitable to occur.

To stay within the law and to avoid criminal prosecution, the decision to withhold treatment or to "pull the plug" on persons in deep continuous comas (persistent vegetative states) should be made only when the following can be shown:

1. Terminally ill patients who are mentally competent can instruct that treatment or life-support systems be withdrawn. Courts have held that the individual's right to refuse treatment must come before the interests of the state in keeping the individual alive.

2. Life-support systems or treatment may be withheld from patients who are comatose or in a persistent vegetative state if one of the following is clearly shown:
    a. That the patient left prior explicit written instructions that this be done (a *living will*) or
    b. That the patient had legally appointed another adult to make such health care decisions, should the patient be unable to do so (*medical power of attorney*), or
    c. Clear and convincing evidence is presented to a court showing that the withdrawal of treatment or of a life-support system is in accordance with the patient's own wishes or best interests.[3]

The population in the United States is growing older. The Census Bureau estimates that between the years 2000 and 2050 the percentage increase in the number of people over 65 will be 147 percent, compared to the estimated overall population increase of 49 percent. Aging diseases such as Alzheimer's and dementia can cause many older people to suffer conditions that are not comas, but are nonetheless destructive of the quality of life. For example, many people with these diseases have lost their ability to swallow food, and as a result they are required to be fed by tubes inserted in their bodies, much the same as those actually in a vegetative state. As of 2010, neither courts nor legislatures have clarified the law on prolonging life in this complex, unsettled, and controversial area.

≡ The Causation Requirement

Causation and Proximate Cause

Causation and proximate cause are discussed in Chapter 3 of this text. Causation is an essential element of all crimes. The state must show that what the defendant did (or failed to do) was the direct and proximate cause of the harm that occurred. The following two examples illustrate the law of causation:

EXAMPLE 1: After loading a gun with live ammunition, X points the gun at Y and pulls the trigger. The firing pin comes down hard on the back of the live cartridge that X has placed in the chamber of the gun. The blow of the hammer detonates the primer in the cartridge, and the primer detonates the powder in the cartridge. The powder burns so rapidly that hot gases immediately build up tremendous pressure in the chamber of the gun. This pressure forces the propellant (the bullet) out of the muzzle of the gun at a high rate of speed. Because of rifling in the barrel of the gun and the direction in which X is pointing the gun, the bullet travels through the air and strikes Y in the head, killing Y immediately.

EXAMPLE 2: After being shocked by seeing the defendant smash her door open and then rip her telephone cord out of the phone, an elderly woman died of a heart attack. The defendant argued that he wanted to burglarize the woman's home but had no intention of harming her.

A jury can easily conclude in Example 1 that X intended the natural and probable consequences of the deliberate act; it would then find that X intended to kill Y. In Example 1, X's acts were the direct and proximate cause of Y's death. The chain of events that occurred after X pulled the trigger was expected and desired by X. Therefore, X can be held criminally responsible for Y's death.

In Example 2, the Nebraska Supreme Court affirmed the defendant's conviction for felony murder in the case of *State v. Dixon*, 387 N.W.2d 682 (1986), holding:

> Dixon admitted to Detectives Circo and Wade that Jourdan was alive when he entered the house. The implosion of window glass and part of the wooden kitchen door would startle the most imperturbable individual. Seeing Dixon coming through the doorway into the kitchen probably would stir one to "stare" at him, visual fixation founded in fear intensified by Dixon's ripping the "cord out of the phone." All that unfolded before Susan Jourdan, 76 years old and living alone. What total terror likely seized and constricted Susan Jourdan's heart may be beyond another's comprehension. What the jury did understand was Dr. Roffman's explanation of the cause of Susan Jourdan's death, "emotional trauma of having her door kicked in and stimulating her heart to beat abnormally, causing her collapse and ultimate death."

The Year-and-a-Day Rule

The year-and-a-day rule is also discussed in more detail in Chapter 3. The common law rule stated that a person could not be convicted of a murder unless the victim died within a year and a day from the time of the wrongful act. The Michigan Supreme Court pointed out in 1982 that the year-and-a-day rule dates back to 1278 and that the "original rationale for the rule was probably tied to the inability of 13th century medicine to prove the cause of death beyond a reasonable doubt after a prolonged period of time."[4]

Common law rules became part of a new state's criminal law because virtually all states included in their constitution a clause that adopted the "common law of England" in place when the United States was formed. Subsequent changes to that common law, usually by state legislatures, were called "abrogations" of the common law. Courts also possess the power to abrogate a common law rule, which many have in the case of the year-and-a-day rule.

The Michigan Supreme Court and many other state courts or legislatures have abolished this rule. When the common law rule is abrogated by a state supreme court, the court must determine whether to make the abrogation retroactive, or only prospective. In *State v. Picotte*, 661 N.W.2d 381 (Wis. 2003), the Wisconsin Supreme Court abrogated the common law year-and-a-day rule but made the abrogation prospective. As a result, the defendant's conviction for reckless homicide of a victim who died more than one year after the crime occurred was reversed.

A few courts have not abolished the rule. In *Ex Parte Key*, 890 So. 2d 1056 (Ala. 2003), the Alabama Supreme Court reversed a conviction of a defendant for murder of a victim who died 18 months after the injury. The court held that the year-and-a-day rule was still part of the common law in Alabama.

Some states continue to use a variation of the rule. For example, Title 8, Section 194 of the California Penal Code provides that "To make the killing either murder or manslaughter, it is not requisite the party die within three years and a day after the stroke received or the cause of death administered. If death occurs beyond the time of three years and a day, there shall be a rebuttable presumption that the killing was not criminal."

≡ Murder

The first murder to be reported in the American colonies occurred ten years after the Pilgrims landed at Plymouth Rock. In 1630, John Billington, one of the original band of 102 Pilgrims to come over on the *Mayflower*, fired his blunderbuss at a neighbor and killed the man at close range. John Billington was charged with the common law offense of murder under the English law and, after a prompt trial and conviction, was hanged.[5]

Only one degree of murder existed under the common law, and it was punishable by death. After the American Revolution, some state legislative bodies began creating other degrees of murder. They were probably motivated by a desire to separate murder to be punished by death from murder that they did not want to be punished by death.

By the year 1900, virtually all the states had two or three degrees of murder. At that time, the degree system was a useful and meaningful method of distinguishing murder that was punished by capital punishment and that which was not. With the decline in the use of the death penalty in this century and its virtual nonuse in the 1960s and 1970s, the utility of the degree system declined considerably.

The degree system is still meaningful today, when first-degree murder carries a mandatory life imprisonment sentence or the death penalty. The degree system is also used as part of plea bargaining when the state finds advantage in allowing the defendant to plead guilty to second-degree murder or to some other lesser offense if a reduction is appropriate.

State murder statutes vary in how they define first- and second-degree murder. An example of a first-degree murder statute that incorporates the common law "malice" requirement is Nebraska Revised Statute Section 28–303: "A person commits murder in the first degree if he kills another person (1) purposely and with deliberate malice...." Second-degree murder is defined in Section 28–304: "A person commits murder in the second degree if he causes the death of a person intentionally, but without premeditation."

The Illinois statute is an example of a statute that has a broader definition of first-degree murder:

(a) A person who kills an individual without lawful justification commits first degree murder if, in performing the acts which cause the death, (1) he either intends to kill

---

CLASSIFICATIONS OF COMMON LAW MURDER

- *Intent-to-kill murder*: The most common murder, the intentional killing of another human being, is considered the most serious offense in the criminal law.
- *Intent-to-do-serious-bodily-harm murder*: In this type of murder, the defendant intended to do serious bodily harm short of death, but his or her acts resulted in death.
- *Depraved-mind or depraved-heart murder*: When a death results from conduct that shows a wanton disregard for human life and when there is a high probability the conduct will result in death, the homicide is classified as this type of murder.
- *Felony murder*: At common law, one who caused another's death while committing a felony was guilty of felony murder. However, when the doctrine was created, only eight felonies were recognized, and all were punished by death. Because states now have many felonies that do not carry the death penalty, the felony murder rule is generally limited to crimes of violence.

---

or do great bodily injury to that individual or another, or knows that such acts will cause death to that individual or another; (2) he knows that such acts create a strong probability of death or great bodily harm to that individual or another, or (3) he is attempting to commit a forcible felony other than second degree murder.[6]

Second-degree murder is then defined as doing an act that constitutes first-degree murder, but under intense passion caused by serious provocation, or under an unreasonable belief that the killing was justified.

Intent-to-Kill and Premeditated Murder

The unlawful, intentional, premeditated killing of another human being is considered the most serious criminal offense. It is in most states called first-degree or capital murder. The weapon used to implement the murder can be anything from a firearm to bare hands. The type of weapon used or the manner in which the fatal blow is delivered is not necessarily significant. Rather, the presence or absence of the specific intent to take the life of another human being separates this crime from all other degrees of homicide. The type of weapon and the manner in which it is used, however, may give rise to the legal inference that a person intends the natural and probable consequences of his or her deliberate acts.

murder Unlawful homicide with malice aforethought.

Murder under the common law and as enacted by the statutes of many states as first-degree murder is often defined as an "unlawful homicide with malice aforethought." The phrase *malice aforethought* signifies the mental state of a person who voluntarily, without legal excuse or justification, does an act that ordinarily will cause death or serious injury to another. Although the word *malice* ordinarily conveys the meaning of hatred, ill will, or malevolence, it is not limited to those meanings in "malice aforethought" but can include such motives as a mercy killing, in which the homicide is committed to end the suffering of a loved one. *Aforethought* has been interpreted to mean that the malice must exist at the time of the homicidal act. Courts have held that if the design and intent to kill precede the killing for even a moment, the person can be convicted of first-degree murder.[7]

Other states have defined first-degree murder as causing "the death of another human being with intent to kill that person." The American Law Institute Model Penal Code, § 210, uses the words *purposely* and *knowingly* causes the death of another person as the basis for a charge of murder.

Section 18 U.S.C. § 1111 of the federal criminal statutes defines "murder" as follows: "Murder is the unlawful killing of a human being with malice aforethought." If the killing is done by poison, during the commission of certain identified crimes, or is "willful, deliberate, malicious and premeditated," it is murder in the first degree. All other murders are murder in the second degree. The following case addresses the meaning and application of the federal statute:

CASE CLOSE-UP

United States v. Begay
Ninth Circuit Court of Appeals 2009
567 F.3d 540

On March 28, 2002, Kendrick Begay was driving his truck around the Navajo Indian Reservation in Greasewood, Arizona. After passing another vehicle, Begay stopped his truck next to the other vehicle, and walked over to the driver's side window. After a one-minute conversation, Begay walked back to his truck and pulled out a rifle he kept under the front seat. He walked to the passenger side of the other vehicle and fired 8 or 9 shots through the passenger window, killing both passengers.

Begay was arrested and charged with first-degree murder under the federal murder statute, 18 U.S.C. § 1111 (although Begay was an Indian and the killings took place on Indian Country land, the Indian Major Crime Act, 18 U.S.C. § 1153, permitted federal authorities to charge him under the general federal murder statute; see Chapter 2). The jury convicted him of two counts of first-degree murder, as well as two counts of using a firearm in the commission of a felony. Begay was sentenced to two life imprisonment terms for the murders, and 35 years for the firearm convictions.

On appeal, Begay contended (1) there was insufficient evidence to support the jury's verdict of first-degree murder, and (2) if the first-degree murder conviction was reversed, the government could not retry him on any other charge because it failed to ask the appellate court to find Begay guilty of the lesser-included offense of second-degree murder.

A Ninth Circuit Court of Appeals panel of three judges agreed with Begay. It concluded the prosecution did not present sufficient evidence to support a first-degree murder conviction. It interpreted § 1111's requirements for first-degree murder, "willful, deliberate, malicious, and premeditated," to require proof of "premeditation." The court said "willful" referred only to a requirement that there be specific intent as opposed to general intent. "Malicious" referred to 1111's requirement of "malice aforethought," which was required for both first and second-degree murder. Both were present in this case, the court stated. However, "deliberate" and "premeditated," which the court said amounted to the same thing, were not proved, the court held.

The court said premeditation requires that "at some point *after* the defendant forms the intent to kill the victim, he has the time to reflect on the decision to commit murder, that he in fact does reflect on that decision, and that he commits the murder with a 'cool mind' after having engaged in such reflection." 567 F.3d, at 546. The court concluded the evidence did not support the jury finding of premeditation. It noted that Begay had no previous relationship with either victim, he had no shown motive for the killings, he engaged in no planning activity, and he didn't have a "cool-head," because even though he was a skilled marksman, he missed with many of the rifle shots from a short range, which showed he was agitated and excited. The court therefore reversed his conviction for first-degree murder.

The court also noted that while the normal course would be to reduce Begay's conviction to the lesser-included offense of second-degree murder, it could not do that in this case because the prosecution failed to request that on appeal. The court therefore vacated the conviction for murder, and affirmed only the firearm convictions.

In January 2010 the Ninth Circuit Court of Appeals ordered a rehearing *en banc* of the panel's decision in Begay's case. 591 F.3d 1180 (9th Cir. 2010). Oral argument was heard on March 23, 2010. What issues will likely be considered in the rehearing? What should be the result on those issues?

The "Deadly Weapon" Doctrine

Committing a crime by use of a "deadly weapon," such as assault with a deadly weapon, is commonly a separate and more serious crime. In a murder case, the use of a deadly weapon can also be used to prove "malice" or other intent. Because direct evidence is rarely available to show the actual intent of a person charged with a crime, the fact finder, judge or jury, must draw inferences about intent from the conduct of the accused and the circumstances surrounding the crime to determine if the intent to kill existed. The use of a deadly weapon creates an inference of the user's intent. For example, if a defendant pointed a weapon he or she knew to be loaded at another person and pulled the trigger, no direct evidence of intent exists, but intent can be inferred by the defendant's conduct.

The "deadly weapon" doctrine is related to and part of the inference that a person intends the natural and probable consequences of his or her deliberate acts. A loaded revolver is certainly a deadly weapon when aimed and fired at close range. Under such circumstances, a jury can easily infer an intent to kill, because the natural and probable consequences of this act are death or serious bodily harm.

Determining what constitutes a deadly weapon depends on the object used and the circumstances that existed at the time of the homicide. One area where courts are split on this question involves human body parts—fists, feet, or teeth—as deadly weapons. See *Parts of the Body as Dangerous Weapons*, 8 ALR 4th 1268 (1981; 2010 Cum. Supp.) Some jurisdictions hold that parts of the body cannot be a deadly weapon for purposes of conviction of crimes requiring the presence or use of a deadly weapon. For example, in the 2010 case of *McMillian v. State*, 2010 WL 415240 (Ala. Crim. App.), the defendant used his teeth to bite out his girlfriend's left eye. The court held that using teeth to injure another cannot be use of a "deadly weapon" for purpose of a domestic assault statute. That appears to be the position of the Model Penal Code, § 210.0 (4).

On the other hand, in *Dasher v. State*, 676 S.E.2d 181 (Ga. 2009) and *State v. Wallace*, 676 S.E.2d 922 (N.C. App. 2009), the courts held that fists or feet can be deadly weapons depending on how they were used, and the relative size of the assailant and victim. Most courts do agree that if an assailant is wearing heavy boots during an assault, the boots themselves are an extra-body object and can thus be a deadly weapon. See, e.g., *Com. v. Rumkin*, 773 N.E.2d 988 (Mass. App. 2002).

Therefore, in determining what a deadly weapon is, a jury considers the instrument used, who used it, and how it was used. Some items, such as knives, clubs, or guns, are almost always considered deadly weapons because of the potential harm they can cause. Other instruments, such as automobiles, have to be viewed in light of their uses. The U.S. Supreme Court ruled in the 1895 case of *Allen v. United States* that a lower court erred when it withdrew the question of self-defense from a jury on the ground that sticks and clubs were not deadly weapons.[8] Sticks and clubs can be deadly weapons, depending on their size, who is using them, and how they are used.

Juries and judges have held the following objects to be deadly weapons under the circumstances in which they were used:

- Cowboy boots used to "stomp" a grown man's girlfriend's head into the pavement. *People v. Carter,* 423 N.E.2d 30 (1981)
- A floor against which the defendant struck an infant's head, causing fatal injuries. *Stanul v. State,* 870 S.W.2d 329 (Texas 1994)
- An automobile used to run down a victim of a robbery attempt. *Jackson v. State,* 662 So. 2d 1369 (Fla. 1995)
- A nail gun, when used to threaten robbery victims. *Toy v. State,* 855 S.W.2d 153 (Texas 1993)

Transferred Intent

If a killer is a poor shot and misses the intended victim but hits and kills another person, he or she could argue that there was no intent to kill that person. If there was a mistake of identity and the killer kills the wrong person, the same argument could be made. Defense lawyers have used these arguments for hundreds of years, arguing that because there was no ill will and malice toward the victim killed by accident, the defendant should not be convicted of intent-to-kill murder but, at the most, negligent or reckless homicide.

To accept such arguments would allow killers to benefit because of their poor marksmanship or because they killed the wrong person in a mix-up. The common law rejected that argument by creating the doctrine of **transferred intent**. This doctrine became part of the common law before the American Revolution and was recognized as early as 1766

transferred intent A doctrine used when the intention to harm one individual inadvertently causes a second person to be hurt instead. The individual causing the harm will be seen as having "intended" the act by means of the "transferred intent" doctrine.

Gladden v. Maryland

Maryland Court of Special Appeals (1974) 20 Md. App. 492, 316 A.2d 319

In a dispute over a bad batch of heroin, Gladden emptied a revolver, firing wildly at the heroin pusher. He did not hit the man he was shooting at but instead hit and killed an innocent 12-year-old boy. The defendant appealed his conviction of intent-to-kill murder. In affirming the conviction, the court held:

The doctrine of "transferred intent" has long been recognized at common law. Sir Matthew Hale, in 1 History of the Pleas of the Crown (published posthumously in 1736), said, at 466: "To these may be added the cases abovementioned, viz. if A. by malice forethought strikes at B. and missing him strikes C. whereof he dies, tho he never bore any malice to C. yet it is murder, and the law transfers the malice to the party slain; the like of poisoning."

Forty years later, Sir William Blackstone, in 4 Commentaries on the Laws of England, reiterated the common law rule according to Hale; at 200–201: "Thus if one shoots at A. and misses him, but kills B., this is murder; because of the previous felonious intent, which the law transfers from one to the other. The same is the case where one lays poison for A.; and B., against whom the prisoner had no malicious intent, takes it, and it kills him; this is likewise murder."

* * *

The appellant contends that he should not have been convicted of murder, since he bore no malice toward the victim. He urges upon us that the common law doctrine of "transferred intent" should not be received into Maryland, although he acknowledges that this is the law in the overwhelming majority of common law jurisdictions. We have no difficulty in deciding that "transferred intent" is, and should be, a part of the common law of this State.

by Blackstone in 4 *Commentaries* 200–201. The following case illustrates the transferred intent doctrine:

It does not alter the "transferred intent" doctrine if the killer manages to kill both the intended victim and another person. In *People v. Bland*, 48 P.3d 1107 (Cal. 2002), the defendant fired into a car with three passengers, intending to kill one of them. He killed one and critically wounded the other two. The California Supreme Court held that even if the defendant succeeded in killing his intended target, the doctrine of transferred intent would apply to the other persons shot, if they had died. However, the court also held that transferred intent does not apply to charges of attempted murder. The defendant could be convicted of attempted murder only if he in fact had such an intent.

Premeditation Mental determination to unlawfully kill another person after planning or reflection on actions causing death.

The transferred intent doctrine may be used to prove the required "premeditation" for a first-degree murder conviction. Thus, if A aims a gun at B in a premeditated act to kill B, but instead strikes C, A can be convicted of the **premeditated murder** of C. See Wayne R. LaFave, 2 *Substantive Criminal Law*, § 14.7 (a) (2nd Ed. 2003). However, the transferred intent doctrine **by itself** cannot be used to prove premeditation if the defendant in fact intended to kill the person who died. In such a case, the defendant's premeditated intent to kill another does not "transfer", because the defendant had some kind of actual intent with respect to the actual victim. The nature of that intent must be proved by the prosecution. In the case of *State v. Hall*, 722 N.W.2d 472 (Minn. 2006), the defendant left an apartment with a gun, saying he planned to kill three unidentified people. In fact, the defendant walked to gas station and fired 4 shots point-blank at the station clerk. The trial court instructed the jury that under the transferred intent doctrine the premeditation to kill the three unidentified people satisfied the premeditation requirement for the killing of the clerk. The Minnesota Supreme Court reversed, saying that because there was no evidence the clerk was an unintended victim, the prosecution needed to prove the defendant premeditated the clerk's death.

Intent-to-Do-Serious-Bodily-Harm Murder

English courts under the common law long ago decided that a death at the hands of one who intended to do only serious bodily harm was nevertheless murder. The following famous English cases illustrate this type of murder:

Rex v. Errington

2 Lew.C.C. 148, 217 (1838)

The defendants covered a drunken man, who was sleeping, with straw, on which they threw a shovel of hot cinders. The man burned to death in the fire that resulted. The court instructed the jury that if they found that the defendants intended to do any serious harm to the deceased, the crime was murder under the common law; if the defendants' only intent was to play a joke or frighten the deceased, the crime was manslaughter.

Holloway Case

79 Eng. Rep. 715 (K.B.1628)

The defendant tied a boy to a horse's tail and hit the horse to make it run. The boy was killed. The defendant was convicted of murder even though it was found that there was no intent to kill.

Many states follow this common law approach, and include "intent-to-do-serious-bodily-harm" as a class of murder. For example, in *Thornton v. State*, 919 A.2d 678, 699 (Md. 2007) the Maryland Supreme Court noted that in Maryland murder remains a common law crime, and that second-degree murder includes the "serious bodily injury" crime. That crime requires that the "State must prove intent to injure the victim so severely that death would be the likely result even though the defendant did not intend the victim should die."

State murder statutes vary on the inclusion of "serious bodily injury" as a class or type of murder. Those that retain that class generally include it as second-degree murder, although Illinois continues to include it in the first-degree murder statute, 720 ILCS 5/9-1. The Model Penal Code, § 210.2 omits any reference to "intent to do serious bodily harm" in the classification of murder. Rather, the fact that a defendant intended to inflict serious harm would be a factor in showing the kind of "extreme indifference to the value of human life" that is included in the definition of murder.

Depraved-Mind or Depraved-Heart Murder

This classification, in some states called second-degree murder, is similar in some aspects to the intent-to-do-serious-bodily-harm murder. The primary difference is that the depraved-mind murder includes no specific intent to injure or harm. However, if the conduct of the defendant was so reckless as to create a high risk of death, he or she would, in many instances, be found guilty of depraved-heart or reckless-conduct murder.

The California and New Mexico Supreme Courts pointed out in the following cases that malice may be implied when a person, knowing that his or her conduct endangers the life of another, deliberately continues to act in a manner that shows a conscious disregard for life.

People v. Watson

Supreme Court of California (1981) 30 Cal. 3d 290, 179 Cal. Rptr. 43, 637 P.2d 279

After drinking a large volume of beer in a bar, the defendant drove through a red light and avoided a collision with another car, late at night, only by skidding to a halt in the middle of the intersection. After the near collision, the defendant drove off at a high rate of speed (twice the 35 miles per hour speed limit). On approaching another intersection, the defendant again applied his brakes, but he struck a Toyota sedan, killing the driver and her 6-year-old daughter. The defendant's blood-alcohol content one-half hour after the collision was 0.23 percent, which was twice the 0.10 percent then necessary to find a person legally intoxicated.

The issue before the California Supreme Court was whether the defendant could be charged and forced to go to trial on two counts of second-degree murder instead of the usual charges of homicide by intoxicated use of a vehicle or of vehicular manslaughter. In holding that the conduct of the defendant was sufficient to support a probable cause finding of implied malice to justify charging and trying the defendant for second-degree murder, the court stated:

> We have said that second degree murder based on implied malice has been committed when a person does "an act, the natural consequences of which are dangerous to life, which act was deliberately performed by a person who knows that his conduct endangers the life of another and who acts with conscious disregard for life." People v. Sedeno.... Phrased in a different way, malice may be implied when defendant does an act with a high probability that it will result in death and does it with a base antisocial motive and with a wanton disregard for human life....
>
> Based upon our independent review of the record, we believe that there exists a rational ground for concluding that defendant's conduct was sufficiently wanton to hold him on a second degree murder charge.

> ### State v. Ibn Omar-Muhammad
>
> Supreme Court of New Mexico (1985) 102 N.M. 274, 694 P.2d 922
>
> In fleeing from arrest by law enforcement officers (a crime in itself), the defendant tried to run police officers off the road. He ran roadblocks at high rates of speed. He was charged with depraved-mind murder when he killed a man while fleeing from the police. The court held that he was properly convicted of depraved-mind murder instead of the lesser offense of vehicular homicide because the defendant knew the risk involved in his conduct.

Felony Murder

felony murder Most states and the federal government have felony murder statutes that punish as murder the causing of death of another while the defendant is committing a felony of violence. A felony murder conviction does not require a showing of malice or deliberate intent to kill.

The **felony murder** rule became part of the common law of England many years ago. The rule initially stated that if a death occurs while a defendant is committing or attempting to commit any felony, the defendant could be convicted of felony murder even if the death was unintended and accidental. The theory behind the rule was that the intent to commit the underlying felony sufficed to show the intent to kill.

In the United States, courts and legislatures have limited the scope of the felony murder rule. The most frequent method of limiting the rule is illustrated by the federal murder statute, 18 U.S.C. § 1111. That statute includes as murder only a killing that occurs during the commission of certain enumerated crimes, such as arson, robbery, or sexual assault. If a person is killed during the commission of a felony not listed in § 1111, it is not murder **solely** because of the felony committed. In such a case, the prosecution would need to prove the required intent.

Other methods of determining when the felony murder rule is appropriate include a requirement that the killing was the "natural and direct consequence" of the felony, or that the act that caused the death occurred while the felony was in progress. In *People v. Klebanowski*, 852 N.E.2d 813 (Ill. 2006) the Illinois Supreme Court held the felony-murder rule, which applied to killings that occurred "during the commission" of a felony, applied when one of two robbers was killed by the victim (an off-duty police officer) during the robbers' attempt to escape. In *State v. Beach*, 67 P.3d 121 (Kan. 2003) the Kansas Supreme Court held that unless the defendant showed an intervening force caused a death during the commission of a crime, there was no duty on the prosecution to prove otherwise that the death was a "direct result" of the commission. The court reasoned that the absence of an intervening force by itself established the causal connection between the felony and the killing.

The Model Penal Code's definition of murder in section 210.2 omits any reference to the felony murder rule. Instead, that section states that if a homicide occurs during one of the listed crimes (e.g., robbery, rape, arson, kidnapping) it is presumed that it was the result of "extreme indifference to the value of human life" and thus constitutes murder under § 210.2(b). Some state murder statutes, such as the statute in Kentucky, KRS § 507.020, follow the Model Penal Code and drop the felony murder rule, instead using the "extreme indifference" language of the MPC.

In some states, though not all, it has been held that the death of a person, including a co-felon, that occurred during a felony but is caused by a third person—such as a person who was the intended victim, a passerby, or a police officer who confronts a felony in progress—does not qualify as felony murder. Thus, if two robbers are confronted by the police, and the police kill one of the robbers, the other robber is not guilty of felony murder. In New York, Penal Law § 125.25 states the felony murder rule applies when the defendant or "another participant" in the crime kills another person "other than a participant."

In other states, as the *Klebanowski* case discussed earlier shows to be the result in Illinois, the death of a co-felon makes the remaining felon guilty of felony murder. The Florida Appellate Court reached the same conclusion in *State v. Presley*, 389 So. 2d 216 (1980). This also appears to be the rule in prosecutions under 18 U.S.C. § 1111. In *United States v. Garcia-Ortiz*, 528 F.3d 74 (1st Cir. 2008) the court held that a defendant could be convicted of felony murder when an accomplice was killed by a third party.

In those states that do not apply the felony murder rule to the death of a co-felon by a third party, a co-felon could be charged with provocative act murder. That doctrine

FELONY MURDER RULE

Conduct	Finding	Case
Defendant kicked in door of elderly woman's home, tore telephone from wall, and burglarized home.	"[E]motional trauma of having door kicked in and stimulating her heart to beat abnormally, causing her collapse and ultimate death."	*State v. Dixon*, previously presented to illustrate proximate cause
Defendant tied up his victim during a robbery.	Medical testimony established the cause of victim's death as a heart attack "brought on by the emotional stress resulting from the action of the defendant."	*State v. Spates*, Connecticut Supreme Court, 176 Conn. 227, 405 A.2d 656 (1978)
Armed robberies (and one burglary) of victims who died of heart attacks after crimes (in burglary, victim exchanged gunfire with burglar).	Medical testimony that victims died of "cardiac arrest caused by … the stress of events before the victim's death."	*Durden v. State*, 250 Ga. 325, 297 S.E.2d 237 (1982); *People v. Stamp*, 2 Cal. App.3d 203, 82 Cal. Rptr. 598 (1969); *Booker v. State*, 386 N.E.2d 1198 (Ind. 1979); *State v. Atkinson*, 298 N.C. 673, 259 S.E.2d 858 (1979)
Death of firefighters while fighting blazes started by defendants (deliberate arsons).	Felony murder convictions affirmed.	*State v. Leech*, 114 Wash. 2d 700, 790 P.2d 160 (1990); *People v. Zane*, 152 A.D.2d 976, 543 N.Y.S. 2d 777 (1989); *Bethea v. Scully*, 834 F.2d 257 (2d Cir. 1987)
Felons fleeing at high speed killed innocent people in traffic fatalities in their attempt to get away after robberies.	Because fleeing from a crime scene is part of the crime, felony murder convictions were affirmed.	*People v. Jonson*, 1992 WL 73337 (Cal. App. 1992); *Whitman v. People*, 420 P.2d 416 (Colo. 1966); *People v. Fuller*, 150 Cal. Rptr. 515 (Cal. App. 1978)
During an armed robbery, the victim shot and killed one of the robbers. Defendant was convicted of killing the other robber.	*Conviction reversed*: "It is clearly the majority view (that) the doctrine of felony murder does not extend to a killing … (by one other than) those associated with him in the unlawful enterprise."	*State v. Canola*, New Jersey Supreme Court, 73 N.J. 206, 374 A.2d 20 (1977)

applies if the co-felon took some action that was likely to provoke the third party into using deadly force. For example, in *People v. Concha*, 218 P.3d 660 (Cal. 2009) the California Supreme Court held a defendant could be convicted of first-degree murder under the "provocative act" murder doctrine when the victim of an attempted murder killed a co-felon. The court stated that in California even though a co-felon could not be guilty of felony murder of either the death of another felon or death caused by a third party, if the underlying crime was the proximate cause of the death the provocative act murder doctrine applied. Moreover, rejecting the defendant's argument to the contrary, the court held that if a jury found the attempted murder was premeditated, than the resulting death of the co-felon would be first-degree murder.

≡ Manslaughter

Definition of Manslaughter

manslaughter Criminal homicides other than murder. Most states provide for two degrees of manslaughter, voluntary and involuntary.

Manslaughter was defined by common law as a classification of criminal homicide that is less than murder. The common law divided manslaughter into two categories: voluntary and involuntary. Most U.S. jurisdictions follow the common law classifications, but a few states have created three categories. For example, Section 192 of the California Penal Code creates the three classifications of voluntary, involuntary, and vehicular manslaughter. A few states have only one degree of manslaughter. A form of classification other than voluntary and involuntary manslaughter is that of identifying manslaughter by degrees (first, second, and so on).[9]

Reasons given for a manslaughter conviction rather than a murder conviction are as follows:

1. The victim may have provoked the killing, or his or her unlawful conduct set into motion a chain of events that resulted in the killing.
2. The killings are not bad enough to be charged as murder, but the criminal conduct should be punished.
3. In some cases, the jury cannot unanimously agree on a finding of murder and compromise on a manslaughter conviction.

Manslaughter is a crime that is generally considered to be separate and distinct from murder. Because the penalties are less severe than for murder, defense lawyers who are unable to obtain an acquittal for clients seek a conviction of manslaughter rather than murder.

Voluntary Manslaughter

The following example is used to illustrate voluntary manslaughter:

EXAMPLE: When Robert Lee Moody was 18 years old, he killed his father with a shotgun and then went to a California police station to turn himself in, stating what he had done. The prosecutor charged Moody with voluntary manslaughter because of the following reported conduct of the father: he had seduced his two teenage daughters, had begun fondling his 11-year-old daughter, had forced his wife into prostitution to help pay for a pleasure boat, was a child and wife beater, and had opened his older son's head with a screwdriver (the son was committed to a mental hospital). After the trial court convicted Moody of voluntary manslaughter, the court received more than 700 letters, most of which urged a lenient sentence for Moody. The sentence handed down in 1984 was five years of probation, with two of the years to be served in "Peace Corps–like" missionary work.[10]

EXAMPLES OF MANSLAUGHTER

Heat of Passion Manslaughter

Example: Defendant and his wife were separated. Defendant went to the home where the wife and child lived and found his wife having sexual intercourse with another man. Defendant shot and killed the other man and was convicted of first-degree murder. Reversed to voluntary manslaughter.

Heat of passion manslaughter was the finding in this case because:

1. There was adequate provocation, which caused
2. Extreme anger and rage ("In our opinion, the passions of any reasonable person would have been inflamed and intensely aroused by this sort of discovery"),
3. There was no opportunity to cool off, and
4. There was a causal connection between the provocation, anger, and the fatal act.

State v. Thornton, Tennessee Supreme Court, 730 S.W.2d 309 (1987)

Involuntary Manslaughter (Also Called Unintended Manslaughter)

Example: Defendant repeatedly allowed vicious dogs to run loose. The dogs killed a jogger. *State v. Powell*, 426 S.E. 91 (N.C. App. 1993). (See this chapter and Chapter 3 for material on involuntary manslaughter.)

Imperfect Self-Defense Manslaughter

Example: Defendant and his brother became involved in a fight outside a Baltimore bar. When the defendant believed the other man had a knife, he pulled out a handgun and fired, killing the other man. The victim did not have a knife. The trial court did not submit the imperfect self-defense issue to jury. Reversed for new trial.

In a long decision tracing the history and cases on manslaughter, the court used the honest but unreasonable belief rule. Faulkner produced evidence sufficient to generate a jury issue as to whether he had a subjectively honest but objectively unreasonable belief that he was in imminent danger of death or serious bodily injury, and the trial court should have granted his requested instruction on imperfect self-defense. *State v. Faulkner*, Court of Appeals of Maryland, 301 Md. 482, 483 A.2d 759 (1984).

Manslaughter Conviction That Caused a Riot

Example: After losing his job, Dan White sneaked a gun into City Hall in San Francisco, where he shot Mayor Moscone four times. He then reloaded the gun and shot Supervisor Harvey Milk, a leader of the gay community, six times. Both victims died. Dan White used the "Twinkie" defense, claiming that excessive junk food diminished his capacity to form the required intent. White was convicted of two counts of voluntary manslaughter, causing San Francisco gays to riot, taking over the downtown area, burning cars, and breaking windows. *People v. White*, California Court of Appeals, 117 Cal. App. 3d 270, 172 Cal. Rptr. 612 (1981).

In the *Moody* case, the killing was voluntary and intentional. The shocking, unlawful conduct of the victim provoked his own death, and made the charge of murder inappropriate. However, because the killing was not justified as an act of self-defense or defense of another (see Chapter 6 of this text), some criminal charge had to be made. Manslaughter is the crime halfway between murder and excusable homicide.

Heat of Passion Manslaughter

Another form of voluntary manslaughter is heat of passion manslaughter. This crime is commonly charged when the actions of the victim cause the defendant to become enraged and angered to the point of losing normal self-control and, in the heat of passion, killing.

To reduce murder to manslaughter, courts generally hold that the following four requirements be met:

1. There must be adequate provocation.
2. The killing must have been in a heat of passion (anger, rage, or emotional disturbance).
3. There must have been no opportunity to cool off.
4. There must be a causal connection between the provocation, the rage or anger, and the fatal act.

In *People v. Mills*, 228 P.3d 276 (Cal. 2010) a defendant convicted of capital murder appealed, contending the jury lacked sufficient evidence to find he had the required malice aforethought for a murder conviction. The defendant contended the killing occurred in a heat of passion, and he should only have been convicted of manslaughter. The Supreme Court affirmed his conviction and death sentence, finding that evidence the defendant went out sightseeing and snowboarding with his friends two days after the killing supported the jury's verdict. The jury could have concluded that "a person acting under the influence of a passionate impulse would not have behaved in so cavalier a fashion so recently after committing such a violent act."

Sufficient and Adequate Provocation   Sufficient provocation naturally and instantly produces in the mind of an ordinary person the highest degree of exasperation, rage, anger, sudden resentment, or terror. The provocation must be of such a nature and be so great as to overcome or suspend an ordinary person's exercise of good judgment. The provocation must be such as to cause the person to act uncontrollably. The killing must occur immediately during or after the provocation and during the intense heat of passion. Only a few categories of provocation have been recognized by the law as legally sufficient and adequate to justify reduction of a murder charge to that of manslaughter.

In the United States, there is an almost uniform rule that words and gestures are never sufficient provocation to reduce a charge of murder to that of manslaughter. The U.S. Supreme Court stated in the 1895 case of *Allen v. United States* that "mere words alone do not excuse even a simple assault. Any words offered at the time [of the killing] do not reduce the grade of the killing from murder to manslaughter."[11]

CRIMINAL HOMICIDE IN THE UNITED STATES

The criminal homicide that kills the most people	Drunk and drugged drivers kill over 12,000 people each year. Lower blood alcohol standards (0.08) and tougher enforcement have helped reduce that number.
The highest number of murder victims in one day	More than 2,800 people died in the terrorist attacks of September 11, 2001; 168 people died in the Oklahoma City bombing in 1995.
The nation's deadliest serial killer	Gary Ridgway (called the "Green River Killer") pleaded guilty in December 2003 to killing 48 women in the Seattle area over a 21-year period. This exceeds other serial killers: John Wayne Gacy (33, Chicago area, 1972–78), Ted Bundy (30, Washington State and Florida, 1970s), and Jeffrey Dahmer (17, Milwaukee area, 1978–92).
The 2003 convictions of the Washington, D.C., snipers	Two men, John Muhammad and Lee Malvo, were convicted in 2003 of sniper killings in four states and the District of Columbia.

Although words and gestures alone are never sufficient provocation, if other acts, such as a battery, accompany the verbal provocation, then it might be held to be sufficient. In *People v. Rice*, the deceased slapped the defendant's child and a quarrel resulted.[12] This was held to be sufficient provocation. In the 1928 Georgia case of *Lamp v. State*, a minor and technical battery accompanied with words was held to amount to a sufficient provocation to justify reducing the conviction from murder to manslaughter.[13] But in *Commonwealth v. Cisneros*, the Pennsylvania Supreme Court arrived at an opposite conclusion.[14]

Many U.S. courts have held that when a married person finds his or her spouse in an act of adultery, this amounts to sufficient provocation if it causes a genuine heat of passion.[15] However, this rule may not apply if a girlfriend is caught cheating on her boyfriend (or vice versa).[16]

Trespass, like battery, depends on the facts and circumstances in each particular case. A homeowner certainly does not have sufficient and adequate provocation to kill someone who walks across a lawn, yard, farm, or field in the middle of an afternoon. But snowmobilers who broke onto a farmer's land in Wisconsin and were circling the farmhouse at midnight caused a Wisconsin prosecutor to charge manslaughter when the farmer, in a terrible anger and rage, shot and killed one of the trespassers.

Courts often hold that mercy killing is not a defense to a murder charge (see the euthanasia section in this chapter). In a similar way, courts have also held that a request by a dying person to be killed is not adequate provocation to support the reduced charge of manslaughter. See *State v. Michaud*, 611 A.2d 61 (Me. 1992).

Heat of Passion and the Test of the Reasonable Person   The test of sufficiency or adequacy of provocation must be made in view of how the average or reasonable person would react to such provocation. Some people have extraordinary self-control and could endure much provocation before an uncontrollable rage would cause them to use deadly force. Others have short tempers and fly into a rage with little provocation.

A jury cannot give any special considerations to a defendant who has an extraordinarily bad temper. If the provocation is such that it would not cause the average reasonable person to explode in a sudden outburst of rage, it is not adequate or sufficient provocation to reduce murder to manslaughter. California courts have quoted the 1917 case of *People v. Logan* as follows:

> The fundamental … inquiry is whether or not the defendant's reason was, at the time of his act, so disturbed or obscured by some passion—not necessarily fear and never of course the passion of revenge—to such an extent as would render *ordinary men of average disposition* liable to act rashly or without due deliberation and reflection, and from this passion rather than from judgment.[17] [Emphasis added.]

The case of *Bedder v. Director of Public Prosecutions* received considerable attention throughout the English-speaking world.[18] The defendant, who knew that he was impotent, attempted to have sexual intercourse with a London prostitute in a quiet courtyard. She jeered when he was unsuccessful and attempted to get away from him. He tried to hold her, and she slapped him in the face and punched him in the stomach. When he grabbed her shoulders, she kicked him in the groin. He took a knife from his pocket and stabbed her twice, killing her. The House of Lords affirmed both the finding of the jury that there was not sufficient or adequate provocation and the following jury instruction given by the trial court:

> The reasonable person, the ordinary person, is the person you must consider when you are considering the effect which any acts, any conduct, any words, might have

to justify the steps which were taken in response thereto, so that an unusually excitable or pugnacious individual, or a drunken one or a man who is sexually impotent is not entitled to rely on provocation which would not have led an ordinary person to have acted in the way which was in fact carried out.

Cooling of the Blood Cooling of the blood, also known as *cooling time* or *reasonable time to cool off*, is a factor that must be considered if there is an interval between the provocation and the killing. Assume that after Y provokes X into a heat of passion, X, who has lost his self-control, runs to get his gun. If it took X two minutes to get his gun, was this sufficient time for X to cool off? If it took X a half hour or an hour to obtain his gun, was this sufficient time for the heat of passion to cool off? These questions would have to be answered by a court and jury that would consider the type and degree of the provocation that caused the heat of passion.

Imperfect or Unlawful Force in Self-Defense Charged as Manslaughter

perfect self-defense A homicide in which the killer not only subjectively believes that his or her conduct was necessary and reasonable and that, by objective standards, it was lawful and complied with the requirements of the law. The homicide is either justifiable or excusable, and it carries no criminal liability.

imperfect self-defense A homicide in which the killer subjectively, but unreasonably, believes that his or her conduct was necessary. It may be unlawful if the killing was done with excessive or unnecessary force. An unnecessary killing in self-defense, in defense of another, or to prevent or terminate a felony of violence could be imperfect self-defense.

Homicide in **perfect self-defense** is either justifiable or excusable, and it carries no criminal liability. Perfect self-defense requires that the killer not only subjectively believes that his or her conduct was necessary and reasonable but also that, by objective standards, it was lawful and complied with the requirements of the law.

To use deadly force in self-defense, a person must be in fear of *imminent* (right now) death or great bodily harm. If the threat is not imminent and the person has other options available, deadly force is not legally justified.

In **imperfect self-defense**, the killer subjectively believes that his or her conduct was necessary. But if the killing was done with excessive or unnecessary force in self-defense, it is unlawful. An unnecessary killing in self-defense, in defense of another, or to prevent or terminate a felony of violence could be imperfect self-defense.

The fact that a killing was through imperfect self-defense would cause it to be reduced from murder to manslaughter because

- The deceased victim provoked the killing by his or her conduct (however, the killing was not legally justified).
- The killer believed that his or her conduct was lawful and therefore possessed no "malice."

The following case received national attention and is used to illustrate imperfect self-defense (voluntary manslaughter):

State v. Norman

Supreme Court of North Carolina (1989) 324 N.C. 253, 378 S.E.2d 8

John Norman and his wife had been married for 25 years and had five children. John seldom worked and forced his wife to prostitute herself to support him. Norman beat his wife "most every day," especially when he was drunk and when other people were around, to "show off." If his wife made less than the minimum of $100 per day in prostitution, he beat her.

Norman made numerous threats on his wife's life. He called her names and tried to humiliate her in many ways. After a particularly horrible two days of drinking, beating, name-calling, and acts seeking to humiliate his wife, Norman lay down to take a nap. His wife obtained a handgun and shot Norman three times in the head. The jury convicted Mrs. Norman of voluntary manslaughter after the trial judge refused to give the jury an instruction on perfect self-defense. Mrs. Norman appealed, arguing that the trial judge erred in failing to give the perfect self-defense instruction to the jury.

The North Carolina Supreme Court affirmed the conviction for voluntary manslaughter and the six-year sentence of imprisonment, holding:

> *Our law has recognized that self-preservation under such circumstances springs from a primal impulse and is an inherent right of natural law....*
>
> *The right to kill in self-defense is based on the necessity, real or reasonably apparent, of killing an unlawful aggressor to save oneself from imminent death or great bodily harm at his hands.*
>
> * * *
>
> *In North Carolina, a defendant is entitled to have the jury consider acquittal by reason of perfect self-defense when the evidence, viewed in the light most favorable to the defendant, tends to show that at the time of the killing it appeared to the defendant and she believed it to be necessary to kill the decedent to save herself from imminent death or great bodily harm....*
>
> *That belief must be reasonable, however, in that the circumstances as they appeared to the defendant would create such a belief in the mind of a person of ordinary firmness. Id. Further, the defendant must not have been the initial aggressor provoking the fatal confrontation. Id. A killing in the proper exercise of the right of perfect self-defense is always completely justified in law and constitutes no legal wrong.*
>
> * * *
>
> *The defendant in the present case was not entitled to a jury instruction on either perfect or imperfect self-defense. The trial court was not required to instruct on either form of self-defense unless evidence was introduced tending to show that at the time of the killing the defendant reasonably believed herself to be confronted by circumstances which necessitated her killing her husband to save herself from imminent death or great bodily harm. Id. No such evidence was introduced in this case, and it would have been error for the trial court to instruct the jury on either perfect or imperfect self-defense.*

An example of a case where the defense of imperfect self-defense was held properly put before the jury is *People v. Vasquez*, 39 Cal. Rptr. 3d 433 (Cal. App. 2006). There, the defendant shot a man who was choking him, but only after the defendant was the initial aggressor, negating a "perfect" self-defense. The court held that the jury should have been instructed on imperfect self-defense, even though the defendant's conduct set in motion the victim's attack.

Involuntary Manslaughter

Involuntary manslaughter—sometimes called *unintentional* or *unlawful act manslaughter*—was discussed in Chapter 3 in relation to proximate cause or causation.

Involuntary manslaughter is often charged when extreme negligence or wanton or reckless conduct by the defendant brings about an unintended or accidental death. Two 2004 examples of cases in which defendants were charged and convicted of involuntary manslaughter follow. (For further cases on involuntary manslaughter, see Chapter 3).

- *Extreme negligence and failure to act:* A Manassas, Virginia, father was convicted of involuntary manslaughter when he left his 2-year-old daughter strapped in her car seat for 7 hours during the heat of the day.

WHEN MANSLAUGHTER CONVICTIONS HAVE BEEN OBTAINED

Conduct of Defendant	Resulting Harm	Case
Repeated incidents of allowing horses to escape because of rotted fences.	Horses ran on public highway, and motorist was killed in collision with a horse.	*Sea Horse Ranch, Inc. v. Superior Court*, 30 Cal. Rptr. 681 (Cal. App. 1994)
Furnishing heroin or cocaine to victim, who dies of an overdose.	Could also be charged under the Len Bias laws of some states or as felony murder if supplying the drug was a felony.	*Commonwealth v. Perry*, 1993 WL 28569 (Mass. App. 1993); *People v. Patterson*, 46 CrL 1007 (Sup. Ct. Calif. 1991)
Both men were intoxicated in a bar when defendant struck victim once in the face. Victim fell straight back, struck his head, and died.	Defendant's felony murder conviction was reversed because defendant was entitled to a jury instruction on involuntary manslaughter. Jury could find defendant did not intend to kill or do great bodily harm. The fall rather than the blow killed the victim.	*People v. Taylor*, 570 N.E.2d 1180 (Ill. App. 1991)
A San Francisco husband and wife kept two large dogs that repeatedly threatened and frightened neighbors. The husband wrote in a letter, "Neighbors be damned.... They can move."	The dogs killed a woman at the door to her apartment in a prolonged attack. After 30 witnesses testified to the increased threatening behavior of the dogs, the defendants were found guilty of involuntary manslaughter. They are also liable for civil damages.	Both defendants were sentenced to four years in prison, and both were released on parole after serving two years of the sentence. See the *New York Times* article "Parole for Woman Whose Two Dogs Killed," January 2, 2004.
Three men were playing Russian roulette.	One man died, and the other two were charged with involuntary manslaughter.	Convictions affirmed because game involved an unreasonably high risk of death. *Commonwealth v. Atencio*, 189 N.E.2d 223 (1963)

- *Reckless conduct:* A congressman from South Dakota with a history of careless driving was convicted of involuntary manslaughter when traveling 16 miles per hour over the speed limit he ran a stop sign, and he struck and killed a motorcyclist.

Most states have a vehicular manslaughter crime that can be charged when a person operates a vehicle in a grossly negligent manner and people are killed. In 2004, an 87-year-old man slammed his car into a Santa Monica, California, farmers' market, killing ten people and injuring sixty-three others. He was charged with ten counts of violating the California vehicular manslaughter law.

The box "When Manslaughter Convictions Have Been Obtained" gives examples of other fact situations in which manslaughter convictions were obtained.

≡ Suicide, Assisting Suicide, and Euthanasia

In common law, suicide was considered to be self-murder and was a felony. Because the person who committed such a crime was beyond the reach of the law, the punishment was forfeiture of the deceased person's estate to the king and burial off the highway.

euthanasia A killing of a terminally sick or injured individual with only a short time to live. Also called mercy killing.

Assisting a suicide is a crime in most states. A person could assist another to commit suicide by conduct (or words) that a trial judge or a jury finds to amount to "assisting."

Euthanasia—or mercy killing—is murder. However, the motive for the murder is love, or concern for the suffering of the victim. In the 1987 case of *State v. Forrest* (362 S.E.2d 252), the defendant was convicted of first-degree murder and sentenced to life imprisonment for the mercy killing of his terminally ill father, who was suffering from a number of untreatable illnesses. In such cases, appeals are made to the governor of the state for clemency, which is frequently granted after a number of years.[19]

Murder, Assisted Suicide, or Neither?

When one person participates in the death of another, that participation may constitute the crime of murder or assisted suicide. It may not be a crime at all, depending on the degree of participation and the laws of the state having jurisdiction over the acts.

assisting suicide The act of furnishing the means of a suicide, pursuant to a statute that permits such assistance.

The difference between murder and **assisting suicide** was explained by the California Supreme Court in *In re Joseph G.*, 667 P.2d 1176 (1983), as follows:

The key to distinguishing between the crimes of murder and of assisting suicide is the active or passive role of the defendant in the suicide. If the defendant merely furnishes the means, he is guilty of aiding a suicide; if he actively participates in the death of the suicide victim, he is guilty of murder.[20]

The difference between participation that constitutes the crime of assisting suicide and participation that is not criminal is harder to draw. A doctor who, at the patient's or family's request, removes a life-support machine obviously hastens death but does not furnish the means of that death. On the other hand, a doctor who, like Dr. Jack Kevorkian, furnishes a person with a "suicide machine" clearly has furnished the means. Kevorkian admitted in 1997 to "being present" at more than 100 deaths.[21]

So-called passive euthanasia in hospitals does not fall easily into either category. A doctor who "sends a patient home" with a morphine drip and stops all other treatment is, in one sense, only letting nature take its course. On the other hand, the doctor knows that the morphine will shorten the patient's life, so that in prescribing large doses of the morphine he or she is providing the means for death.

Because of the ambiguities surrounding physician-assisted suicide, and because many patients asserted a "right" to choose physician-assisted suicide, various constitutional attacks on state-assisted suicide statutes have been made. In *Washington v. Glucksberg*, 117 S. Ct. 2258 (1997) and *Vacco v. Quill*, 117 S. Ct. 2293 (1997), the U.S. Supreme Court upheld the constitutionality of statutes in New York and Washington making physician-assisted suicides criminal. The Court rejected the contention that the Fourteenth Amendment prohibited states from making such conduct criminal. The concept of "liberty" in the Constitution, which spawned the right to marry, to have children, or to an abortion, does not, the Court held, include a right to assistance in choosing the time and manner of one's death.

The Internet has played a role in this controversy. Among the many so-called "chat" rooms accessible on the Internet are sites where groups provide information and assistance on both sides of the assisted-suicide issue. Some "rooms" provide information about preventing suicide, while others share thoughts and information about suicide.

On April 23, 2010, Minnesota authorities charged William Melchert Dinkel with two counts of assisted suicide. Dinkel, a former nurse who had his Minnesota license revoked in 2009, was obsessed with suicide, and under various identities participated in suicide chat rooms. While there, he often both provided information on committing suicide, and encouraged others to commit suicide. He was charged in the deaths of Mark

Drybrough, 22, of Coventry, England, and Nadia Kajouji, 18, of Brandon, Ontario. Dinkel urged both people to commit suicide by hanging, and in the case of Kajouji attempted to convince her to do so with a webcam filming the event. Kajouji instead drowned herself in a river in Ontario. Dinkel told investigators he was a party to at least 10 suicide "pacts," and that to his knowledge 5 of the other participants actually killed themselves.

In the case of *Baxter v. State*, 224 P.3d 1211 (Mont. 2009), the Montana Supreme Court held that it was not a criminal homicide for a physician to assist a terminally ill patient by giving him a prescription for a lethal drug. Because suicide is not a crime in Montana, the court said assisting the patient to do so was not a crime. Although section 45-5-102(1) MCA made it a crime to unlawfully "cause" another person's death, section 45-2-211(1) provided consent of the "victim" was a defense, unless such consent was against public policy. The court held consent of a mature, aware, terminally ill patient was not against public policy.

The Oregon "Death with Dignity" Law

Most states make assisting a suicide a crime. Oregon, however, enacted the Oregon "death with dignity" law, which became effective in November 1997. The controversial law, which permits assisted suicides, is the first of its kind in the United States. The state of Washington followed with a similar law in 2008.

To qualify under the either state's law, a patient must be found to be terminally ill and have less than six months to live. Patients must have the mental capacity to fully understand the situation that confronts them. There is a 15-day waiting period after the patient applies and is found to have qualified for physician-assisted suicide. A physician may then prescribe drugs to end the patient's life, but the physician does not administer the drugs. The physician is granted immunity from liability for her or his role in the process. Since it was enacted, about 30 people a year have used the provisions of the Oregon law. Each year about 30,000 people die in Oregon. There have been no serious efforts to repeal the law.

The Clinton administration decided not to challenge the Oregon "death with dignity" law, but the Bush administration moved to overturn it, contending physicians acting under the law were doing so in violation of the Federal Controlled Substances Act (CSA). In 2004, the Ninth Circuit Court of Appeals upheld the law, noting that the CSA was designed to fight drug abuse, not to regulate medicine and physicians.[22] On review, the U.S. Supreme Court upheld the Oregon law, reasoning that the CSA was directed at drug abuse and that treating a physician writing a prescription for a mercy killing as "drug abuse" was unreasonable.[23]

Summary

- *Corpus delicti* means the body of the crime. It must be proved by the prosecution before a defendant can be convicted of a crime.
- The year-and-a-day rule was adopted as a "bright line" rule of causation in homicide cases. A death beyond that period was not "caused" by the criminal acts. Today, medical science makes proving the connection between actions and a resulting death much easier and clearer, so most states have dropped the year-and-a-day rule.

- The "born alive" requirement under the common law excluded the death of unborn children as murder. Many states have dropped the requirement, and make the death of an unborn child a crime separate from murder. In those states that still have the requirement, a fetus must by born "alive," that is, show some signs of brain function, before its death can be murder.
- Under the doctrine of transferred intent, the intention formed by the perpetrator of a homicide as

to an intended victim is "transferred" to the killing of an unintended victim, thereby satisfying the intent requirement of the applicable homicide statute.

- Involuntary manslaughter and reckless homicide do not require proof of intent to kill. Second-degree murder based on intent to do serious bodily injury does not require specific intent to kill. In felony murder convictions, the intent to commit the underlying crime satisfies the intent requirement for murder.

- In all states, the death of the victim of a listed felony, and a third person killed by the felon, constitute felony murder. In some, but not all, states, innocent persons killed by a third party or co-felons killed by a third party do not constitute felony murder.

- In voluntary manslaughter, the killing was intended, but occurred under circumstances where, though not excused, is not as culpable as murder. In involuntary manslaughter the death was not intended, but arose out of severely reckless conduct.

- A charge of murder could be reduced to manslaughter if provocation existed to cause the criminal conduct, or if insufficient evidence exists to prove malice or premeditation.

- The state of Oregon has the power to determine what conduct is criminal in that state, unless it contravenes some federal law. The U.S. Supreme Court held that the Death with Dignity Law did not violate the Federal Controlled Substance Law, and thus was a permissible exercise of state power.

Key Terms

homicide, p. 250
"born alive" requirement, p. 254
feticide, p. 254
murder, p. 258

transferred intent, p. 261
premeditation, p. 262
felony murder, p. 264
manslaughter, p. 266

perfect self-defense, p. 270
imperfect self-defense, p. 270
euthanasia, p. 273
assisting suicide, p. 273

Case Analysis and Writing Exercises

1. Several members of the Vatos Locos were sitting in or standing near a car parked in South Minneapolis, part of the "territory" of the Surenos 13 gang. The defendant Cruz, a member of the Surenos 13 gang, arrived as a passenger in another car, and upon exiting asked "Que barrio," meaning, "what gang are you." Before anyone could answer, Cruz pulled out a semi-automatic pistol and began firing at everyone. One person, Hernandez-Leon, was killed, and three others wounded. What homicide crimes did Cruz commit? Can Cruz, in reliance on *State v. Hall*, discussed in this chapter, successfully contend the doctrine of "transferred intent" does not apply to prove the necessary intent for a murder conviction? Why or why not? See *State v. Cruz-Ramirez*, 771 N.W.2d 497 (Minn. 2009).

2. On April 5, 2007, FBI Special Agent Barry Bush was killed by an accidental discharge of another agent's weapon while the agents were in a shootout with three bank robbery suspects. Can the bank robbers be charged with felony murder? Does

any theory of felony murder exist that would support such a charge? Do you think the theory is sound? See *State v. Sophophone*, 19 P.3d 70 (Kan. 2001).

3. Steele and another security guard working for a nightclub scuffled with a customer in the club's parking lot. The customer got in a car with other people in it and took a gun out of the glove compartment. He pointed the gun at the back window, where Steele was standing. Steele shot into the car, killing one of the passengers. What homicide, if any, can Steele be convicted of? See *Steele v. State*, 852 So. 2d 78 (Miss. App. 2003), *cert. denied* 870 So. 2d 666 (Miss. 2004).

4. Should the defendants in the following cases be charged with murder, manslaughter, a lesser offense, or no crime at all?

   1. During a domestic argument, a wife taunted her husband with words that enraged the man. He killed his wife. See *Girouard v. State*, 321 Md. 532, 583 A.2d 718 (1991).

2. The victim threw a glass of beer at the defendant and swore at him. The defendant knocked the victim to the ground and kicked her repeatedly until she died. See *Commonwealth v. Vanderpool*, 367 Mass. 743, 328 N.E.2d 833 (1985).

3. The victim threw a glass figurine at the defendant and then began to stab at the defendant with a knife. In the struggle, the victim was stabbed and died. See *State v. Rhodes*, 63 Ohio St. 3d 613, 590 N.E.2d 261 (1992).

4. The defendant forced his way into his girlfriend's apartment and threatened to kill the woman if she did not get out of his way. As he opened the door to the bedroom, he began shooting into the dark room, killing her male guest. See *State v. Tatum*, 824 S.W.2d 22 (Mo. App. 1991).

5. The defendant was angry because of the victim's past abuses of his sister and killed the man. See *State v. Hanson*, 286 Minn. 317, 176 N.W.2d 607 (1970).

6. A 13-year-old girl jumped from a moving car when the defendant attempted to sexually assault her. The victim died the next day of multiple injuries. See *State v. Statum*, 390 So. 2d 886 (La. 1980), *review denied* 450 U.S. 969, 101 S. Ct. 1489.

Notes

1. See the *Newsweek* article, "Death of the Innocent," August 17, 1998, the *New York Times* article, "Mother Goes from Martyr to Defendant in Infanticides," August 7, 1998, and the *Chicago Tribune*, p. 20, September 25, 1997.

2. *Swafford v. State*, 421 N.E.2d 596 (Ind. 1981).

3. Of the many court cases of brain-dead victims, two young women received a great amount of public attention. Nancy Cruzan received severe injuries in an auto accident, and Karen Ann Quinlan was brain-dead because of a drug overdose. After years in vegetative states, the parents of both young women went into courts to obtain permission to withdraw life-support systems. In both cases, the parents carried the burden of showing that their incompetent daughters would not have wanted to go on living in vegetative states. See *In re Quinlan*, 70 N.J. 10, 355 A.2d 647 (1976), *review denied* 429 U.S. 922, 97 S. Ct. 319 (1976) and *In re Cruzan*, (497 U.S. 261, 110 S. Ct. 2841 (1990).

   In the 1990 *Cruzan* case, the U.S. Supreme Court held that states could establish standards such as the Missouri "clear and convincing" evidence requirement showing that Nancy Cruzan would have wanted to die. The state of Missouri, which was paying about $112,000 per year to keep Cruzan alive in a "persistent vegetative state," had opposed efforts by her parents to have life-support systems withdrawn. In a hearing after the Supreme Court's decision, a Missouri court heard new evidence presented by three of Cruzan's co-workers, who testified that Nancy had stated she would never have wanted to live "like a vegetable." Cruzan's doctor testified that her existence was a "living hell." After eight years on life-support systems, the feeding tube was removed, and Nancy Cruzan died.

4. *People v. Stevenson*, 416 Mich. 383, 331 N.W.2d 143 (1982). See also *State v. Hefler*, 60 N.C. App. 466, 299 S.E.2d 456 (1983), *affirmed* 310 N.C. 135, 310 S.E.2d 310, 34 CrL 2374 (1984), in which the North Carolina court stated: "For the courts to remain judicially oblivious of these advances [in medical science] when considering whether to extend an ancient common law rule would be folly."

5. See Jay Robert Nash, *Bloodletters and Badmen: A Narrative Encyclopedia of American Criminals from the Pilgrims to the Present* (New York: M. Evans & Co., 1974).

6. 720 ILCS 5/9–1.

7. In a case in which the defendant shot a 15-year-old gasoline service station attendant in the head, neck, and back six times, the Minnesota Supreme Court held:

   Extensive planning and calculated deliberation need not be shown by the prosecution.

The requisite "plan" to commit a first-degree murder can be formulated virtually instantaneously by a killer.... Moreover ... premeditation can be inferred from either the number of gunshots fired into the victim ... or the fact that a killer arms himself with a loaded gun in preparation. State v. Neumann, *262 N.W.2d 426, 22 CrL 2465 (Minn. 1978).*

8. 157 U.S. 675, 15 S. Ct. 720 (1895).
9. See the New York Penal Code, Section 125.20.
10. See the *Newsweek* article, "Sentence by Public Opinion?" March 5, 1984.
11. 157 U.S. 675, 15 S. Ct. 720 (1895).
12. 351 Ill. 604, 184 N.E. 894 (1933).
13. 38 Ga. App. 36, 142 S.E. 202 (1928). In this case, the deceased used profane and insulting language, with threats to cut the defendant's throat.
14. 381 Pa. 447, 113 A.2d 293 (1955).
15. Years ago, Texas, New Mexico, and Utah enacted laws that provided that if a husband killed a man caught in an act of adultery with his wife, the killing was a justifiable homicide. Critics of these statutes argued that this permitted an "open shooting season" on paramours if they were caught by husbands in the act of adultery. Women's groups in these states angrily demanded that the statutes be either repealed or amended to give wives the same rights. All three states have repealed these statutes and probably have gone back to the common law rule.
16. In a case where a fiancée was killed after she admitted infidelity, and in another case where a spouse was killed after confessing to adultery, the question before two state supreme courts was whether "mere words" justified reducing murder charges to voluntary manslaughter. Neither the Ohio Supreme Court nor the Michigan Supreme Court would reduce the murder charges to manslaughter because of mere words. See for Ohio *State v. Shane* (590 N.E. 2d 272) and for Michigan *State v. Pouncey* (471 N.W. 2d 346).
17. 175 Cal. 45, 164 P. 1121 (1917).
18. House of Lords, 2, All Eng. R 801 (1954).
19. The *Roswell Gilbert* case caused a national debate on euthanasia in 1985. Mr. Gilbert killed his wife, who was suffering from terminal debilitating diseases. He was 76 years of age at the time and received a sentence of 25 years' imprisonment without parole. After serving five years, he was granted clemency by the Florida governor and returned to Fort Lauderdale.
20. In the case of *In re Joseph G.,* a minor (Joseph G.) and his friend made a mutual suicide pact. The two males drove a car over a cliff to carry out the suicides. Joseph G. survived, but his passenger was killed. The California Supreme Court reversed the first-degree murder conviction, holding that Joseph G. should be charged with assisting a suicide.
21. In April 1999, when he was 70 years old, Dr. Kevorkian was convicted of the crime of murder by a Michigan jury and sentenced to 10-25 years in prison, with the possibility of parole after six years and eight months. He was released in 2007.
22. *Oregon v. Ashcroft*, 368 F.3d 1118 (9th Cir. 2004).
23. *Gonzales v. Oregon*, 546 U.S. 243 (2006).

Assault, Battery, and Other Crimes Against the Person

Johannes Kroemer/Getty images

This sleeping baby is completely dependant on the care and attention of parents or other responsible adults. Persons charged with the care of a child have a duty to act responsibility; failure to do so can be a violation of the criminal laws. Leaving a child alone in a car can lead to injury or death of the child, and result in the criminal prosecution of the child's parents or other person caring for the child.

LEARNING OBJECTIVES

In this chapter we examine assaults and related crimes against the person. The learning objectives for Chapter 11 are:

- Identify the different elements that must be proved for conviction of an assault or a battery.

- Know what kind of nonconsensual touching constitutes an assault or a battery.

- Describe circumstances that warrant a charge of aggravated assault or battery

- List the various laws designed to protect children from assaults and other similar crimes.

- List some of the defenses available to a charge of assault or battery.

- Identify the "movement" requirement for a kidnapping conviction.

- State how the crime of hostage taking differs from kidnapping.

On August 26, 2009 a woman calling herself "Alyssa," together with two other girls, ages 12 and 15, walked into the office of Phillip Garrido's parole officer. After questioning, the parole officer discovered that "Alyssa" was in fact Jaycee Lee Dugard, who was abducted from her home in South Lake Tahoe, California, on June 10th, 1991 when she was 11 years old. Her abductors were Garrido and his wife Nancy. The two girls with her were her daughters with Garrido.

Garrido was on parole for a conviction on a kidnapping and rape that occurred in 1977, when he abducted and raped a young girl. That abduction also occurred in South Lake Tahoe. Garrido served 11 years in Leavenworth Federal Prison, where he met and subsequently married Nancy Bocanegra. He was released on parole in 1988, and he moved to Antioch, California.

The Garridos kept Jaycee at their home in Antioch for 18 years, during which time she lived in tents or outbuildings located at the rear of the Garridos' property. She bore Garrido's daughters, and at times she represented to others that the girls were her sisters. During Jaycee's captivity, in 1997 Garrido served 7 months in prison for parole violations. Also, at various times during Jaycee's captivity, California corrections officers were given several tips and leads about a young girl living in the Garridos' backyard, none of which were vigorously pursued by the corrections department.

The Garridos have been charged with kidnapping and false imprisonment, and Garrido has been charged with rape. Jaycee has custody of her two daughters, and she has been reunited with her mother and stepfather. On July 1, 2010, the California legislature passed a bill that allocated $20 million for settlement of claims Jaycee and her parents may assert against the California Department of Corrections.

In this chapter we will study the rules governing assault, as well as other crimes against the person such as kidnapping and domestic violence.

≡ The Crime of Assault

assault In many instances, an assault is an attempt to commit a battery, but many states also make other conduct an assault. It could be combined with a charge of battery to constitute the crimes of "assault and battery."

battery A successful assault, in which the victim is actually and intentionally (or knowingly) struck by the defendant.

Under common law, **assault** and **battery** were two separate crimes. Today, however, the phrase *assault and battery* is sometimes used to indicate one offense. Because an assault is often an attempt to commit a battery, the California courts point out that an assault is an attempt to strike, whereas a battery is the successful attempt. A battery cannot be committed without assaulting a victim, but an assault can occur without a battery.

Most states have codified the common law crime of assault. Included in the crime of assault today are (1) an attempt to commit a battery in which no actual battery or physical injury resulted, and/or (2) an intentional frightening (such as pointing a loaded gun at a person or menacing with a fist or knife). Generally, in an assault, the state must show apprehension or fear on the part of the victim if no blow, touching, or injury occurred.

In many states, the crime of assault also includes batteries. The state of New York does not have a crime of battery.[1] Therefore, in New York, a person who swings a knife at another with intent to cause serious physical injury is guilty of first-degree assault if successful but is guilty only of attempted assault if no injury occurs. (See New York *Commentaries*, Art. 120, p. 331.)

Section 240 of the California Penal Code (enacted in 1872) defines *assault* as "an unlawful attempt, coupled with a present ability, to commit a violent injury on the person of another." Chapter 38, Section 12-1, of the Illinois Statutes provides that "a person commits an assault when, without lawful authority, he engages in conduct which places another in reasonable apprehension of receiving a battery."

In some states (including California), the lack of "present ability" to commit the injury or battery is a defense to an assault charge.[2] The defendant in the 2002 case of

People v. Miceli attempted to use this defense.[3] He used a semi-automatic rifle to club a victim. When charged with "assault with a firearm," the defendant contended he could not be guilty of an assault, because the firearm was not loaded, and as a result he lacked the "present ability" to injure that victim. The court disagreed, both because evidence existed that the firearm might have been loaded, and in any case the firearm was used as a club, which satisfied the "present ability" requirement.

Other, perhaps most, states, and the Model Penal Code § 211.1, have adopted the common law definition of assault. Under that definition, an assault occurs *either* when one does an overt act that is intended to inflict bodily harm, *or* when the overt act is intended to put another person in fear of bodily harm. The present ability requirement applies only to the first type of assault. The Virginia Supreme Court applied that definition of assault in the case of *Carter v. Com*, 606 S.E.2d 839 (Va. 2006). A police officer stopped a motorist for speeding. When the officer approached the vehicle, the driver suddenly pulled up his right hand, pointed it at the officer, and said "pow." The officer reached for his weapon, but then realized the driver's hand was empty. The driver was charged with assault on a police officer under Va. Code § 18.2-57 (c). The Virginia Supreme Court affirmed his conviction, holding that while the assault statute did not define "assault," under the common law definition of assault used in prior cases acts that put another in fear of bodily injury constitute assault, even without the present ability to inflict injury. The trial court held the belief by that officer that the driver might inflict bodily injury was reasonable, and the Supreme Court agreed.

Under the present Federal Criminal Code, the crime of assault is directed toward certain situations over which the federal government has jurisdiction, such as assaults on a federal officer or assaults on a federal reservation. In the most general assault statute, assault within the territorial jurisdiction of the United States, assault also includes an actual battery; 18 U.S.C.A. Section 113(a) (4) forbids "assault by striking, beating, or wounding." Thus, in addition to the two common law aspects of assault discussed above (present ability or fear of infliction), the statute includes a third aspect, in which the crime of assault is committed by actually inflicting injury on another person.

Other federal assault statutes address assaults to specific federal officials. For example, the following federal prosecution under 18 U.S.C. 351, assault on a member of Congress, illustrates one such statute:

United States v. Masel [4]

U.S. Court of Appeals, 7th Circuit (1977) 563 F.2d 322, 22 CrL 2065

During a campaign for the presidency of the United States, defendant Masel became angry at U.S. Senator Henry Jackson and spat in his face. The defendant was charged with assaulting a member of the U.S. Congress and was convicted in a jury trial. The Federal Court of Appeals affirmed the conviction, holding:

> *[I]t is clear that Congress intended to include "battery" within the term "assault." Accordingly, the district court instructed, in effect, that if the jury found a battery had been committed, defendant should be convicted of the charge of assault.... We also note that every battery must include or be the culmination of an assault (in the sense of attempt).*

Assault with a Deadly or Dangerous Weapon

A simple assault is a misdemeanor or ordinance charge. The criminal charge of assault with a deadly or dangerous weapon is a felony charge. A gun or a dangerous knife is certainly a deadly weapon if it is used to threaten or harm.

As pointed out in Chapter 10, the issue of what is a dangerous or deadly weapon is a question of fact for the fact finder (jury or judge). New York courts have held that something as common as a handkerchief can, under certain circumstances, be a deadly weapon, and many courts have also held that hands can be dangerous or deadly weapons, even if the assailant has no training in martial arts or boxing.

The relative size and strength of the assailant as compared with the victim, the manner and duration of the assault, and the severity of the injuries are all facts that must be taken into consideration in determining whether hands are dangerous or deadly weapons. Fact finders would surely find the hands of an adult man who punched a baby to be dangerous or deadly weapons under the circumstances.[5]

The defendant in *State v. Zangrilli* broke his ex-wife's jaw in two places, grabbed her by the throat and strangled her until she could feel her "eyes bulge," dragged her through several rooms in her house, punched her several times in the face and neck, and shoved her into a bathtub.[6] The Rhode Island Supreme Court affirmed his conviction of assault with a dangerous weapon, quoting the trial judge's holdings:

> The manner in which he used his hands on her throat constituted use of his hands in such a way that it could easily have led to her death.
>
> For that reason, I have concluded that his assault upon her was done with a dangerous weapon. As I say, hands are not per se dangerous weapons, but they are a means to produce death. And they were used, even though briefly, in a manner and in such circumstances as could be reasonably calculated to produce death.

"SIMPLE ASSAULT" IN THE FEDERAL CRIMINAL CODE

In recent years Congress has amended some of the various federal assault statutes, such as the general assault statute, 18 U.S.C. § 113, and assault on a federal officer, 18 U.S.C. § 111, to treat as felonies and increase the penalty for "all other assaults" that are not "simple assaults." The term *simple assault* is not specifically defined in those amendments, requiring the lower federal courts to determine when an assault is a "simple assault" or one that falls into the "all other" class.

Most federal courts have relied on the language of 18 U.S.C. § 113(a) and have interpreted "simple assault" to apply to any assault that does not involve physical contact. "All other" assaults include those that involve physical contact, or assault with the intent to murder, or assault with a deadly weapon.[a]

The Circuit Courts of Appeal appear to be split on whether section 111 applies to conduct that is not an assault. The statute states that whoever "forcibly assaults, resists, impedes, or interferes" with a federal officer is guilty of a crime. However, the statute also states that where the "acts constitute only simple assault" the crime has a one-year imprisonment penalty, but if physical contact is made the penalty can be up to eight years in prison. One federal court has held that the above language means that for a defendant to be convicted of "impeding" under section 111, his actions must also constitute an assault. *United States v. Chapman*, 528 F.3d 1215 (9th Cir. 2008). Others have held that any deliberate actions in resisting or impeding the work of a federal officer constitute violations of section 111, whether or not they constitute an assault under federal law. *United States v. Gagnon*, 553 F.3d 1021 (6th Cir. 2009).

[a]See *United States v. Hathaway*, 318 F.3d 1001 (10th Cir. 2003).

A rubber-soled tennis shoe was held to be a dangerous weapon in the 1991 case of *State v. Munoz*, 575 So. 2d 848 (La. App.). An eyewitness testified that the defendant kicked the victim so hard in the head that the victim's body was lifted off the ground. The attending physician also characterized the attack by the defendant as brutal.

Some states have created a separate crime of committing a felony while armed with a dangerous weapon, whereas other states enhance (increase) penalties of people who commit a felony while armed. What constitutes "armed" is most often a question of law.

A person who actually carries a pistol on his or her person is armed. However, it is less clear if one who commits a felony with a pistol in his or her *vicinity* is armed. The following two Illinois cases illustrate this problem.

In *People v. Board* [7] an appeals court upheld a conviction for armed violence in which the defendant was sitting on a sofa that had a gun under one of the cushions. Although the defendant made no attempt to get the gun, the court held that its accessibility sufficed to support the armed violence conviction. Conversely, in *People v. Shelato*,[8] the court reversed a conviction for armed violence when the defendant's gun was in the same room with the defendant but hidden in a zippered bag underneath 60 bags of marijuana. The court stated that it "defied common sense" to believe the defendant could have gotten this gun under the "watchful eyes of several police officers" and vacated the conviction.

≡ Battery

For an offense to constitute assault, the victim must ordinarily be apprehensive of the impending harm or danger. This is not necessary in a battery. A blow from behind is a battery whether or not the victim is aware that it is coming. Battery is a crime that, like murder and manslaughter, is defined in terms of the conduct of the offender and also in terms of the harm done.

Most state battery statutes define battery to include either physical conduct or actual bodily injury. For example, Florida's battery crime, F.S.A. § 784.03, states a person commits battery if he either (1) "actually and intentionally touches or strikes another person against the will of the other" or (2) "intentionally causes bodily harm." Many other states have a statute similar to the Kansas battery law, K.S.A. 21-3412. It includes as a battery "intentionally or recklessly" causing bodily injury. However, the "physical contact" form of battery must be done in "a rude, insulting or angry manner." Thus, if one intentionally causes another bodily harm, whether by directly striking the person, or indirectly doing so by acts like throwing an object at the person, the crime of battery has been committed. Batteries can be committed with fists, feet, sticks, stones, or other objects used to inflict injury. Under some circumstances, dogs or other animals could be used to commit a battery if they are used to injure another person illegally.[9] If there is physical contact without bodily injury, the contact must be offensive, or unwanted.

Section 211 of the Model Penal Code combines the common law crimes of assault and battery under the crime of assault. That section does not include "offensive touching" without bodily injury. The MPC limits simple "physical contact" to sexual offenses, as discussed below.

All states that make battery a crime require that the act to commit a battery must be intentional (or must be done knowingly), because an accidental physical contact or injury is not a battery. However, most states, as in the Kansas statute quoted above, include recklessly causing bodily injury in the definition of battery.

Offensive Touching Under Sexual Assault and Sexual Battery Statutes

offensive touching
Unpermitted physical contact with another person, usually limited to "private" or genital parts.

Many states have enacted sexual assault statutes to replace or add to their old rape statutes. These statutes generally provide three or four degrees of sexual assault. In addition to defining sexual intercourse broadly, these statutes also forbid and punish **offensive touching**.

Before the enactment of the sexual assault statutes, offensive touching was ordinarily charged under the general assault statute or as a battery or disorderly conduct. Although offensive touching may continue to be charged under the old statutes, the sexual assault statute is now available. However, under the sexual assault statutes, the offensive touching generally must be of an "intimate part" or "private part" of the body and for the purpose "of arousing or gratifying sexual desire of either party" (§ 213.4 Model Penal Code).

The rape charge in the case of *People v. Margiolas* was dropped because of lack of evidence of resistance. However, the defendant admitted that he unbuttoned the victim's blouse, despite her verbal as well as physical objections. The defendant was convicted of sexual battery in forcibly unbuttoning the blouse.[10] Under such a statute, a prosecutor with a weak case might also issue a sexual battery charge when it is apparent that the rape charge has defects that might be insurmountable. (See Chapter 12 for more material on sexual assault and sexual battery statutes.)

Sports Injuries When Force Exceeds the Rules of the Game

A hard tackle in football or a blow to the jaw in boxing would be within the rules of the sport being played. Players in body contact sports consent to such conduct as part of the game. This is commonly referred to as the "voluntary participant" rule.

But if the conduct is beyond the rules of the game—such as a deliberate elbow to the face or a knee to the groin in basketball, the deliberate use of spikes by a runner in baseball, eye gouging in football, or other violence that causes unnecessary injuries—is it a battery or an assault? In one recent case, the Washington Court of Appeals held that an assault was committed when, during a game, one basketball player intentionally punched another player.[11] In *State v. Floyd*, 466 N.W.2d 919 (Iowa 1990), the court upheld the conviction for assault where the defendant was sitting on the bench when a fight broke out on the basketball court. The defendant attacked two players on the opposing team who were also on the sidelines. The court said the "voluntary participant" rule did not apply, since neither the defendant nor the victims were involved in the game when the assault occurred.

Spectator violence and sometimes parental rage are occasionally a problem at sporting events. Angry words between two fathers at a kids' pickup hockey game led to blows and the death of one of the men. A Massachusetts prosecutor charged the other man with manslaughter.

Other Physical Contact Without Consent

Pushing, pinching, biting, scratching, touching, kissing, punching, spitting, and tackling are all forms of physical contact in which the person initiating the contact could be acting in a friendly, joking, or loving manner, or the contact could be hostile, angry, or belligerent.[12]

If such contact were intentional (not accidental) and done without any legal justification, it could cause a great amount of anger or concern by the person not consenting to such physical contact. If the physical contact were made in an obviously hostile or belligerent manner, the physical contact could provoke a verbal or physical reaction.

If it is shown that the conduct provoked or tended to provoke a disturbance or a disorder, the offender could be charged with disorderly conduct.

EXAMPLE: A strange man roughly grabs a woman or a girl in a public place and kisses or touches her in the presence of her husband, boyfriend, or other member of her family or friends. Because such conduct is highly likely to cause a public disturbance or disorder, it can be charged as disorderly conduct (or disorderly person).

Defenses to a charge of touching or physical contact could be that the touching was accidental. Implied consent could also easily be inferred if the touching was done to pull a victim away from danger or if mouth-to-mouth resuscitation was necessary to restore breathing to a victim of an accident. The defense of necessity could also be used if the physical contact was necessary to prevent and avoid a greater harm.

menacing Intentionally placing or attempting to place another in fear of immediate serious physical injury.

Some states have enacted the crime of **menacing**, which is defined as follows in Public Law 120.15 of New York:

> By physically menacing, intentionally placing or attempting to place another person in fear of imminent serious physical injury. (New York class B misdemeanor)

Other states have extended the scope of the crime of assault to include intentional scaring or menacing if a victim is apprehensive of immediate bodily harm.

A fierce look with intent to frighten would not amount to menacing or intentional scaring. Section 211.1 of the Model Penal Code provides:

> (1) Simple Assault ... (c) attempts by physical menace to put another in fear of imminent serious bodily injury.

The crimes of jostling and menacing are both listed in W. J. Williams's *Moriarty's Police Law*,[13] the handbook of British police officers. Jostling is listed under obstruction of public ways and is defined as pushing and shoving in a way that obstructs and blocks the use of a public street, building, sidewalk, and so on. Victims whose passage is blocked are likely to react in anger and violence, which causes the conduct to be charged as disorderly conduct (or disorderly person) in the United States.

Most cities and states have not passed jostling statutes. However, New York City has done so in response to the pick pocketing problem that exists in crowded public places such as subways. The procedure used by most pickpockets is to bump or shove (or have a partner distract by bumping and shoving) to permit entry into a pocket or purse for the theft. Jostling is defined by Public Law 165.25 in New York as follows:

> In a public place, intentionally and unnecessarily:
>
> 1. Placing one's hand in the proximity of a person's pocket or handbag, OR
> 2. Jostling or crowding another person at a time when a third person's hand is in the proximity of such person's pocket or handbag.

≡ Felonious and Aggravated Assaults and Batteries

aggravated assault Assault made more serious by presence of a firearm or as part of intent to commit a felony.

Misdemeanor assault and misdemeanor batteries are classified as class A or B misdemeanors in most states. The degree of these crimes and the penalties are increased with aggravating factors used by state legislatures. All states have enacted "**aggravated assault**"

DEFENSES TO AN ASSAULT OR BATTERY CHARGE

The Aggressor Defense

That the other party was the aggressor, and the defendant acted in self-defense. Perfect or imperfect self-defense can then be argued by attempting to show that force was necessary and the amount of force used was reasonable.

The Mutual Combat Defense

That mutual combat occurred. *Mutual combat* is defined as a "fight or struggle in which both parties enter willingly, or two parties engage in sudden quarrel, in hot blood, and mutually fight on equal terms."[a]

When seeking to avoid the defenses that the other party was the aggressor or that mutual combat occurred, police and prosecutors are likely to charge disorderly conduct. This usually avoids long trials and long arguments that the other party consented to fight in mutual combat or that because the other party was the aggressor, self-defense was justified.

Other Defenses

- That the other party consented within the rules of the sport being played.
- That it was reasonable discipline of a child by a parent, guardian, or a person acting in place of the parent.
- That in an "offensive touching" battery, the touching was accidental, or consented to, or necessary under the circumstances.
- That the conduct was necessary and lawful:
  - in the accomplishment of a lawful arrest.
  - when necessary to lawfully detain or hold a person in custody.
  - when necessary to prevent an escape of a person lawfully in custody.
  - when necessary to prevent a suicide.
  - for any other reason when the conduct is privileged by the statutory or common law of that state.

[a]See *People v. Dower*, 578 N.E.2d 1153 (Ill. App. 1991), in which the defendant used the defense of mutual combat. The defendant (a big man) shot a woman (5 feet 2 inches and 120 pounds) in the head from less than 2 feet away. The woman was unarmed, and defendant admitted she never threatened him. The defense was rejected.

---

aggravated battery A battery that causes serious bodily injury or is committed with a deadly weapon.

or "**aggravated battery**" statutes, which increase an assault or battery from a misdemeanor to a felony. In the case of assaults, the aggravating factors usually are (1) use of a firearm or (2) intent to commit a felony. *See* F.S.A. §784.021.

The most common aggravating factors for battery charges are (1) causing serious bodily injury or (2) using a deadly weapon in the battery. Vernon's Texas Penal Code, § 22.02, is an example of such a statute. In some states circumstances in addition to the two just stated constitute aggravated battery. For example, Florida F.S.A. § 784.045 makes it aggravated battery if the victim of a battery is pregnant and the defendant knew of should have known that fact. In Kansas, K.S.A. § 21-3414 makes it aggravated battery to cause physical contact in a rude or insulting manner with a deadly weapon. Oregon's statute, O.R.S. § 163.175, adds as an aggravating circumstance "recklessly" causing serious physical injury under circumstances that demonstrate "extreme indifference to human life."[14] In applying that statute to injuries arising out of an automobile accident the Oregon Supreme Court stated:

Witnesses testified that prior to the accident defendant was swerving across the road, tailgating so closely he almost hit the car in front of him and passing on a curve. The overwhelming weight of the evidence indicated that the accident occurred because defendant was across the center line in the oncoming lane of traffic. He sideswiped the first oncoming vehicle, bounced or swerved into his own lane and then swerved back across the center line into the second oncoming vehicle, causing serious injury to the passenger. Defendant had a blood alcohol content of .24 percent two hours after the accident. He was belligerent at the scene of the accident, threatening to hit the passenger of the first car he sideswiped. Because of his intoxication he was not only unable to assist the victim, but at one point interfered with the assistance. The degree of intoxication, defendant's erratic driving and his conduct at the scene of the accident are circumstances the jury could properly consider in determining whether defendant was extremely indifferent to the value of human life.

We hold that the circumstances which exist in this case suffice to establish defendant's extreme indifference to the value of human life.[15]

Aggravated assault/battery cases often are complicated by an assertion of self-defense. Using force is justified for self-defense purposes, but only under certain circumstances. A person is not entitled to use force for self-defense if he is engaged in a crime when confronted by force. This has sometimes led to confusion in aggravated assault cases. For example, in the 2005 Florida case of *Williams v. State*,[16] a defendant charged with aggravated battery under the Florida statute cited above contended he struck the victim in self-defense. The trial court instructed the jury that self-defense was not available if the defendant used force while committing an aggravated battery. The Florida Appeals court reversed the conviction, stating that the instruction negated the self-defense claim, because if self-defense was proper the defendant was not guilty of aggravated battery.

Mayhem and Malicious Disfigurement

mayhem and malicious disfigurement Willfully inflicting an injury on another so as to cripple or mutilate the person

Mayhem and malicious disfigurement (or malicious wounding) have been distinguished by federal courts as follows: "[M]ayhem involves disablement of normal functioning of a human body, by contrast with malicious disfigurement which focuses on willful permanent disfigurement."[17]

Lorena Bobbitt was convicted of malicious wounding in Virginia when, in a rage, she cut off her husband's penis and threw it in a field. Believing Mrs. Bobbitt to be a battered woman, a Virginia jury found her not guilty under Virginia's insanity test. She spent four weeks in a Virginia mental hospital and was released on the condition that she receive therapy.

States also follow the common law definition of mayhem, which is the unlawful and violent depriving of the victim of full use of any functional member of the body (hand, arms, feet, eyes, legs, and so on) that would make the victim less able to defend himself or herself.

Article 1166 of the Texas Penal Code provides that "whoever shall willfully and maliciously cut off or otherwise deprive a person of the hand, arm, finger, toe, foot, leg, nose, or ear, or put out an eye or in any way deprive a person of any other member of his body shall be confined in the penitentiary not less than two nor more than ten years."[18]

Hate Crime Laws   The U.S. Supreme Court has repeatedly held that states may not silence "speech on the basis of its contents,"[19] as was done in the flag-burning and cross-burning U.S. Supreme Court cases (see Chapter 9). But states may enact hate crime laws that enhance and increase penalties for crimes if it is proved that the defendant intentionally selected the victim because of the victim's race, religion, color, disability, sexual orientation, national origin, or ancestry.

An example of a hate crime law is the New York Hate Crime Act of 2000, N.Y. Penal Law § 485.05. That act makes it an enhanced crime with added penalties to commit any of several specified crimes if the defendant "intentionally selects" the victim "in whole or in substantial part" because of the defendant's "belief or perception" of the victim's race, religion, gender, age, national origin, sexual orientation, or disability. The specified crimes include virtually all the crimes against the person, as well as many crimes against property.

Proving that the defendant actually "hated" the victim is not generally an element of a hate crime offense. Under the New York law cited above, the prosecution must only prove that the race, religion, or one of the other listed characteristics, was a "substantial" factor in the decision to commit the crime. In this sense, the New York statute is drafted to make the "hate" feature part of the elements of the crime, which under the *Apprendi* decisions discussed in Chapter 8 means the prosecution must prove the "hate" element beyond a reasonable doubt.

Section 485.05(2) states that proof that the victim possessed one of the listed characteristics does not "by itself" satisfy the "people's burden" to prove the elements of a hate crime. Some other corroborating evidence is thus required. In *People v. Fox*, 844 N.Y.S. 2d 627 (Sup. Ct. 2007) the court found the required corroborating evidence in the fact the defendants used Internet chat rooms used by gay men to lure a victim to the robbery location.

Hate crimes laws can be useful tools for prosecutors. For example, the District Attorney for Queens, New York uses the hate crime law in prosecutions against criminals who single out old people, become their "friend," and then steal their life savings. Prosecutors have found that using the enhanced penalties in the hate crime law gives them extra

Mike Stewart/Sygma/Corbis

On October 28, of 2009 President Obama signed the Matthew Shepard and James Byrd, Jr. Hate Crimes Prevention Act. This Act was named in honor of Matthew Shepard, pictured above, a gay man, and James Byrd, Jr., a Black man, who were killed in separate hate crimes in 1998 that received national attention. The act makes it possible for federal prosecutors to expand the use of existing hate crime laws. The HCPA makes several additions to the federal hate crime laws, among them removing the previous requirement that the victim be engaged in some federally protected activity, like voting or attending school. It also gives federal prosecutors the ability to investigate suspected hate crimes that local authorities may not want to pursue. Finally, it requires the FBI to maintain statistics on hate crimes involving transgender victims.

HATE CRIMES 2008

In a Justice Department Report by the Federal Bureau of Investigation, Uniform Crime Reporting Program, the FBI provided the following hate crime statistics for 2008, the most recent year for which statistics are available; 12,417 law enforcement agencies reported 9,691 single-bias incidents in 2008:

Why? (motivation)	Where? (place of crime)	Type of Crime Committed	Victims' Characteristics
Race 51%	Residence 30%	Intimidation 48.8%	Black 72.9%
Religion 17.9%	Highway/street 18.3%	Simple assault 32.1%	White 16.8%
Sexual orientation 17.6%	School/college 13.5%	Aggravated assault 18.5%	Asian 3.4%
Ethnicity 12.7%	Parking lot 6.6%	Murder, rape 0.2%	Multiple race 5.6%
Victim disability 0.9%	Church/synagogue 4.3%	(7 murders, 11 rapes)	Native American 1.3%

Sexual Orientation Crimes (1,706 victims)
Anti-male homosexual 57.5%
Anti-homosexual 27.3%
Anti-female homosexual 11.6%
Anti-bisexual 2.0%
Anti-heterosexual 1.6%

Religious Bias Crimes (1,732 victims)
Anti-Jewish 66.1%
Anti-Islam 7.5%
Anti-Catholic 5.1%
Anti-Protestant 3.6%
Multiple religions 12.8%
Anti-atheists 0.8%

Source: U.S. Department of Justice, 2008.

leverage in plea bargaining, and makes sure the criminals get stiffer jail sentences. See *New York Times*, June 23, 2010, "A Novel Twist for Prosecution of Hate Crimes."

The Wisconsin hate crime statute was challenged on constitutional grounds in 1993. The U.S. Supreme Court upheld the constitutionality of the statute in the following case:

Wisconsin v. Mitchell

Supreme Court of the United States, 508 U.S. 476, 124 L. Ed. 2d 436 (1993)

A group of black youths including Mitchell viewed a scene from the motion picture *Mississippi Burning*, in which a white man beat a young black boy who was praying. The group then moved outside and Mitchell asked if they were "hyped up to move on some white people." When a white boy was seen, Mitchell said, "There goes a white boy; go get him." The group ran after the boy, beat him severely, and stole his tennis shoes. The victim was in a coma for four days.

Mitchell was convicted of aggravated battery in a trial before a jury. The maximum penalty for the crime of aggravated battery was two years. But because the jury found that the defendant had intentionally selected his victim because of the victim's race,

> the trial judge imposed a sentence of four years of imprisonment under the Wisconsin penalty-enhancement statute, known as the hate crime statute.
>
> The U.S. Supreme Court affirmed the conviction and defendant's sentence, upholding the Wisconsin hate crime statute. The Court pointed out that the ordinance struck down in the hate crime case of *R.A.V. v. St. Paul* (112 S. Ct. 2538) was "explicitly directed at expression (i.e., speech or message) ... where the statute in this case is aimed at conduct unprotected by the First Amendment." Finally, the Supreme Court held that in the *Mitchell* case, there was no First Amendment violation on the basis of a "chilling effect" on protected speech (overbreadth).

If a defendant selects a victim based on a prejudice against the perceived race of the victim, it is not necessary that the victim in fact be a member of that race. In *Martinez v. Texas*, 980 S.W.2d 682 (1998), the court affirmed a hate crime sentence enhancement of a defendant who killed a child, believing the child to be part African American. The court said if prejudice against a particular race of people caused the defendant to select the child as a victim, it did not matter that the child was in fact not a member of that race.

≡ Child Abuse and Neglect

Child abuse, child neglect, and sexual abuse are serious problems throughout the United States. In 2006 the National Child Abuse and Neglect Data System issued a report in which it estimated 1,490 children die each year from child abuse or neglect. It also noted that estimate was probably low, because many child deaths are not reported as resulting from abuse or neglect. The report stated that 45 percent of the deaths were children under 1 year old, and 81 percent were children under 4 years old. Some 35 percent were attributable to neglect alone, and 28 percent to physical abuse alone. Eight percent were attributed to sexual abuse alone.

Thousands of children in the United States suffer head injuries; broken bones from beatings; burns from cigarettes, stoves, and hot liquids; ruptured internal organs (such as liver, spleen, kidneys, and bowels) from blows to the abdomen; missing teeth; multiple scars; knife and gunshot wounds; and bruises and lacerations.

People who inflict such injuries on children may be charged with assault, battery, assault with a dangerous weapon, aggravated battery, and other offenses in the criminal code of the state in which the offense occurred. Criminal codes also have child abuse statutes and statutes forbidding the neglect of children. These statutes seek to protect children from injury and trauma inflicted on them by parents, stepparents, paramours, relatives, babysitters, and other adults.

Parents and others responsible for children have a duty to protect children and provide food, clothing, shelter, medical care, education, and a reasonable physical and moral environment for them. Child neglect is the failure to provide adequate food, clothing, shelter, sanitation, medical care, or supervision for a child. In extreme cases of child neglect, criminal laws are violated.

Religious beliefs that cause parents to refuse to obtain medical treatment for a child are controversial. In some states, parents can be charged under criminal homicide laws. For example, in 2009 a Wisconsin couple was convicted of reckless homicide in the death of their 11-year-old daughter. The child was suffering from diabetes, but rather than obtain medical treatment the parents relied on "faith-healing." See *Milwaukee Journal-Sentinel*, October 8, 2009, "Wisconsin Couple Sentenced in Death of Their Sick Child." In some states, statutes have carved out an exception to prosecutions for neglect

---

CRIMINAL AND CIVIL LAWS THAT SEEK TO PROTECT CHILDREN

Under early Roman law, children were considered to be the property of their father, who could discipline them as he saw fit: he could sell them or even condemn them to death.

This law changed slowly over the years, and by the early 1800s, mothers were the primary custodians of their children when a divorce occurred. The *tender years presumption* held that only a mother has the nurturing qualities needed to love and care for a child through the early part of the child's life, or the tender years.

The tender years presumption also changed, and today more than 30 states offer joint custody and shared parenting arrangements with parents who are divorced or have never married. Most criminal laws seek to protect all parties (children and adults alike). States seek to provide additional protection to children by the enactment of most (if not all) of the following statutes:

Laws Forbidding	Statute # in Your State
■ child abuse	_____
■ child neglect	_____
■ abandonment of a child	_____
■ contributing to the delinquency of a child	_____
■ child snatching from the lawful custody of a guardian of the child	_____
■ child endangerment	_____
■ child enticement	_____
■ exposing children to sexually harmful material	_____
■ sexual exploitation of a child	_____
■ statutory rape (children cannot consent to sexual intercourse or sexual contact) under age _____ is (crime) _____	_____
■ other	_____
Compulsory School Attendance Laws	_____
■ imposing duty on parents until age _____	_____
■ making student offense of skipping school truancy	_____
■ authorizing police to take truant into custody	_____

of a child, if the parents had a good-faith belief in healing by spiritual means or prayer. See, e.g., Minn. Stat. Ann. § 609.378, construed in *State v. McKown*, 475 N.W.2d 63 (Minn. 1991), but even in those states the exception does not apply if the child dies. See Oregon R. Stat. § 163.206.

The child abuse that generally appears in courts is physical abuse, such as deliberate injuries inflicted on children. Such injuries could result from excessive and unreasonable force used in disciplining children. The U.S. Supreme Court pointed out in *Ingraham v. Wright* that parents and people taking the place of parents may use force "reasonably believed to be necessary for [the child's] proper control, training, or education."[20] What is "reasonable" is determined in view of the child's age and sex; the physical, emotional, and mental health of the child; and the conduct that prompted the punishment.

Unfortunately, most children who are victims of abuse are under age 5 and are helpless in protecting themselves.

Child abuse as a crime has both an active and a passive element. Physical abuse—hitting, burning, cutting, kicking—of children is obviously the active part of child abuse crimes. But action is not always required for child abuse convictions. Most states have statutes making it a crime for one responsible for a child's welfare to endanger the life of the child. This can be done by failing to adequately feed or clothe a child, by leaving a child unattended at home, by leaving a child in an automobile on a hot day, or by failing to intervene when the child is being sexually molested.[21]

In response to the national problem of child abuse, the following have occurred:

- *Mandatory reporting laws* have been enacted by all states to require doctors, nurses, teachers, day care workers, and other people coming in contact with children to report suspected child abuse. It is likely there is still tremendous underreporting of abuse.
- *Increased authority to social workers* by some states to permit them to interview children without notifying their parents. Increased numbers of trained social workers are needed to handle growing caseloads.
- *New criminal laws* have been enacted, such as Washington's homicide by abuse statute, which makes child abuse resulting in death the equivalent of first-degree murder. Under this statute, prosecutors no longer have to prove premeditation or intent to kill for a conviction. Instead, the state must show that the defendant displayed "extreme indifference to human life." The writer of the bill stated, "Premeditation in child abuse cases is almost impossible to prove. This [law] gets around that oft-heard defense—'I didn't mean to kill the boy; I just wanted to discipline him.' "

Sexual abuse and sexual exploitation of children are discussed in Chapter 12. Sexual abuse may be combined with physical abuse or child neglect. Abuse or neglect in any form may have a severe emotional and psychological effect on a child, causing behavioral problems that could have great impact on the child's life.

≣ Offenses Against the Liberty of a Person Kidnapping

Kidnapping and Hostage Taking

Kidnapping was a crime in common law, punishable by life imprisonment. All states and the federal government with some variations have enacted statutes making kidnapping a crime. Section 212.1 of the Model Penal Code defines **kidnapping** in part as follows:

kidnapping False imprisonment coupled with movement of the victim.

> A person is guilty of kidnapping if he unlawfully removes another from his place of residence or business, or a substantial distance from the vicinity where he is found.

The most common motive for kidnapping is to obtain money ransom, as occurred in 1976, when an entire school bus with 26 children in Chowchilla, California, was taken. Other kidnappings occur as part of crimes of rape, robbery, murder, and other felonies. Kidnappings have also taken place to terrorize, blackmail, or obtain a hostage for escape.

As the M.P.C. section quoted above states, kidnapping requires that the victim unlawfully be "removed" from his residence or place of business, or a "substantial distance" from where he was found. This "moving" aspect of the kidnapping crime has frequently been an issue in kidnapping prosecutions, as the cases discussed here illustrate.

Two recent decisions involved one aspect of the "movement requirement" in kidnapping statutes, that is, what does it mean to "move" a victim. In a 2010 decision, *State v.*

OFFENSES AGAINST THE LIBERTY OF A PERSON

Offense	Usual Definition	Usual Motivation and Use of Offense
False imprisonment	False imprisonment is the unlawful restraint of another and is committed when a person is detained unlawfully.	False imprisonment most often occurs when a retail store employee makes an improper detention for shop lifting or an improper arrest is made by a law officer. These incidents are brought in civil courts and often are called "false arrest" lawsuits.
Kidnapping	Kidnapping is a false imprisonment that is aggravated by the movement of the victim to another place.	Motives could be to obtain ransom or as part of rape, robbery, or murder; to terrorize; to blackmail, and so on. Kidnapping is punished severely, as it is one of the most serious crimes against a person.
Hostage taking	Used to gain an advantage and compel others to comply with demands.	"Taking hostage" is often a tactic used as part of an escape attempt. The crime does not require forcible movement of the victim "some distance."
Parental kidnapping or child snatching (includes former live-ins, lovers, and family)	This crime is often a kidnapping by a parent who has lost (or will lose) custody of the kidnapped child.	This serious crime is committed to retaliate, to harass, to use as leverage in determining support payments, and to control and maintain custody of the child. Some children are never seen again by the other parent.
Abduction	The English enacted the first abduction statute in 1488. For many years, the crime forbade taking a female for any sexual purposes.	States using abduction as a crime generally limit it to a natural parent taking a child from a person having lawful custody.
Slavery and involuntary servitude	The Thirteenth Amendment forbids "slavery … [and] involuntary servitude, except as a punishment for crime."	Slavery, serfage, peonage, debt bondage, and exploitation of children still exists in parts of the world. In 1988, the U.S. Supreme Court affirmed the convictions of Michigan men for the crime of involuntary servitude of two mentally retarded men who were held as slaves for at least eleven years. *United States v. Kozminski*, 487 U.S. 43.

Mejia, 227 P.3d 1139, the Oregon Supreme Court affirmed the kidnapping conviction of a defendant who entered his former girlfriend's apartment and held her there for 90 minutes. The defendant contended he did not "move" the victim and thus could not be convicted of kidnapping. The Oregon Supreme Court rejected that argument. It held that under the Oregon kidnapping statute, Ore. Rev. Stat. Ann. § 163.225(1)(a), the crime is committed when a person "moves" or "constrains" another person "with the intent to interfere with another person's personal liberty." It is this interference that the statute makes criminal, the court said. The act of moving a person a "substantial distance" against her will is required only when no other evidence exists showing the intent to interfere with another's personal liberty. When, as the court found was the case there, other evidence showing that intent is present, the statute's "act" requirement is satisfied with any movement, including from room to room.

In a 2009 decision, *State v. Latham*, 219 P.3d 280, the Arizona Court of Appeals held that the "moving" requirement under the Arizona kidnapping statute, A.R.S. § 13-1304, was satisfied even though the kidnapper did not physically move the victim. The defendant entered a married couple's home and held a gun to the husband until the man's wife returned from work. The defendant then said he would shoot the husband if the wife did not go to the bank and cash a check for $10,000. The wife did so, and after arrest the kidnapper was charged with several crimes, including kidnapping the wife. The court of appeals affirmed the conviction, noting that no other case had been found with similar facts, but that the concept of "moving" the victim under the kidnapping statute applied when the victim "moved" because of the kidnapper's threat to kill her husband if she did not "move".

Another aspect of the "movement" requirement that has come before many courts is whether movements of short distances incident to the commission of such crimes as rape or robbery constitute kidnapping. According to California Jury Instruction 652:

> To constitute the crime of simple kidnapping, … there must be a carrying, or otherwise forceful moving, for some distance of the person who, against his will, is stolen or taken into custody or control of another person, but the law does not require that the one thus stolen or taken be carried or moved a long distance or any particular distance.

In interpreting "some distance," the California courts have held that "movement across a room or from one room to another" is not sufficient movement to justify a kidnapping conviction.[22] The general rule seems to be that movement "merely incident to the commission of the robbery [or rape]" is not kidnapping.[23]

In *People v. Washington*, 127 Cal. App. 4th 290 (Cal. App. 2005) the court reversed a conviction for kidnapping during a bank robbery. The defendant took the teller and bank manager away from their posts to the bank vault room, a distance of 15 and 25 feet respectively. The manager opened the vault, the robbers took the money, and left the bank. The court said that under the California kidnapping statute, Cal. Penal Code § 209, the movement of a victim in a robbery must be more than incidental to the commission of the robbery, and must increase the risk of harm to the victim. Here, the court said, the only reason the manager and teller were moved to the vault area was to enable them to gain access to the cash in the vault. Moreover, the risks to the victims were not increased by this movement. However, in *People v. Hernandez*, 2010 WL 2857046 (Cal. App. 2010) the court affirmed a conviction of kidnapping during the robbery of a Chevron store. The court found the requirements of § 209 satisfied by the movement of the store clerk to a back room, because there the robbers assaulted the clerk and robed him of his personal money. Taking the clerk to the back room, which could not be seen by the public, the court said dramatically increased the risk that harm would come to him.

In 2006 the California Supreme Court attempted to eliminate some of the uncertainty surrounding the amount or kind of movement necessary to support a kidnapping conviction in other contexts. In *People v. Dominquez*, 47 Cal. Rptr. 3d 575 (2006), a defendant was convicted of rape, kidnapping to commit rape, and felony murder. The defendant took the victim against her will from a street to an orchard located about 25 feet from the street but that was visible from the street. There the victim was raped by the defendant and killed by either the defendant or by another man present at the scene but who had since died. The court of appeals reversed the kidnapping conviction, holding that the movement of the victim to the orchard was incidental to the rape. The Supreme Court disagreed. It held that movement of the victim is sufficient to support a kidnapping charge if the movement is substantial and increases the risk that the underlying crime might occur. Because the orchard provided the defendant with an easier site to commit the rape, even though visible from the street, movement of the victim to that site increased the risk of harm and was enough to support the kidnapping charge.

In the case of *State v. Masino*, the defendant dragged his victim from her car and down an embankment, out of sight from passersby, before sexually assaulting her.[24] The New Jersey Supreme Court affirmed the convictions of sexual assault and kidnapping.

hostage taking The use or threat of use of force to restrain or confine a person with the intent to use the person as a hostage to compel another person to perform some act.

In 1982, the Florida Supreme Court stated that there is a "definite trend" toward allowing a kidnapping conviction "where the purpose in confining or moving another person is to use that person as a hostage." In *Mobley v. State*, the defendants were inmates in a jail.[25] They took two guards and an attorney captive in the course of an escape attempt. In affirming the convictions of the defendants for kidnapping and other offenses, the Florida Supreme Court held that the "confinement was not incidental to the attempted escape once [defendants] began using [the victims] as hostages and threatening physical harm."

Because kidnapping requires a forcible movement of the victim "some distance" or a "substantial distance," some states have created the crime of "taking hostage" to eliminate those requirements. A movement of the victim is not required to prove this offense. In creating this new offense, the state legislature can require all the elements of the serious felony of kidnapping except movement of the victim. They can require the state to prove "intent to use the person as a hostage."[26]

Because taking hostage is a serious and dangerous offense, it can be made a class A or B felony. To encourage offenders to release victims unharmed, the offense can be reduced to a class B or C felony if the hostages are released "before the actor's arrest." In *State v. Warfield*, 728 N.W.2d 374 (2007) the Wisconsin Court of Appeals held that a defendant who held 4 children hostage in an attempt to compel their mother to assist in a robbery of the check-cashing business where she worked was not entitled to the benefit of the "release" provision of the Wisconsin Hostage Statute. It rejected the defendant's arguments that he "released" the boys when he escaped from the house when police arrived. The court said the decision to escape is not the same as releasing the hostages.

False Imprisonment

false imprisonment Unlawful restraint or detention of a person.

Under the common law, **false imprisonment**[27] was also a crime that, like kidnapping, was punishable by life imprisonment. Many states have enacted statutes making false imprisonment a crime. The usual elements are as follows:

1. The defendant must have confined or restrained the liberty or freedom of movement of another.
2. Such act must have been intentional and without the consent of the victim.
3. The defendant had no lawful authority to confine or restrain the movement of the victim.

False imprisonment differs from kidnapping in that, in kidnapping, the victim must be moved to another place. In false imprisonment, the confinement or restraint may be at the place of the false arrest or unlawful detention of the victim. Under the old common law, it was also required that kidnapping be done secretly; this is not required for false imprisonment. However, the requirement of secrecy for kidnapping has probably been eliminated by most state statutes.

Many false imprisonment actions today are civil actions alleging false arrest or the improper detention of a person. Law enforcement officers and retail store employees should not interfere with the liberty of a person unless authority exists that justifies the restraint of a person. Many civil false imprisonment lawsuits concern detention of people believed to be shoplifters. Chapter 13 presents the law governing detentions and arrests in shoplifting cases.

Parental Kidnapping or Child Snatching

Child snatching is the abduction of a child by one parent without the consent of the other parent. It could occur before the parents had commenced a divorce action, while a divorce action was pending, or after a divorce judgment had been granted. Child snatching is also known as parental kidnapping, child abduction, or child stealing.

Thousands of children disappear each year as a result of parental kidnapping. Although the offending parent may state that he or she seeks to protect the child's welfare, other motives for child snatching are

- Retaliation against and harassment of the other spouse
- As a means to bargain for reduced child support or reduced division of property in the divorce settlement
- An attempt to bring about a reconciliation of the marriage

Children who are kidnapped by a parent experience changes that may lead to emotional damage. First, the child is often told that the parent who had custody is either dead or no longer loves the child. Second, in most instances, the child begins a lifestyle in which he or she grows up with only one parent. Third, the child is frequently exposed to life on the run, because parental kidnapping is a felony in most states. The pain, fear, guilt, anger, and anxiety from these experiences can cause severe, irreparable psychological harm.

Most states are generally prepared to extradite the offending parent back to the state in which the offense was committed, if he or she can be located. Before the passage of the Uniform Child Custody Jurisdiction Act (UCCJA), a fleeing child snatcher could run to another state, where residence would be established, and a custody order would be sought from the courts of the new state. Under UCCJA, the home or resident state would continue to have jurisdiction.

Because the federal kidnapping statute (the Lindbergh Act)[28] specifically excludes parents from its scope, a federal Parental Kidnapping Prevention Act was passed by Congress in 1981. This act facilitates interstate enforcement of custody and visitation determinations. The act also declares that the Fugitive Felon Act applies in state felony parental kidnapping cases, giving the FBI jurisdiction when the child snatcher crosses state lines.[29]

The Missing Children's Assistance Act

Because of increasing concern about child kidnapping by strangers, there are voluntary programs to fingerprint children for identification throughout the nation. The parents or legal guardians retain the fingerprint cards for use if the child, at a later date, gets lost or is missing.

The Missing Children's Assistance Act of 1984[30] requires the U.S. attorney general to "acquire, collect and preserve any information which would assist in the location of any missing person (including children, unemancipated persons as defined by the laws of the place of residence) and provide confirmation as to any entry [into FBI records] for such a person to the parent, legal guardian or next of kin." The act thus gives parents, legal guardians, or next of kin access to the information in the FBI National Crime Information Center's (NCIC) missing person file.

MISSING CHILDREN IN THE UNITED STATES

The U.S. Department of Health and Human Services estimates that more than 1.5 million children disappear from their homes each year. Studies show that the missing-children problem is really "a set of at least five very different, distinct problems."[a] These problems, which are reported to law enforcement agencies, are identified as follows:

- *Family Abductions:* Those abductions in which a family member took (or failed to return) a child in violation of custody rights or an agreement. More than 150,000 family abductions are reported each year in which a child was absent at least one night. Most of the missing children were under age 11. About half the abductions involved an unauthorized taking, whereas half were a failure to return a child after an authorized visit. Sexual abuse was reported in 1 percent of the cases, whereas neglect or abandonment of the child was a greater concern. The motive for taking the children was generally for revenge and retaliation. Family abductors were not limited to parents but also included other family members, lovers, and former live-ins. To deal with this growing problem, the Parental Kidnapping Prevention Act was passed by Congress in 1980.
- *Runaways:* Runaway age does not commence until 9 or 10. Physical or sexual abuse in the home could cause the runaway. Home conditions could be deplorable, or the child could have become involved in crimes, drugs, sexual relations, or a gang (sometimes all). Most of the reported runaways return home after being missing for one night or more. Runaways from juvenile facilities tend to be more serious than household cases. More than half leave the state, one-third are picked up by the police, and about one-tenth are jailed.
- *Throwaways:* These children are abandoned, deserted, told to leave the home, not allowed to return to the house, or no effort is made to locate them. These children experience more violence within the family and more sexual and physical abuse away from the home. Shelters for runaway and throwaway children report a high rate of exposure to AIDS and other diseases.
- *Lost:* Generally children so young that they cannot identify themselves or give a home address. However, older children could be lost in a rural or wooded area, causing extensive searches. A "lost" child could be a runaway, a throwaway, or the victim of an abduction. Lost children in most cases are found and returned home.

A survey conducted by the U.S. Senate Subcommittee on Investigations shows that more than 85,000 children were missing in 25 of the largest American cities in 1981. Tragically, at the end of the year at least 7,000 of the cases remained unsolved. Law enforcement officers report that few stranger-abducted children are recovered alive.

- *Abduction by Strangers or Victims of Other Crimes:* From 200 to 300 children are kidnapped by strangers every year in the United States. Criminal homicides of children average up to 147 per year. However, it is also estimated that 2,000 to 5,000 unidentified bodies are buried each year in the United States in John or Jane Doe graves, with approximately half of the unidentified being children. Strangers who steal children are broadly categorized by the Behavioral Science Department of the FBI Academy as follows:

  a. *The Pedophile:* The pedophile abducts a child primarily for sexual purposes. The Center for Child Advocacy and Protection states that pedophiles are generally young and middle-aged men who seek to control children rather than injure them. They will, however, murder children and perhaps make up the largest group in this category.
  b. *The Serial Killer:* The killings of 29 young blacks in Atlanta, after abduction, shocked the nation. Wayne Williams was convicted for the murders of two of the older victims.
  c. *The Psychotic:* The psychotic is usually a woman who has lost a baby or cannot conceive. To solve her problem, she abducts another family's child.
  d. *The Profiteer:* This person seeks to make money by stealing children. The child may be used by a baby adoption ring, pornographers, or, in rare instances, as a kidnapping for ransom.

[a]See the *National Incidence Studies on Missing, Abducted, Runaway, and Thrownaway Children in America: The Parental Abduction Prosecutor's Handbook*, available at the National Center for Prosecution of Child Abuse, 1033 N. Fairfax Street, Alexandria, VA 22314; and see the May 2000 report, 'Children as Victims' by the U.S. Department of Justice (NCJ 180753)

The act does not confer on the FBI any new investigative jurisdiction. The FBI can enter parental kidnapping cases through the Fugitive Felon Act if the following conditions exist:

1. A state arrest warrant has been issued charging the parent with a felony violation.
2. Law enforcement officers have evidence of interstate flight.
3. A specific request for FBI assistance must be made by state authorities, who agree to extradite and prosecute.
4. A U.S. attorney must authorize issuance of an unlawful flight warrant.

The National Center for Missing and Exploited Children coordinates efforts to recover missing children. A telephone hotline and other facilities are available to aid in these efforts.

≡ Family Violence and Disturbances

A study conducted for the National Institute of Mental Health concluded that "physical violence occurs between family members more often than it occurs between other individuals or in any other setting except wars and riots." The disturbance is often a quarrel between family members. It may start with a few angry words, or it could be a simmering dispute that explodes into violence. Destruction, damage, or taking of property may occur. One or both (or all) the parties may be under the influence of alcohol or drugs. Job stress or unemployment may contribute to the situation.

Hitting, pushing, choking, or wrestling, combined with other abusive behavior, may occur. Insulting and offending language is almost always used. Injuries range in severity from minor to critical and life-threatening.

Both parties could be at fault, or one party could be the agitator and the offender. The offender may have a prior record of violence and may be under a court order (divorce) or restraining order (criminal) forbidding such conduct. Or the offender may be on probation or parole, and his or her domestic conduct may violate the terms of that

---

RESPONSES TO DOMESTIC VIOLENCE

The following are some of the responses available to violent family situations:

1. Arrest of the offending person (or people)
   - If the state or city has a mandatory arrest law
   - Or at the discretion of the officer (or under the policy of the officer's department)
2. Obtain a protective court order under the statutes of that state
3. Seek shelter for the victim (spouse, children, parent, or others) under the shelter program available in that community
4. Divorce action and obtaining immediate (and also permanent) court orders that could protect by
   - Removing offending spouse from premises
   - Forbidding communication or contact by offending spouse
   - Restricting visitation rights with children and enforcing other restrictions
5. Issue (or threaten to issue) a civil citation with a substantial money fine
6. Use of the emergency detention section of the state mental health act (if applicable) to place the offending party into custody for observation
7. Revocation of probation or parole if the offender has violated terms of a probation or parole agreement

probation or parole. The offender's presence on the premises may be in violation of a court order or a condition of probation or parole. In addition to these violations, the offender may also be a trespasser.

Family units include not only the traditional family relationships but also homosexuals and unwed heterosexual couples. The disturbance or violence could include not only adults but also children within the family unit.

Past experience has demonstrated that family-trouble calls can be dangerous for law enforcement officers. Approximately one-fifth of police deaths and almost one-third of assaults on officers occur when they respond to family quarrels and domestic disputes in which a weapon is used.

In past years, unless serious injury occurred or a clear violation of a court order or probation (or parole) existed, an arrest would ordinarily not be made. Police officers would attempt to mediate the dispute. However, studies by the Police Foundation have shown that police arrests sharply reduce violence in the home. The police commissioner of New York City stated that because of this study and because of his own experience as a "cop on the street," he concluded that past police efforts to mediate have done little to stop what has been a growing problem.

The commissioner stated that arresting violent members of a household would be more effective in protecting other family members and would help to safeguard police officers who are called to intervene in situations where violence could occur.

Some states have responded to domestic violence by passing criminal laws that address domestic violence directly. The terms of these statutes vary, but the following three state laws are representative. Nevada's domestic violence statute, N.R.S. 200.485, makes it a misdemeanor for a person to commit an assault or battery against a spouse, former spouse, a person living with the person, or a person in a dating relationship. The first offense is a misdemeanor with limited penalties; the second offense within 7 years is also a misdemeanor, but penalties are enhanced. The third and subsequent offenses within 7 years are felonies. The statute also provides that if the penalty is greater under the general assault and battery statutes—for example, because of the seriousness of the injury—the defendant can be sentenced under those statutes.

Indiana Code § 35-42-2-1.3 incorporates common law assault and battery language, and it defines domestic violence to include "touching" in a "rude or insulting manner" that causes bodily injury. Persons covered by the statute include spouses, former spouses, persons who are cohabiting, or a person with whom the person charged has had a child. First-offense domestic violence is a misdemeanor. Subsequent offenses are class D felonies. It is also a class D felony if the domestic violence occurs in the presence of a child under 16 years of age.

Idaho Code § 18-918 defines domestic violence as committing an assault or battery as defined in the general criminal statutes for those crimes against a "household member," which includes a spouse, former spouse, a person living with the person charged, or a person with whom the person charged has a child. Assaults are punished as misdemeanors. If a battery results in a "traumatic injury" it is a felony. If not, it is a misdemeanor. "Traumatic injury" means any wound, or any "external or internal injury," regardless of how serious the injury is, caused by physical force.

In past years, it was not uncommon for police departments to receive calls from women asking for protection from men who had threatened them or from wives who expected to be beaten by their husbands when they came home from a tavern. Threats to injure can be the basis of a criminal charge. If the threat was made over a telephone, the charge of unlawful use of a telephone may be made.

Because of the battered woman problem, crisis counseling centers and shelters have been established throughout the United States to assist victims and their families. These centers provide shelter when needed, counseling, support, and emergency food and clothing. Shelter locations are generally not disclosed to the public to avoid further confrontation of the victim by the offender.

CASE CLOSE-UP

United States v. Hayes
United States Supreme Court, 2009
129 S. Ct. 1079

Domestic violence is predominantly regulated by state criminal laws. The federal government has limited powers to pass laws that do not have multi-state consequences, and most domestic disturbances would not have that effect. Congress has nonetheless expressed a desire to enter the domestic violence field, as illustrated by the Violence Against Women Act, discussed later in this chapter. The domestic violence crimes identified in that Act, however, all must include some interstate activity, that is, the crimes must involve conduct in more than one state.

In 1996 Congress again passed a statute aimed at domestic violence, though indirectly. 18 U.S.C. § 922(g)(9) makes it a federal crime to possess a firearm if one has been previously convicted of a "misdemeanor crime of domestic violence." Congress has made possession of firearms by convicted felons a crime since passage of the Gun Control Act of 1968, 18 U.S.C. § 921, and that act is recognized as a proper use of the power granted Congress under the Commerce Clause. Section 922 (g)(9) is the first action by Congress to connect firearm possession and domestic violence. Randy Edward Hayes, the defendant in this case, was convicted under section 922(g)(9), and appealed his conviction through the federal court system, culminating in this decision.

Hayes was arrested in 2004 by West Virginia law officers, who were responding to his house because of a domestic violence call. While there, officers searched Hayes's house with his permission, finding several rifles that Hayes admitted belonged to him. Investigators subsequently discovered that Hayes had been convicted in 1994 of a misdemeanor battery of his then-wife, but the conviction was under the West Virginia general battery statute, which makes no reference to any relationship between the accused and the victim. Based on this information, in 2005 a federal grand jury indicted Hayes for violation of section 922(g)(9), and he was convicted on three counts under that statute.

Hayes appealed to the Fourth Circuit Court of Appeals, which reversed his conviction. That court held that in order for a previous misdemeanor battery conviction to serve as the "predicate offense" under section 922(g)(9), the conviction must have been for an offense in which the domestic relationship between the accused and the victim was "an element" of the offense." Because Hayes had been convicted of a misdemeanor battery under a statute that made no reference to his relationship with the victim, the conviction was not the kind of "misdemeanor crime of domestic violence" covered by the act.

The U.S. Supreme Court granted certiorari to resolve a conflict among the courts of appeal, noting that nine other circuits had reached the opposite conclusion and held that any prior misdemeanor battery conviction sufficed the "to be the predicate offense," so long as the victim was in fact the defendant's spouse or other protected person. The question, the Court said, was what Congress meant when it defined "crime of domestic violence."

The definitions section of the Gun Control Act, 18 U.S.C. § 921(a) (33)(A), defines "misdemeanor crime of domestic violence" as an offense that is a misdemeanor under state, federal, or tribal law, and has, "as an element, the use of ... physical force,... committed by a current or former spouse" against that person's spouse. (The definition covers other kinds of domestic relationships, but in this case Hayes's prior conviction involved his then-wife).

Hayes contended the words "as an element" meant that prior conviction was a "predicate crime" only if the statute under which the conviction occurred made the relationship between Hayes and the victim "an element" of the offense. For example, a statute making it a crime to commit battery against a "household member" would require proof that the victim was in fact a household member with the defendant. Because Hayes was convicted under the general battery statute, which requires no proof of relationship, he contended the "predicate crime" had not occurred, and he thus did not violate section 922(g)(9).

The Supreme Court rejected his contention and affirmed his conviction. The Court found that the term *as an element* modified only the phrase *use of force*, and not "committed by a current or former spouse." Thus, while violation of section 922(g)(9) required proof that the victim of the prior battery was a former or current spouse (or one of the other relationships specified in the statute), it was not necessary for that relationship to be "denominated an element of the predicate offense."

Writing for the majority, Justice Ginsburg also stated that the Court's interpretation seemed more in line with congressional purpose in adopting the statute. She concluded, "Given the paucity of state and federal statutes targeting *domestic* violence, we find it highly improbable that Congress meant to extend §922(g)(9)'s firearm possession ban only to the relatively few domestic abusers prosecuted under laws rendering a domestic relationship an element of the offense."

Domestic Violence and Women

Physical abuse of women, usually by husbands, ex-husbands, or boyfriends, is a crime that is likely to go unreported and, if reported, not prosecuted. Frequently, the victim refuses to press charges against the abuser. Although in theory the prosecutor may continue to prosecute a case even after the complainant wants charges dropped, in practice such cases become hard to prove and are usually dismissed.

FBI studies show that refusals by the battered spouse to cooperate with prosecutors rarely lead to better relations with the abusive spouse. This is because domestic abuse follows a familiar cycle of violence. In the first phase, the tension-building phase, the abusive spouse becomes hostile and belligerent and heaps verbal abuse on the partner.

This phase almost always leads to the next phase, the acute-battering phase. Injury and death can be the result in this phase. Following a severe battering, the abusive spouse will shower the partner with flowers, affection, and contrite behavior. This is called the honeymoon phase, but like all honeymoons, it always ends. The next phase is the tension-building phase, and the cycle continues from there.[31]

In 1994, Congress passed the Violence Against Women Act (VAWA).[32] This law created new federal domestic violence crimes and also provided millions of dollars for battered woman shelters and child care. The following cases illustrate prosecutions under VAWA:

- *United States v. Bailey:*[33] Bailey beat his wife, placed her in the trunk of his car, and drove back and forth between West Virginia, Kentucky, and Ohio for several days. He was convicted under VAWA and sentenced to life imprisonment.
- *United States v. Steele:*[34] Steele beat his girlfriend in Oregon, then forced her to drive with him to California. While she was attempting to escape, Steele dragged her dangling from the car door. Steele was convicted of interstate domestic violence and sentenced to 87 months in prison.
- *United States v. Dowd*, 417 F.3d 1080 (9th Cir. 2005), *cert. denied* 126 U.S. 816 (2005): A defendant was convicted under the VAWA, usually referred to as the *interstate domestic violence* statute, for forcing his girlfriend to accompany him on an extended, three-state trip, in which he abused her both physically and psychologically.

Abuse of the Elderly

In 1990, the House Subcommittee on Health and Long-Term Care on Aging reported that an estimated 1.5 million elderly Americans (5 percent of all older Americans) are abused each year, often by their own children. The report points out that older people often are ashamed to admit that their families abuse them, or they fear reprisals if they complain.

The report also states that "elder abuse has been virtually ignored by the federal government." However, with the increase in the number of elderly people in the United States, the number of cases of elder abuse reported has increased. An *FBI Law Enforcement Bulletin* article entitled "Elder Abuse" (February 1994) called elder abuse a "national tragedy" and quoted the congressional subcommittee on aging as stating, "1 out of every 25 Americans over the age of 65 (is suffering) from some form of abuse, neglect, or exploitation." A July 2001 report of federal and state inspections of the nation's 17,000 nursing homes showed that 30 percent were cited over a two-year period for physical, sexual, or verbal abuse of residents. About one in ten of the citations was a serious incident that either put the victim at great risk of harm or killed the patient. The report contained examples of nursing home residents being punched, choked, or kicked by staff members or by other residents.[35]

THE BROOKE ASTOR CASE

In 2007 Brooke Astor died at the age of 105. She was the heir to a $200 million fortune she inherited from her third husband, Vincent Astor, who died in 1959. He in turn had inherited from his father, who died on the Titanic in 1912. The Astor family owed its wealth to their famous ancestor John Jacob Astor, a 19th-century industrialist who was, when he died in 1848, the United States' wealthiest person. From 1959 to the end of the 20th century Brooke Astor famously lived as a socialite/philanthropist in New York City.

During the last five years of her life Brooke Astor suffered from Alzheimer's disease and was under the financial care of her son, Anthony Marshall. In 2009 Marshall, then 85, and his attorney were convicted of elder abuse and fraud in New York. While managing Brooke Astor's affairs they stole millions of dollars from her investments and fraudulently changed her will to increase her son's share of her estate. Marshall and his attorney were each sentenced to 1-3 years in prison for their crimes.

Many states have enacted laws aimed at various kinds of abuse, including elder abuse. An example of these laws is the Nebraska Adult Protective Services Act (Neb. Rev. Stat. § 28-348-387). This act broadly defines *elder abuse* as act or omission by a caregiver that causes physical injury, cruel punishment, sexual abuse, confinement, or denial of essential services to a vulnerable adult. The act treats violations as class V felonies. It also requires those who treat elderly people, such as physicians and nurses, to report evidence of abuse. Law enforcement agencies are then required to investigate such reports and take steps to protect the elderly person being abused.

California has been a leader in responding to elder abuse. Its law states that it is a crime, a misdemeanor, or a felony, depending on the dangerousness of the situation, for any person charged with the duty of caring for an elder person to "willfully cause or permit the elder or dependent adult to be placed in a situation such that his or her person or health is endangered."[36]

In *People v. Heitzmann*,[37] a daughter was convicted under this statute when her 68-year-old father died from neglect. Although the father lived with the defendant's brothers, the court held that she knew the brothers were not caring for her father but did nothing about it.

The Crime of Violation of a Court Order (or Court Injunction)

Many court orders or injunctions are issued every year in the United States. They are issued in divorce cases in which one of the parties requests such an order (or orders).

They are issued when serious harassment causes the victim to go to a court for protection. The injunction could order a husband (or wife) or a boyfriend not to contact or harass a former spouse or live-in partner. The order could forbid the person against whom it is issued from going into or near the residence or the place of employment of the person the order seeks to protect. The order may forbid harassment, violence, or contact with a person or people.

An increasing number of states are making the violation of such court orders crimes in themselves, because so many of these orders have been violated, because tragedies sometimes occur, and because there is no other practical way of enforcing such orders. Other statutes could also make a person who violates a court order subject to immediate arrest without the necessity of an arrest warrant or another court hearing.

When a court order is issued under these new laws, the person against whom it is issued is informed in the court order that any violation of the order could result in immediate arrest.[38]

If a violation does occur, law enforcement officers are generally called by the person the court order seeks to protect. The person should be able to produce a copy of the order for the law enforcement officers. The order will generally show that it has been personally served on the defendant.

EXAMPLE: A court order is issued against a former live-in boyfriend, ordering him (among other things) not to go near or into the place of employment of his former girlfriend. The police are called when the man enters the store or office that the order forbids him to enter. The police detain the man until they have viewed and read the copy of the court order. When it is clear that he has violated the order, the police then arrest the man and charge him with the crime of violation of the court order.

The Violence Against Women Act discussed earlier has a provision that makes criminal the "interstate violation of a protection order."[39] If a wife travels to another state from her home state and obtains a protection order against her husband, any violation of the order by the husband will be a crime under the federal law and the law of the state that issued the order.

SCHOOL SHOOTINGS

From 1927 to 2010 there have been several instances of school-related shootings in the United States. While schools at all levels have generally been safe for students and faculty members, these events are especially tragic because of the children involved. The following list chronicles the major fatal shootings in the past 80 years:

- *1927—Bath, Michigan:* A school official killed his wife and then blew up the town's school, killing 40 people.
- *1966—Austin, Texas:* Known as the Texas Tower killings, a recent graduate of the University of Texas barricaded himself in a tower on the UT campus, and for 96 minutes fired his rifle at passing pedestrians, killing 14 and injuring 31 before being killed by police.
- *1997—Paducah, Kentucky:* A 14-year-old boy killed three classmates and injured five others at a high school prayer meeting.
- *1998—Jonesboro, Arkansas:* Two cousins, ages 13 and 11, dressed in camouflage, killed 4 girls and a teacher, and wounded 11 others, outside a middle school. The killers were released from juvenile corrections in 2005 and 2007. The older boy was recently arrested for carrying a loaded weapon, a pistol.
- *1998—Springfield, Oregon:* After being suspended from school for bringing a gun to school, a 15-year-old boy killed 3 and wounded 23 other students before other students subdued him, and the police arrested him.
- *1999—Littleton, Colorado:* Two Columbine High School students, ages 17 and 18, killed 12 students and a teacher, and wounded 23 others, before killing themselves.
- *2005—Red Lake, Minnesota:* A 16-year-old boy killed his grandparents, five fellow students, a teacher, and a security guard before killing himself on a Native American reservation.
- *2006—Nichol Mines, Pennsylvania:* A 32-year-old man entered an Amish school and shot 11 girls—killing 4 and wounding 7—before killing himself.
- *2007—Blacksburg, Virginia:* A Virginia Tech student killed 32 students and teachers in a university building on the 26,000-acre campus of Virginia Tech. The student then killed himself. This was the worst mass shooting in the United States since 1991, when George Hennard killed 23 people in a cafeteria in Killeen, Texas.
- *2008—DeKalb, Illinois*: A 27-year-old student at Northern Illinois University killed himself and 5 other students, and wounded 16 others. In *Baton Rouge, Louisiana*, a nursing student opened fire in a classroom at a technical college, killing two women students before killing herself. The campus of Seton Hall University in New Jersey was locked down after a man killed himself after unsuccessfully trying to gain access to a student. These incidents all occurred within a month of each other.
- *2009—Coral Gables, Florida*: A 17-year-old student was stabbed to death at 9:00 a.m. in the school courtyard by another student. In *Tyler, Texas* a 16-year-old student stabbed to death a special education teacher in the classroom.
- *2010—Madison, Alabama*: A 9th-grade student was shot and killed in the school hallway by another 9th-grade student.
- *2010—Huntsville, Alabama*: A female faculty member who was bitter at being denied tenure at the University of Alabama killed three colleagues at a faculty meeting, and wounded three others.

≡ Violence in the Workplace

The U.S. Department of Justice reports that each year 1 million people become victims of violent crimes while at work. Most of such victims are robbed, are victims of felonious assault, or are raped.[40]

While newspapers and television depict scenes of crazed co-workers or fired employees coming back to wreak carnage, statistics show that about a thousand people are killed by violence in the workplace each year.

Is the workplace violent? Should we fear our fellow workers? Statistics show that we have little to fear. For example, in 1993, 1,063 people were killed at work, but only 59 of those killings were committed by fellow workers. Thus, out of a national workforce in 1993 of 120.8 million, only 1 in 2.1 million was killed by a co-worker. The odds of getting hit by lightning each year are about 1 in 600,000. For additional information about workplace violence, log on to the FBI's National Center for the Analysis of Violent Crime, http://www.fbi.gov/publications/violence.pdf.

≡ Road Rage: Violent Aggressive Driving

Vehicle traffic-related injuries and deaths are the ninth leading cause of death worldwide, and combined with the crime of driving while under the influence of alcohol they are the leading cause of criminal homicide in the United States. Moreover, common driving violations create the greater frequency of aggressive driving, known as "road rage."

The National Highway Traffic Safety Administration reported to the U.S. Congress that "violent aggressive driving" had increased 7 percent a year during the late 1990s. Violent aggressive driving was described as aggressive behavior like tailgating, weaving through busy traffic lanes, honking, screaming at other drivers, exchanges of insults, gunfire, and even murder.

Driving violations lead to accidents, which often can help trigger road rage. For example, a 2006 study by the University of Wisconsin showed that in the city of Milwaukee there were more than 1,000 vehicle accidents caused by drivers running stop signs or traffic lights. To combat this problem, about one-half the states have laws permitting red-light cameras, which photograph vehicles and their license plates.

In the 2002 Texas case of *Feldman v. State* (71 S.W.2d 738), a motorcyclist became enraged when a trucker passed him on the highway and nearly hit him. The motorcyclist chased the trucker, pulled up alongside the truck, and shot the driver. The motorcyclist was convicted of murder.

In 2007 motorists became so enraged at delays caused by construction work on a California state highway that they began verbally abusing, throwing objects, and even firing BB guns at the workers. The state highway department finally closed the highway until completion of the construction.[41]

The National Highway Safety chief told members of Congress that road rage was present in two-thirds of the 41,907 highway deaths of 1996 and in one-third of the non-fatal crashes that resulted in 3 million injuries.

The U.S. House Transportation Committee also heard the testimony of other highway safety experts, including a California psychologist who has studied the "road rage disorder" and has treated "road ragers." "It is curable," stated Dr. Arnold Nerenberg, "but first, 'road ragers' must acknowledge that they have a problem" and then "say to themselves, it's just not worth it."

≡ Duty to Report Laws

One recurring problem in assault-related crimes is the failure to report the crimes when they happen. In many cases, because the victim is a child or a spouse, the victim lacks the means or opportunity to report the incident. In other cases, the person who learns of the offense has some relationship with the victim or the assailant and is reluctant to make a report. To deal with this, most states have a variety of reporting laws that require people to report knowledge they have acquired that may show violation of a criminal law. Often, failure to make a report when required is itself a crime. The following are some of the many situations where reporting laws require a person to make a report:

- Physical or sexual abuse of a child;
- Physical or sexual abuse of an elderly person, or a mentally incapacitated person;
- Deaths that (a) occurred under suspicious or unexplained circumstances, (b) are homicides, (c) followed an abortion, (d) are due to poisoning, (e) followed an accident, (f) did not have an attending physician within 30 days of the death and spiritual means or prayer were used for healing, (g) a physician has refused to sign a death certificate or cannot be obtained to sign a death certificate within 6 days after death occurred, and (h) was caused by diseases such as AIDS, N1N1, or sexually transmitted diseases.
- In some jurisdictions, there is a common law duty to report the threat of harm to another, such as a threat made by a violent or dangerous patient and known to those providing medical or psychological treatment to the patient. The leading case of *Tartsoff v. Regents of the University of California*, 551 P.2d 334 (1976) held that medical professionals who learn of a threat made by a dangerous and violent patient against an identified person have a duty to "take reasonable steps to protect ...(that person) from the threat of harm" by the patient.

Summary

- An assault conviction requires acts intended to cause bodily injury, or instill fear of such injury. Using a weapon to cause fear is an assault. A battery conviction requires intentional infliction of bodily harm or unlawful touching in a rude or offensive manner.
- Virtually any kind of physical contact can constitute a battery, so long as it is done in a manner that is non-consensual and in a hostile or belligerent manner.
- An assault or battery becomes aggravated if a deadly weapon is used to commit an assault or a battery, or there is an intent to commit a felony. In the case of a battery, if serious bodily injury results it is aggravated battery. Sometimes other circumstances, such as the fact that the victim is pregnant, make a battery aggravated.
- All states have laws that focus on child abuse, neglect, or endangerment. It is also a crime to expose a child to sexually harmful material, or involve a child in sexual activities. Contributing to the delinquency of a child can be used to include other forms of child neglect.
- Self-defense is a common defense asserted in assault and battery charges. Under some circumstances, the conduct may be justified, as in the case of a law enforcement officer using force. In some activities, like sports, consent is given to some use of force.
- Most states require that a kidnapping victim be "moved" as part of the crime. Generally, the movement must be substantial, and not just moving a person from one room to another. However, where it is clear the purpose of the action was to constrain the victim against that person's will, any movement of the victim will suffice.
- Hostage taking differs from kidnapping in that it lacks a "movement" element. The crime does require that a victim be held against his will in some fashion, and that the purpose of doing so is to force another to take some act, like pay a ransom, or allow the criminals to escape.

Key Terms

assault, p. 280
battery, p. 280
offensive touching, p. 284
aggravated assault, p. 285

menacing, p. 285
aggravated battery, p. 286
mayhem and malicious
    disfigurement, p. 287

kidnapping, p. 292
hostage taking, p. 295
false imprisonment, p. 295

Case Analysis and Writing Exercises

1. When a riot occurs in a prison, the inmates sometimes seize a guard or other prison employee and hold that person during the period of the riot. Not all the inmates will directly participate in seizing or holding the guard, even if they otherwise participate in the riot. When the riot is quelled, what charges can be brought against the inmates? What should the government have to prove to convict an inmate of these charges? See *Comm. v. Spearin*, 846 N.E.2d 390 (Mass. 2006).

2. In those states, and there are many, that include "recklessly" in their aggravated assault or aggravated battery statutes, there is generally a requirement that the "reckless" behavior show an "extreme indifference to the value of human life." Wyoming has such a statute, Wyo. Stat. Ann. § 6-2-502(a)(1). When does a fight between kids out for a night of "cruising" around town become a violation of the statute? What should a trial judge instruct a jury on this issue? See *O'Brien v. State*, 45 P.3d 225 (Wyo. 2002). What were the important factors that convinced the Wyoming Supreme Court that the crime had occurred?

3. A woman sued a former boyfriend, seeking the return of personal property held by the boyfriend. The lawyer representing the boyfriend stated that a judgment against the boyfriend would be no good, because "she (the lawyer) didn't know where he was living." The woman poked the lawyer in the shoulder, stating that the lawyer did in fact know where the boyfriend was living. The police observed the incident, and defendant was charged with simple assault. The state statute defines simple assault as an "unprivileged touching"; the defendant argued that the statute was too broad because it would make a simple pat on the back an assault. Do you agree? See *State v. Burke*, 897 A.2d 996 (N.H. 2006).

4. Parental kidnapping usually involves a noncustodial parent running off with a child while visiting with the child. In such a case, the retention of the child is kidnapping because the parent has no right to continued custody of the child. Can a parent who has joint custody, with the other parent, of a child pursuant to a divorce decree be guilty of parental kidnapping? When and how? Can someone, such as a second spouse, who helps the parent, be guilty of parental kidnapping? See *State v. Froland*, 874 A.2d 568 (N.J. 2005), *review granted* 899 A.2d 304 (2006). Do you agree with the court's decision? For the outcome on appeal, see State v. Froland, 936 A.2d 947 (N.J. 2007).

Notes

1. A few states (including Wisconsin) have not statutorized the common law crime of assault. Disorderly conduct and attempt to commit a battery are substituted for assault in charging.

2. Probably all states have passed statutes that criminalize the conduct of pointing an unloaded gun at a victim who does not know if the gun is loaded or unloaded and becomes apprehensive and frightened. The New York crime of menacing (Section 120.15) by placing "or attempting to place another in fear of imminent serious physical injury" is an example of such criminal statutes.

3. 104 Cal. App. 4th 256, 124 Cal. Rptr. 2d 888 (2002).

4. See also *U.S. v. Frizzi*, 491 F.2d 1231 (1st Cir. 1974), in which the defendant spat in the face of a mail carrier and then hit the carrier in the face when he demanded an apology. The court affirmed the defendant's conviction of assaulting a federal officer in the performance of his duties.

5. In the 1991 case of *Ray v. State* (580 So. 2d 103), the Alabama Court of Appeals quoted another court as to an adult man's fists being used to beat a baby:

   Certainly the use of an adult man's fists to beat a seventeen month [old] child may appropriately allow those fists to be classified as a deadly weapon or a dangerous instrument.

6. 440 A.2d 710 (R.I. 1982).

7. 534 N.E.2d 312 (Ill. App. 1989).

8. 592 N.E.2d 585 (Ill. App. 1992).

9. Other batteries and assaults include a running leap onto a woman's back as assault in *Russell v. State*, 814 S.W. 2d 871 (Tex. App. 1991); poking a teacher in the chest as assault in *People v. Dunker*, 577 N.E.2d 499 (Ill. App. 1991); a profane threat of physical violence as assault in *Wells v. State*, 418 S.W.2d 437 (Ga. App. 1992); grabbing the victim by his coat and punching him in the face as assault in *State v. Waltrip*, 484 N.W.2d 831 (Neb. 1992); holding the victim against her will as battery in *Barnette v. State*, 217 S.W.2d 20 (1949); head-butting the victim as disorderly conduct and assault in *State v. McKenzie*, 605 A.2d 72 (Maine 1992); attempting to film under victim's dress with camcorder as simple battery in *Fitzgerald v. State*, 411 S.E.2d 102 (Ga. App. 1991); and throwing rocks at moving cars on highway as several counts of assault, battery, and malicious destruction in *Ford v. State*, 603 A.2d 883 (Md. 1992).

10. 117 Ill. App. 3d 363, 73 Ill. Dec. 17, 453 N.E.2d 842. The Illinois Appellate Court cited the following:

   > Other instances of conduct held to be simple battery based solely on insulting or provoking physical contact [include]: *People v. Hamilton*, … 401 N.E.2d 318 … (where defendant reached around the female complainant and placed his hand over her mouth); *People v. Siler*, … 406 N.E.2d 891 … (where defendant lifted up complainant's dress during a confrontation having sexual overtones).

11. *State v. Shelly*, 929 P.2d 489 (Wash. 1997).

12. The Federal Aviation Act of 1958, 49 U.S.C.A. § 1472(j), forbids assault, intimidation, or threatening of a flight crew member and punishes such conduct by imprisonment for up to 20 years.

   In the 1991 case of *U.S. v. Tabacca*, 924 F.2d 906 (9th Cir.), the defendant continued to smoke a cigarette after airline flight attendants requested that he extinguish the cigarette. After vulgar language to the attendant, Tabacca grabbed her arm "and jerked and twisted her arm, causing her to strike the bulkhead of the seat across the aisle." The defendant's conviction was affirmed.

13. W. J. Williams, *Moriarty's Police Law*, 21st ed. (London: Butterworths, 1972).

14. *State v. Boone*, 294 Or. 630, 661 P.2d 917 (1983).

15. Id.

16. 901 So. 2d 899 (Fla. App. 2005)

17. *Whitaker v. U.S.*, 616 A.2d 843 (D.C. App. 1992).

18. Vernon's Penal Code of the State of Texas Annotated.

19. 508 U.S. 476 (1993).

20. 429 U.S. 975, 97 S. Ct. 481 (1976). The 1997 U.S. Department of Justice publication *In the Wake of Child Abuse and Childhood Maltreatment* states that more than 3 million children are reported to Child Protective Services each year as being abused. Of these 3 million reported cases, 1 million are found to be abused children. The majority of abused children (85%) are under age 5, and nearly half of the victims (45%) have not reached their first birthday. More than three children die each day as a result of parental maltreatment. Abuse is the most common cause of death (48%), followed by neglect (37%), and a combination of abuse and neglect (15%). Child abuse is a crime that cuts across all walks of life and all social classes.

21. In *Commonwealth v. Miller*, 600 A.2d 988 (Pa. Super. 1992), the court discussed the endangerment statutes requirement that the defendant "knowingly" endangered a child's welfare. The court said the defendant must know he or she has a duty to care for the child, is aware the child is in a dangerous situation, and has either failed to act or has acted in so meager a way that it could not reasonably be believed the actions would be effective. Thus, a mother who leaves her child unattended while she goes out to a nightclub can be convicted of endangerment of a child, but a mother who believes, wrongly and perhaps unreasonably, her boyfriend's statement that another person is watching her child probably would not.

22. See *People v. Daniels*, 71 Cal. 2d 1119, 80 Cal. Rptr. 897, 459 P.2d 225 (1969).

23. See *People v. Williams*, 2 Cal. 3d 894, 88 Cal. Rptr. 208, 471 P.2d 1008 (1970).

24. 94 N.J. 436, 466 A.2d 955 (1983).

25. 409 So. 2d 1031 (Fla. 1982).

26. Section 940.305 Wisconsin "taking hostage" felony.

27. The tort of false imprisonment is sometimes called *false arrest*. False arrest is a wrongful arrest made either by a law enforcement officer or a private person. Arresting, detaining, and holding a person in custody without authority is false imprisonment and gives the victim the basis for a civil lawsuit to recover for the false arrest and false imprisonment. In a civil lawsuit (tort action) for false arrest, the

plaintiff alleges that there was no authority or legal justification for the defendant to interfere with the plaintiff's freedom of movement.

28. 18 U.S.C.A. § 1201.

29. 18 U.S.C.A. § 1073.

30. In October 1984, President Ronald Reagan signed the Missing Children's Assistance Act (36 CrL 3063), which provides for the operation of a national toll-free telephone line for exchanging information on missing children through a national resource center and clearinghouse. The administrator of the program will "facilitate effective coordination among all federally funded programs relating to missing children." Section 406(a) of the act provides:

> The Administrator is authorized to make grants to and enter into contracts with public agencies or non-profit private organizations, or combination thereof, for research, demonstration projects, or service programs designed—(1) to educate parents, children, and community agencies and organizations in ways to prevent the abduction and sexual exploitation of children; (2) to provide information to assist in the locating and return of missing children; (3) to aid communities in the collection of materials which would be useful to parents in assisting others in the identification of missing children; (4) to increase knowledge of and develop effective treatment pertaining to the psychological consequences, on both parents and children.

31. *FBI Law Enforcement Bulletin*, July 1, 1996, p. 15.

32. 18 U.S.C.A. § 2261–2266. In the May 2000 case of *U.S. v. Morrison*, the U.S. Supreme Court declared the civil remedy provisions of the Violence Against Women Act unconstitutional. Just as in the Gun-Free School Zones Act case of *U.S. v. Lopez* (115 S. Ct. 1624), violence against women and firearms in a school zone do not affect interstate commerce, and therefore the federal government has limited authority to enact the civil law portions of laws. Courts commonly uphold the criminal portions of the VAWA, which specifically require movement of the victim in interstate commerce. All states have criminal laws forbidding violence against women, and most states have gun-free school zone laws.

33. *U.S. v. Bailey*, cited in the *Prosecutor*, June 1996, p. 23.

34. *U.S. v. Steele*, cited in ibid.

35. See *Milwaukee Journal Sentinel* article, "30% of Nursing Homes Cited for Abuse," July 31, 2001.

36. California Penal Code Section 368(a).

37. *People v. Heitzmann*, 54 CrL 1019 (1993).

38. A Texas Court of Appeals held that prior actual knowledge of the protective order is an essential element of the crime of violating a court order: *Small v. State*, 809 S.W.2d 253 (Tex. App. 1991). In the 1993 case of *State v. Haley*, 629 A.2d 605 (Me. 1993), the highest court in Maine held that a former husband's repeated telephoning of his former wife, asking her to take him back and threatening to kill himself if she did not, did not violate the protective order forbidding him from "abusing" his former wife and minor children.

39. 18 U.S.C. § 2262.

40. NCJ 148199, U.S. Department of Justice, July 1994.

41. See *Milwaukee Journal Sentinel* article, "Road Rage Closes California Highway," July 27, 2007.

Sexual Assault, Rape, Prostitution, and Related Sex Crimes

Eliot Spitzer, former governor of New York, was forced to resign that office in 2008 when it was revealed he was a "customer" of an expensive prostitution ring called the Emperor's Club VIP. Prior to his election as governor Spitzer was the New York Attorney General, the chief law enforcement officer in the state.

OUTLINE

LEARNING OBJECTIVES

In this chapter we discuss sexual assault crimes and crimes related to sexual conduct. The learning objectives for Chapter 12 are:

- Identify the degrees of sexual assault, and the conduct that distinguishes them.

- Learn the areas of questioning of a sexual assault victim that are prohibited by the rape shield law.

- List two exceptions to the rape shield law's prohibitions.

- State the *mens rea* requirement for a conviction for statutory rape.
- State the conditions that must be shown for civil commitment of a sexual predator.
- List ways a person could be convicted for pimping for prostitution.

- Explain the reasons child pornography laws have been found unconstitutional.
- State the current status of federal acts such as the Child Online Protection Act.

On March 28, 2010, a 15-year-old girl babysitting her 7-year-old stepsister was invited by some men to come to a party. She did, and brought the 7-year-old with her. At the party the babysitter allowed several of the men and some boys to have sex with her for money. She then allowed, for money, the same men and boys to "touch" the child. That soon changed to more violent sexual contact, and ultimately all 7 men and boys had sex with the 7-year-old girl, holding her down and covering her mouth to prevent her from screaming. By April 4th 2010, all seven men and boys had been arrested and charged with aggravated sexual assault and child endangerment.

In this chapter we will study the elements of sexual assault crimes, in particular the rape of women. We will also learn about the rules and procedures put in place to preserve the reputation and emotional well-being of the victim, such as the rape shield laws.

Sexual Relations in the United States Today

Sexual relations (nonmarital) become a crime in the United States if

- There is a lack of consent.
- They are with a minor incapable of legally consenting.
- They are with a mentally deficient person or an adult incapable of consenting.
- They are performed in public.
- They are performed for profit (prostitution).
- They are between a therapist and a patient and in violation of the laws of that state.

Rape or Sexual Assault

Sex crimes occur often in the United States. The term *sex crime* includes a broad classification of offenses that range from serious offenses to nuisance offenses and private offenses between consenting adults. Historically, the term *rape* was used to identify the crime of nonconsensual sexual relations by force or threat of force. The National Institute of Justice (NIJ), the research and development branch of the U.S. Justice Department, defines **rape** as vaginal, oral, or anal penetration achieved through the use of force or threat of force. Rape includes penetration of the vagina or anus by penis, finger, tongue, or some other object manipulated by the rapist. Many state criminal codes use a similar definition.

rape Anal, vaginal, or oral penetration by force or threat of force.

The criminal codes of the 50 states use the terms *rape*, *sexual assault*, or *sexual battery* when dealing with what the common law called rape and do so in a variety of ways. All the states probably treat "ordinary" rape in much the same way as did the common law, though often listing ordinary rape as a second-degree offense and punishing it as a class B felony.

Aggravated rape, however, is handled differently in different states. For example, "gang" rape, rape committed by multiple offenders, is an aggravated offense under the Florida Sexual Battery statutes. Section 794.0233 of the Florida Statutes provides for enhanced penalties and punishes the offense as a first-degree felony (life felony). Other states simply classify gang rape as a first-degree felony.

Other factors that states use as aggravating factors to elevate a rape or sexual assault to a first-degree or class A felony include inflicting serious bodily harm on the victim, using a deadly weapon such as a knife or gun in the rape, causing the victim to become pregnant, infecting the victim with AIDS or other sexually transmitted disease, anal penetration, or raping a very young child.

sexual assault The crime in most states that includes the crime of rape, as well as other lesser degrees of assault.

The NIJ has estimated that rape (or first-degree **sexual assault**) with female victims occurs over 300,000 times each year, and nearly 93,000 with male victims. In the 2006 National Violence Against Women Survey, the results of which were published by the NIJ,[1] telephone interviews conducted nationwide with 8,000 women and 8,000 men disclosed the following information:

- In the United States, one out of every six women experienced rape or attempted rape at some time in her life; one out of every thirty-three men experienced rape or attempted rape at some time in his life.
- Rape or attempted rape more frequently involves younger victims, with most victims being under the age of 12 when the rape occurred.
- Most rape victims are women, and most offenders are men.
- When the victim of rape or attempted rape is 18 years of age or older, physical injury is caused to 31.5 percent of female victims and 16.1 percent of male victims.
- Only 19.1 percent of the female victims of rape or attempted rape, and 12.9 percent of male victims, over the age of 18, reported the incident to the police.
- The reasons given for failure to report a rape or attempted rape were "fear of retaliation by the offender," "too ashamed or embarrassed," "thought the matter was a minor incident," or "not a police matter."
- Where female victims reported the rape or attempted rape, 37 percent resulted in prosecutions, with convictions in 46.2 percent of the prosecutions. Thirteen percent of the female victims sought and obtained restraining orders against the offenders; 69.9 percent reported that the restraining order was violated.

In 2008 the Federal Bureau of Justice Statistics, National Crime Victimization Survey, reported that based on a broader sample than that used in the 2006 study cited above, the incidence of rape and domestic violence is increasing. The Crime Victimization survey interviewed 73,600 individuals in 41,500 households about domestic and sexual violence. It concluded that reported rapes increased 25% over 2006.

The Importance of Corroborative Evidence in a Rape Case

Today, in virtually every state, a rape conviction can rest solely on the uncorroborated testimony of the victim.[2] However, **corroborative evidence** (evidence affirming and supporting statements of the victim) is very important in most cases.

corroborative evidence Physical evidence or witness testimony other than from the victim that supports the claim that a crime occurred.

Statistics show that in as many as 40 percent of the cases that come into the offices of prosecutors in large cities, rape charges are not issued. Lack of corroborating evidence is probably the principal reason. Statements of the complaining witness can be corroborated and affirmed by the following:

- Scratches, bruises, injuries, torn clothing, or blood stains from either the victim or the suspect.
- Witnesses who heard screams or the sounds of a struggle, or observed either party before, during, or immediately after the assault.
- Color photographs of bruises, black-and-blue marks, lacerations, cuts, scratches, or other injuries to either party, as these injuries will disappear within a few days through the healing process.

- Blood, semen, saliva, or nail scrapings taken from the victim or suspect, as well as pubic and head hair obtained at the scene of the crime and from the bodies of the victim and suspect. Such genetic material could result in a positive DNA identification of the offender.
- Weapons or instruments that may have been used to force the victim to submit to the assault.
- Buttons, torn clothing, or other items that the victim or suspect may have lost in the struggle.
- Soiled or stained clothing of the suspect and victim that contains blood, seminal stains, or other evidence of the crime.
- Fingerprints found at the scene of the sexual assault or elsewhere that can be used to corroborate or to identify the suspect.
- Observations by doctors and nurses and samples of fluids from vagina, rectum, or oral cavity showing that forcible intercourse had occurred.
- If DNA evidence from blood, semen, saliva, and so forth is available, it could prove the identity of the offender almost conclusively.

In a rape case, whether the state has a strong or a weak case in going to trial depends on the physical evidence available and the ability of the complaining witness to testify. Lack of corroborative physical evidence and/or the inability of the complaining witness to testify effectively could cause the case to be viewed as weak.

Possible Responses to a Threat of Rape

Studies show that most women, especially young women, fear rape more than any other crime. How should a woman respond to an imminent threat of rape?

- *Should she scream, fight back, and try to escape?* Studies show that women who resist decrease the odds of completed rape by 80 percent. But they increase the likelihood of being physically injured. Experts say that it is better to be raped than to risk being permanently injured or killed.
- *Should she try to talk the man out of it?* Women have tried many different tactics in trying to avoid rape. They have pretended to be pregnant, or have stated they have a sexually transmitted disease, or have AIDS. They have fainted, cried hysterically, acted insane or vomited, urinated, or acted very ill.
- *Should she grit her teeth and bear it?* This is an available option that the victim might choose. Or the victim may be able to combine one or both of the above two in an effort to avoid being raped.

An *FBI Law Enforcement Bulletin* article entitled "RAPE: The Dangers of Providing Confrontational Advice" (June 1986) discussed the question of a woman's response to rape and provided the following advice:

Different motives operate in different offenders and, therefore, what might be successful in dissuading one type of assailant might, in fact, only aggravate the situation with a different type of offender.

Victims must tailor their type of resistance to the environment in which the attack is occurring.

[T]he success of resistance behavior depends largely on the victim's ability to apply it.
We suggest to those who speak publicly on [this] subject to avoid offering single solutions to their audiences.

Different Sexual Assault Statutes Require Different Degrees of Proof

Sexual assault and rape statutes in the 50 states are worded in many different ways. Prosecutors must be prepared to prove beyond a reasonable doubt all the essential elements of the crime that they have charged.

Under "threat of force" and "forcible compulsion" statutes, prosecutors must show that the victim's resistance was overcome by the threat of the use of force, causing the victim to submit to the rape. It must be shown that the victim had a genuine and real fear that imminent force would be used. In some states, sexual assault is defined generally to include any sexual penetration obtained "against the will" of the victim. If force is used, the sexual assault is classified as a more serious felony. The Colorado sexual assault statute, Col. Stat. § 18-3-402 (4)(a), is such a statute. In *People v. Keene*, 226 P.3d 1140 (Colo. App. 2009), the court held that the defendant's own body weight can be the "physical force" that triggers the increased severity of the assault, if in fact the victim struggled and the weight prevented her from escaping.

The California courts have held that

> While generally the woman has the power to determine for herself the extent to which she feels she can safely resist, ... her conduct must always be measured against the degree of force manifested and each case must be resolved on all of the circumstances present.[3]

In both of the following two cases, the victims knew the defendants. The defendants in both cases used little or no force.

Case and State	Facts of the Case	Wording and Requirement of the State Statute
People v. Iniguez, Supreme Court of California, 872 P.2d 1183 (1994)	While the victim was asleep in the defendant's house, he took her clothes off. She testified that she froze when she woke up and "just laid [sic] there" and submitted because she feared he would become violent if she did not submit. The conviction was affirmed.	The wording of the state statute that was charged required a showing that the rape was "accomplished against a person's will by means of force, violence, or fear of immediate and unlawful bodily injury" (no requirement of proof of actual resistance by victim).
Commonwealth v. Berkowitz, Supreme Court of Pennsylvania, 641 A.2d 1161 (1994)	Just repeatedly saying "no" was not enough under this statute. In a college dorm room, the defendant closed the door, placed the victim on the bed, and raped her as she repeatedly said "no." No physical or threatening force was used in removing her clothes and raping her. The victim did not testify that she feared violence if she did not submit.	The rape statute required "forcible compulsion" in achieving sexual intercourse rather than terms of nonconsent. Pennsylvania has an indecent assault crime that has no requirement of forcible compulsion and is defined as indecent contact without consent. This should have been the criminal charge for the facts in this case.

CASE CLOSE-UP

Where a rape or sexual assault statute requires proof of the use of force or physical resistance by the victim, questions can arise about when and how those elements of the statute can be proved. The following two cases illustrate how consent, force, and physical resistance can become issues in a sexual assault or rape case.

State v. Grimes
New Hampshire Supreme Court
876 A.2d 753 (2005)

A defendant was charged with Aggravated Felony Sexual Assault (AFSA) under New Hampshire RSA 632-A: 2. Under this statute, a sexual assault is proved if sexual intercourse occurs under a number of specified circumstances, including if the victim was "physically helpless to resist." The defendant was convicted of AFSA and appealed.

Evidence at the trial disclosed that the defendant and the victim were playing a variation of checkers, during which each time a piece was lost the loser was required to drink a shot of alcohol. Unknown to the victim, the defendant was filling her shot glass and convincing her she had "forgotten" to drink it after her last loss. The victim testified she became drunk and sick and told defendant she needed to lie down. She awoke to find the defendant in bed with her, touching her breasts. She told him to stop, but when he did not, she testified that she "felt numb from the neck down" and lacked the strength to push him away. She passed out again and awoke to find the defendant having intercourse with her. She told him to stop but lacked the strength to push him off her body. The jury convicted the defendant of AFSA.

The defendant argued on appeal that the evidence was insufficient to prove an element of the crime—that is, that the victim was "physically helpless to resist." He argued that the fact the victim woke up and objected to his actions showed that she wasn't physically helpless to resist, and as a result her failure to resist made that element of the statute unproved. He directed the court to cases in other jurisdictions that had limited the "helpless to resist" language to victims who were asleep, unconscious, or "for any other reason unable to communicate unwillingness to do an act."

The New Hampshire Supreme Court rejected the defendant's argument. It reasoned that "physically helpless" under the New Hampshire statute required only a finding that the victim lacked the physical ability to resist the defendant's acts, even if she had the verbal ability to object to them. Because the victim testified that she felt "numb" from the waist down, the court concluded the prosecution introduced ample evidence to prove she was "physically helpless to resist" the defendant's acts. The defendant's conviction for AFSA was affirmed.

Sulliveres v. Comm.
Supreme Judicial Court of Massachusetts
865 N.E.2d 1086 (2007)

The defendant was charged with rape under Mass. G.L. 266, §22, which requires proof of sexual penetration "by force and against the will" of the victim. At his trial the evidence disclosed that late one night the defendant entered the bedroom the victim shared with her boyfriend, the defendant's brother. The defendant began initiating sexual contact with the victim, who responded by calling the defendant by his brother's name. They completed the sexual acts, with the victim continuing to believe the defendant was his brother. When she discovered otherwise, she informed the police and the defendant was charged with rape.

The jury was unable to reach a verdict in defendant's trial, and the judge declared a mistrial. Before the prosecution could begin a new trial, the defendant moved to dismiss the charges against him. He argued that the prosecution could not produce any new evidence against him relating to the "use of force" requirement and that the existing evidence would not support a guilty verdict. Because of this, the defendant contended a second trial would violate the Massachusetts common law double jeopardy rules. The trial court overruled his motion, and the defendant appealed.

The Supreme Judicial Court reversed the trial court, and ordered the dismissal of the charges on double jeopardy grounds. The court stated that in an earlier decision, *Comm. v. Goldenberg*, 155 N.E.2d 187 (1959), it held that a defendant could not be convicted of rape when he tricked the victim into having sex with him. In that case, a woman went to a psychotherapist for an abortion. The therapist told the woman she would have to have sex with him in order to make the abortion procedure more effective. The court held his actions did not amount to "force" under the Massachusetts rape statute. Because that decision was reached almost 50 years before the prosecution in this case, and the legislature had not changed the language of the rape statute, the court refused to reconsider the holding in *Goldenberg* and ordered the charges against the defendant be dismissed under the Massachusetts common law double jeopardy rules.

The Maryland Court of Appeals has noted that the "vast majority of jurisdictions have required that the victim's fear be reasonably grounded in order to obviate the need for either proof of actual force on the part of the assailant or physical resistance on the part of the victim."[4] Pointing out that the reasonableness of a victim's apprehension or fear was plainly a question of fact for a jury to determine, the Maryland Court of Appeals held:[5]

> It was for the jury to observe the witnesses and their demeanor, and to judge their credibility and weigh their testimony. Quite obviously, the jury disbelieved Rusk [defendant] and believed Pat's [victim] testimony.
>
> * * *
>
> Just where persuasion ends and force begins in cases like the present is essentially a factual issue, to be resolved in light of the controlling legal precepts. That threats of force need not be made in any particular manner in order to put a person in fear of bodily harm is well established…. Indeed, conduct, rather than words, may convey the threat.
>
> * * *
>
> That a victim did not scream out for help or attempt to escape, while bearing on the question of consent, is unnecessary where she is restrained by fear of violence.

Defenses in Acquaintance Rape or After-the-Date Rape

More than half of the forcible rapes that are reported are committed by friends, acquaintances, or relatives. The after-the-date rape (or dates who rape) case can be particularly difficult to prove unless evidence of actual physical violence exists. Because of the friendly and sometimes close relationship that existed between the parties, defendants could use the following arguments in court:

Yes, the Parties Had Sex, but ...

She consented ...	and her conduct shows she consented (after all, she invited me up to her apartment, or she came up to my apartment late at night).
I honestly thought she consented....	"It is a defense to a charge of forcible rape that the defendant entertained a reasonable and good faith belief that the female person voluntarily consented to engage in sexual intercourse" (California Jury Instruction 10.23).[6]
She never did say "no" ...	and I thought that because she didn't say "no," she was consenting.
She consented, then changed her mind during the sex ...	and did not clearly communicate her change of mind.
The manner in which the woman dressed was sexy and provocative, as well as her conduct (such as placing her hand on the defendant's upper thigh), ...	led the defendant on, and she did not object until things got out of hand (a well-known professional football player was acquitted in a 1987 rape trial using this defense).
She consented, but later developed guilt feelings and regretted what she did, ...	but before and during the sex, she consented. (This defense is sometimes used with the "groupie" defense. Athletes and performers charged with rape often use this defense, arguing that the victim pursued and pestered them.)

Convictions for Lesser or Other Offenses in Weak Rape Cases

A rape case can be classified as a weak case if there is a lack of corroborating evidence, if the woman is an ineffective witness or becomes so upset that she cannot testify effectively, or if the woman's conduct had been such that it could be interpreted as giving consent to the sex. Other factors that should also be considered are the effectiveness and persuasive abilities of the defense lawyer and the type of witness that the defendant might be.

In anticipation of such problems, prosecutors could file a number of lesser charges to fall back on. Examples of such charges are as follows:

- *Sexual Battery or Sexual Assault:* For example, see the case of *People v. Margiolas*, in which the rape charge was dropped because of lack of evidence of resistance, and the defendant was convicted of a misdemeanor sexual battery, because he admitted that he forcibly unbuttoned the woman's blouse despite her verbal as well as physical objections.[7]
- *Burglary:* As an unlawful entry into a building or dwelling with intent to commit an offense (in some states a felony) or intent to steal, burglary convictions were sustained in the following cases in which the male defendants had no right to enter the premises of the women:
  a. *State v. Felt*, 816 P.2d 1213 (Ore. App. 1991), in which a former lover had forced intercourse after a date.
  b. *State v. Weber*, 814 S.W.2d 298 (Mo. App. 1991), in which the defendant kicked in the door and entered the victim's home for the purpose of committing rape.
  c. *Cladd v. State*, 398 So. 2d 442 (1981), in which the Supreme Court of Florida sustained the conviction of burglary when the separated husband broke into the wife's home twice, severely beating the wife on the first break-in.

The Report of Rape Rule and the Effect of Delay in Reporting

After a sexual assault, the victim could be confused and fearful of her assailant. This could result in a delay in reporting the crime. A long delay could raise questions of the credibility of the victim, it could substantially diminish the possibility of obtaining physical evidence of the rape, and it could prevent the person receiving the report of rape from testifying as to the statements and circumstances. The Model Penal Code, Section 213.6 (4) (the report of rape rule), states that no prosecution may be brought if the complainant fails to report the sexual assault within three months of its occurrence or, if the victim is less than 16 years old, within three months of the time a parent or other competent adult learns of the assault.

A person to whom a rape victim has excitedly reported a rape can testify as to the statements and circumstances under the report of rape or excited utterance exceptions to the hearsay rule.[8] Such testimony is important corroborative evidence in proving a rape charge.

Because a child may delay for some time in reporting a sexual assault, state statutes and court decisions give children more time in reporting sexual assaults. Failure to make an immediate report is generally not relevant in such cases. However, where the length of time since the sexual assault is extremely long, courts sometimes permit evidence of the delay to be admissible on the issue of the credibility of the complainant.

For example, in *State v. P.H.*, 803 A.2d 661 (N.J. App. 2002), the appellate court reversed a conviction for sexual assault on a child because the trial court instructed the jury that it must disregard the child's delay in reporting the assaults when evaluating the child's credibility. In that case, the child testified the defendant sexually assaulted her on six or seven occasions between 1984, when she was 6, and 1990, when she was 12 years old. She did not report these assaults until 1996. The court stated that the Confrontation Clause and Due Process Clause of the U.S. Constitution prohibited the trial judge from instructing the jury to disregard the delay.

The FBI Uniform Crime Reports states that "a national average of 15% of all forcible rapes reported to police were determined by our investigations to be unfounded. In other words, the police established that no forcible rape offense or attempt occurred." Of course, sexual assault is not the only offense subject to false reporting. About the same percentage of burglaries and auto thefts are also falsely reported, primarily for the purpose of obtaining insurance money. Armed robberies of single-employee businesses are sometimes falsely reported to the financial benefit of that employee, and one can only speculate about the number of homes, businesses, and other buildings that are destroyed in "accidental" fires.

The fact that an alleged victim of a sexual assault has made false reports of sexual assaults in the past can be an issue under a Rape Shield law, as discussed in the next section.

Rape Shield Laws

rape shield laws Laws passed by many states to limit the extent to which defense attorneys in a rape case can inquire into the victim's past sexual life.

Most states have enacted **rape shield laws** that forbid the use of evidence of a rape victim's past sexual conduct with others and evidence of her reputation. Under the protection of rape shield laws, victims appearing as witnesses in a sexual assault case therefore do not have to defend their reputations or past sexual conduct.

Rule 412 of the Federal Rules of Evidence is an example of a rape shield law and is similar to many such laws adopted by states. It provides that in a criminal trial of a sexual assault charge, evidence (1) offered to prove the victim engaged in other sexual behavior, or (2) offered to prove the victim's sexual predisposition, is inadmissible. There are three exceptions to this rule: evidence is admissible if it is (1) evidence of specific sexual behavior of the victim offered to prove another person was the source of semen or other physical evidence, (2) evidence of specific past sexual contact between the victim and the accused, if offered to prove consent, or (3) evidence the exclusion of which

NATIONAL PROBLEMS IN THE SEX CRIME AREA

Reports of Sexual Assaults and the Anonymous Reporting Option

It is generally agreed by those involved with domestic violence and sexual assault that a very high percentage, perhaps as much as 80%, of rapes and other sexual assaults go unreported. Many victims of sexual assaults are afraid or too embarrassed to inform law enforcement officers of the assault. The failure to report is a problem for law enforcement, both because the sexual assailant remains at large and may commit more sexual crimes, and because the failure to make a prompt report can result in lost evidence of the sexual assault, in particular DNA evidence. To alleviate victims' concerns and facilitate more reports of sexual assaults, Congress as part of the Violence Against Women Act, 18 U.S.C. § 2261 *et seq.*, requires states to make forensic medical exams available to victims of sexual violence and establishes a grant program to provide funds to pay for the medical examinations. Victims taking these examinations have no obligation to report the sexual assault or the examination's results to law enforcement, but they may do so on a voluntary, anonymous basis. A formal investigation by law enforcement will be undertaken only if the victim requests such an investigation. See the May 2010 *FBI Law Enforcement Bulletin*, "Options for Reporting Sexual Violence," at the FBI website, www.fbi.gov.

Failure of States to Test Rape Kits

When a sexual assault victim receives medical attention, medical professionals are trained to collect forensic evidence in "rape kits," which are then forwarded to the police to aid in their investigation of the sexual assault. For a variety of reasons, most states have a huge backlog of these kits, which remain untested. A report of the Human Rights Watch published July 7, 2010, states that in Illinois, of 7,494 rape kits turned over to police since 1995, only 1,474 have been tested, which suggested that 80% of rape kits are not being tested. In Los Angeles, a city audit conducted in 2009 found over 7,000 untested rape kits in the LAPD freezer, many of them more than 10 years old.

Failure to use the evidence in rape kits has a direct effect on arrests and convictions, studies show. In Illinois, the arrest rate for sexual assault crimes was about 11%. In New York City, once a mandatory rape kit testing rule was put in place, the arrest rate climbed from 40% to 70%. In July 2010 the Illinois legislature passed the 2010 Sexual Assault Evidence Submission Act, PL 096-1011. Effective October 15, 2020, police departments must within 10 days of the receipt of a rape kit submit it for tests, and the tests must be performed and results reported within 180 days.

Sexual Assaults in Prisons

In response to the growing problem of sexual assaults in prisons, in 2003 Congress passed the Prison Rape Elimination Act, 42 U.S.C. § 15602. The stated purpose of the Act was to provide the means and funds to reduce the incidence of

would violate the constitutional rights of the accused. In *United States v. Pumpkin Seed*, 572 F.3d 552 (8th Cir. 2009), the court upheld a trial court's decision to exclude evidence that the defendant was not the source of semen and pubic hair found on the victim. The court reasoned that since the prosecution did not offer the semen or pubic hair as evidence of the rape, that evidence was not relevant to any issue in the trial.

Before rape shield laws, a victim's reputation was deemed "fair game" by defense lawyers, and the victim could be forced to defend her entire sexual history. Rape shield laws were enacted to encourage the reporting of sexual assaults and to forbid evidence that would prejudice a jury. Such evidence is also irrelevant to the issue of guilt or innocence before the court. Rape shield laws apply to male victims as well as female victims. Evidence offered to prove that the victim was a homosexual, or had engaged in past homosexual acts, would be inadmissible under most rape shield laws.[9] In the 2010 case of *State v. Rackliffe*, 2010 WL 2901620 (Maine 2010), the court rejected the contention of a sexual assaults in prisons in the United States. Based on studies done in 2007 under this Act, in March of 2008 the Department of Justice's National Institute of Justice published a report of the Bureau of Justice Statistics. (NIJ # 259). The report concluded that over 60,500 sexual assaults occurred in U.S. prisons every year and that about 6,500 of these assaults were reported to prison officials. Of the reported cases, 47% involved assaults by other inmates, and 53% were assaults by corrections staff members. The report had several recommendations, including training programs for prison officers, and methods of facilitating corroboration of assaults, a major problem for inmates who do report assaults.

Monitoring Sex Offenders in the United States

Since the first sex offender registration acts were passed (see discussion in this chapter), the number of persons required to register has mushroomed each year. In a June 2010 report the Center for Missing and Exploited Children stated that 716,750 individuals had registered as sex offenders. The number of sex offenders on state lists makes the lists almost useless: a state the size of Georgia might have as many as 18,000 individuals on its list, including rapists, kidnappers, flashers, or even juveniles who had consensual sex. Each state requires all sex offenders to register, and it also requires persons on the list to give the state a new address when they move. The federal SORNA Act requires all registered sex offenders who move from state to state to register in a new state; it is a crime punishable by up to 10 years in prison to fail to register. Notwithstanding these requirements, it is estimated that over 100,000 paroled sex offenders have failed to register or have given false information. It has been a sometimes overwhelming task for local law enforcement agencies to keep track of these sex offenders. See the 9/2/09 *New York Times* article, "Plenty of Data on Offenders, but Little on Its Effects."

Sex Offenders and State Licensing Laws

One question sex offender registration laws present to state officials is the effect, if any, sex offender status has on the granting of state licenses. Millions of work and professional licenses are granted each year, including security guards, locksmiths, real estate brokers, barbers, funeral directors, lawyers, and medical professionals. In some professions, such as physicians, elaborate licensing provisions help answer that question. The Missouri physician license statute, V.A.M.S. § 334.100, permits the licensing agency to deny a physician's license if the applicant has been convicted of a sexual offense. This section was used to deny a license to a physician in the case of *State v. Hartenbach*, 216 S.W.3d 158 (Mo. App. 2007). In many other areas, the licensing criteria make no mention of sex offender status or convictions; as an example, the South Carolina license requirements for a funeral director's license, Code 1976, § 40-1-140, make a prior criminal conviction the basis for license denial only if the crime related to the profession. It is questionable whether denial of a license without specific statutory or regulatory reference to sex offender status is permitted.

defendant convicted of sexual assault on a male victim that proof of the victim's sexual orientation was relevant on the issue of consent to the sexual assault.

However, exceptions are made in rape shield laws to allow the introduction of relevant, probative evidence at trial. In the U.S. Supreme Court case of *Olden v. Kentucky*, 488 U.S. 227, 109 S. Ct. 480 (1988), the defendant sought to prove that the victim made up her charge of sexual battery against him in order to protect her relationship with her boyfriend. The U.S. Supreme Court reversed the defendant's conviction, holding that his Sixth Amendment right to conduct reasonable cross-examination had been violated.

In *State v. Baker*, 679 N.W.2d 7 (Iowa 2006), the Iowa Supreme Court stated it was joining the majority of state courts that permitted a defendant in a rape case to offer evidence that the victim had in the past made false rape claims against others. Since such evidence is not about past sexual behavior, the court held the rape shield law inapplicable. A similar result was reached in *In Re K.W.*, 666 S.E.2d 490 (N.C. App. 2008),

OLD RAPE LAWS AND NEW SEXUAL ASSAULT LAWS

Under Old Rape Laws and the Common Law	**Statutory Changes Enacted in Most States Since the 1970s**
■ Only females could be the victims of rape.	■ Any person (male or female) may be a victim.
■ Only a male could directly commit the crime.	■ Any person (male or female) can directly commit the crime. See the 1986 case of *State v. Stevens*, 510 A.2d 1070 (Me.), in which the court held that an adult woman could be charged with having sexual intercourse with a 13-year-old boy.
■ A husband could not rape his wife (under the common law, however, the husband could be charged with assault and battery).	■ A husband can be charged with the rape of his wife under the law of states that have made this change from the common law.
■ Rape was defined in one (or at most a few) degree.	■ A variety of degrees of criminal conduct are defined in more specific language. "Ordinary" rape, which could be second-degree rape, is the most common criminal charge, while "aggravated" rape, such as gang rape or rape with use of a deadly weapon, or rape resulting in physical injury or pregnancy, is usually first-degree sexual assault.
■ Rape was defined only as the insertion of the penis into a vagina by force and against the will of the female.	■ Sexual intercourse is broadly defined not only as vaginal intercourse but also as "cunnilingus, fellatio, anal intercourse, or any other intrusion, however slight, of any part of a person's body or of any object into the genital or anal opening of another, but emission of semen is not required." See Section 940.225(5)(c) of the Wisconsin Criminal Code.
■ Common law rape did not include the crime of offensive touching (however, this could be charged either as disorderly conduct or assault and sometimes battery).	■ Many modern sexual assault laws include the offense of offensive touching in that they forbid "sexual contact"(intentional touching of an intimate part of another person's body without consent for sexual gratification). (See, e.g., Neb. Rev. Stat. § 28–319.)
■ "Utmost resistance" and resistance were required under the old common law.	■ "Utmost resistance" is no longer required for the crime of rape. Instead, many states require proof that the sex act was done "without consent" and "against the will" of the victim. Wisconsin, for example, eliminated the requirement of utmost resistance in the 1970s.
■ Rape was classified as a crime against sexual morality.	■ Sexual assault is more often classified as a crime against a person.

where the court interpreted the North Carolina Rape Shield law to be inapplicable to evidence of false rape reports. Colorado's Rape Shield Law, C.R.S.A. § 18-3-407, specifically provides that evidence of past false reports is admissible. However, in *People v. Weiss*, 133 P.3d 1180 (Colo. 2006), the Colorado Supreme Court held that such evidence must be proof that the past rape reports were determined to be false. It reversed the decision of a trial court that permitted a defendant to introduce evidence of previous rape reports by the victim, holding that just because no charges were filed based on the reports did not make them false under the rape shield exception.

Exceptions vary from state to state, and the rape shield law of each state must be consulted to determine the exact nature of the exceptions.

Statutory Rape

statutory rape Sexual intercourse with a minor female under a certain age, usually 18. Consent and, generally, mistake as to age are not defenses to this crime.

All states have statutes that make sexual intercourse with a female who is not the wife of the perpetrator a criminal offense if the female is under the age stated by the state criminal code. This crime is called **statutory rape**.

The origin of current U.S. statutes goes back to the English statute of 1275, when the age of consent was set at 12 years. In 1576, the age was reduced to 10 years. California, for example, enacted its first statute in 1850 making the age 10. In 1913, it was fixed at 18, where it remains.

In 1981, the California statutory rape statute was challenged before the U.S. Supreme Court when it was alleged that the statute unlawfully discriminates on the basis of gender, because men alone were criminally liable under the statute. The Court upheld the power of the states to enact such statutes in the case of *Michael M. v. Superior Court of Sonoma County*,[10] holding:

> We are satisfied not only that the prevention of illegitimate pregnancy is at least one of the "purposes" of the statute, but that the State has a strong interest in preventing such pregnancy. At the risk of stating the obvious, teenage pregnancies, which

---

OTHER TYPES OF RAPES OR SEXUAL ASSAULTS

Type of Rape	Characteristics	Most Common Defense Used
Rape in which the victim was mentally defective or diseased and incapable of giving consent	This type of criminal statute seeks to protect people who are mentally incompetent and incapable of giving consent to sexual acts. The offense usually requires that the state show that the defendant knew or had reason to know of the mental incapacity of the victim. See, e.g., *Comm. v. Fuller*, 845 N.E.2d 434 (Mass. App. 2006), *cert. denied* 848 N.E.2d 1211 (2006).	Defendant denies that he knew of the mental incapacity of the victim or that any sex act occurred.
Rape by use of a date rape drug	Rohypnol ("roofies") and GHB are odorless, nearly tasteless, and potentially lethal to a victim. They are slipped into a drink to drug and sexually assault women.	The woman has no memory of what happened, and most often there are no other witnesses. With no witnesses, it is important to obtain a urine sample immediately to prove the presence of a date rape drug.
Sexual intercourse obtained by threats other than threats of violence, which would be forcible rape	In the few states that have enacted a statute such as this, the threat might be to disclose information that the victim did not want disclosed, or it could be a job-related threat that the victim would be fired or lose a promotionif she refused to have sex. Employment and sexual harassment laws also provide civil remedies for such acts.	No threat was made or implied, or no sexual act occurred.

SEXUAL MISBEHAVIOR OR A FELONY?

An 18½-year-old high school senior has a 15-year-old girlfriend. They have sex together, with both parties consenting. Is this a case of "kids will be kids," in which both parties are sexually active? Some law enforcement officers, prosecutors, and judges point out that young men have been doing this going back to the horse-and-buggy days. Are they correct? Do such comments condone and approve of such behavior?

If the girl's parents discover what is going on and angrily demand prosecution, should a prosecutor charge the young man with a felony? If high school officials come upon the couple during a sex act and demand that an example be set, should the young man (an adult) be charged with the felony of having sex with a minor?

If the girl did not consent to the sex, the case would uniformly be charged as rape (or forcible sexual assault). However, when the parties are both young and both consent, few of the cases are charged criminally.

Should such cases be left to the discretion of parents, law enforcement officers, and prosecutors, as they have been in past years? Or should state legislative bodies provide additional laws governing such situations? An example of such a proposed enactment provides:

Criminal charges cannot be issued if the child consents and the offender is no more than four years older than the victim (for example, a 19-year-old has sexual relations with a 16-year-old).

have increased dramatically over the last two decades, have significant social, medical and economic consequences for both the mother and her child, and the State. Of particular concern to the State is that approximately half of all teenage pregnancies end in abortion. And of those children who are born, their illegitimacy makes them likely candidates to become wards of the State.

We need not be medical doctors to discern that young men and young women are not similarly situated with respect to the problems and the risks of sexual intercourse. Only women may become pregnant and they suffer disproportionately the profound physical, emotional, and psychological consequences of sexual activity. The statute at issue here protects women from sexual intercourse at an age when those consequences are particularly severe.

Honest mistake as to the age of the minor is not permitted as a defense in most states that forbid statutory rape. See, for example, *State v. Jadowski*, 680 N.W.2d 810 (Wis. 2004), where the court held that even if the child intentionally misleads the defendant about her age, it is no defense to a charge of statutory rape. Nor is consent by the child a defense, even if investigation shows that the child was a willing participant in the sex acts.

≡ The Crime of Incest

incest Sexual relations between persons closely related.

The crime of **incest** may be committed by adults within a family, but the public concern and prosecution are generally for cases involving children. Like statutory rape, the crime does not require a showing that force was used (or threatened) or that the victim did not consent.

Incest was not a crime under common law, nor was it statutorized in England until 1908. Before that time, the offense was dealt with by ecclesiastical (religious) courts. Today, probably all the states have statutes making the offense a crime. Generally, incest in the first degree involves sexual intercourse. Incest in the second degree involves sexual contact without penetration. Generally, incest is limited to sexual relations with a descendent, ancestor, brother, or sister of the offender. The category of "descendant" usually includes adopted children or stepchildren.

An article entitled "Incest: The Last Taboo" in the *FBI Law Enforcement Bulletin* (January 1984) states:

> One thing every State has in common is the prohibition of marriage between parents and children, between siblings, between grandparents and grandchildren, uncles and nieces, and aunts and nephews.
>
> Incest is usually defined as sexual exploitation between persons so closely related that marriage is prohibited by law. While this definition indicates that there is sexual intercourse, it is important to note that not all incestuous relationships involve intercourse. The term *intercourse* refers specifically to sexual activity between two individuals of the opposite sex. Beyond this usual definition are two other types of sexual child molestation that are closely related to incest and share some common features.

The article also points out that an estimated 60,000 to 100,000 female children are sexually abused annually and that 80 percent of sexual abuse is not reported. It is believed that incest affects more than 10 percent of all American families, with at least 5,000 cases of father–daughter incest.

Penalties for incest, the article reports, range from 90 days to life imprisonment. Enforcement, however, is practically impossible unless a member of the family cooperates. Unfortunately, the credibility of the child victim is often attacked and severely questioned.

In 90 percent of cases, the victim is female, and the abuse may commence while the child is too young to realize the significance of the problem. When the child becomes knowledgeable about what has happened, or is happening, the child is apt to feel guilt, betrayal, confusion, and fright.

As stated above, incest is similar to statutory rape in that consent is not a defense, nor is use of force required for conviction. Unlike statutory rape, however, in most states the incest statute requires proof that the defendant knew the person was related to the defendant in the statutory manner. Thus, a reasonable belief that the other person is not related to the defendant would be a defense to a charge of incest. This belief must relate to the absence of a biological relationship between the defendant and the other person.

In *State v. Hall*, 48 P.3d 350 (Wash. App. 2002), the court affirmed a conviction for second-degree incest of the defendant with his biological daughter. The court rejected the defendant's argument that because he had surrendered his parental rights when the girl was 4 years old, he did not believe she was his daughter, and thus he lacked the knowledge required by the incest statute. The court said all the statute required was knowledge that the girl was his biological daughter, because that fact made her the defendant's descendant.

≡ H.I.V. and AIDS-Related Crimes

H.I.V. is the virus that causes AIDS. When AIDS first became known to the medical establishment in the 1970s, there were few medications or treatments for AIDS patients, and in most cases death occurred within a few months of diagnosis of the disease. During the AIDS epidemics of the 1980s and 1990s, widespread fear of the spread of this disease led many states to enact criminal laws specific to the spread of the disease.

However, in the past 10 to 15 years, knowledge and treatment of AIDS and H.I.V. have improved substantially, and the fear of infection has subsided somewhat. Notwithstanding those medical changes, the criminal laws adopted by more than 30 states remain on the books and continue to be enforced.

In virtually all states, knowingly, recklessly, or (in some) negligently exposing or infecting another person to the AIDS virus is a felony. This is often charged under a specific AIDS or H.I.V. statute; an example is Louisiana's Intentional Exposure to AIDS Virus statute, LSA-R.S. 114:43.5. In other states, the offense is charged as an "assault with a deadly weapon" or similar crime. In *State v. Price*, 834 N.E.2d 847 (Ohio App. 2005), the court upheld the assault with a deadly weapon conviction of a hemophiliac defendant who spat on a police officer during an altercation. The court said that because of his condition, the defendant's saliva carried blood cells, and the saliva contained the AIDS virus. This, the court said, made the defendant's "whole body" a deadly weapon.

In 2010 a man in Florida was charged with a first-degree felony after police learned he had sex several times with another man without telling that man he was H.I.V. positive. See the 4/12/10 *New York Times* article titled "Equestrian Is Facing H.I.V.-Related Felony Charge."

The U.S. Center for Disease Control and Prevention states in its "Basic Information About HIV and AIDS" publication that H.I.V. is primarily spread through sexual contact or the exchange of blood. That publication states that the virus cannot be transmitted through tears, sweat, or saliva. It also states that as of the publication date of March 2010, "There has been no documented case of H.I.V. being transmitted by spitting." Severe bites can transmit the virus, but only if the bites involve severe trauma and include the presence of blood. The publication states that H.I.V. cannot be spread if the skin is not broken.

States continue to prosecute AIDS carriers who spit on others. In a *New York Times* article of 5/16/08 titled "Prison for Man With H.I.V. Who Spat on Police Officer," it was reported that a Dallas, Texas, homeless man was sentenced to 35 years in prison for spitting in the mouth and eyes of a police officer. The man was sentenced as a habitual offender, since this was the third time he had fought with officers, biting the officers in the prior arrests.

≡ Laws that Require Registration for Sex Offenders (Megan's Law)

In the 2002 case *McKune v. Lile*, the U.S. Supreme Court stated:

> Sex offenders are a serious threat in this nation.... Between 1980 and 1994 the population of imprisoned sex offenders increased at a faster rate than for any other category of violent crime.... Victims of sexual assault are most often juveniles ... nearly 4 in 10 violent sex offenders said their victims were 12 or younger. [When released from prison] sex offenders are more likely than any other type of offender to be re-arrested for a new rape or sexual assault.[11]

Megan's laws Laws passed in many states requiring convicted sex offenders to register with a state or local registration office. Named after a young girl killed by a convicted sex offender.

In response to these grim statistics, in the 1990s states began passing registration laws for sexual offenders. These laws, called **Megan's laws** after the name of a child killed by a sexual offender in 1994, require sex offenders to register their name and address when released from prison. In 2006 Congress passed the federal Sex Offender Registration and Notification Act (SORNA), 42 U.S.C. § 16913, and 18 U.S.C. § 2250 authorizes up to a 10-year prison sentence for failure to register.

State laws usually list offenses for which registration is mandatory and those for which registration is within the discretion of a sentencing judge. Such laws commonly include some or all of the following features:

- Sex offenders are prohibited from living in a residence located within a specified distance from schools, day care facilities, or other places where children gather; zoning or other local laws might have a similar restriction.
- Sex offenders are required to personally notify authorities when they change their place of employment or change their address. Failure to give this notification is a crime.

SEXUAL INCIDENTS THAT RECEIVED NATIONAL ATTENTION

Three Duke University lacrosse players charged with rape in 2006

A nightclub dancer claimed she was sexually assaulted by the students at a team party. Her claims were found to be "faulty and unreliable," and when the district attorney prosecuting the case failed to check and provide the defense with contradictory evidence, the attorney general of North Carolina intervened and ordered the charges dismissed.

Sexual violence as a weapon and tool of war

It is now recognized that sexual violence has been used for many years as a weapon of terror and a tool of war. Thousands of women were forced into prostitution and sexual enslavement by Japan during World War II, but the crime of sexual slavery was not charged until February 2001 when the Hague War Crimes Court convicted three Bosnian Serbs of rape and sexual enslavement.

Clergypersons, therapists, and doctors

These cases continue to make the news for sex acts committed while providing pastoral or medical services or counseling. Many states make it a criminal offense for a therapist to have sex with a patient. See 812 P.2d 797 (N. Mex. 1991); 499 N.W.2d 31 (Minn. 1993); 397 S.E.2d 1 (Ga. 1991).

The longest and most expensive criminal trial in U.S. history

The McMartin Preschool case ended in 1990, when a California jury acquitted a 62-year-old woman and her 31-year-old son after six years and costs estimated at $13.5 million. The charges of sodomy, rape, and oral copulation were based on statements of 4- and 5-year-old children.

No-name DNA arrest warrants

DNA evidence (genetic fingerprints) is used to convict sex offenders and also to clear and free the innocent. Prosecutors are obtaining no-name arrest warrants to stop statutes of limitations from running when DNA evidence is available, but the identity of the offender continues to be unknown. The no-name warrants can be held for years until a suspect somewhere in the United States matches up with the genetic code of the guilty person.

Parental liability for sexual assaults by minor child

A Wisconsin civil jury found a 15-year-old boy's conduct was "willful and wanton" in making sexual contact with a 10-year-old girl on 20 occasions. Because Wisconsin limits parental liability to $2,500 per incident, the judgment against the boy's parents was limited to $50,000. See *N.E.M. v. Strigel* (95–0755, Supreme Court of Wisconsin).

College rapes and sexual assaults

In an April 2002 report, the National Institute of Alcohol Abuse and Alcoholism estimated that an average of 192 students every day are raped by their dates or sexually assaulted after drinking. See the *New York Times* article "Study Calculates the Effects of College Drinking in the U.S." (April 10, 2002).

The 33-year-old case of Roman Polanski

Roman Polanski, a film director, was indicted in 1977 for six felonies including rape, sodomy, and giving alcohol and a Quaalude to the victim, a 13-year-old girl. The rape and sodomy charges were dropped as part of a plea bargain in which Polanski pled guilty to one count of having sex with a minor. Before he could be sentenced, Polanski fled to Europe, and resided in France. He settled a civil lawsuit with the victim's family. In 2009, while in Switzerland, he was arrested and prosecutors sought extradition back to the United States. After a protracted legal battle, Swiss authorities refused to extradite Polanski. See the article in the *New York Times* of 7/13/2010 "Swiss Reject U.S. Request to Extradite Polanski."

- Sex offenders are required to provide a DNA sample to authorities to be placed in a state and national DNA database.
- An Internet website is to be accessible to the public that includes current information about sex offenders registered in the system. In 2006 Congress created the National Sex Offender Registry, 42 U.S.C. Section 16919. This law requires the FBI to maintain a national registry available to law enforcement and the public that contains the names and addresses of all persons required to register in any state's sex offender registration system.

At least one state, Utah, includes in the sex offender registration requirements that a sex offender must list all "Internet identifiers" used by the offender in any "Internet communication," such as a chat room. Utah Code § 77-27-21.5(14)(i)(j). In *Doe v. Shurtleff*, 2009 WL 2601455 (D. Utah 2009) a federal court upheld this part of the Utah sex offender registration law against a claim it violated the First Amendment, noting that information placed in the registry could only be used in investigation of sex offenses.

In hearings on the National Sex Offender Registry Act, the House Judiciary Committee of the U.S. Congress reported that there were 500,000 convicted sex offenders in the United States but that 100,000 of these offenders were not currently registered or were missing and could not be located.[12] Some prosecutors have stated that state registration laws have caused an increase in the number of sex offenders who disappear, leaving no information about their whereabouts. This creates an increased burden for law enforcement, who must under state and federal laws track down released sex offenders and obtain the required information.

≡ Civil Commitment of Sexually Dangerous Offenders

For many years states have had in place laws that permit the state to bring civil commitment proceedings for the involuntary, temporary commitment of persons who pose a threat to themselves or others. For example, a man who attempted suicide could be temporarily held for mental observation based on the demonstrated danger to his own life. If long-term civil commitment were needed, these laws required a court hearing to determine the need and justification for such commitment.

As an additional response to the threat posed by sexual predators, in the 1990s some states enacted sexual predator laws. These laws permitted the state to obtain civil commitment of convicted sexual offenders after the offenders were released from prison.[13] In *Kansas v. Crane*, 534 U.S. 407, 413 (2002), the U.S. Supreme Court held that before a state could commit a sex offender under a civil commitment statute, it must prove that not only was the offender dangerous and likely to commit more sex crimes but also that the offender had "serious difficulty in controlling [his] behavior." The Court noted that pedophilia was a mental abnormality that made it difficult for an offender to control his behavior and would thus properly be a basis for civil commitment.

In 2006 Congress passed 18 U.S.C. § 4248, which authorizes civil commitment of sexually dangerous prisoners following the expiration of their prison sentence. That section was upheld by the U.S. Supreme Court in the 2010 case of *United States v. Comstock*, 130 S. Ct. 1949.

In 2007 about 2,700 pedophiles, rapists, and other sexual offenders were being held indefinitely under sexual predator laws enacted in 19 states. Because the goal of the commitment was to furnish treatment to the sex offender, rather than punish him for criminal conduct, it is generally held that these civil commitments do not violate the Double Jeopardy Clause or Ex Post Facto Clause of the U.S. Constitution.[14]

Once committed under these programs, many sex offenders are never released. In a study of these programs published in the *New York Times*,[15] it was reported that virtually all those committed were men; only three women have been committed to date. The costs of commitment under these programs averaged more than four times the cost of keeping an inmate in prison. Ages of those committed varied greatly; under Wisconsin's sexual predator law, the youngest of the 283 persons committed was 18, and the oldest 102.

In 2007 New York became the twentieth state to enact a sexual predator law with civil commitment. Critics of the law contended that treatment under the law nearly always failed and that money spent treating the worst sexual offenders would be better spent pursuing the dangerous sexual offenders who continue to abuse at will.[16]

≡ Prostitution

prostitution Providing sex for money or other value.

The crime of **prostitution** can be one of at least three nonmarital acts:

1. Engaging in sexual relations with another person for a fee or something of value
2. Offering (or soliciting) to engage in sexual relations with another person for a fee or something of value
3. Requesting (or agreeing) to pay a fee or something of value to another person for sexual services and acts

The fee or something of value is most often money. Members of either sex may now be convicted of prostitution, as distinguished from the past, when only women could be convicted. Most (if not all) state prostitution statutes forbid males from selling sexual services to other males. Males who offer to pay a woman to engage in sex acts may also be charged with the crime.

Prostitution is often referred to as the world's oldest profession and is described in history's earliest written records. The Bible, for instance, makes many references to whores and whore-mongering. Prostitution is an activity that grows and recedes,

---

JUVENILES WHO COMMIT SEX OFFENSES AGAINST CHILDREN

A 2009 Department of Justice Juvenile Bulletin, www.ojp.usdoj.govlojjdp, reported statistics from recent studies of sex offenses generally and sex offenses targeting children. Children, boys and girls, are the victims of nearly 70% of all sex crimes committed each year. Older children commit more than 25.8% of all reported sex offenses, and 35.6% of sex offenses against children. The report also stated:

- The criminal incidents in the study were rape (26.4%), sodomy (11.9%), sex assault with object (4.2%), fondling (47.2%), and non-forcible sex offenses (10.5%)
- 88% of the offenders were between the ages of 12 and 18.
- The offenses occurred mostly in a home/residence (68.1%); 12.1% occurred at a school.
- Of the victims, 64.5% were acquainted with the offender; 23.8% were family members.
- The juvenile offenders differed from the adult offenders in that (1) they were more likely to offend in groups, 24% versus 14%, (2) more likely to have male victims, 25% versus 19%, and (3) were more likely to target younger children as victims, 59% versus 39%.
- Most juvenile offenders were male; only 7% of juvenile offenders were female.
- Juvenile offenders commit more than one in four of all sex offenses, and more than one in three of sex offenses against children.

depending on the changing mores and morals of a particular civilization. Many believe that, like the poor, it will always be with us.

Throughout the world, efforts have been made to suppress, control, organize, or discourage prostitution, with varying degrees of success. Prostitutes range from the common streetwalker to the privately kept woman or man. In the United Kingdom and France, prostitution is legal, but publicly soliciting customers is against the law. In some countries, particularly in Asia, government-inspected houses of prostitution are allowed.

Efforts to decriminalize prostitution in the United States have met with little success. Only one state (Nevada) has legalized prostitution. In Nevada, each county has the option to legalize prostitution. Fifteen of Nevada's seventeen counties have decided to remove the legal restraints against prostitution.

The Crimes of Procuring, Promoting, and Pimping for the Practice of Prostitution

Many prostitutes operate without pimps or other people procuring or promoting for them. Some prostitutes, however, have pimps, who procure customers and provide protection and bail as needed. In addition to pimps, other people could obtain money by procuring and promoting prostitution.

procuring, promoting, and pimping Actions taken to provide services of a prostitute.

Procuring, promoting, and pimping for prostitution are forbidden by state criminal codes. Because of financial gains, these people have a motive to encourage and coerce young people into prostitution. They increase the volume and extent to which prostitution is practiced and often gain a vicious hold over the prostitutes who work for them.

Following are a few of the many procuring, promoting, and pimping prostitution cases that have come before appellate courts:

- The owner of a hotel who rented out rooms, knowing that rooms were being used for prostitution, could not be convicted of solicitation for this conduct alone. See *State v. Alveario*, 381 A.2d 38 (N.J. Super. 1977).
- A defendant could be convicted of pimping for prostitution by proof that the defendant lived off the earnings of a person known by the defendant to be a prostitute, even if no specific act of prostitution solicited by the defendant is shown. *People v. Chamberlain*, 2007 WL 128281 (Cal. App. 2007), *review denied* April 13, 2007.
- Under the federal Travel Act (Mann Act), prosecutors must show that the escort service violated state law and used interstate facilities for an unlawful activity (prostitution business). See *United States v. Jones*, 909 F.2d 533 (D.C. Cir. 1990).

Crimes That Require Proof That the Crime Was Committed in a Public Place

Private sex acts between consenting adults are rarely charged as crimes, even if they violate specific sections of criminal codes. In the 2003 case of *Lawrence v. Texas*, 539 U.S. 558, the U.S. Supreme Court struck down a Texas statute that made it a crime for two male adults to have prohibited sex acts in the privacy of their home.

Public sex acts, however, are charged as criminal conduct, and the statute defining the crime often requires proof that the crime was committed in a public place. The following cases illustrate the concept:

- The Supreme Court of Arkansas quoted other state courts in defining a public place as a place where the forbidden conduct "could be seen by a number of persons if they were present and happened to look"; see *State v. Black*, 545 S.W. 2d 617 (1977). If proving that the crime was committed in a public place is a problem, there

OLD OFFENSES THAT ARE NO LONGER CRIMES OR ARE SELDOM CHARGED

Offense	Definition	History
Bigamy (or polygamy)	Marriage to two or more spouses at the same time.	Statutorized in 1604 (prior to that time, it was an ecclesiastical crime in England). In recent years, it has seldom been prosecuted in the United States.[a]
Adultery[b]	Voluntary sexual intercourse in which one or both parties are married to another person (parties not married to each other). About half the states continue to make adultery a crime, but these old laws are rarely enforced.	Goes back in history to old Roman law. A Wisconsin woman admitted in a contested divorce hearing in 1990 that she had had an affair; she received national attention when she was charged with the two-year felony crime of adultery. Charges were later dropped.
Homosexuality	Sexual relations between persons of the same sex.	For many years, this was a crime in all states. In *Lawrence v. Texas*, 123 S. Ct. 2472 (2003), the U.S. Supreme Court held a Texas sodomy statute unconstitutional because individuals have a right to engage in private consensual sexual conduct without government intervention.
Fornication	Voluntary sexual intercourse between two unmarried people.	Formerly a crime in all states. Most states have removed this offense from their criminal codes.
Seduction	Enticement by a male of an unmarried woman of prior chaste character to have sexual intercourse.	Was a crime in early English law and in many states.
Miscegenation	Intermarriage (and in some states living together) of people of different races (generally white and black).	Was a crime in some of the states. Such statutes were declared unconstitutional by the U.S. Supreme Court. See the case of *Loving v. Virginia* in Chapter 1.
Buggery (or sodomy)	Any type of sexual intercourse with an animal.	A statutory offense in England until 1967.
Abortion	Causing the expulsion of a human fetus prematurely.	Previously a crime in all states. States may not now make abortion a crime until the third trimester of pregnancy. Some states no longer have a crime of abortion.
Blasphemy, profanity, and indecent language	Cursing or reviling God; unbecoming, indecent, or impious language.	Can no longer punish for language violations unless the language falls within one of the crimes listed in Chapter 9.
Crimes against transgenders	The term *transgenders* covers cross-dressers, homosexual drag queens, and persons who believe they are both male and female.	An assortment of criminal laws were used in past years against transgenders (persons who either believed they were born in the wrong body or are intersexed).

[a]Utah banned polygamy as a required precondition to becoming a state in 1890, but over the years the practice of polygamy in Utah has never completely disappeared. See the *New York Times* article, "A House, 10 Wives: Polygamy in Suburbia," December 11, 1997, and also the *Newsweek* article, "Secrets in the Desert," August 10, 1998.

[b]Adultery remains a crime in the U.S. armed forces, Art. 134 U.C.M.J. Dismissal from the service is often the punishment. In *U.S. v. Orellana*, 62 M.J. 595 (N.M. Ct. Crim. App. 2005) *review denied*, 63 M.J. 295 (2006), a Marine corporal was convicted of adultery for having consensual sex with a woman while married to another woman. The court rejected the defendant's argument that *Lawrence v. Texas* (cited above) rendered Art.134 of the U.C.M.J. unconstitutional.

PROSTITUTION (MALE AND FEMALE)

Type of Operation	Type of Complaint Received by Law Enforcement Agencies
Streetwalkers (and prostitutes who operate out of taverns and bars)	This is the form of prostitution most visible to the public. It is also the most dangerous for women because they are exposed to violence and robbery by strangers and to arrest by police. Female and male police decoys have been very effective in apprehending "Johns" soliciting for sex with males or females.
Public toilets and parks	When complaints of loitering for prostitution are received, police sometimes set up "sting" operations. In 2007 police did so at the Minneapolis/ St. Paul Airport. During a three-month period, 40 men including a U.S. senator were arrested and charged with crimes. The senator pled guilty to disorderly conduct and interference with privacy, gross misdemeanors. Others pled guilty or were convicted of loitering or indecent exposure.
Call girls (or boys) and other organized prostitution services	This could involve the crime of pandering through pimps, bartenders, cab drivers, and others who refer customers to call girls. A 1988 *FBI Enforcement Bulletin* noted that the crimes of theft, robbery, assault, battery, and illegal drug transactions are frequent products of organized criminal prostitution.
Online, Internet, escort services, and massage parlors	Online prostitutes say the Internet is a natural medium for selling sex because it is anonymous and connects with many potential customers. The Cook County (Chicago) sheriff filed a civil lawsuit against Craigslist in 2009, charging that the popular online ad site promoted and facilitated prostitution on a huge basis. Many law enforcement agencies are using Craigslist in sting operations, where they often make more arrests than in street prostitution. One online escort business, Emperor's Club V.I.P., charged up to $4,300 per hour for its prostitution services. Eliot Spitzer, the governor of New York, resigned from office after it was disclosed he used prostitutes from that service. See "4 Arrests, then 6 Tumultuous Days That Ended in a Governor's Resignation," *New York Times*, 3/13/08.
"Sex-for-drugs" prostitution	Public health officials are very concerned about the spread of disease linked to sex-for-drugs prostitution.
Brothels and houses of prostitution	State laws forbid houses of prostitution. In the case of *State v. Mueller*, 671 P.2d 1351 (1983), one woman was selling sex in her apartment with no street or public solicitation and only consenting adults involved. She argued that she had a right of privacy in her home to do as she wished. The Supreme Court of Hawaii affirmed her conviction, holding she had no right to practice prostitution.
Combining prostitution with con games, robbery, extortion, theft of money, credit cards, and so on	*FBI Law Enforcement Bulletin* article, "Knock-Out Dates: Flirting with Danger," January 1993, describes women who pick up men in hotels, restaurants, and bars to rob them or steal from them after placing a drug in their drink to incapacitate them. For an example, see the case of *U.S. v. Pasucci*, 943 F.2d 1032 (9th Cir. 1991),where a businessman was caught by an extortion ring.

© Sean Murphy/Getty Images

A young woman, perhaps only a teenager, engages in the dangerous business of street prostitution.

generally are one or more alternative offenses in a state criminal code that do not have the requirement of public place.[17]

- The defendant appeared nude in the presence of a female babysitter in the bedroom and bathroom of his home. The Georgia Court of Appeals held that the defendant's behavior converted his bedroom and bathroom from a private zone into a public place in affirming his conviction under the Georgia public indecency statute. See *Greene v. State*, 381 S.E.2d 310 (1989).

BECAUSE PROSTITUTION FUELS THE ILLEGAL DRUGS TRADE, CITIES USE ONE OR MORE OF THE FOLLOWING TO DISCOURAGE THE CRIME

- Increased fines and jail sentences for prostitutes and johns.
- Cracking down on male johns to discourage this activity.
- Increased use of the "loitering to solicit prostitution" ordinance or statute.
- Filing a civil lawsuit against people with five or more prostitution or loitering for prostitution arrests, as was done in San Diego and Milwaukee. The civil court would then declare loitering by such people in certain areas of the city to be a public nuisance and also forbid them from flagging down cars and loitering at bus stops throughout the city. Violations would lead to a civil forfeiture of up to $2,000 or jailing if the forfeiture was not paid. One of the people in Milwaukee had 18 arrests for prostitution and 124 arrests for loitering for prostitution. Police in San Diego reported that the lawsuit virtually eliminated street prostitution in specific areas of San Diego.
- Confiscation of the johns' cars under forfeiture statutes.
- City placing newspaper ads listing names of prostitutes and johns (a few cities also place pictures of the johns in the ads).
- Compulsory AIDS tests for convicted prostitutes and johns (a California statute mandating the testing of people convicted of prostitution for AIDS was upheld in the 1990 case of Love v. Superior Court, 226 Cal. App. 3d 736, 276 Cal. Rptr.).

- A court officer in charge of a female prisoner had sex with the prisoner in a holding cell in the basement of a courthouse. A closed-circuit camera covered the courthouse, including the holding cell. The court held the sex occurred in a public place. See *Com. v. Merrill*, 864 N.E.2d 1235 (Mass. App. 2007).
- Defendants were seen having sex in a car parked on a well-lit public street so that the interior was readily visible to passersby. The highest court in New York affirmed the convictions for public lewdness, holding that the interior of the car was a public place when casual passersby could see and were likely to see the partial nudity and the sex acts. See *People v. McNamara*, 585 N.E.2d 788 (1991).

≡ Touching or Other Conduct Done to Arouse Sexual Desire

Touching a private part of another person's body could be (1) accidental, (2) consented to by the other person (children are not capable of consenting to sexual touching), or (3) necessary in the care of the person or for medical reasons. Touching could be in a friendly, joking, or loving manner, or the contact could be to discipline a child (spanking) or in a hostile or angry manner.

REGULATION OF NUDITY BY STATES OR MUNICIPALITIES

Nudity by itself is not obscene, lewd, or indecent but may be regulated by specific statutes and ordinances as follows:

Place of Nudity	Manner in Which Nudity May Be Regulated
Public nudity (public beach or public place, such as street)	May be forbidden or regulated by a specific statute or ordinance.
Nude entertainment or nudity in a place licensed to serve alcoholic beverages	May be forbidden or regulated under the authority given to states by the Twenty-First Amendment of the U.S. Constitution to regulate the sale and use of alcohol. The U.S. Supreme Court stated that "the broad sweep of the 21st Amendment has been recognized as conferring something more than the normal state authority over public health, welfare, and morals"; *see California v. LaRue*, 409 U.S. 109, 93 S. Ct. 390 (1972).
Nudity in a private place (a nudist camp, for example), a stage play, or a movie (the musical *Hair*, the play *Oh! Calcutta!* and the opera *Salome* have nude performers)	May not be regulated unless the conduct or display is obscene. Nudity, by itself, is not obscene, lewd, or indecent.
Nudity used for sexual gratification	For example, see the case of *People v. Garrison*, 82 Ill. 2d 444, 45 Ill. Dec. 132, 412 N.E.2d 483 (1980), in which the defendant stood behind a storm door in his home exposing his penis to a woman standing outside. The Supreme Court of Illinois held that this was not private conduct and that the defendant had no right of privacy. If a jury found that the defendant exposed his body "with intent to arouse or to satisfy (his) sexual desire," the defendant could be found guilty of the Illinois public indecency statute.

Sexual crimes, such as sexual touching, require the state to show that the touching was for sexual gratification. Lewd and lascivious conduct or behavior with a child statutes often require showing that the defendant "had the specific intent to arouse or gratify either child's sexual desires or his own."[18]

Following are examples of crimes that require showing that the conduct was intended to arouse sexual desire:

- The California lewd and lascivious acts with a child statute requires that the touching be done "with the specific intent to arouse, appeal to, or gratify the sexual desire of either party"; see *People v. Carson*, 890 P.2d 1115 (1995). The California Supreme Court also held that lewd touching can occur through the victim's clothing and does not require contact with the bare skin or with "private parts" of the defendant or victim. See *People v. Martinez*, 1995 WL 641969 (1995).
- Most state statutes include the buttocks as an intimate part of a person's body. To be a sexual battery or disorderly conduct or another sex crime, it must be shown that the touching was intentional, was without consent, and was for purposes of sexual gratification. See, for example, *State v. Osborne*, 808 P.2d 624 (N. Mex. 1991).
- The defendant offered a teenage boy a ride, made sexually suggestive inquiries of the boy, and then pressed his entire hand on the inner thigh of the boy in a manner suggestive of an intimate massage. The Massachusetts Court of Appeals affirmed the conviction of the defendant for indecent assault and battery. See *Commonwealth v. Lavigne*, 676 N.E.2d 1170 (1997).

≡ Protecting Children Against Sexual Exploitation: Child Pornography

The U.S. Supreme Court has repeatedly held that states have a compelling interest in "safeguarding the physical and psychological well-being of a minor" and that "the use of children as subjects of pornographic materials is harmful to the physiological, emotional, and mental health of the child."[19]

child pornography Movies, pictures, or drawings that depict children in explicit sexual relations. Unlike adult pornography, child pornography need not be obscene to be criminal.

pornography Movies, pictures, writings, and other expressions that are intended to arouse sexual incitement and have no artistic merit or redeeming social value.

Because of these reasons, **child pornography** is treated differently from adult **pornography**. Adult pornography is sold openly in many communities throughout the United States, but child pornography is outlawed by the federal government and most states.

The child pornography laws of the majority of states and the federal government do not require obscenity as an element of the crime.[20] If an actual child or children are depicted in a photograph or video as engaged in sexually explicit conduct, possession is such material is a crime under the federal pornography law and the laws of most states, even if the photograph or video would not meet the obscenity test applicable to adult pornography.

Five categories of conduct and attempted conduct are made crimes under the federal law and the laws of most states. The crime of child pornography broadly includes the following:[21]

- Production of child pornography (for example, filming a child or children engaged in sexually explicit conduct)
- Advertising child pornography
- Possession of material, knowing that it depicts minors in sexually explicit conduct
- Trafficking in child pornography (importation, distribution, sale, loan, gift, exchange, receipt, or transportation of material, knowing that it depicts minors engaged in sexually explicit conduct)
- Procurement of child pornography (buying, selling, or transporting child pornography or inducing, coercing, or kidnapping a minor for the purposes of producing child pornography)

FIGHTING THE INTERNATIONAL CHILD SEX TRADE

Representatives of 134 countries met in Yokohama, Japan, in December 2001 to fight the fast-growing world sex trade in children. The first international meeting was held in Stockholm in 1996. UNICEF estimates that every year 1 million children (girls and boys) are forced into the sex trade.

Most of these children are from poor countries or are poor illegal immigrants living in industrial countries. Using the Internet and cell phones, pedophiles can reach the children online. The governments of the 134 countries pledged increased efforts to stamp out the thriving sex trade by tougher laws and by coordinating police efforts against the child sex trade.

In the United States, in 2003 Congress passed as part of the PROTECT Act (discussed in this chapter) 18 U.S.C §§ 1591 and 2423, which are directed at international "sex trafficking" and "sex tourism." Section 1591 is aimed at "trafficking" and makes any person who entices or transports a child under 18 in interstate or foreign commerce knowing the child will be forced to engage in a commercial sex act guilty of the crime. In *United States v. Chang Da Liu*, 538 F.3d 1078 (9th Cir. 2008) the federal government used this statute to shut down a "Tea House" operated by the defendants in the Northern Mariana Islands, a territory within the jurisdiction of the federal government by virtue of an agreement between the United States and the Islands. The defendants lured Chinese girls to the Islands, promising them work as waitresses, and charging them $6,000 "broker fees." When the girls arrived, they were forced to engage in commercial sex. The Ninth Circuit upheld their conviction.

Section 2423 identifies three so-called sex-tourism crimes. Subsection (a) applies to a person who knowingly "transports" a child under 18 across state of international borders for the purpose of engaging in "illicit sexual conduct," which means sex with a child under 18 that would be illegal under federal law, or any commercial sexual act with a child under 18. Subsection (b) applies to persons who travel in interstate or foreign commerce with the purpose of engaging in illicit sexual conduct with a child under 18. Subsection (c) applies to any U.S. citizen who travels interstate or to a foreign country and engages in illicit sexual conduct with a child under 18. Subsections (a) and (b) are similar to prior law and require only that the defendant have the purpose of engaging in illicit sexual conduct. It is not a defense to prosecutions under either section that the individual the defendant intended to have illicit sex with was not under 18; it is enough the defendant believed that was the case. *United States v. Spurlock*, 495 F.3d 1011 (8th Cir. 2007), *cert. denied* 552 U.S. 1054 (2007).

Section 2423 (c) represents a change from former law and is expressly directed at "sex tourists." Under subsection (c), the government need not prove the defendant traveled to a foreign country for the purpose of having illicit sex. Thus, in the 2010 case of *United States v. Pendleton*, 2010 WL 427230, the defendant was convicted under § 2423 (c) when he traveled to Germany from the United States, and while in Germany he was arrested for having sex with a 14-year-old boy. When the defendant finished a two-year prison sentence in Germany, he was deported to the United States in January of 2008; in March of 2008 he was arrested and charged under 2423 (c) and was convicted.

The section also has what is called an "extraterritorial" effect on U.S. citizens. In *United States v. Clark*, 435 F.3d 1100 (9th Cir. 2006), a retired U.S. military member who resided in Cambodia but traveled between the United States and Cambodia was charged under § 2423(c) when he was arrested by Cambodian police having sex with two 14-year-old boys and extradited to the United States. The court held that under the statute, all the government needed to prove was the illicit sexual conduct and the citizenship of the defendant.

More than two dozen states have passed criminal laws aimed at local brothels and sweatshops that bring people into the country, including children, and force them to work as sex slaves or in sweatshops. Most federal legislation in this area is directed at organized trafficking rings.

Child pornography could be depicted in magazines, books, motion pictures, videos, and by other means. Most state statutes forbid live performances, and some specifically forbid the use of computers. The federal government and some states forbid visual depictions or advertisements of child pornography "by any means including by computers."

Schools and libraries using federal funds are obligated to use computer filters to block pornographic material available on the Internet. Such filters are also available for parents to use on computers used by children. Child pornography from many countries, including the United States, Russia, and others, is available on websites and can be accessed from anywhere in the world. The National Center for Missing and Exploited Children estimates that the number of child pornography websites increased by 400 percent between 2001 and 2005.

Federal legislation directed at use of the Internet to exploit children has met with attacks on the legislation's constitutionality. In response to the use of the Internet for dissemination of pornography and the effect of such pornography on children, Congress passed two significant pieces of legislation in 1996: the Communications Decency Act (CDA) of 1996 (47 U.S.C. § 223) and the 1996 Child Pornography Prevention Act (CPPA) (18 U.S.C. § 2256). The CDA prohibited any use of the Internet to post material that was "indecent" or "patently offensive" and made available to children. The CPPA prohibited Internet use to post any picture "that appears to be" of a minor engaged in sexually explicit conduct. Both laws were found to be unconstitutional by the U.S. Supreme Court:

- In *Reno v. American Civil Liberties Union*, 521 U.S. 844 (1997), the Court held that the CDA was unconstitutional because it failed to clearly identify what constituted "indecent" or "patently offensive" material and as a result prohibited speech that was protected under the First Amendment.
- In *Ashcroft v. Free Speech Coalition*, 122 S. Ct. 1389 (2002), the Supreme Court held that the CPPA was overbroad and unconstitutional. The Court concluded that the CPPA did not limit its prohibition to only obscene materials but included all depictions of sexual conduct between children, including depictions that were "simulated sex" between children. It noted that the movie *Traffic*, which won an Academy Award, had depicted sexual conduct of a 16-year-old girl.

In response to these decisions, Congress passed legislation designed to eliminate the problems in the earlier legislation. The Child Online Protection Act (47 U.S.C. § 231 of 1998) (COPA) prohibits any commercial Internet communication that is "harmful to minors." *Harmful to minors* is defined in a manner that tracks the obscenity test of *Miller v. California* (discussed in Chapter 9), including the "community standards" test. In *ACLU v. Gonzales*, 478 F. Supp. 2d 775 (E.D. Pa. 2007), a federal judge held that the COPA statute was unconstitutional because it did not use the least restrictive means to achieve the desired result. The Third Circuit affirmed that decision in 2008 (534 F.3d 181), and the U.S. Supreme Court denied certiorari, 129 S. Ct. 1032 (2009).

In 2003 Congress passed the PROTECT Act, 18 U.S.C. § 2252A(a)(3), which included several specific crimes directed at children through the Internet. In *United States v. Williams*, 444 F.3d 1286 (11th Cir. 2006), a federal court of appeals held the "pandering" provision of the PROTECT Act unconstitutional because it was vague and overbroad and did not solve the problems presented by the earlier statutes. The U.S. Supreme Court granted review of this decision, 127 S. Ct. 1874 (2007). In the following Case Close Up, the Supreme Court upheld the child pornography provisions of the PROTECT Act.

CASE CLOSE-UP

United States v. Williams
Supreme Court of the United States
553 U.S. 285 (2008)

18 U.S.C. § 2252(A) of the 2003 PROTECT Act added a new pandering and solicitation section to the child exploitation provisions of that Act. It makes it a crime for any person to knowingly advertise, promote, present, distribute, or solicit through the mails or the Internet any material in a manner "that reflects the belief, or that is intended to cause another to believe" that the material contains (a) an obscene visual depiction of a minor engaged in sexually explicit conduct, or (b) a visual depiction of an actual minor engaged in sexually explicit conduct. In other words, the Act made it a crime to "pander" *obscene* child sexual depictions, whether or not the child pictured was an actual child or a simulated child. It also made it a crime to "pander" *any* image of a child, actual or simulated, engaged in sexually explicit conduct if the person pandering the image believes it to be an actual image of a child, or intends another to have such a belief.

The legislative history of the Act made it clear Congress was concerned that the decision in *Ashcroft v. Free Speech Coalition,* which seemed to limit non-obscene child pornography prosecutions to material that involved only actual children, would make it impossible to prosecute many pornographers who would allege their "depictions" were made by "virtual" imaging. To address this concern, Congress did not in the Act attempt to prohibit the possession of "virtual" child pornography. Rather, it prohibited a person from "pandering" material he believed to be either **obscene** virtual child pornography (which can always be prohibited) or depictions of **actual** children engaged in sexually explicit conduct (which can be prohibited only if not overbroad). It was the pandering provision that was under review in this case.

The defendant Williams conducted an online conversation in an Internet chat room with a person calling herself "Lisa n Miami." Lisa was in fact a Secret Service Agent working undercover. Williams posted a message that said "Dad of toddler has good pics of her" for swap of "your toddler pics, or live cam." The agent exchanged some non-pornographic pictures with Williams. After some discussion, in which Williams demanded proof in the form of additional pictures which the agent refused to furnish, Williams posted a message stating "I CAN PUT UP CUZ IM FOR REAL" that contained a hyperlink that when followed led to seven pictures of actual children engaging in explicit sexual conduct. The Secret Service then obtained a warrant, seized Williams's computer, and found at least 22 pornographic images of actual children. He was charged with possession of child pornography under § 2252A(a)(5)(B) and pandering under § 2252A(a)(3)(B). After conviction under both statutes, Williams appealed only the pandering conviction, alleging the statute was overbroad. The court of appeals agreed, and reversed his conviction under that section.

On review, the Supreme Court upheld the statute, and reversed the court of appeals. It said that the pandering section is directed at persons who are attempting to engage in an illegal transaction, and such conduct is not protected by the First Amendment:

> *Offers to engage in illegal transactions are categorically excluded from First Amendment protection....One would think that this principle resolves the present*

case, since the statute criminalizes only offers to provide or requests to obtain contraband-child obscenity and child pornography involving actual children, both of which are proscribed.....and the proscription of which is constitutional, see Free Speech Coalition, *553 U.S., at 245-246, 256.*

Williams, 553 U.S. 285, at 297.

Since the conduct proscribed, distributing or soliciting material believed to be depictions of actual children, was not protected, the Supreme Court said the circuit court was wrong to hold the statute up to the "strict scrutiny" test. That test only applies if a statute attempts to regulate protected speech or conduct. The Supreme Court also stated that the statute does not, unlike the statute in *Ashcroft v. Free Speech Coalition*, impinge on legitimate depictions of child sexual conduct, such as advertisements for mainstream Hollywood movies that depict underage characters having sex. The Court thought it "implausible" that either the producers or the distributors either "believed" the scenes depicted actual children having sex, or "intended to cause" others to believe that was the case. The Court stated that the "average person" knows sex scenes in movies use non-child actors or depict sex scenes in a way that does not rise to the explicit level covered by the statute. Id., at 301, 302.

≡ Movies, Videos, and Photographs

X-rated videos are a multibillion-dollar business in the United States. European and Asian producers also have large sales throughout the world. Are producers of X-rated videos and films, who pay adults to perform sexual acts that are filmed for movies and videos, engaged in the business of prostitution? This issue was before the courts in the case of *California v. Freeman*, 758 P.2d 1128 (Cal. 1988), *cert. denied* 109 S. Ct. 1133 (1989).

Freeman was convicted of pandering under the California Criminal Code for hiring adults to perform sex acts, which he filmed and sold. The Supreme Court of California reversed the conviction, holding that Freeman's conduct was not prohibited by the California prostitution and pandering laws. The court held that hiring actors to perform sexual acts to be filmed in a private place is not "procuring" prostitution, because the payment to the actors was not made for the purpose of sexual gratification, a necessary part of the definition of prostitution. The court also noted that the film made was not obscene, and thus the prosecution under the pandering statute amounted to an improper "end run" around the First Amendment.

Because a new law expanding the California pandering and prostitution statute has not been enacted, California has become the capital of the United States for X-rated and pornographic films and videos.[22]

"Sexting," and Nude Photos of Children Taken by Family Members

Many family photo and video collections have pictures of young nude children. But when children are no longer babies and have begun to develop sexually, are pictures taken by parents and stepparents sexual abuse? This question has been before a number of U.S. courts, with results similar to the following case.

The defendant took color photos of his physically mature, 14-year-old stepdaughter, showing her fully exposed breasts. He was convicted in a jury trial and sentenced to 10 years in prison. The Massachusetts Supreme Judicial Court reversed the conviction, holding the statute to be overbroad. The U.S. Supreme Court vacated the Massachusetts Supreme Court ruling and remanded the case for further hearings. On remand, the Massachusetts Supreme Judicial Court upheld the defendant's conviction, holding that although his photographs were not obscene, the state had a legitimate interest in protecting minors from such practices and that interest was more compelling than the defendant's "restrictive speech" interest under the First Amendment.[23]

Convictions of other defendants in similar situations were affirmed. In *Perry v. State*, 568 So. 2d 339 (Ala. Cr. App. 1990), the defendant photographed not only his 15-year-old daughter but also her 14-year-old friend. In *Brackins v. State*, 578 A.2d 300 (Md. App. 1990), the conviction for child sexual abuse was affirmed in the semi-nude photographing of a 12-year-old stepdaughter.[24]

Nude home photos can also result in prosecution under the federal child pornography statutes, including the PROTECT Act. In a 2010 case the Sixth Circuit Court of Appeals upheld the conviction under 18 U.S.C.§ 2251 and 2252 of a defendant charged with possession of child pornography based on home pictures. The defendant took nude photographs of his 10-year-old daughter and her friends. He did not distribute the photographs or show them to other people. Because the pictures showed actual children in sexually suggestive positions, the court said the pictures were child pornography and violated the statutes. The court also held that Congress had power to regulate the activity under the Commerce Clause because of the possibility that home-made child pornography would hinder the purpose Congress has in regulating national child pornography.[25]

In the July 2010 issue of the *FBI Law Enforcement Bulletin,* an article entitled "Sexting: Risky Actions and Overreactions" discusses the problems related to juveniles "sexting" naked or near-naked pictures of themselves to others. Sexting is defined as "sending or posting sexually suggestive messages and images, including nude or semi-nude photographs, via cellular telephones or over the Internet." The article suggests that juveniles consider the consequences of sexting, and offers this advice:

> Before hitting send, remember that you cannot control where this image may travel;
>
> If you forward a sexual picture of someone underage, you are responsible for this image as the original sender;
>
> Think about the consequences of taking, sending, or forwarding a sexual image of yourself or someone else under age.

One of those consequences could include criminal charges. In the 2009 case of *State v. Canal*, 773 N.W.2d 528 (Iowa 2009), the Iowa Supreme Court upheld the conviction of an 18-year-old man who sent a cell phone picture of his erect penis to a 14-year-old girl. He was convicted under a statute that made it a crime to send obscene material to a minor.

≡ Voyeurism and Other Criminal Invasions of Privacy

Until recent years, Peeping Toms who trespassed or were not in a public place were often charged as a disorderly person (or with disorderly conduct). Many states now have voyeurism or invasion of privacy laws in their criminal codes. An example of such law is Ohio Criminal Code Section 2907.08(A), which reads:

> No person, for the purpose of sexually arousing or gratifying himself or herself, shall commit trespass or otherwise surreptitiously invade the privacy of another, to spy or eavesdrop upon another.

These laws have been toughened in many states by provisions forbidding video voyeurism or video stalking. The terms *upskirting* and *downblousing* describe offenses that are charged under invasion of privacy statutes. Examples of conduct charged under these laws are as follows:

- A California man videotaped three different women at three different times as he had sex with them. The women did not know and did not consent to the filming. Police learned of the tapes when the man showed the videos to friends. He was convicted under California's invasion of privacy law, which forbids filming or recording confidential communications without the consent of participants. See *People v. Gibbons*, 263 Cal. Rptr. 905 (1989).
- An apartment manager secretly installed a video camera in a shower used by college women living in his building. After several months of filming the women taking showers, the camera was discovered, and the man was criminally charged under the Wisconsin Criminal Code.

▤ The Crime of Harassment

The crime of harassment can be committed in many ways, such as the use of a telephone,[26] cell phone, fax, e-mail, voice mail, regular mail, or any other means of communication. Section 250.4 of the Model Penal Code defines harassment, in part, as "(c) making repeated communications anonymously or at extremely inconvenient hours, or in an offensively coarse language." Convictions under harassment statutes usually require a showing that the defendant made the communications with the intent to harass the recipient. Because the First Amendment's free speech protection does not apply to speech made with the intent to harass, harassment statutes have been held constitutional.[27]

Harassment need not have as its purpose harm to the recipient. Repeated unwelcome communications can be enough for a conviction. In *City of Montgomery v. Zgounas*, 953 So. 2d 434 (Ala. App. 2006), the court held that a defendant's frequent, unwelcome visits and telephone calls to a woman at her place of work satisfied the requirements of the Alabama harassment statute, even if the defendant did not intend to harm or injure the woman.

Sexual Harassment

sexual harassment
Unwelcome sexual advances, with or without physical contact; in the workplace, creation of a "hostile environment," such as belittling or embarrassing an employee or co-worker who has refused sexual advances, can be sexual harassment.

Sexual harassment can be a criminal or civil offense. It is defined as unwelcome sexual advances or requests for sexual favors that may be combined with other verbal or physical conduct of a sexual nature. Ordinarily, women and girls are the victims of sexual harassment, but occasional cases concern men who are the victims of unwelcome sexual advances that amount to sexual harassment.

Workplace sexual harassment could occur when

- The boss expects submission by an employee to sexual harassment as an explicit or implicit term or condition of employment
- Pay raises, promotions, type of work, and so forth are used as a reward for submission to sexual harassment and providing sexual favors
- Such conduct interferes with work performance or creates an intimidating, hostile, or offensive working environment

The U.S. Supreme Court held in 1986 that sexual harassment that caused a hostile or abusive work environment violated Title VII of the Civil Rights Act of 1964 (42 U.S.C. §§ 2000e-1–2000e-17). In the case of *Meritor Savings Bank v. Mechelle Vinson*, the female bank employee was subjected to public fondling and sexual demands, to which she allegedly submitted out of fear that she would lose her job.[28]

The U.S. Supreme Court ruled in 1993 that harassment need not result in a "tangible injury" but that it had to be more than "merely offensive" conduct or words. Holding that there could not be "a mathematically precise test," the Court held that a "hostile or abusive" environment violates the law (*Harris v. Forklift Systems, Inc.*, 114 S. Ct. 367).[29]

In two 1998 cases, the U.S. Supreme Court held that corporations and other employers are potentially liable for the conduct of supervisors, whether the employer was aware of it or not. The cases held that an employee who refused unwanted sexual advances but suffered no job consequences may still bring a lawsuit. The cases are *Burlington Industries v. Ellerth* (118 S. Ct. 2257) and *Faragher v. City of Boca Raton* (118 S. Ct. 2275).

Summary

- Most states divide sexual assault into two or more degrees. Factors that can increase the degree of the crime include force used, a weapon used, or bodily injury inflicted.
- Rape shield laws prohibit questioning of a rape victim if the purpose of the questions is to expose the victim's previous sexual history.
- Rape shield laws do not prevent the introduction of evidence of past sexual conduct of the victim if it is offered to prove either consent of the victim, or that another person was the source of semen or other physical evidence used as part of the case against the defendant.
- Statutory rape requires no specific intent to have sex with a minor. It is not a defense to the charge that the defendant reasonably believed the person was not a minor.
- Civil commitment is permissible only if it can be shown the person is a dangerous sexual predator

who poses a substantial threat to commit sexual offenses in the future, and that the person cannot control his behavior.
- Pimping includes not only securing clients for a prostitute but also living off the prostitute's illegal earnings.
- Child pornography can be regulated either because it is obscene, and thus prohibited even if it didn't involve a child, or because it depicts actual children in sexually explicit conduct. The federal and state governments have a legitimate interest in keeping children away from such sexual conduct.
- The Child Online Protection Act has been found unconstitutional by a circuit court of appeal, and the Supreme Court has denied review of that decision. Provisions of the PROTECT Act that apply to child pornography have been upheld by the Supreme Court.

Key Terms

rape, p. 312
sexual assault, p. 313
corroborative evidence, p. 313
rape shield laws, p. 319
statutory rape, p. 323

incest, p. 324
Megan's laws, p. 326
prostitution, p. 329
procuring, promoting, and
   pimping, p. 330

child pornography, p. 335
pornography, p. 335
sexual harassment, p. 341

Case Analysis and Writing Exercises

1. Consent by the victim is often raised as a defense to charges of sexual assault or rape. When must that consent exist? If consent is once given, can it be retracted? What should the rules be for retraction of consent? See *State v. Bunyard*, 133 P.3d 14 (Kan. 2006).

2. New Jersey passed a sexual predator law in 1998 that provides for civil commitment of convicted sexual offenders. In *In re Commitment of W.Z.*, 801 A.2d 205 (N.J. 2002), the New Jersey Supreme Court remanded a case to the trial court to decide if the defendant could be committed under the statute, as controlled by the Supreme Court's opinion in *Kansas v. Crane*. What must the prosecution prove on remand, in order to comply with the requirements set forth in the *Crane* case?

3. A man is parked in his car on a city street at night. A woman approaches the car and gets in without being invited. Inside the car the woman offers to perform a sex act for money. Can the woman be prosecuted under the following statute? A person who "solicits or accepts a solicitation to engage for hire in sexual penetration or sexual contact while in a public place" shall be guilty of a misdemeanor? If so, can the man? See *State v. White*, 692 N.W.2d 749 (Minn. App. 2005). Do you agree with the result in the case? Does it represent the majority view?

4. In *State v. Bacon*, 2005 WL 758065 (Conn. 2005), the defendant was convicted under Connecticut's child pornography laws. Based on the U.S. Supreme Court decisions discussed in this chapter, what issues would you expect the defendant to raise on appeal? How did the court resolve those issues? Was the court's resolution correct under the Supreme Court's decisions?

Notes

1. The title of this report is "Extent, Nature, and Consequences of Rape Victimization: Findings from the National Violence Against Women Survey," NCJ 210346 (2006).

2. See *Gilmore v. State*, 855 P.2d 143 (Okla. Cr. 1993); *Cole v. State*, 818 S.W.2d 573 (Ark. 1991); *Wealot v. Armontrout*, 740 F. Supp. 1436 (W.D. Mo. 1990); and *Case v. State*, 458 N.E.2d 223 (Ind. 1984).

3. *People v. Hunt*, 72 Cal. App.3d at 194, 139 Cal. Rptr. at 676 (1987).

4. *State v. Rusk*, 289 Md. 230, 424 A.2d 720 (1981).

5. See also *State v. Reinhold*, 123 Ariz. 50, 597 P.2d 532 (1979); *People v. Hunt*, 72 Cal. App.3d 190, 139 Cal. Rptr. 675 (1977); *State v. Dill*, 3 Terry 533, 42 Del. 533, 40 A.2d 443 (1944); *Arnold v. United States*, 358 A.2d 335 (D.C. App. 1976); *Doyle v. State*, 39 Fla. 155, 22 So. 272 (1897); *Curtis v. State*, 236 Ga. 362, 223 S.E.2d 721 (1976); *People v. Murphy*, 124 Ill. App.2d 71, 260 N.E.2d 386 (1970); *Carroll v. State*, 263 Ind. 86, 324 N.E.2d 809 (1975); *Fields v. State*, 293 So. 2d 430 (Miss. 1974); *State v. Beck*, 368 S.W.2d 490 (Mo. 1963); *Cascio v. State*, 147 Neb. 1075, 25 N.W.2d 897 (1947); *State v. Burns*, 287 N.C. 102, 214 S.E.2d 56 (1975), *cert. denied* 423 U.S. 933, 96 S. Ct. 288 (1975); *State v. Verdone*, 114 R.I. 613, 337 A.2d 804 (1975); *Brown v. State*, 576 S.W.2d 820 (Tex. Cr. App. 1978); *Jones v. Commonwealth*, 219 Va. 983, 252 S.E.2d 370 (1979); *State v. Baker*, 30 Wash. 2d 601, 192 P.2d 839 (1948); *Brown v. State*, 581 P.2d 189 (Wyo. 1978).

6. However, "if as a result of self-induced intoxication, the defendant believed that the female was consenting, that belief would not thereby become either reasonable or in good faith" (California Jury Instruction 4.20).

7. 117 Ill. App.3d 363, 453 N.E.2d 842 (1983). See also *Florida v. Meyers*, 466 U.S. 380, 104 S. Ct. 1852, 35 CrL 4022 (1984), in which the defendant was convicted of sexual battery. The conviction was affirmed by the U.S. Supreme Court.

8. Report of rape could also be made to a medical professional and be admissible under statements for the purposes of medical diagnosis or treatment. Report of rape is also known as the *fresh complaint* or the *outcry rule.*

9. See, e.g., *Comm. v. Battista*, 1995 WL 864097 (Pa. App. 1995).

10. 450 U.S. 464, 101 S. Ct. 1200 (1981). Most states probably make their statutory rape statutes applicable to both females and males. There certainly is a justifiable need for states to protect children from adults, whether the child is a girl or a boy.

11. 536 U.S. 24, 32 (2002).

12. See the *Milwaukee Journal Sentinel* article, "Sex Offender Database Passes House," July 26, 2006.

13. U.S. Supreme Court cases on sex offenders found to be sexual predators include *Kansas v. Crane*, 122 S. Ct. 867 (2002); *Kansas v. Hendricks*, 521 U.S. 346 (1997); *Conn. v. John Doe*, 123 S. Ct. 1160 (2002); *Foucha v. Louisiana*, 112 S. Ct. 1780 (1992); *Smith v. Doe*, 538 U.S. 84 (2003).

14. *Hendricks v. Kansas*, 521 U.S. 346 (1997).

15. *New York Times*, March 4–March 6, 2007.

16. See *New York Times* article, "Wrong Turn on Sex Offenders," March 13, 2007.

17. In states where public intoxication is a crime or ordinance violation, it must be shown that the person was intoxicated in a public place. The Supreme Court of Iowa pointed out that a "right of public access is the touchstone of the … definition of a public place" (476 N.W.2d at 56).

    The majority of state courts hold that a motor vehicle on a street or highway is a public place for criminal statutes such as public intoxication, soliciting an act of prostitution, and public indecency in which the state must show "public place."

18. *State v. Rollins*, 581 So. 2d 379 (La. App. 1991).

19. *Osborne v. Ohio*, 110 S. Ct. 1691 (1990).

20. In 1977, the U.S. Congress enacted the federal Protection of Children Against Sexual Exploitation Act (18 U.S.C.A. § 2252). The federal child pornography law was upheld as constitutional by the U.S. Supreme Court in the case of *U.S. v. X-Citement Video, Inc.*, 115 S. Ct. 464, and the state of New York child pornography law was upheld in the case of *New York v. Ferber*, 458 U.S. 747, 102 S. Ct. 3348 (1982).

21. This material is adapted from the U.S. Department of Justice publication entitled *Child Sexual Exploitation: Improving Investigations and Protecting Victims* (1995).

22. In the 1990 Arizona case of *State v. Taylor* (808 P.2d 314), the Arizona courts distinguish between "prostitution and theatre." The defendant was convicted of four counts under the Arizona prostitution statute for paid performances in which "sexual contact" occurred. The Arizona case distinguishes this case and statute from the California *Freeman* case.

    In defending a criminal or civil obscenity case, defense counsel often use pay-for-view sex movies available at local hotels, erotic films available from cable or satellite providers, the number and location of X-rated video stores, X-rated material available on the Internet, and local nightclubs that feature nude or semi-nude entertainment as a way to prove the "contemporary community standards" requirement.

23. *Massachusetts v. Oakes*, 109 S. Ct. 2633 (1989); *on remand* 551 N.E.2d 910 (1990).

24. See the *New York Times* article, "Family Photos or Pornography? A Father's Bitter Legal Odyssey," January 30, 1995, which tells of a 45-year-old businessman who was arrested, handcuffed, and taken from his home. The man took 110 photographs of his nude 6-year-old daughter for an art class he was taking. The article tells of similar incidents in Ohio and California.

25. *United States v. Bowers*, 594 F.3d 522 (6th Cir. 2010).

26. In addition to statutes forbidding abusive, harassing, or obscene telephone calls, federal statutes also forbid other abusive use of the telephone, such as the Consumer Credit Protection Act (Public Law 95–109 Statute 877), which prohibits debt collectors from "placing telephone calls without meaningful disclosure of the caller's identity"; from "engaging any person in telephone conversation repeatedly or continuously with intent, to annoy, abuse, or harass any person at the called number"; and from "us[ing] obscene or profane language or language the natural consequence of which is to abuse the hearer or reader."

27. See, for example, *Commonwealth v. Hendrickson*, 724 A.2d 315 (Pa. 1998).

28. 413 U.S. 15, 93 S. Ct. 2607 (1973).

29. The Paula Jones lawsuit against President Bill Clinton was settled by an out-of-court payment to Paula Jones. Proceedings in the case had commenced when the U.S. Supreme Court held that the lawsuit for alleged sexual advances against a sitting president of the United States could not be deferred until the president's term of office ended. See *Clinton v. Jones*, 137 L. Ed. 2d 945, 1997.

Theft

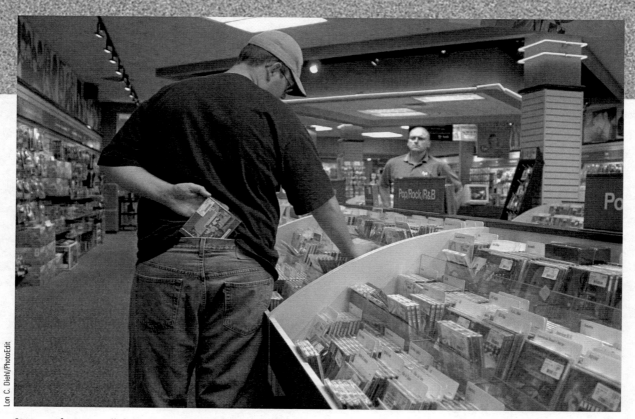

Lon C. Diehl/PhotoEdit

Someone forgot to tell this shoplifter about the surveillance camera.

OUTLINE

LEARNING OBJECTIVES

In this chapter we discuss the various forms of larceny or theft. The learning objectives for Chapter 13 are:

- List the property concepts that underlie property theft crimes.

- State the "money" rule and why it is an exception to general property rules.

- List four ways the taking element can be proved.

- Define "property of another" as it applies to theft of jointly owned property.

- Identify ways the taking requirement can be met in shoplifting.

- Advise a hypothetical merchant on how best to proceed when a suspected shoplifter is identified.

- Explain the ways credit card theft can be proved.

- Distinguish between forgery and uttering a forged instrument.

- Describe how a check-kiting scheme works.

Timothy Maynard had a friend who was receiving disability checks from the Social Security Administration. To help his friend out, Maynard often drove him to the post office where the checks were mailed to the friend's post office box. The friend was incarcerated in 2006, which under Social Security rules would have caused the termination of his benefits. However, Maynard took his friend's post office box key and began cashing the Social Security checks by forging his friend's signature, and they continued to arrive each month. This went on for nearly two years, until the Social Security Administration discovered the friend's incarceration. Maynard was caught forging a check in the ensuing investigation, and in 2010, after pleading guilty to theft of government money, he was sentenced to 6 months in jail followed by 5 years' probation.

In this chapter we will learn about several property crimes committed against individuals, government, or business, such as shoplifting, fraudulent use of credit cards, and check forgery. We will also learn about the rise of computer-related crimes and the use of computers in committing crimes. In shoplifting cases we will learn the rules that determine when a business is justified in detaining and questioning a suspected shoplifter and the risks associated with such a decision that turns out not to be justified.

≡ General Property Concepts

Understanding the criminal law as it relates to property or interests in property requires some understanding of property law concepts. The following paragraphs illustrate some of these concepts.

- *Property* is divided into two types: real property and personal property. Real estate is real property; everything else is personal property.
- Two important rights to property are (1) the right of ownership and (2) the right of possession of the property. A person may have the lawful possession of property but not necessarily be its owner. Possession of personal property is presumptive evidence of ownership if no evidence to the contrary is shown. Possession accompanied by the exercise of the complete acts of ownership for a considerable period is strong evidence of the ownership of property.[1]
- Property ownership may be in the form of sole ownership. It could also be in the form of joint ownership, as between husband and wife, business partners, or friends or relatives. The property may be owned by a corporation or a business partnership. Property ownership may be vested in a government unit, such as a city, a county, a state, or the national government.
- Lawful possession of property takes many forms. The owner may have the possession of property or may permit another person to have lawful possession and use of the property. An employee or agent of the owner of the property may have possession.

    Bailees and pledges also have the lawful possession of property that belongs to others. A bailment exists, for example, when people take their car into a garage for repairs. The owner of the car retains title and ownership to the vehicle but gives possession to the garage so the repair work may be done. State statutes give the garage a right to a lien on the vehicle in the amount of the work that was done on the car. The garage then has a superior right of possession of the vehicle until the owner satisfies the amount lawfully due the garage. In many states, the owners of the property could be charged with theft if they intentionally and unlawfully take possession of such property from a pledgee or bailee who has a superior right of possession.[2]
- A thief has neither the lawful right to possession nor ownership of stolen property. Therefore, in almost all situations, a thief cannot convey lawful title to stolen property to another person, even if that person is an innocent good-faith purchaser of the property. Known by the Latin phrase *nemo dat quod non habet* ("one cannot give what one does not have"), this principle, together with the phrase *caveat emptor* ("let the buyer beware") requires the innocent purchaser to be very wary of buying from strangers, as the following case illustrates.
- One exception to the *nemo dat* rule involves the transfer by a thief of stolen money or negotiable securities, such as bearer bonds, which are securities payable to any person in possession of the bonds. Called the "money" rule, it provides that a person who receives money in good faith and for value given takes title to the money. For example, in *City of Portland v. Berry*,[3] a thief stole nine $1,000 bills and eighteen $500 bills

> ### *Greek Orthodox Church of Cyprus v. Goldberg* et al.
>
> Court of Appeals of the United States, Seventh Circuit (1990) 917 F.2d 278
>
> Peg Goldberg, an art dealer, was in Europe on a buying trip. She "fell in love" with four early Christian mosaics that she was told were "found" in the rubble of an "extinct" church in northern Cyprus and were exported to Germany with the permission of the Cyprus government. Goldberg made some inquiries about the mosaics and then borrowed money to purchase them for U.S. $1,080,000. After she shipped the mosaics to the United States, she was informed that the sixth-century mosaics had been stolen from the Greek Orthodox Church. Possession of the mosaics was awarded to the Church, with the Court concluding:
>
> > *[W]hen circumstances are as suspicious as those that faced Peg Goldberg, prospective purchasers would do best to do more than make a few last-minute phone calls. As testified to at trial, in a transaction like this, "All the red flags are up, all the red lights are on, all the sirens are blaring." ... (quoting testimony of Dr. Vikan). In such cases, dealers can (and probably should) take steps such as a formal IFAR search; a documented authenticity check by disinterested experts; a full background search of the seller and his claim of title; insurance protection and a contingency sales contract; and the like. If Goldberg would have pursued such methods, perhaps she would have discovered in time what she has now discovered too late: the Church has a valid, superior and enforceable claim to these Byzantine treasures, which therefore must be returned to it.*

from her employer and took them to her bank, where she converted the large bills to bills of smaller denomination. When the theft was discovered, the bank still had possession of the large bills, and the owners sought their return. The court said no, because the bank had given value for the bills in good faith; that is, it had no reason to suspect the bills were stolen.

The justification for the "money" rule has been stated as follows:

It is absolutely necessary for commerce and business to continue that one who receives money, cashier's checks or money orders is not put on inquiry as to the source from which the funds have been derived. It is generally impossible or impractical to discover the source of money, and for this reason one who receives money in good faith for valuable consideration prevails over the victim.[4]

≡ Theft or Larceny[5]

theft or larceny Stealing property of another with the intent to deprive the owner of possession.

taking The act of obtaining physical possession or control of another's property. The key to taking is that the thief exercises unauthorized dominion over the property.

Historically, the common law recognized a broad and often confusing number of theft of property crimes. Today, virtually all states have consolidated these many crimes under the heading of **theft or larceny**.[6] A great number of these crimes remain, however. The federal government alone has more than 100 separate statutes in Title 18 of the U.S. Code that deal with theft or theft-related activity.[7]

A typical theft or larceny statute today would require an unlawful (1) taking of (2) property of another with (3) intent to deprive the owner of possession thereof. In this section, these requirements are discussed in detail.

The Taking

Taking refers to the act of obtaining physical possession or control of another's property. A taking can occur by acts of a stranger, by a trusted employee, or even by a spouse.

It can be by one having no right to possess the property or by one with limited rights to that possession. The key to taking is that the thief exercises unauthorized dominion over the property.

Direct Taking   The most easily understood taking is direct taking, where the thief directly takes physical possession of another person's property. Examples of this include purse snatching, pickpocketing, shoplifting, and car theft. This kind of taking requires the thief to obtain actual physical possession of the property, even if for a short time.

EXAMPLE: A stranger walks into your backyard and up to your locked bike. He attempts to break the lock, but before he can do so, he is stopped by a passing police officer. He has not yet taken the bike and is not guilty of theft.

EXAMPLE: The same facts, except that the stranger breaks the lock. While he is turning to wheel the bike out of your yard, the police stop him. Even if he has moved only a few feet, he has taken the bike and is guilty of theft.

The common law and some states today require both a taking ("caption") and carrying away ("asportation") of the stolen property. Carrying away requires that the property be moved in some manner. However, even the slightest change of position of the property satisfies this requirement. Thus, in the example, in a state that retains a carrying away requirement, the smallest movement of the bike would be sufficient.[8]

The Taking of Lost and Mislaid Goods or Goods Delivered by Mistake   A taking may also occur where the initial physical possession of the property of another is not unlawful but where the person in possession acts in a manner showing an intent to deprive the owner of ownership rights.

EXAMPLE: A woman finds a purse under a bush near a walking path. Inside the purse she finds $500 in cash. The woman puts the cash in her pocket. At this point, she has not taken the cash, because her possession is not yet unlawful. Later, she uses the cash to buy herself a new coat. At this point, she has taken the cash.

EXAMPLE: A man deposited a federal income tax return check in the amount of $1,907 into his checking account. His bank mistakenly credited his account in the amount of $10,907. When he discovered the mistake, the man withdrew over $7,000 of the money. He was convicted of theft.[9]

EXAMPLE: A man leaving the U.S. Army was to receive a severance check for $183, but to his surprise, the check he received was for $836,728.19. The man immediately deposited the money and began spending it. After the error was discovered, action was taken against the man.[10]

Sometimes in situations like these examples, the person in possession of lost or misdirected property does nothing about it. For example, the owner of a checking account does nothing when he discovers that his bank has credited his account with too much money. Proving a taking in those cases may be difficult, even though the account's owner plans to wait and see if the bank discovers the mistake and, if not, keep the money. Some states have followed the Model Penal Code's approach to this problem. Section 223.5 makes one guilty of theft if "with purpose to deceive the owner thereof, he fails to take reasonable measures to restore the property to a person entitled to it." Other states, following the common law rules, find the person guilty of theft only if at the time the person learned of the mistake he or she formed the intent to appropriate the funds. In those states, the taking must occur at the same time the intent to steal is formed.[11]

A person who finds lost property and makes an attempt to return it to the true owner is not guilty of theft, even if he or she tries to obtain a reward for the return of the property. (Under some circumstances, the person might be guilty of extortion; see the discussion of extortion in Chapter 14.)

However, if the property is not lost, and the person takes it and subsequently demands a reward for its return, a taking does occur. For example, in *People v. Stay*, 96 Cal. Rptr. 651 (Cal. App. 1971), a defendant was convicted of theft when he collected shopping carts owned by various supermarkets that customers had removed from the owners' premises. The defendant then offered to return the carts, upon payment of a "finder's" fee. If the fee was not paid, the defendant sold the carts. The court held that because the carts were left within a few blocks of each store, in front of customers' houses, the markets knew where they were and routinely collected them. The carts were not lost, and therefore the defendant had no right to a finder's fee. The defendant was convicted of grand theft.

Taking by Trick, Deception, or Fraud   Taking has been achieved by the use of many tricks, deceptions, and **fraud**. The owner of the property may be deceived by false representations that cause the owner to give up possession of the property. Con games fall into this category. Modern theft and larceny statutes specifically define these forms of taking as elements of the crimes of theft and larceny.

fraud Use of deceit or trickery to obtain profit or advantage.

Confidence games and schemes (con games) have been used for hundreds of years. The pigeon drop was reportedly used more than 1,000 years ago in China. The deception has always been the same. The con man or woman wins the confidence of the victim, talking fast enough to keep the victim confused while dangling enough temptation to appeal to the victim. Unfortunately, a large percentage of the victims are elderly.

Phone call thefts are also common in the United States. The Federal Trade Commission (FTC), which monitors and investigates interstate telemarketing scams, reported that Americans lose nearly $1 billion each year in phony telemarketing schemes. The FTC reported that telephone swindlers are increasingly defrauding the elderly in telephone frauds. The chance of victims' recovering their money from con games and phone call thefts, unfortunately, is low.

The following cases illustrate only two of the many ways used to commit theft by fraud:

People v. Rohlfs

Court of Appeals of Illinois, 752 N.E.2d 499 (2001)

While in jail on similar charges, the defendant made telephone calls to elderly women, telling them he was a relative in need of cash. One of these women sent the defendant a $1,500 money order made out to him. Western Union delivered the money order to the defendant in jail, where he endorsed it. Before he could cash the money order, jail officials seized it. The court held that he "obtained" money by deception and convicted him of that crime.

> ### *Lambert v. State*
>
> Supreme Court of Wisconsin (1976) 73 Wis. 2d 590, 243 N.W.2d 524
>
> The defendant obtained substantial amounts of money from different women by promising to marry them. The Supreme Court of Wisconsin affirmed the convictions of the defendant for six charges of theft by fraud. (Broken promises are punished in only a minority of the states as theft by fraud.) The Wisconsin jury found in this case that Lambert made false promises meant to deceive so that he could obtain money from his victims by fraud (in breach of promise cases, promises are genuine and are then broken).

FORMS OF TAKING AND TYPES OF THEFT

Shoplifting (Retail Theft) or Price Altering
- Shoplifting—the most common form of theft in retail stores—is the taking by concealment to avoid payment for goods.
- Price altering avoids payment of the full price of an object by lowering the amount on the price tag.

Taking by Employee, Bailee, or Trustee
- Employee theft of money and other objects causes large losses in business places.
- Embezzlement of funds or negotiable securities that are in the custody of employees, bailees, or trustees.

Snatch and Run
- The taking is observed, and the offender flees to avoid apprehension.

Till Tap
- Thief opens cash register unobserved and takes cash and coins.
- While store employee has cash drawer open, money is grabbed, and the thief flees (snatch and run).

Taking by Trick, Deception, or Fraud (Stings, Scams, or Swindles)
- Con games and operations.
- Deceptions and tricks to obtain property illegally.
- Obtaining property by false pretense.

Taking from a Person
- Purse snatching (a form of snatch and run).
- Pickpocketing.
- Rolling a drunk (taking from a person incapacitated by alcohol, drugs, or other means).
- Taking from a corpse.

Taking of Lost or Mislaid Goods or Money

Taking of Objects or Money Delivered by Mistake
- Example: a check for too much money is mailed to a person by mistake.

Looting
- Taking property from or near a building damaged, destroyed, or left unoccupied by tornado, fire, physical disaster, riot, bombing, earthquake, and so on.

Embezzlement[12]   Many employees have money and property that belong to their employer. Lawyers, stockbrokers, business partners, and bailees also have money or property that belongs to clients and business associates. Because bank clerks and cashiers in restaurants and stores already have possession of money belonging to their employers, they do not have to take the money in the legal sense in order to steal.

To fill in this large gap left in the criminal codes, the crime of **embezzlement** was created by statutes in England and the United States. It forbids a person already in lawful possession of money or property from fraudulently converting the money or property to his or her own use.

Many states have also solved this problem by expanding the "taking" in their theft or larceny statutes to include "uses, transfers, conceals or retains possession." Under such a

embezzlement To wrongfully appropriate money or property entrusted to one for that person's own use.

Taking by Failure to Return a Leased or Rented Object
- Example: failure to return a rented car or videotape within the time specified by state statutes or city ordinance.

Taking by Illegal Entry into Locked Coin Box
- Vending machine, pay telephone, parking meter, and so on.

Smash and Run
- A store or other window is broken, and after snatching objects, the thief runs to avoid apprehension. (This can also be charged as burglary.)
- Women drivers waiting at stoplights are sometimes subjected to this tactic. The thief breaks the car window, takes the woman's purse from the front seat, and runs.[a]

Taking by Illegally Obtaining or Using Information
- Such as the insider trading scandals. See the 1987 U.S. Supreme Court case of *Carpenter v. United States* (108 S. Ct. 316). One of the defendants in the case was the co-author of a *Wall Street Journal* column.

Taking by Illegal Use of a Credit Card or Credit Card Number
Taking from a Person with a Superior Right of Possession
- People may acquire a superior right of possession over the owner of property because of a bailment, pledge, or contract. State criminal codes may make taking from a person with a superior right of possession a crime.

Theft by Possession of Stolen Property
- See 832 P.2d 337 (Idaho 1992), 473 N.W.2d 84 (Nebraska 1991), and 419 S.E.2d 759 (Georgia 1992).

Ordinary Theft
- Taking occurs observed or unobserved by owner or other people.

[a]The "bump" technique is also used. An expensive car with only a driver occupant is usually picked as the victim. While the victim is waiting at a stoplight, the victim's car is bumped intentionally. When the victim gets out of the car to view the damages, one of the thieves distracts the victim while the other thief sneaks around to get into the victim's car. Because the victim generally leaves the keys in the ignition, the thief drives off in the victim's car. The other thief jumps in his or her car and also speeds away, leaving the victim stranded.

statute, a stockbroker, lawyer, or cashier who stole money could be charged with theft or larceny.

Defining What Property Can Be Stolen

Under the common law, only tangible personal property could be stolen. Real estate and items attached to the land could not be stolen, because of the "asportation," or "carrying away" requirement. Documents such as stocks, bonds, checks, or promissory notes were not subject to theft, because they are intangible personal property.

All states and the federal government have broadened the original common law definition of property that can be stolen. Some modern criminal codes include any sort of property of value that can be moved. Illinois defines *property subject to theft* as "anything of value," including real estate, money, commercial instruments, tickets, and written documents.[13] Minnesota defines *property* to include documents and things growing on or affixed to land.[14] Section 223.2 of the Model Penal Code defines "theft by unlawful taking or disposition" as

1. *Movable Property:* A person is guilty of theft if he takes, or exercises unlawful control over, movable property of another with purpose to deprive him thereof.
2. *Immovable Property:* A person is guilty of theft if he unlawfully transfers immovable property of another or any interest therein with purpose to benefit himself or another not entitled thereto.

As the above definition of "immovable property" suggests, in order to convict a person of theft of real estate there must be a "transfer" of the property, or an interest in the property. Because an interest in real estate is transferred by the owner signing a deed, the theft offense is usually committed by the thief deceptively persuading the owner to sign a deed transferring the property. For this reason, most state theft statutes that include theft of real estate define theft to include obtaining property by deception. See, e.g., Cal. Pen Code § 484(a). However, executing a purported deed by forging the owner's signature and recording the deed is not theft, since absent a lawful deed nothing has been taken. The California Court of Appeals reversed a conviction under the theft statute based on a forged deed, holding that forged deed cannot convey title. The person forging the deed could be charged with forgery, or fraudulently recording a forged deed, the court said.[15]

Not only may documents be stolen but also information from computers, files, and other places may be stolen.[16] Under fraud statutes and other specific statutes, telephone and computer services may be stolen. In a 2008 case, the Wisconsin Court of Appeals held that the Wisconsin theft statute, WSA 943.20(2)(b), applied to theft of phone services. An inmate serving a 133-year term in a Wisconsin prison set up several telephone accounts in fictitious names and then used the telephone numbers to make collect calls totaling over 40,000 minutes. The court held that the definition of "property" in the theft statute included "electricity," and that electricity includes telephone service. The court also held that the defendant could be prosecuted under the general theft statute, even though Wisconsin has a specific statute, WSA § 943.45, for telecommunications theft.[17] Contraband, such as illegal drugs, can be stolen, even though people losing such property are not likely to report such thefts to the police. In *Ceballos v. State*, 2009 WL 1478000, the Arkansas Court of Appeals held that the Arkansas theft statutes included contraband. The defendant broke into a residence to steal illegal marijuana held there by the residence's owner. When charged with theft, the defendant argued illegal contraband is not "property of another," because no one can own contraband. The court disagreed, stating that the theft statutes define "property" as anything of value that can be possessed, and that illegal marijuana satisfies both of those requirements.

Value of Property   If the property has no intrinsic value, a prosecution for theft or larceny would be hard to sustain. A single sheet of paper worth a penny or less has little intrinsic value. If, however, a signed promissory note for $1,000 were on the sheet of paper, the value of the paper would increase considerably. In charging theft or larceny, the state must introduce evidence showing the value of the property alleged to have been stolen.

The value of the property stolen, in most instances, determines whether the charge is a misdemeanor or a felony. The value of the property must be determined by the court or jury. Statements by the owner concerning what he or she paid for the property, how long it was possessed, its replacement cost, and its condition are admissible in determining value. Evidence of the value of comparable property in comparable condition is admissible to show the value of the property at issue. Experts and appraisers may, in some instances, be called into court to testify as to value. (Sentimental value can generally not be considered.)

In the New York case of *People v. Harold*, the defendant was convicted of grand larceny for the theft of a water pump that had been purchased five days before the theft. However, the pump had been damaged before the theft by two men, Crego and Terpening, who had attempted to install the pump. In ordering a new trial, the court stated:

> The question presented by this appeal pertains to the value of the stolen pump.... [T]he market value of a stolen item is to be measured by what the thief would have had to pay had he purchased the item instead of stealing it.... In the instant case, the value of the pump must be reduced to reflect the mechanical prowess of Crego and Terpening. Additionally, an allowance must be made for the fact that the pump, when taken, was no longer new.
>
> Many state statutes provide that *value* means the market value at the time of the theft or the cost to the victim of replacing the property within a reasonable time after the theft. The replacement value to a retail store is the replacement cost to the store, not the retail price of the item.[18]

As the New York court pointed out in the *Harold* case, the value in New York would be "market value" or "what the thief would have to pay had he purchased the item instead of stealing it." Colorado[19] and many other states also follow this rule in determining value. Other states use the replacement value rule—the replacement cost to a retail store to replace a stolen item.

Property of Another

To prove theft or larceny, the state must show that the property belonged to another, whether that is an individual, a corporation, or a governmental unit. Because the consent of the owner would constitute a total defense in a theft or larceny charge, the owner (or a representative of the owner) must testify that the taking was without his or her consent. A showing that the owner did not consent to the conduct of the defendant is also necessary in criminal damage to property, in trespass, and in arson of either real property or personal property.

Under modern law, a husband and wife are not treated as a single entity for many purposes, including the criminal law of theft. As a result, one spouse can be guilty of theft of the other spouse's property, because that property qualifies as "property of another." However, the property must belong to the spouse from whom it is taken, and it cannot be the kind of property that is "normally accessible" to both spouses. A refrigerator, for example, even if bought by one spouse, cannot be stolen by the other spouse if the couple is still living together.

An example of theft by a spouse is *State v. Krinitt*,[20] a 1991 decision of the Supreme Court of Montana. In *Krinitt*, a husband was convicted of stealing his wife's trust fund check. The husband had a history of wasting the couple's finances, so the wife instructed the trust fund to send the check to her attorney. When the check was delivered to their home by mistake, the husband cashed it and spent the money. He was convicted of theft because the trust fund check was not "accessible" to both spouses.

Many people hold property jointly with others. Suppose a business partner steals $1,000 from the partnership checking account and uses it for his personal needs. Or suppose a wife runs off with another man and takes $500 out of a savings and loan account that is in the name of her husband and herself. Is this stealing the property of another? Whether this constitutes theft or larceny would be determined by the statutes of that jurisdiction in defining the property of another.

The Model Penal Code Section 233 (7) defines "property of another" to include property in which the defendant has an interest, so long as the interest of the other person is one the defendant "is not privileged to infringe." Although each partner in a partnership, or each holder of a joint checking account, may have access to partnership funds or the checking account, they are not privileged to infringe on the others' rights and can be guilty of theft. In *State v. Mora*, 43 P.3d 38 (Wash. App. 2002) the court upheld a theft conviction of funds in a checking account. The defendants convinced the mother of one of them to place their names on her checking and savings accounts. They then withdrew more than $50,000 from those accounts. When charged with theft, they contended that they did not steal property of another, because they were authorized to make the withdrawals. The court rejected their defense, stating that while a good faith belief that a person had a right to take property was a good defense, the defendants could not have that belief based only on the fact their names were on the accounts. They knew the funds belonged to the mother, and that she had no intention of giving them any interest in the funds.

The question of the meaning of "property of another" came up in the Michigan case of *People v. Young*. In that case, the defendant took back from a prostitute the $10 he had paid the woman for her sexual services. In affirming the conviction for the crime of larceny from the person, the court stated:

> On appeal defendant Young's only argument is that his actions did not constitute a crime since the agreement he made to purchase sexual services was illegal and so his forcefully taking back the $10 was not a crime.
>
> We are not persuaded by that argument. The trial court did not enforce any contract legal or otherwise. The agreement had been completed and both parties had received the agreed-upon consideration. Defendant Young then forcefully took back the $10 which by that time belonged to the woman. Such action constituted the crime of larceny from a person. "Public policy requires that courts should lend active aid in punishing persons who obtain money or property from others by criminal means, and it is no defense that the complaining witness was himself engaged in an illegal transaction." Glenn Gillespie, *Michigan Criminal Law and Procedure* (2d ed.), § 29, p. 49 (St. Paul, Minn.: West, 1953)[21]

Difficulties in Identifying Property   Some property is difficult for owners to identify. Diamonds and other valuable stones are an example. Valuable stones may be easily identified by their settings, but once they are removed, they are difficult to distinguish. The four Cs of the diamond business—cut, clarity, carat, and color—provide only the roughest means of identification. An owner's testimony of "it looks like my property, but I am not sure" is not sufficient identification. Because of the difficulty of identification, in some situations the police have been forced to return property to a known thief because of lack of evidence that the property was stolen.

The stolen property must be identified by introducing evidence showing no reasonable doubt as to its identity. For this reason, law enforcement agencies urge marking property in such ways that the identification marks cannot be easily removed or obliterated.

Abandoned Property   If the property has been abandoned or if the owner of the property cannot be located, then theft or larceny cannot be proved. *Abandonment* has been defined as the relinquishment or surrender of property or the rights to property. In 1952, the U.S. Supreme Court considered the case of *Morissette v. United States.*[22] Morissette was charged with the theft of scrap metal from an old bombing range. His defense was that he honestly thought that the property had been abandoned.

Because the trial court would not allow the jury to determine whether the property had been abandoned or whether Morissette honestly, but mistakenly, believed that the property was abandoned, the conviction was reversed.

Intent to Steal

Theft or larceny requires a specific intent to deprive the owner of possession of the property. The intent to steal may be proved by direct evidence or by circumstantial evidence. Generally, the fact finder (jury or judge) concludes and infers an intent to steal from the conduct and acts of the defendant. In the following shoplifting case, the California Court of Appeals directed that the described California jury instructions on intent to steal be given to the jury.

Frequently, defendants attempt to defeat the intent to steal requirement by contending that they intended only to borrow the property. In many cases, the jury gives little credence to this defense, sensibly concluding that the defendants' actions show a different intent. However, if true, an intent to return the property negates guilt of theft, unless

People v. Jaso

Court of Appeals of California (1970) 4 Cal. App.3d 767, 84 Cal. Rptr. 567

The defendant was walking toward the parking lot and his car when he was stopped with unpaid merchandise in a shopping bag from a Sears store. The defendant stated that he left his wallet in the glove compartment of his car because he was wearing tight Levi's. He stated that he was going to get his wallet and would pay for the merchandise, but when the security officer held him and would not let him go, he struggled with the security officer. Defendant was subdued and placed in handcuffs. A new trial was ordered after the defendant was convicted at the first trial. The court of appeals held that the trial court had failed to give the following California jury instruction:

In the crime of [theft], there must exist in the mind of the perpetrator the specific intent to [take the property of another], and unless such intent so exists that crime is not committed. (CALJIC Instruction 71.11) The specific intent with which an act is done may be manifested by the circumstances surrounding its commission. But you may not find the defendant guilty of the offense charged in Count [II] unless the proved circumstances not only are consistent with the hypothesis that he had the specific intent to [take the property of another] but are irreconcilable with any other rational conclusion. (CALJIC Instruction 27-A) the return date is unusually far in the future. For example, taking a neighbor's lawn mower in April and intending to return it in November may be enough to prove theft, unless the theft statute of that state requires a showing that the taker intended to permanently deprive the owner of possession.

In some states, the "borrowing" problem has been solved by establishing a separate theft offense for taking property without the intent to deprive the owner of "permanent" possession. For example, the Kansas "Criminal deprivation of property" statute, KSA § 21-3705, makes a theft crime of any "obtaining or exerting unauthorized control over property of another, with the intent to deprive the owner of the temporary use thereof." In Texas, VTCA Penal Code § 31.01 includes within the meaning of "deprive another" of property keeping the property for "So extended a period of time that a major portion of the value...of the property is lost to the owner."

In some cases, even short-term borrowing can be a crime. Many states have statutes that make it a crime to use or operate another person's automobile, motorcycle, or other motor-propelled vehicle without permission of the owner, even if the person intends to return the vehicle after a short joyride. The Model Penal Code, Section 223.9, makes this conduct a misdemeanor.

☰ Shoplifting

Theft has always been a problem for retail stores in the United States. Annual studies done jointly by the National Retail Federation and the University of Florida indicate that the cost of retail theft and fraud every year in the United States runs into billions of dollars. Preliminary results from the most recent survey, released by the National Retail Federation on June 15, 2010, show national retail inventory "shrinkage" (inventory losses) was $33.5 billion for 2009, down from $36.5 billion in 2008. Of that total, employee theft accounted for $14.4 billion, or 43 percent of the total. Shoplifting was responsible for $11.7 billion, or 35 percent. The balance of the shrinkage was due to administrative error ($4.9 billion), and vendor fraud ($1.3 billion).[23]

The most common form of employee fraud and theft is called "sweethearting," which occurs when cashiers fail to scan goods or ring up sales for goods brought through a check-out line or to a register by friends or relatives. Stealing from the till continues to be a problem, as do manipulation of store computers to issue gift cards or other fraudulent schemes. When stolen or fake credit cards are used to purchase inventory, the retail store owner can suffer losses if the credit card company does not honor the credit card.

shoplifting Stealing goods from retail stores by concealment, generally on the person of the defendant. Commission does not require removal of the goods from the store.

The crime of **shoplifting**, or retail theft, is a form of theft and larceny. Shoplifting has the same essential elements as theft and larceny: (1) a taking and carrying away (2) of the property of another (3) without consent and (4) with intent to steal and deprive the owner of possession of the property.

Taking and Carrying Away in Shoplifting

In modern self-service stores, customers are invited to examine merchandise on display. Garments may be taken to dressing rooms and tried on. Customers carry about merchandise either in their hands or in shopping carts provided by the store. The New York Court of Appeals pointed out in the case of *People v. Olivo* that stores therefore consent "to the customer's possession of the goods" for limited purposes.[24]

Stores do not consent, however, to concealment of their merchandise by customers. The merchandise is offered for sale, and if customers are not going to purchase an object, they are obligated to return the merchandise to the display counter in good condition.

CASE CLOSE-UP

State v. Goodman
915 A.2d 79 (N.J. Super. A.D. 2007)

Proving the charge of shoplifting, just as with other crimes, requires proof of every element of the offense. As stated above, shoplifting has the same elements as other theft crimes. In this case a defendant was charged with violation of the New Jersey shoplifting statute, N.J.S.A. Section 2C:20–11(b). That statute defines shoplifting as:

> *For any person purposely to take possession of, carry away, transfer or cause to be carried away or transferred, any merchandise displayed, held, stored, or offered for sale by any retail mercantile establishment with the intention of depriving the merchant of the possession, use or benefit of such merchandise or converting the same to the use of such person without paying the full retail value thereof.*

Defendant left some film to be developed by a Walgreens store. When he picked up the finished prints, he refused to pay the $9.75 charge, stating that the price was different from that advertised, and also he asked for double prints and got only single prints. The store manager disagreed, and the defendant left the store with the prints, leaving his name and telephone number where he could be contacted to "settle the billing dispute." The store manager filed a complaint with the police, and the defendant was charged with violation of the shoplifting statute.

The defendant was tried in a municipal court and convicted of shoplifting and sentenced to pay a $150.00 fine, pay restitution to the store of $9.75, and perform 10 days of community service. He appealed to the Law Division (the first appellate level in New Jersey), which affirmed the conviction. That court stated, "The defendant was not entitled to leave the store with merchandise being offered for sale without payment because defendant felt he was being overcharged."

The defendant then appealed to New Jersey Superior Court, Appellate Division. That court reversed the conviction, stating that the shoplifting statute contained a "fatal ambiguity" and did not cover defendant's actions. The court said that the statute prohibits taking or carrying away "merchandise" held or offered for sale. The court said that the term *merchandise* refers to inventory held by a retail store for sale to the public, and the prints taken by the defendant were not "goods displayed, held, stored or offered for sale" to the public. Because the defendant owned the film being developed, the store could not legally sell the prints to the public, the court said, which prevented the prints from being "merchandise" as required by the statute. Moreover, the court said, as to the defendant the Walgreens store was not a "mercantile establishment" as required by the statute, but simply a bailee for services.

The court also refused to interpret the words *held* or *stored* to include the prints. Those terms related to merchandise in a retail store, which the prints were not. The court also said that even if the terms could be interpreted as including the prints, they would be ambiguous, and in criminal statute an ambiguity cannot be resolved by expanding the conduct covered by the statute.

Finally, the court found another element of the offense unproved. The statute requires the taking to be done "purposely" with the intent to deprive the merchant of the goods taken without payment of the "full retail value thereof." Because the defendant simply disputed what the "full retail value" was, and he was willing to pay the price once it had been fairly determined, the court said the prosecution failed to prove he had the intent to deprive Walgreens of the "full retail value" of the prints. The defendant's conviction was reversed.

If customers take the merchandise, they have a legal obligation to pay the purchase price. The highest court in New York State held in the *Olivo* case:

> If the customer exercises dominion and control wholly inconsistent with the continued rights of the owner, and the other elements of the crime are present, a larceny has occurred. Such conduct on the part of a customer satisfies the "taking" element of the crime.
>
>   * * *
>
> A taking of property in the self-service store context can be established by evidence that a customer exercised control over merchandise wholly inconsistent with the store's continued rights. Quite simply, a customer who crosses the line between the limited right he or she has to deal with merchandise and the store owner's rights may be subject to prosecution for larceny. Such a rule should foster the legitimate interests and continued operation of self-service shops, a convenience which most members of the society enjoy.[25]

Proving the Crime of Shoplifting When the Suspect Has Not Left the Store

There is a common belief that shoplifting has not occurred until the merchandise has been taken from the store premises. The Criminal Court of the City of New York discussed this belief in *People v. Britto*:

> There are a number of myths about the criminal law, comfortably shared and nourished by those in the street, the business community and sometimes, the courts. One of these is the belief that an observed shoplifter acts with impunity unless and until he or she leaves the store with the goods. So strong is this belief that the majority of store detectives are instructed to refrain from stopping the suspect anywhere inside the premises; although the likelihood of apprehension is thus enormously decreased.[26]

Courts are virtually unanimous in holding that goods need not leave the store for theft to occur. The New York Court of Appeals explained that result as follows:

> Case law from other jurisdictions seems unanimous in holding that a shoplifter need not leave the store to be guilty of larceny.... This is because a shopper may treat merchandise in a manner inconsistent with the owner's continued rights—and in a manner not in accord with that of a prospective purchaser—without actually walking out of the store.[27]

Inconsistent actions might include hiding the goods under the shopper's coat or other clothes. As the Maryland Court of Special Appeals held in *Lee v. State*, if merchandise is secreted under clothing, it meets the requirement of concealment, and it does not matter if the concealment was for a short time or if the shopper did not leave the store.[28]

The Requirement of Probable Cause Based on Personal Knowledge

Private security officers and retail store employees are often told, "If you have not seen it, it has not happened." Customers are not to be treated like shoplifters until hard, first-hand information demonstrates that shoplifting has occurred. The Criminal Court of New York emphasized the **probable cause** requirement in *People v. Britto*:

probable cause
Reasonable grounds to believe.

> It must be emphasized that this court's holding in no way lessens the burden of proof on the People in shoplifting cases. On the contrary, there is, and should be, a higher standard of proof upon the People in self-service situations than in other larceny cases, because the mere fact of possession may not be used to demonstrate larceny.

This remains true even when such possession is accompanied by suspicious or equivocal actions, such as placing unpaid goods directly into the defendant's shopping bag (see *Durphy v. United States*, 235 A.2d 326 [D.C. App. 1967]). It is only when the trier of fact concludes, beyond a reasonable doubt, that defendant's actions were totally inconsistent with and clearly adverse to the owner's interests that a conviction may lie. If the facts are sufficient to support such a conclusion *before* the defendant leaves the store, the fact that he has not left is wholly irrelevant and should not absolve him from the consequences of his acts.[29]

The U.S. Supreme Court defined *probable cause* as "facts and circumstances within their knowledge and of which they had reasonable trustworthy information [that] were sufficient in themselves to warrant a man of reasonable caution in the belief" that the suspect had committed a crime.[30] The Supreme Judicial Court of Massachusetts held:

> Historically, the words "reasonable grounds" and "probable cause" have been given the same meaning by the courts.
>
> * * *
>
> The Oregon Supreme Court construed the meaning of the words "reasonable grounds" in its "shoplifting statute" as having the same meaning as they have in a statute authorizing arrest without a warrant and applied the probable cause standard to the facts before it.[31]

EXAMPLE: On a hot July day, a woman customer stated to a clerk in a large food store, "I suspect that young man of shoplifting." She pointed at a young black man wearing a jogging suit. The clerk relayed the statement to the assistant manager of the store, who confronted the young man, accusing him of shoplifting in a voice overheard by other people. The young man was detained, and the police were called. Did probable cause exist to justify this action?

When the police arrived, they questioned the store employees and the woman customer. The woman customer stated that she had not witnessed a shoplifting but had only "suspected" that a theft had occurred. The police then realized that probable cause did not exist from the facts known to the store employees, and they released the young man. In the civil lawsuit that followed, a jury awarded the young man money damages for false imprisonment and **defamation** (slander).

Merchants who detain or prosecute suspected shoplifters face the possibility of large damage awards if they are found to have acted unreasonably, as the following cases held:

defamation Wrongful injury to another's reputation.

malicious prosecution Initiating a judicial action with knowledge the claims made in the action are without merit.

- An employee who drank a soft drink in a damaged can was prosecuted for shoplifting by the employer; after acquittal, the employee sued the employer for **malicious prosecution** and won a $30,000 verdict. See *Bi-Lo Inc. v. McConnell*, 404 S.E.2d 327 (Ga. App. 1991).
- After a court held there was a "total lack of probable cause" to detain him, Clark sued a Kroger Food Store and was awarded $83,500 in compensatory damages and $1 million in punitive damages. See *Clark v. Kroger Food Stores, Inc.*, 587 N.E.2d 1084 (Ind. App. 1992).
- After a search disclosed no stolen merchandise, a security guard continued accusations of theft. The defendant was awarded $75,000 in actual damages and $100,000 in punitive damages. See *Caldwell v. Kmart Corp.*, 410 S.E.2d 21 (S.C. App. 1991).
- The *New York Times* article, "Woman Wins $1.56 Million in Department Store Bias Case," December 11, 1997, tells of black shoppers who won large money awards in

HANDLING A SHOPLIFTING INCIDENT

1. Make sure you have probable cause and a good solid case before you restrain the freedom of movement of a person for shoplifting. Probable cause (or "reasonable grounds to believe") must be based on personal knowledge (firsthand information) by you or another reliable adult employee. Remember: "If you did not see it, it did not happen. When in doubt, let them go."

2. Observing a person concealing "something" or putting "something" in his or her pocket or purse is not sufficient to establish probable cause. The person may be putting a handkerchief or glasses back in a pocket. You must have "reasonable grounds to believe" (probable cause) that the object is unpaid merchandise and that the item belongs to the store. If you do not have probable cause, you may
   - Keep the person under observation.
   - Engage in voluntary conversation ("May I help you?" "Are you looking for something?").
   - Ask the person what they put in his or her pocket, or whether the person has a receipt for merchandise in his or her possession, under circumstances in which there is no restraint of their freedom of movement.

3. After a person is observed shoplifting, the following options are available to store employees or a security officer:
   - Confront the person immediately, and ask that he or she produce the item. Always ask if the person has a receipt showing that he or she paid for the item. Under these circumstances, you may seek only recovery of the item and deterrence, rather than prosecution in court.
   - You may be under instructions to allow the person to go beyond the last pay station (or, in some cases, even out of the store). Under these circumstances, the person should be kept under surveillance. A person who becomes aware of your surveillance may attempt to discard the shoplifted item or pass it onto another person. If you fail to observe the "discard" or "pass-on," you may then be unable to explain why the stolen property was not recovered. If it appears that the person may outrun you and other store employees, it may be wise to position yourself between the exit door and the person.

4. If your state has a civil settlement of shoplifting law, you should know the requirements of this law and also any guidelines that your employer has established for using the law.

5. Shoplifting cases are handled by your local law enforcement agency (police or sheriff), prosecutor, and judge. Consult a knowledgeable official to determine whether any specific standards are required, such as
   - Whether the local judge requires that the person observed shoplifting be allowed beyond the pay station (or out of the store) before being detained. (A young man in gym shoes who gets near a door or out of the store is going to outrun most store security people.)
   - Whether cases will be prosecuted when
     - The value of the merchandise stolen is small (what is the minimum for prosecution?).
     - The merchandise or item stolen has not been recovered.
     - The offender is very young or very old.
     - Other factors are considered.

6. Absolute defenses to civil suits are
   - That the person either voluntarily stayed in the area or that the restraint of movement was made in good faith on probable cause based on personal knowledge.
   - That if any force was used, it was necessary and reasonable either
     - In self-defense.
     - To detain the person.
     - To prevent the theft of the property.

federal lawsuits when juries found that store security officers discriminated against black customers in shoplifting stops and searches without probable cause. An award of $1.56 million was rendered against Dillard's department store in Kansas City, Kansas, and $3 million was awarded against an Eddie Bauer store in Greenbelt, Maryland (a suburb of Washington, D.C.).

To give some protection to store owners in cases like these, some states have enacted statutes called Shoplifting Detention Acts. An example of such an act is Indiana Code Section 35-33-6-2. It grants immunity from civil prosecution if the detention is authorized by the act. The act permits a merchant with probable cause who believes shoplifting has occurred to detain the suspect, demand identification, search the suspect, and inform the suspect's parents of the detention.[32]

Criminal or Civil Prosecution of Shoplifters?

Shoplifting cases can be handled in a variety of different ways, depending on the circumstances of the case. Following are some of the alternative options in handling shoplifting cases:

- When the amount stolen is very small or the offender is very young or very old, a scolding and warning might be used. Parents of children could be called, or the police could take the child home and inform the parents of the problem. Many states have laws making parents liable in a civil action for goods damaged or taken by a minor in a theft.
- More than 30 states have passed laws giving merchants and retailers authority to extract payments and fines from thieves they catch in the act. The offender could sign an agreement under a civil settlement of shoplifting law, acknowledging guilt and agreeing to make the payments to the merchant. In this way, the merchant can save time and expenses by bypassing the police and the courts. The advantages to the shoplifter are that a criminal record is avoided and the incident is taken care of without a court appearance.
- Because criminal courts are very crowded, shoplifting cases are not ordinarily charged criminally unless the amount taken is very large. Civil citations are issued in many cases, and offenders can pay the fine in the same way as parking tickets are paid. Or the offender can be ordered to appear in a municipal court, where the case is heard by a judge in the same way speeding and other traffic violations are heard.
- Criminal charges are likely to be issued in shoplifting cases when

  - The shoplifter commits a serious assault or battery in resisting detention or in attempting to escape. Assault on a law enforcement officer is a felony in probably all states.
  - Escape is made from a law enforcement officer while the defendant is in custody, which is a crime. Some states also forbid escape from a merchant who has lawfully detained a shoplifter. See *State v. Hughes*, 598 N.E.2d 916 (Ohio 1992).
  - The shoplifter has a concealed weapon or illegal drugs on his or her person. Or the shoplifter is in possession of a criminal tool or a shoplifting device. See *State v. Lee*, 586 N.E.2d 190 (1990), in which the defendant had a girdle as a shoplifting tool.
  - The shoplifter causes considerable damage to the merchant's property in an effort to escape. Many states make criminal damage to property a crime if the damage is done either "intentionally" or "recklessly."
  - The shoplifter obstructs and hinders a law enforcement officer by giving the wrong name and date of birth, as in the case of *State v. Caldwell*, 454 N.W.2d 13 (Wis. App. 1990), or obstructs by refusing to obey a law enforcement officer.

See the case of *Mathis v. State*, 391 S.E.2d 130 (Ga. App. 1990), in which the defendant refused to get into the patrol car and struggled with officers.

- The shoplifter has a long prior record of theft and/or has a serious drug or alcohol problem, which the person is stealing to support. (Prosecutors can encourage such people to enter drug treatment programs by threatening jail sentences.)
- The shoplifter commits other crimes. For example, in the case of *State v. Santilli*, 570 So.2d 400 (Fla. App. 1990), the defendant was convicted of robbery when, after shoplifting a greeting card, he backed his car into a law enforcement officer in attempting to escape.

Other Retail Theft Crimes

- *Tag Switching:* A lower price tag is placed on a store item. In the case of *State v. Nguyen*, 584 So.2d 256 (La. App. 1991), tags were switched on a dress and blouse. The state would have to show the switching was done by the defendant and was not a mistake by a store employee or done by another person.
- *Undercharging by Checkout Clerk* (under ringing schemes): The checkout clerk undercharges a friend or co-conspirator. See *Wal-Mart v. Medina*, 814 S.W.2d 71 (Tex. App. 1991).
- *"Storming" or Mass Shoplifting:* Two or many more people storm an all-night or late-night convenience store, take items, and then leave. If force is used or threatened, this could be charged as robbery.
- *Till Tapping:* Reaching into a cash register after distracting the employee, or grabbing money from an open cash register ("snatch and run").
- *Boosting:* This is an organized form of shoplifting used by gangs, in which goods in large quantities are placed in booster bags and then sold by the gangs at huge discounts.

≣ Fraudulent Use of Credit Cards

Credit cards are a means of extending short-term credit. The three parties ordinarily involved in a credit card transaction are (1) the issuer of the credit card, which could be a bank or an organization, such as American Express or MasterCard; (2) the credit card user, who is the holder of the card and the person purchasing the merchandise or service; and (3) the seller of the merchandise or provider of the services.

A person holding a valid credit card signs for the receipt of the goods and commits himself or herself to pay for the service or the property that has been received. The

---

STAY WITHIN THE LAW WHILE PREVENTING SHOPLIFTING

In acting to prevent shoplifting and apprehend shoplifters, merchants and their employees must obey the law. Failure to do so could result in civil lawsuits such as the following:

- False imprisonment, false arrest, or malicious prosecution because of failure to have probable cause to make forcible detention. See *Lazarus Dept. Store v. Sutherlin*, 544 N.E.2d 513 (Ind. App. 1989).
- Slander and false imprisonment because after customer opened her purse to show that no merchandise was taken, guard continued to accuse her in a voice overheard by others in *Caldwell v. K-Mart Corp.*, 410 S.E.2d 21 (S.C. App. 1991), and *Wal-Mart Stores, Inc. v. Dolph*, 825 S.W.2d 810 (1992).
- Wrongful detention in *Taylor v. Dillards Dept. Stores, Inc.*, 971 F.2d 601 (10th Cir. 1992).

merchant or business organization supplying the goods or services is then reimbursed for the amount of the billing by the issuer of the credit card. The credit card issuer then bills the credit card holder.

Credit Card Theft and Obtaining Credit Cards and Bank Cards for Fraudulent Use

Credit card theft occurs when a credit card is stolen, and every state has a statute directed at such theft. The Maryland statute is illustrative of these credit card theft statutes. Section 8-204 of the Maryland Code (2002) makes it a crime to either (1) take a credit card from another without the owner's consent or (2) receive a credit card knowing it was stolen and with the intent to use the card.

The methods of obtaining credit cards for fraudulent use are many and varied. They can be stolen by burglars, pickpockets, or robbers. They can be retained by workers in gas stations or restaurants or stolen from the mail. They can be counterfeited or altered. In the 2009 case of *Gheorghiu v. Com.*, 682 S.E.2d 50, the Virginia Court of Appeals upheld the conviction under the credit card theft statute of a defendant who produced fake credit cards using a laptop computer and a "remagger" device. The device enabled the defendant to place stolen credit card numbers on a fake card, and encode the number onto the magnetic bar used when a credit card is "swiped."

The credit card itself need not be stolen; if a thief uses the card number unlawfully, it is credit card theft.[33] Many states have credit card abuse laws that make it a crime to use a revoked or canceled credit card to fraudulently obtain property.[34]

Thieves obtain credit cards to commit crimes in the following ways:

- Counterfeiting cards (29%)
- Stealing credit cards (22.4%)
- Obtaining lost and mislaid credit cards (16.4%)
- Theft from the mail (13.7%)
- Making fraudulent applications for credit cards (3.2%)
- Placing telephone and mail orders with false cards (9.3%)[35]

It is generally held that a defendant can be convicted under a credit card fraud statute even without possession of the credit card. In *Robinson v. State*, 780 N.E.2d 849 (Ind. App. 2002), the defendant handed an invalid credit card to a merchant to "swipe" in the card reader. When the card would not register, the defendant took the card back and "read" the numbers to the merchant. In fact, the defendant was reading numbers from credit cards the defendant had seen when used by their owners. The court held that the defendant could be convicted under the credit card statute even though he never had the credit card in his possession.

It is also generally held that possession alone of a stolen credit card constitutes credit card theft, even if the card had not been used. In *State v. Jernigan*, 209 P.3d 153 (Ariz. App. 2009) the court upheld a credit card theft conviction even though the prosecution offered no proof the defendant used or intended to use the cards. The defendant knowingly had lost or stolen cards in his possession for over two weeks, which the court said satisfied the "appropriating" requirement of the statute, ARS § 13-1802, since the defendant was both depriving the true owner of possession, and was holding the credit cards for his own use, whatever use that was.

Criminal Use of Bank Cards and Credit Cards

Fraudulent charges using stolen, counterfeit, and lost credit cards are made more frequently during the Christmas season than at any other time of the year. Merchants and salesclerks are busy and probably do not take the precautions they would at other times of the year.

Purchasing goods and services is the principal type of credit card and bank card fraud in the United States. Automated teller machines (ATMs) also present another means of theft and fraud.

A large ATM fraud occurred with one bank card in 1995. The machines are supposed to give no more than $200 per day to any single card. However, because of a program changeover, thieves were able to obtain $346,770 from a single card by making 724 withdrawals from many different machines.[36]

☰ Check Violations

Most checks that bounce are the result of negligence, mistakes, or bad bookkeeping. Persons writing NSF (nonsufficient funds) checks or ISF (insufficient funds) checks generally make the checks good within the period provided by the statutes of that state. For example, Florida Statutes, Section 832.07, require that a bad check be made good within seven days or a criminal prosecution may be commenced, and the writer of the check is liable in a civil action for triple the amount of the check.

Bad checks are a constant problem for retail businesses and banks, as the crime is easy to commit and the money losses are huge.[37] Not only are the money losses growing every year, but an *FBI Law Enforcement Bulletin* article of 1996 pointed out that half of all check fraud in the United States is committed by professional and organized groups.[38] The article pointed out that even street gangs are using sophisticated means to commit check fraud.

The problem of bad checks overwhelms most local law enforcement agencies. The sheer volume of bad checks limits the number that can be investigated and prosecuted. Debit cards, where funds from the card's use are taken directly out of the card owner's bank account, are similar to both checks and credit cards. Theft and use of a debit card can be prosecuted under many states' credit card theft statutes, though in some states existing credit card theft statutes had to be amended to cover debit cards. See, for example, *Withers v. State*, 218 S.W.2d 386 (Ark. App. 2005), where the court held the defendant could not be convicted of theft of a debit card under the existing credit card statute.

The Crime of Uttering

forgery Wrongfully signing a writing or instrument in the name of the person who issued the writing or instrument, or to whom it was payable.

uttering Putting into circulation a check known to be worthless.

When a person signs a false name in the presence of a bank clerk to a check that does not belong to him or her, the felony crime of **forgery** has been committed. The bank clerk can then testify in court that he or she witnessed the forgery. When a forged check is presented for payment, the felony of **uttering** has been committed. The Supreme Court of Virginia defined the crime of uttering:

> Under our bad-check statute, the gravamen of the offense is the intent to defraud, and the offense is complete when, with the requisite intent, a person utters a check he knows to be worthless.... A check is uttered when it is put into circulation; for example, when it is presented for payment.... The presentment is more than a request for payment; it constitutes an implied representation that the check is good. The statute itself dispenses with proof of an extrinsic representation.
>
> * * *
>
> It need not be shown that the implied representation was relied upon or that anything was received in return for the check; indeed, the discovery by a payee that a check is worthless before a purchase transaction is completed does not preclude a conviction under the statute.... And, while we have stated that the statute is "specifically aimed to discourage the giving of bad checks for what purports to be a cash

purchase," ... such a purchase is not the only transaction proscribed; the statute clearly encompasses a worthless check given to obtain cash.[39]

The crime of uttering a forged instrument is most often committed when a person presents a forged instrument for payment. In the case of *England v. State*, the defendant handed a forged check to a bank teller without saying anything.[40] In affirming the defendant's conviction for uttering a forged instrument, the Supreme Court of Indiana held: "We conclude the offering of the check to the teller with no instructions, when this act is generally construed in the banking industry as a request to exchange said check for cash, is sufficient conduct to warrant the jury to believe that the appellant intended to cash a forged instrument." In the 1989 case of *State v. Tolliver*,[41] the defendant deposited a forged check into his own checking account through the use of an ATM. A Wisconsin Court of Appeals affirmed his conviction for uttering, holding that the defendant's act introduced the forged check "into the stream of financial commerce." The crime of uttering can be committed with a forged check or with a bad check that is not forged but is known to be worthless.

The crime of uttering can also be committed with counterfeit money or "raised" bills. In the 1991 case of *United States v. Brown*,[42] the defendant was convicted of connecting parts of different money bills and uttering the altered bills (defendant "raised" $1 bills to $20 bills and then uttered them).

The Crime of Forgery

Documents and writing are important in the functioning of a modern society. The crimes of forgery and uttering are offenses created primarily to safeguard confidence in the genuineness of documents and writing. Forgery is committed when a person with an intent to defraud falsely makes or alters a writing or document. Forgery may be committed by

- Creating a wholly new false writing or document
- Altering an existing document (raising the amount of a check, for example)
- Endorsing a check or other instrument with another person's name (example: X steals Y's check and cashes the check by endorsing Y's name on the back of the check)
- Filling in blanks over a signature of another, either without authority or with unauthorized terms

When a check is presented either for cash or in payment for goods, there is an implied representation that the check is good. A common business practice is to request people presenting a check to either endorse or sign the check in the presence of the person who is about to honor the document. If the presenters of the check (the bearers) know that the check is forged, they have committed the crime of uttering in presenting the forged document. If they sign a false name to the check, they have then committed the crime of forgery in the presence of the person who is about to honor the check.

The many types of forged documents include driver's licenses, identification cards, credit cards, passports, and residency cards for people illegally in the United States.

With checks, the forgery could be done by hand. However, the many desktop computers have created a new industry. Forgery and counterfeiting of documents, including checks, is a fast-growing problem throughout the United States. The American Bankers Association states that desktop counterfeiting is the number-one crime problem facing banks.[43]

Operations of Check-Forging Rings

Check-forging rings operate in all large cities in the United States. Some of their blank checks are obtained as the result of burglaries or thefts from business firms. Other checks are the product of a desktop computer, which is a new tool for making false copies of checks and other documents.

SAFEGUARDS IN HANDLING CHECKS

- Do not endorse checks in blank (with just your name), as the check then becomes a bearer instrument that can be cashed by any person obtaining possession.
- Do not sign blank checks, as any person obtaining possession of the checks could fill in the amount and cash the checks.
- In sending checks through the mail, make the checks payable to a specific person or corporation. Make bank deposits payable to "deposit only" or "for deposit to account number."

The checks are often forged by using names found on stolen identification cards and papers. Such identification can be obtained by purse snatching and pickpocketing. The thief looks for a victim with the same general appearance as the person who will utter (pass) the check. With a good set of identification cards and with checks that have all the appearance of payroll checks, the check-forging ring goes to work.

To minimize the possibilities of being apprehended, professional criminals often recruit other people to commit the actual uttering and passing of the checks. This can be done by selling the checks made out in whatever amount and name the person wishes, or the criminal transaction can be done under an agreement to share the criminal loot.

If a criminal is apprehended while attempting to pass a forged check, he or she is likely to attempt to eliminate the evidence of the crime by eating the check or destroying it in some other way. Should the offender be successful, he or she can then be charged with the offense of destroying (or attempting to destroy) evidence of a crime.

Passing Forged Checks and Other Counterfeit Securities in Interstate Commerce

In the 1930s, the U.S. Congress became concerned about the use of fraudulent securities in interstate commerce. The Congress amended the National Stolen Property Act (58 Statute 1178) by also forbidding "falsely made, forged, altered or counterfeit securities" to be used and passed in interstate commerce. The U.S. Supreme Court recognized that the "general intent" and "broad purpose" of Congress was to "curb the type of trafficking in fraudulent securities that often depends for its success on the exploitation of interstate commerce."[44]

The National Stolen Property Act, therefore, makes it unlawful to transport not only stolen property in interstate commerce but also fraudulent securities, which include forged or "falsely made" checks. The following U.S. Supreme Court cases illustrate the enforcement of law:

United States v. Sheridan

Supreme Court of the United States (1946) 329 U.S. 379, 67 S. Ct.332

The defendant was convicted under the National Stolen Property Act for cashing checks at a Michigan bank, drawn on a Missouri account, with a forged signature. The Supreme Court held:

Drawing the [forged] check upon an out-of-state bank, knowing it must be sent there for presentation, is an obviously facile way to delay and often defeat apprehension, conviction, and restoration of the ill-gotten gain. There are sound reasons therefore why Congress would wish not to exclude such persons (from the statute's reach), among them the very case with which they may escape the state's grasp.

> ### McElroy v. United States
>
> Supreme Court of the United States (1982) 455 U.S. 642, 102 S. Ct.1332
>
> The defendant used blank checks that had been stolen in Ohio to buy a car and a boat in Pennsylvania. The Supreme Court held that the defendant circulated fraudulent security in violation of the National Stolen Property Act and that Congress's general purpose was "to combat interstate fraud."

Check Kiting

check kiting Creating multiple checking accounts at multiple banks for the purpose of writing fraudulent checks from one account and depositing them in another, and then withdrawing funds from the deposit bank.

Check kiting can be compared with a shell game at a carnival, in that manipulations are used in both to deceive. The most common reason for the deception in check kiting is to create a false bank balance from which to draw and run off with money that does not belong to the person. The U.S. Supreme Court used the following example to explain a check-kiting scheme in the 1982 case of *Williams v. United States:*

> The check kiter opens an account at Bank A with a nominal deposit. He then writes a check on that account for a large sum, such as $50,000. The check kiter then opens an account at Bank B and deposits the $50,000 check from Bank A in that account. At the time of deposit, the check is not supported by sufficient funds in the account at Bank A. However, Bank B, unaware of this fact, gives the check kiter immediate credit on his account at Bank B. During the several-day period that the check on Bank A is being processed for collection … the check kiter writes a $50,000 check on his account at Bank B and deposits it into his account at Bank A. At the time of the deposit of that check, Bank A gives the check kiter immediate credit on his account there, and on the basis of that grant of credit pays the original $50,000 check when it is presented for collection.
>
> By repeating this scheme, or some variation of it, the check kiter can use the $50,000 credit originally given by Bank B as an interest-free loan for an extended period of time. In effect, the check kiter can take advantage of the several-day period required for the transmittal, processing, and payment of checks from accounts in different banks.[45]

A check kiter can build up a big "float" by using many bank accounts in different banks and then running off with all the money. In *United States v. Payne*,[46] used car dealers exchanged checks for the sale of automobiles between themselves and used the immediate credit to operate their businesses. One nonexistent car was sold seven or eight times a week for a four-month period. The Court concluded:

> Payne and Fountain successfully managed a kite for four months with a float that rose to $178,000. They obtained that credit, advance, and loan only by falsely representing the worthless checks as worth their face value. 18 U.S.C. § 1014 makes their misrepresentation a federal offense when the injured bank is insured by the FDIC.

In 1985, the stock brokerage firm of E. F. Hutton & Co. pleaded guilty to 2,000 felony counts of check kiting (federal mail and wire fraud). E. F. Hutton agreed to pay a $2 million fine and also to make restitution to the many banks cheated by their scheme. Investigations showed that three techniques were used by some of the top E. F. Hutton managers to obtain maximum illegal interest on huge sums of money.

After E. F. Hutton pleaded guilty to massive check-kiting charges in 1985, federal prosecutors sought criminal indictments against the company in 1987 for allegedly helping organized-crime figures launder hundreds of thousands of dollars illegally.[47] (See Chapter 18 for material on the crime of money laundering.)

The banking system in the United States has begun the process of electronically debiting checks, rather than sending the paper through the banking system. This results in an immediate debit on the account on which a check is drawn, rather than the three to seven days it takes to send a check through the system. "Floats" are likely to become a thing of the past when full electronic debiting comes into existence, and crimes such as check kiting may also decrease.

Summary

- The owners of property hold both the right to title and possession of the property. Therefore, when a thief takes possession of the property the owner's rights have been violated. Because one cannot acquire rights in property except through consent of the owner, a thief generally acquires no rights in stolen property, and cannot transfer rights in that property.

- The "money" rule, which permits good faith purchasers for value of money or certain negotiable securities to obtain title unless they knew or should have known the money was stolen, is necessary to make sure money is freely negotiable.

- Taking can occur by direct acts, by appropriating lost or mislaid goods, by deception, or by embezzlement.

- A joint owner "takes" the property of the other joint owner if the taker had no right to use or keep the property and doing so infringes on the rights of the joint owner.

- Hiding retail goods on the person, taking the goods out of the store, or otherwise exercising control over the goods inconsistent with the right of a shopper to possess goods prior to sale can constitute taking in a shoplifting crime.

- A suspected shoplifter in the store may be stopped and questioned, and a shoplifter outside the store may be followed to discover the person's identity. In some states, a merchant or security officer with probable cause can detain a suspected shoplifter, and search for stolen goods.

- Credit card theft can be proved by showing the defendant was in actual possession of a stolen card, or by showing the defendant caused purchases to be made with the number taken from another person's credit card.

- Forgery occurs when, with the intent to defraud another, a person creates or alters an instrument or document by signing with a fictitious name or another person's name. Uttering occurs when a forged instrument is presented for payment.

- A check-kiting scheme works by establishing an account at one bank, and then writing a large check on that account, which is deposited in a second account at another bank. While the check is going through the clearing process, which can take days, money is fraudulently withdrawn from the second account.

Key Terms

theft or larceny, p. 349
taking, p. 349
fraud, p. 351
embezzlement, p. 353

shoplifting, p. 358
probable cause, p. 360
defamation, p. 361
malicious prosecution, p. 361

forgery, p. 366
uttering, p. 366
check kiting, p. 369

Case Analysis and Writing Exercises

1. Most states have consolidated the various common law larceny offenses into a general theft offense. Where that has happened, under what circumstances, if any, may a defendant be charged and convicted of separate offenses for "taking," "retaining," or "disposing of" stolen property? See *State v. Cox*, 82 P.3d 619 (Or. 2003).

2. A state statute makes it a crime to steal a "financial transaction device." Can a defendant who takes credit card numbers from receipts he sees at his job be convicted under this statute? See *State v. Rhea*, 636 N.W.2d 364 (Neb. 2001).

3. A defendant invited a few of his friends out for a fancy dinner. The tab was $20,000. The defendant did not pay the bill. What should the charge be, theft of services or theft of goods? What must the prosecution prove to convict the defendant? See *People v. Wilson*, 751 N.Y.S.2d 720 (N.Y. 2002), and *State v. Hogrefe*, 557 N.W.2d 871 (Ia. 1996).

4. The parents of two children in the custody of state authorities stopped a van in which the children were passengers and at gunpoint expelled the state officers from the van. They drove the van a short distance and abandoned it. Can they be convicted of theft of the van? See *State v. Christine*, 93 P.3d 82 (Ore. App. 2004).

Notes

1. A 22A *Corpus Juris Secundum* (Criminal Law), Section 597.

2. For cases in which the owners of cars were convicted of theft when they took their car from a person with a superior right of possession, see *State v. Pike*, 826 P.2d 152 (Wash.1992) (car taken from mechanic without paying for repairs, but the conviction was reversed when it was shown that a written repair estimate was not provided as required by state law); and *Courtney v. Rice*, 546 N.E.2d 461 (Ohio App. 1989) (car towed to police lot after a parking violation; defendant was convicted of theft and the parking violation, but both convictions were reversed on appeal).

3. 739 P.2d 1041 (1987).

4. *Transamerica Ins. Co. v. Long*, 318 F. Supp. 156 (W.D. Pa. 1970).

5. *Theft* and *larceny* are interchangeable terms for the crime of stealing. Some states use the term *theft*; other states use *larceny*. The Model Penal Code uses *theft* (Article 223).

6. Nebraska Revised Statutes Section 28–510.

7. "Working Papers of the National Commission on Reform of Federal Criminal Laws," 2: 913.

8. See *State v. Johnson*, 432 So. 2d 758 (Fla. App. 1983), where forcing the store clerk to put money in paper bag and place it on the store counter satisfied the carry-away requirement.

9. *People v. Schlicht*, 709 P.2d 94 (Colo. App. 1985).

10. See the *Chicago Tribune* article, "$836,000 Check for GI Triggers Row," October 23, 1993. For criminal cases on the taking of mislaid or lost property, see *State v. Evans*, 807 P.2d (Idaho App. 1991) and *State v. Getz*, 830 P.2d 5 (Kan. 1992).

11. See LaFave, *Criminal Law*, 4th ed., pp. 930–931 (Belmont, Calif.: West, 2003).

12. LaFave and Scott, *Criminal Law*, 2nd ed. (Belmont, Calif.: West/Wadsworth, 1986), discusses the following on pp. 729–739: (a) Embezzlement by a person in lawful possession of money or property (an employee; a person who found the money or property; or a person who obtained it by mistake), (b) what is called fraudulent embezzlement, and (c) embezzlement by public officials.

  The crime of "breaking bulk" is sometimes classified as an embezzlement crime. It is committed when a person takes a portion of goods that have been temporarily placed in his or her custody by the owner. This could be done by a warehouse employee or a common carrier in charge of transporting a shipment of goods. (For example, dockworkers loading cases of beer into a railroad car remove many bottles from cases for their own consumption.) Some states have statutorized the common law crime of breaking bulk (or breaking bale). Other states have made the offense that of larceny or embezzlement; still others include it as larceny by bailee.

13. Illinois Revised Statutes, Chapter 38, Section 15–1.

14. Minnesota Statutes Annotated Section 609.25.

15. *People v. Sanders*, 79 Cal. Rptr. 2d 806 (1998).

16. See *U.S. v. Riggs*, 739 F. Supp. 414 (N.D. Ill. 1990).

17. *State v. Howard*, 760 N.W.2d 183 (Wis. App. 2008), *review denied*, 775 N.W.2d 100 (2009).

18. 22 N.Y.2d 443, 293 N.Y.S.2d 96, 239 N.E.2d 727 (1968).

19. See *People v. Schmidt* (1996 WL 350878), in which the Colorado Court of Appeals pointed out that Colorado has a statute that makes price tags attached to a stolen item prima facie evidence of the item's value in a theft prosecution, unless the price is commonly subject to negotiation, as a motor vehicle would be.

20. 823 P.2d 848 (1991). Also, in the case of *People v. Wallace*, 434 N.W.2d 423 (Mich. 1989), a Michigan Court of Appeals held that a chain given to a wife during the marriage was her property and not the jointly owned property of the husband and wife.

21. 25 Mich. App. 371, 181 N.W.2d 551 (1970). In the 1983 case of *U.S. v. Perez*, 707 F.2d 359 (8th Cir. 1983), the defendant stole an exhibit of the government that was being used in a criminal case against him and others for the distribution of cocaine. The exhibit consisted of fifteen $100 bills. The Court of Appeals affirmed the conviction, holding: "We have little difficulty holding that here the United States had sufficient possession and control, if not actual title, to the property." The property had been seized when the defendants were arrested.

22. 342 U.S. 246, 72 S. Ct. 240 (1952). This case is also discussed in Chapter 7.

23. The preliminary results from the survey may be viewed online at www.ncf.com/lp10.

24. 420 N.E.2d 40 (1981).

25. In affirming the convictions of three different defendants in the *Olivo* case, the New York court held:

> In *People v. Olivo*, defendant not only concealed goods in his clothing, but he did so in a particularly suspicious manner. And, when defendant was stopped, he was moving towards the door, just three feet short of exiting the store. It cannot be said as a matter of law that these circumstances failed to establish a taking.
>
> In *People v. Gasparik*, defendant removed the price tag and sensor device from a jacket, abandoned his own garment, put the jacket on, and ultimately headed for the main floor of the store. Removal of the price tag and sensor device, and careful concealment of those items, is highly unusual and suspicious conduct for a shopper. Coupled with defendant's abandonment of his own coat and his attempt to leave the floor, those factors were sufficient to make out a prima facie case of a taking.
>
> In *People v. Spatzier*, defendant concealed a book in an attaché case. Unaware that he was being observed in an overhead mirror, defendant looked furtively up and down an aisle before secreting the book. In these circumstances, given the manner in which defendant concealed the book and his suspicious behavior, the evidence was not insufficient as a matter of law.

26. 93 Misc. 2d 151, 402 N.Y.S.2d 546 (1978).

27. 438 N.Y.S. at 246 (1981).

28. 59 Md. App. 28, 474 A.2d 537 (1984).

29. 402 N.Y.S.2d at 548 (1978).

30. *Carroll v. United States*, 267 U.S. 132, 45 S. Ct. 280 (1925).

31. *Coblyn v. Kennedy's, Inc.*, 359 Mass. 319, 268 N.E.2d 860 (1971).

32. See *Wal-Mart Stores Inc. v. Bathe*, 715 N.E.2d 954 (Ind. App. 1999).

33. In *State v. Morgan*, 985 P.2d 1022 (Alaska App. 1999), a former boyfriend gave his girlfriend's credit card number to the defendant, who used it to place $3,669 worth of long-distance calls. The court held his use of the card number was obtaining a credit card by fraudulent means.

34. See *Nolan v. State*, 629 S.W.2d 940 (Tex. App. 1982).

35. MasterCard International and the *New York Times* article, "Guarding Credit Cards from the Latest Scams," July 2, 1994.

36. See the *New York Times* article, "Missing Bank Card Brings Overwithdrawal of $346,770," February 12, 1995.

37. Even the Congress of the United States had a "bad check" scandal in 1992. More than 100 members of the House of Representatives had written bad checks in a year's time on the House Bank. One member of Congress wrote 996 bad checks in a three-year period. See the *New York Times* articles, "Adding Up the Casualties in the House Bank Scandal" and "The House Is Getting Jittery over Bad-Check Disclosures," March 12, 1992. All the bad checks were made good, but at the time they were written there were insufficient funds to cover the checks.

38. See the *FBI Law Enforcement Bulletin* article, "Check Fraud: A Sophisticated Criminal Enterprise," August 1996.

39. *Warren v. Commonwealth*, 219 Va. 416, 247 S.E.2d 692 (1978).

40. 249 Ind. 446, 233 N.E.2d 168 (1968).

41. 149 Wis. 2d 166, 440 N.W.2d 571 (Wis. App. 1989).

42. 938 F.2d 1482.

43. See the *New York Times* article, "New Breed of Check Forgers Exploit Desktop Publishing," August 15, 1994.

44. See *Moskal v. United States*, 111 S. Ct. at 466 (1990).

45. 458 U.S. 279, 102 S. Ct. 3088 (1982).

46. 602 F.2d 1215 (5th Cir. 1979), *review denied* 445 U.S. 903, 100 S. Ct. 1079, 26 CrL 4209 (1980).

47. See the *FBI Law Enforcement Bulletin* article, "Check Kiting: Detection, Prosecution and Prevention," November 1993.

Robbery, Burglary, and Related Crimes

A bank teller's worst nightmare. This is a surveillance camera photograph of a masked bank robber. Unlike the majority of persons who rob banks, who simply hand a note to the bank teller demanding money and threatening violence, this masked robber is armed with a handgun. While armed bank robbers present more of a threat of death or injury, statistics show that the most likely gunshot victim of a bank robbery is the bank robber.

OUTLINE

LEARNING OBJECTIVES

In this chapter we discuss the theft crimes of robbery and burglary, as well as the related crimes of extortion and trespass.. The learning objectives for Chapter 14 are:

- Describe what facts separate robbery from common theft.

- State when robbery becomes armed or aggravated robbery.

- List the requirements for home invasion robbery.

- State when purse snatching or pickpocketing can become robbery.

- Distinguish robbery from extortion.

- List the elements of the general burglary offense.

- Describe ways current state criminal codes modified the common law burglary offense.

- Distinguish criminal trespass from defiant trespass.

On July 17, 2010, a heavily made-up woman with long black hair walked into a bank in Hamilton, Maryland. The woman handed a teller a note that demanded cash and threatening violence if the teller did not comply. The teller gave the woman cash, and as the woman left the bank, the teller engaged an electronic "man-trap" that locked the exterior and interior doors of the bank. The robber was trapped between the two doors. FBI agents stated that while trapped between the doors the robber's make-up begin to run, and she unsuccessfully tried to break the glass doors. Police arrested her while she was still trapped.

The FBI identified the woman as Darion Jeanina Randle, 27, who is the suspect in six other bank robberies committed in the Baltimore area. Randle faces criminal charges under both state and federal laws.

In this chapter we learn the elements of many of the crimes involving theft or other taking of property. Crimes against property occur in a variety of ways, with or without the presence of violence. And the manner in which the crime occurs can change the name of the crime or the punishment for it.

For example, the value of the property taken is often important in determining if the crime is a felony or misdemeanor. In the case of burglary, the time when the crime occurs (night or day), or the manner of gaining entry to the premises where the burglary occurs (breaking a door or window or walking through an unlocked door) can aggravate the crime and resulting punishment.

We will study many of these different elements in this chapter.

≡ Robbery

Robbery Forcible stealing.

Robbery is forcible stealing. It is one of the most frequent crimes of violence in the United States. The common law crime of robbery was defined before the early English courts had defined larceny. The Model Penal Code, § 222.1, defines robbery as follows:

(1) <u>Robbery Defined</u>. A person is guilty of robbery if, in the course of committing a theft, he:

(a) inflicts serious bodily harm upon another; or

(b) threatens another with or purposely puts him in fear of immediate serious bodily injury; or

(c) commits or threatens immediately to commit any felony of the first or second degree.

An act shall be deemed "in the course of committing a theft" if it occurs in an attempt to commit theft or in flight after the attempt or commission.

The usual elements incorporated into robbery statutes by the states include:

- A taking and carrying away (only a slight movement of the property is needed)[1]
- of the property of another
- with intent to steal
- from the person or from the presence of the victim
- by the use of force against the person, or
- with the threat of the use of imminent force, to compel the victim to acquiesce in the taking and carrying away of the property.

Armed or aggravated robbery Forcible stealing combined with the use of a deadly or dangerous weapon, or which results in serious bodily injury to another.

Simple robbery, also called strong-arm robbery or mugging, is distinguished in probably all state statutes from the aggravated form of robbery, commonly called *armed robbery*. Armed robbery carries penalties that are more severe than those for simple robbery. Some of the statutory distinctions various states use in distinguishing between armed robbery and simple robbery are the following:

- That the perpetrator was armed with a "dangerous" or "deadly" weapon
- That the perpetrator intended to kill or wound if the victim resisted
- That the perpetrator did actually inflict a bodily injury[2]

State statutes differ on what is required for a conviction of armed robbery or aggravated robbery, where the presence or use of a "weapon" or "deadly weapon" is the basis for increasing the crime from simple robbery to armed robbery. The issue arises when a robber either (1) brandishes a toy or simulated weapon, like a starter pistol, or (2) states that he has a weapon, but does not actually show the weapon, and it later turns out the robber did not have a weapon.

One approach, called the objective approach, requires that the defendant actually possessed a deadly weapon during the robbery. An example of that approach is the definition of *weapon* for purposes of the Montana armed robbery statute, MCA § 45-2-101 (76). That section has been interpreted as requiring proof that the defendant actually possessed a weapon, something "readily capable of producing death or serious bodily injury." See *In re L.S.*, 977 P.2d 967 (Mont. 1999).

More commonly, states have adopted the subjective approach, which requires proof only that the defendant appeared to have a deadly weapon, such as a firearm. The Georgia armed robbery statute, Ga. Code Ann. § 16-8-41(a), states that the crime occurs if the defendant has a weapon, or "any replica...or device having the appearance of such a weapon." In *Kirk v. State*, 610 S.E.2d 604 (Ga. App. 2005), the court held that the defendant must give some physical manifestation of a weapon, but it was the reasonable apprehension by the victim that determined if it appeared a weapon was being used. In *State v. Wren*, 32 P.3d 717 (Kan. App. 2001), the Court interpreted the Kansas armed robbery statute, KSA § 21-3427, as requiring that the victim reasonably believed the robber had a firearm or dangerous weapon.

It is generally held that some indication or representation of a weapon is needed to make a crime armed robbery. In *State v. Muldrow*, 559 S.E.2d 847 (S.C. 2002), the defendant walked into a convenience store and handed the clerk a note that said "give me all your cash or I'll shoot you." He did not show a gun. The court reversed his conviction under the South Carolina armed robbery statute, which defined armed robbery as "alleging...he was armed while using a representation of a deadly weapon." The court said, "[w]ords alone are not sufficient" to support a conviction for armed robbery.

The Illinois legislature resolved the "actual" weapon problem by enacting both an armed robbery statute, 720 ILCS 5/18-2(a), which requires carrying an actual weapon, and an aggravated robbery statute, 720 ILCS 5/18-5(a), which only requires that the robber "indicate" he has a weapon, whether or not he actually does. See *People v. Gray*, 806 N.E.2d 753 (Ill. App. 2004), *appeal denied*, 823 N.E.2d 694 (Ill. 2002).

Finally, it is clear that the fact that a firearm used by a robber is unloaded is not relevant to a conviction for armed robbery. In *McLaughlin v. United States*, 476 U.S. 16 (1986), the U.S. Supreme Court held that the "dangerous weapon" requirement in the federal bank robbery statute, 18 U.S.C. § 2113(d), was satisfied by an unloaded gun.

Changes in Bank Robbery

In 2009 about 5,500 bank robberies occurred in the United States, which was about a 20% decrease from 2008. About $45 million in cash was taken in those robberies, and $8 million was recovered. Most robbers were males (2,796) and only a few were female (177). The predominant method was presentation of a demand note (3,269), accompanied by the threat of the use of a weapon (2,553). However, in only 1,619 cases was a weapon actually brandished by a robber. There were 140 people injured in bank robberies, and 21 people died. All 21 of those deaths were perpetrators. See Crime In America, FBI Bank Crime Statistics for 2009, March 23, 2010.

The image of the gun-wielding, masked bank robber forcing all the bank employees to lie on the floor while the bank vault is opened is one of the most common images of the crime of robbery. In fact, as a method of bank robbery, that image has changed, as the statistics stated above show. Most bank robberies are, like the story that opened this chapter, "note" jobs, where the robber presents a note to a bank employee demanding money under a threat of violence.

The identity of the robber also has changed from the classic image of a violent, career criminal. Perpetrators of note jobs included a New York housewife, a 91-year-old man in Texas, a Florida golf pro, and a former college basketball player and his pre-med student girlfriend. Law enforcement officers have speculated that these "amateurs" have turned to bank robbery as a way to solve financial problems because they know bank tellers have been told to surrender money from their cash drawers on demand. The average take in a note job is between $2,000 and $3,000; banks lose about $50 million a year to bank robbers. By contrast, banks lose about $700 million each year to check fraud schemes.

More than half of all bank robbers are apprehended each year. Better bank surveillance cameras, more undercover guards, and dye packs that explode and color stolen

CASE CLOSE-UP

United States v. Kelley
Eleventh Circuit Court of Appeals, 412 F.3d 1240 (2005)

The defendant was charged with bank robbery under 18 U.S.C. § 2113 (a).

Evidence at his trial disclosed that two female tellers at a Bank of America branch located within a grocery store noticed the defendant and another man walking in front of the bank. When one of the tellers left her position to make a phone call, the two men jumped over the counter, grabbed money from the teller's cash drawer, and ran out of the store. None of the tellers made any attempt to interfere with the robbers, although one teller was standing within arm's length of the defendant when he grabbed cash from the absent teller's drawer.

After his first trial resulted in a hung jury, the defendant was convicted of bank robbery in his second trial and sentenced to 84 months in jail. He appealed his conviction, arguing that the prosecution introduced insufficient evidence to satisfy the requirements of the federal bank robbery statute. Section 2113 (a) states, "Whoever, by force and violence, or by intimidation, takes ... from the person or presence of another" any property of a bank is guilty of bank robbery. The defendant argued the evidence did not show he used intimidation, nor did it show he took property from "the person or in the presence of another." The defendant, relying on *United States v. Wagstaff*, 865 F.2d 626 (4th Cir. 1989), argued that because he did not have a weapon and made no demand upon the tellers, he cannot be said to have "intimidated" either of the tellers. The court disagreed. Unlike the defendant in *Wagstaff*, the court said, who never got within eight feet of a teller, here the defendant was close enough to touch one of the tellers. Moreover, the court said, the way the defendant jumped over the counter was loud and sudden, which, according to the testimony of the tellers, frightened them. The court thought the case was closer to *United States v. Caldwell*, 292 F.3d 595 (8th Cir. 2002), where the court held that leaping over a counter toward a bank teller constituted actions that a reasonable person would find intimidating.

The defendant also argued the evidence did not establish that he took money "from the person or presence of another," as required by Section 2113 (a). The court also rejected that argument, relying on interpretations of similar language in 18 U.S.C. § 2119, the federal crime of vehicle theft in interstate commerce. Cases interpreting the "presence of another" under that statute required only proof that the property was so within the victim's reach that the victim, but for the force or intimidation, could have retained possession of the property. Because one of the bank tellers was close enough to the cash drawer from which the money was taken to "retain possession" of the money but for the defendant's intimidation, the court held that this element was also satisfied. The defendant's conviction was affirmed.

money have all contributed to the increased number of bank robbers captured. The most recent advance has been the implantation of global positioning devices in the money given to robbers, which enables investigators to follow the money with their laptops. These devices were used in only 372 of the 2009 robberies.

The *Chicago Police Department Training Bulletin* lists the following factors that favor a robber:

- He or she can carry out the crime swiftly.
- He or she will usually leave few clues that would lead to his or her arrest.
- The robbery is committed in such a short period that the victim and witnesses sometimes do not have sufficient time and composure to view the offender so as to furnish an accurate description to the police.
- The probability of interruption is limited because of the short time.[3]

Distinguishing Robbery from Theft or Larceny

Robbery differs from theft or larceny because, in charging the crime of robbery, it must be shown that

- Property was taken from the victim or taken from the presence of the victim.
- The use of force or the threat of force was used in the taking.

If no force or threat of force is used, the crime of robbery has not been committed, and a lesser crime such as theft or larceny should be considered.

Where State Courts Differ on What Constitutes Robbery

In ruling whether the crime of robbery has occurred, state courts differ in the following areas:

1. When force is not used in the taking of property, but is used to keep the property and to escape:

Majority View[4]	**Minority View**
Held that a robbery occurred even though a bottle of wine was taken without the use of force. Force was then used to prevent the store owner from recovering the wine, and a knife was waved to make the escape. *People v. Hovenec*, 596 N.E.2d 749 (Ill. App. 1992). Also *People v. Pham*, 1993 WL128504 (Cal. App. 1993), and *State v. Handburgh*, 830 P.2d 641 (1992), in which the Supreme Court of Washington called this view the majority view in the United States.	Held that to be robbery, force must be used at the time of taking and concurrent with the taking. After the victim discovered his money was taken, he attempted to get it back. The defendant then pulled a gun and threatened. The court held that the crime was not that of robbery. *State v. Lewis*, 1993 WL 564208 (N.M. App. 1993). Also *Royal v. State*, 490 So. 2d 44 (Fla. 1986). In response to the *Royal* decision, the Florida legislature amended the robbery statute to include force used in fleeing after a theft. F.S.A. Section 12.13(3)(a)(b).

2. In the U.S. Supreme Court case of *Ashe v. Swenson,* 90 S. Ct. 1189 (1970), masked gunmen robbed six men playing poker and took money from all six of the men. The defendant in that case was charged with six counts of robbery. (See Chapter 7 for the case.)

However, courts are divided on multiple charges of robbery when a business is robbed, and employees of the business are also robbed:

Holding That Robbery Is an Offense Against the Person Assaulted	Holding That Robbery Is an Aggravated Form of Theft
The defendant threatened two clerks with an axe and stole money from a store's cash register. Two counts of robbery affirmed. *People v. Borghesi*, 66 P.3d 93 (Colo. 2003). Also see *State v. Green*, 833 P.2d 311 (Or. App. 1992).	The Supreme Court of Hawaii held that only one count of robbery could be used for a conviction, even though money was taken from five different Ramada Inn employees. See *State v. Faatea*, 648 P.2d 197 (1982). Also held to be single robbery when money belonging to both a restaurant and the manager was taken. *Harris v. State*, 399 S.E.2d 284 (Ga. App. 1990).[5]

Carjacking: A New Name for an Old Crime

Thieves have been stealing cars from their owners or occupants by force or fear of force for years. These cases did not fit easily into theft or robbery criminal statutes because the thief often did not intend to keep the car permanently. (Figure 14.1 describes the various types of car and vehicle theft.) As the October 1993 issue of the *FBI Law Enforcement Bulletin* stated, more than 90 percent of the vehicles taken in carjackings were returned.

carjacking Forcibly taking possession of a motor vehicle in the possession of another against his or her will with intent either to permanently or temporarily deprive the person of possession.

To remedy this, most states and the federal government passed statutes making **carjacking** a separate offense. The Anti-Car Theft Act of 1992, 18 U.S.C. 2119, was passed by Congress in response to the more than 35,000 carjackings completed or attempted each year in the United States. An example of a carjacking statute is the following California law:

> Carjacking is the felonious taking of a motor vehicle in the possession of another, from his or her person or in the immediate presence ... against his or her will and with the intent to either permanently or temporarily deprive the person ... of his or her possession, accomplished by force or fear.[6]

Carjacking statutes have presented several problems concerning the requisite elements of the offense. Some of these are the following:

- A taking occurs even if the true owner of the car remains in the car during the carjacking. See *People v. Duran*, 106 Cal. Rptr. 2d 812 (2001).
- The true owner is in "possession" of the car even if he is alighting from the car when the carjacking occurs. See *State v. Mobley*, 681 A.2d 1186 (Md. App. 1996).
- In *People v. Lopez*, 79 P.3d 548 (Cal. 2003), the California Supreme Court reversed earlier decisions under the carjacking statute, see *People v. Montero*, 56 Cal. Rptr. 2d 303 (1996), and held that movement of the car was an element of the crime. Florida's statute, FSA §812.133, has been interpreted as not requiring movement of the car. *Price v. State*, 816 So. 2d 738 (Fla. App. 2002).[7]
- At least one state, Maryland, has interpreted its carjacking statute as requiring no specific intent to deprive the owner of possession. This means that intoxication or drugged condition, which can be a defense to specific intent crimes (see Chapter 7) is not a defense to carjacking. See *State v. Harris*, 728 A.2d 180 (Md. App. 1999).
- A carjacker may also be convicted of kidnapping, if the owner of the car is kept in the car and the car is moved a substantial distance from the vicinity of the carjacking. Movement of the car owner merely as "incidental" to the carjacking is not kidnapping. See *People v. Medina*, 161 P.3d 186 (Cal. 2007).

FIG-14.1 Car and Vehicle Theft in the United States

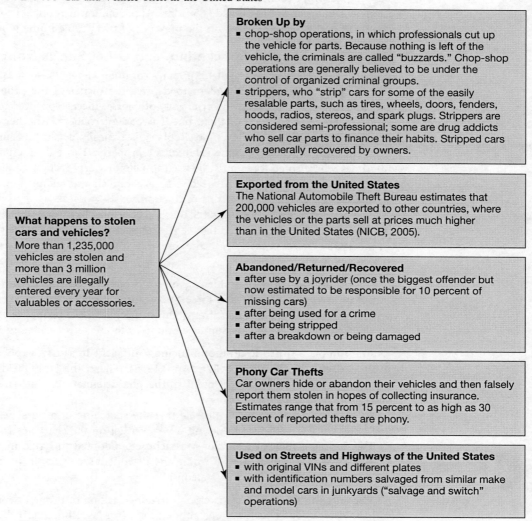

What happens to stolen cars and vehicles?
More than 1,235,000 vehicles are stolen and more than 3 million vehicles are illegally entered every year for valuables or accessories.

Broken Up by
- chop-shop operations, in which professionals cut up the vehicle for parts. Because nothing is left of the vehicle, the criminals are called "buzzards." Chop-shop operations are generally believed to be under the control of organized criminal groups.
- strippers, who "strip" cars for some of the easily resalable parts, such as tires, wheels, doors, fenders, hoods, radios, stereos, and spark plugs. Strippers are considered semi-professional; some are drug addicts who sell car parts to finance their habits. Stripped cars are generally recovered by owners.

Exported from the United States
The National Automobile Theft Bureau estimates that 200,000 vehicles are exported to other countries, where the vehicles or the parts sell at prices much higher than in the United States (NICB, 2005).

Abandoned/Returned/Recovered
- after use by a joyrider (once the biggest offender but now estimated to be responsible for 10 percent of missing cars)
- after being used for a crime
- after being stripped
- after a breakdown or being damaged

Phony Car Thefts
Car owners hide or abandon their vehicles and then falsely report them stolen in hopes of collecting insurance. Estimates range that from 15 percent to as high as 30 percent of reported thefts are phony.

Used on Streets and Highways of the United States
- with original VINs and different plates
- with identification numbers salvaged from similar make and model cars in junkyards ("salvage and switch" operations)

Source: The National Insurance Crime Bureau, 2005.

Home Invasion Robberies

home invasion robbery
Robbery of persons inhabiting a dwelling.

Home invasion robbery differs from similar crimes, such as burglary or breaking and entering, in how the crime is defined. For example, the Illinois Criminal Code defines home invasion as an unlawful entering of a dwelling by a person who knows someone was present therein, and armed with a dangerous weapon either uses or threatens use of force or injures someone inside the home.[8]

In some states, this difference means that a defendant can be convicted of both home invasion and another crime, such as armed violence during residential burglary, based on one unlawful entry. See *People v. Cunningham*, 851 N.E.2d 653 (Ill. App. 2006). Other states hold that conviction of home invasion bars conviction of related crimes such as residential burglary based on one unlawful entry. See *Perez v. State*, 951 So. 2d 859 (Fla. App. 2006). Florida courts also hold that only one conviction on a count of home invasion may be obtained, even if more than one person is in the home. *Schulterbrandt v. State*, 984 So.

2d 542 (Fla. App. 2008). Other courts have reached the opposite result. See, for example, *Com. v. Antonmarch*, 874 N.E.2d 665 (Mass App. 2007), which upheld convictions on two counts of home invasion based on the presence of two people in the home.

Purse Snatching, Pickpocketing, and Other Thefts from a Person

The crimes of robbery and theft have many common elements, such as the requirement that there be a "taking" with intent to deprive the owner of the property stolen. One principal difference between the crimes is, of course, the use of force to accomplish the "taking." Force is not part of theft, but it is part of robbery. Another difference is the penalty that results from the crime. Robbery is typically a felony, while theft can be a misdemeanor, depending on the value of the property. Those distinctions are important in crimes where some force must be used to take property from another person, but the force does not go beyond that needed to accomplish the taking. Purse snatching and similar crimes are examples of this distinction.

The majority rule in the United States is that crimes like purse snatching are not robberies unless some force is used that is greater than that needed to take the purse is used. In the 1991 case of *State v. Sein*,[9] the Supreme Court of New Jersey stated the majority rule as follows:

> [A] simple snatching or sudden taking of property from the person of another does not of itself involve sufficient force to constitute robbery, though the act may be robbery where a struggle ensues, the victim is injured in the taking, or the property is so attached to the victim's person or clothing as to create resistance to the taking.

An example of force in a purse snatching sufficient to satisfy a robbery conviction is *Jones v. Com.*, 496 S.E.2d 668 (Va. App. 1998). There, the court held that grabbing a woman's shoulder to jerk her around so that the defendant could snatch her purse was enough force to constitute robbery.

A few courts have adopted the rule that the snatching of a purse without the use of any other force is sufficient to permit a jury verdict on the charge of robbery.

The Supreme Judicial Court of Massachusetts adopted this rule in the 1972 case of *Commonwealth v. Jones*.[10] In affirming the defendant's conviction of unarmed robbery for a purse snatching, the court stated:

> The question whether the snatching or sudden taking of property constitutes robbery has arisen in other jurisdictions although not in Massachusetts. In Kentucky, the rule is that snatching, without more, involves the requisite element of force to permit a jury verdict on a charge of robbery. See *Jones v. Commonwealth*, 112 Ky. 689, 692–695, 66 S.W. 633; *Brown v. Commonwealth*, 135 Ky. 635, 640, 117 S.W. 281. According to the rule prevailing in most jurisdictions, however, snatching does not involve sufficient force to constitute robbery, unless the victim resists the taking or sustains physical injury, or unless the article taken is so attached to the victim's clothing as to afford resistance....
>
> We prefer the Kentucky rule on purse snatching. The majority jurisdiction rule, in looking to whether or not the victim resists, we think, wrongly emphasizes the victim's opportunity to defend himself over the willingness of the purse snatcher to use violence if necessary.

Sudden snatching A form of robbery where force is not used beyond that needed to take property from another person

In some states this issue is resolved by adding "**sudden snatching**" to the general robbery statute. Georgia's robbery statute, Ga. Code Ann. § 16-8-40, defines robbery in the usual manner as taking by use of force, but includes a taking "by sudden snatching." Florida addressed the force issue by passing a "robbery by sudden snatching" statute, FSA § 812.131, which explicitly does not require any use of force beyond that needed to take the property, and does not need any showing the victim resisted the taking. It is a third-degree felony, unless the perpetrator carried a firearm, in which case it is a second-degree felony. In *Walker v. State*, 933 So. 2d 1236 (Fla. App. 2006), the court reversed a conviction under the robbery by sudden snatching statute, holding that a conviction under the statute required that the victim knew her purse was being snatched.

Even if not treated as a robbery, theft from the person is punished more severely than ordinary theft, and it is a felony in most states, whether the amount taken is very small or very large. State legislative bodies and courts are well aware that injury can easily occur to a victim who is often startled by the theft and may seek to protect his or her property.

Common forms of theft from a person are pickpocketing and purse snatching. However, theft of a purse from a shopping cart was also held to be theft from the person when the victim's hand was on the cart.[11]

Extortion

extortion Obtaining property by threats of future harm. Differs from robbery in that robbery requires threat of immediate harm.

Extortion is a crime of threatened force, fear, or violence. The name comes from the Latin *torquere*, which means "to wrench or twist." The term *torture* also can be traced to this Latin root. State statutes have different definitions of extortion, but they all make it a crime to obtain "property" (usually money) of another by causing that person to consent to transfer the property because of fear or threats that the extortionist will take some action in the future. The nature of the threat varies from state to state. New York's extortion statute, McKinney's Penal Law § 155(e), lists nine kinds of threats used in "instilling a fear" of extortionate acts. The most common kinds of threats listed in state statutes are bodily injury or death, damage to property, false criminal accusations, exposure of a secret that would subject the victim to contempt or ridicule, or economic harm.

Robbery and extortion are similar in that they are both methods used to obtain money or property illegally. Extortion differs from robbery in these ways:

- There is a threat to inflict a future harm (extortion) rather than an immediate harm (robbery).
- In robbery, the victim must immediately comply with the criminal demand, or violence will immediately occur. In extortion, future compliance is demanded to avoid future harm to a third party or to the victim.
- Robbery must be committed in the presence of the victim, whereas extortion can be committed over the telephone or by mail (such conduct, however, immediately makes the offense also a federal violation).
- The harm that is threatened differs also. In robbery, immediate force is threatened or used against the owner or victim to compel the victim to acquiesce in the taking of the property. In extortion, the victim must pay the amount demanded to avoid
- Destruction of property (bombing a restaurant or business place has been a standard practice of organized crime that could result in a serious loss of life and injuries if the restaurant or business place were open for business).
- Kidnapping or injuries to the victim or the victim's family or friends.
- Accusations of crime, and so forth.
- Damaging the good name or business reputation of the victim or the victim's family.
- Exposing a secret or failing of the victim or family.[12]

Cases illustrating the crime of extortion are as follows:

- In 2009 David Letterman, the talk-show host, was told by a blackmailer that if he did not pay $2 million, Letterman's extramarital affairs would be made public.

Letterman went to the police, who arranged a sting operation to verify the story and collect evidence. A phony $2 million check was given to the blackmailer, who was arrested when he tried to cash the check. The man pled guilty to second-degree grand larceny. See the 3/10/10 *New York Times* article "Love, Bad Behavior, and the Consequences."

- Threats to tamper with soft drinks unless money was paid. See *United States v. Hummer*, 916 F.2d 186 (4th Cir. 1990).
- To drive a service station out of business by illegal means. See *United States v. Penn*, 966 F.2d 55 (2d Cir. 1992).
- Threats to collect a legitimate debt by illegal means. See *United States v. Goode*, 945 F.2d 1168, 50 CrL 1060 (10th Cir. 1991).
- Threats to kill unless hospital administrator had criminal charges against defendant dropped. See *People v. Discala*, 379 N.E.2d 187 (N.Y. 1978).
- Strong-arm tactics and threats used by a wholesale meat distributor to collect money owed by customers for products. See *United States v. Lima et al.*, 914 F.2d 967 (7th Cir. 1989).

When Congress enacted the Hobbs Act, the statute was aimed primarily at gangsters who were extorting protection money from businesses. That is, the business would not be bombed or receive other violence if the protection money was paid.

The Hobbs Act (18 U.S.C.A. 1951(b)(2)) defines extortion as "the obtaining of property of another, with his consent, induced by wrongful use of actual or threatened force, violence, or fear."

Extortion by Intimidation

Extortion is often accomplished by threats of violence, but other kinds of threats or coercive tactics can constitute extortion. For example, in *State v. Gant*, 597 N.W.2d 501 (Iowa 1999), a defendant was charged with extortion under the Iowa extortion statute, Iowa Code Section 711.4(6). That section states that a person commits the crime of extortion if the person takes certain actions for the purpose of obtaining anything of value from another person. Among the prohibited actions is "threatens to testify or provide information or to withhold testimony or information with respect to another's legal claim or defense." In *Gant*, a garage owner had tools and equipment stolen. Gant told the owner he could provide information concerning the location of the stolen goods but would do so only if the owner paid him $200. The court found this to be a threat to withhold information about the owner's claim to the stolen goods and affirmed the defendant's conviction for extortion.

The threat must be wrongful; that is, it must threaten some action that is not legally protected. It would not be extortion, for example, to threaten to sue a debtor if the debtor did not pay a debt on time. However, if the person making the threat is not privileged to do so, it can be extortion. In *State v. Pauling*, 69 P.3d 331 (Wash. 2003), the court held that a former boyfriend who threatened to publish nude photographs of his former girlfriend if she did not repay a debt could be charged with extortion. Publishing the photographs was not protected as free speech, because its only purpose was to threaten the girlfriend.

However, the crime of extortion does require a threat, and the receipt of property from another without a threat is not extortion. For example, in *People v. Hesslink* [13] the court reversed the conviction of a defendant who, posing as a police officer, forced a prostitute to perform oral sex on him. The prostitute also gave the defendant money in the hope he would not arrest her, and based on that payment he was charged with extortion. The court held that because the defendant did not demand money under threat of "arrest," the money paid by the prostitute was not the result of a threat and could not sustain a conviction for extortion.

In some states extortion can be charged based on threats of future economic harm. In *Rendelman v. State*, 947 A.2d 546 (Md. 2008), the Maryland Supreme Court held that under the Maryland extortion statute, CL § 3-701(a), threatening to file a lawsuit unless a "settlement" payment was made on a "claim" was not extortion, even if the claim was made in bad faith. The court reasoned that while a threat to file a meritless lawsuit is a threat to inflict economic harm, the extortion statute states that the threat must be "wrongful." Because it is not illegal to file a lawsuit, even in bad faith, the court concluded the threat to do so cannot be a "wrongful threat of economic injury." The court noted that this is also the result reached by federal courts in prosecutions under the Hobbs Act based on filing frivolous civil lawsuits, citing *United States v. Pendergraft*, 297 F.3d 1198 (11th Cir. 2002).

≣ Burglary

burglary Unlawful entry into the premises of another with intent to steal or commit a felony. Two hundred years ago in England, an illegal entry into the home of another by force and at night was punishable by death if the entry was done to steal or commit a felony.

Burglary is among the most frequently committed major crimes in the United States, with more than 3.5 million burglaries committed every year. Because burglary is a crime of stealth and opportunity, the national clearance rate, as reported by the Uniform Crime Report, is low, at approximately 15 percent. (That is, arrests are made in only approximately 15 percent of the burglaries reported.)

Burglary is a crime committed by both amateurs and professionals. It is committed against residences (homes and apartments) and nonresidences (offices, business places, and so on). It is committed not only at night but also during the day.

Under the old common law, burglary was punished by death. Because of the severe penalty, burglary required a breaking under the common law. It was also limited to the dwelling house of another, at night, and with intent to commit a felony.

All states have modified and changed the definition of burglary in their jurisdictions, resulting in differences in the definitions of burglary in the United States.[14] The Uniform Crime Reporting Program defines burglary as "the unlawful entry of a structure to commit a felony or theft. The use of force to gain entry is not required to classify an offense as burglary."

Breaking

Under common law, a "breaking" or a "breach" was required to constitute the crime of burglary. An entry through an open door or window without the consent of the person living in or controlling the building was not a breaking. All states have abolished the requirement of breaking in their general burglary statutes. For example, the Texas burglary statute, VTCA Penal Code § 30.02, defines burglary as "entry" into a residence or building that is not open to the public without consent and with intent to commit a felony, theft, or assault. In *Clark v. State*, 667 S.W.2d 906 (Tex. App. 1984) the court held that entry through an open door can be burglary, if not open to the public and occurs without the owner's consent. In *Martinez v. State*, 304 S.W.3d 642 (Tex. App. 2010), the court said the "entry" occurs as soon as some part of the burglar's body, such as a hand or a foot, crosses the home's threshold.

Today, a good percentage of burglaries occur when someone leaves a window or door unlocked or open. In *McCovens v. State*, 539 N.E.2d 26 (Ind. 1989), the court affirmed a conviction of burglary, stating the defendant committed a breaking when he climbed over a fence surrounding a business.

Some states, however, continue to use an act of "breaking" to gain entry as an aggravated form of burglary in addition to their regular or simple burglary statutes.

Unlawful Entry into Premises

Because burglary is a form of trespass, an unlawful entry into the premises must take place. An entry could be made by inserting a hand or arm (or even the tip of a screwdriver) into the premises. For example, suppose X threw a brick through a jewelry store window and then inserted his hand and arm through the broken window to obtain watches and rings from the window display. This would be an unlawful entry that would justify a conviction of X for burglary of the jewelry store.

Suppose that instead of using his arm, X inserted a cane and began removing watches and rings by hooking them with the cane. Would this be an entry that justifies a conviction of burglary? Most courts would hold that this was an entry, because the cane was an extension of X's body inserted into the store to carry out a criminal purpose.[15]

In the 1983 case of *People v. Tingue*, the defendant entered a New York church that was open at all hours for the public to pray and meditate.[16] However, instead of praying, the defendant stole the amplifier system from behind the altar rail and entered a room of the church not open to the public, where he attempted to force the lock of a safe. The defendant was charged with burglary. In his first trial, the state failed to "muster sufficient evidence" to prove unlawful entry, and the case was dismissed. The state tried again and in the second trial obtained a conviction for burglary. (The appellate court reversed the conviction, because double jeopardy forbade the second trial and conviction.)

Any element of a crime may be proved by circumstantial evidence. In the U.S. Supreme Court case of *United States v. Edwards*, someone had burglarized a U.S. post office using a pry bar on a window.[17] The defendant had in his possession property stolen from the post office. Direct evidence of the break-in could not be shown, because no witnesses were available. However, crime lab tests showed paint and wood fragments on the defendant's clothing similar to the paint and wood on the post office window. A jury held that this evidence proved unlawful entry, and the defendant's conviction was affirmed.

In the case of *State v. Tixier*, police officers responded to a triggered burglar alarm within a minute.[18] They found a small hole near the door-opening mechanism of a garage. The defendant was found hiding among tires stacked near the door. The piece of the door that had been removed was found near the defendant. It was concluded that the defendant had used an instrument to penetrate the building. In affirming the defendant's burglary conviction, the court held:

> Evidence of a break-in by use of an instrument which penetrates into the building is, in our opinion, evidence of entry into the building. The sufficiency of this evidence is

---

EXAMPLES OF DIFFERENT THEFT CRIMES

- **Theft:** A man lays his ring on the edge of a sink while washing his hands. Another man takes the ring and runs off while the owner is not looking (felony if value is more than amount determined by state statute).
- **Theft from Person:** A ring is taken from a pocket by a pickpocket or taken in a purse by a purse-snatcher (felony in most or all states, regardless of value of ring).
- **Simple Robbery (Mugging):** A woman is accosted in an alley by a menacing robber who threatens to beat her if she does not give the thief the ring on her finger (felony regardless of value of ring if she gave up the ring out of fear).
- **Armed Robbery:** A woman is held at gunpoint by a robber who demands that she give him the ring on her finger (higher felony than mugging).

not destroyed by a failure to prove that the instrument was used to steal something from the building or to commit another felony. Such proof is unnecessary because burglary does not depend upon actions after the entry; the crime is complete when there is an unauthorized entry with the requisite intent.

In the case of *Champlin v. State*, the defendant entered a hotel lobby open to the general public 24 hours a day and removed a television set and a cash register.[19] Instead of charging the defendant with theft, a prosecutor charged the defendant with burglary. In reversing the conviction for burglary, the court pointed out that the defendant's conduct, although illegal, was not burglary, because the premises were open to the general public.

The Dwelling House of Another

A "dwelling house" is a place where people live and sleep. Under the common law, unlawful entry into and theft from a business place would not be a burglary, because a business place is not a dwelling house. Hotel rooms and apartments are dwelling houses, because people live and sleep in such places. A new building into which no one has yet moved has been held not to be a dwelling house.[20]

All the states and the federal government have changed the common law restricting burglary to only dwelling houses. Today, virtually all buildings are contained within the scope of the crime of burglary (and some states, such as California, also include vehicles). Many states punish the burglary of an inhabited building more severely than that of an uninhabited building. In the case of *People v. Lewis*, the court held that the question of "inhabited" or "uninhabited" turns not on the immediate presence or absence of people in the building but rather on the character of the use of the building.[21]

Nighttime

The common law required that burglary be committed at night, which was defined as the time between sunset and sunrise. An entry into a dwelling house with an accompanying theft during the day could not be charged as a burglary under this definition. The defendant, however, could be charged with the separate crimes of trespass, stealing, and, depending on the circumstances, criminal damage to property. Today, about half the burglaries in the United States are committed during the day, and all jurisdictions recognize daylight burglaries. Some states impose more severe penalties for nighttime burglaries.

INTENT TO STEAL IN A BURGLARY CHARGE

The general rule of law is that intent to steal cannot be inferred from the single fact of an unlawful entry into a building. Additional circumstances must be considered, such as:

- Type of Entry: Was it forcible?
- Manner of Entry: Was there a breaking or splintering?
- Place of Entry: Was it the rear or side of the building?
- Type of Building: Did the building contain items that a thief would be interested in stealing?
- Time of Entry: Was it the middle of the night or the middle of the day?
- Conduct of the Defendant When Interrupted: Did he or she attempt to hide or escape?

Source: This material is adapted from a chart originated by the Supreme Court of Wisconsin in the case of *State v. Barclay*, 54 Wis. 2d 651, 196 N.W.2d 745 (1972).

Intent to Commit a Felony

Old common law burglary required proof of intent to commit a felony. Most states and the federal government have broadened this element of burglary. Some states now require that the state prove an intent to steal or commit a felony. Others provide that the intent must be to commit a crime (misdemeanor or felony). Other state statutes specify crimes, whereas still others require that an intent to commit a larceny or theft or other felony be shown.

Whether the state must prove an intent to commit a specific crime depends on the language of the statute, courts hold. For example, in *State v. Mesch*, 574 N.W.2d 10 (Iowa 1997), the Iowa Supreme Court held that the Iowa burglary statute, which required a showing that the defendant entered with "the intent to commit a felony" meant that the state must prove what specific crime a defendant was intending to commit. On the other hand, because a New Jersey burglary statute required only that the defendant entered with a "purpose to commit an offense," the court in *State v. Robinson*[22] held that the state need not prove that any specific crime was intended. General intent can be inferred from the circumstances of the break-in itself.

A defendant who is apprehended in a warehouse in the middle of the night with an armful of merchandise leaves little question concerning intent in that particular situation. With respect to proving intent for burglary when there is no evidence of stealing or of any other crime, the Supreme Court of Illinois stated in the case of *People v. Johnson*:

> Intent must ordinarily be proved circumstantially, by inferences drawn from conduct appraised in its factual environment. We are of the opinion that in the absence of inconsistent circumstances, proof of unlawful breaking and entry into a building which contains personal property that could be the subject of larceny gives rise to an

WHAT IS THE STATE OBLIGATED TO PROVE?			
In addition to the intent or mental element of each crime …			
In order to charge	**That there was a stealing (taking and carrying away)?**	**The value of the property taken?**	**Elements other than the crime of stealing?**
Theft/Larceny	Yes	Yes	No
Robbery	Yes	Not necessary as long as the property was something of value	Yes, (1) that the taking was by force or threat of force and (2) that the taking was from the victim's person or presence
Burglary	No, only an intent to steal or to commit a felony as required by the statutes of that state	Not necessary as long as the property was something of value (or there was an intent to steal)	Yes, requires a showing of an unlawful entry into a dwelling or building (or an unlawful remaining after closing)

inference that will sustain a conviction of burglary. Like other inferences, this one is grounded in human experience, which justifies the assumption that the unlawful entry was not purposeless, and, in the absence of other proof, indicates theft as the most likely purpose. This conclusion is supported by the decisions of other courts.

In the 1973 Pennsylvania case of *Commonwealth v. Muniem*, the defendant, who had been found in an empty warehouse about noon, was convicted of burglary.[23] The door was half open and the defendant was walking out when the police arrived. He was cooperative, did not run, and had nothing in his possession. The owner testified that nothing was missing. The defendant stated that he had to go to the toilet and had looked for a lavatory in the empty building. The defendant was 33 years old, employed, and married, and he had no prior record. In reversing the conviction and ordering the defendant discharged, the court stated:

> In the instant case, the only evidence produced against the appellant is his presence, perhaps as a trespasser, in a vacant building in daylight at about noontime. When found by the police, he was walking to the open door by which he testified he entered the building. The owner of the building testified that nothing was missing and there

FORMS OF THEFT

Theft/larceny	Theft from the person	Robbery[a] (theft[b] by force or threat of force)	Burglary (trespass with intent to steal or to commit a felony)
▪ Ordinary theft (usually done secretly)	▪ Purse snatching	▪ Mugging or yoking (strong-arm robbery)	▪ Ordinary burglary (some states punish burglary committed at night more severely)
▪ "Snatch and run" theft	▪ Pickpocketing	▪ Armed robbery (weapon shown or not shown)	▪ Armed burglary
▪ Shoplifting	▪ "Rolling a drunk" (taking valuables from an intoxicated person or person in a stupor)	▪ Carjacking	▪ Burglary in which an occupant of the building is injured
▪ Theft from autos		▪ Burglaries that turn into robberies	
▪ Theft from buildings			▪ "Break and run" burglary (breaking store window and running off with property)
▪ Theft by fraud (con game)	▪ Taking valuables from injured, dead, or disabled people	▪ Purse snatching and pickpocketing in which such force is used against the person that it constitutes strong-arm robbery	▪ Newspapers use the term car burglary. Some states do have this crime. See *State v. Subin*, 536 A.2d 758 (N.J. 1988), and *State v. Martinez*, 832 P.2d 331 (Idaho App. 1992).
▪ Embezzlement			
▪ Theft by bailee		▪ Home invasion robbery	
▪ Fraud on innkeeper, restaurant			
▪ Looting—taking property from building that has been destroyed by disaster, riot, bombing, fire, tornado, and so on			

[a]Depending on the laws of the state, sentences could be enhanced (increased) when there is concealment of identity (mask), a bulletproof garment is used, or a police scanner radio is used during the commission of the crime.
[b]In robberies of banks and stores, the terms *counter-jumpers* and *take-over robberies* (as distinguished from "single teller" or "single clerk" robberies) are sometimes used to describe the methods used by the robbers.

was no evidence of a forcible entry, or possession of any burglary tools, other tools or anything else.

Each case must stand on its own facts in determining whether the Commonwealth has sustained its burden of proof. At best, the evidence of the Commonwealth may give rise to suspicion and conjecture of guilt but most certainly does not have such volume and quality capable of reasonably and naturally justifying an inference of a willful and malicious entry into a building with the intent to commit a felony so as to overcome the presumption of innocence and establish guilt beyond a reasonable doubt of the crime of burglary.

Proof of Burglary When Other Crimes Are Committed

As a trespass offense, burglary is most often committed by a defendant who steals or who has an intent to steal. Criminals, however, enter private premises for criminal purposes other than to steal. Offenders have entered the premises of others with intent to commit rape, arson, or other serious felonies. In *Commonwealth v. Bibbo*, 740 N.E.2d 1024 (Mass. App. 2001), the court affirmed a conviction of burglary, holding that evidence of the prior act of stalking the dwelling's occupant supported the finding that the defendant intended to commit the felony of stalking when he entered the victim's house.

The charge of burglary is sometimes one of multiple serious charges against a defendant who went on a criminal rampage in a private home or business place. The charge of burglary also offers prosecutors an alternative charge when doubt exists as to whether the state can prove attempted rape, murder, arson, or another crime. If X broke into W's apartment with the intent to rape her but found that she was not home, X could be charged with burglary if the state could prove his intent to commit a felony. The following case illustrates:

Mitchell v. State

Court of Criminal Appeals of Oklahoma (1971) 489 P.2d 499

Evidence showed that at approximately 1:30 a.m., the defendant drove his fist through the screen door of a house and unlatched it after he tore the screen door off the facing. After gaining entry, he choked the 79-year-old woman who lived in the house. He demanded $25 from her and struck her in the face. He then discharged a firearm into the floor of the house. He left after an hour, demanding that the woman give him $100 by the following morning or he would come back and kill her. He received no money from the woman, who called the sheriff as soon as the defendant left. The conviction for first-degree burglary and the sentence of 15 years' imprisonment were affirmed by the Court of Criminal Appeals of Oklahoma.

Trespass

In its broad sense, the word *trespass* means an unlawful act against a person, property, or right of another. For example, court decisions today continue to speak of the trespassory taking of property, meaning that the property was wrongfully taken. Murder, assault, and battery are trespassory acts because they are wrong and unlawful acts that violate the rights of other people.

trespass A wrongful intrusion on the land or into the premises of another person.

However, in its usual and more common use, **trespass** refers to a wrongful intrusion on the land or into the premises of another person. All states have statutes that reflect this usual and common concept of the offense, and when newspapers use the word, they usually mean it in this limited sense. The Washington statute, RCWA 9A.52.070, defines criminal trespass as follows: "a person is guilty of criminal trespass in the first degree if he knowingly enters or remains unlawfully in a building."

A variety of trespass statutes can be found in criminal codes and municipal ordinances. The trespass to land statutes make the unlawful entry on land (when the land has been posted or the person notified to stay off) a criminal offense if the entry or the remaining on the land is without the consent of the owner or the person in lawful possession. Trespass to dwelling statutes and ordinances forbid entry into homes and residences without the consent of an occupant.

Other trespass statutes and ordinances forbid entry into specific places, such as schools with classes in session, unless the person has legitimate business or is a parent. Trespass statutes generally have a section dealing with entry and also a section pertaining to "failure to depart."

The Crime of Defiant Trespass

defiant trespass A person remains in a place where he or she is not privileged to remain even after notice of trespass is given.

In the case of *Commonwealth v. Groft*, 623 A.2d 341 (Pa. 1993), the defendant (a 56-year-old man) refused to leave the home of his mother after repeatedly being told to find another place to live. He was convicted of **defiant trespass**, which the court described as follows:

> The crime of defiant trespass occurs when a person remains in a place where he is not privileged to remain after notice of trespass is given…. The offense is defined by statute as follows:
>
> (b) Defiant trespasser.—(1) A person commits an offense if, knowing that he is not licensed or privileged to do so, he enters or remains in any place as to which notice against trespass is given by: (i) actual communication to the actor; or (ii) posting in a manner prescribed by law or reasonably likely to come to the attention of intruders; or (iii) fencing or other enclosure manifestly designed to exclude intruders.

Summary

- Robbery differs from common theft in that force or threat of force must be used to take property from the victim. Theft can occur without force and outside the victim's presence.
- Armed or aggravated robbery occurs when a deadly weapon is used in a robbery, or when a victim suffers serious bodily injury. In most states, the threat of the presence of a deadly weapon satisfies the statute, though in many the weapon must in some manner be shown.
- Home invasion requires unlawful entry of the dwelling of another with intent to commit a crime, with persons present in the home, and the use force or threat of force to commit a crime. In most states, a home invasion while armed with a dangerous weapon carries an increased penalty.

- Purse snatching becomes robbery when force more than that needed to take the property is used in the crime. Grabbing the victim and turning her around to get at the purse is sufficient to make the crime robbery.
- Robbery involves a taking of property by the present threat of use of force; extortion is the unlawful taking of property by threat of force or other harm in the future, if the victim does not comply with the demand.
- Under the common law, burglary was defined as breaking into a residence of another at night with the intent to commit a felony.
- Under modern statutes, burglary is usually defined as the unlawful entry, with or without a breaking, of a residence or building, either during the day or at

night, with the intent to commit a crime therein. In some states the statute requires the intent to commit a felony; in others, specific crimes are listed.

• Criminal trespass occurs when a person unlawfully and knowingly enters the land or building of

another. Defiant trespass occurs when the person unlawfully entering is given notice of the trespass, but refuses to leave the premises.

Key Terms

robbery, p. 376
armed or aggravated robbery,
    p. 376
theft by sudden snatch, p. 382

carjacking, p. 380
home invasion robbery, p. 381
sudden snatching, p. 382
extortion, p. 383

burglary, p. 385
trespass, p. 391
defiant trespass, p. 391

Case Analysis And Writing Exercises

1. The defendant had brief sexual affairs with several men. In each case after the affair was over, she wrote to the man and demanded money, or she would make a criminal complaint against him charging sexual assault. In some cases she did in fact make such a complaint. Can her conviction for extortion be sustained? Is it a defense to a charge of extortion that the threats she made, to make a criminal complaint, were true? See *People v. Umana*, 41 Cal. Rptr. 3d 573 (Cal. App. 2006).

2. Defendant went to the victim's house supposedly to look at and buy a rifle owned by the victim. When the victim gave the rifle to the defendant to inspect, he turned the rifle on the victim and refused to give the rifle back. Can he be convicted of robbery? What argument can he make that he cannot be so convicted? Is it a good argument? See *Jacobs v. United States*, 861 A.2d 15 (D.C. 2004). For the result on appeal, see *United States v. Jacobs*, 886 A.2d 510 (D.C. 2005).

3. Washington State has a statute making robbery of a "financial institution" a crime. The defendant was convicted of robbing a bank. On appeal he argued his conviction must be reversed because the prosecution presented no evidence that the robbery took place at a business that met the definition of financial institution in the statute. Should his conviction be reversed? Why or why not? See *State v. Liden*, 156 P.3d 259 (Wash. App. 2007).

4. The defendant entered the home of a man he believed had drug money hidden. He held a gun on the man and a woman seated next to him and demanded the money. When the man refused, the defendant shot him. He then demanded the woman find the money. While searching, the woman escaped. Can the defendant be charged with one count of armed robbery, or two? See *State v. Bernal*, 146 P.3d 289 (N.M. 2006).

Notes

1. The asportation or carrying away requirement in robbery is usually easily met. For example, in *State v. Johnson*, 432 So. 2d 758 (Fla. App. 1983), the court found asportation complete when the defendant forced a store clerk to put money in a paper bag and set it on the counter near the defendant, even if the defendant never touched the bag. In *Lattimore v. U.S.*, 684 A.2d 357 (D.C. 1996), asportation was found when the defendant took a wallet from the victim, saw only a payroll check in the wallet, and threw the wallet back at the victim.

2. Many states also make concealing identity while committing a crime such as robbery conduct for which the degree of the crime and the penalty may be increased. The Supreme Court of Wisconsin has held that if one robber concealed his identity and the other did not, the second robber could be a party to the crime of concealing identity: *Vogel v. State*, 96 Wis. 2d 372, 291 N.W.2d 838 (1980).
3. Volume IX, No. 27, July 1, 1968.
4. Other majority view cases include the following: although the taking may be without force, the offense is robbery if the departure with the property is accomplished by use of force: *People v. Sanders*, 28 Mich. App. 274, 184 N.W.2d 269 (Ct. App. 1970); a woman who saw the defendant run from her house with her purse and bag of money called for help; her grandson, who pursued the defendant, gave up the chase when the defendant fired a gun: *Hermann v. State*, 239 Miss. 523, 123 So. 2d 846 (1960); the defendant asked a service station attendant to fill up his gas tank, then displayed a rifle in a threatening manner and drove away without paying: *State v. Bell*, 194 Neb. 554, 233 N.W.2d 920 (1975).
5. See *State v. Canty*, 469 F.2d 114 (D.C. Cir. 1972), holding that the robbery of each of four bank tellers did not constitute a separate taking within the meaning of the federal bank robbery statute, and therefore the defendant could not be convicted on four counts of robbery based on a single incident; *Rogers v. State*, 272 Ind. 65, 396 N.E.2d 348 (1979), holding that the defendant was improperly convicted on two counts of robbery of a grocery store despite the fact that money was taken from two employees; *Williams v. State*, 271 Ind. 656, 395 N.E.2d 239 (1979), holding that an individual who robs a business establishment, taking that business's money from four employees, can be convicted of only one count of armed robbery; *State v. Potter*, 285 N.C. 238, 204 S.E.2d 649 (1974), holding that when the lives of all employees in a store are threatened and endangered by the use or threatened use of a firearm incident to the theft of their employer's money or property, a single robbery is committed; *State v. Whipple*, 156 N.J. Super. 46, 383 A.2d 445 (1978), holding that the defendant's robbery of a liquor store and its owner constituted but a single transaction, which could not be fractionalized to enhance the defendant's punishment for a single crime.
6. West's Annotated Penal Code, § 215.
7. Courts facing the movement or asportation question under the general robbery statute have reached a different answer. In *State v. Johnson*, 558 N.W.2d 375 (Wis. 1996), the Wisconsin Supreme Court held that the robber must move the car to be guilty.
8. Illinois Revised Statutes 1983, Chapter 38, paragraph 12–11.
9. 590 A.2d 665 (1991).
10. 362 Mass. 83, 283 N.E.2d 840 (1972).
11. See *Alfred v. State*, 659 S.W.2d 97 (Tex. App. 1983).
12. In 1997 Autumn Jackson attempted to extort $40 million from actor Bill Cosby. Jackson alleged she was Cosby's illegitimate daughter, and she threatened to make her claim public if he did not pay her the $40 million. After she began writing letters to companies whose products Cosby endorsed, he went to the FBI and then began tape recording conversations between himself and Jackson. Jackson was subsequently found guilty of extortion. See the *New York Times* articles, "Cosby Describes Requests for Money from 2 Women," July 16, 1997, and "To Ask Is Not Always to Extort: In the Case Involving Bill Cosby, a Troubling Legal Issue," July 18, 1997.
13. 213 Cal. Rptr. 465 (Cal. App. 1985).
14. Florida's burglary statutes, adopted in 1975, provide that "burglary means entering or remaining in a structure or conveyance with the intent to commit an offense therein, unless the premises are at the time open to the public or the defendant is licensed or invited to enter or remain."
15. The New Mexico Court of Appeals held in the 1976 case of *State v. Tixier*, 89 N.M. 297, 551 P.2d 987, that "A one-half inch penetration into the building is sufficient. Any penetration, however slight, of the interior space is sufficient. The fact that the penetration is by an instrument is also sufficient. 2 *Wharton's Criminal Law and Procedure* (1957) § 421; Clark and Marshall, *Crimes*, 6th ed., § 13.04."
16. 91 A.D.2d 166, 458 N.Y.S.2d 429 (1983).
17. 415 U.S. 800, 94 S. Ct. 1234 (1974).
18. See note 15.
19. 84 Wis. 2d 621, 267 N.W.2d 295 (1978).
20. *Woods v. State*, 186 Miss. 463, 191 So. 283 (1939).
21. 274 Cal. App. 2d 912, 79 Cal. Rptr. 650 (1969).
22. 673 A.2d 1372 (1996).
23. 225 Pa. Super. 311, 303 A.2d 528 (1973).

White-Collar Crime, Cyber Crime, and Commercial Crime

Bernard Madoff, shown leaving a federal courthouse, pled guilty in 2009 to 11 counts of violation of federal fraud laws, and was sentenced to 150 years in prison. It is estimated his "ponzi" scheme cost investors more than $65 billion.

OUTLINE

LEARNING OBJECTIVES

In this chapter we discuss nonviolent, mainly economic theft or harm crimes. The learning objectives for Chapter 15 are:

- Define white-collar crime.
- Explain why fraud convictions require action done knowingly.
- Describe the elements of a "scheme or artifice" under federal criminal statutes.
- Explain how bribery and extortion are similar under the federal bribery and extortion statutes.

- List the laws protecting intellectual property.
- Name two federal criminal statutes frequently used to convict white-collar criminals.
- Identify one element making wire fraud different from bank fraud, and state why the element exists.
- Define insider trading.
- State the elements of identity theft crimes.

For years, William Jefferson of Louisiana served as a member of the U.S. House of Representatives. In that role he was instrumental in arranging business relationships between U.S. companies and interests in West African nations.

On August 6, 2009, Jefferson was found guilty on 11 counts of bribery, conflict of interest, and honest services fraud in federal court. The case involved payment of bribes to Jefferson to enlist his help in getting American companies business contracts with West African nations. The prosecution's case famously revealed that Jefferson had $90,000 in bills marked by the FBI in his freezer, allegedly to be used for payment of a bribe. In November of 2009, the former congressman was sentenced to 13 years in prison and ordered to forfeit about $470,000 in funds received as part of the fraud crimes.

Jefferson appealed his conviction to the Fourth Circuit Court of Appeals, and he was permitted to remain free pending that appeal. On June 24, 2010, the U.S. Supreme Court decided *Skilling v. United States* (discussed in this chapter). In that case the Court decided that "honest services fraud" under the federal wire fraud statute covered only bribery and kickback schemes, but it did not cover conflicts of interest. Since Jefferson's convictions for honest services fraud involved, in some parts, conflicts of interest, the court of appeals must consider the effect, if any, of the *Skilling* decision on Jefferson's conviction. One likely result would be to order the case remanded to the district court for hearings on that question. It is also possible that convictions under explicit bribery counts would justify the sentence imposed.

In this chapter we will learn about many crimes that focus on schemes or plans designed to fraudulently deprive another person of money or other property, as well as crimes like arson and trespass that directly injure another person's property.

≡ White-Collar Crime

white-collar crime
A class or type of criminal conduct that has solely economic gain to the criminal as its goal.

The term **white-collar crime** is generally understood to refer to a class or type of criminal conduct that has solely economic gain to the criminal as its goal. While the "white-collar" language suggests the status of the wrongdoer, most definitions of the term focus on the kind of behavior made criminal, not the identity of the criminal. The U.S. Department of Justice, in its 1989 FBI report "White Collar Crime: A Report to the Public,"[1] defined white-collar crime as "those illegal acts which are characterized by deceit, concealment or violation of trust and which are not dependent upon the application or threat of physical force or violence."

The economic cost of white-collar crimes and the other commercial crimes discussed in this chapter is enormous and greatly outstrips the cost of many other crimes. For example, in the 2001 FBI "Crime in the United States Report,"[2] it was estimated that the total economic cost of all robbery, burglary, theft, and car theft crimes in 2001 was $17.2 billion. The estimated loss suffered by Enron investors in the 2001 "meltdown" of that company in 2001 alone was $67 billion.

In this chapter we focus on the many forms of commercial, business, financial, and fraudulent conduct that are made criminal under state and federal laws.

≡ Fraud and Fraudulent Practices

fraud Deceitful means or acts used to cheat a person, corporation, or governmental agency.

Fraud consists of deceitful means or acts used to cheat a person, corporation, or governmental agency. Theft by fraud or larceny by fraud is often the criminal charge used, as fraud can be a form of theft and larceny. Fraud convictions require some form of specific intent, such as acting knowingly or willfully, as distinguished from negligent conduct. In the following materials this chapter examines some of the key criminal laws that target white-collar crimes of fraud.

Bank Fraud

The federal government has an important interest in fraud aimed at banks and other financial institutions. Most of these institutions are federally insured, so that losses suffered by them caused by fraud can end up being paid for by the federal government. Because of this, Congress passed the bank fraud statute, 18 U.S.C. § 1344, which makes it a federal crime to defraud a financial institution that is federally insured. Examples of **bank fraud** that would fall under this statute are check kiting (discussed in Chapter 13), check forgery, false statements on loan applications, unauthorized use of ATM machines, credit card fraud, and student loan fraud. These crimes all require proof that the defendant knowingly executed or attempted to execute a "scheme or artifice" to defraud, or through false statements, obtain money or property from a federally insured financial institution.

bank fraud Fraud aimed at banks and other financial institutions.

The statute does not define "scheme or artifice," but 18 U.S.C. § 1346 states that a "scheme of artifice" includes a scheme to deprive another of the intangible right of honest services (discussed later in this chapter). The federal fraud statutes otherwise leave it to courts to determine whether "a scheme of artifice" exists. A definition that is too specific makes it possible for criminals to manipulate their scheme so that it falls outside the definition. The U.S. Supreme Court has held that any such scheme must include a "material falsehood," that is, one that a person would understand to be important and relied on by another. See *Neder v. United States*, 527 U.S. 1 (1999), where the holding was made applicable to mail fraud and wire fraud statutes as well. These statutes also require proof of a "scheme or artifice."

An example of a bank fraud scheme can be seen in *United States v. Jenkins*, 210 F.3d 884 (8th Cir. 2000). Jenkins started a computer sales business, and he entered into an agreement with his bank that permitted him to withdraw funds from his account based on credit card receipts of computer sales. Jenkins, using his own and other people's credit cards, created receipts showing sales that had actually not occurred. He then presented these receipts to the bank as evidence that payments would be made by the credit card companies. The credit card companies refused to pay, because the sales did not occur. Jenkins was convicted under the bank fraud act.

Health Care Fraud

The federal government has many health care programs, most notably Medicare and Medicaid. These programs rely on statements, claims, and bills sent to program administers by health care professionals, as well as persons served in the programs. False claims under these programs cost the federal government huge amounts each year. A 2007 article states that it has been estimated that the yearly cost of health care fraud is more than $13 billion.[3]

Congress has passed various statutes that address this problem, among them the Medicaid False Claims Statute, 42 U.S.C. § 1320a-7b(a), and the Medicaid Anti-Kickback Statute, 42 U.S.C. § 1320a-7b(b). The false claims statute makes it a crime for any person to make a false statement in any application for a federal health care benefit, if made knowingly and willfully. An example of a crime falling within this statute includes submitting a bill for services or tests that were not performed. The anti-kickback statute is aimed at those who promise or receive payments based on referrals of patients for services paid under federal health care programs. An example of a crime coming under this statute includes accepting a fee for sending a patient to a physician or other provider for medical services. It also includes sending a patient to a health care provider with whom the referring physician has a financial relationship. Violation of these laws can lead to massive fines. In 2001 TAP Pharmaceutical Products, Inc. was fined $875 million, the largest fine ever for health care fraud.

The federal government also has a general "Health Care Fraud" statute, 18 U.S.C. § 1347, which makes it a crime to willfully execute a "scheme or artifice" intended to defraud a "health care benefit" program. One typical prosecution under this statute is found in *United States v. Franklin-El*, 554 F.3d 903 (10th Cir. 2009). The defendants ran an alcohol and drug addiction counseling clinic, which received reimbursement payments under Medicaid for qualified patients. Only diagnosed addicts were qualified patients. The defendants filed 1,331 false claims for reimbursement from Medicaid that totaled over $1.2 million, listing as "addicts" persons who were not addicts, were not enrolled in the defendant's program, or in some cases were children only a few weeks old. The court affirmed their convictions on 52 counts of health care fraud.

Convictions under the health care fraud statute carry both a prison sentence and a fine. In extreme cases, the prison sentence can be for life. In *United States v. Martinez*, 588 F.3d 301 (6th Cir. 2009), a physician operated a "pain-management clinic." Some of the medical services he provided were paid for under Medicaid, Medicare, or the Ohio Bureau of Workers Compensation, each of which qualifies as a "health care benefit" program. Martinez gave his patients "nerve-block" injections, for which he billed these programs. The average number of "nerve-block" injections patients usually received were 2.5 per year; Martinez gave his patients an average of 64 injections per year, with the result many became addicted to the medication and incurred serious bodily injury. Two patients died as a result of Martinez's treatments. He was convicted of health care fraud for claiming reimbursements of more than $14 million for improperly diagnosed and treated medical services. Because his actions resulted in the deaths of two patients, he was sentenced to life in prison under § 1347(2).

Intellectual Property Fraud

Intellectual property generally means property rights in ideas; inventions; artistic works such as books, movies, and songs; and the like. The theft, piracy, or counterfeiting of intellectual property costs its owners billions of dollars each year and has become even more damaging with the rise of Internet thefts. The primary criminal laws aimed at **intellectual property fraud** are the federal copyright and patent acts and federal and state trade secret acts.

intellectual property fraud Theft, piracy, or counterfeiting of ideas, inventions, artistic works, and the like.

Copyright   The copyright act, 17 U.S.C. 506, protects books, movies, and songs once they have been published. Any person who willfully infringes a valid copyright for economic gain violates the statute. Infringing means reproducing or distributing the work without permission. Thus, while it is permitted to use a copyrighted song in a free school production, it is not permitted to use the same song in a production that charges admission. Questions about the permissible use of copyrighted material are decided under the "fair use" doctrine, 17 U.S.C. § 107. "Fair use" includes classroom use, scholarship use, research, teaching, and related uses of the copyrighted materials.

The Internet has presented a great challenge to the "fair use" doctrine. Many software programs available on the Internet enable users to "share" files with other users on a "peer-to-peer" basis, that is, the users' computers communicate directly with one another without using an Internet server. If these files contain copyrighted works, such as songs downloaded from a CD to the user's computer, the songs are being distributed and may be a violation of the copyright law. Individual criminal prosecutions for copyright infringement have not been found. However, in two leading cases, courts have found Internet servers to be in civil violation of the copyright laws, based on the actual "sharing" done by its Internet customers.

In *M.G.M. Studios v. Grokster, LLC*, 545 U.S. 913 (2005), the Supreme Court held that two Internet companies that distributed software to its customers that enabled the customers to share copyrighted works could be found to be in violation of the copyright laws. The software created a network that allowed users to access other computers using the same software program, find designated files, and download them. Since about

90 percent of the files included copyrighted songs, the Court held that the Internet companies could be found in violation of the copyright owners' exclusive distribution and reproduction rights.

In *A & M Records v. Napster*, 239 F.3d 1004 (9th Cir. 2001), the court held that Napster violated copyright laws by creating a network where individual users could create MP3 files of copyrighted songs, list them on the Napster site, and share them on a peer-to-peer basis with others using the Napster software. Whether decisions like these will lead to criminal prosecutions remains to be seen.

The Internet sharing of copyright materials also makes application of the "first sale" defense questionable. It has long been recognized that one who purchases a copyrighted work is entitled to sell that very work once. That is because after this "first sale," the seller no longer has the work to sell and cannot use it for the kind of economic gain the copyright laws are intended to punish. However, if a computer file is "sold" or traded, the seller/trader keeps the file and can do it again. The "first sale" defense does not seem appropriate in that case.

Trade Secrets The federal government and every state have trade secret laws that make it a crime to steal a trade secret. Generally, trade secrets are property characteristics that have been kept a secret by the owner of the property, and the property is made valuable because of the trade secret. The best example of a trade secret is the recipe for Coca-Cola, which is aggressively kept secret by the Coca-Cola Company. The federal government makes it a crime to convert a trade secret for economic gain under the Economic Espionage Act, 18 U.S.C. § 1831–1839.

Fraud and Corruption in Government

Fraud against government is as old as government itself. Reports of fraud and corruption date back to biblical times and early civilizations. The U.S. government today is spending over $3.5 trillion per year in its total budget, so it is not surprising that it has serious fraud and corruption problems.

Losses through fraud and corruption occur in many ways. Fraud can be charged criminally in federal courts as mail fraud (when the U.S. mails are used), wire fraud (when interstate or international communications are used), racketeering, bribery and theft of public funds, fraud and conspiracy to commit fraud, false entries or false statements, fraud in connection with government contracting, equity skimming, false statements and misappropriation of funds, conspiracy to defraud the United States, and interstate transportation of funds obtained by fraud. The following areas account for many of the fraud losses in the federal government.

Contract Fraud and the False Claims Act In the procurement of arms and military supplies, the federal government spends more than $600 billion yearly. Fraud in military procurement contracts has been discovered in the selling of inside information on contract bids, bid rigging, bribes and kickbacks, double billing, falsifying test results or failure to conduct tests, and overcharging for materials and services. The False Claims Act, 18 U.S.C. § 287, makes it a crime to present a claim to the U.S. government that is false or fraudulent and known to be false or fraudulent. The statute was first passed during the Civil War, because of the rampant fraud practiced by contractors providing goods and services to the Union Army.

The False Claims Act applies to any kind of false claim, if its purpose is to obtain payment from the government. For example, in *United States v. Saybolt*, 577 F.3d 195 (3d Cir. 2009), defendants were convicted under § 287 for filing false income tax returns

SCAMS, FRAUDS, AND OFFSHORE BANK ACCOUNTS

White Collar crime can take many forms. The following accounts illustrate some of the ways fraudulent schemes have been uncovered and prosecuted.

ABSCAM: The Scam that Shocked the United States

The trafficking in stolen art was intense in 1979, and the FBI set up a scam in New York City to trap some of the persons dealing in stolen art. FBI agents dressed as wealthy Arab sheiks ("ABSCAM") pretended to be interested in buying stolen art, and then spread word of their interest to persons in the art world.

The FBI was surprised when instead of attracting persons attempting to sell stolen art works, the scam captured six U.S. Congressman and one U.S. Senator in its net. Videotapes made of the meetings between the "sheiks" and the Congressmen showed payments to the Congressmen of $50,000 and more. One Congressman was taped saying to the "sheiks" "I can give you me". All of the Congressman and the U.S. Senator were convicted of bribery and other charges and served time in prison.

The uproar in the U.S. Congress went on for months. Many blamed the FBI for targeting and embarrassing the U.S. Congress. Should members of Congress and other high government officials be off-limits for scams and investigations such as ABSCAM?

Troubled Times and Ponzi Schemes

Troubled times are said to bring more frauds to light. As Warren Buffet, the financial wizard from Omaha, put it "…when the tide goes out, we can see who is swimming naked". New records for fraudulent schemes were set since the financial melt-down of 2008–2009. They include the following massive Ponzi schemes (Ponzi schemes and their origination are described later in this chapter)

For almost 40 years Bernard Madoff was regarded by almost everyone as a brilliant investor and a pillar of the New York and international community. Investors flocked to invest their money with him, and asked few questions about his operations. Madoof paid high dividends, and his monthly statements showed impressive paper profits to his investors, which numbered in the thousands. However, when financial markets collapsed in 2008, it was discovered that in fact Madoff had made virtually no investments with his client's money but had simply used new investors' deposits to pay "investment gains" to existing investors, the classic Ponzi scheme. Madoff, age 70, was convicted of criminal charges such as mail and security fraud, money laundering, and perjury in 2008, and in 2009 was sentenced to 150 years in prison.

Losses from this gigantic fraud totaled more than $64.8 billion. Thousands of people lost their life savings, and schools and charitable institutions that invested with Madoff took huge financial hits.

with the IRS and seeking refunds. They were also convicted under 18 U.S.C. § 286, which punishes conspiracies to defraud the government by false claims.

Program Frauds Billions of dollars are dispersed every year in programs such as Medicaid, Medicare,[4] food stamps,[5] small business loans, subsidy programs, HUD (U.S. Department of Housing and Urban Development), Social Security, and various aid programs. Persons who make false claims for benefits under these programs can be prosecuted under the False Claims Act or, in some cases, under statutes directed at specific programs, such as Medicaid, discussed earlier.

In many federal programs, funds are disbursed by city or state granting agencies to be used for appropriate purposes under the federal funding legislation. The federal program theft statute,18 U.S.C. § 666, applies to theft or bribery by persons who are agents for organizations that receive in one year more than $10,000 of federal funds. A conviction under this statute requires that the defendant (1) be an agent of the organization and (2) that the theft involve property of the organization. For example, an independent

In Europe, thousands of investors who were directed to Madoff through European banks and investment houses also lost billions. However, these overseas investors were able to collect about $15.5 billion from these institutions through civil lawsuits. (See *New York Times*, 5/25/10: "$15.5. Billion for Victims of Madoff Overseas.")

Other Ponzi schemes uncovered during this same period include a scheme targeting Hollywood celebrities that caused $30 million in losses (*New York Times* 6/7/10); a Fort Lauderdale lawyer was charged with operating a $1 billion Ponzi scheme (*New York Times* 12/2/09), in 2021 a Nashville Tennessee man pled guilty to a $11 million Ponzi scheme (*New York Times* 4/14/10).

Secret Offshore Tax Havens and Accounts

The U.S. Treasury Department estimates that the United States loses $100 billion per year because of offshore tax havens, bank accounts, and credit cards. Wealthy Americans can use these offshore bank accounts to hide income and other funds from authorities and thereby avoid paying taxes on those hidden funds. In 2009 Braely Birkenfeld, an American banker who worked for UBS, the largest bank in Switzerland, was sentenced to 40 months in prison for helping American citizens use UBS to hide funds. Birkenfeld provided the Internal Revenue Service with detailed information on how UBS solicited wealthy Americans to use the bank to hide funds and avoid payment of taxes.

The U.S. Justice Department filed civil charges against UBS in 2008, which resulted in UBS paying penalties of $780 million to the United States. UBS also agreed to furnish names and account information on about 4500 Americans who had accounts of over $1 million with UBS. On June 17, 2010 the Swiss Parliament ratified an agreement between Switzerland and the United States that opens the door for the disclosure of imformation about Americans with accounts in Swiss banks.

In 2009 the IRS offered an amnesty program to taxpayers with offshore bank accounts which excused them from criminal charges if they paid back taxes and penalties. About 14,700 persons accepted the amnesty offer (*New York Times* 11/18/09).

The U.S. Justice Department and the IRS state there is increased scrutiny of questionable offshore accounts in many countries in addition to Switzerland, such as Liechtenstein and Hong Kong. In an unusual turn of events, Birkenfeld, in prison in Pennsylvania, has applied for a reward under the American "whistleblower" law. Unde that law, a person who gives information leading to the recovery of unpaid taxes is given a reward of between 15 and 30 per cent of the taxes collected. In the tax haven cases, taxes collected could be more than $4 billion dollars (*New York Times* 11/27/09).

contractor providing services to a regional airport that received federal funds was convicted under § 666 for overbilling the airport for services allegedly provided to the airport. The court held the contractor was an "agent" of the airport and thus was guilty of theft from the organization that received the federal funds. *United States v. Vitillo*, 490 F.3d 314 (3d Cir. 2007). However, not every theft of federal program funds is covered by § 666. In *United States v. Abu-Shawish*, 507 F.3d 550 (7th Cir. 2007), the court held that a defendant who was given a "block" grant of HUD funds by a Milwaukee city agency for development of a community organization could not be convicted for theft of property under § 666. It was not enough that the defendant defrauded the Milwaukee "organization" that disbursed the federal funds; the court said the defendant must be an agent of that organization as well, which the defendant was not. The court stated that the defendant should have been prosecuted under the federal mail or wire fraud acts.

Bribery Offering a gift or payment to another with the specific intent to obtain some unlawful particular *quid pro quo* for the gift or payment

Bribery of agents of an organization that receives federal funds is also covered by § 666. In *United States v. Caro-Muniz*, 406 F.3d 22 (1st Cir. 2005), the mayor of Rincon, Puerto Rico, was convicted for taking bribes to award contracts that were funded by federal grants. In *United States v. Ganim*, 510 F.3d 134 (2d Cir. 2007), the mayor of Bridgeport, Connecticut, was convicted of accepting illegal "gifts" from persons who received city contracts. Often, as was the case in *Ganim*, defendants convicted under § 666 are also charged under the RICO statutes, discussed in Chapter 18. Moreover, public officials like the defendant in *Ganim* could also be prosecuted under state bribery laws such as § 53(a)-148 of the Conn. Gen. Statutes.

Bribery Bribery of federal officials is covered by 18 U.S.C. § 201(b). Federal officials include everyone from members of Congress to food inspectors. In *United States v. Alfisi*, 308 F.3d 144 (2d Cir. 2002), produce inspectors for the U.S. Department of Agriculture were convicted for taking bribes from wholesale produce sellers in exchange for higher quality produce-inspection receipts.

Bribery prosecutions under 18 U.S.C. § 201(b) often are coupled with extortion charges under 18 U.S.C. § 872. A federal officer that "solicits" a bribe in exchange for some official act may also threaten to use his official position to prevent the official act from occurring. The former is a "bribe" under § 201, and the latter is "extortion" under § 872. Moreover, there are similarities between extortion and bribery offenses, as the Supreme Court noted in *Evans v. United States*, 504 U.S. 255 (1992). The Court said in *Evans* that while conviction of extortion under the Hobbs Act, 19 U.S.C. § 1951, requires proof of an exchange of payment for an agreement to perform an official act, it does not require proof that the official took affirmative steps to "induce" the payment. The Court stated that it is no defense to an extortion charge that the facts would also support a bribery conviction. It should be noted that the *quid pro quo* requirement discussed in *Evans* for Hobbs Act cases has typically been interpreted to require only an agreement that the official would "exercise some influence on the payor's behalf as opportunities arise" and does not require an agreement on a specific official act. *United States v. Abbey*, 560 F.3d 513 (6th Cir. 2009).

A case illustrating bribery and extortion charges under federal statutes is *United States v. Valle*, 538 F.3d 341 (5th Cir. 2008). In that case, an Immigration and Customs agent approached a Mexican national being held in a detention facility pending deportation. The agent told the detainee that there were pending criminal charges against the detainee but that the agent would remove them for a payment of $20,000. The detainee told other federal officers about the conversation, and ultimately an undercover FBI officer gave the agent the $20,000 and then arrested the agent. The court affirmed his convictions under both the bribery statute and the extortion statute. It rejected the agent's defense that he never intended to remove any criminal charges because they didn't exist, stating that all either statute required was that the official enter into a "corrupt" agreement to use his official position.

Quid pro quo Giving something of value ("quid") for something else.

Bribery and, to some degree, extortion crimes usually involve a **quid pro quo**, that is, an exchange of some official act for some promised payment. The nature of the *quid pro quo* requirement in the federal bribery statutes was described in the U.S. Supreme Court case of *United States v. Sun-Diamond Growers of California*, 526 U.S. 398 (1999). In that case the defendant was prosecuted under 18 U.S.C. § 201 (c), the crime of giving an official an illegal gratuity. The trial court had instructed the jury that the crime included giving an official a gift "simply because of his position," without tying the gift to any particular official act. The Supreme Court reversed the conviction, holding that § 201(c) required proof of a link between the gratuity and some official act.

In the course of its decision in *Sun-Diamond,* the Supreme Court made this statement about the federal bribery statute, § 201(b): "[b]ribery requires intent to 'influence' an official act {the bribe-giver] or to be 'influenced' in an official act [the public official bribe receiver].... In other words, for bribery there must be a *quid pro quo*—a specific intent to give or receive something of value in exchange for an official act." 526 U.S. at 404–405.

Bribery convictions under § 201 (b) thus have as an element of the offense a showing that the bribe was given or solicited as part of an agreement to exchange some official action for the bribe. Courts addressing the *quid pro quo* issue in prosecutions under 18 U.S.C. § 666, the federal program bribery statute, have reached a different conclusion. Those courts hold that there need be no showing of payment for a particular official act, but only that the payment was made to influence the official "in connection" with transactions under the federal programs. *United States v. McNair*, 605 F.3d 1152 (11th Cir. 2010).

Bribery was traditionally a crime committed by or with officials, and as a result many state bribery statutes are specifically addressed to official misconduct. The Georgia bribery statute, OCGA § 16-10-2, makes it a crime to (1) offer to give an official anything of value in order to influence the official in performance of official acts and (2) solicit anything of value from another by "inducing the reasonable belief" that giving the thing of value will result in influencing the performance of official actions. Most states also have bribery statutes that are directed at persons other than public officials. One example is in sports bribery cases. As a result of famous "point-shaving" basketball scandals and other sports bribery incidents, many states have passed bribery statutes aimed directly at sports participants. Louisiana's statute, LSA-RS 14-118.1, and North Carolina's NC GSA § 14-373 are examples of these statutes.

Stock Market and Financial Market Frauds

The stock markets and financial markets of the United States and other industrial countries are important to their economic development in creating jobs and providing for economic security. Among the crimes that infect this field is insider trading. People who obtain inside information on the plans of large corporations can often make huge profits by insider trading or by selling the information illegally.

The federal criminal securities laws applicable to crimes like insider trading are generally contained in regulations promulgated in Section 10(b) of the Securities Exchange Act of 1934, 15 U.S.C. § 78j. Section 78j makes it a crime for any person to use a "manipulative or deceptive device or contrivance" in connection with the purchase or sale of a security, such as a share of stock. This includes insider trading.

Insider trading often involves a person with some fiduciary responsibility, such as a corporate officer, using information known only to corporate "insiders" to profit from the information by buying or selling corporate stock in advance of public acquisition of the information. Insider trading also includes the so-called tippee situation, where an "outsider" acquires information from an insider and uses it to his advantage. If the tippee knew the information came from an insider in breach of a fiduciary duty, the tippee can be convicted under § 78j. See *United States v. Evans*, 486 F.3d 315 (7th Cir. 2007).

Determining exactly what constitutes a "manipulative" devise under the securities laws can be difficult. In *United States v. Finnerty*, 533 F.3d 143 (2d Cir. 2008), the court held that the so-called interpositioning practice used by a trader on the New York Stock Exchange did not violate the securities laws. "Interpositioning" refers to the practice of a trader taking a position in a stock transaction between two customers, one wishing to buy a stock and one wishing to sell. Stock Exchange rules state that in such a case, the

In 2010 Angelo Mozilo, the former CEO of Countrywide Financial Company, was fined $22 million by the Securities Exchange Commission based on insider trading violations committed by Mozilo. In addition, Mozilo was ordered to disgorge $45 million received by him as a result of the illegal insider trades. Mozilo sold about $140 millon in Countrywide stock when the company was trading at its peak price, even though Mozilo knew the company was in fact in financial difficulty because of the number of undervalued, "subprime" mortgage securities the company owned. In 2008 Countrywide, near bankruptcy, was purchased by the Bank of America Company for $2.2 billion. Mozilo is famous for having made favorable loans to many public figures, including members of Congress, known as "Friends of Angelo".

trader is required to "match" the buyer with the seller. In interpositioing, the trader trades separately with each customer, thereby taking advantage of any gap that existed between the two orders. The court said that while the trader was acting wrongly for his own gain, he did not deceive or manipulate his customers.

Stock market and corporate fraud reached unprecedented heights during the period 1990 to 2004. Although there have been previous instances of scandal and greed in American economic markets, nothing comes close to those in recent years. The bankruptcy of the energy giant Enron Corporation alone cost investors and employees billions of dollars. In February 2001, Enron stock sold for $90 per share; when it filed for bankruptcy 10 months later, those same shares were selling for pennies. Many of Enron's executives made millions of dollars selling their shares at a time when employees were unable to sell their shares. In 2006 Jeffrey Skilling and Kenneth Lay, chief executive officers of Enron during the period Enron misrepresented its financial condition to investors and banks, were convicted of fraud and conspiracy. Skilling was sentenced to 24 years in prison; Lay died before he could be sentenced. Skilling appealed his conviction on various grounds; the court of appeals affirmed his convictions in 2009, but the U.S. Supreme Court reversed and remanded the case in a 2010 decision.

Skilling was charged with violations of federal fraud statutes, including "honest services" fraud under the mail and wire fraud acts. The term "honest services" was derived from federal court cases where courts interpreted the "scheme or artifice" language of the mail and wire fraud statutes as including actions that didn't directly deprive a victim of money or property, but were nonetheless fraudulent. An example would be a mayor who takes a bribe or kickback to give a city contract to a friend. Even if the contract price is fair, so that no money is fraudulently "taken" from the city, the city has been deprived of the "honest services" of the mayor. Federal courts were frequently affirming convictions under the mail and wire fraud statutes for bribery and kickback schemes.

In 1987 the U.S. Supreme Court held in *McNally v. United States*, 483 U.S. 350, that the "scheme or artifice" language of the wire and mail fraud acts applied only to direct frauds, where victims were deprived of money or other property by the fraudulent actions. "Honest services" fraud was not covered by the statutes, the Court held. The next year Congress passed 18 U.S.C. § 1346, which stated that for the mail and other fraud statutes a "scheme or artifice" included depriving another of the "intangible right of honest services".

Courts began applying section 1346 to various kinds of fraudulent actions, if, as the result of these actions, a defendant acted dishonestly. For example, making false representations about a company's financial situation, as in the Enron case, or acting with a conflict of interest, as in the Jefferson case discussed at the beginning of this chapter, were actions treated by federal prosecutors and courts as covered by the mail and wire fraud statutes.

In *Skilling v. United States*, 130 S. Ct. 2896 (2010) the Supreme Court held that section 1346 didn't include under the language "honest services" fraudulent actions that didn't directly deprive a victim of money or property, except for bribery or kickback schemes. Since Skilling had been convicted of "honest services" fraud without any evidence he took a bribe or received a kickback, the Court reversed and remanded his case for consideration of whether he should receive a new trial on all of the counts of his indictment.

Other Fraud Statutes in the Federal Criminal Code

Each state has fraud statutes in its criminal code to punish fraudulent conduct that takes place within that state. Because most large fraud schemes involve criminal conduct that crosses state lines, Congress has power to punish these crimes under the Interstate Commerce Clause. Also, because many fraud schemes use the banking system, the stock market, or other large financial institutions regulated by federal law, Congress has passed several federal fraud crime laws, and violators are frequently charged under these laws.

False Statements Act In 18 U.S.C. § 1001, the federal government makes it a crime to give a false statement to a federal officer or relating to a matter within federal jurisdiction. This statute is frequently used in conjunction with other federal-criminal statutes, since many white-collar crimes include the criminal's lying to federal officers investigating other suspected crimes. For example, in the investigation in the Martha Stewart case, the initial investigation concerned possible insider trading violations. Stewart was ultimately convicted of conspiracy and making false statements to federal investigators.[6] As of 2005, most of the convictions for violation of the terrorism provisions of the Patriot Act were for making false statements.

Convictions for making false statements can include withholding information. The statute also applies to statements made to state agencies, if they are under federal jurisdiction. The recent case of *United States v. Moore*, 446 F.3d 671 (7th Cir. 2006),

NATIONAL FRAUD FACTS

Which fraud case is the largest on record?	The 2009 conviction of Bernie Madoff marked the end of a $64.8 billion Ponzi scheme that defrauded hundreds of investors. Madoff maintained elaborate books that showed investment returns on his clients' money, when in fact those investments did not exist. The 1998 accounting fraud on the Cendent Corporation, by Walter Forbes, is believed to be the next largest fraud on record, at $19 billion. After lengthy litigation, Forbes was convicted of securities fraud in 2007. See *United States v. Forbes,* 2007 WL 141952. It is likely the Enron collapse cost shareholders and other investors more than that amount. The WorldCom accounting fraud in 2004, in which the CEO, Bernard Ebbers, received a 25-year prison sentence, cost investors $11 billion.
Which fraud case led to the most criminal convictions?	The Enron case resulted in the convictions of 10 executives and guilty pleas from 16 others. Only one executive was acquitted, and one trial resulted in a hung jury.
What were the most common charges in the largest fraud cases?	Securities fraud, wire fraud, conspiracy, false statements, mail fraud, bank fraud, insider trading, and theft were the criminal charges in these frauds.
How often are government employees convicted of corruption charges?	While most government employees are honest, the FBI reports that about 500 city, state, or federal employees each year are convicted of corrupt practices. Former Illinois Governor George Ryan, former Congressman Randall Cunningham, and mega-lobbyist Jack Abramoff were among those convicted. See the *New York Times*, "FBI Focus on Public Corruption Includes 2000 Investigations," May 11, 2006.
Which computer-related crimes are prosecuted in state courts?	The type of crimes prosecuted, from the highest number to the lowest, are credit card fraud, bank card fraud, identity theft, child pornography, computer forgery (altering documents), cyber stalking (sending threatening or harassing e-mails) hacking (unauthorized access), computer sabotage (placing worms, viruses, or logic bombs—hidden programs "detonated" by a specific date or event), and theft of computer data (copyright infringement).

illustrates this aspect of the federal false statement statute. In *Moore*, Rose Cameron was the director of a community group that received block grants from HUD, a federal agency. One of the requirements for receiving the grants was that no director of the recipient have a conflict of interest with persons awarding the grants. Cameron ran for and was elected an alderwoman on the Milwaukee Common Council, where she was a member of the committee that awarded HUD grants. Her daughters succeeded her as directors of the community group but used different names when communicating with the council. The daughters and Cameron on several occasions failed to disclose the relationship between them, which violated HUD rules. They were all convicted under the federal false statements statute by intentionally concealing their relationship. Because the false statements were made to a city official acting under the jurisdiction of HUD, the federal statute applied.

Mail and Wire Fraud and the Travel Act   Many federal crimes have a broad scope and are used in prosecutions for violations of the particular statute and also in both fraud and RICO violations (see Chapter 18). They include:

Mail Fraud Act

18 U.S.C. § 1341. This act has been amended to include all interstate carriers such as FedEx and UPS.	"To prove mail fraud, the government must show that the defendant (1) intentionally participated in a scheme to defraud, and (2) used the mails to execute the fraudulent scheme; … conviction for mail fraud need not rest on the success of the fraudulent scheme." *United States v. Bailey,* 123 F.3d 1381 (11th Cir. 1997). The scheme need not such as to deceive a reasonable person; even one directed at the naïve or ignorant is a violation. *United States v. Svete*, 556 F.3d 1157 (11th Cir. 2009).

Wire Fraud Act

18 U.S.C. § 1343	The same elements as mail fraud, plus the wire communication must cross state lines. The Commerce Clause gives the federal government jurisdiction over wire communications, whereas the mail fraud statute stems from the Constitution's grant of power to Congress over the postal service.

The Travel Act

18 U.S.C.A. § 1952	To prove a violation of the Travel Act, the government must show "(1) travel in interstate or foreign commerce, or use of telephone, mail, or other facility in interstate or foreign commerce; (2) with intent to facilitate the promotion, management, establishment, or carrying on of any unlawful activity, and (3) thereafter performs an additional act in furtherance of the specified unlawful activity." *United States v. Long*, 949 F.2d 1370 (5th Cir. 1991). In 2007 the football player Michael Vick was charged with violation of the Travel Act, as well as other crimes.

The Major Fraud Act

18 U.S.C. § 1031	Any person who executes a scheme or artifice to defraud the United States or obtain property under false pretenses based on a contract or grant from the United States in excess of $1,000,000 is guilty of major fraud.

Fraudulent Schemes Under State Law   Every state has enacted statutes that make fraud a crime under certain circumstances. In many states, the general fraud statute follows the language of the federal acts, such as mail or wire fraud. Arizona's statute, ARS § 13-2310, makes it a crime to execute a "scheme or artifice" intended to fraudulently deprive another person of property. Some states also have specific statutes aimed at "confidence games" or related trickery. New York's statute, titled "Fraudulent accosting," Penal Law § 165.30, is an example of such a statute. It makes it a crime to obtain property of another by trick, deception, or confidence game. Finally, many states have statutes aimed at schemes to obtain money by false pretenses. See, e.g., W. Va. Code § 61-3-24.

The Crime of Identity Theft and False Identification Documents

A February 24, 2010, report released by the Federal Trade Commission stated that identity theft complaints in 2009 totaled 288,078, by far the highest form of consumer complaint made to the FTC. Countless other incidents of identity theft went unreported. In 2009 the FTC estimated identity theft caused losses in excess of $50 billion in the United States.

identity theft Theft based on stealing a real person's identification information (true name) or theft based on creating a fictitious person's identification (synthetic identity).

Identity theft can be both "true name" and "synthetic identity" theft. In true name theft, an actual person's identity—his or her name, address, Social Security number, or credit card number—is stolen. In synthetic identity theft, a fictitious person's name or Social Security number are used to commit the theft. It is reported that the number of synthetic identity thefts exceeds the number of true name thefts.

Because it is common to use stolen identity documents or numbers in computers, the mail system, or over telephone lines, many identity theft prosecutions are under federal laws. The principal federal statutes are 18 U.S.C. § 1028, identity theft; and 18 U.S.C. § 1028(A), aggravated identity theft. Section 1028 makes it a crime to "knowingly" possess, transfer, use, or produce a false identification document or authentication feature of a document, or use, possess, or transfer an identification document of another person. Section 1028(A) makes it an aggravated offense punishable by an additional two-year prison term to use or possess the identification document of another person as part of any of the crimes listed in § 1028(a).

Prosecutions under § 1028 include production of false identification documents, as well as theft of identification documents. The statute prohibits production of identification documents that appear to be issued by an agency of the United States. However, it is not necessary for the prosecution to prove a false document makes reference to an actual U.S. agency, like the FBI or the U.S. Marshall's Office. In *United States v. Fuller*, 531 F.3d 1020 (9th Cir. 2008), the court upheld the conviction of a defendant who produced an identification allegedly issued by the "United States Special Response Department Anti-Terrorism Unit." The court stated that the statute is violated when a false identification appeared to be issued by an agency of the United States, whether or not such an agency actually exists.

Prosecutions for theft of an identification document or number, at least under § 1028(A) for aggravated identity theft, require the prosecution to prove the defendant knew that the document or number used belonged to an actual person. In *United States v. Flores-Figueroa*, 129 S. Ct. 1886 (2009), discussed in Chapter 3, the U.S. Supreme Court held that a conviction for use of the identification document of another required proof the defendant knew the identity card belonged to another person. This may also be the case for a conviction under § 1028, which employs the same "knowingly" language, though the Court did not expressly consider the requirements under that statute.

The prosecution may prove the knowledge requirement under § 1028(A) by inference. In *United States v. Holmes*, 595 F.3d 1255 (11th Cir. 2010), the court held that the fact the defendant had previously successfully used another person's name to obtain a drivers license and passport was sufficient evidence for a jury to infer she knew the name belonged to an actual person. Nor does the name have to belong to a living person. In *United States v. Maciel-Alcla*, 2010 WL 2836992 (9th Cir. 2010), the court held that the prosecution need not prove that "another person" under § 1028(A) was living at the time the defendant used that person's identification documents. Finally, in *United States v. Blixt*, 548 F.3d 882 (9th Cir. 2008), the court held that a forged

IDENTITY THEFT

Identity theft has grown rapidly to the point where, according to the U.S. Federal Trade Commission, over 15 million people were victims of identity theft in 2009. These thefts cost the victims and businesses an estimated $50 billion.

To commit the crime a thief needs	Your name, date of birth, Social Security number, and an estimate of your annual income.
How would a thief obtain this information?	Steal (or find) a purse or wallet, steal your mail, or go through your trash looking for credit or bank card statements. Old or recent tax returns also have this information. It can be obtained from the databases of some businesses.
A thief can then	Open a new credit card account or bank account in your name. Use the credit card (or cards) to obtain goods. Write bad checks on your bank account. Open charge accounts with retail stores. Establish telephone or wireless service in your name. Use your identity and credit to obtain many items of value.
To avoid immediate detection, the thief can	Use a change-of-address form and divert your mail and the bills to another address.

To protect your family and yourself, take the following precautions: (1) keep an eye open for missing mail, as a change of address filed by a clever thief will send bills and credit card statements to another address, (2) reveal only such personal information as is necessary, and (3) check your credit file every year or two to make sure a thief is not borrowing money in your name.

In theft of identity, thieves seek to profit in the following ways:

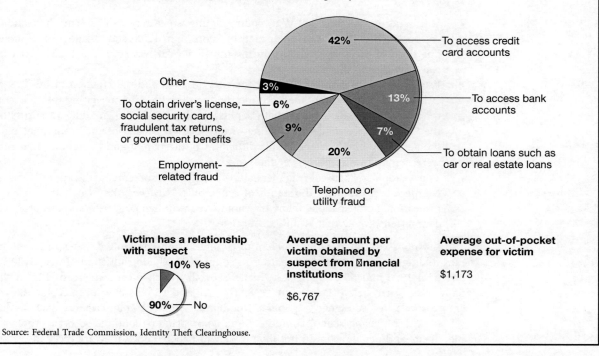

Source: Federal Trade Commission, Identity Theft Clearinghouse.

signature on a check was a "means of identification" of another person and was a violation of the aggravated identity theft statute.

Most states have identity theft statutes similar to the federal statutes, though often with broader definitions of the crime. The Wisconsin identity theft statute, Wis. Stat.

§ 943.201(2) (c), includes using another person's identification information to cause harm to that person's reputation. In *State v. Baron*, 769 N.W.2d 34 (Wis. 2009), the court held the statute applied to a defendant who gained access to his employer's e-mail account and learned the employer was having an extramarital affair. The defendant sent out an e-mail to several persons, purporting to come from the employer, which made the affair public. The next day, the employer committed suicide. The court rejected the defendant's argument that the statute violated his First Amendment rights.

In *State v. Hardesty*, 213 P.3d 745 (Kan. App. 2009), the Kansas Court of Appeals held that "another person" in the Kansas identity theft statute, KSA 21-4018, includes a deceased person. Perhaps in response to that decision and the U.S. Supreme Court's decision in *Flores-Figueroa*, the Kansas legislature amended the identity theft statute in 2010 to state expressly that (1) theft of a deceased person's identification is covered by the statute and (2) it is not a defense that the thief did not know the identification belonged to an actual person. However, it appears the decision in *State v. Vargas*, 24 P.3d 155 (Kan. App. 2001), that the statute requires proof that the identification information actually belonged to another person is still accurate.

☰ Counterfeiting of Money and Commercial Products

Counterfeiting of Currency

Counterfeiting of currency is a serious federal offense that could have a severe economic impact on society. The history of counterfeiting in the United States can be summarized as follows:

- Until and during the Civil War, counterfeiting was a serious problem; thousands of various legal bills were being printed by more than 1,500 state banks. An estimated one-third of the currency used during the Civil War was counterfeit. Counterfeiting was easy during that period.
- Establishment of a single national currency in 1863 and the creation of the U.S. Secret Service immediately made counterfeiting difficult. Counterfeiting the new currency required skilled people with sophisticated equipment. The diligent efforts of the Secret Service made the pooling of the necessary material and equipment plus the necessary highly trained skills difficult. Counterfeiting and alteration of currency were kept at a minimum over the years.
- Today, sophisticated color copiers allow what law enforcement officers call "casual counterfeiters" to print thousands of crude bills. However, the principal problem is professional craftspeople, many of whom live in foreign countries and are producing counterfeit money that is difficult to detect.

In response to the growing problem of counterfeiting, the United States began issuing new folding money that is much harder to counterfeit. The introduction of new $100 bills began in 1996 and $50 bills in 1997. The $20 bill, which most Americans use in their daily lives, began being replaced in 1998. The $10 and $5 bills have been replaced, and a "more modestly redesigned" $1 bill is to follow. Amateur counterfeiters such as high school students using school computers and color printers continue to be a problem to merchants and people who do not look closely at paper money they are receiving.[7]

Other Counterfeiting Problems

Counterfeited designer jeans, compact discs, recordings of movies, electronic components, computers, books, circuit relays, and drugs are sold extensively in the United

States. Many of the counterfeited products are manufactured in foreign countries, where they are also sold under the well-known label. Usually, the counterfeit product is a cheap or inferior copy of the real thing. However, the phony label deceives many dealers and consumers, who believe that they are buying the name-brand product.

Importation, manufacture, or sale of a counterfeit product in the United States could result in (1) prosecution under the criminal code of a state, which would probably treat the offense as a misdemeanor; (2) civil suit and sanctions in federal or state civil courts; or (3) federal prosecution under the mail fraud statute (18 U.S.C.A. § 1341), the wire fraud statute (18 U.S.C.A. § 1343), the Food, Drug and Cosmetic Act (21 U.S.C.A. §§ 301, 321, and so on), or other federal statutes.

Countries where most counterfeiting piracy occurs are China (which far exceeds all other countries), Russia, Italy, Mexico, and Brazil. See the *New York Times* article, "With Piracy Blooming in Mexico, U.S. Industry's Cries Get Louder" (April 20, 1996).

Counterfeiting of driver's licenses and other documents has become a serious problem in the United States. This crime might be committed by private individuals, both within and outside of the United States, but also by state employees, who have access to the necessary forms for counterfeiting official documents. In the late 1990s California discovered several employees of the Department of Motor Vehicles had sold counterfeit driver's licenses; it was feared the number of such counterfeits might reach 25,000.

≡ Computer or Cyber Crime

The rise of computer use and ownership has seen a corresponding rise in the use of computers in criminal activity. Computers as tools in crime make many aspects of criminal behavior easier and more efficient. Even an illegal drug gang must keep records of sales and purchases, and computers no doubt make that task easier. Computers can also be the object of criminal activity, where computer hardware of software is stolen. Finally, computers can be the subject of a crime, as where information on a computer file is stolen or damaged. The phrase **cyber crime** generally refers to the last two kinds of crimes involving computers, where computers are used to access, or are accessed through, the Internet.

cyber crime Criminal acts implemented through use of a computer or other form of electronic communication.

The earliest forms of Internet attacks on computers involved amateur hackers who invaded a computer just to prove they could. However, as use of the Internet exploded, computers began being used in a wide variety of crimes, including fraud, money laundering, extortion, software theft, corporate espionage, and child pornography (discussed in Chapter 12).

Most states have modified their criminal codes to account for the rise in computer use in criminal behavior. Many states have, for example, made it a crime to use computers for online harassment; see Texas Penal Code § 42.07 (a)(2) (Vernon 2003). Some states have passed specific statutes making it a crime to use a computer unlawfully to obtain money or property. For example, in *Damaio v. Com.*, 621 S.E.2d 696 (Va. App. 2005), *affirmed* 636 S.E.2d 456 (2006), a defendant was convicted under the Virginia computer theft statute, § 18.2-152.3. The defendant quit his job as human resources director and transferred over 829 employee files to a third-party server only he could access. He told his employer he would return the files only if a debt he owed the employer would be canceled. He was convicted of computer theft under the statute.

California has passed a law, California Penal Code § 502(c)(1), directed at unlawful access to a computer system for altering or using data on the system for the purpose of advancing a scheme to fraud or extort money or property.

WHITE-COLLAR CRIMES IN THE NEWS

For a variety of reasons, white-collar crimes are frequently reported in the national press. This may be because of the identity of the criminals or because of the nature of a fraudulent scheme. The following is a list of some of the crimes that received national attention.

- *Price Fixing*: Federal law, in the form of the Antitrust Act, prohibits price fixing. In 2006, South Korean suppliers of computer memory chips were found guilty of conspiring with others to fix prices on computer chips. Several individual defendants received fines and jail sentences; one company agreed to pay a fine of $160 million.[a]
- *Insider Trading*: It is a crime to use inside information acquired in one's position at a company or investment firm to profit from stock trades. In the *New York Times* article, "Insider Trading Case with a B-Movie Plot" (April 30, 2006), David Pajcin, a 29-year-old employee of an investment firm, used inside information on the sale of Reebok International to Adidas to make more than $6 million for himself and his family. He set up accounts in family member names, including his aunt, a seamstress in Croatia, and bought stock futures in Reebok before the sale became public. Investigators caught on when they discovered that 80 percent of the futures trades made in Reebok just prior to the announcement of the sale were by Pajcin. Pajcin cooperated with the government, and his guilty plea was sealed. Others involved received prison terms of up to four years.[b]
- *Industrial Espionage:* Stealing a company's ideas or trade secrets is a crime, and it can be done by competitors, foreign companies or governments, or trusted employees. In 2006 the Hewlett-Packard Company was experiencing leaks of corporate information. The CEO, in an effort to discover the source of the leaks, unlawfully monitored employees' personal telephones, e-mails, and Internet activities. When her actions were uncovered, she lost her position as CEO.[c]
- *Eavesdropping*: This old English crime takes its name from trespassing on another's property and listening to conversations under the eaves of a house. In 2007 seven Wall Street brokers were charged with eavesdropping when they secretly listened in on conversations of others on "squawk boxes" (intercoms) in their offices. After a seven-week trial, they were acquitted of the eavesdropping and other securities charges, but because the jury deadlocked on a conspiracy charge, the brokers will be retried.[d]
- *Mortgage Fraud*: Mortgage fraud is one of this country's fastest-growing fraud crimes. The FBI estimates it cost lenders over a billion dollars in 2005. Mortgage fraud often involves borrowers who greatly overstate the value of mortgaged property or their ability to repay loans. During the housing boom of 2001 to 2006, the rise of "no document" mortgage loans contributed to the problem. In these loans, the borrower was not required to produce documents to prove statements made on loan applications. These loans were often "sub-prime" loans, which in 2007 began to experience high default rates.
- *Movie and Television Show Piracy*: Wrongful sale of bootlegged copies of copyrighted movies and television shows violate the copyright and trade secrets laws. In the February 19, 2007, *New York Times* article, "Hollywood Gets Tough on Movie Copying in Canada," it was reported that 30 to 40 percent of the bootlegged DVDs sold in the United States were made in Canada.
- *Theft of Trade Secrets*: A secretary who worked for the Coca-Cola Company attempted to sell the secret recipe for Coke to the Pepsi-Cola Company for $1.5 million. Pepsi officials notified Coca-Cola, and the secretary was convicted of stealing trade secrets and sentenced to up to 10 years in prison.[e]
- *Check Kiting*: An NYU student was sentenced to over three years in prison for bank and wire fraud in 2006. In an elaborate check-kiting scheme, the student deposited millions of dollars in a New York bank using fake check and then transferred funds to a hedge fund he controlled and ultimately withdrew money from the fund. The student's mother was sentenced to two years in jail for her role in the scheme.[f]
- *Payola*: Under federal law, and in many states, it is a crime to pay broadcasters to play specific songs on the radio unless the payment is disclosed to listeners. These laws stemmed from the 1950s and 1960s,

when rock-and-roll radio DJs had enormous influence on the popularity of a given song or artist. In 2006, EMI Recording Company agreed to pay a fine of $3.75 million to settle payola charges brought against it and four other corporations.[g]

■ *Misbranding:* It is a federal crime to place false or misleading information on a drug, or in ads used to sell a drug, or to promote it for unapproved use. The corporate producer of the drug OxyContin in 2007 pleaded guilty to misbranding and paid fines totaling $600,000. Individual defendants pleaded guilty to misdemeanors and were also fined. The company failed to disclose to physicians prescribing the drug and users of OxyContin the addictive nature of the drug.

■ *Kickback Schemes:* It is a crime under every state's law for employees of a government unit like a state or city, or employees of a corporation, to accept kickbacks for making contracts with persons providing goods or services to the government unit or corporation. In an unusual case, New York authorities indicted the former mayor of Sao Paulo, Brazil, charging him with receiving kickbacks in excess of $11 million from a highway project in Brazil. The kickback money was transferred through a New York bank, giving New York jurisdiction over the crime. The New York attorney general stated that New York would not become the "Cayman Island" of the United States.[h]

■ *Bid Rigging:* This crime occurs when persons with power to award bids—frequently state, city, or federal employees—direct bids to persons or companies with whom they are in a fraudulent partnership. In 2007 Army Reserve officers were charged with receiving more than $1 million in cash and gifts as payment for giving bids on reconstruction work in Iraq.[i]

■ *Con Games:* One of the oldest forms of theft or fraud is the confidence game, so named because it requires gaining the confidence of the intended victim. One famous con game, the "Ponzi"[j] or pyramid scheme, operates by enticing participants to pay money to the scheme's organizers, with the promise of enormous payouts if they in turn sell the scheme to more participants. The Federal Trade Commission monitors businesses closely if their marketing resembles a pyramid scheme. In the last 10 years the FTC has shut down 17 national pyramid schemes and returned over $90 million to victims of these frauds. The FTC recently filed a complaint against a business in California that was selling rights to operate an online digital music store, a scheme that in fact paid off only if participants could entice others to buy such rights.[k]

■ In March of 2010 a group of computer experts was indicted under federal wire fraud and computer statutes for using computer programs to buy concert and sports event tickets and reselling them at a huge profit. The group, calling itself "Wiseguys Tickets Inc.," resold over 1.5 million tickets before being arrested and charged. The indictment states they acted fraudulently by using a computer program to circumvent rules limiting how many tickets a corporate entity could buy.[l]

[a]See the *New York Times* article, "4 to Plead Guilty to Chip Pricing," March 2, 2006.
[b]*Fortune Magazine*, October 2, 2006.
[c]See the *Chicago Tribune* article, "Boss, Infighter, Leakbuster, Spy," September 13, 2006.
[d]See the *New York Times* article, "Ex-Brokers Face Retrial in Eavesdropping Case," May 5, 2007.
[e]See the *Wall Street Journal* article, "Former Coke Secretary Sentenced in Trade-Secret Case," May 24, 2007.
[f]See the *New York Times* article, "Ex-N.Y.U. Student Pleads Guilty to Fraud in Hedge Fund Scheme," June 7, 2006.
[g]See the *New York Times* article, "EMI Agrees to Fine to Resolve Payola Case," June 16, 2006.
[h]See the *New York Times* article, "Brazilian Politician Indicted in New York in Kickback Scheme," March 9, 2007.
[i]See the *New York Times* article, "State Reservist Among Four Charged in Bid-Rigging Scheme," February 8, 2007.
[j]The pyramid scheme, or the Ponzi swindle, has a long history in the United States. Immigrants are particularly vulnerable to the swindle because crooks within their own group gain their confidence and cheat them. Carlo Ponzi engineered one of the first great frauds in the early 1920s in Boston. Ponzi took advantage of his fellow Italians, including family members and his parish priest. He then reached beyond Italian immigrants to defraud more than 20,000 people of more than $10 million before his scheme collapsed. Ponzi fled to Brazil, where he died a pauper. See the *New York Times* article, "Immigrants Swindle Their Own, Preying on Trust," August 25, 1992, telling of the problems of modern immigrants who are cheated by people within their own groups.
[k]See FTC Report, June 12, 2007.
[l]See March 3, 2010 article in the *Wall Street Journal,* "Four Charged in Bid to Buy, Resell Tickets."

computer trespass
Unlawful access to a computer or computer system with intent to commit a crime, or unlawful access to a computer or computer system maintained by a government unit.

Most states have a statute similar to § 9A.52.110 of the Washington Criminal Code, which prohibits computer trespass. **Computer trespass** is defined as unlawful access to a computer or computer system with intent to commit a crime or unlawful access to a computer or computer system maintained by a government unit. Most states also have a statute similar to the Maryland Code, Criminal Law, § 7–302, the "anti-hacking" statute. This law makes it a crime to enter a computer system without permission with intent to alter or damage the system or data stored in the system.

The federal government uses the Computer Fraud and Abuse Act, 18 U.S.C. § 1030 (CFAA), to target computer crime. Under this statute, a wide variety of cyber crimes are prohibited, from unlawful access to computers (the anti-hacking law) to unlawfully obtaining information from a financial institution, as the following cases illustrate.

In *United States v. Phillips* , 477 F.3d 215 (5th Cir. 2007), the court affirmed a conviction of a University of Texas student under the CFAA. The student was granted access to the UT computer system when he enrolled as a freshman. He then used a technique called "port scanning" to find other computers on the network that could easily be accessed. The student gained access to many computers this way, and he stole information. He also found a secure UT web server called "TXClass" and by using a "brute force" attack (a program that sends multiple possible passwords to enter a computer) was able to make multiple entries into the TXClass server. Once there, he collected data and information, such as Social Security numbers of students and faculty. The Secret Service investigated the intrusions into the UT system, which were damaging the system and making it crash repeatedly. The student was arrested and charged with a violation of the CFAA. He was convicted, sentenced to five years probation and 500 hours of community service, and ordered to pay $170,000 in restitution to UT.

The student appealed, contending the prosecution had not proven "unauthorized access" under § 1030. The court of appeals rejected his contention, stating that, under § 1030, unauthorized access included no authority to access a computer, hacking, and exceeding authorized use. While the student did have authority to access the UT computer system, the court held he clearly did not have authority to use a brute force attack to gain entry to a secure server, and the court affirmed his conviction.

In *United States v. John*, 597 F.3d 263 (5th Cir. 2010), the court considered another violation of the CFAA. In *John* an employee of Citigroup Company accessed computer accounts of customers of Citigroup. She then gave the information gained from that access to confederates, who made fraudulent charges against those accounts. She was arrested and charged with violating CFAA, convicted on several counts, and sentenced to 108 months in prison. On appeal she contended she could not be convicted of unauthorized access under § 1030, because in her position at Citigroup she was authorized to access the accounts and view the information in the accounts. As a result, she argued, her access was not "unauthorized." The court disagreed, and it affirmed her conviction. It stated that "unauthorized access" includes accessing a computer with the fraudulent intent to take information from the computer and use it in a scheme to defraud the computer account holders.

In addition, many of the existing federal crimes, such as mail and wire fraud and the National Stolen Property Act, have been held to apply to crimes involving computers or their use. An example of use of the mail fraud statute is *United States v. Susel*, 429 F.3d 782 (8th Cir. 2005). There, an employee of a software manufacturer stole some copyrighted software programs and sold them on eBay. He then mailed the software on discs to the buyers. He was convicted of violating the mail fraud act.

☰ The Crime of Trafficking in Stolen Goods

The crimes of trafficking in stolen goods are defined by the statutes of each state and ordinarily include (1) receiving (a single act), (2) concealing and possessing (continuing acts) and, in some states, (3) buying and transferring. In determining the statute of limitations for these offenses, the Supreme Court of Minnesota held in the 1981 case of *State v. Lawrence*, 312 N.W.2d 251:

> The crime commonly known as "receiving stolen property," when used in a short-hand sense, is a misnomer, since it includes a number of different legal concepts in addition to and separate from receiving. The offense includes not only receiving, but concealing; … it includes buying; and … it also includes possessing and transferring.
>
> The issue here is whether any of these terms may be deemed continuing in nature. The two most likely descriptions of defendant's conduct are possession and concealment. Does either, or both, apply? In answering this question we should keep in mind that a crime is not continuing in nature if not clearly so indicated by the legislature….
>
> Both possessing and concealing are distinguishable from receiving in that the latter connotes a single act. Behind possessing and concealing, however, is the notion that property is being kept from someone in violation of a duty to return and this duty to return continues. One of the reasons for including possessing and concealing as crimes is to be able to prosecute even though the time has run out on receiving. Surely this serves the purpose of the statute, which is to deter trafficking in stolen goods.
>
> * * *
>
> We hold, therefore, that either concealing or possessing stolen goods is a continuing offense for the purpose of the statute of limitations. We hold this defendant may not assert the statute of limitations as a bar where he kept the goods he stole in his house and garage, thereby not only possessing the goods but making their discovery more difficult for the owner.

To convict of trafficking in stolen goods, the state is ordinarily required to prove

- That the property involved was stolen property.
- That the defendant received, concealed, possessed, purchased, or transferred the property as forbidden by the statutes of that state.
- That the defendant knew the property was stolen. "Stolen" means that the property was obtained as a result of a theft, burglary, robbery, or any other form of theft crime, such as shoplifting or obtaining property by deception.

The Fence and Fencing Stolen Property

fence A person who traffics in stolen property (receiving, concealing, possessing, buying, transferring, and so on).

A **fence** is a person who traffics in stolen property (receiving, concealing, possessing, buying, transferring, and so on).[8] A fence acts as a middleperson and pays the thief for stolen property, which the fence in turn attempts to merchandise at a profit. The compensation paid by the fence to the thief is usually a small fraction of the value of the goods. The report of the President's Commission on Law Enforcement and Administration of Justice makes the following observations regarding fencing in the United States:

> Nearly all professional theft is undertaken with the aim of selling the goods thereafter. Although the thief himself may retail his stolen merchandise, he probably will

prefer to sell to a fence. He thereby increases his safety by reducing the risk that he will be arrested with the goods in his possession, or that they will be stolen in turn from him. He also avoids the dangers associated with the disposal process itself. In addition, large quantities of goods which may be perishable or otherwise quickly lose their value, or for which there is a specialized demand, will require a division of labor and level of organization beyond the capacity of an individual thief operating as his own retailer. The professional thief thus needs a "middleman" in the same way and for some of the same reasons as the farmer, manufacturer, or other producer.

* * *

Some fences engage in fencing as a supplement to their legitimate businesses, often on a more or less regular basis. The consultants learned of clothing and appliance dealers who regularly serve as outlets for stolen goods. The major outlets for stolen jewels in one of the cities studied were reported to be legitimate jewelry merchants. Other fences deal primarily or wholly in stolen goods and are therefore professional criminals themselves.

Some narcotics pushers act as fences, taking stolen goods instead of cash for narcotics. While dealing with addicts is generally regarded as more dangerous than dealing with nonaddicts, it is also more profitable. The addict in need of a "fix" does not bargain well.

When Property Loses Its Character as Stolen Goods

United States v. Monasterski
United States Court of Appeals, Sixth Circuit (1977) 567 F.2d 677, 22 CrL 2357

Three juveniles were caught attempting to steal tires from a railroad boxcar. The juveniles cooperated with FBI agents and delivered some of the tires to the defendant, whom they identified as their prospective fence. The defendant was convicted of receiving stolen property (the tires). In reversing the defendant's conviction, the Sixth Circuit Court held that once the thieves were caught, the tires lost their character as stolen goods and could no longer support the defendant's conviction. The court further held:

> In accord with the common law rule, one cannot be convicted of receiving stolen goods when actual physical possession of the stolen goods has been recovered by their owner or his agent before delivery to the intended receiver. We further hold, also in accord with the common law rule, that the term "agent" means any person with a right to possession or control over the goods.

The Alabama Supreme Court followed the common law rule that goods that had never been stolen or goods that had lost their stolen character could not support a conviction of the crime of receiving stolen property.[9]

Florida, however, changed the common law and enacted a law taking away this defense from a person charged with the crime of dealing in stolen property. Florida Statute (1995), § 812.028(3), permits criminal convictions in Florida for endeavoring to traffick in stolen property without proof by the state of Florida that the property was actually stolen.[10]

Possession of Criminal or Burglary Tools

All states probably have statutes making the possession of criminal or burglary tools a criminal offense.[11] The usual elements of this crime are as follows:

- The defendant had a device or implement in his or her possession.
- This device or implement was suitable or was capable of being used in committing burglary.[12]
- The defendant intended to use this device or implement to break into a building, dwelling, or depository with the intent to steal.

Like the crime of receiving stolen property, possession of burglary tools is also difficult to prove. The difficult element to prove in receiving stolen property is knowledge by the defendant that the property was stolen. In possession of burglary tools, the difficult element is intent by the defendant to use the tool for purposes of burglary. Possession of ordinary work tools is not ordinarily sufficient to justify a conviction for possession of burglary tools; there must be additional evidence of intent to use them to commit burglary.

Cases in which most convictions have been obtained can be divided into the following categories:

- The defendant was apprehended while committing or attempting to commit a burglary with the tool or had the tool in his or her actual or constructive possession.
- The defendant was in the possession of a specifically designed or adapted tool under circumstances in which a judge or jury could infer the tool's use for an illegal purpose of entry.

≡ Destroying or Damaging the Property of Another

No U.S. city, town, or village escapes the physical and psychological disfigurement vandalism brings to public and private property. Vandalism is a serious problem in most public transport systems, and it costs millions of dollars in large cities. Schools are often hit hard, with broken windows, break-ins, damaged property, and spray-painted walls.

Veteran law enforcement officers observe that vandalism (criminal damage to property) occurs in cycles. In the summertime, public parks are hit. Benches are piled up, debris is thrown into lagoons, and beaches are littered. If buildings are left vacant, they sometimes are vandalized to the point where they must be razed. Criminal damage to private property varies considerably and is a constant source of citizen complaints to law enforcement agencies.

Many states and cities have passed laws making parents of minors responsible for damage their child causes. Kansas imposes liability on the homeowner's insurance company, which gives the owner of damaged property the right to collect damages from the insurance company.[13]

In 1990, one 18-year-old did more than $500,000 damage by graffiti vandalism in Los Angeles. The Los Angeles city attorney said that it was "the worst case of graffiti vandalism we have seen in Los Angeles ... or anywhere else in the nation [by a single individual]." Near Tampa, Florida, three teenagers pulled down more than a dozen traffic stop signs for kicks one night. Other teenagers driving home after bowling were killed when their car drove into an intersection and was hit broadside, killing the occupants. The teenagers who took down the stop sign were convicted of three counts of manslaughter.[14]

☰ Arson

One of the first concerns of a fire investigator is the fire's origin. Fires can be classified by their causes as accidental fires, natural fires (caused without human intervention), **arson** (fires of incendiary origin), and fires of unknown origin.

Many fires are started accidentally, when children play with matches or people are careless with cigarettes, cigars, or pipe ashes. Some fires are of natural origin and occur without human intervention because of spontaneous combustion, defective heating units, faulty electrical appliances or wiring, and the like.

Arson is a person's deliberate, willful, and malicious burning of a building or personal property. Arson is the easiest of the major crimes to commit, the most difficult to detect, and the hardest to prove in court.

In most states, arson has several degrees or grades of commission, with gradations depending on whether the property destroyed is a residence or other kind of structure. An example of a common form of arson statute is Idaho Code § 18-802-805. First-degree arson under § 802 includes unlawfully and willfully damaging by fire or explosives a dwelling or a structure where people are commonly present or any structure in which the arsonist has reasonable grounds to believe a person might be present. Second-degree arson under § 803 is damaging any structure not covered in § 802. Third-degree arson under § 804 is damage to any other real or personal property. Finally, Idaho, like most states, has an "aggravated arson" statute, § 18-805, under which the penalty for arson is greatly increased if a person, including a firefighter, is killed or suffers serious bodily injury as a result of the fire.

The United States has an arson statute, 18 U.S.C. § 844(f), that applies to any malicious damage by fire or explosives to any property owned by or leased to the United States, an agency of the United States, or any organization receiving financial assistance from the United States. In *United States v. Hersom*, 588 F.3d 60 (1st Cir. 2009), the court held that the federal arson statute applied to arson of four buildings owned by a private company but which were undergoing renovations with financial assistance provided by block grants from HUD.

Essential Elements of Arson

All states have enacted statutes that define arson. In general, most statutes require that the state prove the following elements:

- That there was a fire and that some part of the building or personal property was damaged. Some courts require an actual burning of part of the property. In the 1992 case of *State v. Williams*, 600 N.E.2d 962, the Indiana Court of Appeals held that soot and smoke constituted "damage" within the meaning of the Indiana arson statute. Attempted arson or conspiracy to commit arson may also be possible criminal charges.[15]

- That the fire was of incendiary origin and was willfully and intentionally set. This is the required proof of corpus delicti (that a crime was in fact committed). For a fire inspector to testify in court that he or she "suspected" arson or that the fire was of "unknown origin" is insufficient to prove corpus delicti.[16] An expert witness is usually required to testify that arson did occur and support the statement with specific evidence.

- That the accused committed or was party to the crime of arson charged. Like all other crimes, the evidence required to convict a person of arson is proof beyond a reasonable doubt.

≡ Product Tampering

Since 1982, product tampering has cost the lives of at least 12 people in the United States. The offense of poisoning over-the-counter drugs and food products was described by a high-ranking federal official as "an insidious and terrible crime. It is a form of terrorism not unlike planting a bomb in some public place to gain media attention, notoriety, or some sick sense of control over human life."

During a one-year period in 1986, the federal Food and Drug Administration (FDA) was involved in nearly 1,700 cases of actual tampering or hoaxes. The FBI investigated more than 300 of these incidents. Although it is rare that a product is actually contaminated or poisoned, crimes related to product tampering include the following:

- *Extortion:* After seven people died in the Chicago area in 1982 from cyanide-laced Extra-Strength Tylenol, James Lewis tried to use the killings in attempting to extort $1 million from the manufacturer of Tylenol. Lewis was convicted in a federal court in 1983.
- *Threats to Tamper and/or Threats to Allege Tampering:* Another form of extortion attempts to obtain money from manufacturers, who incur huge costs and loss of market and sales in tampering cases.
- *Attempts to Create the Basis of a Civil Lawsuit:* A person fakes a tampering case to make it appear that a person in a family has been the victim of random tampering.
- *Covering Up a Murder by Attempting to Make It Appear That the Victim Was Killed by Random Tampering:* A Seattle woman was convicted in 1988 under the 1984 Federal Consumer Tampering Act. She laced Excedrin capsules with cyanide to kill her husband and collect $176,000 in life insurance. Then she planted other cyanide-laced Excedrin capsules in stores to make it appear that her husband was the victim of a random killer. Unfortunately, an innocent victim also died from the poison. The Seattle woman was convicted of two counts of homicide under the Consumer Tampering Act and three other counts of placing cyanide in three other Excedrin bottles.

The Federal Consumer Tampering Act, 18 U.S.C.A. § 1365, also forbids tampering that reduces the efficacy of a drug designed to save a life or alleviate bodily injury, as well as tampering that turns a drug into a poison. In *United States v. Cunningham,* 103 F.3d 553 (7th Cir. 1997), a nurse was convicted of tampering when she used the painkiller Demerol belonging to a hospital allegedly to feed her addiction and substituted a harmless liquid without informing anyone.

The crime of consumer product tampering receives a great deal of attention and concern because all societies are vulnerable to such acts. Millions of dollars have been invested in tamper-proof packaging. Most consumers are well aware of the remote possibility that the product they purchase may have been tampered with in a way that could seriously hurt them or someone in their family.

Federal statutes and the laws of most (if not all) states also make the following conduct criminal:

- Tampering (altering) or destroying evidence of a crime
- Tampering (altering) a financial document such as a check or another document such as a will or a mortgage
- Tampering (altering) an odometer of a motor vehicle that is to be sold to another person
- Tampering with a witness or potential witness by telling the witness what to say or what not to say

Summary

- White-collar crime refers to criminal offenses that have only economic gain as the criminal goal.
- Fraud is in essence a crime of deceit, and therefore it must be shown that the defendant's actions were intended to be deceitful. One cannot normally be negligently deceitful.
- A "scheme or artifice" in federal criminal statutes is an intentional act that has as a goal fraudulent and unlawful gain, and includes a material falsehood one would understand to be important and would be relied on by others. It specifically includes depriving another of the intangible right to honest services.
- Bribery under the federal statute is similar to extortion because it is not necessary in an extortion prosecution to prove an official threatened to use his official authority if the extortion amount was not paid. Thus, the receipt of unlawful payment to the official may prove extortion and also could prove bribery.
- The principal laws protecting intellectual property are the federal copyright, patent, and trademark laws, as well as state trade secret laws.
- The federal bank fraud act and the wire fraud act are frequently used to convict white-collar criminals.
- A communication under the wire fraud act must cross state lines. This is necessary to give Congress jurisdiction over the crime under the Commerce Clause. By definition, use of the U.S. mails involves interstate commerce.
- Insider trading includes using information acquired by an insider and not available to the public to profit in a sale of securities. It also includes use of such information by a person not an insider, if the person acquired the information knowing it came from an insider and was not available to the public.
- A conviction under the federal identity theft statute requires proof that a person produced a false identification document or possessed or used an identification document that belonged to another person. The federal statute requires that the defendant know the identification document belongs to another person, though some state statutes do not have this requirement.

Key Terms

Case Analysis and Writing Exercises

1. Some states distinguish between illegal pyramid schemes and illegal lotteries, making the penalties higher for lottery convictions than for pyramid convictions. Can a participant in a pyramid scheme, a misdemeanor, be charged under the felony lottery statute? If so, when? When would the state be prevented from charging the higher crime? See *State v. Croy*, 813 So. 2d 993 (Fla. App. 2002).

2. A technician working in a Maine veterinary research lab wanted to move to another job. She contacted a Wyoming veterinarian, who was CEO of a Wyoming company that in some areas competed with the Maine research company. In the course of several months of e-mail and letter communications between the two, the Maine technician supplied confidential information to the Wyoming vet. What crimes, if any, can these people be convicted of? What must the prosecution prove? See *United States v. Martin*, 228 F.3d 1 (1st Cir. 2000).

3. The police arrested a thief in possession of three stolen car radios. The police returned the radios to the car dealer that owned them. The thief informed the police he was planning on selling the radios to the defendant. The police returned to the car dealer, picked up the three radios, and eleven more, and gave them to the thief with instructions

to sell them to the defendant. He did, and the defendant was arrested and charged with possession of stolen property. Can he be convicted of that crime? Would it have been better if the police sent only the three radios stolen earlier? Why or why not? See *Ex Parte Walls*, 711 So. 2d 490 (Ala. 1997).

4. The defendant, an illegal alien, was charged with various crimes, including "knowingly transferring" a document that contains another person's identification. The defendant had purchased what he knew to be fake alien identification and Social Security cards, but argued he did not know the cards actually contained numbers given to other people. He therefore argued he could not be convicted under the identity theft statute. Is he right? See *United States v. Montejo*, 442 F.3d 213 (4th Cir. 2006, *cert. denied* 127 S. Ct. 366 (2006)). The court held, *inter alia*, that the doctrine of "lenity" did not apply. What is that doctrine, and when does it apply?

Notes

1. U.S. Department of Justice, 1989, p. 3.
2. U.S. Department of Justice, October 28, 2002.
3. See *Health Care Fraud*, 44 Am. Crim. L. Rev. 633, 635 (2007).
4. Investigating fraud in Medicaid and Medicare programs is discussed in two *FBI Law Enforcement Bulletins*: "Medicaid Fraud Control" (October 1992) and "Health Care Fraud" (October 1992).

   See the *New York Times* editorial, "Fraud and Waste in Medicare," August 1, 1997, and other news articles reporting that federal auditors estimate $23 billion in fraud and mistake loss in Medicare payments in 1996. These losses fell into the following categories: (1) "raw fraud," which for the most part was services not provided; (2) a gray area requiring the exercise of judgment; and (3) the anti-kickback provision forbidding payment for referrals.
5. See the *New York Times* article, "Agents Uncover Rampant Food Stamp Fraud," September 11, 1994, which estimates that in a $24 billion program, $2 billion is used for fraudulent purposes.
6. See *United States v. Stewart*, 433 F.3d 273 (2d Cir. 2006).
7. See the *New York Times* article, "Teens Accused of Using Computers to Counterfeit," February 17, 1997.
8. Many states and cities require pawnbrokers to register and comply with requirements seeking to prevent pawnbrokers from dealing in stolen goods. Following is the Indiana Loan Broker Act (see 602 N.E.2d at 1066):

   IC 23–2–5–4 (1988) requires that "[a]ny person desiring to engage or continue in business of loan brokering shall apply to the commissioner for registration under this chapter," while IC 23–2–5–16 (1988) provides, "[a] person who knowingly violates this chapter commits a Class D felony." Thus, a violation of the Act consists of "(1) knowingly, (2) engaging or continuing in the business of loan brokering, (3) without having registered with the securities commissioner."
9. See *Ex Parte Walls*, 711 So. 2d 490, 1997.
10. See *Capaldo v. State*, 679 So. 2d 717 (1996).
11. The British refer to this offense as "going equipped for stealing." See J. W. Williams's *Moriarty's Police Law*, 21st ed. (London: Butterworths, 1972).
12. See 33 A.L.R.3d 798 (1970).
13. See *Catholic Diocese of Dodge City v. Farmers Insurance Co.*, 825 P.2d 1144 (Kan. App. 1992), in which the property damage was more than $18,000.
14. See the *Milwaukee Journal Sentinel* article, "Three Friends Get 15 Years for Fatal Stop-Sign Prank," June 21, 1997.
15. If the completed crime of arson cannot be proved beyond a reasonable doubt, the state may then consider charging attempt to commit arson (or in an appropriate situation, conspiracy to commit arson).
16. See *Hughes v. State*, 6 Md. App. 389, 251 A.2d 373 (1969), in which the court pointed out that mere presence of the accused at the scene of a fire is not proof beyond reasonable doubt that the fire was willfully and maliciously set. In *Hughes v. State*, a fire chief testified that he could not determine the cause of the fire. The court reversed the defendant's conviction, holding that the evidence was legally insufficient to establish the corpus delicti of the crime of arson.

CHAPTER 16

Drug Abuse and Alcohol-Related Crimes

Mike Grandmaison/All Canada Photos/Alamy

A vast marijuana field in Manitoba, Canada. Much of the illegal marijuana sold in the United States is imported from foreign countries, though because of the Mexican crackdown on drug cartels, illegal marijuana is being grown on public lands in the United States.

OUTLINE

Controlled Substances Used in Religious Ceremonies

Drug Rip-Off Cases and Simulated Drugs

Criminal Liability for Drug-Induced Deaths

Possession or Sale of Drug Paraphernalia

Alcohol-Related Crimes

Alcohol's Relation to Crimes and Deaths

Alcohol and Drug Problems of Prison Inmates

Drunk Driving: The Criminal Homicide Causing the Most Deaths

Elements and Defenses in Drunk-Driving Prosecutions

"Booze It and Lose It" Laws

When Is a Person Driving, Operating, or "in Physical Control" of a Vehicle?

LEARNING OBJECTIVES

In this chapter we discuss crimes related to drugs, drug abuse, and alcohol abuse. The learning objectives for Chapter 16 are:

- List the ways a person can violate the Uniform Controlled Substances Act.
- Identify the elements of the crime of possession of an illegal drug with intent to deliver.
- State the current status of state medical-use-of-marijuana statutes.

- Explain the rationale of the Supreme Court's holding in *Gonzales v. Raich*.
- Identify the elements that must be proved for a conviction under a state drug-induced death statute.
- Learn the statistics for alcohol-related deaths among college students.
- Learn the statistics for alcohol-related motor vehicle deaths.
- Identify what must be shown to prove a person was operating a motor vehicle.

Luis F. Alarid served as a U.S. Marine in Iraq, and on return he joined the U.S. Customs and Border Protection agency as a customs inspector, stationed at the Mexican border. In December 2009 he was convicted of federal crimes based on his involvement with a Mexican drug cartel, in which many of his family were members. Alarid was paid over $200,000 in exchange for permitting several truck loads of marijuana to cross the border at his checkpoint.

Border agency officials are concerned that the Mexican drug cartels, facing increasing pressure within Mexico from federal police officers and stiffer border protection efforts by the United States, are attempting to corrupt border agents like Alarid. The amount of money available to the cartels to tempt U.S. agents is staggering, agency officials state.

In this chapter we will study the many ways the criminal laws are used to combat the illegal drug problem in the United States. We will also study the relationship of the abuse of alcohol to criminal behavior and government's attempts to control that behavior.

☰ Drug Abuse

The Frightening Drug Problem

The possession, sale, and use of illegal drugs are a problem of epic proportion in the United States. Illegal drugs have shattered many lives, led to suicides and murders, and caused serious health problems in many people. Sections of many American cities where illegal drugs are readily available have become seriously disrupted; where drugs are available other crimes follow.

Drug lords all over the world have become rich and powerful. Gangs and organized criminals in the United States find selling drugs to be an easy way to make money and gain power, which in turn leads to even greater lawlessness. For example, where criminals have huge amounts of cash available, the crime of bribery becomes more common. On October 25, 2006, the *Los Angeles Times* reported that bribery of federal and local officials along the 2,000-mile border between Mexico and the United States was "rising sharply."

Illegal smuggling goes both ways on the United States-Mexico border. Going North is the largest, constant flow of illegal drugs in the world. In addition, illegal immigrants seeking work in the United States are also a steady flow across the border, along with smuggled counterfeit goods, money, medical drugs, and electronic products.

Going South are smuggled American dollars to purchase illegal drugs. The Drug Enforcement Agency (DEA) estimates that $18 billion to $39 billion crosses the border each year. In 2008 alone the DEA seized $138 million of illegally smuggled money. (New York Times, 12/26/09 "Torrent of Illegal Cash Flows Where the U.S. and Mexico Meet"). More than 16,000 vehicles cross the border each day in Laredo, Texas alone, making policing the border almost impossible.

Also going South are smuggled firearms. Mexican drug gangs are a fertile market for sales of illegal weapons. There reportedly are about 6,600 American gun dealers along the Mexican border, and these dealers sell high-powered pistols and military rifles to the drug gangs. In 2008 over 20,000 illegal guns were seized by border patrol officers. (New York Times, 2/26/09, "U.S. Is a Vast Arms Bazaar for Mexican Drug Cartels: Easy Flow of Weapons to Mexican Drug Gangs".) In 2008 more than 8,000 Mexicans died in gang warfare; in one drug raid by Mexican police in 2008 eight officers were killed because the police were unprepared for the fire power the drug gangs possessed.

The year 2006 marked renewed efforts in the "war on drugs." In the United States, billions of dollars were allocated to increasing border security and hiring more border and customs agents. In Mexico, President Felipe Caldron launched a "federal assault" on drug cartels, using federal police to attack drug cartels in areas of Mexico where they operated.

The results on illegal drug smuggling and production since 2006 are mixed. While marijuana is harder to smuggle across the border with Mexico, the increase in production in the United States is dramatic. The Drug Enforcement Agency (DEA) reports that Mexican drug cartels are now sending members to the parks and forests of the United States to plant and harvest the drug. The DEA also reports that 80 percent of the marijuana grown in the United States is grown on state or federal land.

The production and import of methamphetamine has also increased over 2006 levels, according to the Justice Department's National Drug Intelligence Center. In the 2010 Methamphetamine Threat Assessment released by the Center, the supply of methamphetamine is the highest since 2005, the quality is the best, and the price is the lowest. Domestic manufacture in small "one pot" operations is also at a high level. In 2009 drug enforcement agencies seized 5,308 of these small operations, up from 3,096 in 2007. As an additional problem, Mexican drug cartels are frequently producing methamphetamine using nonephedrine-based methods. Both the United States and Mexico have passed laws making it harder to obtain ephedrine and pseudoephedrine, the base chemicals used in the preferred manufacturer of methamphetamine. This method produces drugs with the highest potency. Mexican drug cartels are now producing the drug by the "P2P" method, which produces drugs with lower potency, and then using other chemicals, such as tartaric acid, to increase the potency.

National or international figures on methamphetamine production are not known. However, based on the number of lab seizures made by Mexican and United States authorities in 2009, and the quantity of the drug seized by border officials, 5,187 kilograms in 2009, the Threat Assessment concludes that traffic in and use of methamphetamine will increase in 2010.

The "war on drugs" has had tragic consequences for Mexican border towns. Since the crackdown efforts commenced in late 2006, more than 25,000 people have been killed by drug cartel gunmen, or in gunfights between federal police and drug cartels. One border city, Ciudad Juarez, which shares a border with El Paso, Texas, has been especially hard hit by the killings. On July 17, 2010, the Mexican drug gang La Linea exploded a car bomb in a trap set for federal police, killing three officers. In the weeks preceding the car bomb attack, 14 police officers were killed by drug gunmen. In Juarez alone, 4,000 people have been killed since 2006 in drug cartel–related killings.

Heroin production and use has increased since 2005. Opium, a product derived from certain kinds of poppy plants, was produced in amounts significantly greater than previous years starting in 2006: Afghanistan, which produces about 90 percent of the world's opium, produced about 6,100 metric tons of opium in 2006, a 49 percent increase over the previous year. The 2007 crop was about 8,300 metric tons. The volume dropped in 2008, when opium having a value of about $3.4 billion was exported from Afghanistan. In 2009 exported opium dropped again, when $2.8 billion was exported. Based on crops planted in 2010, the United Nations believes opium production will drop again in 2010, which would mean a 1/3 drop since the highs of 2007.[1] Of the opium grown in Afghanistan, 80 percent comes from villages controlled by Taliban force, according to the United Nations. The proceeds from the sale of the illegal opium is believed to be a source of money to fund the insurgents and terrorists fighting the UN forces seeking to establish a stable, democratic government in Afghanistan.

With virtually unlimited sources, illegal drugs have become readily available to anyone seeking them. Not only are the drugs available, they are cheaper and of a better

"METH: A CHEMICAL TIME BOMB AND THE MOST HIGHLY ABUSED DRUG IN THE WORLD"

In 2006 the United Nations reported that methamphetamine ("meth") was the most highly abused hard drug in the world, with almost as many addicts as cocaine and heroin combined. Huge quantities of Meth are smuggled into the United States each year by gangs and organized criminals. Increasingly, meth is also being produced in the United States by small "one-pot" or "shake and bake" operations.

Meth "labs" have always presented risks for both producers and law enforcement officers. An article in the April, 2000 FBI Law Enforcement Bulletin stated that raiding a meth (also known as crack, ice, or poor man's cocaine) lab "…has become one of the most dangerous operations a law enforcement officer can undertake." The labs also present a danger to third parties who encounter waste or trash from the site of a meth lab.

A meth lab contains highly volatile chemicals used in the manufacture of the drug. These can include battery acid, drain cleaner, Coleman fuel, kerosene, lacquer thinner, mineral spirits, Heet, denatured alcohol, and Epson salts. A 2007 article in the FBI Law Enforcement Bulletin described the risks of fire and explosions in the use of the toxic mixtures of these volatile chemicals.

The key ingredient in meth operations is pseudoephedrine, which can be found in over-the-counter drugs such as Sudafed and Contac. In 2005 Congress passed the Combat Methamphetamine Epidemic Act, 21 U.S.C. § 830, which requires retail sellers of ephedrine or pseudoephedrine products to keep them "behind the counter", to demand identification from purchasers, and report sales figures to the government. Most states have similar laws regulating sales of products that contain pseudoephedrine. Two states, Oregon and Mississippi, require a prescription for the purchase of such products. In a letter to the New York Times, published 4/23/10, Ron Wyden, a U.S. Senator from Oregon, stated the results of requiring a prescription appear to be good. Prior to the law, police in Oregon raided over 500 meth labs per year. In 2009, after the law was passed, they raided only 10 labs.

Despite the intense efforts by state and federal legislatures and law enforcement agencies, home-based meth labs continue to flourish. The demand for meth is huge, the production easy, and the profits are immense. Recently, new methods of producing meth have surfaced. In a 4/15/10 article in the New York Times titled "With Cars as Meth Labs, Evidence Litters Roads" law enforcement officers report that the "mobile method has grown in popularity because it is easier, cheaper, and harder to get caught than making (meth) indoors….most of the cooks are addicts themselves, not dealers or distributors." It is reported that for every pound of meth produced in these small labs, 5 or 6 pounds of toxic, flammable, corrosive waste is generated, and left as litter on back roads and highways.

quality, making them attractive to the poor and the young. The Partnership for a Drug-Free America points out that

- Americans spend billions of dollars yearly for the purchase of illegal drugs.
- Many organized criminal groups, gangs, and terrorists depend on drug money. Police surveys show that there are now more than 30,000 gangs in the United States, with more than 800,000 members. (See Chapter 18.)
- Each year, more than 25 million Americans use illegal drugs.

Illegal Drug Users

The war against illegal drugs is being fought on the supply side and on the demand side. Cocaine, heroin, crack, and marijuana are produced and grown for the most part outside the United States. Great efforts are being made to prevent illegal drugs from entering the United

States. However, efforts to win the supply-side war have been going on since the 1950s with what is estimated as 90 percent of the illegal drugs getting into the United States.

The demand-side problem is that millions of Americans are willing to pay billions of dollars yearly for illegal drugs. More money is spent annually in the United States on illegal drugs and legal alcohol than is spent for clothing.[2] The United States is the biggest market in the world for illegal drugs and the profits are huge, therefore criminals take great risks to bring the illegal drugs into the country. The users of illegal drugs can be classified as follows:

- *The "Situational" Drug Abuser:* A person who uses illegal drugs for a specific or "situational" purpose, such as to accomplish some other objective. A person who is under a great deal of stress or tension might use a drug such as marijuana to relax. A performer or a truck driver might use a stimulant, or an upper, to stay awake.
- *The "Party" or the "Weekend" User:* A drug abuser who might use drugs for kicks or just for the experience. These users and the "casual user" are great sources of profits for drug pushers.
- *The Drug Addict:* A person who is physically and/or psychologically dependent on drugs. He or she cannot perform daily without drug support. Addicts have a "monkey on their back," which could be very expensive to support. To raise the money for the daily supply of drugs ($50, $100, or even $150 per day), addicts steal, break into cars, commit burglaries, rob, snatch purses, or push drugs. Women or men who trade sex for drugs are among those most susceptible to disease, including AIDS.

Today, common forms of drug abuse include so-called street drugs, such as marijuana, cocaine or crack, methamphetamine, heroin, and other drugs; prescription drugs, whether obtained legally through a prescription, or by theft of the drugs or a prescription to obtain the drugs; and over-the-counter substances, such as cold medicines or inhalants that produce a "high." Combining any of these drugs with each other, or with alcohol, creates the risk of stroke, seizure, coma, or even death. Accidental drug overdoses doubled in the period from 1999 to 2004 and in 2007 became the nation's second leading cause of accidental deaths, behind only automobile accidents. Drug overdoses now number about 20,000 per year in the United States.

Abuse of prescription drugs, mainly pain killers, has also risen markedly over the past few years. A July 15, 2010, report by the Substance Abuse and Mental Health Services Administration concluded that prescription pain killer abuse increased by 400 percent in the last 10 years. The percentage of hospital admissions for substance abuse of pain killer medications increased from 2.8 percent in 1998 to 9.8 percent in 2008. Admissions for cocaine and alcohol abuse during the same period went down, the report stated.

In a June 3, 2010, report the Center for Disease Control stated that in 2009 it conducted its National Youth Risk Behavior Survey, and for the first time it obtained data on high school students' use of prescription drugs without a prescription. It found that one in five high school students have used prescription drugs like OxyContin, Percocet, Vicodin, or Adderall. Adderall is a prescription psycho-stimulant that is commonly prescribed for person with Attention Deficit Hyperactivity Disorder. It has become popular on college campuses as a stimulant used during testing and "cramming" periods. While college students generally regard the drug as harmless, it is a Schedule II drug under the Controlled Substances Act, which means that while it has accepted medical usages it carries a high potential for addiction.

≡ Drug Laws in the United States

The first law enacted in the United States was an anti–opium smoking ordinance passed in San Francisco in 1875 because of the opium problem there.[3] This was one of the few restrictions in the United States at that time.

In the 1880s and 1890s, people in the United States could concoct and sell to the American public practically any drug or drug compound they wished. Drugs were available in stores, through mail-order catalogs, and from traveling vendors and peddlers. Little was known at that time about the effects of drugs on human beings. Drug promoters claimed the drugs cured sickness and other human problems.

A German firm, for example, marketed a newly discovered drug in the 1890s as a cough suppressant. The name the firm gave the drug is well known today—heroin.

Heroin did a wonderful job of suppressing coughs, but years passed before people realized the terrible problems of addiction to heroin. Other drugs and compounds that often contained either cocaine or heroin were advertised and promoted as cures for everything from ingrown toenails to cancer. Medications were sold that guaranteed sex rejuvenation, new hair for bald people, breast enlargement, a cure for arthritis, and more.

Cocaine was used in Coca-Cola, a very popular soft drink even in those days. Cocaine was not replaced by the drug caffeine in Coca-Cola until 1906.

With the use of cocaine and heroin in some everyday products, U.S. President William Howard Taft stated in 1910 that "the misuse of cocaine is undoubtedly an American habit, the most threatening of the drug habits that has ever appeared in this country." In 1906, the federal Pure Food and Drug Act was enacted because of the concern over heroin addiction. In 1914 the federal Harrison Narcotics Act was passed.

The Food and Drug Administration (FDA) now requires a firm or person who wishes to market and sell a drug in the United States to show that

- The drug or medication is not harmful to humans.
- The drug or medication will do what it is advertised to do.

The Uniform Controlled Substances Act

Uniform Controlled Substances Act model act identifying illegal drug crimes, drafted by a national conference of uniform law commissioners and adopted by the states and the federal government.

Today, the federal government and all of the states have enacted the **Uniform Controlled Substances Act,** which was approved by the National Conference of Commissioners on Uniform State Laws in 1970.[4] The purposes of this act have been stated as follows:

> This Uniform Act was drafted to achieve uniformity between the laws of the several States and those of the Federal government. It has been designed to complement the new Federal narcotic and dangerous drug legislation and provide an interlocking trellis of Federal and State law to enable government at all levels to control more effectively the drug abuse problem. (Uniform Controlled Substances Act, 9 U.L.A., Commissioners' Prefatory Note, 1979, p. 188)

controlled substance A drug that may be possessed or sold only as permitted by state or federal law.

In their uniform **controlled substance** acts, most states forbid and make it criminal conduct to

- Manufacture[5] or deliver a controlled (forbidden) substance
- Possess with intent to manufacture or deliver a controlled substance
- Create, deliver, or possess with intent to deliver a counterfeit substance
- Offer or agree to deliver a controlled substance and then deliver or dispense a substance that is not a controlled substance
- Possess a controlled substance
- Knowingly keep or maintain a store, dwelling, building, vehicle, boat, or aircraft, or other place resorted to by persons illegally using controlled substances
- Acquire or obtain possession of a controlled substance by misrepresentation, fraud, forgery, deception, or subterfuge

FIVE SCHEDULES OF CONTROLLED SUBSTANCES

Schedule	Abuse Potential	Examples of Drugs Covered	Some of the Effects	Medical Use
I	Highest	Heroin, LSD, hashish, marijuana, methaqualone, designer drugs	Unpredictable effects, severe psychological or physical dependence, or death	No accepted use; some are legal for limited research use only
II	High	Morphine, PCP, codeine, cocaine, methadone, Demerol, Benzedrine, Dexedrine	May lead to severe psychological or physical dependence	Accepted use with restrictions
III	Medium	Codeine with aspirin or Tylenol, some amphetamines, anabolic steroids	May lead to moderate or low physical dependence or high psychological dependence	Accepted use
IV	Low	Darvon, Talwin, phenobarbital, Equanil, Miltown, Librium, diazepam	May lead to limited physical or psychological dependence	Accepted use
V	Lowest	Over-the-counter or prescription compounds with codeine, Lomotil, Robitussin A-C	May lead to limited physical or psychological dependence	Accepted use

The Uniform Controlled Substances Act has five schedules of controlled substances according to their potential for abuse, degree of accepted medical use, and relative physical danger to the abuser. These schedules are summarized by the U.S. Bureau of Justice Statistics, in *1992 Report on Drugs, Crime and the Justice System*, as shown in the box.

Types of Possession of Controlled Substances

The most common criminal (or ordinance) illegal drug charge is that of possession of a controlled substance.[6] Possession must be proved to sustain the arrest and conviction. The Controlled Substances Act defined the possession offenses to include a *mens rea* requirement, that the person knowingly or intentionally possess the controlled substance. The federal controlled substances law, 21 U.S.C. § 841 (a) (1) has a "knowingly" requirement. See *United States v. Abdulle*, 564 F.3d 119 (2d Cir. 2009). As a result, when states adopted the Controlled Substances Act, they usually included the requirement that the possession must be done "knowingly." Texas statute VTCA § 481.115, as an example, states, "Except as authorized by this Chapter, a person commits an offense if the person knowingly or intentionally possesses a controlled substance listed in Penalty Group I...."

Some states make the simple fact of possession a crime. The Washington Supreme Court held in *State v. Bradshaw*, 98 P.3d 11990 (Wash. 2009), *cert. denied*, 544 U.S. 922 (2005) that because the Washington state legislature omitted the "knowingly" language when it adopted the Controlled Substances Act, mere possession of a controlled substance is made criminal. The *Bradshaw* court stated that there is "no mens rea" in RCWA 69.50.4013, the Washington illegal possession statute.

It is uniformly held in both state and federal courts that as long as a defendant knew he possessed *some* kind of controlled substance, the prosecution need not prove he knew the exact nature and kind of drug possessed. For example, in *United States v. De La Torre*, 599 F.3d 1198 (10th Cir. 2010) the court held that a defendant carrying a backpack that he knew contained marijuana could be convicted of possession of methamphetamine that was also in the backpack, whether or not the defendant knew that fact.

In some kinds of controlled substances, which are not as well known as marijuana or cocaine, proof of knowledge of possession can be more difficult. Khat is the name for an African plant commonly chewed in African countries as a stimulant. Khat is not a controlled substance. After harvest khat contains a chemical called catherinone, a Schedule I controlled substance. However, over a short time, the plant decays and the catherinone is replaced by a different substance, cathine, a Schedule IV controlled substance. A person in possession of khat may thus be in possession of catherinone, or cathine, depending on how long the plant has decayed. In *United States v. Hassan*, 542 F.3d 968 (2d Cir. 2008) the court reversed a conviction of a defendant charged with conspiracy to possess with intent to distribute catherinone. The court said that it was not enough to prove the defendant intended to import khat. The government needed to prove the defendant knew khat contained catherinone, and that he intended to import khat that had catherinone.

Proof of possession may be satisfied by either of the following:

- *Actual possession* is possession on the person of the defendant, or within an area of his or her immediate control and reach. Actual possession may be within a container (e.g., purse, package, or suitcase) that the defendant may be carrying or has within reach. Actual possession may also occur in a vehicle when the controlled substance is under the seat of the person or in the glove compartment of the vehicle owned or driven by the defendant.
- *Constructive possession* of a controlled substance occurs when illegal drugs are in a place immediately accessible to the accused and subject to his or her domination and control. Examples of constructive possession would be drugs found in the trunk of a car the defendant owned or was the driver of, or in a home or business place controlled and dominated by a defendant, to such an extent that a strong inference of possession could be drawn by a judge or jury.

To Convict of Possession of an Illegal Drug, Must the State Present a "Usable Amount" as Evidence?

State courts differ on the question as to whether a "trace" amount of an illegal drug (that is, an amount so small that it is unusable) will sustain a conviction for possession of that drug.

In the case of *People v. Mizell*,[7] the highest court in the state of New York followed the "majority" of the states and held that "any amount of an (illegal drug) is sufficient to sustain a conviction for possession." In the *Mizell* case, cocaine "residue" found on the sides of vials was used to support the criminal charge and conviction for possession. The conviction was affirmed, with the court holding that the "cocaine residue—though unusable—is nevertheless a controlled substance" under the criminal code of the state of New York.[8]

In *Beeler v. State*, 807 N.E.2d 789 (Ind. App. 2004) the court found that possession of an electronic scale with minute quantities of cocaine residue satisfied the requirements for illegal "possession" of a controlled substance. The defendant contended that he could

CASE CLOSE-UP

United States v. Heredia
Ninth Circuit Court of Appeals
483 F.3d 913 (2007)

The defendant Heredia was charged with violation of 21 U.S.C. § 841(a)(1), possession of a controlled substance with the intent to distribute. She was arrested at a border checkpoint as she drove a vehicle from Mexico to Arizona. Border agents noticed a strong "perfume" smell in the vehicle driven by Heredia, and a search of the car discovered 349 pounds of marijuana covered by dryer sheets to disguise the odor.

At her trial Heredia testified that she did not know the trunk contained marijuana and that the car belonged to her aunt, who told Heredia the "perfume" odor came from a bottle of Downy fabric softener the aunt spilled in the car a few days earlier. Heredia testified she believed her aunt's explanation. Heredia also testified she began to suspect drugs were in the trunk, but not until she was driving on a highway near the border checkpoint, and at that time she was afraid to stop and check the trunk to confirm her suspicions.

Because 18 U.S.C. § 841(a)(1) prohibits only the "knowing" possession of a controlled substance, the trial judge gave the jury what is called the "deliberate ignorance" instruction. In that instruction, the jury is instructed to find the defendant "knowingly" possessed a controlled substance if the defendant (1) was aware of a high probability of the presence of drugs in the vehicle and (2) deliberately chose to ignore that high probability. Simple being careless would not satisfy the "knowing" requirement.

The jury convicted Heredia of possession of a controlled substance with the intent to distribute, and she appealed. A panel of the circuit court of appeals reversed her conviction, stating the "deliberate ignorance" instruction was not a permissible method of establishing the "knowing" requirement of § 841(a)(1), 429 F.3d 820. The court of appeals granted rehearing *en banc* (where all the members of the circuit court review the decision of the panel) and reversed the panel's decision, thereby affirming Heredia's conviction in the trial court.

Heredia's claims in the appellate court were (1) deliberate ignorance was not a permissible method of proving knowledge under § 841 and (2) even if it was, the trial court's instruction was deficient because it failed to instruct the jury it could find deliberate ignorance only if Heredia's motive in choosing to ignore the probability of drugs in the car was to provide her a defense to any subsequent criminal charges.

The full court rejected her claims. It noted that the deliberate ignorance rule originated 30 years ago in *United States v. Jewell*, 532 F.2d 697 (9th Cir. 1976), and since that date virtually every circuit court had adopted the rule, and Congress did nothing to change § 841 to indicate it did not think "knowing" could be satisfied by deliberate ignorance. The court agreed with Heredia that many subsequent decisions added a third prong to the deliberate ignorance instruction, which required the jury to determine the motive for the defendant's choice to remain ignorant. See, for example, *United States v. Puche*, 350 F.3d 1137 (11th Cir. 2003). However, the court concluded that deliberate ignorance under § 841 was not limited to those who chose to be ignorant only to provide a defense to a subsequent prosecution. Any choice to ignore the high probability of drugs in a vehicle, so long as the choice was made freely, satisfied the knowing requirement.

Four judges dissented, arguing that the *Jewell* rule should be discarded, and let Congress determine if "knowing" could be satisfied with anything less than actual knowledge. The U.S. Supreme Court denied certiorari in 2007, 128 S. Ct. 804.

POSSESSION OF A SMALL AMOUNT OF MARIJUANA

The offense of possession of a small amount of marijuana is charged in different ways throughout the United States.

Criminal Offense

If the person is charged and convicted under a statute and could receive a jail sentence, the conviction is a criminal conviction and the person has been convicted of a crime.

Civil Offense

If the only penalty that can be imposed after conviction is a monetary fine, the conviction is for a civil offense and is similar to a speeding ticket or a parking ticket. Under these circumstances, the offense of possession of a small amount of marijuana has been "decriminalized" as it is no longer charged as a crime.

Legalizing This Conduct

If neither criminal nor civil punishment is imposed for possession of a small amount of marijuana, the conduct has then been legalized and is no longer a crime or a civil offense. The Alaska Supreme Court has held that under the Alaska Constitution's right of privacy, adults may possess up to four grams of marijuana in their homes. See *State v. Crocker,* 97 P.3d 93 (Alaska App. 2004).

not "knowingly" possess a miniscule amount of a drug and thus could not be convicted under the Indiana statute, Ind. Code § 35-48-4-6. That statute, like other possession statutes in most states, prohibits one from "knowingly or intentionally" possessing a controlled substance. The court said that circumstantial evidence, such as the admitted use the defendant panned for the scale, was sufficient to prove he "knew" the residue was a controlled substance.

usable amount In contrast to a useless trace amount, a quantity of an illegal drug sufficient to be used.

However, other courts follow the "usable quantity" rule and hold that a blackened residue or a useless trace amount is not a **usable amount** and will not sustain a criminal conviction for possession of an illegal drug. Courts holding that a usable quantity of drugs must be presented include California[9] and Florida, at least where the trace amount of the substance is found on a commonly exchanged object, such as a dollar bill.[10]

Delivery of Controlled Substances

The acts that are prohibited under the Uniform Controlled Substances Act, as illustrated in Florida's Criminal Code Section 893.13, include:

[I]t is unlawful for any person to sell, purchase, manufacture, or deliver, or possess with intent to sell... a controlled substance.

Delivery of an illegal drug can be either an actual delivery, or it could be the crime of possession of a controlled substance with intent to deliver (sell or transfer).

In most of the actual delivery cases that come into criminal courts throughout the United States, the government presents evidence showing that the accused sold (delivered) illegal drugs to an undercover law enforcement officer. In other actual delivery cases, the state proves its case by producing a witness to the illegal drug transaction (either the receiver of the drugs or an observer of the delivery). Videotapes or a film of the delivery can also be used as evidence.

possession with intent to deliver A criminal case in which the state presents evidence showing that the accused had possession of a large amount of an illegal drug, meaning more than the accused would personally use.

In the typical criminal case of **possession with intent to deliver** (sell), the state presents evidence showing that the accused had possession of a large amount of an illegal drug (more than he or she would personally use). A combination of the following evidence is also generally presented: that the accused also possessed scales and/or small plastic bags with evenly weighed-out illegal drugs, a large amount of money, a pager, or a cellular phone. Evidence that the accused did not have a job but lived very well and drove an expensive car could also be presented.

The evidence presented by the government must be sufficient to justify a conclusion by the fact finder (jury or judge) that the accused possessed the illegal drug with intent to deliver (sell or transfer) it to another person. To do this, the U.S. Supreme Court requires that there must be a "rational connection"[11] between the facts presented and the conclusion drawn by the fact finder.

State–Federal Clash Over the Medical Use of Marijuana

In 2010 New Jersey became the 14th state to pass a "Compassionate Use Medical Marijuana" statute. Under these statutes, doctors may prescribe the personal use of marijuana for pain management for people with serious illnesses who do not respond to other treatments. These laws, such as the California Compassionate Use Act of 1996 (California Health & Safety Code, Section 11362.5), created what is termed a "medical use" exception to the state's drug laws.

The federal government did not initially challenge these laws, but beginning with President George W. Bush's first administration, the attorney general began directing federal prosecutors to prosecute, under the Federal Controlled Substances Act (CSA), persons distributing prescribed marijuana. In *United States v. Oakland Cannabis Buyers' Cooperative,* 532 U.S. 483 (2001), the Supreme Court held that the CSA had no "medical use" exception and that as a result manufacturers and providers, such as the cooperative, of marijuana for medical use could be prosecuted under the CSA. The Court did not specifically hold that *users* of marijuana for medical purposes could be prosecuted under the CSA, but it did suggest as much in a footnote: "nothing in our analysis, or the statute, suggests that a distinction should be drawn between the prohibition on manufacturing and distributing and the other prohibitions in the Controlled Substances Act" (532 U.S., at 495).

After *Oakland,* several seriously ill persons using marijuana brought an action to declare the CSA unconstitutional, alleging that prosecutions of *users* of marijuana was not permitted because their use did not affect interstate commerce. That being so, they alleged, Congress had no constitutional authority to prohibit the medical use of marijuana.

In *Raich v. Ashcroft,* 352 F.3d 122 (9th Cir. 2003), the Ninth Circuit Court of Appeals agreed, holding that medical use of marijuana "does not have any direct or obvious effect on interstate commerce." (See Chapter 2 for a discussion of the Commerce Clause as authority for federal laws.) In 2005 the U.S. Supreme Court reversed the Ninth Circuit Court, holding that because the in-state use of marijuana might have an effect on the interstate market for marijuana, the federal government had the power under the Commerce Clause to prohibit the use of marijuana for medical purposes. See *Gonzales v. Raich,* 545 U.S. 1 (2005).[12]

In the years immediately following the decision in *Raich* federal law enforcement agencies conducted many "raids" on medical-use marijuana suppliers and users. However, on October 19, 2009, U.S. Attorney General Eric Holder announced that prosecutions of medical-use marijuana suppliers and users would be relaxed, with law enforcement focusing on large-scale marijuana operations. See the *Washington Post,* October 20,

2009. However, in an announcement made October 15, 2010, Holder stated that if California voters vote in November 2010 to approve a measure making possession of marijauna legal, the federal government will act to enforce provisions of the federal Controlled Substances Act which make such possession illegal under federal law. In July 2010 the House of Representatives passed a bill that changes the sentencing structure for "crack" cocaine convictions. Under the present law, possession of 5 grams of crack triggers the mandatory five-year prison sentence rule, while for powder cocaine the triggering amount is possession of 500 grams. Because crack convictions overwhelming involve black defendants, many persons and organizations objected to the sentence disparity for creating racial distinctions in sentencing decisions. Under the new law, which the Senate passed earlier in 2010, the amount of crack needed to trigger the 5-year mandatory sentence has been raised to 28 grams. The powder cocaine amounts remain the same.

Controlled Substances Used in Religious Ceremonies

When Congress adopted the Controlled Substances Act, the issue of religious use of substances included in the schedules of controlled substances arose. An immediate exception to the Act's prohibitions was made for the use of peyote by members of the Native American Church. In 1994, Congress passed 42 U.S.C. § 1996a(b)(1), which made this exception applicable to all Indian tribes.

Other religious groups had no specific exception to the Controlled Substances Acts' prohibitions. Moreover, the Supreme Court had held that the Free Exercise Clause of the constitution did not require judges to consider the burden placed on religious exercise by facially constitutional laws, such as the Controlled Substances Act. See *Employment Div. Dept. of Human Resources of Ore. v. Smith*, 494 U.S. 872 (1990). However, in 1993 Congress passed the Religious Freedom Information Act, 42 U.S.C. § 2000bb. Section 2000bb-1(a) of the Act prohibits the government from placing a "substantially burden" on the exercise of religion, even if the "burden results from a rule of general applicability" (such as the drug laws), unless the government can show a compelling interest in doing so. This section has been used by religious groups to resist federal prosecutions under the Controlled Substances laws.

The U.S. Supreme Court considered the application of the Religious Freedom Restoration Act in *Gonzales v. O Centro Espirita*, 546 U.S. 418 (2006). In that case the government sought to use the Controlled Substances Act to prohibit a practice followed by a religious sect located in the United States but with ties to a Christian Spiritist sect in Brazil, with origins in the Amazon rainforest. That sect had a ceremonial "tea" drink called "hoasca," which contained a substance called DMT, which was a Schedule I controlled substance. The Supreme Court said that since the government agreed the group using the "hoasca" was sincere in its religious significance, it could prohibit that use only if it could show some "compelling interest" for doing so. The Court rejected the government's argument that the fact DMT was a controlled substance by itself justified the prohibition. Because the government made no other showing of a compelling interest, the Court said it was barred from prosecuting the religious sect.

The original Religious Freedom Restoration Act applied to the states as well as the federal government, but in *Boerne v. Flores*, 521 U.S. 507 (1997), the Supreme Court held that Congress lacked the power to make the law effective against the states. As a result, state prosecutions for use of a controlled substance in a religious ceremony are possible, unless the state has made its own exception to state controlled substances laws. Some have: Arizona has a statute, ARS § 541-1493.01, that is similar to the federal Religious Freedom Restoration Act. Other states have specific exceptions for the Native American

Church for use of peyote; Wis. Code § 161.115 is such a statute. The Utah Supreme Court has held that the federal exception for the Native American Church was incorporated into the Utah Controlled Substances Act. See *State v. Mooney*, 96 P.3d 420 (Utah 2004).

Drug Rip-Off Cases and Simulated Drugs

In *State v. Glover*, 594 A.2d 1086 (Me. 1991), the defendant planned to "rip off" a buyer of illegal drugs. Instead of cocaine, the defendant delivered two bags of baking soda to the buyer, at $50 a bag. His conviction for attempted trafficking in cocaine was affirmed. Glover's buyer was an undercover police officer.

Other states, among them Iowa, have statutes that make the delivery or possession of a "simulated controlled substance" a crime. A simulated controlled substance is a substance "represented to be [an illegal drug]... and because of its nature, packaging, or appearance would lead a reasonable person to believe it to be a controlled substance" (Iowa Statute 204.401(1)).

In *State v. Henderson*, 478 N.W.2d 626 (Iowa 1991), the Iowa Supreme Court affirmed the defendant's conviction of possession of a simulated controlled substance. Georgia has a similar statute, which makes it a crime to sell an uncontrolled substance that the seller has represented to be a controlled substance. (See Georgia Code Annotated § 16-13-30.1.) In *Brown v. State*, 581 S.E.2d 35 (Ga. 2003), the court held that a defendant who sold a fake "rock" of crack cocaine to an undercover agent could be convicted under the statute.

Criminal Liability for Drug-Induced Deaths

Drug overdose cases occur regularly in every city in the United States, as drugs have become purer, cheaper, and easier to obtain. Cocaine is particularly dangerous because it is an unpredictable killer that can cause life-threatening complications that are not related to the dose taken, the length of use, or the manner in which the drug is taken. Swallowing an "eight ball" of cocaine (one-eighth of an ounce) can easily cause acute cocaine intoxication and death.[13]

A number of states have enacted laws that make people who illegally manufacture, distribute, or dispense illegal drugs strictly liable for a death that results from the injection, inhalation, or ingestion of such a drug.[14] Such laws are often called *Len Bias laws*. Len Bias was a basketball star at the University of Maryland. Shortly after being drafted by an NBA team, he died as the result of using cocaine. The following cases illustrate prosecutions under these laws.

People v. Boand

Court of Appeals of Illinois (2005) 838 N.E.2d 367, *review denied* 838 N.E.2d 809 (2006)

The defendant brought a woman home to his house, based in part on her insistence on obtaining some cocaine. The woman had a history of drug abuse and suicide attempts. At his house the woman ingested some methadone prescribed for the defendant to deal with his heroin addiction. She also smoked marijuana. Later in the evening the woman collapsed and died on the defendant's couch. The court held that the evidence was sufficient to convict the defendant under the Illinois drug-induced death statute, 720 ILCS 5/9-3.3.

> ### State v. Ervin
>
> Superior Court of New Jersey (1990) 242 N.J. Super. 584, 577 A.2d 1273
>
> Ervin purchased cocaine, which he and his girlfriend shared. She died as the result of using the cocaine. He was charged not only with possession of cocaine but also with possession with intent to deliver and causing a drug-induced death, in violation of NJSA 2C: 35-19, the New Jersey Len Bias law. In sustaining the conviction for the drug-induced death, the court held:
>
> > *The New Jersey Legislature has determined that manufacturing, distributing and dispensing certain illegal drugs, including cocaine which is the substance involved in the present case, are criminal activities which, like the crimes enumerated in the felony murder statute, pose inherent dangers to others including those who use the drugs. Defendant has shown us no basis upon which to conclude that that determination is irrational.*
> >
> > * * *
> >
> > *We hold that the absolute or strict liability feature of N.J.S.A. 2C:35-9, limited as it is to deaths which are the proximate consequences of inherently dangerous illegal activities, does not violate due process of law.*

Possession or Sale of Drug Paraphernalia

drug paraphernalia
Objects that are primarily intended or designed for use with illegal drugs.

State criminal codes and the federal government make the possession or sale of **drug paraphernalia** a crime. The Federal Criminal Code defines *drug paraphernalia* as "any equipment, product or material of any kind which is primarily intended or designed for use" with illegal drugs.[15]

Some products have only one use, and that is as drug paraphernalia. For example, bongs, which are water pipes used for the smoking of marijuana, were called "hardcore paraphernalia by virtue of (their) physical features… (because bongs have) no alternative uses."[16]

An example of an item that has more than one use is inositol, an optically inactive alcohol. Inositol is a common cocaine-cutting ingredient. Because inositol has dual purposes, the government must establish that the inositol was "primarily intended" as drug paraphernalia in order to convict a defendant under the statute.[17]

SNIFFING, BAGGING, AND HUFFING INHALANTS

Inhalants are chemicals that give off fumes or vapors that slow the body's reactions and cloud thinking when breathed in. Many common household products are inhalants. Common products available to kids that will produce a high include glue, gasoline, correction fluid, and felt-tipped markers. The Partnership for a Drug-Free America estimates that more than 1,200 products available to kids are capable of producing highs and states that the use of inhalants has become an "epidemic."

Inhalants can be "sniffed" (inhaling the substance into the nose directly from the container), "bagged" (dumping the substance into a bag and inhaling the fumes), or "huffed" (soaking a rag with a mixture, putting the rag to the mouth, and inhaling the fumes).

Inhalants can cause suffocation, heart attack, or even death. Common symptoms in a child (or an adult) of inhalant use are staggering gait and uncoordinated walk and movement; delirium; slurred speech; chemical odor on breath, body, or clothes; loss of appetite; intoxication; nausea and/or vomiting; belligerence; or impaired hearing.

For further information, call or write the National Clearing House of Alcohol and Drug Addiction.

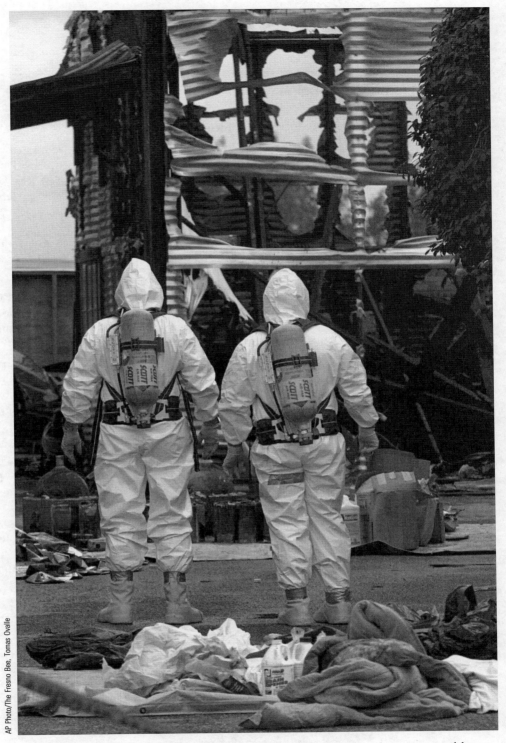

Fresno Meth Task Force investigators inspect the charred ruins of a methamphetamine super lab near Madera, California. The lab exploded when investigators attempted to remove some remaining combustible red phosphorus chemicals. Methamphetamine is a highly addictive central nervous system stimulant. Meth is one of the few illegal drugs that people without any chemical expertise can manufacture on their own. In 2006 the United Nations reported that meth was the most widely abused hard drug in the world, with almost as many addicts as cocaine and heroin combined.

OTHER STATUTES AND LAWS USED IN THE WAR ON DRUGS

Subject Matter of Law	Problem Addressed by Law
"Drug kingpin" statutes	The federal government and many states have created a separate crime of being the leader of a narcotics trafficking network. Many criminal codes punish this offense with life imprisonment. New Jersey is one of the states that does and defines *drug kingpin* as follows in New Jersey Statute 2C-35-3: *A person is a leader of a narcotics trafficking network if he conspires with others as an organizer, supervisor, financier or manager, to engage for profit in a scheme or course of conduct to unlawfully manufacture, distribute, dispense, bring into or transport in this State any substance classified in Schedule I or II, or any controlled substance analog thereof.*
Additional imprisonment for using or carrying a firearm during and in relation to a drug-trafficking crime	The Federal Criminal Code (18 U.S.C.A. § 924(c)) and the statutes of most (if not all) states provide for additional punishment for a person using or carrying a firearm during and in relation to a drug-trafficking crime.[a]
Nuisance laws and drug house abatement statutes and ordinances	Landlords are often warned that if they allow tenants to sell drugs from the landlord's property, an abatement or nuisance proceeding could be started against the property. Drug houses could also be taken over by a state or local government because of failure to pay taxes, or they could be condemned because of fire or code violations.
Forfeiture of property	Under the Controlled Substances Act and other forfeiture statutes, the following may be seized under court order: (1) instruments of the crime (such as vehicles or watercraft used to commit the crime), (2) profits of the crime (money from drug dealing, stolen goods, and so on), and (3) proceeds of the illegal act (homes, condos, yachts, farms, or other luxury goods purchased from profits of the crime). If the offender did not pay taxes on the profits of drug dealing, the Internal Revenue Service may take action against drug traffickers.
Use of communications facility to further a drug violation	The use of a communications facility to commit or facilitate a drug violation is a crime itself under federal law if the defendant has a prior conviction for

Drug paraphernalia charges and convictions are most often obtained when the item or paraphernalia is seized along with drugs such as marijuana and cocaine. In the 1994 case of *People v. Feld* (641 N.E.2d 924), an Illinois appellate court held that the state failed to establish that boxes and small wooden pipes were drug paraphernalia. The defendant, a manufacturer, was not apprehended using the boxes and wooden pipes in drug use.

The federal Mail Order Drug Paraphernalia Control Act (21 U.S.C.A. § 857) was upheld in *Posters 'N' Things Ltd. v. United States*, 969 F.2d 652, 51 CrL 1369 (1992), *cert. granted* 113 S. Ct. 1410 (1993). The defendant in this case sold scales and substances commonly used by cocaine dealers to dilute cocaine. The defendant advertised the products for such use, and purchases were made in such large quantities that it showed that dealers rather than other users were buying the items.

Subject Matter of Law	Problem Addressed by Law
	a felony drug violation. (See the 1998 case of *United States v. Mankins,* 1998 WL 65317 (5th Cir. 1998).)
Possession of wiretapping devices, illegal bugs, and eavesdropping equipment	Title 18, Chapter 119, of the Omnibus Crime and Safe Streets Act makes it illegal to own, manufacture, or sell eavesdropping and wiretapping equipment specifically designed for "the surreptitious interception of wire, oral or electronic communications." Only law enforcement agencies are permitted to buy or use such devices and then only with a court order. Some drug dealers and other criminals illegally possess and use these devices.
"Schoolyard" or "School-house" laws	In an attempt to keep drugs from schoolyards and neighborhoods, "schoolyard" laws were passed that increase jail time for dealing drugs within 1,000 feet of an elementary or secondary school.
Loss of financial aid and the loans for a year for students who are found guilty of simple possession of an illegal drug such as marijuana	More than 9,000 students lost financial aid in the year 2000 under a law enacted by Congress in 1998. Federal college aid can be lost for longer periods for repeat or more serious drug offenses.
Laws punishing the sale of counterfeit medical drugs	Medical personnel report an increase in counterfeit drugs for the treatment of diseases such as tuberculosis, AIDS, and malaria, and for antibiotics. The World Health Organization has reported that labs in China produce most of these counterfeit drugs, which cause thousands of unnecessary deaths each year.[b]
"Doctor shopping" as violation of Controlled Substances Act	Obtaining multiple prescriptions from different doctors for the same drug. Police affidavits state that Rush Limbaugh, the radio commentator, received 2,000 painkillers from four different doctors in a six-month period.

[a]In the 1995 case of *Bailey v. U.S.* (116 S. Ct. 501), the U.S. Supreme Court held that to violate § 924(c), the weapon had to be actively deployed and not just left sitting in a closet or nightstand drawer. In the 1997 case of *Muscarello v. U.S.* (118 S. Ct. 1911), Muscarello was convicted of dealing marijuana. He kept his gun in the locked glove compartment of his pickup truck.
[b]See the *New York Times* article, "In the World of Life-Saving Drugs: A Growing Epidemic of Deadly Fakes," March 15, 2007.

≡ Alcohol-Related Crimes

Alcohol is a drug used by an estimated 95 million Americans in some form and in varying amounts. It is a mood-altering drug many people use as a tranquilizer. It has been observed that if alcohol were discovered today for the first time, the FDA would be obligated by law to forbid its over-the-counter sale without prescription. Alcohol is an addictive drug, and it is toxic—it is a poison. However, alcohol has, for a long time, been part of our economic, social, and cultural environment. Because of the beverage's long history of social acceptance and our society's economic dependence on it, it continues to be sold openly on the market.

Alcohol's Relation to Crimes and Deaths

British and U.S. studies of accidental deaths in the 1980s and a National Institutes of Health study in 2002 showed that alcohol has a high relationship to deaths caused by drowning, choking, burns and fires, and falls.[18] A pedestrian who is intoxicated was reported 3.5 times more likely to be killed or injured in a traffic accident.

Alcohol is the most widely abused and misused drug in America and in many other countries. Alcoholism is one of the biggest health problems in the United States, just behind heart disease and cancer. Excessive use of alcohol is also a factor causing heart disease and cancer.

When public drunkenness was prosecuted as a crime throughout the United States, it was always high on the yearly list of crimes.[19] Alcohol continues to be an important factor in many disorderly conduct, battery, assault, rape, child abuse, domestic relations disputes, and criminal damage to property cases in the United States every year. The movement from other drugs to alcohol is sometimes condoned by parents who, in their relief that their children are not involved in the use of other forms of drugs, do not recognize the dangers of alcohol.

The 2002 National Institutes of Health study surveyed drinking among the 8 million college and university students in the United States. The study showed that most students drink moderately or not at all, but 44 percent of students drink in binges.

Alcoholic-related student deaths numbered 1,445 students a year—four per day. An additional 1,370 students suffered injuries (some very serious) tied to drinking, and an estimated 192 students each day are raped or sexually assaulted after drinking.[20]

Alcohol and Drug Problems of Prison Inmates

The majority of the over 2 million prisoners in U.S. jails and prisons have substantial alcohol and drug abuse problems. A national study released in 1998 found that illegal drugs and alcohol helped lead to the imprisonment of 80 percent of U.S. prisoners.[21]

The report released by the National Center on Addiction and Substance Abuse at Columbia University found that 80 percent of the prisoners had been high when they had committed their crimes, had stolen to support their habits, or had a history of drug and alcohol abuse that led them to commit crimes. The study reported that alcohol was the drug most closely associated with the violent crimes of murder, rape, assault, and child and spousal abuse.

Twenty-one percent of state prisoners were convicted of a violent crime while under the influence of alcohol alone, 3 percent were high on crack or powder cocaine, and 1 percent were on heroin.

Drunk Driving: The Criminal Homicide Causing the Most Deaths

Almost 50 people are killed every day in the United States because of driving under the influence. In addition, about 1 million people are injured annually. The National Highway Traffic Safety Administration estimates the yearly costs of drunk driving to be $45 billion. It also estimates that at least 9 million Americans each year drive while under the influence of illegal drugs. A survey done in Florida in 2000 showed that about one-third of all people stopped for driving erratically or speeding who failed a field sobriety test were not drunk on alcohol but were high on illegal drugs.

Tougher laws and enforcement, taking more blood alcohol tests of suspected drunk and drugged drivers, and increased efforts to educate students and the public on the dangers of drunk and drugged driving are being used to decrease the dangers on our streets and highways. The punishment for drunk driving has been increased, and some states

DRIVING AND ALCOHOL

Does Your State Regulate the Following Conduct or Have the Following Laws?

Conduct	Statute
Driving a vehicle while under the influence of alcohol or drug. (Does "vehicle" include watercraft, aircraft, moped, etc.?)	
First offense	_____
Second offense	_____
Third offense	_____
The legal drinking limit is	_____
Drinking and driving age is	_____
"Booze it and lose it" statute (administrative license revocation laws that give police the right to seize licenses of drivers who fail or refuse sobriety tests)	_____
Punish refusal of driver to take Breathalyzer or other test when lawfully requested	_____
Ban open containers of alcohol beverage in motor vehicles	_____
While driving under the influence:	
▪ causes property damage	_____
▪ causes serious injury to another person	_____
▪ causes the death of another person	_____
Leaving scene of accident (failing to stop and report):	
▪ property damage	_____
▪ injury to person	_____
▪ fatal accident	_____
Can law enforcement agencies in your state set up sobriety checkpoints?	_____

have enacted laws forbidding or curbing happy hours by taverns and clubs. Victims of drunk driving are reminded that they may commence lawsuits in most states under "dram shop"[22] laws (a dram being a small drink of liquor) that permit civil lawsuits under some circumstances against bars and individuals who furnish or sell the alcoholic drinks.

Debates have occurred in the legislatures of all states as to what the blood alcohol limit should be in that state. Organizations such as MADD (Mothers Against Drunk Driving) urge that the limit of 0.10 percent be reduced to 0.08 percent and point out that the lower limit is still higher than in most European countries and Japan. Insurance companies and the American Medical Association join MADD in noting that alcohol can unravel driving skills subtly and insidiously, long before people look and act drunk.

Experts now point out that it is the driver with a drinking or drug problem who is the problem. Too many people with severe alcohol and/or drug problems continue to drive while impaired and under the influence. Problem drinkers continue to drink and drive even after their licenses have been revoked. They are generally the danger on the highway.

Elements and Defenses in Drunk-Driving Prosecutions

Drunk driving statutes differ from state-to-state, but most follow a format similar to the following statute, Neb. Rev. Stat. § 60-6,196:

It shall be unlawful for any person to operate or be in the actual physical control of any motor vehicle:

(a) While under the influence of alcoholic liquor or of any drug;
(b) When such person has a concentration of eight-hundredths of one gram or more by weight of alcohol per one hundred ten liters of his or her blood; or
(c) When such person has a concentration of eight-hundredths of one gram or more by weight of alcohol per two hundred ten liters of his or her breath.

Most states also increase the penalty for a conviction based on a blood-alcohol count appreciably higher than the statutory limit, and for subsequent convictions. See, e.g., NJSA § 39:4-50 (a) (1), (2), and (3). At some point, repeated violations can be treated as felonies.

Under the most common type of statute, the prosecution can prove the violation either by evidence the driver was under the influence of alcohol or drugs, or by use of either a blood or breath test. Blood tests are more reliable, but they are more expensive, time-consuming, and not always available. As a result, breath tests on a Breathalyzer machine are often used to prove the violation.

A prosecution based on evidence of impairment due to drugs or alcohol, where no results from breath or blood tests are available, usually includes police evidence from **field sobriety tests.** These tests, done according to guidelines established by the National Highway Traffic Safety Administration (NHTSA), are given by officers in the field who suspect a motorist they have stopped is impaired by alcohol or drugs. Because alcohol can cause **nystagmus,** a condition in which the eye demonstrates abnormal and involuntary movement, Horizontal Gaze Nystagmus (HGN) testing can be used as evidence of alcohol impairment. While there has been some controversy about the reliability of HGN testing, most courts conclude the results are admissible. See, e.g., *People v. McKown*, 924 N.E.2d 941 (Ill. 2010). Observation of the other two field tests can be combined with results from the HGN testing and can be used as evidence of impairment, if the tests are conducted according to NHTSA guidelines. Most states require that the NHTSA guidelines be strictly or substantially followed for the test results to be admitted. See, e.g., *State v. Boczur*, 863 N.E.2d 155 (Ohio 2007). Prosecutors will usually have additional observed evidence of impairment, such as the suspect's physical condition, the smell of alcohol on the breath, slurring of words, and so forth. This evidence can be sufficient to convict a defendant of driving while intoxicated, or driving while impaired as it is called in some states.

Breathalyzer test results are also generally admissible, so long as the person administering the test follows proper procedures. Currently, two machines, the Datamaster and the Intoxilizer, are commonly used by law enforcement agencies. The sophistication of Breathalyzer machines has increased over the years. In 2003 New Jersey began using a new computer-operated machine called the Alcotest. In 2008 the New Jersey Supreme Court upheld the reliability of the machine and stated that results from the machine could be used to prove a drunk driving charge, if the machine's procedures were followed. *State v. Chun*, 943 A.2d 114 (N.J. 2008).

With all Breathalyzer machines, defenses in DUI cases can turn on the operation of the machine and how the machine has been maintained. Procedures for routinely

Field sobriety tests Field tests used to evaluate a motorist's alcohol or drug impairment. They include HGN testing, the walk-and-turn test, and the one-leg stand test.

Nystagmus A persistent, rapid, involuntary, side-to-side eye movement.

checking the machine for reliability are required to guarantee its accuracy, and law enforcement agencies must keep detailed records of maintenance checks. Many DUI defense arguments are based on the absence of such records or checks. See, e.g., *Blazier v. Vincent*, 204 S.W.2d 658 (Mo. App. 2006).

"Booze It and Lose It" Laws

"booze it and lose it" laws In more than 30 states, laws that give the police the authority to immediately seize the driver's license of people who fail or refuse sobriety tests.

More than 30 states have passed **"booze it and lose it" laws**, which give the police the authority to immediately seize the driver's license of people who fail or refuse sobriety tests. After these new laws became known to the drinking public, nighttime fatal crashes dropped dramatically. The National Safety Board estimated that if all 50 states adopted such laws, 2,000 lives could be saved in the United States each year.

Many states have laws that take away the driver's licenses of motorists under age 21 who drive after drinking even a small amount of alcohol.

When Is a Person Driving, Operating, or "in Physical Control" of a Vehicle?

States forbid operating motor vehicles, watercraft, snowmobiles, and aircraft while under the influence of alcohol or of a controlled substance. In most drunk driving cases, either a police officer or a witness testifies to seeing the defendant drive a vehicle while intoxicated. However, when no witnesses are available to testify about the driving, courts have ruled as described in the following list in answer to the question of when a person is driving, operating, or "in physical control" of a vehicle. All of the following defendants were under the influence:

- *Defendants Who Were Found Asleep Behind the Wheel of Their Vehicle:*
  Yes, engine was running. See *State v. Dey*, 798 S.W.2d 210 (Mo. App. 1990).
  No, vehicle was in a ditch with engine off. See *State v. Block*, 798 S.W.2d 213 (Mo. App. 1990).
  No, key was in the "off" position. See *Stevenson v. City of Falls Church*, 416 S.E.2d 435 (Va. 1992).
  No, engine was running but vehicle was "parked." See *State v. Mordacq*, 585 N.E.2d 22 (Ind. App. 1992).
- *Defendant Turned on the Ignition of Vehicle:*
  Yes. See *State v. Hines*, 478 N.W.2d 888 (Iowa App. 1991).
- *Defendants Were Sitting Behind the Wheel of Their Vehicle, the Engine Was Off, but They Were Intoxicated:*
  Yes, in the two Minnesota cases of *State v. Starfield*, 481 N.W.2d 834 (1992), and *State v. Nelson*, 483 N.W.2d 739 (1992).
- *California Requires "Volitional Movement of Vehicle."* See *Mercer v. Department of Motor Vehicles*, 809 P.2d 414 (Calif. 1991).

Summary

- All states and the federal government have enacted the Uniform Controlled Substances Act of 1970. Under this law, which is part of the criminal code of your state, the following are crimes:

1. Manufacture or delivery of an illegal drug
2. Possession with intent to deliver an illegal drug

3. Delivery or possession with intent to deliver a counterfeit substance
4. Offering or agreeing to deliver an illegal drug and then delivering a substance that is not a controlled substance
5. Possession of an illegal drug
6. Knowingly allowing a store, dwelling, building, vehicle, boat, aircraft, or other place to be used by people using illegal drugs
7. Obtaining possession of an illegal drug by misrepresentation, fraud, forgery, deception, or subterfuge

- Intent to deliver illegal drugs can be proved by showing a "rational connection" between the facts of possession, such as the large quantity of the drug, and an intent to sell the drugs.
- Medical use of marijuana is permitted in 14 states, if done as prescribed treatment for listed illness or conditions. While medical users can be prosecuted under federal laws, in 2010 the Justice Department stated it would not do so.
- In *Gonzales v. Raich* the court reasoned that private use of marijuana might have an adverse impact on federal drug laws, and thus Congress had the power under the Commerce Clause to regulate even purely intrastate use of marijuana.
- The state must show only that the defendant provided the drugs to the victim, and that the victim died as a proximate result of the defendant's actions. That means no other intervening event must have caused the death.
- A suspect can be found to have been operating a motor vehicle by being behind the wheel of a car with the keys in the ignition, with a showing it had recently been operated.

Key Terms

Uniform Controlled Substances Act, p. 428
controlled substance, p. 428
usable amount, p. 432

possession with intent to deliver, p. 433
drug paraphernalia, p. 436
Field sobriety tests, p. 442

Nystagmus, p. 442
"booze it and lose it" laws, p. 443

Case Analysis and Writing Exercises

1. The defendant and another man went to a part of town where illegal drugs were sold. They pooled their cash and bought some heroin. They ingested the heroin, and the other man died. The defendant was charged with a drug-induced death under the New Jersey drug-induced death statute. Can he be convicted? Why or why not? See *State v. Morrison*, 902 A.2d 860 (N.J. 2006).

2. The police find a car or truck parked on or near a road. Looking inside, they see a person sitting or lying in the car. They open the door, and it is clear the person in the car is intoxicated. Under what circumstances can the person be charged with drunk driving? What must the prosecution prove? Compare *State v. Kincaid*, 614 N.E.2d 1112 (Ohio App. 1992) with *City of*

Independence v. Clark, 2001 WL 127736 (Ohio App. 2001).

3. The defendant was found with a "crack pipe" in his possession. It was of the type that could be used for smoking crack cocaine, but it could also be used for other purposes. Can the defendant be convicted of possession of drug paraphernalia? Would it matter whether he bought the pipe or made it himself? Why or why not? See *People v. Reeves*, 762 N.E.2d 1124 (Ill. App. 2002).

4. The defendant was sitting in the passenger seat another man's car. A police officer approached the car and asked the driver a question. The driver put a plastic bag that contained marijuana on the center console of the car, and the officer saw the bag. Both the driver and the passenger

were arrested and charged with possession of marijuana. What must the prosecution prove to convict the defendant of the possession charge?

What facts did the court say supported the prosecution's case? See *State v. Proctor*, 901 So. 2d 477 (La. App. 2005).

Notes

1. See the February 10, 2010, report of the United Nations Office of Drug Control.

2. A UN report in 1997 estimated that the illegal drug trade makes up 8 percent of world trade. This illegal industry is estimated at between $400 billion and $1 trillion worldwide. It is as large as the worldwide trade in textiles and bigger than the sales of iron or steel. See the *Pensacola New Journal* article, "U.N. Report: Social Costs of Drug Abuse About $120 Billion," November 16, 1997.

3. The Opium War, which Great Britain waged against China from 1839 to 1842, was conducted to force China to permit the importing of opium into China. China had silk and many other goods to sell to the world but would not buy goods from Britain and other nations. As a result, the British ran up a huge trade deficit. To pay off this deficit, the British commenced selling opium to the Chinese and established a British colony at Hong Kong. When the Chinese government tried to stop the sale of opium, the Opium War began.

   To supply the opium trade, opium was grown in the British colony of India and shipped to China to be traded for Chinese exports. By 1850, India's largest export was opium, exceeding the export of Indian cotton textiles.

   American shippers also brought opium into China to sell in exchange for goods from China. The biggest American trader was Warren Delano (the grandfather of President Franklin Delano Roosevelt). Delano became a very wealthy man in the trade with China. But this trade created thousands of opium addicts and was denounced in churches and in newspapers throughout the United States. After trading in opium was forbidden, illegal shipping and trading in opium continued to supply this deadly drug. See the *New York Times* articles, "The Opium War's Secret History" and "Hong Kong's Colonial Ghosts," June 22, 1997. Also see Martin Booth, *Opium: A History* (New York: St. Martin's Press, 1998).

4. This act replaced the 1933 Uniform Narcotic Drug Act and the 1966 Model State Drug Abuse Control Act.

5. A designer drug is a drug that is cheaply made from chemicals and is sometimes similar to a commonly known illegal drug. New designer drugs come on the market regularly. To prevent the invention, manufacturing, and distribution of designer drugs before they are permanently scheduled in the Uniform Controlled Substances Act, the U.S. Congress enacted a law permitting the quick and temporary placement of a new designer drug in the federal Controlled Substances Act. If this law had not been passed, a new designer drug could be sold throughout the United States for up to a year before it was permanently made a part of the Uniform Controlled Substances Act. The U.S. Supreme Court unanimously upheld the quick scheduling of new designer drugs in the 1991 case of *Touby v. U.S.* (111 S. Ct. 1752).

6. Many courts hold that a person cannot be convicted of possession of a drug solely because the drug is in the person's body. See *State v. Thronsen*, 809 P.2d 941 (Alaska App. 1991) and *State v. Vorm*, 570 N.E.2d 109 (Ind. App. 1991). However, people with an illegal drug in their bodies could be charged with the crime of "being under the influence of a controlled substance." See *Junior v. State*, 807 P.2d 205 (Nev. 1991).

7. 532 N.E.2d 1249 (N.Y. 1988). Surprisingly, tests done by the Argonne National Laboratory in 1997 showed that many $1 and $2 bills circulated in Chicago, Miami, and Houston were tainted with microscopic traces of cocaine. The chemists conducting the tests stated that $1 and $2 bills are used to wrap "rocks" (chunks of solid cocaine

chipped off a cocaine brick). The rock is then sold. Paper money is used instead of newspaper because the money does not transfer ink to the cocaine as newspaper does. Dollar bills are also rolled into tubes and used to snort cocaine powder.

Defense lawyers have used these findings in cocaine possession cases. The report also states that people who handle cocaine-tainted money do not show traces of cocaine on their person except when money comes into contact with large amounts of cocaine immediately before a person handled it. See the *New York Times* article, "Cocaine Turns Up in Many $1 and $2 Bills," September 23, 1997.

8. The Court of Appeals of South Carolina held that ordinarily a measurable quantity is necessary, but when the cocaine was the "remnant of a larger amount previously possessed in the past," the conviction was affirmed. The cocaine residue was in a crack pipe; *State v. Robinson,* 411 S.E.2d 678 (1991). In *State v. Wood,* 1994 WL 250015 (N.M. App. 1994), the cocaine residue was in syringes (conviction sustained).

9. *People v. Rubacalba,* 859 P.2d 708 (Calif. 1993).

10. *Lord v. State,* 616 So. 2d 1065 (Fla. App. 1993). In *Gilchrist v. State,* 784 So. 2d 624 (Fla. App. 2001), the court suggested that the holding in *Lord* applied only to common objects like dollar bills. Where the trace amounts are on a device used to ingest the drug, as was the case in *Gilchrist,* the usable quantity rule does not apply.

11. See *County Court of Ulster County v. Allen,* 442 U.S. 140, 99 S. Ct. 2213 (1979).

12. A spokesperson for the California attorney general's office stated in 2005 that there was now "a sort of détente" between federal and state law enforcement agencies over medical use of marijuana. He stated that federal law enforcement agencies for the most part are targeting individuals who seem clearly to be using marijuana for purposes other than medical treatment, something the state of California was doing also. Nine other states have passed laws permitting the medical use of marijuana.

13. See the *Harvard Medical School Heart Letter* article, "Cocaine: An Unpredictable Killer," April 1992. The article points out that until 1914, cocaine was an ingredient in many cough syrups and home remedy medications sold in the United States. The article also notes that cocaine was used in Coca-Cola until it was replaced by caffeine in 1906. The Harrison Narcotics Act of 1914 classified cocaine as a narcotic in 1914 and limited its use to prescription medical purposes. The article states that cocaine "then went underground, where it remains (today)."

14. If a person was committing a felony in supplying an illegal drug that directly caused a drug-induced death, a prosecutor could issue a criminal charge of felony murder in addition to other criminal charges if the case met the requirements of the felony murder law of that state. (See Chapter 10 of this text for a discussion of the crime of felony murder.)

15. 21 U.S.C.A. § 863(d).

16. *U.S. v. Dyer,* 750 F. Supp. 1275 (E.D. Va. 1990).

17. *United States v. Mishra,* 979 F.2d 301 (3d Cir. 1992).

18. *Harvard Medical School Health Letter* (September 1993) citing *British Medical Journal* and *Southern Medical Journal.* The April 2002 report is entitled *A Call to Action: Changing the Culture of Drinking at U.S. Colleges.* The study was done by the National Institute of Alcohol Abuse and Alcoholism, which is a branch of the National Institutes of Health. (See the *New York Times* article, "Study Calculates the Effects of College Drinking in U.S.," April 10, 2002.)

19. Although many states have decriminalized public drunkenness, other states continue to make public drunkenness a crime. In cities and states where public drunkenness is not a crime, a person who is intoxicated in a public place is often ignored if not getting into trouble or endangered. If such people are a problem, they could be taken to a detoxification center (if available) or a homeless shelter. Such people could also be arrested for disorderly conduct or another offense.

20. A survey done in 2002 by the National Institute on Alcohol Abuse and Alcoholism found that 2 percent of the 400,000 students questioned stated they had sex while they were too drunk to give consent. When this number is added to the number of reported cases of sexual assault, the report estimates that each day about 192 students are sexually assaulted.

21. The former head of the White House national drug policy, General Barry R. McCaffrey, stated that the 1998 study was consistent with recent U.S. Justice reports showing that more than 60 percent of adult males arrested in the United States for felonies had tested positive for at least one illegal drug. See the *New York Times* article, "Alcohol or Drug Link Found in 80 Percent of U.S. Prisoners," January 9, 1998.

22. Most states have dram shop liability laws under which taverns and bars can be liable to innocent victims of alcohol-related accidents and crimes. Social hosts who provide alcohol can also be liable under the laws of some states. Providing alcohol to an underage intoxicated minor creates the greatest dram shop liability.

CHAPTER 17

Terrorism

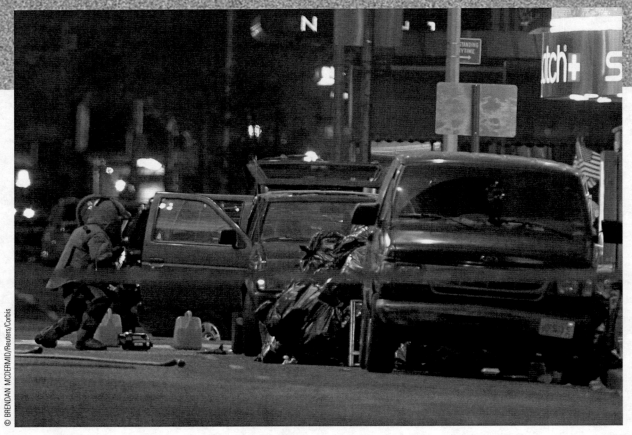

Bomb Squad officers search and secure an automobile used by Faisal Shahzad in his unsuccessful attempt to detonate a bomb in Times Square in New York City. Had he been successful the explosion would likely have caused multiple deaths and immense destruction, since Times Square is one of the most crowded, busiest spots in the country. Street vendors observed the automobile and became suspicious and informed the police before any damage could be done. At his sentencing on October 5, 2010 to life in prison Shahzad, an immigrant from Pakistan, told the court he did not regret his actions, and that the United States should expect many more attacks by others like himself.

OUTLINE

The Crime of Terrorizing (Terrorism by Threats)

The 804 Terrorism Prosecutions from 2001–2009

Financing Terrorism: Where Does the Money Come From?

Moving Money Into and Out of the United States

International Criticism of Aspects of the U.S. War Against Terrorism

LEARNING OBJECTIVES

In this chapter we discuss criminal statutes aimed at punishing and preventing terrorism. The learning objectives for Chapter 17 are:

- Attempt to write a working definition of terrorism.

- Explain why federal criminal statutes must define terrorism.

- Explain one method by which a group can be identified as a terrorist group.

- List the elements of the crime of terrorism under most state laws.

- Define a terrorist threat under state criminal laws.

- Explain the concept of the rules of war.

- List ways terrorists obtain financial support for their terrorist actions.

- List ways money is sent into and out of the United States by terrorist supporters.

- Identify when a seizure is an extraordinary rendition.

The common image of a terrorist is that of an angry and radical militant brandishing a weapon or wearing a suicide bomb. However, the definition of a terrorist is much broader than that common image. For example, both FBI regulations and the USA Patriot Act include in the definition of terrorism "domestic terrorists." Domestic terrorists are those persons in the United States who use unlawful force or violence with the intention of intimidating others, or coercing government policy.

Joseph Stack might have been a domestic terrorist. On February 18, 2010, Stack flew his Piper PA-28 into an office building in Austin, Texas, that included offices of the IRS. The attack killed an IRS employee and injured 13 other individuals. Stack died in the attack. In a suicide note posted in a website the morning of the attack, Stack railed against the federal government and the IRS, and he urged others to revolt against the government and its policies.

In this chapter we will study the many forms terrorism takes and the criminal laws passed by governments to punish terrorism. We will learn the criminal laws enacted to address both terrorist acts committed by U.S. citizens and those committed by citizens of other countries.

Terrorism

Terrorists are criminals who use force and violence in the pursuit of extreme political, ideological, or religious goals. They are willing to take innocent lives to make their statements. Terrorists may be domestic or international. They may be stateless (acting on their own), or they may be domestic (homegrown) acting against their own people and government. They might be acting for a nation, backed by a nation, or supported by people within a nation.

terrorism The use of force and violence in the pursuit of extreme political, ideological, or religious goals, without regard to the innocent lives that may be lost.

Terrorism can be cheap and relatively easy. Terrorists use surprise and vulnerability to their advantage. A handful of dedicated individuals can cause great harm. Timothy McVeigh and Terry Nichols killed 168 people in seconds by blowing up the Alfred P. Murrah Federal Building in Oklahoma City. Fewer than a hundred foreign terrorists killed thousands on September 11, 2001.

Terrorism has existed for ages. The term *terrorism* comes from the Latin word *terere*, which means "to frighten." The word *zealot* originates from militant Jews in the first century when they used terrorism to fight the Roman occupation of Israel. The word *assassin* comes from the name of a group of Shiite Muslims who used terrorism against Persia in the twelfth century. In 1901 an American president, William McKinley, was killed by an American terrorist. Four European heads of state were assassinated by terrorists between the years 1894 and 1900.

Terrorists can be religious or ethnic zealots. They might be people seeking to avenge a perceived wrong or maniacs who get their kicks out of violence. They are sometimes oppressed people angry or desperate enough to use bombs and guns.

Terrorism is a tactic—a means of striking out suddenly, using surprise. The goal is to intimidate and coerce a civilian population, or influence or punish a government. It has put governments around the world on the defensive, forcing them to spend billions of dollars to protect their civilian populations.

While terrorism has existed for centuries, the international community has yet to agree on a definition of the term. The term first appeared during the French Revolution in 1789 and was used to describe the actions of the Republican government, mainly Prime Minister Robespierre, in executing more than 17,000 people. In subsequent years the term came to be applied to specific kinds of crimes, where the criminal had a political motivation.

The United Nations has never defined international terrorism. Rather, it has adopted several international agreements, called "Conventions," which member nations must follow. For example, after the bombings of civilian aircraft in the 1960s and 1970s, the UN adopted the Tokyo and Montreal Conventions against attacks on civilian aircraft. As part of these Conventions, every member nation was required to make the specified acts criminal under their domestic law.

Similar Conventions have been adopted to deal with nuclear terror, financing terrorists, holding hostages, and bombing. These Conventions are aimed at individual terrorists, not at member nations. Their goal is not to identify international terrorism as a specific offense, but rather to identify various kinds of conduct used by terrorists or that supports terrorists and to require member nations to make such conduct criminal.

The United States has a definition of international terrorism in 18 U.S.C. § 2331(1). International terrorism is defined as violent acts that would be crimes in the United States, which are intended to

1. Intimidate or coerce a civilian population
2. Influence government by intimidation or coercion
3. Affect government by mass destruction, assassination, or kidnapping

Because of the constitutional prohibition against vagueness (see Chapter 1), terrorism as an offense must be clearly defined under U.S. law.

Terrorists differ from other criminals because they commit their crimes to send a political or ideological message or to retaliate for a wrong that they believe has occurred. They may seek a change, such as people who wanted to stop abortions by burning down clinics and shooting doctors.

Terrorism is also a form of warfare that has existed since wars have been waged and conducted. Northern Ireland witnessed terrorism for more than a half century. To people who are believers in the cause of the terrorist, the terrorist may be viewed as a hero. To the great majority of the civilized world, terrorists are criminals.

Early Terrorist Acts

Anarchists (people who oppose organized government) historically have used terrorism to convey their political message. In May 1886, after local anarchists printed and distributed fliers calling for workingmen to arm themselves, a bomb exploded at a Haymarket Square rally in Chicago. It killed a policeman and wounded several other people. Two editors of an anarchist newspaper and six other men were convicted of conspiracy in the bombing; four were hanged.

In the years between 1894 and 1900, four European heads of state (the president of France, the prime minister of Spain, the empress of Austria, and the king of Italy) were assassinated by anarchists. President McKinley's assassin, an anarchist, stated in 1901 before his execution, "I don't believe we should have any rulers. It is right to kill them."[1]

World War I was started, in part, by the assassination of Archduke Franz Ferdinand, the heir to the Austrian throne, by a terrorist in 1914 in Sarajevo, Bosnia. That war, which lasted for four years, caused the deaths of more than 20 million people.

Terrorism in Recent Years

Terrorism has become a global problem, and all nations have become vulnerable to terrorist attacks. In September 2004, more than 300 people, mostly children, were killed by terrorists in Beslan, Russia, in a protest against Russian policy in Chechnya. In Madrid, Spain, in March 2004, more than 200 people were killed when terrorists exploded bombs on crowded city commuter trains.

Because of these and other terrorist attacks, police all over the world are on almost constant alert for suspected terrorist activities. The United States in particular is a stated target of the terrorist group al Qaeda, a radical Islamic fundamentalist group.

Other recent terrorist acts include:

- During the 1980s and 1990s antiabortion extremists bombed, shot at, and torched abortion clinics in the United States and Canada, killing six people.
- The Unabomber (Theodore Kaczynski), during a 17-year period, killed 3 people and injured 28 others by sending letter bombs through the mails.
- Deadly anthrax spores were sent through the mails in many eastern U.S. cities in 2001, killing 5 people.

- In 1995, the deadly nerve gas sarin was released in a Tokyo subway, killing 27 people and injuring more than 5,000 others. The leader of a religious cult responsible for the attack was sentenced to death in 2004.[2]
- One month after the Tokyo attack, the Federal Building in Oklahoma City was destroyed by a massive bomb, killing 168 people and injuring more than 500 others. Timothy McVeigh received the death sentence for this crime and was executed in 2001. Terry Nichols was sentenced to life in prison for his role in the bombings.[3]
- In 2007, six Muslim men were arrested and charged with planning an attack on Fort Dix, a federal military base in New Jersey. Using automatic weapons and hand grenades, they planned "to kill as many soldiers as possible." Authorities also thwarted a 2003 plot to blow up the Brooklyn Bridge.[4]

The October 1987 issue of the *FBI Law Enforcement Bulletin* listed extremist groups operating in the United States in that period:

- *Leftist Groups:* Weather Underground, Black Liberation Army, and Black Panther Party were listed as responsible for 21 bombings and 16 terrorist acts.
- *Antigovernment and White Supremacist Groups:* Committed four bombings, armed robberies, assaults, and one murder.
- *Puerto Rican Leftist Groups:* Committed 70 terrorist acts—bombings, assassinations, armed robberies, and rocket attacks—mostly in Puerto Rico.
- *Jewish Extremists:*[5] Committed 20 incidents of terrorism, including extortion and threats against persons deemed anti-Semitic or "overtly supportive of Arab efforts … not in the interests of Israel." Two members of the Jewish Defense League were arrested in Los Angeles in December 2001 and charged with conspiracy to bomb a Los Angeles mosque and the office of a U.S. congressional representative whose grandfather was Lebanese.[6]
- *Supporters of Terrorism in Northern Ireland:* Committed the following crimes in the United States:
  - Illegal purchase and transport of weapons to Northern Ireland
  - Illegal transfers of money to Northern Ireland
  - Assisting in the illegal presence of Irish terrorists in the United States to obtain funds and weapons

The Antiterrorism and Effective Death Penalty Act (AEDPA), 18 U.S.C. § 1332, and the USA Patriot Act, 18 U.S.C. § 2239, make it a federal crime to provide "material support or resources" to an organization that has been designated and named as a foreign terrorist organization in the United States by the State Department. The penalty for violation of these statutes is imprisonment for up to 15 years or, if a death occurs, for life. In addition, triple civil damages may be recovered from any organization that provides support to a terrorist organization that injures or kills a U.S. citizen.[7]

The following terrorist acts were committed by Muslim extremists against the United States:

- Pan Am Air Flight 103 was blown out of the sky over Lockerbie, Scotland, killing all 259 on board the aircraft and 11 people on the ground.
- Seven U.S. overseas buildings were bombed between 1985 and 1998. More than 150 people were killed and more than 2,000 injured. Many of the dead and injured were foreign nationals working for the United States. The locations were U.S. Air Force bases in Spain and Germany, a military training center and barracks in Saudi Arabia, and the U.S. embassies in Kenya, Tanzania, and Peru.
- A truck bomb damaged the New York World Trade Center in 1993, killing six people and injuring more than a thousand. Sheik Omar Rahman and nine other

"THE TORTURE ACT"

In 1988 President Reagan signed the United Nations Convention against Torture (CAT). This international agreement was aimed at persons who, under color of law, torture individuals for political or other reasons. Nations who sign the convention agree to prosecute persons who violate international law by torturing others. In 1994 Congress passed the Torture Act, 18 U.S.C. § 2340-2340A, which punishes any person who subjects another person to torture, defined as the intention, under color of law, to inflict severe pain or suffering. Federal courts are given jurisdiction to try persons charged under this statute for torture that occurred outside the United States if they are U.S. nationals, or were arrested within the United States.

The first person charged under the Torture Act was Charles Arthur Emmanuel, a/k/a Charles Taylor, Jr. Emmanuel was the son of Charles Taylor, a Liberian citizen living in the United States, where Emmanuel was born. In the 1990s Taylor led a revolt that ended with his election to the Liberian presidency in 1997. From 1999 to 2003, when Taylor was forced out of Liberia, Emmanuel was his father's security chief. In that position he tortured and killed Liberian citizens, and he was known as "the demon." After his father left Liberia, Emmanuel returned to the United States in 2006, where he had lived with his mother under the name of Belfast. He was arrested in Florida that year and charged under the Torture Act. He was convicted and sentenced to 97 years in prison. His conviction and sentence were affirmed in *United States v. Belfast*, 2010 WL 2787629 (11th Cir. 2010).

Emmanuel's father, Charles Taylor, was extradited to The Hague, Netherlands, where in the summer of 2010 he was on trial for various charges of violation of international law.

---

militant Muslims were convicted of this attack and also a conspiracy that, if carried out, would have destroyed the United Nations building and many other New York City landmarks.

- The U.S. naval ship *U.S.S. Cole* was seriously damaged in a suicide bombing in the Middle Eastern country of Yemen, killing 17 sailors and injuring 39.
- On September 11, 2001, four U.S. commercial aircraft were hijacked by 19 terrorists. Two planes loaded with jet fuel were deliberately flown into the 110-story twin towers of the New York World Trade Center, causing the towers to collapse. One aircraft was flown into a section of the Pentagon in Washington, D.C., while passengers in the fourth aircraft fought with the hijackers, causing the plane to crash in Pennsylvania. More than 2,800 people died in these attacks. In 2006, Habib Zacarias Moussaoui was convicted in U.S. federal court for conspiring and aiding the 9/11 attacks and was sentenced to life in prison without parole. He is currently incarcerated at the Federal ADX Supermax prison in Florence, Colorado. Khalid Sheikh Mohammed, believed to be the ringleader of the 9/11 terrorists, is in federal custody and awaiting trial on terrorist charges.

≡ Criminal Charges Against Terrorists

After the 1995 terrorist attack that destroyed the Oklahoma City Federal Building, Congress enacted the Federal Antiterrorism Law, 18 U.S.C.A. § 1331, which gives the federal government jurisdiction to act against terrorism toward the United States, whether it occurs in the United States or elsewhere in the world.

Because the federal government has thousands of crimes in the Federal Criminal Code, terrorists have been and will generally be charged under existing federal or state criminal law.

Terrorism and Support of Terrorism Under State Laws

Over the years, states have also enacted many antiterrorism laws and other laws protecting the state and the state government. At least 24 states have adopted antiterrorism statutes. An example of a state statute is Florida Statute Annotated, § 775.30. Many states have adopted a definition of the crime of terrorism closely modeled after the federal definition. For example, the Alabama Criminal Code, § 13-A-10-151, defines the crime of terrorism as an act or acts intended to:

a. Intimidate or coerce a civilian population.
b. Influence the policy of a unit of government by intimidation or coercion.
c. Affect the conduct of a unit of government by murder, assassination, or kidnapping.

Many states passed statutes similar to the Alabama statute, punishing terrorist threats that are directed at civilian populations or governments. Michigan's terrorist threat statute, MCL 750.543m, makes it a crime to threaten to do a "terrorist act." A terrorist act is defined as a (1) violent felony, that (2) is dangerous to human life, and (3) is intended to intimidate or coerce a civilian population or influence a government by coercion or intimidation. In *People v. Osantowski*, 748 N.W.2d 799 (Mich. 2008) the Michigan Supreme Court upheld the conviction under § 750.543m of a high school student who sent e-mails to his 16-year-old girlfriend threatening to commit "mass murder" at his high school with guns and explosives.

States also have enacted statutes making it a crime to make a false report of a bomb or explosive threat with the purpose of frightening a group of people, or causing the evacuation of a building. In *State v. Tanis*, 247 S.W.3d 610 (Mo. App. 2008) the court upheld a conviction under the Missouri terrorist threat act, V.A.M.S. 574.115, of a man who falsely told police he had explosives in his truck and would use it to blow up a college building. The police evacuated the building, but a search of the truck revealed no explosives. The court affirmed his conviction, stating that the statute is aimed at actions which are intended to cause fear, and the evidence showed that was the intent of the defendant in making the false report.

Most state statutes also make it a crime for a person to support a terrorist act or organization. Actions that could constitute support include providing financial support, lodging, training, safe houses, false documents, communications equipment, weapons, lethal substances, explosives, personnel transportation, and other physical assets, except religious of medical material.

Other Possible Criminal Charges Against Terrorists

treason Acting to overthrow one's government, or in violation of allegiance to one's country.

Treason   **Treason** is the only crime defined in the U.S. Constitution. Article III, Section 3, provides:

> Treason against the United States, shall consist only in levying War against them, or in adhering to their Enemies, giving them Aid and Comfort. No Person shall be convicted of Treason unless on the Testimony of two Witnesses to the same overt Act, or on Confession in open Court.

Treason is a difficult crime to prove. In the history of the United States, treason has been charged only some 30 times. Aaron Burr was charged with treason in 1807 and, after a trial, was acquitted on a technicality. After World War II, Tokyo Rose, among others, was convicted of treason and served seven years in prison for urging American military personnel to desert during World War II.

sedition The crime of advocating the forceful overthrow of the established government. In this country, the Smith Act makes such advocacy a crime.

Sedition   All democratic countries have had to pass laws to protect their governments from overthrow by the use of force and violence. The **sedition** law now in effect in the

Zacharias Moussaoui, a conspirator in the 9/11 attacks, is shown at his booking in Culver County, Minnesota. He was charged with federal conspiracy offenses, and after extensive hearings and trial motions, pled guilty to the charges. Jurors determining the prosecution's claim for the death penalty voted to reject that penalty, instead recommending a life sentence. On May 4, 2006, the trial judge sentenced Moussaoui to six life sentences. He is currently a prisoner in the federal maximum security prison located in Colorado.

United States is the Smith Act of 1940, 18 U.S.C. § 2385. It forbids advocating the forceful overthrow of the U.S. government, distributing with disloyal intent materials teaching and advising the overthrow of the government by violence, and organizing or helping to organize any group having such purpose.

The seditious conspiracy statute, 18 U.S.C. § 2384, makes it a crime to conspire with another person to destroy by force the government of the United States. In *United States v. Rodriguez*, 803 F.2d 318 (7th Cir. 1986), *cert. denied* 480 U.S. 908 (1987), the court upheld the conviction under the seditious conspiracy statute of a member of FALN, a terrorist group seeking the independence of Puerto Rico. The court rejected the defendant's argument that the statute violated the Treason Clause, Article III, Section 3, of the U.S. Constitution. That clause limits convictions for treason by requiring proof of overt acts, and corroboration by two witnesses in open court. The defendant contended the seditious conspiracy act was "constructive treason," but the court disagreed, finding it served a different interest than the Treason Clause. The purpose of the conspiracy statute, the court said, was to combat "urban terrorism" and make government property and officials safe. It was not simply directed at those making war on the United States.

ANTITERRORISM LAWS ENACTED BY U.S. CONGRESS

Year	Popular Name/Citation	Purpose of Law
1903 and 1918	Immigration Act of 1903 and Act of 1918	Permitted exclusion of aliens advocating overthrow of government or affiliating with organizations who did so.
1940	Alien Registration Act and Smith Act of 1940	Requires deportation of aliens violating Act of 1918. Forbids advocating the forceful overthrow of the U.S. government, distributing with disloyal intent materials teaching and advising the overthrow of government by violence, and organizing any group having such purpose.
1950	Internal Security Act of 1950, 50 U.S.C.A. § 402	Further regulated actions of resident aliens.
1976	Foreign Sovereign Immunities Act, 28 U.S.C.A. § 1602	Permits civil lawsuits by persons injured by terrorists against nations supporting those terrorists.
1978 and 2000	Foreign Intelligence Surveillance Act of 1978 as amended by the Act of 2000	Gives government broad power to conduct electronic and other surveillance of suspected terrorists.
1984	Hostage Taking, 18 U.S.C.A. § 1203	Makes it a federal crime to take an American citizen hostage anywhere in the world if purpose is to coerce person or government.
1996	Antiterrorism Act of 1996, 18 U.S.C.A. § 2332(d)	Makes it a crime for U.S. citizens to support any group listed as a foreign terrorist organization by either money or with other meaningful assistance. Also makes it a crime to enter into a financial transaction with a nation designated as a supporter of terrorism.
1996	Iran and Libya Sanctions Act of 1996, 50 U.S.C. § 1701	Places sanctions on persons or nations that engage in trade with Iran or Libya.
2001	USA Patriot Act of 2001, 18 U.S.C. § 1993	
	Title III	Criminal penalties and forfeiture rules for money laundering by or for terrorist organizations.
	Title IV	New rules for protecting U.S. borders.
	Title V	Removes obstacles to investigating terrorism; pays rewards and uses DNA to identify terrorists.
	Title VI	Payments to victims of terrorism.
	Title VIII	Strengthens criminal laws against terrorism. New crimes governing attacks against mass transportation systems, harboring terrorists, or providing support to terrorists.
2006	18 U.S.C. § 2709 (as amended in 18 U.S.C. § 3511)	Requires communication systems, such as Internet servers, to give FBI access to records of communications by suspected terrorists.

The U.S. Supreme Court affirmed the conviction of an officer in the American Communist Party in the 1951 case of *Dennis v. United States*.[8] At that time, Communist literature distributed in the United States urged the violent overthrow of the U.S. government. Following the conviction of Dennis, the Communist Party stopped urging the violent overthrow of the U.S. government and now advocates change through peaceful and lawful means.

sabotage The crime of damaging or injuring national defense material or utilities with the intention of interfering with national defense.

Sabotage   **Sabotage** is made a crime by 18 U.S.C.A. § 2155. The offense forbids damaging or injuring national defense material or national defense utilities "with intent to injure, interfere with, or obstruct the national defense." In the 1987 case of *United States v. Johnson* (41 CrL 2205), the defendant was convicted of sabotage when he put a bolt in an airplane's engine intake because he was "angry," "upset," and "thinking about all of my problems." The defendant was an airman with the U.S. Air Force.

A person can be convicted under 18 U.S.C. § 2155 for any acts that obstruct or interfere with any national defense installation or material. In *United States v. Platte*, 401 F.3d 1176 (10th Cir. 2005) three Sisters of the Dominican Order were convicted under the statute for breaking into a Minutemen III Missile Site in Colorado. The defendants cut through a chain fence surrounding the property, and using ball-peen hammers they pounded on the rails that held the blast doors on nuclear missile silos. The court rejected their contentions that they did nothing that would have prevented the missiles from launching, stating that the statute required only that their actions interfere with or obstruct the national defense. Because the national defense includes training, the fact that the defendants' actions forced the virtual shutdown of the missile base for a period meant that their actions violated the statute.

▤ The Crime of Terrorizing (Terrorism by Threats)

The term *terror* means a state of extreme fear, dread, or fright. Crimes that create such a condition are sometimes labeled "terrorist" crimes or the **crime of terrorizing** in state criminal codes. (See discussion of assault crimes in Chapter 11.) Examples are:

crime of terrorizing A crime that creates a state of extreme fear, dread, or fright.

- The *California Street Terrorism Enforcement and Prevention Act* prohibits willful threats to commit a violent crime if the threat "on its face and under the circumstances in which it is made [is] so unequivocal, unconditional, immediate, and specific as to convey ... a gravity of purpose and an immediate prospect of execution." See *People v. Dias*, 1997 WL 18994(1997).
- The *Working Papers for the Proposed Federal Criminal Code* explains § 1614 and § 1616 (menacing in which a defendant uses threats to deliberately put another in fear):

The threat may be a prank, or may be made in anger; while there may be no intent to inflict actual injury, such acts can be intended to cause fear. Such deeds have been traditionally punishable as misdemeanors.

But there can be deeds deliberately designed to instill fear in a large number of people, or to so affect an individual as to disrupt normal life patterns. In short, the proposal conceives of a type of assault, in form of threat, which warrants more than a misdemeanor punishment.

Present Federal law already recognizes that some forms of threat can be quite serious.... These laws make no distinction, however, between the relatively harmless expression of anger and a threat more serious in its impact. The proposed statutes would permit differentiation between a serious and a relatively minor threat against an individual.

... [I]t is the making of such threats that will be illegal under the proposed statute, regardless of whether the defendant actually plans to carry out the threat.

THE CONTINUING BATTLE AGAINST TERRORISM

The many national and international incidents of terrorism, both attempted and successful, force authorities all over the world to maintain a constant state of vigilance against these attacks. The following reports show some of the incidents that received national and international coverage, the ways terrorists can be prosecuted, and international concerns about future terrorist attacks:

Failed Attempts to Ignite Explosives

In 2010 a terrorist parked a van loaded with explosives in New York's Times Square, and triggered the device. The explosives smoldered, but did not ignite. Nearby vendors noticed the van, and informed police, who broke into the van and disarmed the explosives. The driver of the van was quickly apprehended, and after talking freely to the police about his terrorist goals, pled guilty to criminal charges.

In 2009 a passenger on a commercial airplane attempted to ignite explosives he had concealed in his clothing. While other passengers heard a series of loud pops, the explosives did not ignite.

In 2008 a passenger traveling by airplane from Europe to New York attempted to trigger explosives concealed in his shoes. There was smoke but no explosion.

Incidents of International Terrorism

Nations all over the world have been the victims of attacks by terrorists groups. In one of the most deadly since 9/11, in 2008 10 Pakistani terrorists attacked India's largest city, Mumbai (formerly called Bombay), illustrating the brazen and deadly tactics terrorists employ. Armed with assault rifles and grenades, the terrorist entered the city on small boats, and for 3 days launched attacks against hotels and other targets in the city, killing as many as 164 people, including 6 Americans, before 9 of the terrorists were killed by police. A Chicago man, David Headley, pled guilty in March of 2010 to providing surveillance support to the terrorists. In exchange for an agreement not to seek the death penalty or extradite Headley to India, prosecutors obtained his cooperation in investigations of other terrorist actions.

In one of the longest, costliest, and most serious trials in English history, in 2008 a London jury convicted three terrorists of plotting to use liquid explosives to bring down in one day at least 7 airliners traveling from England to the United States or Canada. Other members of the conspiracy were convicted in 2010. The suicide bombers planned to carry "liquid bombs" made by injecting liquid explosives into soft drink containers to be carried unto the airplanes. London police discovered the plot only days before the men planned the attacks. Worldwide airport security was changed to adjust to this new threat.

Prosecutions for making terrorist threats under state criminal codes generally require proof that the defendant threatened violence against another, with the purpose of terrorizing that person. An example of the application of a terrorist threat statute in a terrorist threat prosecution is *Cobble v. State*, 603 S.E.2d 86 (Ga. App. 2004). The defendant stood outside his former girlfriend's house and shouted obscenities at her, in violation of a protective order obtained by the woman. Police were called and arrested the defendant. The defendant struggled with the arresting officers and was subdued by pepper spray, which required his hospitalization. While he was in the hospital, in the presence of officers, the defendant stated that when he was released he "would kill" the woman. He was then charged with making terrorist threats and was convicted. On appeal the defendant argued that he could not be convicted under the Georgia terrorist threat statute for two reasons: first, because the threat was never communicated to the victim, and second, because the statute specifically stated a conviction could not be based solely on the uncorroborated testimony of the person to whom the threat was communicated.

Prosecuting Terrorists

Both federal and state courts could have jurisdiction to try terrorists, if the terrorist conduct was a violation of their respective criminal codes. Most terrorist crimes are tried in federal courts, since federal procedures offer more flexibility in determining venue, or bringing in witnesses. Moreover, because federal courts have a long and successful history of trying difficult and complex cases such as espionage or those involving highly classified information, federal officials believe federal courts to be a 'good fit" for these cases.

Military courts may also be used to try these cases, where they involve a member of the military. Nidal Hasan, the army major charged with killing 13 people at Fort Hood in 2009, will be tried in military courts. Prosecutors have indicated they will seek the death penalty. Military commissions created to try "enemy combatants" may also try these kind of case, but not if the defendant is a citizen of the United States.

Placing Terrorists on the "Kill List"

The Central Intelligence Agency is permitted under federal law to maintain a list (called the "kill list") of enemy targets, and is authorized to mount attacks against those targets, This includes names of persons found to be enemies of the United States. If the person placed on the list is a United States citizen the CIA must get approval from the White House. Anwar al-Awlaki, an American born cleric hiding in Yemen has been placed on this list, based in part on his statements that "it is a religious duty to attack the United States." Anwar al-Awlaki is believed to have actively plotted and supported violence against the United States, and has been involved in more than a dozen terrorist plots, including the recent failed Times Square bombing plot. He is known to have had contact with Nidal Hasan, the army major discussed above, and in a statement posted on an internet web page praised Hasan's actions.

Concern Over Future Terrorist Attacks

The National Intelligence has stated that the United States, and other democracies, faces an enemy that has "no scruples about employing any weapon or tactic". This could include nuclear weapons. At a 2010 nuclear summit meeting President Obama and other world leaders voiced great concern about the prospect of terrorists using stolen or homemade nuclear devices to kill thousands of civilians in major cities.

The Georgia Court of Appeals disagreed. It held that it did not matter if the victim did not actually hear the threat; it was enough if the defendant made the threat under circumstances where he intended or knew the threat would be communicated to the victim. It also held that the defendant's actions in violation of the protective order were sufficient corroboration of his intent to carry out his threat.

≣ The 804 Terrorism Prosecutions from 2001–2009

In 2010 the Center on Law and Security of New York University School of Law published an excellent study entitled "The Terrorist Trial Report Card, 2001-2009". The study analyzed the public records or 804 terrorist prosecutions conducted during that 8 year period, and reached conclusions from those records. Some of the findings of the study appear below following the Rules of War box, used with the kind permission of the Center on Law and Security. A copy of the full study may be obtained by contacting www.lawandsecurity.org.

RULES OF WAR

Rules of war are a body of customs, practices, treaties, and agreements that most nations subscribe to for the conduct of wars openly declared against sovereign nations. President Abraham Lincoln began the codification of these rules in 1864, and since that time most nations have signed the international conventions adopting these rules. Under these rules, combatants in a war are liable for the violation of ordinary criminal laws, such as rape or theft, even if carried out pursuant to orders from a superior. Such combatants can be charged with violation of their own nation's laws or the laws of the nation where the crimes took place. Saddam Hussein, the former president of Iraq, was tried and convicted in an Iraqi court for violations of these laws.

The rules of war create three categories of crimes:

- *Crimes Against Peace*: These laws forbid the planning, commencement, and conduct of an aggressive war. The United Nations recognizes only wars fought in self-defense as lawful wars. Hermann Goering and other Nazi leaders were convicted at the Nuremberg war crimes trials of violation of this law.
- *Crimes Against Humanity*: These laws forbid deportation, enslavement, persecution, and extermination of groups of people based on their race, religion, or ethnic origin. These laws were the result of the concentration camps and slave labor camps used by the Nazis during World War II.
- *Traditional War Crimes*: These are traditional laws concerning rules of conduct of the combatants toward prisoners of war and toward civilians living in the war zone. After World War II, Japanese General Yamashita was convicted and executed for "failing to provide effective control" over Japanese troops who raped and killed Philippine civilians.

Where did the 804 persons charged come from and what was the conviction rate? The persons charged came from at least 47 different countries (there was no information on the home countries of about 20% of the defendants). The largest group indicted (273) were persons with U.S. citizenship. Next was Colombia, South America (98), Pakistan (60), the Palestinian Territories (22), Jordan (18), Iraq (14), Egypt (13) and the United Kingdom (12). The remainder came from a group of 39 countries.

What were the most common categories of criminal charges brought by the prosecutors? The crime of terrorism was charged in 244 of the cases, followed by racketeering (127), national security or hostage taking (102), fraud and false statements (77), drug charges (60), commercial fraud, embezzlement and theft (54), immigration violations (43) obstruction charges (9), and violent crimes (4).

What conduct constituted a violation of a "terrorist statute"? 244 of the defendants were convicted under terrorism statutes, which required proof of involvement with terrorism, which included terrorist conduct, knowingly or intentionally aiding a "terrorist organization", or acting in furtherance of a terrorist objective.

What conduct constituted violation of "national security statutes"? 102 prosecutions were brought under hostage talking, sabotage (including destruction of national defense material, premises or utilities), or possession or use of chemical weapons.

Were terrorism actions used for sentence enhancement purposes? Terrorism was also used for sentence enhancement in convictions under the following principal crimes: immigration violations (1); obstruction of an investigation (1); crimes of terrorism or national security (20).

What conduct did the study include under "domestic terrorism"? In this study "domestic terrorism" focused on white supremacy advocates, anti-abortion activists, animal liberation , and environmental terrorism.

How many prosecutions involved weapons of mass destruction (WMD)?   161 prosecutions alleged WMD charges. Under Federal law, 18 U.S.C.§ 2332a, WMD includes a broad list of weapons, such as "destructive devices" like explosives, grenades, or other explosives and poison gases. This list is larger than what the general public considers WMD to include, which is probably limited to nuclear, chemical, radioactive, or biological weapons.

Many of the violations occurred overseas against American military targets. Groups behind these violations were al Qaeda (22), FARC (71), Cambodian Freedom Fighters (1), the Free Papua (New Guinea) Movement (1), Ku Klux Klan (1), and Tamil Tigers (5). In 57 of the cases no affiliation was found. Narco-terrorists, covered by 21 U.S.C. § 960, were briefly mentioned in the study, and limited to 4 persons in Afghanistan charged with narco-terrorism.

≡ Financing Terrorism: Where Does the Money Come From?

Terrorists need money to operate. INTERPOL (the International Criminal Police Organization, located in Lyon, France) has said: "The frequency and seriousness of international terrorist acts are often proportionate to the financing that terrorist groups might get."

The 9/11 Commission Report[9] issued in 2004 found no evidence of any foreign government knowingly helping to finance the 9/11 attack. The 9/11 Commission found that most of the $400,000 to $500,000 used to finance that operation came from donations to "charitable organizations," which then funneled the necessary funds to the terrorists.[10] At least 19 terrorists lived and trained in the United States for a period of 18 months to two years before the 9/11 attack. Organizations that knowingly provide aid to terrorists violate 18 U.S.C. § 2339B, and also can be sued for civil damages under 18 U.S.C. § 2333(a) of the Anti-Terrorism Act.[11]

The shortage of financial support can affect the scope of a terrorist attack. In the February 2007 issue of the *FBI Law Enforcement Bulletin,* the 1993 attack on the World Trade Center is used to illustrate this fact. The terrorists in that first attack on the World Trade Center had plans to use larger bombs and also chemical and biological weapons that would hamper rescue efforts and increase fatalities. Because of a shortage of funds, they were unable to execute the attack as planned, which greatly limited the harm caused and casualties inflicted.

Terrorists frequently use other criminal activity to finance their terrorism, the FBI article states. So-called low-risk, high-reward crimes are favored by terrorists. These include drug trafficking ("if we can't kill them with guns, we kill them with drugs"), theft, and fraud crimes, such as identity theft, credit card, Social Security, welfare, and insurance fraud. In one instance, the theft of baby formula netted a terrorist ring $18 million during an 18-month period. Intellectual property crimes were also committed by terrorists, such as counterfeiting watches, selling fake driver's licenses, and pirating software. One terrorist group made $750,000 in one year smuggling cigarettes.

Stopping the flow of funds to terrorists is an extraordinarily difficult task. One major obstacle is the international source of funds. The 9/11 Commission stated that Saudi Arabian charities alone funneled hundreds of millions of dollars to jihad groups and al Qaeda cells over the last few years. There is little the United States can do to prevent such transfers.

For groups with assets within the United States, the Trading With the Enemy Act, 50 U.S.C. § 1702(a)(1)(b), permits the president to establish a "Specially Designated Terrorist List" and freeze assets of those groups or those who contribute financial support to the groups. The USA Patriot Act, passed after 9/11, includes a provision permitting the president to block assets held by any group or person being investigated for involvement with terrorist attacks.

Moving Money Into and Out of the United States

Moving funds into and out of the United States happens on a massive scale each business day and can be part of a lawful banking or business activity. However, it can also be illegal money laundering, or movement of funds in illegal operations, or transferring funds to terrorist groups for future operations.

Funds can be transferred by human couriers, a time-honored custom in many parts of the world, or it could be moved through high-tech electronic wire transfers of funds. Web pages on the Internet can be used to solicit funds, which can then be sent to terrorist groups. One large fund, the Benevolence International Foundation, used a website that appealed to Muslim donors to send money to the foundation. The director of the foundation, Enaam Arnaout, pleaded guilty to a count of racketeering in 2003, admitting he sent money from the foundation to support Muslim "fighters" in Bosnia and Chechnya. He was sentenced to 10 years in prison, and the foundation has been banned everywhere in the world.

Funds can also be transferred through the use of so-called informal value transfer systems (IVTS). An example of an IVTS is the ancient system, originating in India, known as Hawala. In a Hawala transaction a person in one location gives money to a representative of the network. The money is not physically or electronically transferred. Instead, a representative of the system in the location where the sender wants the money to go gives funds to the intended recipient. The advantages of the Hawala system are that the cost of the transaction can be lower than more traditional transfer methods, and there is virtually no paper trail for the transaction. The 9/11 Commission Report stated that al Qaeda cells used the Hawala system for moving funds in and out of Afghanistan, the headquarters of al Qaeda.

Illegal use of the Hawala system violates federal money laundering laws and could also violate provisions of antiterrorism laws. The case of *United States v. Anvari-Hamedani*, 378 F. Supp. 2d 821 (N.D. Ohio 2005), illustrates use of the Hawala system in violation of these laws. An Iranian doctor living in Ohio was indicted for money laundering and violating the federal International Emergency Economic Powers Act (IEEPA) based on transfers of money and goods to Iran. In Executive Order 13059, the president placed Iran on the list of designated countries that support terrorism and made any investment in business in Iran or commitment of funds to groups in Iran a violation. The defendant instructed Merrill Lynch to send funds from an account he had with that brokerage firm to persons in Iran. Merrill Lynch filed a Suspicious Financial Activity Report, as required under federal law, detailing the transaction. The FBI investigated and found that the defendant also sent funds to Iran through a Halawa system.

International Criticism of Aspects of the U.S. War Against Terrorism

The war against terrorism has been in some ways an international effort. The United Nations has adopted a number of Conventions aimed at specific kinds of terrorist acts, such as attacks on civilian aircraft or kidnapping of government officers. Member nations are expected to pass local laws to implement these Conventions. Prior to 9/11 the United States was mainly content to participate in these internationally sponsored efforts.

But after 9/11, the United States, together with some of its allies, began fighting terrorism without the formal cooperation of the United Nations. Some of the actions taken by the U.S. government have received criticism from other nations and their governments; chief of these is the war in Iraq. Other actions have also engendered controversy. They include:

- *Kidnapping and Abductions:* In 2007 both Italy and Germany issued criminal complaints and warrants against 39 Americans working in a U.S. program called "extraordinary renditions." Under this program, first used pursuant to a presidential directive by President Clinton in 1995, suspected terrorists are seized by U.S. agents and are transported to another country for interrogation. Many of the pre-9/11 "ghost detainees" were suspected al Qaeda operatives, and they were sent to Egypt

LAW ENFORCEMENT NEEDS CITIZENS' HELP TO DETER HOMEGROWN TERRORISTS

Timothy McVeigh, the man who masterminded the bombing of the Federal Building in Oklahoma City in 1995, appeared to be a "regular guy." He was a U.S. Army veteran who served with great distinction. He held a regular job after leaving the service and seemed like a man who believed in the ideals upon which the United States was founded. In fact, McVeigh had become deeply bitter about the role of federal agents in the Waco, Texas, action against the Branch Davidians, a religious sect, in which several members died, and the Ruby Ridge action against a separatist group that caused the death of a woman and a 14-year-old girl.

In 1995, McVeigh, with the help of Terry Nichols, constructed a massive fertilizer bomb and blew up the Federal Building in Oklahoma City. The attack killed 168 innocent people and injured more than 500 others. During the Vietnam War, radical students used a similar device to blow up buildings on the campus of the University of Wisconsin.

Constructing these bombs required the purchase of large amounts of materials that are known to be capable of destructive power. Nonetheless, no one reported anything unusual to the authorities until after the bombs were detonated.

In 2006, a Circuit City employee in New Jersey became concerned about a video he saw that showed men apparently training for combat. He called the police, and the FBI were able to place an informant with the group, which was, in fact, planning a terrorist attack on the soldiers at Fort Dix. After 16 months of investigation, in 2007 the FBI arrested the men and stopped the terrorist plan before it could be executed.

Also in 2006 the FBI received a tip on its web site that lead it to place two New Jersey men under surveillance for suspected terrorist plans of a "jihad" against the United States. The men were arrested in 2010.

Both tips were essential to the success of the investigations and that future help from the public in spotting "homegrown" terrorists is "not something that we would like. It is something that we absolutely need."

Because extremists like McVeigh can come from a large and varied pool of disaffected people, the help of the public in identifying potential terrorist threats is vital to the success of law enforcement efforts to curb "homegrown" terrorists.[a]

[a]See the *Chicago Tribune* article, "FBI Says Domestic Extremists Big Threat," May 13, 2007.

for interrogation. Since 9/11, persons detained under this program have been sent to several countries for interrogation, including Jordan, Syria, Morocco, and Uzbekistan. Critics of the program say it permits the United States to indirectly use torture to interrogate detainees, something forbidden under U.S. law and the United Nations Convention Against Torture. Supporters of the program contend it makes sense to send detainees to countries that know the detainees' language and cultural background.[12]

- *Secret Over-Flights of European Countries:* A European Union Parliament committee has objected to flights by U.S. military and civilian government aircraft over European airspace without prior approval from the countries affected. The committee stated that at least 1,245 secret CIA flights were made over Europe from 2003 to 2007.

- *Canadian Citizen's Treatment:* Canada, historically a U.S. ally, in 2003 participated with American agents in the seizure of a Canadian citizen in New York by American agents and transferred to Syrian authorities. The man was held for more than 10 months in Syria, where he stated he was subjected to torture. Though Canadian authorities denied any knowledge that the United States was planning to send the man to Syria, Canadian intelligence officials acknowledged they sent a list of questions for the man to American agents. The man ultimately was returned to Canada, where he was awarded $9.75 million in damages for his wrongful detention.[13]

Summary

- Terrorism is the use of unlawful force to coerce or intimidate persons or governments in the pursuit of political, social, or religious goals.
- International law did not clearly define terrorism. When the United States became a signatory on international conventions that addressed specific terrorist acts, Congress passed laws to implement those conventions. Because of the vagueness limitation on statutes, Congress was required to clearly define the acts that constituted terrorism and condemned under the conventions.
- The State Department is authorized to identify groups or organizations as terrorist organizations.
- The crime of terrorism under most state laws requires proof that a defendant took acts intended to (1) intimidate or coerce a civilian population, or (2) influence a government by intimidation or coercion, or (3) affect the conduct of government by intimidation or coercion.
- A terrorist threat is a threat to (1) commit a violent felony that (2) is a danger to human life, and is made to (3) intimidate or coerce a civilian group or a government.
- Rules of war are customs and practices followed by most nations in wartime and now the subject of

international conventions. They create three classes of crimes: crimes against peace, crimes against humanity, and traditional war crimes.
- Terrorists raise money for their actions both directly and indirectly. Some countries contribute directly to terrorists organizations. The U.S. presidents have the power to identify such countries and place them on a list of countries that support terrorism. Individuals contribute indirectly to terrorist organizations by giving money and support to phony "charitable" groups that support terrorists.
- Money can be sent out of the United States through normal banking channels, or by funneling the cash through international business organizations. It can also be sent by human carrier, such as the Hawala system used for centuries in the Middle East.
- An extraordinary rendition occurs when a person is seized in one country and then transported to another country for interrogation. The country to which the person is transported often has a relationship with the person, or the country permits interrogation procedures not permitted by the country where the seizure occurred.

Key Terms

terrorism, p. 450
treason, p. 454

sedition, p. 454
sabotage, p. 457

crime of terrorizing, p. 457

Case Analysis and Writing Exercises

1. How does government obtain a court order to identify electronic communications, such as cell phone use, of a suspected terrorist? Has the procedure changed since 9/11? See *In Re Application by U.S. For Order for Prospective Cell Site Location*, 460 F. Supp. 2d 448 (S.D. N.Y. 2006).
2. Since 9/11, federal law permits suspected terrorists/enemy combatants to be detained indefinitely by military authorities, usually without review by

civilian courts. (See Chapter 2.) What does it take to be an enemy combatant? Can an alien seized shortly after 9/11 be detained in a military prison without judicial review? See *al-Marri v. Wright*, 487 F.3d 160 (4th Cir. 2008). For the subsequent, and contentious, history of this case see *al-Marri v. Pucciarelli*, 534 F.3d 213 (4th Cir. 2008), and *al-Marri v. Spagone*, 129 S. Ct. 1545 (2009).

3. Federal law enforcement officers have the option of deportation when investigation leads to an alien in the United States providing support to a terrorist group. One threatened with deportation may bring his or her case before the Board of Immigration Appeals. What must the government (or the alien) prove if the charge is providing support to a terrorist organization? See *Singh-Kaur v. Ashcroft*, 385 F.3d 293 (3d Cir. 2004).

4. One frequent defense in a deportation case rests on the United Nations Convention Against Torture, to which the United States is a signatory. What must be shown by the alien threatened with deportation if this Convention is urged as a basis for nondeportation? See *Zheng v. Ashcroft*, 332 F.3d 1186 (9th Cir. 2003). Does that Convention make it possible for one held by the U.S. military to sue for alleged treatment in violation of the Convention? See *Renkel v. United States*, 456 F.3d 640 (6th Cir. 2006).

NOTES

1. After McKinley's death, President Theodore Roosevelt stated that anarchism was "a crime against the whole human race." The United States passed immigration laws that excluded anarchists from entry into the country.

2. See the *New York Times* article, "How Japan Germ Terror Alerted World," May 26, 1998. The article states that one of the Japanese cultists testified that the cult's plan was to kill millions of people throughout Tokyo and also at nearby American military bases, where thousands of American service people and their families live.

3. A jury found McVeigh guilty of all charges against him, which were the federal crimes of (1) conspiracy to use a weapon of mass destruction, (2) use of a weapon of mass destruction, (3) destruction by an explosive, and (4–11) the eight counts of the murders of the eight federal law enforcement officers killed in the blast. All three men were charged in federal courts for federal crimes.

   The third man, Michael J. Fortier, pleaded guilty to four federal charges and was sentenced to 12 years in prison. Because of his cooperation, this sentence was a reduction from the longer sentence he would have received. One of the federal criminal charges was "misprision of a felony." Fortier had known of the planned bombing but had not warned anyone. See Chapter 19 on the federal crime of misprision of a felony.

4. See the *New York Times* article, "Men Arrested in a Terror Plot Against Ft. Dix," May 9, 2007.

5. The Jewish group known as Kahane Chai was designated a foreign terrorist group by the U.S. secretary of state. In *Chai v. Department of State*, 466 F.3d 125 (C.A.D.C. 2006), the District of Columbia Court of Appeals upheld that designation, finding that the group was connected to murders of Arabs and to the bombing of an Arab school, and it was responsible for death threats against police officers investigating the school bombing.

6. See the *New York Times* article, "Followers of Rabbi Kahane Subjects of Terror Inquiry," December 16, 2001.

7. See *Boim v. Quranic Literacy Inst. & Holy Land Foundation*, 291 F.3d 1000 (7th Cir. 2002).

8. 341 U.S. 494, 71 S. Ct. 857 (1951).

9. The 9/11 Commission Report: Final Report of the National Commission of Terrorist Attacks Upon the United States (Washington, D.C., 2004).

10. See the article, "Dealing with Hawala" in the February 2007 issue of the *FBI Bulletin*, and the 9/11 Report.

11. See *Weiss v. Westminster Bank PLC*, 453 F. Supp. 2d 609 (E.D. N.Y. 2006).

12. See the *New York Times* article, "Italy Indicts 26, Many From C.I.A. in '03 Abductions," February 17, 2007.

13. See the *New York Times* article, "Canadian Court Limits Detention in Terror Cases," February 24, 2007.

CHAPTER 18

Organized Crime and Gangs

LUCAS JACKSON/Reuters/Landov

Street gang members in Los Angeles, California. The distinctive clothes and hand signals are factors that under most state laws can result in a finding that a defendant is a member of a "criminal street gang", and used as a sentence enhancement factor for crimes committed.

OUTLINE

Newburgh, New York, is a city of about 29,000 residents located just north of New York City. While it has called itself the "sixth borough," it was better known as "crack alley" in the 1980s for its incidence of drug use and crimes. That tradition has continued, and the city now leads New York in per capita homicides from drug- and gang-related activity.

In the early morning of May 13, 2010, more than 500 federal, state, and local law enforcement officers staged dozens of raids on residences of suspected gang members. After the raids, the U.S. Attorney for the Southern District of New York announced indictments on drug and gang charges against 60 suspected members of the Bloods gang, and 18 suspected members of the Latin Kings gang.

Gangs in Newburgh have been responsible for all but 2 or 3 of the 16 homicides committed in that city in the past 2½ years.

In this chapter we will study the state and federal criminal laws enacted to give prosecutors the tools to go after criminals who engage in criminal acts but who are protected by the nature of an organization engaged in a criminal enterprise. We will also see how those laws can be used to prosecute individuals like the gang members indicted in Newburgh, who commit criminal acts as part of a plan to further a criminal enterprise. Finally, we will study the limitations the Constitution places on those uses.

☰ Organized Crime and Criminal Gangs

Gangs of organized criminals have operated in the United States for over 200 years, and in Europe for much longer. Bands of criminals soon realized that working together greatly increased their chances of success.

In most periods of American history, the character of gangs was dictated by the environment. In the Wild West of the late nineteenth century, outlaw gangs traveling around on horseback specialized in cattle rustling or stagecoach robbery. At the same time, in the infamous Five Points section of New York (what is now Lower Manhattan's Chinatown), various gangs of Irish, Italian, or German immigrants practiced murder, prostitution, theft, and extortion. With the rise of the automobile in the 1920s and 1930s, gangs became mobile and could travel about the country, robbing small-town

---

ATTEMPTS BY CITIES AND STATES TO REGULATE GANG ACTIVITY

Cities and states have used a variety of laws in attempts to curb gang violence:

- Nuisance laws, both civil and criminal, are used to seize and tear down crack and other drug houses and to prosecute landlords who permit drug use by gangs in rented premises.
- Laws against the crimes of unlawful assembly, rioting, stalking, and curfew violation (see discussion in Chapter 9) are used to curb gang activity.
- Injunction laws are used to deter gang action. Because of its serious gang problems, the city of Los Angeles is seeking injunctions (court orders) against gang members that forbid a specific gang to gather, even in groups as small as two, in specified public places. In defending these injunctions, a Los Angeles city attorney states: "People deserve protection.... Gang members are terrorizing our communities." Penalties for violating the injunction include up to a year in jail.[a]
- Graffiti laws, cruising laws, and laws making membership in a gang a crime (found in a few states) are used.
- If the offense was committed by gang members, laws to increase criminal penalties can be used.
- Laws punishing parents for the gang behavior of their children.
- Laws making parents civilly liable for the criminal behavior of their children may be applied.
- Laws forbidding intimidation and threats (discussed in Chapter 9).
- Forfeiture laws such as those found in the Uniform Controlled Substances Act permit the government to seize the proceeds and profits of a crime, as well as cars, boats, airplanes or real estate used in the commission of crimes. In Los Angeles prosecutors have seized homes and businesses owned by members of the 18th Street gang which were shown to be the proceeds of or instrumentalities used in drag crimes, extortion, money laundering, and related crimes.
- Deportation of those who enter the United States illegally, or commit crimes while in the United States.
- Street gang terrorism and drug conspiracy laws may be used, such as Illinois Comp. Stat. Ch. 720, Section 5/12–6 (1998).

Many state and city loitering laws and ordinances criminalize specific acts, such as "overt acts or evidence of criminal intent" or "loitering for the purpose to engage in drug-related activities," which have been upheld in state courts. However, in *City of Chicago v. Morales,* 527 U.S. 41 (1999), the U.S. Supreme Court struck down the Chicago gang congregation ordinance as unconstitutional because it was too vague and did not give citizens fair notice of what was required of them to comply with the law. (See Chapter 1 on the "void for vagueness" doctrine.)

[a]See the *New York Times* article, "Gangs Without Borders, Fierce and Resilient, Are Confronting the Law," September 26, 2004.

banks. Indeed, it was the inability of the local police to coordinate efforts to apprehend gangs like the Dillinger gang that played a significant role in the creation of the FBI as a national crime-fighting agency.

The Prohibition period helped the spread of the most notorious gang in the twentieth century, the mafia. While the mafia had its roots in a much earlier period in Italy and Sicily, controlling the market in illegal alcohol sales during Prohibition made it possible for the mafia to branch out and control many other criminal endeavors.

In 2002, the U.S. Department of Justice, with the participation of about 2,000 law enforcement agencies, published a study of gangs in the United States.[1] The study, which was prompted by a 1996 report that identified more than 30,000 gangs with more than 800,000 members, focused on the nature and growth of violent gangs in the past 20 years.

The study concluded that most law enforcement agencies distinguished between "gangs" and "organized crime" associations by the nature of their organizations. Organized crime generally involved a highly structured leadership arrangement, designed in part to insulate those at the top from criminal accountability. These organizations generally have a chief or "don" who makes policy and issues orders, which are carried out by captains, lieutenants, and soldiers, all of whom are sworn career criminals.

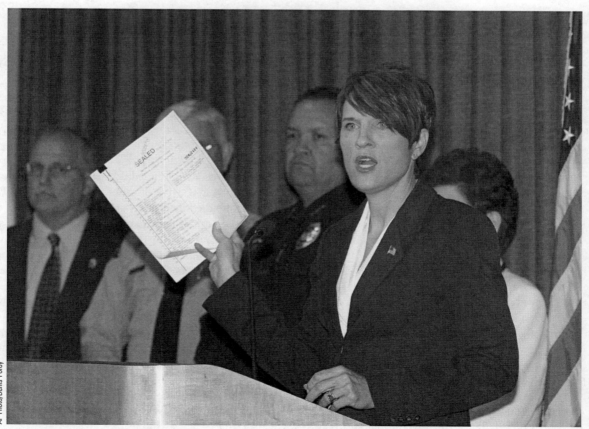

Laura Duffy, the United States Attorney in San Diego, California, appears at a news conference on July 23, 2010 to announce the indictment on conspiracy charges of 43 defendants for violation of federal RICO laws. The indictment that U.S. Attorney Duffy holds in her hand represents the results of an extensive investigation into the defendants' alleged criminal activities involving border violence on the American-Mexican border, and illegal drug trafficking.

Gangs, the study found, tended to be a far looser affiliation of criminals:

Most gangs are loosely knit coalitions of small, autonomous cliques. Apart from a general commitment to their "hood" and the gang lifestyle, the only unifying force is combat with outsiders. Gang leadership is usually decentralized, nonhierarchical, even situational; it is more a function of individual prowess and reputation than a formalized structure for making collective decisions. Leadership changes rapidly and may vary by activity.... The type of gang leadership varies from gang to gang and by geographical area.

Some gangs, and most groups of organized criminals, have long histories of criminal activities as groups. Others are recent entries into organized crime. The Russian mafia is an example of the latter group; the FBI in 2004 identified it as the fastest-growing criminal organization in the United States. Terrorist groups would probably be classified as criminal organizations because they generally have more structured leadership organizations.

Law enforcement agencies participating in the study reported that

the delinquent gang was the most typical gang in their jurisdiction ... consisting primarily of juveniles who engaged in vandalism and other delinquent behavior.... Yet police reported that most gangs, regardless of type, participated in many different types of crimes.

WILL THE MOB EVER GET OUT OF THE CRIME BUSINESS?

The criminal organization known as the mafia in most parts of this country has many different names. In Chicago, it is called the outfit. In New York it is called the family; in Italy and Sicily it is known as la cosa nostra ("our thing"). In other areas, it is referred to as "bent noses," or simply thugs. The mob is perhaps a suitable generic name for this band of criminals.

Over the years, large American cities such as New York and Chicago have experienced hundreds of mob-related killings, most of them unsolved. In 2005, indictments were handed down against top Chicago mobsters, charging them with 18 Chicago-area murders. In June 2007, five of these mobsters went to trial for these murders; of the others indicted, six pleaded guilty, one died, and one was too ill to be tried.

The trial received national attention, as hit men, bookies, career burglars, gamblers, pornographers, and other street associates of the defendants testified about their dealings with the outfit. A key witness was Nick Calabrese, a "made" member of the outfit. He confessed to participating in 14 of the murders, and he testified against his brother, Frank Calabrese, and other defendants. For this reason, the press labeled the trial as "The Family Secrets Case."[a]

It took years and millions of federal and state dollars to put this case together. Regardless of how it ends, many of the top Chicago mobsters will be removed from the positions of power. Will this be the end of the Chicago mob? Law enforcement experts say no. Younger up-and-coming members of the outfit will quickly replace the older members who disappear. An FBI spokesman stated that the outfit continues to have influence in vice rackets, labor unions, and political corruption and will continue to function in Chicago, though perhaps in a smaller capacity.[b]

The Italian government reported that mafia-related killings in that country declined to 121 in 2006, down from a high of 340 per year ten years previously. Authorities believe stronger law enforcement has forced the mafia to shift its criminal efforts to less violent crimes, such as money laundering.[c]

[a]See the *Chicago Tribune* article, "Mob Secrets Go to Trial: Murder, Juice Loans, Pornography and Street Gambling," June 17, 2007.
[b]See the *Chicago Tribune* article, "Younger Mobsters Ready to Take Over for Outfit's Old Guard," June 17, 2007.
[c]See the *New York Times* news release, "Italy: Mafia Killings Decline," June 21, 2007.

The membership and location of gangs varied greatly, the report found. Street gangs made up of delinquents were found in inner cities, suburbs, rural areas, and small towns. Gangs organized along ethnic or racial lines included Asian, Hispanic, Jewish, Russian, African American, and Irish. The nature of the activity, such as drug dealing, sometimes served as the identifying feature of a gang. Shoplifting, purse snatching, check forging, insurance fraud, and identity theft are examples of these kinds of gangs.

The report found that most gangs began as local groups that, if successful, expanded to nearby cities and states. If a gang was involved with illegal drugs or weapons, expansion included violence to achieve dominance. Criminal networks crossing state lines can be formed, which the report stated could use "modern weapons, communication technology, and transportation in their operations to control and expand their operations more effectively." Fights and violent clashes accompany these expansions ("turf wars"); in 2001 half of all the homicides in Los Angeles and Chicago were gang-related.

The waves of immigrants coming to the United States since the 1970s, especially from Asian, Latin American, and eastern European nations, have changed the membership of old gangs and caused the creation of many new gangs.

The youth gang known as the Bloods has demonstrated that recruiting new members is possible, including from the populations in prisons and jails. The name Bloods reflects the fact that blood must be spilled for one to become a new member, and blood will be spilled if a member tries to leave the gang. The blood spilled is frequently that of an innocent passerby, slashed by a gang member in a random act of violence.

Some gangs are extremely large. The Black Gangster Disciples (BGD) gang, for example, is reported to have as many as 30,000 members heavily involved in drug trafficking. The Latin Kings have an estimated membership of 5,000 to 15,000. Gangs continue to grow despite the criminal convictions or deaths of key leaders.

In January 2009 the Department of Justice published the 2009 National Gang Threat Assessment, based on statistics gained from law enforcement jurisdictions from all 50 states. Based on those reports, the Threat Assessment concluded:

- There are about one million gang members nationwide. Of those, about 900,000 are in communities, and 147,000 incarcerated.
- 58 percent of law enforcement agencies reported that gangs were active in their jurisdictions in 2008.
- Gang members are leaving urban centers and expanding into suburbs. They are also becoming more active in the southeastern United States.
- In the Pacific region of the country, which includes Los Angeles, there are about 6,900 gangs, with 237,000 members. Police reports show that in some parts of that region, gangs are responsible for 80 percent of all criminal activity.

In 2008 the city of Chicago launched a concentrated attack on gangs and gang-related crime, including the hiring of 400 officers to form a special unit to work with communities to reduce violence. While these efforts resulted in the arrest and conviction of many gang leaders, the approximately 70 gangs located in Chicago still have an estimated 100,000 members. Moreover, these members tend to be younger, most under 20 years of age, and more violent. In 2009, over 60 percent of the homicides in Chicago were gang-related. One part of the South Side of Chicago has been called "kill town" because of a recent rash of gang killings.

The Police Department of the city of Los Angeles reported that in 2008 there were 6,877 gang-related crimes committed in Los Angeles; 167 of those crimes were homicides. Recruiting younger members from schools and illegal immigration has helped make gangs like the Mara Salvatruchas and the 18th Street Gang two of the fastest growing gangs in the United States, with branches and operations as far east as Washington,

D.C., New York State, and North Carolina. Former Los Angeles Police Chief William J. Bratton refers to gangs as "domestic terrorists" and urges that gang problems receive top priority from state and federal authorities.[2]

Federal and State Laws Passed After 1970 to Fight Organized Crime

Prior to 1970, federal and state criminal codes did not have effective laws to penetrate the code of silence that insulated organized crime leaders from prosecution. Because lower-ranking gang members actually committed most crimes under orders from above, the lack of success in linking crimes to the leaders meant that they were rarely prosecuted. Indeed, the long-time director of the FBI, J. Edgar Hoover, went so far as to deny the existence of the mafia, a denial that mystified much of the population that saw and read reports of horror stories of mafia crime.

A well-known mafia leader, Al Capone, enjoyed a reputation as a vicious killer, yet he was ultimately convicted not of murder but of income tax evasion, and he was sentenced to 11 years in prison.[3] Other crime leaders saw the danger presented by prosecutions for tax evasion, and instituted what we now call money laundering (which was made a separate crime in 1986) to obscure or eliminate any paper trail linking illegal gains to the crime bosses who reaped those gains.

In the federal and state fight against organized crime, 1970 marked the beginning of a concentrated effort against criminal organizations like the mafia. Two important federal statutes were the **Racketeer Influenced and Corrupt Organizations Act (RICO)** and the **Continuing Criminal Enterprise Statute (CCE)**. The state laws often had similar titles, such as Organized Crime Control Act or Offenses Concerning Racketeering.

The RICO laws, and the similar state laws commonly known as "little RICO" laws, were drafted to enable prosecutors to focus on the conspiratorial nature of organized crime. That is, the statutes made individuals, groups, and organizations criminally liable for multiple criminal acts that established a pattern of criminal activity.

The federal and state RICO laws generally require the government to prove that the defendants committed or conspired to commit acts of racketeering, called "predicate acts." The list of criminal acts that qualify as predicate acts is very long in both federal and state RICO statutes, including drug trafficking, violent crimes, witness tampering, mail or wire fraud, and illegal gambling. To obtain a RICO or "little RICO" conviction, the prosecution must prove:

- That the enterprise existed and was engaged in racketeering activity
- Two or more incidents of racketeering conduct "that have the same or similar intents, results, victims, or methods of commission" (Fla. Stat. § 895.02)
- That the defendants in the criminal action were members of the racketeering enterprise
- That the racketeering conduct by the defendants was committed for the purpose of maintaining or advancing their positions in the racketeering enterprise

The RICO and CCE laws, both federal and state, are written very broadly and permit convictions for more than a half dozen separate and distinct racketeering crimes.[4] Each year hundreds of criminal and civil prosecutions under the RICO laws are brought in the United States, for a wide variety of criminal violations. RICO has been successfully used to stop illegal activities by anti-abortion groups, violations by brokers and traders on stock exchanges, Taft-Hartley violations, porn shop violations, Medicare and public assistance frauds, and many other illegal acts.

RICO The Racketeer Influenced and Corrupt Organizations Act. Passed by Congress to enable prosecutors to charge all people engaged in unlawful activity who own or invest in an enterprise that affects interstate commerce.

Continuing Criminal Enterprise Statute (CCE) Federal law making prosecution possible for those whose actions enable a criminal enterprise to function, whether or not those same people can be proved to have performed specific criminal acts.

MAKING GANG MEMBERS PAY

Crime, it is said, doesn't pay. Most states have statutes that try to do the same for gang membership by increasing the penalty for crimes that are committed by gang members. The following cases are illustrative of these statutes:

- New York has a "gang assault" statute which elevates an assault into a class B felony if the assault is "aided by two or more persons actually present" and causes serious physical injury. In *People v. Sanchez*, 921 N.E.2d 570 (NY 2009) the court upheld a conviction under the gang assault statute even though the prosecution did not prove the persons aiding the defendant intended to cause serious bodily injury.
- Most states have statutes that elevate the seriousness of an offense if the defendant is a member of a "criminal street gang." The Texas statute VTCA Penal Code § 71.02 elevates the offense to the next level if it is proved the defendant was a member of a criminal street gang. See *Coleman v. State*, 2010 WL 2741534 (Tex. App. 2010). California's statute, Cal. Penal Code § 186.22, provides for sentence enhancements of 1 to 10 years, depending on the nature of the underlying offense, if the defendant is a member of a criminal street gang, or acts to further the interests of a criminal street gang. Both state statutes define "criminal street gang" in a similar manner: a criminal street gang is a group of 3 or more persons who have a common name or symbol, have as a primary purpose the commission of crimes, and who have a pattern of criminal activity. In *People v. Bragg*, 75 Cal. Rptr. 3d 200 (Cal. App. 2008) the court upheld sentence enhancements under the statute for a defendant who attempted to murder a rival gang member. The court said the prosecution need not prove the defendant was a current member of the gang, but only that his actions were taken to further the interests of the gang.
- Minnesota § 609.229 provides for sentence enhancements of up to 10 years if the underlying offense is a felony and was committed "for the benefit of a gang," with a definition of gang similar to the definition of a criminal street gang in the Texas and California statutes.
- Street gang membership is also relevant in juvenile courts. Under Florida law, F.S.A. § 985.433, a court making a disposition order for a juvenile adjudicated a delinquent must take into consideration the fact that the juvenile is a member of a street gang.

RICO laws target membership in a "criminal enterprise." In *Boyle v. United States*, 129 S. Ct. 2237 (2009) the U.S. Supreme Court considered the meaning of "enterprise" for a conviction under the federal RICO law, 18 U.S.C. § 1962. The defendant was one of a group of criminals who robbed bank night deposit boxes. They did this over a period of several years. However, the group had no leader, no hierarchy, no long-term plan, and no formal structure. The defendant appealed his conviction under § 1962, claiming he did not belong to a "criminal enterprise."

The Supreme Court concluded he did. While the Court agreed an "enterprise" under the RICO act must have an ascertainable structure, it need not have a formal or business structure. It was enough that a group was an "association in fact" with a common purpose, and with some longevity. The Court rejected the defendant's claim that to be an "enterprise" the group must have a leader or a manager. It compared the RICO act to the illegal gambling act, 18 U.S.C. § 1955(b) and the Continuing Criminal Enterprise act, 21 U.S.C. § 848 (c), which each have a requirement that the enterprise have an owner, supervisor, or other manager. Because the RICO act says nothing about owners or organizers, the Court concluded a "criminal enterprise" includes an informal group with a common purpose, even if no structural hierarchy exists within the group.

Limits on Federal Jurisdiction and RICO Prosecutions

The federal RICO statute permits federal prosecutions based on criminal acts that would normally fall under state criminal jurisdiction. (See Chapter 2 of this text.)

Federal jurisdiction is possible under RICO if the underlying acts affect interstate commerce, because Congress has the authority to pass laws, including criminal laws, to regulate interstate commerce. However, if the underlying predicate acts do not affect interstate commerce, the federal government has no jurisdiction over those crimes and cannot charge defendants under the RICO law. *Waucaush v. United States*, 380 F.3d 251 (6th Cir. 2004), is an example of a case where a Federal Court of Appeals held the predicate acts did not affect interstate commerce.

The defendant Waucaush was a member of a Detroit, Michigan, street gang called the Cash Flow Posse (CFP). In CFP's effort to control its turf from encroachment by rival gangs, the government alleged that members of the CFP murdered members of those other gangs. Waucaush and other gang members were charged with violation of the RICO laws. The indictment identified the gang as the criminal enterprise but included only the murders and other acts of violence as the predicate acts.

Waucaush initially pleaded guilty to the RICO charges, but after his conviction, two U.S. Supreme Court decisions were announced that potentially placed restrictions on the ability of Congress under the Commerce Clause to make the RICO laws applicable to criminal acts. In *United States v. Morrison*, 529 U.S. 598 (2000), the Court held that Congress could pass a law regulating conduct that did not have a direct interstate element only if the conduct had an economic effect on interstate commerce. In *Jones v. United States*, 529 U.S. 848 (2000), the Court held that the arson of a private residence did not affect interstate commerce, even though it was insured by an out-of-state entity. Based on these decisions, Waucaush sought to retract his guilty plea and have the charges against him dismissed. Charges against other defendants, who had not been sentenced when these decisions came down, had already been dismissed.

The court of appeals held that the murders and other violent acts were not by themselves sufficient to sustain federal jurisdiction under the Commerce Clause. Where a gang is not involved in economic activity, RICO requires a criminal enterprise that substantially affects interstate commerce, the court held.

Violent crimes can be prosecuted under RICO only if they are done for the purpose of furthering the criminal enterprise. Because the CFP was engaged in no proven economic activity, such as drug dealing, gambling, or credit card fraud, the murders were not undertaken to further an enterprise that affects interstate commerce.

The court agreed that every person's death has an effect in some way on interstate commerce—"a corpse cannot shop"—but "we may not 'follow the but-for causal chain from the initial occurrence of violent crime (the suppression of which has always been the prime object of the States' police power) to every attenuated effect upon interstate commerce.'"

After *Waucaush* was decided, the Supreme Court issued its opinion in *Gonzales v. Raich*, 545 U.S. 1 (2005) (discussed in Chapter 2). In this decision the Court suggested that the Commerce Clause should be read broadly to give Congress power to pass laws regulating interstate commerce. That decision has persuaded at least one federal circuit court to reject the reasoning of the *Waucaush* court. In *United States v. Nasceminto*, 491 F.3d 25 (1st Cir. 2007), *cert. denied* 552 U.S. 1297 (2008), the court upheld a RICO conviction of gang members who, like the gang members in *Waucaush*, were not engaged in economic activity but merely focused on violence against other gangs. The court held that the activities of the gang had a de minimis effect on interstate commerce, in part because one of the gang members bought a gun in another state and brought it into his

MEXICAN DRUG CARTELS AND THEIR AFFILLIATES

Since 2006, when the President of Mexico announced increased efforts to stamp out drug cartels, Mexican drug cartels have waged violent battles with one another and the Mexican government to determine who will control the lucrative drug and contraband smuggling market into the United States. The U.S. Department of Justice stated in 2009 that the Mexican drug cartels "represent the greatest organized crime threat to the United States." The Justice Department also identified 230 cities in the United States and Canada (up from 100 cities in 2006) where the Mexican drug cartels and their affiliates "maintain drug distribution networks or supply (illegal) drugs to their distributors."

The Mexican government stated in 2010 that over 28,000 people have been killed since the drug crackdown was started by the government in 2006. Of those killed, 2076 were Mexican local, state, or federal police officers. The Mexican government has offered rewards of up to $2 million for information leading to the arrest of any of the known top drug kingpins, and up to $1 million for similar information on any of 13 named lieutenants.

Violence has spread north over the borders. Officials in Vancouver, Canada believe that drug traffickers are responsible for the increased shootings in that city. There have also been increased kidnappings and home invasions in border states like Arizona, as well as increased violence in other American cities, such as Birmingham Alabama, where several murders have been linked to drug cartels. In 2010 three American diplomats were murdered by drug terrorists in Ciudad Juarez, which is "ground zero" in the battle against drug cartels. See the New York Times of 3/15/10.

The Mexican government has thousands of federal troops in addition to the other law enforcement officers fighting the drug cartels in northern Mexico. On the American side of the border, thousands of Border Patrol officers, state and local police officers, and National Guard troops seek to enforce laws and maintain public order. States from Texas to California are affected by the turmoil, with Arizona suffering the most violence. Truly, as the New York Times opined in a 5/28/10 editorial, "Mexico is in a vicious fight to the death with drug cartels.

---

home state and that a de minimis effect was sufficient to satisfy the interstate commerce requirement. The court accordingly rejected the requirement of "substantial effect" applied by the *Waucaush* court.

≡ The Federal Witness Protection Program and the Crime of Witness Tampering

Organized crime leaders were often insulated from the violent crimes they ordered committed. As a result, prosecutors needed the testimony of witnesses familiar with the leaders' role in the organization to charge and convict those leaders. Moreover, the Sixth Amendment's Confrontation Clause required that a defendant be permitted to be "confronted with the witnesses against him."

Obtaining witnesses to testify against gang and organized crime figures has always been a problem, both because in many cases the witnesses were themselves gang or organized crime members who had sworn a blood oath of silence and also because of real fears of reprisal against the witness or his or her family. Threats of violence, bribery of witnesses, and extortion of witnesses and their family members were common methods criminals used to prevent witnesses from testifying.

In an effort to break these barriers to prosecution, Congress passed significant legislation in 1970 and 1982. As part of the Organized Crime Control Act of 1970,[5] Congress

witness protection program Established as part of the Organized Crime Control Act of 1970, this program provides new identities and relocation for witnesses and their families in both state and federal criminal prosecutions of organized crime.

witness tampering Criminal interference with someone who plans to testify in either a criminal or a civil trial.

established the **witness protection program**. This program provides new identities and relocation for witnesses and their families in both state and federal criminal prosecutions of organized crime. Since its creation, this program has protected more than 7,500 witnesses and 9,500 family members from fear of reprisals, enabling them to safely testify against gang and organized crime figures.

In 1982, Congress passed the Federal Victim and Witness Protection Act of 1982. This statute created the crime of **witness tampering** and punishes any person who by any means tampers with a witness, victim, or informant.[6] Tampering is a crime, whether the witness plans to testify in a criminal trial or a civil trial. The U.S. Supreme Court has held that the duty to testify and give information in both civil and criminal cases is inherent in being a citizen of the United States, even when witnesses fear for their lives because of such testimony.[7] These and other federal laws are designed to make it possible for witnesses to perform their duties and to convict gang and organized crime members.

In October 2004, Dustin Honken, a methamphetamine dealer, was convicted in the Federal District Court for Iowa of murdering five people: two were witnesses the government planned to have testify against him in a drug charge, one was the girlfriend of one of the witnesses, and two were the girlfriend's small children. He was charged with the murders as furtherance of a continuing criminal enterprise and witness tampering, both federal laws that permit imposition of the death penalty. Even though Iowa is one of twelve states that does not have the death penalty, the jury sentenced Honken to life imprisonment for the murders of the adults and sentenced him to death for the murders of the children. The Eighth Circuit Court of Appeals upheld his sentence, and the U. S. Supreme Court denied certiorari in December 2009, 130 S. Ct. 1011.

≡ The Crime of Money Laundering

money laundering The crime of disguising money obtained illegally by channeling it through legitimate commercial and financial transactions.

Money laundering is defined by the U.S. Department of the Treasury as "the process by which criminals or criminal organizations seek to disguise the illicit nature of their proceeds by introducing them into the stream of legitimate commerce and finance."[8] The Bank Secrecy Act of 1970[9] was the first attempt by Congress to prevent criminals from concealing or laundering money through banks or other financial institutions. The Money Laundering Control Act of 1986 created the crimes of money laundering and knowingly helping money laundering of the proceeds of criminal activities.[10] Because terrorists must conceal and launder money to achieve their criminal purposes, the USA Patriot Act of 2001[11] toughened laws prohibiting the concealment of money and laundering money for criminal purposes. U.S. banks dealing with foreign customers are held accountable under this law, sentences for cash smuggling are increased, and both civil and criminal penalties for violation of the law are enlarged.

Money laundering has been called the world's third largest business. Drug dealers, terrorists, and organized crime figures need to have money moved undetected through the world's financial systems. "Following the money" is one effective way for investigators to find the criminals who made the money. The International Monetary Fund estimates that money laundering activities account for between 2 and 5 percent of the world's gross domestic product, or about $600 billion annually.[12]

In addition to laundering money through legitimate businesses owned or controlled by them, criminals also use several other methods. In the July 2006 issue of the *FBI Law Enforcement Bulletin*, the article "Breaking the Bank" listed the following methods of money laundering and transfer used by drug dealers:

… some of the more common laundering methods include: the Black Market Peso Exchange, cash smuggling (courier or bulk cash shipments), gold purchases, structured deposits to or withdrawals from bank accounts, purchases of monetary instruments (e.g., cashier's checks, money orders, traveler's checks), wire transfers, and forms of underground banking, particularly the Hawala system.

The article points out that while drug money is the leading source of money laundering, persons laundering money gained from other criminal activity can also be prosecuted under federal law.

Transactions Covered by the Federal Money Laundering Statutes

Title 18 of the United States Code prohibits the following money laundering activities, among others:

- Section 1956: "intending to transport or transfer monetary funds knowing that the property represents the proceeds of unlawful activity."
- Section 1957: "knowingly engaging in a monetary transaction involving criminally derived property valued at more than $10,000."

Prosecutions under 18 U.S.C. § 1957 require only that the defendant engage in a transaction where he knew the money being transferred was over $10,000 and came from criminal activities. In *United States v. Johnson*, 450 F.3d 366 (8th Cir. 2006), the court affirmed the conviction of a defendant who accepted over $10,000 from a person to use in a down payment on a house, knowing the money came from illegal drug transactions.

Recent court decisions by the United States Supreme Court and Federal Courts of Appeals have addressed some of the issues raised in prosecutions under 18 U.S.C. § 1956, the principal money laundering statute. In *Whitfield v. United States*, 543 U.S. 209 (2005), the Supreme Court held that convictions for conspiracy to violate the money laundering statute did not require proof of an overt act. While the general federal conspiracy statute, 18 U.S.C. § 371, does require proof of the commission of an overt act in furtherance of the conspiracy, the Court held that when Congress leaves out that specific requirement, as it did in the money laundering statutes, it intended to exclude the necessity of proof of that element.

Prior to 2008, the Federal Courts of Appeals were split on the elements the prosecution must prove for a conviction under the transportation part of the money laundering statute. Section 1956(a)(2)(B)(i) states that it is a crime to transport certain funds into or out of the United States with a design "to conceal or disguise the nature, the location, the source, the ownership, or the control of the proceeds of specified unlawful activity." Some courts interpreted this provision as requiring proof that the defendant intended to give the transported funds "the appearance of legitimacy." See *United States v. Morales-Rodriguez*, 467 F.3d 1 (1st Cir. 2006). These courts reasoned that the "classic" example of money laundering was schemes designed to make illegal money look legal, using a "disguise" of some sort.

Other federal courts disagreed. In *United States v. Ness*, 466 F.3d 79 (2d Cir. 2006), the court of appeals held that conviction under the "transportation" money laundering statute did not require proof that the defendant intended to give the transported funds the appearance of legitimate wealth. The defendant, who operated an armored car company, transported proceeds from illegal drug sales to persons outside the country. He contended that he made no effort to pass the money as legal wealth and thus could not be guilty of "concealing" under the statute. The court disagreed, finding that the concealment element was satisfied because the defendant used "elaborate" methods attended by a high degree of secrecy in transporting the money.

The U.S. Supreme Court settled the split in the Circuits in *Cuellar v. United States*, 128 S. Ct. 1994 (2008). There, the defendant was caught in Texas on his way to Mexico carrying $81,000 of illegal drug money in a concealed compartment of his car. He was convicted under the transportation part of § 1956. On appeal, the Fifth Circuit affirmed his conviction, concluding that evidence the defendant made an elaborate attempt to conceal the money satisfied the money laundering requirements of a "design" to transfer funds to conceal their unlawful source. The defendant appealed to the Supreme Court, contending the prosecution did not prove he made any attempt to give the money the "appearance of legitimate wealth."

The Supreme Court held the prosecution was not required to prove the defendant tried to give the money the appearance of legitimate wealth. However, it also held that the prosecution under § 1956 had to prove that the defendant knew the purpose of the transportation of the money to Mexico was to conceal its unlawful origin. Simply proving the defendant concealed the money did not suffice to prove he knew the purpose of the transportation to Mexico was to conceal its source. "There is a difference between concealing something to transport it, and transporting something to conceal it." 128 S. Ct. at 2005. Because the prosecution offered no evidence on the defendant's knowledge of the purpose of the transportation, all the elements of § 1956 were not proved, the Court said, and reversed the conviction.

The Supreme Court also remanded the *Ness* case back to the Second Circuit Court, 128 S. Ct. 2900, and that court reversed the convictions under the money laundering statute, 565 F.3d 73 (2d Cir. 2009). In the later case of *United States v. Garcia*, 587 F.3d 509 (2d Cir. 2009) the court held that the financial transaction part of the money laundering statute, § 1956 (a)(1), also required proof that the defendant knew the purpose of the transaction was to conceal the unlawful origin of the money transferred.

18 U.S.C. § 1956 expressly prohibits using the "proceeds of specified unlawful activity" in financial transactions or transportation transactions. In *United States v. Santos*, 128 S. Ct. 2020 (2008) the Supreme Court held that the term *proceeds* in the money laundering statutes covers "profits" from unlawful activity, not "receipts." In *Santos* a defendant ran an illegal lottery in Indiana. He used receipts from persons "playing" the lottery to pay expenses, such as winning tickets, and kept the profits. He was convicted under the federal money laundering statute based on transactions where he used receipts from the unlawful activity to pay expenses. The government contended these transactions qualified as money laundering because the funds transferred were "proceeds" of the illegal lottery, and thus were "proceeds" under § 1956. The Supreme Court rejected the government's position, and reversed the conviction under the money laundering statute. Congress did not define "proceeds" in the money laundering statute, and the Court concluded either "receipts" or "profits" would fit within the meaning of "proceeds" as used in the statute. That being so, "Under a long line of our decisions, the tie must go to the defendant. The rule of lenity requires ambiguous criminal laws to be interpreted in favor of the defendants subjected to them." 128 S. Ct. at 2024. The Court also reasoned that because there were 250 "predicate" offenses that could produce unlawful proceeds, every time a criminal paid the costs of committing one of those crimes (such as thief renting a car to move his stolen property) a money laundering violation would occur. The Court did not think that was the intended result of the money laundering legislation.

Currency Transaction Reports and the Crime of Smurfing

With drug-trafficking revenues as high as $300 billion a year, many drug dealers and other criminals reap huge profits. A large amount of such criminal profits is spent purchasing expensive cars, homes, condos, jewelry, furs, clothing, and other luxuries.

Businesses and financial institutions in the United States are required to report cash transactions of $10,000 or more under the Currency Transaction Reporting Act (31

CASE CLOSE-UP

United States v. Haddad
Seventh Circuit Court of Appeals
462 F.3d 783 (2006)

Defendant Haddad operated a "mom and pop" grocery store in Chicago, R&F Grocery. Pursuant to an agreement with the U.S. Department of Agriculture (USDA), R&F participated in the USDA food stamp program. Under this program, eligible recipients exchanged food stamps for specified groceries. Recipients were issued a "LINK" card that operated as a debit card. At the first of each month a recipient's account with the USDA was credited with the amount of food stamps for which that person qualified. This LINK card could be presented to a participating grocery store, where a special point-of-sale machine would debit the recipient's account for the amount of groceries purchased. The USDA would then credit a designated account maintained by the store accepting the food stamps. Participating stores agreed not to exchange food stamps for cash.

After investigation by Chicago police, R&F was discovered to be exchanging food stamps for cash. Police observed long lines of customers standing at the entrance to R&F on midnight of the first day of the month, the time when their LINK cards were credited with the food stamp amounts. These customers entered the store and emerged later without groceries, but with cash.

Subsequent investigation of the bank account used by R&F showed that during a 30-month period more than $1,117,000 was deposited in that account. Expert analysis by a federal officer determined that all but $345 of the deposits were from the USDA, and that during the period of the deposits R&F sold only $45,000 worth of groceries to food stamp recipients. Thus, over a million dollars in the account came from illegal exchanges of food stamps for cash, the expert concluded. Haddad wrote checks to himself from that account in excess of $708,000.

Haddad was charged with money laundering under 18 U.S.C. § 1957, which makes it a crime to knowingly engage in a monetary transaction in criminally derived property over the value of $10,000, derived from certain specified unlawful activity, which included misappropriating money under the food stamp program. To satisfy Section 1957, the prosecution introduced two checks in the amounts of $15,000 and $16,000 drawn on the R&F account and payable to Haddad. He was convicted, and he appealed, contending the prosecution failed to prove the money laundering charge, because it failed to prove the two checks contained only funds from the unlawful activity.

The court of appeals affirmed the conviction. It noted that based on the evidence, it was clear that virtually all the funds in the R&F account on the dates the two checks were written came from unlawful cash exchanges. Moreover, the court held, even if other funds were commingled in that account with funds from illegal transactions, the government did not have to prove the actual source of each dollar taken from the account and transferred to Haddad. It was clear from the evidence that some part of the two checks constituted funds from unlawful exchanges, and that was sufficient to satisfy the requirements of Section 1957.

CTRs (currency transaction reports) Reports that businesses, banks, and financial institutions are required to file for cash transactions of more than $10,000. CTRs can help determine whether tax fraud or money laundering is occurring.

U.S.C.A. § 5311). The **CTRs (currency transaction reports)** filed by businesses, banks, and other financial institutions are used to determine whether tax fraud or money laundering is occurring. Further investigation could then uncover illegal drug dealings and racketeering.

Unfortunately, businesspeople who want to make profits sometimes cooperate with drug dealers and other criminals seeking to hide cash transactions. Car dealers, real estate agents, and jewelers sometimes illegally agree to structure a transaction. In a structured transaction, the buyer makes a series of payments in cash or cashier's checks of under $10,000 over a period of weeks. When the sales price is reached, the dealer or real estate agent turns the car or condo over to the buyer. For a $50,000 car, six or seven payments under $10,000 would be the structured transaction. This illegal practice is sometimes called "smurfing" and is made a crime by the Federal Money Laundering Control Act of 1986 (31 U.S.C. § 5324).

Section 5324(a)(3) prohibits "structured transactions" involving financial institutions. It states that "No person shall, for the purpose of evading the reporting requirements of section 5313(a) ... structure or assist in structuring ... any transaction with one or more domestic financial institutions." The U.S. Supreme Court defined "structuring" in *Ratzlaf v. United States*, 510 U.S. 135, 136 (1994) as any plan "to break up a single transaction above the reporting threshold into two or more separate transactions for the purpose of evading a financial institution's reporting requirement." In *United States v. Morales-Rodriguez*, 467 F.3d 1 (1st Cir. 2006) the court affirmed the conviction under § 5324(a)(3) of a vice president of a non-profit organization that provided benefits to police officers and fire fighters. The defendant received monthly checks from the organization's 18,000 members and deposited them in bank accounts. He then had the banks issue him hundreds of checks made out to cash for just under $10,000. Over a two-year period he received about $1.2 million dollars in this manner, none of which was reported anywhere.

Title 31 of the United States Code, which contains rules for monetary recording and reporting, requires in Section 5316 that a CMIR (currency or other monetary instruments report) be filed when more than $10,000 is taken out of or brought into the United States. Because illegal drugs are a major source of profit for many criminals and criminal organizations, law enforcement officers look not only for importation of illegal drugs but also for the money making the narcotics deals possible. These statutes enable law enforcement officers to "follow the money," if it is laundered in legal entities, and prosecute those engaged in the laundering activities.

Failing to file a report, or filing a false report, is a violation of Section 5316, and under Section 5317 the funds taken out of the country can be confiscated.[13]

☰ Other Criminal Laws Used to Fight Gangs and Organized Crime

The Travel Act

Travel Act Legislation that can be used to prosecute those involved in criminal activities that cross state borders or involve foreign commerce.

Title 18 of the United States Code, Section 1951, titled the **Travel Act**, can be used to prosecute those involved in criminal activities that cross state borders or involve foreign commerce. That act prohibits traveling in interstate or foreign commerce or use of the mail or any facility in interstate or foreign commerce with intent to:

1. Distribute the proceeds of any unlawful activity; or
2. Commit any crime of violence to further any unlawful activity; or
3. Otherwise promote, manage, establish, carry on, or facilitate the promotion, management, establishment or carrying on of any unlawful activity

Felony convictions for violations of the Travel Act have been obtained for interstate travel as part of a scheme to

- Bomb a homosexual bar[14]
- Travel with the intent to violate state law[15]
- Place illegal gambling wagers using telephones, which are included in the meaning of a "facility" under the act[16]
- Demand the payment of a ransom for the release of a person held unlawfully using a telephone[17]
- Travel to facilitate an illegal narcotics transaction[18]

Extortion

Both the federal government and the state governments have statutes making extortion criminal. The federal statute, known as the Hobbs Act (discussed in Chapter 14), permits prosecution under that act if the extortion can be shown to interfere with interstate commerce. The Hobbs Act defines *extortion* as "obtaining of property of another, with his consent, induced by wrongful use of actual or threatened force, violence, or fear, or under the color of official right" (18 U.S.C. § 1951).

A common example of extortion used by gangs or organized crime members is the threat of violence against a business that does not pay "protection" money. Often, a business owner is forced to pay one gang extortion money to protect the business from another gang. An example of the use of the "color of official right" is the city health inspector who threatens to charge a business with serious sanitation violations unless the official is paid off.

Bribery

Bribery has always been a problem for society. Using money, property, or "favors" to influence a public or private official to act in some agreed manner is a crime in all the states and under federal statutes. The problem has been acute in recent years because of the huge amounts of money controlled by criminal organizations. The presence of this money not only encourages criminals to approach officials to attempt to buy their actions but also serves as an illegal incentive for corrupt officials to solicit such payments.

An example of a state bribery law is Chapter 838 of the Florida Criminal Code, which makes it a crime to offer a bribe to any state, county, or city employee or official, or any employee or official of any political subdivision in the state. Both the person offering the bribe and the person taking the bribe can be charged under the statute. It is also the crime of bribery to offer money to "fix" an athletic contest (§ 838.12). The crime of "commercial bribery" (§ 838.15) is committed when a bribe is offered to any employee or agent of a business or another person; a trustee, guardian, or other fiduciary; a lawyer, physician, accountant, appraiser, or other professional advisor; an officer, director, or manager of an organization; or an arbitrator, adjudicator, or referee.

Bribery is a specific intent crime, and to obtain a conviction the prosecution must prove the bribe was offered with "corrupt intent," that is, with intent to influence the actions of the person to whom the bribe was paid. It is not necessary that the bribe be offered to influence a specific official act, but only that its purpose is to cause favorable results in the future. Thus, in *State v. Lopez*, 522 So. 2d 997 (Fla. App. 1988), a contractor's conviction for bribery of a building inspector under the Florida bribery statute was affirmed, even though the contractor asked only for "timely, prompt and cooperative efforts" on the part of the building inspector.

ILLEGAL GAMBLING IN THE UNITED STATES

During Prohibition in the United States (1919–1933), organized crime made huge profits selling illegal beer and alcohol to the many people who wanted to drink.

With the legalization of alcoholic drinks, organized crime turned to other illegal activities. It is widely believed that until the 1970s, illegal gambling was the greatest moneymaker for organized crime.

With the legalization of many forms of gambling in the United States and with the effective use of RICO, profits from gambling dropped rapidly, while the risks in illegal gambling went up. Illegal gambling is no longer as attractive to criminals as it previously was. Today, some forms of gambling continue to be illegal.

Distinguishing Illegal Gambling from Friendly Gambling

For a game of chance or a lottery to be illegal, it must violate a specific law or ordinance. Illegal gambling is often distinguished from legitimate commercial promotions by the fact that illegal gambling or lotteries have (1) a prize, (2) consideration, and (3) chance elements.

Therefore, a company that wishes to run a promotion can offer a prize if the customer does not have to buy anything or pay anything (no consideration). Or the contest can be legal if, instead of a chance element, there is a skill element (writing an essay or naming a new product, for example).[a]

The Federal Crime of Gambling: 18 U.S.C.A. § 1955

(b) *As used in this section—*

   (1) "illegal gambling business" means a gambling business which—
      (i) is a violation of the law of a State or political subdivision in which it is conducted;
      (ii) involves five or more persons who conduct, finance, manage, supervise, direct, or own all or part of such business; and
      (iii) has been or remains in substantially continuous operation for a period in excess of thirty days or has a gross revenue of $2,000 in any single day.

The Federal Professional and Amateur Sports Protection Act (Public Law 102-559) Prohibiting Sports Gambling

Section 3702 makes it unlawful for states or individuals to sponsor, operate, advertise, promote, or license a lottery, sweepstakes, or betting on one or more competitive games in which amateur or professional athletes participate.

Several exemptions are provided, including betting on parimutuel animal racing, jai alai, and some casino betting.[b]

---

[a]When is gambling a "social game" between friends, between neighbors, or in an office or factory pool? The court in the 1991 case of *State v. Hansen*, 816 P.2d 706 (Or. App.), cited Oregon Statute 167.117(4)(c):

"Social game" means:
   (a) A game, other than a lottery, between players in a private home where no house player, house bank or house odds exist and there is no house income from the operation of the social game; and
   (b) If authorized pursuant to ORS 167.121, a game, other than a lottery, between players in a private business, private club or place of public accommodation where no house player, house bank or house odds exist and there is no house income from *the operation of the social game.*" ORS 167.117(13). [Emphasis added.]

Friendly gambling (office or factory football pool, neighborhood poker game, and so on) can be distinguished from commercial gambling by some or all of the following factors:

- Where the game is played and who the players are
- Size of the pot
- Whether the house takes a percentage of each pot
- Whether the players bet against the house and the house acts as the banker, and whether the house acts as the dealer in such games as blackjack and craps
- Other factors such as the type of game played

[b]Sports betting is a big business in the United States, with billions of dollars wagered each year. Much of the betting is legal, but some of the betting could be in violation of state and/or federal law, and it also could be in violation of the National Collegiate Athletic Association rules.

Gambling scandals occurred in 1994 at Northwestern University and in 1996 at Boston College, where 13 football players were suspended.

In some states the prosecution must prove the bribed official was actually influenced by the bribe. See, for instance, Nebraska Revised Statutes § 28–917 (Reissue of 1995), though even there the defendant can be convicted of attempted bribery if the official action is not in fact influenced by the bribe; see *State v. Kao,* 531 N.W.2d 555 (Neb. App. 1995). Attempted bribery is often the charge, because in many cases of bribery of officials the official is a law enforcement officer posing as the official, or the actual official is cooperating with the police. For example, in the case of *United States v. Caceres,* 99 S. Ct. 1465 (1979), a defendant was convicted of attempted bribery of a federal tax agent. The agent was carrying a recording device that recorded the bribe and transmitted it to other law enforcement officials.

The Federal Foreign Corrupt Practices Act of 1977, 15 U.S.C. § 78, prohibits U.S. companies and individuals from making payments to win contracts from foreign governments. This law was enacted after it was disclosed that the Lockheed Corporation had paid the prime minister more than $1.9 million so that Japan would purchase Lockheed jet aircraft.

Kickbacks

It is not uncommon for parties in a sales transaction to agree that some part of the purchase price paid by the buyer would be returned to the buyer. In new car sales, for example, this practice goes under the name of a "factory rebate" or "dealer participation"

THE ADVANTAGES OF FEDERAL PROSECUTIONS

A December 2003 publication of the U.S. Department of Justice titled "Fighting Urban Crime: The Evolution of Federal-State Collaboration" (NCJ #197040) discussed the following advantages of federal over state prosecutions of criminals:

- *Federal Grand Jury:* This body can be called at any time, can be kept in action for as long as three years, can hear hearsay evidence, and is armed with national subpoena power. State grand juries have a shorter duration, "no hear-say" rules, and limited subpoena power.
- *Immunity:* Limited immunity for a grand jury witness conferred by federal prosecutors does not impede later prosecution of the witness for perjury, obstruction of justice, or contempt. Most states have only blanket transactional immunity, which provides less flexibility and leverage against potential witnesses.
- *Search Warrants:* Federal standards for obtaining a search warrant are generally lower than those of most states.
- *Preventive Detention:* The federal bail statute provides for preventive detention in a range of circumstances. State laws do not have such provisions.
- *Electronic Surveillance:* Most states require a higher burden of proof for wiretaps than the federal government.
- *Witness Protection:* In contrast to the well-developed federal witness protection program, most states do not have such a program.
- *Accomplice Testimony:* Federal rules permit conviction on the basis of an accomplice's uncorroborated testimony. State rules generally do not.
- Discovery: Federal rules provide that a statement by a government witness need not be made available to the defense until the witness has testified at trial. Also, the defense has no entitlement to a witness list before trial or to interview government witnesses prior to trial. Most state rules provide otherwise.

It should also be recognized that federal prosecutors generally have much more money than state prosecutors to spend on investigations and trials.

bonus. A bank may agree with a car dealer that if the car dealer sends credit customers to the bank for new car loans, then part of the interest charged to the customer will be returned to the car dealer. These agreements, commonly called kickbacks, are not all illegal, but many of them are.

In one famous case, Spiro T. Agnew, then vice president of the United States, was forced to resign the vice presidency because of kickback schemes he was involved in as governor of Maryland. Agnew forced engineering firms seeking government contracts to kick back a percentage of the contract amount to various people, including him. He also required every vendor selling cigarettes in the state capitol building to kickback five cents on every pack sold. In addition to being forced to resign, Agnew pleaded guilty to income tax evasion because of his failure to report the kickbacks as income.

Kickbacks can be charged under a state bribery law because the person receiving the kickback is soliciting payment to influence her or his actions. Kickbacks are covered under the Foreign Corrupt Practices Act of 1977 discussed previously, and kickback agreements between a contractor and a federal procurement officer or other employee are prohibited under the federal bribery and anti-gratuity statute, 18 U.S.C. § 201. However, any payment received by the official must be made "for an official act." In *United States v. Valdes*, 475 F.3d 1319 (D.C. Cir. 2007), the court held that a gratuity is an unlawful payment "for an official act" only if it was paid in order to influence some pending public question. In *Valdes* an FBI agent posing as a judge paid a District of Columbia police inspector $50 to run the names of four fictitious people through a law enforcement database to see if they had any outstanding warrants. The court held that the inspector's use of the government database was not an "official act" under Section 201(c)(1)(B), because it was not intended to have any effect on any pending charge or issue.

Mail Fraud

mail fraud A fraudulent scheme, no matter its purpose or method, that uses either private or public delivery service.

People who commit crimes involving fraud of another person can usually be prosecuted under state criminal fraud laws. However, when they use the U.S. mail or any other interstate delivery system such as Federal Express or United Parcel Service to defraud a victim, they can be prosecuted under the federal mail fraud statute (18 U.S.C. § 1341–1346). In 1994, Congress expanded the **mail fraud** crime to include "any matter or thing whatever to be sent or delivered by private or commercial interstate carrier." Any fraudulent scheme, whatever its purpose or method, that uses any of these delivery services can be prosecuted as a felony under the mail fraud statute.

Incidental use of the mail or other interstate carrier does not violate the mail fraud statute. For example, in *United States v. Maze*, 94 S. Ct. 603 (1974), the Supreme Court held the mail fraud act was not applicable to a defendant who stole his roommate's credit card and made local purchases. The merchants who sold the goods sent their invoices through the mail for payment from the credit card company, and based on this use of the mails, the federal prosecutor charged the defendant under the mail fraud statute. The Supreme Court said the merchants' use of the mail did not trigger the mail fraud statute because the mails were not used to perpetrate the theft or fraud, but were only incidental to the crime.

Honest Services Fraud

wire fraud A fraudulent scheme that uses interstate or international wire or other electronic communications.

The wire fraud act (discussed in Chapter 15) prohibits any scheme to defraud another by use of wire services. A **wire fraud** scheme is defined to include a scheme to deprive another of the "intangible right of honest services." This definition was added to the wire and mail fraud acts because of the Supreme Court's holding in *McNally v. United States*,

483 U.S. 350 (1987), that limited the scope of the fraud statutes to deprivations of money or property. The fraud statutes can thus be used to prosecute persons whose scheme is designed not to take money from another, but to deprive him or her of the right to the "honest services" of some person.

The U.S. Supreme Court limited the scope of honest services fraud in *Skilling v. United States*, 130 S. Ct. 2896 (2010). As a result, prosecutions under the federal mail and wire fraud acts based on deprivations of the right to honest services will be limited to classic property crimes, where the defendant defrauds another out of money or property, and bribery or kickback schemes. Prosecutions for breach only of a fiduciary duty, as was the case in *Skilling*, can no longer be brought under honest services fraud.

Summary

- A RICO conviction requires proof that an enterprise existed that engaged in racketeering activity, that the defendants were members of the enterprise and participated in the activity, and that the enterprise had a pattern of racketeering activity.
- The federal RICO adds the jurisdictional requirement that the racketeering activities affected interstate commerce. Most courts now hold that any effect on interstate commerce satisfies the jurisdictional requirement.
- Money can be laundered by transporting it to another country, buying cash or bearer instruments, passing it through a legitimate business, or using underground banking like the Hawala system.
- The mail fraud act, wire fraud act, money laundering act, and the RICO act are principal federal laws that are used to combat organized crime.

- Money laundering by transporting the proceeds of unlawful activity requires knowledge that the purpose of the transportation is to conceal the origin of the money.
- Proceeds for purpose of the money laundering statutes means profits gained from unlawful activities.
- Because lower-ranking members of crime families were the ones usually arrested with specific crimes such as murder or extortion, heads of organizations could not be prosecuted without testimony from those arrested. Such testimony was rarely given.
- The grand jury system, witness protection program, immunity doctrines, and federal court discovery rules all make prosecution in federal courts advantageous.

Key Terms

Case Analysis and Writing Exercises

1. An unusual case came before the U.S. Supreme Court in 1997. Over a period of time, a sheriff and his deputy were requiring bribes from a prisoner for contact visits with the man's wife and sometimes his girlfriend. The officers were paid $6,000 a month and $1,000 per contact visit, which was twice a week. Because the prisoner was a federal prisoner housed in a county jail for a federal fee, both the sheriff and his deputy were charged and convicted of federal bribery and also the RICO violation of continuing criminal enterprise. Should the convictions be affirmed? Was this a continuing criminal enterprise? See *Salinas v. United States,* 118 S. Ct. 469 (1997).

2. A drug dealer has $50,000 in cash proceeds from the sale of illegal drugs. He gave $30,000 to his wife, with instructions to "hide" the money in a safe deposit box maintained at a bank for that purpose. With the rest, he purchased a used car. Can he be convicted of money laundering for either or both of these actions? If not, of what can he be convicted ? See *United States v. Stephenson*, 183 F.3d 110 (2d Cir. 1999).

3. Two police officers stopped a car, believing the passenger made an obscene gesture to them. They then beat the passenger. When the Police Internal Affairs investigated the beating, the defendants convinced friends to lie about the event, in part by offering them money and paying their attorney fees. At some point, the witnesses determined to tell the truth, and the police officers were charged with both witness tampering and obstruction of justice under federal statutes. Can they be convicted under both statutes? See *United States v. LeMoure*, 474 F.3d 37 (1st Cir. 2007).

4. The gang known as the Mexican mafia, or "the Eme" exerts significant control over the inmates of California prisons, as well as many of the street gangs in Los Angeles. Convicting leaders of crimes can be a problem, since witnesses to crimes of violence may be unwilling to testify against gang leaders. The use of federal laws such as RICO to some degree makes prosecutions possible, if so-called predicate acts can be shown. The case of *United States v. Fernandez*, 388 F.3d 1199 (9th Cir. 2004), *cert. denied* 544 U.S. 1043 (2005), illustrates how the RICO laws can be so used. What must the prosecution prove to get a RICO conviction? How did it do it?

Notes

1. See the 2002 U.S. Department of Justice publication NCJ 190351, "Responding to Gangs: Evaluation and Research."

2. See the *New York Times* article, "Gangs Without Borders, Fierce and Resilient, Confront the Law," September 26, 2004.

3. See Chapter 19 of this book for materials on tax evasion.

4. Most, if not all, state RICO statutes create three distinct crimes: (1) using or investing the proceeds of racketeering activity, (2) acquiring an interest in property or an enterprise engaged in racketeering activity, and (3) conducting or participating in the enterprise. Each of these crimes requires proof of a fact the others do not and can therefore result in multiple convictions without violating the Double Jeopardy Clause. (See Chapter 7 of this book for additional material on the Double Jeopardy Clause.)

Courts have uniformly held not only that the substantive violations may be charged but also that the corresponding conspiracy violations may be charged. In addition, the underlying predicate offenses may also be charged. See *Iannelli v. United States,* 420 U.S. 770 (1975).

5. Public Law No. 91–452, 84 Stat. 938.

6. 18 U.S.C. § 1512.

7. For additional material on witnesses, see Thomas Gardner and Terry Anderson, *Criminal Evidence, Principles and Cases,* 7th ed., Chapter 5 (Belmont, CA: Wadsworth, 2010). The May 2004 *FBI Law Enforcement Bulletin* article, "Hiding in Plain Sight: A Peek into the Witness Protection Program," is an excellent description of the witness protection program.

8. *U.S. Department of the Treasury,* "2000–2005 Strategic Plan," p. 1.

9. 11 U.S.C. § 5311–5332.

10. 18 U.S.C. § 1956.

11. 18 U.S.C. § 5332.

12. In what has been called the biggest drug bust in history, the United States invaded Panama in 1989 to stop the use of Panama as a money laundering center.

13. See *United States v. United States Currency in Amount of Two Hundred Forty-Eight Thousand Dollars,* 2004 WL 958010 (E.D.N.Y. 2004).

14. *United States v. Winslow,* 962 F.2d 1488 (9th Cir. 1992).

15. *United States v. Briggs,* 700 F.2d 408 (7th Cir. 1983), *cert. denied* 103 S. Ct. 2463 (1983).

16. *United States v. Hanon,* 428 F.2d 101 (8th Cir. 1970).

17. *McIntosh v. United States,* 385 F.2d 274 (8th Cir. 1967).

18. *United States v. Bernaugh,* 969 F.2d 858 (10th Cir. 1992).

CHAPTER 19

Immigration Crimes, Contempt, and Other Crimes Against Government

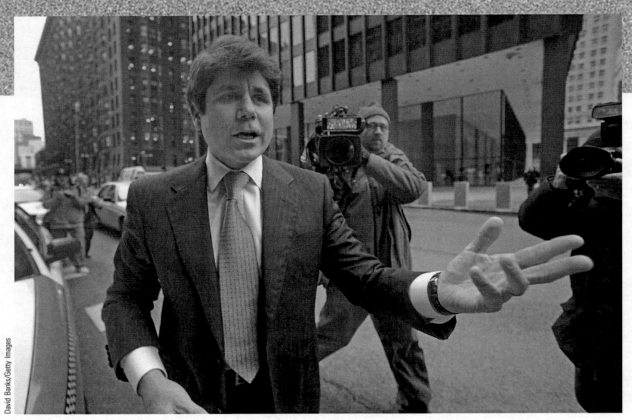

Former Illinois Governor Rod Blagojevich arriving for a hearing on corruption charges. In August, 2010 Blagojevich was convicted on one count of lying to investigators, but the jury could not reach a verdict on the other 23 count filed against him. The prosecutors have stated they intend to retry Blagojevich on the counts on which the jury could not agree. The previous Governor of Illinois, George Ryan, was convicted in 2006 of federal corruption charges and sentenced to 6 years and 6 months in prison.

OUTLINE

LEARNING OBJECTIVES

In this chapter we discuss various crimes in which a government body or court is the complaining party. The learning objectives for Chapter 19 are:

- List the various kind of conduct made criminal under the immigration laws.

- Distinguish civil contempt from criminal contempt.

- Make the connection between a gift and an official act required for conviction under the bribery laws.

- State the intent required for conviction under the federal clean air and clean water acts and explain how that intent can be shown.

- State the limits on summary contempt convictions.

In 2009, Barry Bonds, the holder of the baseball home-run record, was indicted for perjury based on his answers to a grand jury in the federal government's investigation of steroid use by professional athletes. Bonds stated he had never used steroids, but results of urine samples indicated Bonds had tested positive for steroids on some occasions. In 2010, the Ninth Circuit Court of Appeals upheld the trial court's decision that some of these test results could not be used at Bonds's trial. The prosecution must then decide whether a conviction can be obtained with the remaining evidence.

In the summer of 2010, pitcher Roger Clemens was indicted for perjury for giving allegedly false answers to Congress in hearings on the steroid scandal. Clemens also stated he had not used steroids.

In this chapter we will study immigration crimes, because these crimes are essentially crimes against government. We will study civil and criminal contempt and how those charges are used by government. We will also learn about other crimes directed against government, such as perjury, espionage, and tax evasion, where the criminal laws are used to protect the integrity or financial security of governments.

≡ Immigration Crimes

In 1997, the Center for Immigration Studies estimated that there were more than 5 million illegal immigrants in the United States. Ten years later, in 2007, the U.S. government estimated that the number of illegal immigrants living and working in the United States was over 12 million. Despite efforts to secure the borders of the United States, the wave of illegal immigrants is increasing. Most experts believe at least 500,000 and perhaps as many as 1,000,000 illegal immigrants cross the borders each year. The U.S. Congress has passed bills starting in 2006 designed to construct both actual and "virtual" barriers on the 2,000-mile U.S.–Mexico border. Actual walls, varying from chain-link fence to concrete and steel, have been constructed at key points along the border, covering perhaps one-third of the border. Virtual borders, consisting of cameras and other electronic monitoring devices, have also been put in place, though not in the quantity anticipated by sponsors of that barrier.

Comprehensive illegal immigration reform has been debated by Congress, but no legislation has been passed. In 2010, Arizona passed a state statute aimed at illegal immigrants, which permits police to detain persons suspected of being in this country illegally and also requires persons to carry valid immigration documents. In July of 2010, a federal judge issued a preliminary injunction blocking these provisions of the Arizona law, agreeing with the U.S. Justice Department that immigration enforcement laws were the within exclusive power of the federal government. That decision was appealed to the Ninth Circuit Court of Appeals.

Illegal immigrants enter this country through many methods. The United States has thousands of miles of borders with Mexico and Canada, and many illegal immigrants simple walk across the border into the United States. Others are smuggled in ships docking at any of the many ports on the Atlantic and Pacific oceans. Still others arrive under student, visitor, work, or business visas and remain after their visas have expired. It is estimated that 30 percent of all illegal immigrants in this country arrived here legally but then overstayed their visas. Because some of the 9/11 terrorists were in the United States under expired visas, efforts were made by the government to develop a system to monitor persons here under a visa. However, because of the prohibitive cost of such a system, and the lengthy lead time for it to become effective, there is not presently in place a reliable method to track those in the United States under an expired visa.

Illegal aliens generally come to the United States for work. Many "melt" into society and stay in the country for years. Forged green cards and other documents necessary to remain in this country are often used by illegal aliens to secure employment and housing. While many illegal aliens remain in the United States without attempting to change their illegal status, some attempt to obtain legal alien status.

A few become legal residents by marriage to a U.S. citizen or permanent resident. If an illegal alien in the United States marries a U.S. citizen or permanent resident, that person may file an application with the Immigration and Naturalization Service (INS) to change the status of the illegal alien. After review by the INS, the alien can be granted a permanent visa. However, if the INS determines that the marriage is a sham and entered into solely for the purpose of obtaining legal status for the alien, the INS can began immediate deportation proceedings.[1] Moreover, in 2006 the U.S. Supreme Court held that even if the marriage is legitimate, if the illegal alien had been previously deported and had then reentered the United States illegally, the illegal alien can be deported under the provisions of 8 U.S.C. § 1231(a)(5).[2]

The U.S. Congress has in the past granted limited amnesty to some illegal aliens. In 1986 it passed a law granting amnesty and legal resident status to persons who illegally entered the United States prior to 1982. In 2000 the INS released a report that while about 2.7 million aliens were given legal status under that law, the number of illegal

APPREHENDING THE "WORST OF THE WORST" OF ILLEGAL IMMIGRANTS: THE "SECURE COMMUNITIES" PROGRAM

The "Secure Communities" program was begun under the Bush administration, and continued under the Obama Administration. The purpose of the program is to help law enforcement officers identify the "worst of the worst" of violent criminals, drug traffickers, gang members and other dangerous aliens by checking the immigration history of a person arrested. Law enforcement officers holding a person may either contact the Immigration and Customs Enforcement Department (ICE), or have the person's fingerprints run through an immigration database under the "Secure Communities" program. The latter process is much faster, and costs nothing.

As of September, 2010 574 cities and counties in 30 states have used the program. While participation in the program was intended to be voluntary, it was planned to have the entire United States participating in the program by 2013. Because of criticism of the program in 2010, changes in the program may permit states to opt out of the program.

aliens in the United States actually increased. This was in part because family members of those granted legal status entered the country illegally to join their relatives.

In 2007, legislation was introduced in Congress to make it possible for some illegal aliens to obtain legal status. Based on a point allocation method, aliens with certain skills, education, and language ability could apply for permanent resident status. That legislation stalled before coming to vote, and it is now unlikely to be considered for the next several years.

Illegal aliens can place significant economic pressure on state social service programs. In response to this, a few states have passed laws limiting the availability of social services to illegal aliens. Most recently, in 2006 Georgia passed a law that declared illegal aliens ineligible for such services, required employers to verify the legal status of workers before hiring them, and required police to inform the INS when illegal aliens were arrested for crimes.

Criminal Charges for Illegal Immigration Offenses

There are many criminal laws aimed at illegal immigration. Violators of these laws can be charged in criminal courts, or they can be deported after a hearing in an immigration court. In some cases, immigration officials may simply transport the illegal alien to a border and release that person without formal prosecution. The following chart shows some of the various crimes that can be charged for immigration offenses, and the maximum punishments possible if convicted (see 8 U.S.C. § 1301 and the following).

Felonies

- Failure of alien to deport after order to do so (ten years)
- Counterfeiting alien papers or application to enter (five years)
- Bringing in or harboring illegal aliens (five years)
- Illegal entry, second offense (two years)
- Reentry of deported alien (two years)
- Aiding subversive alien to enter (five years)
- Importing alien for immoral purposes (ten years)

Misdemeanors

- Failure to register (six months)
- Failure to notify of change of address (thirty days)
- Making false statements (six months)
- First illegal entry (six months)
- Knowingly hiring an illegal alien (six months)

Deportation laws, now called removal laws, provide for removal of a person from the United States for a variety of reasons. Most directly, 8 U.S.C. § 1225 states that an immigration officer who inspects an immigrant at the place of entry may order the removal of the person if the person is inadmissible for any of the reasons set forth in 8 U.S.C. § 1182. In some situations an immigration judge may hold a hearing on inadmissibility, though in others the decision that a person is inadmissible is not reviewable.

A person within the United States and who is not a citizen or legal resident may be removed for any of the many reasons set forth in 8 U.S.C. § 1227. These include violation of entry conditions, overstaying a visa, helping smuggle in other illegal immigrants, commission of crimes of "moral turpitude," which carry a sentence of one year or more in prison, multiple convictions, or conviction of an aggravated or violent felony. Failing to register as a sex offender, using false documents, trafficking in controlled substances, or committing crimes of domestic violence are also reasons for removal of an illegal immigrant. During the removal process the alien may be detained pending removal, and removal is to occur within 90 days of the removal order.

Many persons removed from the United States subsequently reenter this country, usually illegally. Because of this, a federal statute, 8 U.S.C. § 1231(a)(5), permits immigration officials to reinstate former removal orders where any person reenters illegally. Such reinstatement orders are not subject to review.

Reports show that more than a million people are detained annually for violations of the immigration laws; most of these people are removed to their home countries. In some cases, the illegal alien's home country does not want and will not consent to the return of the alien. Federal Statute 8 U.S.C. § 1231(a)(6) permits immigration authorities to detain an alien after a removal order has been entered. In *Zadvydas v. Davis*, 533 U.S. 678 (2001), the Supreme Court held that such a detention could not extend beyond the "reasonable time" necessary to remove the alien. In *Tuan Thai v. Ashcroft*, 366 F.3d 790 (9th Cir. 2004), the court found that a detention for more than 16 months, with no prospect of removal, was unreasonable and ordered the government to release the alien. In *Suarez-Martinez v. Rozos,* 125 S. Ct. 716 (2005), the Supreme Court held that the reasoning of *Zadvydas* applied also to aliens detained after having been convicted of a crime that would result in deportation, even though the homeland of the detainee would not accept the detainee's return. The Court reasoned that notwithstanding the above, a person cannot constitutionally be detained indefinitely and that a reasonable time to detain an alien while deportation is pending should not exceed six months.

Illegal entry or reentry into the United States accounts for about 40 percent of immigration investigations. Harboring or bringing in foreign citizens with forged or inadequate documents accounts for about 38 percent of the criminal offenses investigated. Misusing visas or permits accounts for approximately 8 percent of the offenses, and fraud and forgery involving passports and other documents comprise another 8 percent, according to the INS.

contempt Failure or refusal to obey a court order (civil contempt), or interfering with the functioning of a court or legislative body (criminal contempt). Criminal contempt that occurs in the presence of the court can be punished summarily; other criminal contempts require the normal prosecution procedures.

It is also a crime under 8 U.S.C. § 1324 for a person to unlawfully assist an illegal alien to enter the United States, to transport such an alien around the United States, or harbor or shield from detection such an alien. In *United States v. Ye*, 588 F.3d 411 (7th Cir. 2010) the court held that a person can violate § 1324 if he takes "any means" to shield the alien from discovery by the government. The court rejected the position of other circuit courts that required a showing that the means used to shield the alien "substantially" facilitated the avoidance of discovery.

≡ Contempt

Contempt is the willful disregard of the authority of a court of law or of a legislative body. Acts that delay, impede, or frustrate the functioning or the dignity of a court or legislative body may be held to be in contempt of that body. The deliberate, willful, and contumacious (obstinate) disobedience of a lawful order is a common reason for finding a person in contempt. Contempt that occurs in the presence of the court, often called "direct" contempt, can be punished summarily, that is, by an immediate finding of contempt and appropriate sentence. However, courts commonly require that the contempt occur completely in the court's presence for this summary action to be upheld. That is because actions taken outside the presence of the court are not personally observed by the judge, and thus must be proved in the usual manner. In that case, the usual procedures for proving facts must be followed. An example of this principle is the case of *Scialdone v. Com.*, 689 S.E.2d 716 (Va. 2010). In that case two attorneys introduced into evidence documents that appeared to have been altered. The trial judge conducted an investigation of how the documents were altered, which included questioning witnesses who may have been involved in the alteration. The judge concluded the attorneys altered the document, and that offering the altered document was criminal contempt. It summarily sentenced the attorneys to short jail terms. On appeal, the Virginia Supreme Court reversed the contempt convictions, holding that because some of the facts needed for the contempt charge did not occur in the presence of the court, the summary finding of contempt was improper.

Civil Contempt

civil contempt This is a remedial form of contempt order used to force people to do what they are lawfully required to do (answer questions, identify themselves, pay support money as ordered by a divorce court, and so on).

criminal contempt This is a criminal charge based on a persons actions in a court case or legislative proceeding and used to punish people by a fine or imprisonment for what they have done.

Contempt is classified as either civil or criminal. **Civil contempt** is used to compel people to do something they are obligated to do. **Criminal contempt** can be used to punish people for what they have done. Civil or criminal contempt is sometimes used in divorce cases, child custody cases, and other matters to compel people to comply with court orders. Following are a few of the thousands of contempt cases that occur every year in the United States:

A contempt order is treated as a civil contempt if the purpose of the contempt is to compel compliance with a court order. In such a case, confinement is permitted until the person confined complies with the order. However, where it becomes clear compliance will not or cannot occur, a civil contempt order of confinement is normally lifted. *See United States v. Winter*, 70 F.3d 655 (1st Cir. 1995).

- Refusal to answer questions before a grand jury after being granted immunity could mean jailing for contempt, as in the Susan McDougal case (21 months) and in the case of *Shillitani v. United States*, 86 S. Ct. 1531 (1966) (two years).
- Failure to comply with a court order, as in the divorce case of *Morgan v. Foretich*, 564 A.2d 1 (D.C. Cir. 1989) (25 months for contempt in hiding a child).
- Newsperson failure to provide information as ordered by court (only a few states have enacted a newsperson privilege law protecting confidential sources of news information).
- An Arizona rancher refused to remove 28 grazing cows from federal land and threatened to shoot federal agents who came near the cows. After spending 13 months in jail for contempt, he was released in 2004 after agreeing to remove the cows, stop threatening federal agents, and not use federal land for grazing purposes.[3]
- Under federal law, 28 U.S.C. § 1826, the usual limit on the period a person can be held in jail for civil contempt for refusal to obey a court order is 18 months, though in one case a defendant was jailed for seven years for refusal to produce $15 million in gold and antiquities unlawfully retained by him.[4]

Criminal Contempt

Criminal contempt is designed to protect the public interest by ensuring the effective functioning of the judicial and legislative systems. In 1968, the U.S. Supreme Court stated in *Bloom v. Illinois* that "criminal contempt is a crime in the ordinary sense; it is a violation of the law, a public wrong which is punishable by fine or imprisonment or both."[5] The Court quoted Justice Oliver Wendell Holmes in stating that "these contempts are infractions of the law, visited with punishment as such. If such acts are not criminal, we are in error as to the most fundamental characteristic of crimes as that word has been understood in English speech."

The defendant in the *Bloom* case was sentenced to 24 months in prison for submitting a falsely prepared will for probate. His demand for a jury trial was denied. In holding that in serious contempt cases the defendant had a right to a jury, the Court stated:

> Prosecution for contempt plays a significant role in the proper functioning of our judicial system; but despite the important values which the contempt power protects, courts and legislatures have gradually eroded the power of judges to try contempts of their own authority. In modern times, procedures in criminal contempt cases have come to mirror those used in ordinary criminal cases.[6]

Criminal contempt is treated as a crime, as stated above, which includes application of the Double Jeopardy Clause. In *United States v. Dixon*, 509 U.S. 688 (1993) the Supreme Court held that a prior conviction of a defendant on a criminal contempt charge for violation of a protection order barred subsequent prosecution by the government for the crime that constituted the violation of the order. However, in a 2010 case the Supreme Court reversed its decision to grant a petition for certiorari on the question of whether a subsequent criminal contempt charge brought by a woman who obtained a protective order violated the Double Jeopardy Clause. In *In re Robertson*, 940 A.2d 1050 (D.C. Cir. 2008) the court upheld a criminal contempt order based on the defendant's assault on the woman who filed the action. In an earlier proceeding the woman had obtained a civil protection order against the defendant, who subsequently violated the order on more than one occasion. The defendant and the government had entered into a plea agreement on criminal charges related to those violations, and the defendant served time in prison. The defendant thus argued that under *Dixon* the criminal contempt prosecution brought by the woman was barred by the Double Jeopardy Clause. The Supreme Court initially granted certiorari on that question, 130 S. Ct. 1011, but subsequently voted to deny certiorari as "improvidently granted," 130 S. Ct. 2184 (2010). Four Justices dissented, believing the subsequent criminal contempt conviction violated the Double Jeopardy Clause.

Other examples of people who were found in criminal contempt include the defendant who hit his defense lawyer in *United States v. Wright*, 854 F.2d 1263 (11th Cir.), and a defendant who gave the judge the finger in *Mitchell v. State*, 580 A.2d 196, 48 CrL 1082 (Md. 1990).

Contempt Is a Specific Intent Crime That Requires Proof of Intentional Wrongdoing

In the 1976 case of *Commonwealth v. Washington*, the Supreme Court of Pennsylvania quoted other courts, holding:

> There is no contempt unless there is some sort of wrongful intent. *Offutt v. United States*, 98 U.S. App. D.C. 69, 232 F.2d 69, 72 (1956), *cert. denied* 351 U.S. 988, 76 S. Ct. 1049, 100 L. Ed. 1501 (1956). "[A] degree of intentional wrongdoing is an ingredient of the offense of criminal contempt." *In re Brown*, 147 U.S. App. D.C. 156, 454 F.2d 999, 1006 (1971). "Willfulness is, of course, an element of criminal contempt and must be proved beyond a reasonable doubt." *United States v. Greyhound Corporation*, 508 F.2d 529, 531 (7th Cir. 1974).[7]

In the *Washington* case, the defendant overslept and failed to appear on time at his trial. In reversing his contempt conviction, the Pennsylvania Supreme Court held:

> Were we to accept the prosecution's argument, any person, judge, attorney, witness, or party, who comes into the courtroom late can be held guilty of contempt of court, regardless of the reason for the lateness. We cannot accept such a conclusion. Unless the evidence establishes an intentional disobedience or an intentional neglect of the lawful process of the court, no contempt has been proven. Such is the case here.
>   Judgment of sentence reversed.

In the 1976 case of *People v. Harris,* the defendant failed to pay a fine imposed for a prior criminal conviction.[8] Although the defendant showed that he had no money and was unemployed, he was found in contempt for failure to pay the fine. The Illinois Court of Appeals reversed the contempt finding, holding that there was no showing that the defendant willfully placed himself in a position to be unable to pay the fine.

Language by a Witness or Attorney That Would Justify a Contempt Finding

While answering a question on cross-examination, a witness used the expression *chicken shit.* As a result, the witness was found to be in direct contempt for the use of this term in a courtroom. The U.S. Supreme Court reversed the defendant's conviction in the case of *Eaton v. City of Tulsa,* holding:

> This single isolated usage of street vernacular, not directed at the judge or any officer of the court, cannot constitutionally support the conviction of criminal contempt. "The vehemence of language used is not alone the measure of the power to punish for contempt. The fires which it kindles must constitute an imminent, not merely a likely,

CONTEMPT

Classification	Type	Procedure Used to Punish
Civil contempt is remedial and is used to force people to do what they are lawfully required to do (answer questions, identify themselves, pay support money as ordered by a divorce court, and so on).	Direct contempt is committed in the immediate presence and view or hearing of the court or legislative body.	Summary process: Only direct contempt may be punished summarily. If the court or legislative body does not act at the time the contempt is committed, notice and an opportunity for a hearing must be given to the person.
"Criminal contempt is a crime in the ordinary sense; it is a violation of the law, a public wrong which is punishable by fine or imprisonment or both." U.S. Supreme Court in *Bloom v. Illinois*, 391 U.S. 194, 88 S. Ct.1477 (1968).	Constructive, or indirect, contempt is committed out of the presence or hearing of the court or legislative body. Although the matter or incident does not occur in or near the presence of a court or legislative body, it obstructs or delays the functioning of the court or the legislative body.[a]	Contempt hearings: Notice and an opportunity for a hearing (plus other due process rights) must be given for constructive (indirect contempt) and for direct contempt when the court or legislative body does not act immediately.

[a]State legislatures and the U.S. Congress have the constitutional power to hold persons in contempt, as well as the authority to issue subpoenas, grant immunity from prosecution, and demand within the law that persons appearing before them answer questions.

threat to the administration of justice." *Craig v. Harney,* 331 U.S. 367, 376 (1947). In using the expletive in answering the question on cross-examination "it is not charged that [petitioner] here disobeyed any valid court order, talked loudly, acted boisterously, or attempted to prevent the judge or any other officer of the court from carrying on his court duties." *Holt v. Virginia,* 381 U.S. 131, 136 (1965); see also *In re Little,* 404 U.S. 553 (1972). In the circumstances, the use of the expletive thus cannot be held to "constitute an imminent ... threat to the administration of justice."[9]

Contempt and the Crime of Failure to Appear (Bail Jumping)

In all states and in the federal court system, a criminal defendant free on bail may be charged with criminal contempt if he or she intentionally fails to appear at a scheduled hearing in his or her criminal case. The penalty for bail jumping is generally determined by the severity of the underlying crime charged. For example, in *Curley v. Comm.,* 895 S.W.2d 10 (Ky. App. 1995), the court reversed a conviction of first-degree bail jumping because the underlying criminal charge had been reduced from a felony to a misdemeanor before the bail jumping occurred. Under most state bail jumping statutes, the crime is committed if the defendant is free on bail as a result of being charged with a crime. If the defendant does not appear at a scheduled hearing on the criminal charge, he or she can be convicted of bail jumping, even if the criminal charge is subsequently dismissed.[10]

Most states provide an affirmative defense to bail jumping if the defendant can show that his or her failure to appear at a scheduled hearing was the result of "uncontrollable circumstances" not created by the defendant. Hospitalization for a serious illness would be an example of this defense.

≡ Crimes by Public Officials

If all people were angels who lived in peace and harmony with one another, then, as James Madison observed in *The Federalist Papers* of the 1780s, there would be no need for governments. But people are not angels, nor are they governed by angels (as Madison also pointed out more than 200 years ago).

The U.S. Supreme Court observed that "nothing can destroy a government more quickly than its failure to observe its own laws, or worse, its disregard of the charter of its own existence."[11] In 1928, Justice Louis D. Brandeis stated in his dissenting opinion in *Olmstead v. United States:* "Our Government is the potent, the omnipresent teacher. For good or ill, it teaches the whole people by its example.... If the Government becomes a lawbreaker, it breeds contempt for law; it invites every man to become a law unto himself; it invites anarchy."[12]

Cicero wrote long ago in *Pro Cluentio 53* that "we are in bondage to the law in order that we may be free." While president of the United States, Calvin Coolidge observed:

> Wherever the law goes, there civilization goes and stays. When the law fails, barbarism flourishes. Whoever scorns the law, whoever brings it into disrespect, whoever connives at its evasion, is an enemy of civilization. Change it if you will ... but observe it always. That is government.

Some Crimes Committed by Public Officials and Others

Some of the many offenses committed by public officials and private individuals are as follows:

- Unauthorized (or excessive) use of force (assault and battery)
- False imprisonment

- Unauthorized wiretapping (federal felony) or bugging (state offense)
- **Perjury**[13] obs**subornation of perjury** (the crime of perjury consists of knowingly and materially testifying falsely while under oath; the crime of subornation of perjury is inducing or knowingly permitting another person to testify falsely). The federal perjury statute, 18 U.S.C. § 1623, makes it perjury to "knowingly" make a "false material declaration" to a court or grand jury. In Bronston v. United States, 409 U.S. 352 (1973) the Supreme Court held that an answer that is literally true, but either unresponsive to a question or that creates a false impression, cannot be perjury. For example, if the president of a corporation is asked "Have you ever had a Swiss bank account," and he answered "The company has never had a Swiss bank account," his answer cannot be perjury even though it created the false impression the president did not personally have such an account. In *United States v. Thomas*, 2010 WL 2853875 (9th Cir 2010) the court held the "literal truth" defense was not available to a professional cyclist who gave false answers to a grand jury investigating BALCO and the distribution and use of steroids by athletes. Called before a grand jury, the defendant was asked if she had ever been "given" steroids by a BALCO representative. She testified "no." She was subsequently indicted for perjury under § 1623, and she raised the literal truth defense. She claimed her answer was literally true, because she paid for the steroids, and thus they were not "given" to her. The court said the defense is not available when the witness understands the meaning of the question in the context it was asked, and the answer is false as to that meaning.
- Official misconduct and misconduct in public office (using the powers of one's office to obtain a dishonest advantage for oneself, or falsifying an entry in a record or report)
- Aiding, assisting, or permitting the escape of a prisoner
- Intimidating witnesses, prisoners, or others
- **Tampering with evidence** or falsifying evidence
- **Misprision of felony**. Some states and the federal government have codified this old common law crime. In 1998, Michael Fortier pleaded guilty to misprision of a felony (and other crimes) because he failed to warn officials of the plot to blow up the Alfred P. Murrah Federal Building in Oklahoma City.[14] *Federal courts define the crime of misprision of a felony as follows:*

  [T]o sustain a conviction ... for misprision of felony it was incumbent upon the government to prove beyond a reasonable doubt (1) that ... the principal had committed and completed the felony alleged; ... (2) that the defendant had full knowledge of that fact; (3) that he failed to notify the authorities; and (4) that he took ... affirmative steps to conceal the crime of the principal.[15]

- Bribery. The U.S. Supreme Court held that to prove a violation of the federal gratuity statute (18 U.S.C.A. § 201(c)(1)(A)), the government must prove a link between the thing of value given to a public official and a specific "official act" for which it was given.[16]

  The federal court in the case of *United States v. Arthur* described the crime of bribery as follows:

  Not every gift, favor or contribution to a government or political official constitutes bribery. It is universally recognized that bribery occurs only if the gift is coupled with a particular criminal intent.... That intent is not supplied merely by the fact that the gift was motivated by some generalized hope or expectation of ultimate benefit on the part of the donor.... "Bribery" imports the notion of some more or less specific quid pro quo for which the gift or contribution is offered or accepted.[17]

perjury The crime of knowingly and materially testifying falsely while under oath.

subornation of perjury The crime of inducing or knowingly permitting another person to testify falsely while under oath.

tampering with evidence Knowingly altering or damaging evidence intended to be used in a court proceeding.

misprision of felony Failing to report knowledge of a felony to the appropriate authorities.

- Extortion by a public official or employee in violation of the Hobbs Act, 18 U.S.C.A. § 1951. The public official or employee obtains payment because of his or her office and by use of "force, violence or fear." In *United States v. Swift,* the defendant was a city sewer director who received payments from a contractor in return for approval of payments made for work done on sewage pumping stations.[18] Another example of extortion under the Hobbs Act is as follows:

  A bail bonds agent who was also an alderman in a small town conspired with members of the police department to extort money from travelers passing through town in exchange for dismissal or reduction of drunk driving charges against the travelers. (See *United States v. Stephens,* 964 F.2d 424 (5th Cir. 1992).)

- Fraud and corruption.

≡ Crimes Against Government

Espionage

espionage Giving or selling national military or defense secrets to a foreign nation.

Spying or being a party to **espionage** is forbidden by all democratic countries. Giving or selling national military or defense secrets to a foreign nation is a serious felony. A shocking number of Americans have been charged with or convicted of spying. Most spies today sell secrets for money.

The Federal Espionage Act forbids disclosing, transmitting, stealing, or receiving information that has been classified. Experience has shown that most of the violators of this Act either work for the U.S. government and have security clearances or are part of a foreign government's spy operation. Espionage cases receiving national attention include:

- *Aldrich Ames* was an alcoholic for years, yet he worked for the Central Intelligence Agency and received regular promotions within the organization. On a civil servant's pay, he bought an expensive home in Washington, D.C., for cash, and he drove a Jaguar.

  To obtain the money to live a luxurious life, Ames delivered vast amounts of highly secret documents and information to the Soviet Union, which paid Ames millions of dollars. Ames betrayed at least a dozen of the United States' best spies working within Russia. All were jailed, and most were executed. Ames and his wife were taken into custody in 1994 after nine years of espionage.

- *Robert P. Hanssen* was convicted in May 2001 of selling highly sensitive national secrets to Russia for 15 years. Hanssen was a high-ranking FBI counterintelligence agent. It is believed that Hanssen also corroborated information that Aldrich Ames provided to the Russians.
- *John A. Walker, Jr.,* headed a spy ring of family members and friends. Officials called it the most damaging espionage conspiracy in decades. Walker received life imprisonment and said the Soviet Union paid $1 million for his information on military communication codes.
- *Jonathan Jay Pollard* provided secret information to Israel that was available to him as a U.S. Navy intelligence analyst. He received a long prison sentence.[19]
- The highest ranking military officer to be convicted of spying was German-born *George Trofimoff,* a retired Army Reserve colonel. He was convicted in September 2001 of selling military secrets to Russia for more than 20 years.

The Federal Espionage Act forbids disclosing, transmitting, stealing, or receiving information that has been classified. Experience has shown that most of the violators of this Act either work for the United States government and have security clearances or are part of a foreign government's spy operation. Robert P. Hanssen, depicted here by actor Chris Cooper in the movie *Breach*, was convicted in May 2001 of selling highly sensitive national secrets to Russia for fifteen years. Hanssen was a high-ranking FBI counterintelligence agent.

- *Ronald A. Pelton* was convicted of selling military secrets from the National Security Agency to Russia.
- *Richard W. Miller,* a former FBI agent, became involved with a Russian woman and provided national secrets to Russia.
- In 2010 10 people who had lived in the United States for more than 10 years as ordinary citizens working ordinary jobs were arrested as "deep-cover" Russian spies. After revealing their true identities they all pled guilty to conspiracy to commit espionage. They were then returned to Russia in a "swap" for the release of four Russian citizens who had been jailed in Russia, accused of spying for England or the United States. Two of the four Russians released under this swap were high-ranking Russian military officers. See the New York Times, 6/29/10 and 7/09/10.

Obstruction of Justice

obstruction of justice
Intentional acts that hinder, corrupt, or impede the functioning of the judicial system.

The offense of **obstruction of justice** was a common law misdemeanor and is now part of the criminal code of the federal government and states. The offense seeks to protect the judicial system, both civil and criminal, from intentional acts that would hinder, corrupt, or impede the functioning of the system. Attempting to influence a juror, destroying or suppressing evidence, and seeking to prevent a witness from testifying or from

CRIMES UNCOVERED BY THE WATERGATE AND WHITEWATER INVESTIGATIONS

Watergate

This burglary led to a White House cover-up that resulted in a presidential resignation. After the botched break-in of the National Democratic Headquarters at the Watergate apartment building, the White House became involved in a cover-up that then led to:

- The resignation of President Richard Nixon
- Eighteen months in prison for former Attorney General John Mitchell for perjury and cover-up conspiracy
- Seven months in prison for Jeb Magruder for perjury and conspiracy to obstruct justice
- Thirty-three months in prison for E. Howard Hunt for burglary, conspiracy, and wire-tapping
- A prison term for James McCord, Jr., for burglary
- Eighteen months in prison for H. R. Haldeman for perjury, conspiracy, and obstruction of justice
- Prison terms also for John Ehrlichman (eighteen months), John Dean (four months), and Chuck Colson (eighteen months)

Whitewater

This was a six-year investigation of the Arkansas business dealings of President Bill Clinton and Hillary Clinton. Neither President nor Mrs. Clinton was accused or found guilty of any wrongdoings, but 14 other people were convicted:

- Former law partner of Mrs. Clinton, Webster Hubbell, pleaded guilty to felonies of tax evasion, mail fraud, and concealment by scheme.
- Former Arkansas Governor Jim Guy Tucker was found guilty by a jury of conspiracy and mail fraud. He pleaded guilty to conspiracy to defraud the IRS.
- Whitewater land development partner of the Clintons, Jim McDougal, was convicted by a jury of 18 felonies in the collapse of his savings and loan, which cost taxpayers $73 million.
- Susan McDougal was convicted by a jury of four felonies, then she served 18 months for failure to answer grand jury questions about Whitewater.
- Former judge, David Hale, pleaded guilty to two felonies.
- Little Rock appraiser, Robert Palmer, pleaded guilty to conspiracy.
- Convicted of felonies: William Marks (one) and Christopher Wade (two).
- Convicted of misdemeanors: Stephen Smith (one), Larry Kuca (one), attorney John Haley (one), banker Neal Ainley (two), Charles Matthews (two), and Eugene Fitzhugh (one).
- White House advisor Bruce Lindsey was named an unindicted co-conspirator in a case that ended in mistrial.

attending a trial are some of the acts that have justified charging the offense of obstruction of justice.

In the early days of the law, resisting, hindering, or obstructing a law enforcement officer was a common form of obstruction of justice. Many states, however, have made this offense a separate offense from obstruction of justice.[20] For example, Chapter 843 of the Florida Criminal Code is entitled "Obstructing Justice." Within Florida Chapter 843 are 18 separate offenses, two of which forbid "resisting an officer." Tampering with evidence (destroying, concealing, or altering) is found in Florida Chapter 918.

A police officer was charged with obstructing justice in 1991 when he pretended to find a bag of cocaine in the vicinity of a person who had just been arrested. An Illinois

Court of Appeals held that the officer could be convicted of obstructing justice for attempting to "frame" the arrested person in the case of *People v. Hollingshead* (210 Ill. App. 3d 750, 155 Ill. Dec. 216, 569 N.E.2d 216). The officer's defense was that he was just joking, and then that he was attempting to obtain a confession from the arrested person.

A Philadelphia doctor was convicted in 1997 of obstruction of justice and harboring a fugitive when he voluntarily changed fingerprints and dramatically altered the appearance of a drug lord wanted by federal officials.[21]

Tax Evasion

To operate and provide services, government needs money. Former U.S. Supreme Court Justice Oliver Wendell Holmes pointed out that taxes are the price we pay for civilization. Much of the money needed to fund government services and activities is obtained through taxes. Deliberate tax evasion and tax fraud are generally punished as crimes. Tax evasion cases that have received national attention include the following:

- In 1973, the vice president of the United States, Spiro T. Agnew, resigned after pleading no contest to tax evasion charges.
- Socially prominent hotel owner Leona Helmsley was convicted of failure to report and pay taxes on $1.8 million in 1990. She was sentenced to four years in prison and fined $7.1 million.
- Former baseball player and manager Pete Rose spent five months in prison in 1990 for tax charges related to gambling and other income earned but not reported. In 2003, it was reported that Rose still owed about $1 million, on which he is making monthly payments.
- In the 1920s, gangster Al Capone and his gang had an extraordinary grip on Chicago. Law enforcement officials were unable to convict Capone of any of the many felonies they believed he had committed, but they were able to convict him of income tax fraud and send him to prison. Capone was one of the first people to be convicted with the use of the "net worth" method (circumstantial evidence). The U.S. Supreme Court affirmed the use of the net worth method in the 1954 case of *Holland v. United States* (348 U.S. 121, 75 S. Ct. 127).

Drug dealers and other criminals who live lavishly as a result of their criminal activities must show "legitimate" income to support their lifestyles. To do this, they must launder dirty money and create sources of "legitimate" income. They then pay taxes to state and federal governments on their declared incomes.

In 1985, a prominent mafia leader was tried. The jury heard a tape recording of the mafia leader talking to a friend in which the mafia leader stated, "I surround myself with accountants and lawyers." The mafia leader had in mind what happened to Al Capone and wanted to avoid being prosecuted in a net worth tax case. He was convicted, however, of other criminal violations.

Environmental Crimes

The United States alone produces approximately 125 billion pounds of hazardous waste annually.[22] If not properly handled and disposed of, this waste can foul air, pollute land, poison water, and seriously affect people, animals, fish, and agriculture.

Until the 1980s, little was done to regulate disposal of hazardous waste. FBI Director William S. Sessions quoted American conservationist Paul Brooks: "In America today [1970s], you can murder land for private profit. You can leave the corpse for all to see, and nobody calls the cops." Sessions pointed out that unfortunately "this was the case 20 years ago. No one could call the police, because no laws had been broken."[23]

In the 1980s and 1990s, laws were enacted to protect public health and the quality of the environment. The U.S. Congress added criminal sanctions to a host of environmental laws and in 1990 enacted the Clean Air Act Reauthorization. Vigorous enforcement of these laws has been said to be a top priority. Criminal prosecutions under the Clean Air Act, and similar kinds of environmental protection laws, require the prosecution to prove that the defendant "knowingly" violated the act.

An example of the meaning of "knowingly" is *United States v. Rubenstein*, 403 F.3d 93 (2d Cir 2005). There, the owners of a commercial building were in the process of restoring the building so that it could be leased. In the process they discovered that many of the pipes in the building were covered by asbestos. They hired workers to remove the asbestos without first complying with Clean Air Act requirements for removal of asbestos. The New York Environment Protection department discovered their actions, and they were charged with violation of the Clean Air Act, 42 U.S.C. § 7413(c)(5)(A). They contended they did not know they were in violation of the act, because their religion kept them isolated from public affairs. As a result, they argued, they did not "knowingly" violate the Clean Air Act. The court disagreed. It found that the defendants knew the pipes were covered in asbestos and that asbestos removal required safety practices to be observed. Knowledge of that was enough to constitute a knowing violation of the act.

The Environmental Protection Agency (EPA) and the Department of Justice's Environmental Crimes Section are among the federal agencies combating environmental crimes. All of the states have enacted laws and authorized agencies within each state to enforce these laws.[24]

Other Criminal Violations

The President's Commission on Law Enforcement reported that the federal government alone has more than 2,800 crimes in the Federal Code. The President's Commission also pointed out that each state has the same number or more crimes in their state statutes.

The following are a very few of the many crimes reported in daily newspapers:

- States often make the failure of an employer to withhold income taxes on employees' wages and salaries a crime. Under California law, employers who fail to withhold can be charged with a felony. (See the May 3, 2001, *New York Times* article, "California Raids a Business that Refuses to Withhold Taxes.")
- State election laws sometimes make it a felony to induce a person to vote if the inducement is worth one dollar or more. A New York woman came to Wisconsin and passed out packages of cigarettes to homeless men as an inducement to vote in the presidential election of 2000. She was fined $5,000. (See the May 4, 2001, *Milwaukee Journal Sentinel* article, "$5,000 Settles Election Case.")
- It is a federal crime to use marriage as a means of evading the immigration laws of the United States. Twenty persons were indicted on charges that they fraudulently obtained marriage licenses to gain permanent resident status for illegal immigrants in Chicago. (See the November 18, 2000, *Milwaukee Journal Sentinel* article, "20 Accused of Marriage to Gain Residency.")
- States often make failure to report for jury duty when summoned a crime. In Wisconsin, the misdemeanor is punished by a $40 fine, and ignorance of the law is not a defense. (See the October 31, 2000, *Milwaukee Journal Sentinel* article, "County Prosecuting Jury Service No-Shows.")
- Bootlegging whiskey has made millionaires of some families in the Appalachian hills of Virginia and West Virginia. Cigarette smuggling is a problem in the Detroit area. Both crimes cause federal and state government to lose tax revenue. The federal government claimed a loss of $2.9 million in unpaid federal taxes for one

moonshiner alone. (See the September 9, 2001, *New York Times* article, "Alleged Bootleggers Face Sobering Case," and the May 20, 1997, *Detroit Free Press* article, "Cigarette Smugglers Busted.")

- Criminal nonpayment of child support is a crime in all states, and is frequently charged. The federal government also makes such nonpayment a crime, primarily as a way to assist states in their efforts to apprehend non-paying defendants who flee a state to avoid prosecution.

- Criminal anti-trust laws, such as the Sherman Anti Trust Act (1890) and the Clayton Act (1914), and the Robinson-Patman Act (1936).. These laws prohibit individuals and corporations from taking actions to create monopolies or engaging in unreasonable restraints of trade, such as discriminatory pricing schemes, market allocation agreements, or agreements to restrict production, output, or competition. These laws have successfully protected consumers from many predatory practices of persons and businesses in the United States.

Summary

- The immigration laws make it a crime to make a false entry into this country, either by illegal crossing or by using false documents, to assist others to make an illegal entry into or stay in this country, to reenter after being removed, or to harbor or hire an illegal alien.

- Civil contempt is punishment used to coerce a defendant into obeying a lawful court order; criminal contempt is punishment for actions that constitute a "public wrong," just like ordinary criminal laws.

- All that is required for a gift to be an illegal gratuity is that the gift was given or received with the specific intent to obtain some favorable treatment for the giver in the future, although the exact nature of the return need not be expressed.

- While one must "knowingly" violate the Clean Water and Clean Air acts, knowledge is sufficient if the defendant knew that his actions were the type made unlawful by those acts, whether or not he knew the provisions of the act.

- Summary contempt is proper only where all the actions making up the contempt occurred in the presence of the judge.

Key Terms

contempt, p. 492
civil contempt, p. 493
criminal contempt, p. 493

perjury, p. 497
subornation of perjury, p. 497
tampering with evidence, p. 497

misprision of felony, p. 497
espionage, p. 498
obstruction of justice, p. 499

Case Analysis and Writing Exercises

1. It is a violation of the immigration laws to "bring" an illegal alien into the United States. Can a defendant who does not actually cross the border with an illegal alien be convicted under these laws? What must the prosecution prove? See *United States v. Arzane-Picasso*, 18 Fed. Appx. 484 (9th Cir. 2001).

2. Judges have the power to issue summary criminal contempt citations where a person's conduct obstructs the judicial process. If the person uses only bad language, but does not otherwise slow down or obstruct the court proceedings, can the person be held in contempt? See *United States v. Marshall*, 371 F.3d 42 (2d Cir. 2004).

3. Pursuant to Executive Order No. 12,543, the president identified Libya as a country to whom shipment of goods from the United States was prohibited. A U.S. resident arranged to ship 50 trailers to Italy, and from there another company was to ship the goods to Libya. United States custom agents discovered the plan and confiscated the trailers. The defendant was charged with illegal sales of goods to Libya, and he defended by contending he could not be convicted under the statute because the goods never arrived in Libya. Is this a good argument? See *United States v. Soussi*, 316 F.3d 1095 (10th Cir. 2002).

4. Federal agents executed a sting operation in Illinois against the defendant Skoczen, in which the agents offered to sell Skoczen stolen, contraband cigarettes. When Skoczen agreed to the deal, the agents crossed state lines and obtained cigarettes from a cigarette manufacturer. They brought the cigarettes into Illinois and delivered them to Skoczen. When he started to pay for the cigarettes, he was arrested and charged with (1) receiving goods stolen in an interstate transaction, and (2) possession of contraband cigarettes.

The applicable federal statute defined contraband as any pack of cigarettes that did not have a state tax stamp on the pack. Skoczen argued he could not be convicted under the stolen property statute because the cigarettes were only in interstate commerce as part of the government sting operation. He also argued that because he was not a distributor under Illinois law, ha had no duty to pay a tax on the cigarettes, and that as a result he could not be in violation of the contraband act. Do his arguments have merit? See *United States v. Skoczen*, 405 F.3d 537 (7th Cir. 2005).

Notes

1. See *United States v. Bithoney*, 631 F.2d 1 (1st Cir. 1980).
2. *Fernandez-Vargas v. Gonzales*, 126 S. Ct. 2422 (2006).
3. See the *New York Times* article, "Rancher Has Change of Heart," May 13, 2004.
4. See *New York Times* article, "In Fraud Case, 7 Years in Jail for Contempt," February 16, 2007.
5. 391 U.S. 194, 88 S. Ct. 1477 (1968).
6. *Bloom v. Illinois*, 391 U.S. 194, 206 (1968). New Jersey courts have held that "before a judge makes a contempt determination the accused should be permitted to speak," 357 A.2d at 276 (1976). In the case of *In re Logan Jr.*, 52 N.J. 475, 246 A.2d 441 (1968), the court held: "The pronouncement of guilt before according that opportunity places the defendant at the disadvantage of trying to persuade a mind apparently already made up, and also puts the judge in the possibly embarrassing position of reversing himself if such persuasion results."
7. 466 Pa. 506, 353 A.2d 806 (1976).
8. 41 Ill. App. 3d 690, 354 N.E.2d 648 (1976).
9. 415 U.S. 697, 94 S. Ct. 1228 (1974). In a dissenting opinion, Justice William H. Rehnquist suggests "a flat rule, analogous to the hoary doctrine of the law of torts that every dog is entitled to one bite, to the effect that every witness is entitled to one free contumacious or other impermissible remark."
10. See *State v. Downing*, 93 P.3d 900 (Wash. App. 2004).
11. *Mapp v. Ohio*, 367 U.S. 643, 81 S. Ct. 1684 (1961).
12. 277 U.S. 438, 48 S. Ct. 564 (1928).
13. In 1968, the President's Commission on Crime noted that perjury has always been widespread and that there must be more effective deterrents against perjury to ensure the integrity of trials. Another writer commented that few crimes "except fornication are more prevalent or carried off with greater impunity." See "Perjury: The Forgotten Offense," *Journal of Criminal Law & Criminology* 65 (1974).
14. See the *New York Times* article, "Sentencing the Man Who Failed to Warn of a Fatal Conspiracy," May 13, 1998.
15. Court in *U.S. v. Stuard*, 556 F.2d 1, 22 CrL 2337 (6th Cir. 1977), quoting *Neal v. U.S.*, 102 F.2d 643 (8th Cir. 1939). See also *Pope v. State*, 284 Md. 309, 396 A.2d 1054 (1979).

16. *U.S. v. Sun-Diamond Growers of California,* 119 S. Ct. 1402 (1999). In other criminal cases concerning the biggest sting operation conducted by the FBI, more than 60 lawyers, bailiffs, judges, and other people in the Chicago court system were indicted for bribery. Operation Greylord was conducted because money was used to buy and fix criminal and civil Chicago court cases. Other criminal charges resulting from Operation Greylord included mail fraud, racketeering, and obstruction of justice.

17. 544 F.2d 730 (4th Cir.). The decision of the court continues as follows:

> This requirement of criminal intent would, of course, be satisfied if the jury were to find a "course of conduct of favors and gifts flowing" to a public official in exchange for a pattern of official actions favorable to the donor even though no particular gift or favor is directly connected to any particular official act. *U.S. v. Baggett* (4th Cir. 1973) 481 F.2d 114, *cert. denied* 414 U.S. 1116 (1973) (Travel Act prosecution involving alleged bribery of Maryland County Commissioner). Moreover, as the Seventh Circuit has held, it is sufficient that the gift is made on the condition "that the offeree act favorably to the offer or when necessary." *U.S. v. Isaacs* (7th Cir. 1974) 493 F.2d 1124, 1145, *cert. denied* 417 U.S. 976 (1974) (construing Illinois statute in a Travel Act prosecution). It does not follow, however, that the traditional business practice of promoting a favorable business climate by entertaining and doing favors for potential customers becomes bribery merely because the potential customer is the government. Such expenditures, although inspired by the hope of greater government business, are not intended as a quid pro quo for that business: they are in no way conditioned upon the performance of an official act or pattern of acts or upon the recipient's express or implied agreement to act favorably to the donor when necessary.

18. 732 F.2d 878 (11th Cir. 1984). In the 1992 case of *Evans v. U.S.* (504 U.S. 255, 112 S. Ct. 1881), the U.S. Supreme Court held that a demand or other act of inducement by the public official was not necessary to convict of extortion under the Hobbs Act.

19. See *United States v. Pollard,* 959 F.2d 1011, *review denied* U.S. Supreme Court, 52 CrL 3033 (1992).

20. An example of "resisting law enforcement" is *Jackson v. State,* 576 N.E.2d 607 (Ind. App. 1991), in which the defendant refused to provide identification under circumstances that obligated him to do so. An example of "interfering with an officer" is *State v. Peruta,* 591 A.2d 140 (Conn. App. 1991), in which a jury found that the defendant, a news cameraman, interfered with law enforcement officers at the scene of a fatal automobile accident.

21. See the *New York Times* article, "Surgeon Is Convicted of Disguising a Fugitive," February 28, 1997.

22. See the *FBI Law Enforcement Bulletin* article, "Environmental Crimes Prosecution," April 1990, and the *FBI Law Enforcement Bulletin* article, "Director's Message," April 1991.

23. One of the largest environmental oil spills was that of the *Exxon Valdez,* an oil tanker that caused an oil spill in Alaska. The Exxon Corporation made the following payments as a result of that spill: for damages, $287 million; for fines, $25 million; for cleanup, $2.2 billion; for restoration, $1 billion.

24. Examples of environmental criminal charges include illegal storage and disposal of hazardous waste (New York, 768 F. Supp. 957, 1991); illegal landfill (New York, 751 F. Supp. 368, 1990); illegally discharging pollutants into navigable waters (993 F.2d 395, 1993); causing hazardous waste to be transported to an unpermitted facility (980 F.2d 27, 1992); discharge of waste water with excessive pollution levels (755 F. Supp. 771, Ill. 1990); unlawful storage and disposal of hazardous wastes (766 F. Supp. 873, Wash. 1991); violations of the Clean Water Act (784 F. Supp. 6, reversed in part 3 F.3d 643, 2d Cir. 1993, N.Y. 1991); and reckless disposal of hazardous waste (586 N.E.2d 1239, Ill. 1992).

APPENDIX
Sections of the U.S. Constitution Related to Criminal Law

(Ratified in 1788)

Preamble

We the People of the United States, in Order to form a more perfect union, establish Justice, insure domestic Tranquility, provide for the common defense, promote the general Welfare, and secure the Blessings of Liberty to ourselves and our Posterity, do ordain and establish this Constitution for the United States of America.

Article I

Section 1 All legislative Powers herein granted shall be vested in a Congress of the United States, which shall consist of a Senate and House of Representatives....

Article II

Section 1 The executive Power shall be vested in a President of the United States of America....

Article III

Section 1 The judicial Power of the United States, shall be vested in one supreme Court, and in such inferior Courts as the Congress may from time to time ordain and establish....

Article IV

Section 4 The United States shall guarantee to every State in this Union a Republican Form of Government, and shall protect each of them against Invasion; and on Application of the Legislature, or of the Executive [when the Legislature cannot be convened] against domestic Violence....

Article VI

This constitution, and the Laws of the United States which shall be made in Pursuance thereof; and all Treaties made, or which shall be made, under the Authority of the United States, shall be the supreme Law of the Land; and the Judges in every State shall be bound thereby, any Thing in the Constitution or Laws of any State to the Contrary notwithstanding....

American Bill of Rights (Ratified in 1791)

Amendment 1

Congress shall make no law respecting an establishment of religion, or prohibiting the free exercise thereof; or abridging the freedom of speech, or of the press; or the right of the people peaceably to assemble, and to petition the Government for a redress of grievances.

Amendment II

A well regulated Militia, being necessary to the security of a free State, the right of the people to keep and bear Arms, shall not be infringed.

Amendment III

No Soldier shall, in time of peace be quartered in any house, without the consent of the Owner, nor in time of war, but in a manner to be prescribed by law.

Amendment IV

The right of the people to be secure in their persons, houses, papers, and effects, against unreasonable searches and seizures, shall not be violated, and no Warrants shall issue, but upon probable cause, supported by Oath affirmation, and particularly describing the place to be searched, and the persons or things to be seized.

Amendment V

No person shall be held to answer for a capital, or otherwise infamous crime, unless on a presentment or indictment of a Grand Jury, except in cases arising in the land or naval forces, or in the Militia, when in actual service in time of War or public danger, nor shall any person be subject for the same offence to be twice put in jeopardy of life or limb; nor shall be compelled in any criminal case to be a witness against himself, nor be deprived of life, liberty, or property, without due process of law; nor shall private property be taken for public use, without just compensation.

Amendment VI

In all criminal prosecutions, the accused shall enjoy the right to a speedy and public trial, by an impartial jury of the State and district wherein the crime shall have been committed, which district shall have been previously ascertained by law, and to be informed of the nature and cause of the accusation; to be confronted with the witnesses against him; to have compulsory process for obtaining witnesses in his favor, and to have the Assistance of Counsel for his defence.

Amendment VII

In suits at common law, where the value in controversy shall exceed twenty dollars, the right of trial by jury shall be preserved, and no fact tried by a jury, shall be otherwise reexamined in any Court of the United States, than according to the rules of the common law.

Amendment VIII

Excessive bail shall not be required, nor excessive fines imposed, nor cruel and unusual punishments inflicted.

Amendment IX

The enumeration in the Constitution, of certain rights, shall not be construed to deny or disparage others retained by the people.

Amendment X

The powers not delegated to the United States by the Constitution, nor prohibited by it to the States, are reserved to the States respectively, or to the people....

14th Amendment, Ratified 1868

Amendment XIV

Section 1   All persons born or naturalized in the United States, and subject to the jurisdiction thereof, are citizens of the United States and of the State wherein they reside. No State shall make or enforce any law which shall abridge the privileges or immunities of citizens of the United States; nor shall any State deprive any person of life, liberty, or property, without due process of law; nor deny to any person within its jurisdiction the equal protection of the laws....

Glossary

accomplice   One who aids another in the commission of a crime. An accomplice is generally treated the same as a principal.

actus reus   The criminal act.

administrative crime   Crime created by government administrative agencies under specific authority and guidelines granted to the regulatory or administrative agency by law of that state or the federal government.

affirmative defense   A defense to a criminal charge in which the defendant generally admits doing the criminal act but claims an affirmative defense such as duress (he or she was forced) or entrapment.

aggravated assault   Assault made more serious by presence of a firearm or as part of intent to commit a felony

aggravating circumstances   A consideration in imposing the death penalty that judges and juries must make a finding of statutory aggravating circumstances to justify the penalty.

aider and abettor   One who provides help to the person who commits a crime, either before or after the crime is committed.

alibi   A defense to criminal prosecution on the grounds that the defendant physically could not have committed the crime because at the time the crime was committed, he or she was at another place.

armed or aggravated robbery   Forcible stealing combined with the use of a deadly or dangerous weapon, or which results in serious bodily injury to another.

arson   A person's deliberate, willful, and malicious burning of a building or personal property.

assault   In many instances, an assault is an attempt to commit a battery, but many states also make other conduct an assault. Could be combined with a charge of battery to constitute the crimes of "assault and battery."

assisting suicide   The act of furnishing the means of a suicide, pursuant to a statute that permits such assistance.

attempt crimes   Acts that are a substantial step toward the commission of a crime that is not yet completed.

bank fraud   Fraud aimed at banks and other financial institutions.

battered woman defense   Evidence of past abuse offered by women charged with violence against their abusers to show its psychological effects as part of their claim of self-defense.

battery   A successful assault, in which the victim is actually and intentionally (or knowingly) struck by the defendant.

benefit of clergy   A medieval limit on capital punishment. People convicted of a capital crime entitled to claim the benefit of clergy (by the fifteenth century, anyone who could read) could not be executed for their offense. By the end of the eighteenth century, the privilege had been eliminated for most crimes.

bill of attainder   Legislative act that inflicts punishment without trial; prohibited by Article I, Sections 9 and 10, of the Constitution.

"booze it and lose it" laws   In more than thirty states, laws that give the police the authority to immediately seize the driver's license of people who fail or refuse sobriety tests.

"born alive" requirement   To be able to charge homicide of a newborn baby, the prosecution must be able to prove that the child was living at the time it was killed.

bribery   Offering a gift or payment to another with the specific intent to obtain some unlawful particular quid pro quo for the gift or payment.

burglary   Unlawful entry into the premises of another with intent to steal or commit a felony. Two hundred years ago in England, an illegal entry into the home of another by force and at night was punishable by death if the entry was done to steal or commit a felony.

capital punishment   Inflicting deadly injury as punishment for criminal conduct.f

carjacking   Forcibly taking possession of a motor vehicle in the possession of another against his or her will with intent either to permanently or temporarily deprive the person of possession.

"castle" doctrine   The doctrine permitting people who have been assaulted in their homes by a trespasser to stand their ground and use such force as is necessary and reasonable to defend themselves.

certiorari   A form of review of lower court decisions by the Supreme Court. Certiorari is discretionary with the Court, and most petitions requesting it are denied. Traditional legal doctrine is that no conclusion can be drawn from a denial of certiorari.

check kiting   Creating multiple checking accounts at multiple banks for the purpose of writing fraudulent checks from one account and depositing them in another, and then withdrawing funds from the deposit bank.

child pornography   Movies, pictures, or drawings that depict children in explicit sexual relations. Unlike adult pornography, child pornography need not be obscene to be criminal.

civil contempt   This is a remedial form of contempt order used to force people to do what they are lawfully required to do (answer questions, identify themselves, pay support money as ordered by a divorce court, and so on).

"clear and present danger" test   The test used to judge government restrictions on speech.

coercion   A person who forces (coerces) another to commit a crime can be charged and convicted of the crime committed in addition to other offenses.

collateral estoppel   The doctrine that prohibits a second determination of a fact, when the fact was earlier judicially determined in a case involving the party who advances the doctrine.

common design or plan   Scope of liability of persons who are party to a conspiracy or other agreement to do an unlawful act.

common law crime   Crime created by judges.

common law   The earliest type of law. Common law was created by judges based on custom, usages, and moral concepts of the people. Most law today is statutory law enacted by legislative bodies.

competency to stand trial   Defendants must have the ability to cooperate with their attorneys and the ability to understand the charges and proceedings against them.

computer trespass   Unlawful access to a computer or computer system with intent to commit a crime, or unlawful access to a computer or computer system maintained by a government unit.

Concurrence   The requirement in crimes requiring proof of mental intent that the forbidden act and guilty mind must occur at the same time or otherwise be linked. For example, trustees, guardians, and lawyers might have possession of another person's money (physical act). For the crime of embezzlement to occur they must intentionally and wrongfully misappropriate this money (forbidden act and guilty mind).

conspiracy crimes   An agreement between two or more persons to engage in unlawful acts.

conspirator   A person who is a party to an agreement to commit an unlawful act.

contempt   Failure or refusal to obey a court order (civil contempt), or interfering with the functioning of a court or legislative body (criminal contempt). Criminal contempt that occurs in the presence of the court can be punished summarily; other criminal contempts require the normal prosecution procedures.

Continuing Criminal Enterprise Statute (CCE)
Federal law making prosecution possible for those whose actions enable a criminal enterprise to function, whether or not those same people can be proved to have performed specific criminal acts.

controlled substance   A drug that may be possessed or sold only as permitted by state or federal law.

corporal punishment   Inflicting nondeadly physical injury as punishment for criminal conduct.

corpus delicti   In all criminal cases, the government must prove that the crime charged was committed (corpus delicti) and that the defendant was party to the crime (committed the crime or was an accomplice).

corroborative evidence   Physical evidence or witness testimony other than from the victim that supports the claim that a crime occurred.

crime of terrorizing   A crime that creates a state of extreme fear, dread, or fright.

criminal contempt   This is a criminal charge based on a persons actions in a court case or legislative proceeding and used to punish people by a fine or imprisonment for what they have done.

criminal liability of corporations   The rules for making corporations liable for actions taken by officers, directors, or employees. Corporations can be vicariously criminally liable for actions of their agents if the offense is minor, a duty is specifically assigned to a corporation, a statute explicitly creates vicarious criminal liability, or the person committing the crime is acting in the interest of the corporation and is a high managerial agent.

criminology   The sociological and psychological study of the causes, development, and control of crime, as well as the conditions under which criminal law developed.

cruel and unusual punishment   Under the Eighth Amendment, a limitation on punishment for criminal conduct.

CTRs (currency transaction reports)   Reports that businesses, banks, and financial institutions are required to file for cash transactions of more than $10,000. CTRs can help determine whether tax fraud or money laundering is occurring.

cyber crime   Criminal acts implemented through use of a computer or other form of electronic communication.

deadly force   Force that is likely to cause or is capable of causing death or serious bodily injury.

defamation   The offense of injuring the character or reputation of another by oral or written

communication of false statements. Defamation consists of libel (written offense) or slander (oral offense).

defamation   Wrongful injury to another's reputation.

defense of   another The elements to evaluate whether an act of force for defense of another is justified include the unlawfulness of the action toward the other, the necessity to defend the other immediately, and the reasonableness of the act of defense under the circumstances.

defiant trespass   A person remains in a place where he or she is not privileged to remain even after notice of trespass is given.

diminished capacity defense   A defense for criminal responsibility based on the fact that because of mental or emotional conditions, the defendant did not possess the required *mens rea* for conviction of crime charged.

disorderly conduct   Loud, obnoxious, or other offensive conduct in a public place.

double jeopardy   A defense, stated in the Fifth Amendment, to prosecution on the grounds that the defendant has been tried before on the same charge, and acquitted.

drug paraphernalia   Objects that are primarily intended or designed for use with illegal drugs.

"dual sovereignty" doctrine   A doctrine that different governments may each file separate criminal actions for the same criminal act.

due process   The constitutional guarantee that criminal arrests and trials must meet certain minimum standards of fairness (procedural due process) and that laws not violate constitutional rights (substantive due process).

duress   A defense to criminal prosecution on the grounds that the defendant was forced to commit the criminal act.

embezzlement   To wrongfully appropriate money or property entrusted to one for that person's own use.

entrapment   The defense that a law enforcement officer used excessive temptation or urging to wrongfully induce the defendants to commit a crime they would not have ordinarily committed.

espionage   Giving or selling national military or defense secrets to a foreign nation.

euthanasia   A killing of a terminally sick or injured individual with only a short time to live. Also called mercy killing.

ex post facto   Criminal law made retroactive to punish prior conduct not criminal when done. Prohibited by Article I, Sections 9 and 10, of the Constitution.

extortion   Obtaining property by threats of future harm. Differs from robbery in that robbery requires threat of immediate harm.

extradition   The surrender of an accused criminal under the provisions of a treaty or statute by one authority to another having jurisdiction.

false imprisonment   Unlawful restraint or detention of a person.

federal enclaves   Federally owned and controlled lands.

felony murder   All states and the federal government have felony murder statutes that punish as murder the causing of death of another while the defendant is committing a felony of violence. A felony murder conviction does not require a showing of malice or deliberate intent to kill.

felony   The most serious grade of crime; usually includes possibility of prison sentence.

fence   A person who traffics in stolen property (receiving, concealing, possessing, buying, transferring, and so on).

feticide   Murder of an unborn child.

Field sobriety tests   Field tests used to evaluate a motorist's alcohol or drug impairment. They include HGN testing, the walk-and-turn test, and the one-leg stand test.

fighting words   Speech that, because it will likely incite immediate violence, is not protected by the First Amendment.

forfeiture   Going back to early English law, the concept and use of seizing the property that was used to commit a crime is a strong deterrent to crime, as is seizing the profits of crime a deterrent in crimes committed for profit.

forgery   Wrongfully signing a writing or instrument in the name of the person who issued the writing or instrument, or to whom it was payable.

frame-up   The defense that usually alleges that a law enforcement officer has planted false evidence, or has altered, substituted, or destroyed evidence, in an effort to convict the defendant of the crime charged.

fraud   Deceitful means or acts used to cheat a person, corporation, or governmental agency.

fraud   Use of deceit or trickery to obtain profit or advantage.f

Good Samaritan laws   Laws that encourage people to come to the aid of another or to defend another against unlawful force or interference.

guilty but mentally ill   A defendant may be found guilty but mentally ill if all the following are found beyond a reasonable doubt: (1) defendant is guilty of offense; (2) defendant was mentally ill at time offense was committed; (3) defendant was not legally insane at time offense was committed.

habeas corpus   A writ that compels the authority holding a person in confinement to explain the basis for that confinement. Used frequently as a method for state and federal prisoners to attack the constitutionality of their imprisonment. Both the federal government and states have some form of a habeas corpus law, often called *post-conviction relief* laws.

home invasion robbery   Robbery of persons inhabiting a dwelling.

homicide   The killing of one human being by another. There are three types of homicide: justifiable, excusable, and felonious.

honest services fraud   Unlawful actions that cause another person to lose the honest services of a person obligated to perform such honest services.

hostage taking   The use or threat of use of force to restrain or confine a person with the intent to use the person as a hostage to compel another person to perform some act.

identity theft   Theft based on stealing a real person's identification information (true name) or theft based on creating a fictitious person's identification (synthetic identity).

immunity   An exemption from criminal prosecution, which can be limited to prosecution for a specific crime (transactional immunity) or for any crime related to the testimony or conduct for which immunity is granted (use immunity). Diplomats and legislators also enjoy immunity from prosecution in many circumstances.

imperfect self-defense   A homicide in which the killer subjectively, but unreasonably, believes that his or her conduct was necessary. It may be unlawful if the killing was done with excessive or unnecessary force. An unnecessary killing in self-defense, in defense of another, or to prevent or terminate a felony of violence could be imperfect self-defense.

in loco parentis (Latin; "in place of the parents")
Any person taking the place of the parents has the duties and responsibilities of the parents and may reasonably discipline a child in his or her care. This category includes legal guardians, foster parents, and public school teachers.

incest   Sexual relations between persons closely related.

inciting   The offense of urging another to commit an unlawful act.

infant (child)   Under the civil law, a person who has not yet reached the age of majority, whether that age is 18, 19, 20, or 21, as determined by the law of each jurisdiction.

inference   A conclusion or deduction that a jury or judge *may* draw from a fact or a group of facts presented to them.

insanity tests   Tests to determine legal and moral liability.

intellectual property fraud   Theft, piracy, or counterfeiting of ideas, inventions, artistic works, and the like.

intent   The mental purpose or design to commit a specific act (or omission).

jurisdiction   Subject-matter jurisdiction is the authority to regulate conduct. Personal jurisdiction is the authority to prosecute and punish an offender.

kidnapping   False imprisonment coupled with movement of the victim.

long-arm statutes   Statutes that extend a state's jurisdiction beyond it's physical borders.

Magna Carta   The document signed by King John in 1215 giving certain rights to his nobles. Successive kings affirmed this charter before Parliament.

mail fraud   A fraudulent scheme, no matter its purpose or method, that uses either private or public delivery service.

"make my day" rules   Rules adopted by some states that put no limits on the use of deadly force by the occupant of a dwelling in response to a trespasser.

malicious prosecution   Initiating a judicial action with knowledge the claims made in the action are without merit.

manslaughter   Criminal homicides other than murder. Most states provide for two degrees of manslaughter, voluntary and involuntary.

maritime jurisdiction   Jurisdiction of the United States over actions within territorial waters of the United States on U.S. ships, or stateless vessels on the high seas.

martial law   A state of military control over civilian populations as declared by state or federal government

mayhem and malicious disfigurement   Willfully inflicting an injury on another so as to cripple or mutilate the person

Megan's laws   Laws passed in many states requiring convicted sex offenders to register with a state or local registration office. Named after a young girl killed by a convicted sex offender.

menacing   Intentionally placing or attempting to place another in fear of immediate serious physical injury.

mens rea   The criminal intent or state of mind.

misdemeanor   Offenses that carry punishment of a degree less than felonies. Usually misdemeanor crimes do not involve prison sentences.

misprision of felony   Failing to report knowledge of a felony to the appropriate authorities.

mistake of law   A claim by a defendant that the defendant did not know the action taken violated the criminal law.

mitigating circumstances   A consideration in imposing the death penalty that judges and juries must make findings of the mitigating circumstances that would weigh against the imposition of the death penalty.

M'Naghten rule   The insanity defense rule requiring proof that because of mental disease or defect defendants did not know the scope or character of their actions.

Model Penal Code (MPC)   Proposed criminal law developed by the American Law Institute, a group of lawyers, judges, and teachers. Many states have modeled their criminal codes on the Model Penal Code.

money laundering   The crime of disguising money obtained illegally by channeling it through legitimate commercial and financial transactions.

motive   The cause, inducement, or reason why an act is committed.

murder   Unlawful homicide with malice aforethought.

necessity   A defense to criminal prosecution on the grounds that the harm to be avoided outweighed the harm caused by the crime committed. Necessity will not justify taking another person's life.

nulla poena sine lege   The principle of legality; no act should be made criminal or punished without advance warning in the form of legislative act.

Nystagmus   A persistent, rapid, involuntary, side-to-side eye movement.

obscenity   Communication that the average person, using contemporary community standards, would find appeals to the prurient interests or depicts sexual conduct in a patently offensive manner and, taken as a whole, lacks serious artistic, literary, political, or scientific value.

obstruction of justice   Intentional acts that hinder, corrupt, or impede the functioning of the judicial system.

offensive touching   Unpermitted physical contact with another person, usually limited to "private" or genital parts.

"overbreadth" doctrine   The constitutional law doctrine that invalidates laws that regulate conduct so broadly as to interfere with individual freedoms.

parties to the principal crime   Under common law, persons who either committed the crime, or aided or abetted the commission of the crime or the persons who committed the crime.

perfect self-defense   A homicide in which the killer not only subjectively believes that his or her conduct was necessary and reasonable and that, by objective standards, it was lawful and complied with the requirements of the law. The homicide is either justifiable or excusable, and it carries no criminal liability.

perjury   The crime of knowingly and materially testifying falsely while under oath.

Pinkerton rule   The rule followed in federal courts that one conspirator is liable for crimes committed by another conspirator, if foreseeable and done in furtherance of the conspiracy.

police power   The inherent power of every state and local government, subject to constitutional limits, to enact criminal laws.

pornography   Movies, pictures, writings, and other expressions that are intended to arouse sexual incitement and have no artistic merit or redeeming social value.

possession with intent to deliver   A criminal case in which the state presents evidence showing that the accused had possession of a large amount of an illegal drug, meaning more than the accused would personally use.

posse comitatus   Latin, meaning "power of the country. In the U.S. it generally refers to the military forces.

post-crime offenses   Actions taken after a crime has been committed with knowledge that it had been committed that provide aid to the person who committed the crime.

preliminary, anticipatory, or inchoate crimes   Criminal acts that lead to or are attempts to commit other crimes.

Premeditation   Mental determination to unlawfully kill another person after planning or reflection on actions causing death.

Preponderance of the evidence   The greater weight of the evidence, though not necessarily the amount needed to remove every reasonable doubt. It is proof sufficient to incline a reasonable person toward one side of an issue rather than the other.

presumption   A rule of law that the trier of fact shall assume the existence of a state of facts without evidence being produced. Presumptions are rebuttable or irrebuttable.

probable cause   Reasonable grounds to believe.

procedural due process   A claim under the Fourteenth Amendment that there is an absence of fair procedures regulating state conduct.

procuring, promoting, and pimping   Actions taken to provide services of a prostitute.

proportionality   An objective evaluation of the appropriateness of a punishment for a particular crime.

prostitution   Providing sex for money or other value.

proximate cause   The ordinary and probable cause of a result.

public law   Criminal law in England and the United States.

Quid pro quo   Giving something of value ("quid") for something else.

rape   Anal, vaginal, or oral penetration by force or threat of force.

rape shield laws   Laws passed by many states to limit the extent to which defense attorneys in a rape case can inquire into the victim's past sexual life.

reasonable doubt   Proof beyond a reasonable doubt means that it is not enough to prove it was more likely than not that an element of the crime was true. The proof must be such that a reasonable person could not conclude the element was not true.

recidivist   One who is a habitual criminal.

res judicata   Ceen judicially determined in a case involving the same parties.

RICO   The Racketeer Influenced and Corrupt Organizations Act. Passed by Congress to enable prosecutors to charge all people engaged in unlawful activity who own or invest in an enterprise that affects interstate commerce.

"right and wrong" test   An insanity test that claims that defendants are not legally responsible for their acts if, due to a defect of the mind, at the time of the crime they were unable to understand the difference between right and wrong.

riot   Under the common law, a tumultuous disturbance of the peace by three or more people assembled with a common purpose to do an unlawful act.

robbery   Forcible stealing.

sabotage   The crime of damaging or injuring national defense material or utilities with the intention of interfering with national defense.

sanctuary   In the Middle Ages in England, sanctuary was a religious place where criminals could take refuge. The concept of sanctuary later broadened to include asylum for refugees.

scienter   A form of specific intent requiring a showing that the actor knew of the existence of certain facts. For example, one cannot be guilty of possession of stolen property if one does not know property is stolen.

sedition   The crime of advocating the forceful overthrow of the established government. In this country, the Smith Act makes such advocacy a crime.

self-defense   The elements to evaluate whether an act of force for self-defense is justified include the unlawfulness of the other's action, the necessity to defend oneself immediately, and the reasonableness of the act of self-defense under the circumstances.

sexual assault   The crime in most states that includes the crime of rape, as well as other lesser degrees of assault.

sexual harassment   Unwelcome sexual advances, with or without physical contact; in the workplace, creation of a "hostile environment," such as belittling or embarrassing an employee or co-worker who has refused sexual advances, can be sexual harassment.

shoplifting   Stealing goods from retail stores by concealment, generally on the person of the defendant. Commission does not require removal of the goods from the store.

solicitation or incitement crimes   Attempting to get another to commit a crime.

specific   intent The intent necessary for one or more elements of an offense. Murder, for example, requires the specific intent that the act be done intentionally or purposely.

stalking   A crime involving activities such as spying on the victim, following the victim, or attempting to communicate with the victim through the telephone or mail. Cyber stalking through the Internet is also a crime.

"stand your ground" laws   Recent laws passed in many states that permit using deadly force in response to an unlawful attack rather than the traditional "duty to retreat" policy.

status crime   Criminal laws that punish a status, such as drug addiction, with no act requirement.

statute of limitations   A defense to a criminal prosecution based on a statute that sets the maximum time the government has to prosecute a violation of a criminal law.

statutory rape   Sexual intercourse with a minor female under a certain age, usually 18. Consent and, generally, mistake as to age are not defenses to this crime.

strict liability crime   Crime that does not require proof of the mental element essential to true crimes.

subornation of perjury   The crime of inducing or knowingly permitting another person to testify falsely while under oath.

"substantial capacity" test   A test to determine criminal responsibility based on whether the defendant could (1) distinguish between right and wrong or (2) conform his or her conduct to the requirements of law.

substantive due process   A claim under the Fourteenth Amendment that state conduct is so brutal, demeaning, and harmful as to shock the conscience.

Sudden snatching   A form of robbery where force is not used beyond that needed to take property from another person

symbolic speech   Nonverbal expressions that convey a belief or idea.

taking   The act of obtaining physical possession or control of another's property. The key to taking is that the thief exercises unauthorized dominion over the property.

tampering with evidence   Knowingly altering or damaging evidence intended to be used in a court proceeding.

terrorism   The use force and violence in the pursuit of extreme political, ideological, or religious goals, without regard to the innocent lives that may be lost.

theft or larceny   Stealing property of another with the intent to deprive the owner of possession.

threats of violence   Statements or actions that unequivocally convey the message that violent actions will be taken.

"three strikes" laws   Laws that impose increased penalties for multiple felony convictions.

tort   A noncontractual civil wrong.

Transactional immunity   Total or full immunity for the criminal offense to which compelled testimony relates.

transferred intent   A doctrine used when the intention to harm one individual inadvertently causes a second person to be hurt instead. The individual causing the harm will be seen as having "intended" the act by means of the "transferred intent" doctrine.

Travel Act   Legislation that can be used to prosecute those involved in criminal activities that cross state borders or involve foreign commerce.

treason   Acting to overthrow one's government, or in violation of allegiance to one's country.

trespass   A wrongful intrusion on the land or into the premises of another person.

trial by ordeal   A test used to determine criminal responsibility in ancient England involving subjecting the individual to a torturous ordeal. These ordeals were essentially appeals to God; surviving the ordeal was viewed as God's judgment of innocence.

true threat   A serious expression of an intent to inflict bodily harm.

Uniform Controlled Substances Act   A model act identifying illegal drug crimes, drafted by a national conference of uniform law commissioners and adopted by the states and the federal government.

United Nations Conventions   An agreement between nations on a specific subject, such as piracy at sea.

unlawful assembly   Under the common law, a gathering of three or more people for any unlawful purpose or under such circumstances as to endanger the public peace or cause alarm and apprehension.

unreasonable   seizure A seizure made by a government officer that is unreasonable under the circumstances and thus violates the Fourth Amendment.

usable amount   In contrast to a useless trace amount, a quantity of an illegal drug sufficient to be used.

Use immunity   Prohibits prosecutorial authorities from using the compelled testimony in a criminal prosecution, but does not make the witness totally immune from prosecution based on evidence other than the witness's testimony and not derived from that testimony.

uttering   Putting into circulation a check known to be worthless.

"void for vagueness" doctrine   The constitutional law doctrine that invalidates criminal laws written in such a manner as to make it unreasonably difficult for a defendant to know whether or not conduct is prohibited by the law.

Wharton rule   The requirement that crimes needing more than one person for commission, such as bigamy, require three or more people for a conspiracy conviction.

"what one did, they all did"   The rule that all parties to a conspiracy or other agreement to perform an unlawful act are liable for every action taken by any party in furtherance of the conspiracy or agreement.

white-collar crime   A class or type of criminal conduct that has solely economic gain to the criminal as its goal.

wire fraud   A fraudulent scheme that uses interstate or international wire or other electronic communications.

witness protection program   Established as part of the Organized Crime Control Act of 1970, this program provides new identities and relocation for witnesses and their families in both state and federal criminal prosecutions of organized crime.

witness tampering   Criminal interference with someone who plans to testify in either a criminal or a civil trial.

Case Index

Subject Index